Managing Customer Relationships

A Strategic Framework

Second Edition

DON PEPPERS
MARTHA ROGERS

WILEY
John Wiley & Sons, Inc.

Published by John Wiley & Sons, Inc., Hoboken, New Jersey.
Published simultaneously in Canada.

For general information on our other products and services or for technical support, please contact our Customer Care Department within the United States at (800) 762-2974, outside the United States at (317) 572-3993 or fax (317) 572-4002.

Wiley also publishes its books in a variety of electronic formats. Some content that appears in print may not be available in electronic books. For more information about Wiley products, visit our web site at www.wiley.com.

Library of Congress Cataloging-in-Publication Data:

Peppers, Don.
   Managing customer relationships : a strategic framework / Don Peppers, Martha Rogers.—2nd ed.
       p.   cm.
   Includes index.
   ISBN 978-0-470-42347-9 (cloth); 978-0-470-93015-1 (ebk); 978-0-470-93016-8 (ebk); 978-0-470-93018-2 (ebk)
   1. Customer relations—Management.   2. Consumers' preferences.   3. Relationship marketing.   4. Marketing information systems.   5. Information storage and retrieval systems—Marketing.   I. Rogers, Martha, Ph.D.   II. Title.
   HF5415.5.P458 2011
   658.8′12—dc22   2010027042

Printed in the United States of America.

10   9   8   7   6   5   4   3

Contents

Preface

In 1993 we published our first book, *The One to One Future: Building Relationships One Customer at a Time* (New York: Currency/Doubleday). We had no way of knowing how or when ubiquitous, cost-efficient interactivity would arrive, but the march of technology was inevitable, and we felt strongly that genuinely interactive media channels would become widely available sooner or later, in one form or another. And when interactivity did arrive, we suggested, the nature of marketing would have to change forever. At the time, marketing consisted primarily of crafting outbound messages creative or noticeable enough to break through the clutter of other one-way messages. These messages promoted standardized, mass-produced products with unique selling propositions that appealed to the most commonly held interests among the widest possible markets of consumers.

In sharp contrast to this model of marketing, we maintained that interactive technologies would compel businesses to try to build relationships with individual customers, one customer at a time. To our minds, this new type of marketing—which we dubbed "one-to-one marketing," or "1to1 marketing"—represented literally a different dimension of competition. We predicted that in the one-to-one future, the battle for market share would be supplemented by a battle for "share of customer"; product management organizations would have to be altered to accommodate managing individual customer relationships as well; and the decreasing returns of production economics would be supplanted by *increasing* returns of relationship economics.

We did not know it at the time, but also in 1993, the first genuinely useful Web browser, Mosaic, was introduced, and by the end of 1994, the World Wide Web had begun making major inroads into business and academia. This meant that interactivity arrived even sooner than we had suspected it would, via a more robust, vibrant technology than we anticipated. But over the next 10 years, our predictions about the nature of marketing in an interactive world proved uncannily accurate, and we were gratified at the popularity our little book enjoyed among the many marketers and information-technology professionals wrestling with the question of how, exactly, to use this new capability for interacting with their customers on the Web. The term "one-to-one marketing" was often used interchangeably with the easier-to-say computer-industry acronym "CRM," standing for "customer relationship management." Some think of CRM as a reference only to the software, but from our standpoint, the 1to1 rose smells as sweet by any other jargon.

By the time the first edition of *Managing Customer Relationships* was written, 10 years later, many other academics, business consultants, and authorities had become involved in analyzing, understanding, and profiting from the CRM revolution. Our goal with the first edition was to provide a comprehensive overview of the background, the methodology, and the particulars of managing customer relationships for competitive advantage. Although we have significantly updated the material in this second edition, we believe this general approach has in fact been confirmed. So we will begin with background and history, move through an overview of relationship theory, outline the *Identify-Differentiate-Interact-Customize* (IDIC) framework, and then address metrics, data management, and customer management and company organization.

Since our first edition of that first book came out, the steady march of technology has continued to change the business environment, bringing us two particularly important developments, each of which requires some treatment in this new edition. One has to do with the increasing influence of social media—including everything from blogging and microblogging, to sharing and collaboration Web sites such as Facebook, MySpace, LinkedIn, YouTube, and Flickr. The other has to do with the increasing proliferation of mobile devices and interactive services for them, including not just broadband Wi-Fi at places like business hotels, Starbucks, and McDonald's, but smart phones that can surf the Web, keep your calendar, deliver movies, and track your location, as well.

Over the last few years, there has also been a major change in the way businesses think about the process of value creation itself, given their new technological capabilities to track and interact with customers, one at a time. Increasingly, companies are coming face-to-face with the question of how to optimize their businesses around individual customers. When you think about it, this is the very central issue when configuring a Web site, or when trying to design the work processes or scripting for a call center, or when outlining new procedures for sales reps or point-of-sale operations. Each of these tasks involves optimizing around a customer, and none of them can be completed adequately without answering the question, "What is the right communication or offer for *this* customer, at *this* time?"

But a business can answer this kind of question accurately only by disregarding its existing, product-based metrics and using customer-based metrics instead. This is because the fundamental issue at stake is how to maximize the value a particular customer creates for the enterprise, a task that contrasts sharply with the financial objective of the old form of marketing (mass marketing), which was maximizing the value that a particular product or brand created for the enterprise. So we have considerably upgraded the financial issues we consider in the metrics discussion in this edition of *Managing Customer Relationships*.

Among other things, we will suggest that a new metric, Return on Customer[SM], is more appropriate for gauging the degree to which a particular customer or group of customers is generating value for a business. Return on investment (ROI) measures the efficiency with which a business employs its capital to create value, and Return on Customer (ROC) is designed to measure the efficiency with which it employs its customers to create value. The ROC metric is simple to understand, in principle, but it requires a sophisticated approach to comprehending and analyzing customer lifetime values and customer equity. With the computer analytics available today, however, this is no longer an insurmountable or even a particularly expensive task. And this kind of customer-based financial metric will ensure that a company properly uses customer value as the basis for executive decisions.[1]

---

[1]Return on Customer[SM] and ROC[SM] are trademarks of Peppers & Rogers Group.

In the years since the first edition of this book was released, we have continued to teach seminars and workshops at universities and in for-profit and nonprofit organizations, and we have collaborated in depth with our own firm's working consultants in various Peppers & Rogers Group offices around the world, from São Paulo to Dubai, and from London to Johannesburg. We have wrestled with the serious, real-world business problems of taking a customer-centric approach to business in all different business categories, from telecom, financial services, and retailing, to packaged goods, pharmaceuticals, and business to business. Over the years, our experience in all these categories has reinforced our belief that the basic IDIC model for thinking about customer relationships is valid, practical, and useful, and that financial metrics based on customer value make the most sense. And, over the years, we have continued documenting these issues, coauthoring a total of seven additional business trade books, in addition to this textbook, with another one on the way.

While we obviously know more about our own work than anyone else's, and this book draws heavily on our fairly extensive direct experience in the work environment, we also continue to believe that a textbook like this should reflect some of the excellent work done by others, which is substantial. So, as with the first edition, you will find much in this edition that is excerpted from others' works or written by others specifically for this textbook.

When it appeared in 2004, *Managing Customer Relationships* was the first book designed specifically to help the pedagogy of customer relationship management, with an emphasis on customer strategies and building customer value. It is because of the wonderful feedback we have had over the years with respect to its usefulness for professors and students that we have undertaken this revised edition. And, while we hope this revised work will continue to guide and teach our readers, we also encourage our readers to continue to teach us. Our goal is not just to build the most useful learning tool available on the subject but to continue improving it as well. To that end, you may always contact us directly with suggestions, comments, critiques, and ideas. Simply e-mail MCR2@1to1.com.

How to Use This Book

The contents pages provide not only a guide to the chapter topics but also a listing of the contributions and contributors who have shared their insights, findings, and ideas.

Each chapter begins with an overview and closes with a summary (which is really more about how the chapter ties into the next chapter), Food for Thought (a series of discussion questions), and a glossary. In addition, chapters include these elements:

- Glossary terms are printed in boldface the first time they appear in a chapter, and their definitions are located at the end of that chapter. All of the glossary terms are included in the index, for a broader reference of usage in the book.
- Sidebars provide supplemental discussions and real-world examples of chapter concepts and ideas.
- Contributed material is indicated by a shaded background, with contributor names and affiliations appearing at the beginning of each contribution.

We anticipate that this book will be used in one of two ways: Some readers will start at the beginning and read it through to the end. Others will keep it on hand and use it as a reference book. For both readers, we have tried to make sure the index is useful for searching by names of people and companies as well as terms, acronyms, and concepts.

If you have suggestions about how readers can use this book, please share those at MCR2@1to1.com.

Acknowledgments

We started the research and planning for the first edition of this book in 2001. Our goal was to provide a handbook/textbook for students of the customer-centric movement to focus companies on customers and to build the value of an enterprise by building the value of the customer base. We have made many friends along the way and have had some interesting debates. We can only begin to scratch the surface in naming those who have touched the current revision of this book and helped to shape it into a tool we hope our readers will find useful.

We are honored to be contributing all royalties and proceeds from the sale of this book to Duke University, where Martha serves as an adjunct professor.

Thanks to Dr. Julie Edell Britton, who team-taught the Managing Customer Value course at Duke with Martha for many years, and to Rick Staelin, who has always supported the work toward this textbook in both editions and the development of this field. Additional thanks to all of the marketing faculty members at Duke, especially Christine Moorman, Wagner Kamakura, Carl Mela, and Dan Ariely, and all those who have used and promoted the book and its topics.

The voices of the many contributors who have shared their viewpoints have helped to make this book what it is; and you will see their names listed on the contents pages and throughout the text. We thank each of you for taking the time to participate in this project and to share your views and insights with students, professors, and other users of this book. And, as big as this book is, it is not big enough to include formally all the great thinking and contributions of the many academicians and practitioners who wrestle with deeper understanding of how to make companies more successful by serving customers better. We thank all of you too, as well as all those at dozens of universities who have used the first edition of the book to teach courses, and all those who have used the book as a reference work to try to make the world a better marketplace. Please keep us posted on your work!

This work has been greatly strengthened by the critiques from some of the most knowledgeable minds in this field, who took the time to review the book in both editions and share their insights and suggestions with us. This is an enormous undertaking and a huge professional favor, and we owe great thanks to Becky Carroll at Petra Consulting; Jeff Gilleland at SAS; Mary Jo Bitner and James Ward at Arizona State; Ray Burke at Indiana; Anthony Davidson at NYU; Susan Geib at MSUM; Rashi Glazer at U.C. Berkeley; Jim Karrh at Karrh & Associates; Neil Lichtman at NYU; Charlotte Mason at UGA; Janis McFaul; Ralph Oliva at Penn State; Phil Pfeifer and Marian Moore at UVA; David Reibstein at Wharton; and Jag Sheth at Emory. Thanks to John Deighton, Jon Anton, Devavrat Purohit, and Preyas Desai for additional contributions, and we also appreciate the support and input from Mary Gros and

Corinna Gilbert at Teradata. And thanks to Maureen Morrin and to Eric Greenberg at Rutgers, who have contributed to the Web site supporting this book, and to John Westman, General Manager of Critical Care, NxStage Medical, Inc., and adjunct professor of the Boston College Carroll School of Management.

Much of this work has been based on the experiences and learning we have gleaned from our clients and the audiences we have been privileged to encounter in our work with Peppers & Rogers Group. Dozens and dozens of the talented folks who have been PRGers over the past years have contributed to our thinking—many more than the ones whose bylines appear on contributions in the book, and more than we are able to list here. Our clients, our consulting partners and consultants, and our analysts are the ones who demonstrate every day that building a customer-centric company is difficult but doable and worthwhile financially. Special thanks go to Hamit Hamutcu, Orkun Oguz, Caglar Gogus, Mounir Ariss, Ozan Bayulgen, Amine Jabali, and Onder Oguzhan for their thinking and support. We also thank Tulay Idil, Bengu Gun, and Aysegul Kuyumcu for research. And to Thomas Schmalzl, Annette Webb, Mila D'Antonio, Elizabeth Glagowski, Jessica Bower, Jennifer Makris, and Ginger Conlon of the 1to1 Media team, our gratitude for a million things and for putting up with us generally. We also appreciate the work Tom Lacki has done toward this book and our thinking. Special additional thanks for ideas in the original edition that have survived to this version to Elizabeth Stewart, Tom Shimko, Tom Niehaus, Abby Wheeler, Lisa Hayford-Goodmaster, Lisa Regelman, and many other Peppers & Rogers Group alumni as well as winners of the 1to1 Impact Awards and PRG/1to1 Customer Champions, who are best in class at customer value building.

Plain and simple, we could not have gotten this book done without the leadership and project management of Marji Chimes, the talented and intrepid leader of 1to1 Media and an integral part of the success of Peppers & Rogers Group, or the dedicated day-to-day help from Susan Tocco. Thanks to you both. And the real secret sauce to finishing the many details has been Amanda Rooker—a truly resourceful researcher and relentlessly encouraging and gifted content editor, who has patiently and capably assisted in winding us through the morass of minutiae generated by a project of this scope.

Our editor at John Wiley & Sons, Sheck Cho, has been an enthusiastic supporter of and guide for the project since day one. As always, thanks to our literary agent, Rafe Sagalyn, for his insight and patience.

We thank the many professors and instructors who are teaching the first Customer Strategy or CRM course at their schools and who have shared their course syllabi. By so doing, they have helped us shape what we hope will be a useful book for them, their students, and all our readers who need a ready reference as we all continue the journey toward building stronger, more profitable, and more successful organizations by focusing on growing the value of every customer.

DON PEPPERS AND MARTHA ROGERS, PH.D.
2011

PART I

Principles of Managing Customer Relationships

The *Learning Relationship* works like this: If you're my customer and I get you to talk to me, and I remember what you tell me, then I get smarter and smarter about you. I know something about you my competitors don't know. So I can do things for you my competitors can't do, because they don't know you as well as I do. Before long, you can get something from me you can't get anywhere else, for any price. At the very least, you'd have to start all over somewhere else, but starting over is more costly than staying with me, so long as you like me and trust me to look out for your best interests.

CHAPTER 1

Evolution of Relationships
with Customers

No company can succeed without customers. If you don't have customers, you don't have a business. You have a hobby.

—Don Peppers and Martha Rogers

By definition, customers are every company's source of revenue. No company will ever realize income from any other entity except the customers it has now and the customers it will have in the future. Thus in many ways a firm's most valuable financial asset is its customer base, and, given our new and unfolding technological capabilities to *recognize*, measure, and manage relationships with each of those customers individually, a forward-thinking firm must focus on deliberately preserving and increasing the value of that customer base. Customer strategy is not a fleeting assignment for the marketing department; rather it is an ongoing business imperative that requires the involvement of the entire enterprise. Organizations must manage their customer relationships effectively in order to remain competitive. Technological advancements have enabled firms to manage customer relationships more efficiently, but technology has also empowered customers to inform themselves and to demand much more from the companies they do business with. The goal of this book is not just to acquaint the reader with the techniques of **customer relationship management**. The more ambitious goal of this book is to help the reader understand the essence of customer strategy and how to apply it to the task of managing a successful enterprise in the twenty-first century.

The dynamics of the customer-enterprise relationship have changed dramatically over time. Customers have always been at the heart of an enterprise's long-term growth strategies, marketing and sales efforts, product development, labor and resource allocation, and overall profitability directives. Historically, enterprises have encouraged the active participation of a sampling of customers in the research and development of their products and services. But until recently, enterprises have been structured and managed around the products and services they create and sell. Driven by assembly-line technology, mass media, and mass distribution, which appeared at the beginning of the twentieth century, the Industrial Age was dominated by businesses that sought to mass-produce products and to gain a competitive advantage by manufacturing a product that was perceived by most customers as better than its closest competitor. Product innovation, therefore, was the important key to business success. To increase its overall market share, the twentieth-century enterprise would use mass marketing and mass advertising to reach the greatest number of potential customers.

As a result, most twentieth-century products and services eventually became highly commoditized. Branding emerged to offset this perception of being like all the other competitors; in fact, branding from its beginning was, in a way, an expensive substitute for relationships companies could not have with their newly blossomed masses of customers. Facilitated by lots and lots of mass-media advertising, brands have helped add value through familiarity, image, and trust. Historically, brands have played a critical role in helping customers distinguish what they deem to be the best products and services. A primary enterprise goal has been to improve brand awareness of products and services and to increase brand preference and brand loyalty among consumers. For many consumers, a brand name testifies to the trustworthiness or quality of a product or service. But brand reputation has become less important among shoppers.[1] Indeed, consumers are often content as long as they can buy one brand of a consumer-packaged good that they know and respect. Whether shopping in a store, online, or from a catalog, consumers are just as satisfied when a retailer carries a trusted store brand or a trusted manufacturer's brand.[2]

For many years, enterprises depended on gaining the competitive advantage from the best brands. Brands have been untouchable, immutable, and inflexible parts of the twentieth-century mass-marketing era. But in the **interactive era** of the twenty-first century, firms are instead strategizing how to gain sustainable competitive advantage from the *information* they gather about customers. As a result, enterprises are creating a *two-way brand*, one that thrives on customer information and interaction. The two-way brand, or *branded relationship*, transforms itself based on the ongoing dialogue between the enterprise and the customer. The branded relationship is "aware" of the customer (giving new meaning to the

> For many years, enterprises depended on gaining the competitive advantage from the best brands. Brands have been untouchable, immutable, and inflexible parts of the twentieth-century mass-marketing era. But in the interactive era of the twenty-first century, enterprises are instead strategizing how to gain sustainable competitive advantage from the information they gather about customers.

---

[1] Peppers and Rogers Group and Institute for the Future, "Forecasting the Consumer Direct Channel: Business Models for Success" (2000), p. 48. This fact is also particularly true for emerging global markets. See Masaaki Kotabe's chapter, "Emerging Markets," in *Marketing in the 21st Century: New World Marketing*, ed. Bruce David Keillor (Westport, CT: Praeger, 2007).

[2] Todd Hale, "Think All Store Brand Buyers Are the Same? Think Again!" (NielsenWire, May 5, 2009), accessed January 25, 2010, available at: http://blog.nielsen.com/nielsenwire/consumer/think-all-store-brand-buyers-are-the-same-think-again/.

term *brand awareness*) and constantly changes to suit the needs of that particular individual.

Roots of Customer Relationship Management

Once you strip away all the activities that keep everybody busy every day, the goal of every enterprise is simply to get, keep, and grow customers. This is true for non-profits (where the "customers" may be donors or volunteers) as well as for-profits, for small businesses as well as large, for public as well as private enterprises. It is true for hospitals, governments, universities, and other institutions as well. What does it mean for an enterprise to focus on its customers as the key to competitive advantage? Obviously, it does *not* mean giving up whatever product edge or operational efficiencies might have provided an advantage in the past. It does mean using new strategies, nearly always requiring new technologies, to focus on growing the value of the company by deliberately and strategically growing the **value of the customer base**.

> What does it mean for an enterprise to focus on its customers as the key to competitive advantage? It means creating new shareholder value by deliberately preserving and growing the value of the customer base.

To some executives, customer relationship management (CRM) is a technology or software solution that helps track data and information about customers to enable better customer service. Others think of CRM, or one-to-one, as an elaborate marketing or customer service discipline. We even recently heard CRM described as "personalized e-mail."

This book is about much more than setting up a business Web site or redirecting some of the mass-media budget into the call-center database or **social networking**. It's about increasing the value of the company through specific customer strategies (see Exhibit 1.1).

- **Acquire**   profitable   **customers.**   **Get**

- **Retain**   profitable   **customers longer.**   **Keep**
- **Win back**   profitable   **customers.**
- **Eliminate**   unprofitable   **customers.**

                                                              Grow

- Upsell   **additional products in a solution.**
- Cross-sell   **other products to customers.**
- Referral   **and word-of-mouth benefits.**
- Reduce   **service and operational costs.**

EXHIBIT 1.1   Increasing the Value of the Customer Base

Companies determined to build successful and profitable customer relationships understand that the process of becoming an enterprise focused on building its value by building customer value doesn't begin with installing technology, but instead begins with:

- A strategy or an ongoing process that helps transform the enterprise from a focus on traditional selling or manufacturing to a customer focus while increasing revenues and profits in the current period and the long-term.
- The leadership and commitment necessary to cascade throughout the organization the thinking and decision-making capability that puts customer value and relationships first as the direct path to increasing shareholder value.

The reality is that becoming a **customer-strategy enterprise** is about using information to gain a competitive advantage and deliver growth and profit. In its most generalized form, CRM can be thought of as a set of business practices designed, simply, to put an enterprise into closer and closer touch with its customers, in order to learn more about each one and to deliver greater and greater value to each one, with the overall goal of making each one more valuable to the firm to increase the value of the enterprise. It is an enterprise-wide approach to understanding and influencing customer behavior through meaningful analysis and communications to improve customer acquisition, customer retention, and customer profitability.[3]

Defined more precisely, and what makes CRM into a truly different model for doing business and competing in the marketplace,

> Enterprises determined to build successful and profitable customer relationships understand that the process of becoming an enterprise focused on building its value by building customer value doesn't begin with installing technology but rather begins with:
>
> - A strategy or an ongoing process that helps transform the enterprise from a focus on traditional selling or manufacturing to a customer focus while increasing revenues and profits in the current period and the long term.
> - The leadership and commitment necessary to cascade throughout the organization the thinking and decision-making capability that puts customer value and relationships first as the direct path to increasing shareholder value.

---

[3] Erik M. van Raaij, "The Strategic Value of Customer Profitability Analysis," *Marketing Intelligence & Planning* 23, no. 4/5: 372–381, accessed January 28, 2010, available at: ABI/INFORM Global (document ID: 908236781); Sunil Gupta and Donald R. Lehmann, *Managing Customers as Investments* (Philadelphia: Wharton School Publishing, 2005); Robert S. Kaplan, "A Balanced Scorecard Approach to Measure Customer Profitability," Harvard Business School's Working Knowledge Web site, August 8, 2005, available at: http://hbswk.hbs.edu/item/4938.html, accessed January 28, 2010; Phillip E. Pfeifer, Mark E. Haskins, and Robert M. Conroy, "Customer Lifetime Value, Customer Profitability, and the Treatment of Acquisition Spending," *Journal of Managerial Issues* 17, no. 1 (Spring 2005): 11–25; George S. Day, *Market-Driven Strategy: Processes for Creating Value* (New York: Free Press, 1999); Frederick Newell, *The New Rules of Marketing* (New York: McGraw-Hill Professional Book Group, 1997); Don Peppers and Martha Rogers, *The One to One Future* (New York: Doubleday Books, 1993); Ronald S. Swift, *Accelerating Customer Relationships: Using CRM and Relationship Technologies* (Upper Saddle River, NJ: Prentice Hall, 2001); Fred Reichheld, *The Loyalty Effect* (Boston: Harvard Business School Press, 1996).

is this: It is an enterprise-wide business strategy for achieving customer-specific objectives by taking customer-specific actions. It is enterprise-wide because it can't merely be assigned to marketing if it is to have any hope of success. Its objectives are customer-specific because the goal is to increase the value of each customer. Therefore, the firm will take customer-specific actions for each customer, often made possible by new technologies.

> An enterprise-wide business strategy for managing customer relationships achieves customer-specific objectives by taking customer-specific actions.

In essence, building the value of the customer base requires a business to *treat different customers differently*. Today, there is a customer-focus revolution under way among businesses. It represents an inevitable— literally, irresistible—movement. All businesses will be embracing customer strategies sooner or later, with varying degrees of enthusiasm and success, for two primary reasons:

1. All customers, in all walks of life, in all industries, all over the world, want to be individually and personally served.
2. It is simply a more efficient way of doing business.

We find examples of customer-specific behavior, and business initiatives driven by customer-specific insights, all around us today:

- Instead of mailing out the same offer to everyone, a company waits for specific trigger behavior from a customer and increases response rates 25-fold.
- A car-rental customer rents a car without having to complete another reservation profile.
- An online customer buys a product without having to reenter his credit card number and address and looks at product reviews from other customers before ordering, significantly reducing the "returns" rate.
- A firm's product-development people turn their attention to a new service or product based on customer feedback captured by the sales force.
- Fans of a product band together on social networking sites and provide service and recommendations to each other.
- An insurance company not only handles a claim for property damage but also connects the insured party with a contractor in her area who can bypass the purchasing department and do the repairs directly.
- A supervisor orders more computer components by going to a Web page that displays his firm's contract terms, his own spending to date, and his departmental authorizations.
- Sitting in the call center, a service rep sees a "smart dialogue" suggestion pop onto a monitor during a call with a customer, suggesting a question the company wants to ask that customer (not the same question being asked of all customers who call this week).

Taking customer-specific action, treating different customers differently, building the value of the customer base, creating and managing relationships with individual customers that go on through time to get better and deeper: That's what this book is about. In the chapters that follow, we will look at lots of examples. The overall business goal of this strategy is to make the enterprise as profitable as possible over time by taking steps to increase the value of the customer base. The enterprise makes itself, its products, and/or its services so satisfying, convenient, or valuable to the customer that she becomes more willing to devote her time and money to this enterprise than to any competitor. Building the value of customers increases the value of the **demand chain**, the stream of business that flows from the customer down through the retailer all the way to the manufacturer. A customer-strategy enterprise interacts directly with an individual customer. The customer tells the enterprise about how he would like to be served. Based on this interaction, the enterprise, in turn, modifies its behavior with respect to this particular customer. In essence, the concept implies a specific, one-customer-to-one-enterprise relationship, as is the case when the customer's input drives the enterprise's output for that particular customer.[4]

A suite of buzzwords have come to surround this endeavor: CRM, one-to-one marketing, Customer Experience Management, Customer Value Management, customer focus, customer orientation, customer centricity, and more. You can see it in the titles on the business cards: Chief Marketing Officer, of course, but also a host of others, including "Chief Relationship Officer," "Customer Value Management Director," and even "Customer Revolutionary" at one firm. Like all new initiatives, this newfangled customer approach (different from the strictly financial approach or product-profitability approach of the previous century) suffers when it is poorly understood, improperly applied, and incorrectly measured and managed. But by any name, strategies designed to build the value of the customer base by building relationships with one customer at a time, or with well-defined groups of identifiable customers, are by no means ephemeral trends or fads, any more than computers or connectivity are.

A good example of a business offering that benefits from individual customer relationships can be seen in today's popular online banking services, in which a consumer spends several hours, usually spread over several sessions, setting up an online account and inputting payee addresses and account numbers, in order to be able to pay bills electronically each month. If a competitor opens a branch in town offering slightly lower checking fees or higher savings rates, this consumer is unlikely to switch banks. He has invested time and energy in a relationship with the first bank, and it is simply more convenient to remain loyal to the first bank than to teach the second bank how to serve him in the same way. In this example, it should also be noted that the bank now has increased the value of the customer to the bank and has simultaneously reduced the cost of serving the customer, as it costs the bank less to serve a customer online than at the teller window or by phone.

Clearly, "customer strategy" involves much more than marketing, and it cannot deliver optimum return on investment of money or customers without integrating individual customer information into every corporate function, from customer service, to production, logistics, and channel management. A formal change in the organizational structure usually is necessary to become an enterprise focused on growing

---

[4]Ranjay Gulati, "The Quest for Customer Focus," *Harvard Business Review* 83, no. 4 (April 2005): 92–101. Also see Don Peppers and Martha Rogers, Ph.D., *One to One B2B* (New York: Doubleday Broadway Books, 2001).

customer value. As this book shows, customer strategy is both an operational and an analytical process. **Operational CRM** focuses on the software installations and the changes in process affecting the day-to-day operations of a firm—operations that will produce and deliver different treatments to different customers. **Analytical CRM** focuses on the strategic planning needed to build customer value as well as the cultural, measurement, and organizational changes required to implement that strategy successfully.

Focusing on Customers Is New to Business Strategy

The move to a customer-strategy **business model** has come of age at a critical juncture in business history, when managers are deeply concerned about declining customer loyalty as a result of greater transparency and universal access to information, declining trust in many large institutions and most businesses, and increasing choices for customers. As customer loyalty decreases, profit margins decline too, because the most frequently used customer acquisition tactic is price cutting. Enterprises are facing a radically different competitive landscape as the information about their customers is becoming more plentiful and as the customers themselves are demanding more interactions with companies and creating more connections with each other. Thus a coordinated effort to get, keep, and grow valuable customers has taken on a greater and far more relevant role in forging a successful long-term, profitable business strategy.

If the last quarter of the twentieth century heralded the dawn of a new competitive arena, in which commoditized products and services have become less reliable as the source for business profitability and success, it is the new computer technologies and applications that have arisen that assist companies in managing their interactions with customers. These technologies have spawned enterprise-wide information systems that help to harness information about customers, analyze the information, and use the data to serve customers better. Technologies such as **enterprise resource planning (ERP)** systems, supply chain management software (SCM), enterprise application integration software (EAI), **data warehousing, sales force automation (SFA)**, marketing resource management (MRM), and other enterprise software applications have helped companies to mass-customize their products and services, literally delivering individually configured communications, products, or services to unique customers, in response to their individual feedback and specifications.

The accessibility of the new technologies is motivating enterprises to reconsider how they develop and manage customer relationships. More and more chief executive officers (CEOs) of leading enterprises have made the shift to a customer-strategy business model a top business priority for the twenty-first century. Technology is making it possible for enterprises to conduct business at an intimate, individual customer level. Indeed, technology is driving the shift. Computers can enable enterprises to remember individual customer needs and estimate the future potential revenue the customer will bring to the enterprise. What's clear is that technology is the enabler; it's the *tail*, and the one-to-one customer relationship is the *dog*.

Traditional Marketing Redux

Historically, traditional marketing efforts have centered on the "four Ps"—product, price, promotional activity, and place—popularized by marketing experts E. Jerome McCarthy[a] and Philip Kotler. These efforts have been enhanced by our greater (and deeper) understanding of consumer behavior, organizational behavior, market research, segmentation, and targeting. In other words, using traditional sampling and aggregate data, a broad understanding of the market has preceded the application of the four Ps, which enterprises have deployed in their marketing strategy to bring uniform products and services to the mass market for decades.[b] In essence, the four Ps are all about the "get" part of "get, keep, and grow customers." These terms have been the focal point for building market share and driving sales of products and services to consumers. The customer needed to believe that the enterprise's offerings would be superior in delivering the "four Cs": customer value, lower costs, better convenience, and better communication.[c] Marketing strategies have revolved around targeting broadly defined market segments through heavy doses of advertising and promotion.

This approach first began to take shape in the 1950s. Fast-growing living standards and equally fast-rising consumer demand made organizations aware of the effectiveness of a supply-driven marketing strategy. By approaching the market on the strength of the organization's specific abilities, and creating a product supply in accordance with those abilities, it was possible for the firm to control and guide the sales process. Central to the strategic choices taken in the area of marketing were the—now traditional—marketing instruments of product, price, place, and promotion—the same instruments that served as the foundation for Philip Kotler's theory and the same instruments that still assume an important role in marketing and customer relations today.

The four Ps all, of course, relate to the aggregate market rather than to individual customers. The market being considered could be a large, mass market or a smaller, niche market, but the four Ps have helped define how an enterprise should behave toward all the customers within the aggregate market:

1. *Product* is defined in terms of the average customer—what *most* members of the aggregate market want or need. This is the product brought to market, and it is delivered the same way for every customer in the market. The definition of *product* extends to standard variations in size, color, style, and units of sale as well as customer service and aftermarket service capabilities.
2. *Place* is a distribution system or sales channel. How and where is the product sold? Is it sold in stores? By dealers? Through franchisees? At a single location or through widely dispersed outlets, such as fast-food stores and ATMs? Can it be delivered directly to the purchaser?
3. *Price* refers not only to the ultimate retail price a product brings but also to intermediate prices, beginning with wholesale; and it takes account of the availability of credit to a customer and the prevailing interest rate. The

price is set at a level designed to "clear the market," assuming that everyone will pay the *same* price—which is only fair, because everyone will get the same product. And even though different customers within a market actually have different levels of desire for the same product, the market price will generally be the same for everybody.

4. *Promotion* has also worked traditionally in a fundamentally nonaddressable, noninteractive way. The various customers in a mass market are all passive recipients of the promotional message, whether it is delivered through mass media or interpersonally, through salespeople. Marketers have traditionally recognized the trade-off between the cost of delivering a message and the benefit of personalizing it to a recipient. A sales call can cost $350 or even more,[d] but at least it allows for the personalization of the promotion process. The CPM or cost per thousand to reach an audience through mass media is far lower but requires that the same message be sent to everyone. Ultimately, the way a product is promoted is designed to differentiate it from all the other, competitive products. Except for different messages aimed at different segments of the market, promotion doesn't change by *customer* but by *product.*

---

[a]E. Jerome McCarthy, *Basic Marketing: A Managerial Approach* (Homewood, IL: Irwin, 1958).

[b]Philip Kotler, *Marketing Management: Analysis, Planning, Implementation, and Control,* 9th ed. (Upper Saddle River, NJ: Prentice Hall, 1997), pp. 92–93.

[c]Philip Kotler, *Kotler on Marketing* (New York: Free Press, 1999), pp. 116–120.

[d]"Hoover's White Paper: How to Convert Prospects to Sales Faster with Pre-Call Planning" (2005), www.hoovers.com, accessed January 2010.

Dr. Philip Kotler, the highly respected marketing academic who, with Jerome McCarthy, is responsible for our understanding and practice of traditional marketing, shares his views of the transition to the customer strategies mandated by new technologies.

The View from Here

Philip Kotler
S. C. Johnson Distinguished Professor of International Marketing, Kellogg School of Management, Northwestern University

When I first started writing about marketing 45 years ago, the Industrial Age was in its prime. Manufacturers churned out products on massive assembly lines, stored them in huge warehouses where they patiently waited for retailers to order and shelve boxes and bottles so that customers could buy them. Market leaders enjoyed great market shares from their carefully crafted mass-production, mass-distribution, and mass-advertising campaigns.

(continued)

(Continued)

What the Industrial Age taught us is that if an enterprise wanted to make money, it needed to be efficient at large-scale manufacturing and distribution. The enterprise needed to manufacture millions of standard products and distribute them in the same way to all of their customers. Mass producers relied on numerous intermediaries to finance, distribute, stock, and sell the goods to ever-expanding geographical markets. But in the process, producers grew increasingly removed from any direct contact with end users.

Producers tried to make up for what they didn't know about end users by using a barrage of marketing research methods, primarily customer panels, focus groups, and large-scale customer surveys. The aim was not to learn about individual customers but about large customer segments, such as "women ages 30 to 55." The exception occurred in business-to-business marketing where each salesperson knew each customer and prospect as an individual. Well-trained salespeople were cognizant of each customer's buying habits, preferences, and peculiarities. Even here, however, much of this information was never codified. When a salesperson retired or quit, the company lost a great deal of specific customer information. Only more recently, with sales automation software and loyalty-building programs, are business-to-business enterprises capturing detailed information about each customer on the company's mainframe computer.

As for the consumer market, interest in knowing consumers as individuals lagged behind the business-to-business marketplace. The exception occurred with direct mailers and catalog marketers who collected and analyzed data on individual customers. Direct marketers purchased mailing lists and kept records of their transactions with individual customers. The individual customer's stream of transactions provided clues as to other items that might interest that customer. For example, in the case of consumer appliances, the company could at least know when a customer might be ready to replace an older appliance with a new one if the price was right.

Getting Better at Consumer Marketing

With the passage of time, direct marketers became increasingly sophisticated. They supplemented mail contact with the adroit use of the telephone and telemarketing. The growing use of credit cards and customers' willingness to give their credit card numbers to merchants greatly stimulated direct marketing. The emergence of fax machines further facilitated the exchange of information and the placing of orders. Soon the Internet and e-mail provided the ultimate facilitation of direct marketing. Customers could view products visually and verbally order them easily, receive confirmation, and know when the goods would arrive. Now that experience is enhanced by the way customers speak to each other. Even companies that don't really understand social networking realize they have to get on board. If 33 million people are in a room, you have to visit that room.[a]

But whether a company was ready for *customer relationship management* depended on more than conducting numerous transactions with individual customers. Companies needed to build comprehensive *customer databases*. Companies had been maintaining product databases, sales force databases, and dealer databases. Now they needed to build, maintain, mine, and manage a customer database that could be used by company personnel in sales, marketing, credit, accounting, and other company functions.

As customer database marketing grew, several different names came to describe it, including individualized marketing, customer intimacy, technology-enabled marketing, dialogue marketing, interactive marketing, permission marketing, and one-to-one marketing.

Modern technology makes it possible for enterprises to learn more about individual customers, remember those needs, and shape the company's offerings, services, messages, and interactions to each valued customer. The new technologies make mass-customization (otherwise an oxymoron) possible.

At the same time, technology is only a partial factor in helping companies do genuine one-to-one marketing. The following quotes about CRM make this point vividly:

> *CRM is not a software package. It's not a database. It's not a call center or a Web site. It's not a loyalty program, a customer service program, a customer acquisition program, or a win-back program. CRM is an entire philosophy.*

—Steve Silver

> *A CRM program is typically 45 percent dependent on the right executive leadership, 40 percent on project management implementation, and 15 percent on technology.*

—Edmund Thompson, Gartner Group

Whereas in the Industrial Age, companies focused on winning market share and new customers, more of today's companies are focusing on **share of customer (SOC)**, namely increasing their business with each existing customer. These companies are focusing on customer retention, customer loyalty, and customer satisfaction as the important marketing tasks and customer experience management and increasing customer value as key management objectives.

CRM and its kindred customer-focused efforts are more than just an outgrowth of direct marketing and the advent of new technology. This approach requires new skills, systems, processes, and employee mind-sets. As the Interactive Age progresses, mass marketing must give way to new principles for targeting, attracting, winning, serving, and satisfying markets. As advertising costs have risen and mass media has lost some effectiveness, mass marketing is now more costly and more wasteful. Companies are better prepared to identify meaningful segments and niches and address the individual customers within the targeted groups. They are becoming aware, however, that many customers are uncomfortable about their loss of privacy and the increase in solicitations by mail, phone, and e-mail. Ultimately, companies will have to move from an

(continued)

(Continued)

"invasive" approach to prospects and customers to a "permissions" approach. On the flip side, customers—now in contact with millions of other customers—have never been more informed or empowered.

The full potential of CRM is only beginning to be realized. Of course every company must offer great products and services. But now, rather than pursue all types of customers at great expense only to lose many of them, the objective is to focus only on those particular customers with current and long-term potential, in order to preserve and increase their value to the company.

---

[a]Juliette Powell, *33 Million People in the Room* (Upper Saddle River, NJ: Financial Times Press, 2009), pp. 8–9.

Managing Customer Relationships Is a Different Dimension of Competition

A lot can be understood about how traditional, market-driven competition is different from today's customer-driven competition by examining Exhibit 1.2(a) and 1.2(b). The direction of success for a traditional aggregate-market enterprise (i.e., a traditional company that sees its customers in markets of aggregate groups) is to acquire more customers (widen the horizontal bar), whereas the direction of success for the customer-driven enterprise is to keep customers longer and grow them bigger (lengthen the vertical bar). The width of the horizontal bar can be thought of as an enterprise's market share—the proportion of total customers who have their needs satisfied by a particular enterprise, or the percentage of total products in an industry sold by this particular firm. But the customer-value enterprise focuses on share of customer—the percentage of this customer's business that a particular firm gets—represented by the height of the vertical bar. Think of it this way: Kellogg's can either sell as many boxes of Corn Flakes as possible to whomever will buy them, even though sometimes Corn Flakes will cannibalize Raisin Bran sales, or Kellogg's can concentrate on making sure its products are on Mrs. Smith's breakfast table every day for the rest of her life, and thus represent a steady or growing percentage

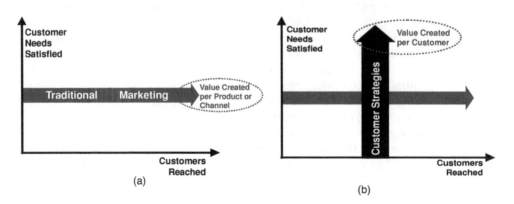

EXHIBIT 1.2   (a) Growing Market Share and (b) Growing Customer Shares

of that breakfast table's offerings. Nissan can try to sell as many Altimas as possible, for any price, to anyone who will buy; or it can, by knowing Mrs. Smith better, make sure all the cars in Mrs. Smith's garage are Nissan brands, including the used car she buys for her teenage son, and that Mrs. Smith uses Nissan financing, and gets her service, maintenance, and repairs at Nissan dealerships throughout her driving lifetime.

Although the tasks for growing market share are different from those for building share of customer, the two strategies are not antithetical. A company can simultaneously focus on getting new customers and growing the value of and keeping the customers it already has.[5] Customer-strategy enterprises are required to interact with a customer and use that customer's feedback from this interaction to deliver a customized product or service. Market-driven efforts can be strategically effective and even more efficient at meeting individual customer needs when a customer-specific philosophy is conducted on top of it. The customer-driven process is time-dependent and evolutionary, as the product or service is continuously fine-tuned and the customer is increasingly differentiated from other customers. The aggregate-market enterprise competes by differentiating products, whereas the customer-driven enterprise competes by differentiating customers. The traditional, aggregate-market enterprise attempts to establish an actual product differentiation (by launching new products or modifying or extending established product lines) or a perceived one (with advertising and public relations). The customer-driven enterprise caters to one customer at a time and relies on differentiating each customer from all the others.

The principles of a customer-focused business model differ in many ways from mass marketing. For one thing, the traditional marketing company, no matter how friendly, ultimately sees customers as adversaries, and vice versa. The company and the customer play a zero-sum game: If the customer gets a discount, the company loses profit margin. Their interests have traditionally been at odds: The customer wants to buy as much product as possible for the lowest price, while the company wants to sell the least product possible for the highest price. If an enterprise and a customer have no relationship prior to a purchase, and they have no relationship following it, then their entire interaction is centered on a single, solitary transaction and the profitability of that transaction. Thus, in a transaction-based, product-centric business model, buyer and seller are adversaries, no matter how much the seller may try not to act the part. In this business model, practically the only assurance a customer has that he can trust the product and service being sold to him is the general reputation of the brand itself.[6]

By contrast, the customer-based enterprise aligns customer collaboration with profitability. Compare the behaviors that result from both sides if each transaction occurs in the context of a longer-term relationship. For starters, a one-to-one enterprise would likely be willing to fix a problem raised by a single transaction at a loss if the relationship with the customer were profitable long term (see Exhibit 1.3).

---

[5]See George S. Day, *Market-Driven Strategy: Processes for Creating Value* (New York: Free Press, 1999), for a useful discussion of the difference between "market-driven" and "market-driving" strategies.

[6]Don Peppers and Martha Rogers, Ph.D., *The One to One Manager* (New York: Doubleday, 1999).

EXHIBIT 1.3   Comparison of Market-Share and Share-of-Customer Strategies

Market-Share Strategy	Share-of-Customer Strategy
Company sees products and brands as the source of all company value.	Company sees customers as—by definition—the only source of revenue.
Product (or brand) managers sell one product at a time to as many customers as possible.	Customer manager sells as many products as possible to one customer at a time.
Differentiate products from competitors.	Differentiate customers from each other.
Sell *to* customers.	Collaborate *with* customers.
Find a constant stream of new customers.	Find a constant stream of new business from established customers.
Company makes sure each product, and likely each transaction, is profitable, even at the cost of a customer's confidence.	Company makes sure each customer is profitable, even if that means losing money on an occasional product or transaction.
Use mass media to build brand and announce products.	Use interactive communication to determine individual needs and communicate with each individual.

The central purpose of managing customer relationships is for the enterprise to focus on increasing the overall value of its customer base—and customer retention is critical to its success. Increasing the value of the customer base, whether through *cross-selling* (getting customers to buy other products and services), *upselling* (getting customers to buy more expensive offerings), or customer referrals, will lead to a more profitable enterprise. The enterprise can also reduce the cost of serving its best customers by making it more convenient for them to buy from the enterprise (e.g., by using Amazon's one-click ordering process or Web banking rather than a bank teller).

> The central purpose of managing customer relationships is for the enterprise to focus on increasing the overall value of its customer base—and customer retention is critical to its success.

Technology Accelerates—It Is Not the Same as—Building Customer Value

The interactive era has accelerated the adoption and facilitation of this highly interactive collaboration between the customer and the company. In addition, technological advancements have contributed to an enterprise's capability to capture the feedback of its customer, then customize some aspect of its products or services to suit each customer's individual needs. Enterprises require a highly sophisticated level of integrated activity to enable this customization and personalized customer interaction to occur. To effectuate customer-focused business relationships, an enterprise must integrate the disparate information systems, databases, business units, customer touchpoints—everywhere the company touches the customer and vice-versa—and many other facets of its business to ensure that all employees who interact with customers have real-time access to current customer information. The objective is to optimize each customer interaction and ensure that the dialogue is seamless—that each conversation picks up from where the last one ended.

> Technology has made possible the mass customization of products and services, enabling businesses to treat different customers differently, in a cost-efficient way.

Many software companies have developed enterprise point solutions and suites of software applications that, when deployed, elevate an enterprise's capabilities to transform itself to a customer-driven model. And as we said earlier, while one-to-one customer relationships are enabled by technology, executives at firms with strong customer relationships and burgeoning **customer equity (CE)** believe that the enabling technology should be viewed as the means to an end, not the end itself. Managing customer relationships is an ongoing business process, not merely a technology. But technology has provided the catalyst for CRM to manifest itself within the enterprise. Computer databases help companies remember and keep track of individual interactions with their customers. Within seconds, customer service representatives can retrieve entire histories of customer transactions and make adjustments to customer records. Technology has made possible the mass customization of products and services, enabling businesses to treat different customers differently, in a cost-efficient way. (You'll find more about mass customization in Chapter 10.) Technology empowers enterprises and their customer contact personnel, marketing and sales functions, and managers by equipping them with substantially more intelligence about their customers.

> The foundation for an enterprise focused on building its value by building the value of the customer base is unique: Establish relationships with customers on an individual basis, then use the information gathered to treat different customers differently and increase the value of each one to the firm.

Implementing an effective customer strategy can be challenging and costly because of the sophisticated technology and skill set needed by relationship managers to execute the customer-driven business model. A business model focused on building customer value often requires the coordinated delivery of products and services aligned with enterprise financial objectives that meet customer value requirements. While enterprises are experimenting with a wide array of technology and software solutions from different vendors to satisfy their customer-driven needs, they are learning that they cannot depend on technology alone to do the job. Before it can be implemented successfully, managing customer relationships individually requires committed leadership from the upper management of the enterprise and wholehearted participation throughout the organization as well. Although customer strategies are driven by new technological capabilities, the technology alone does not make a company customer-centric. The payoff can be great, but the need to build the strategy to get, keep, and grow customers is even more important than the technology required to implement that strategy.

> The firms that are best at building customer value are not the ones that ask "How can we use new technologies to get our customers to buy more?" Instead they are the companies that ask *"How can we use new technologies to deliver more value to our customers?"*

The foundation for an enterprise focused on building its value by building the value of the customer base is unique: Establish relationships with customers on an individual basis, then use the information gathered to treat different customers differently and increase the value of each one to the firm. The overarching theme of such an enterprise is that the customer is the most valuable asset the company has; that's why the primary goals are to get, keep, and grow profitable customers. Use technology to take the customer's point of view, and act on that as a competitive advantage.

What Is a Relationship?

What does it mean for an enterprise and a customer to have a *relationship* with each other? Do customers have relationships with enterprises that do not know them? Can the enterprise be said to have a relationship with a customer it does not know? Is it possible for a customer to have a relationship with a brand? Perhaps what is thought to be a customer's relationship with a brand is more accurately described as the customer's attitude or predisposition toward the brand. Experts have studied the nature of relationships in business for many years, and there are many different perspectives on the fundamental purpose of relationships in business strategies. (You'll find two in-depth discussions on the nature of "relationship" in the next chapter.)

This book is about managing customer relationships more effectively in the twenty-first century, which is governed by a more individualized approach. The critical business objective can no longer be limited to acquiring the most customers and gaining the greatest market share for a product or service. Instead, to be successful going forward, now that it's possible to deal individually with separate customers, the business objective must include establishing meaningful and profitable relationships with, at the least, the most valuable customers and making the overall customer base more valuable. Technological advances during the last quarter of the twentieth century have mandated this shift in philosophy.

In short, the enterprise strives to get a customer, keep that customer for a lifetime, and grow the value of the customer to the enterprise. Relationships are the crux of the customer-strategy enterprise. Relationships between customers and enterprises provide the framework for everything else connected to the customer-value business model. The exchange between a customer and the enterprise becomes mutually beneficial, as customers give information in return for personalized service that meets their individual needs. This interaction forms the basis of the *Learning Relationship*, based on a collaborative dialogue between the enterprise and the customer that grows smarter and smarter with each successive interaction.[7]

Who Is the Customer?

Throughout this book, we refer to *customers* in a generic way. To some, the term will conjure up the mental image of shoppers. To others, those shoppers are *end users* or *consumers*, and the customers are downstream businesses in the distribution chain—the companies that buy from producers and either sell

---

[7]B. Joseph Pine II, Don Peppers, and Martha Rogers, Ph.D., "Do You Want to Keep Your Customers Forever?" *Harvard Business Review* 73:2 (March–April 1995): 103–114.

directly to end users or manufacture their own product. In this book, *customer* refers to the constituents of an organization, whether it's a business-to-business customer (which could mean the purchasing agent or user at the customer company, or the entire customer company) or an end-user consumer—or, for that matter, a hotel patron, a hospital patient, a charitable contributor, a voter, a university student or alum, a blood donor, a theme-park guest, and so on. That means the *competition* is anything a customer might choose that would preclude choosing the organization that is trying to build a relationship with that customer.

Learning Relationships: The Crux of Managing Customer Relationships— *needs/high quality service*

The basic strategy behind Learning Relationships is that the enterprise gives a customer the opportunity to teach it what he wants, remember it, give it back to him, and keep his business. The more the customer teaches the company, the better the company can provide exactly what the customer wants and the more the customer has invested in the relationship. Ergo, the customer will more likely choose to continue dealing with the enterprise rather than spend the extra time and effort required to establish a similar relationship elsewhere.[8]

The Learning Relationship works like this: If you're my customer and I get you to talk to me, and I remember what you tell me, then I get smarter and smarter about you. I know something about you that my competitors don't know. So I can do things for you my competitors can't do, because they don't know you as well as I do. Before long, you can get something from me you can't get anywhere else, for any price. At the very least, you'd have to start all over somewhere else, but starting over is more costly than staying with me, so long as you like me and trust me to look out for your best interests.

This happens every time a customer buys groceries by updating her online grocery list[9] or adds a favorite movie to her online queue. Even if a competitor were to establish exactly the same capabilities, a customer already involved in a Learning Relationship with an enterprise would have to spend time and energy—sometimes a lot of time and energy—teaching the competitor what the current enterprise already knows. This creates a significant **switching cost** for the customer, as the value of what the enterprise is providing continues to increase, partly as the result of the customer's own time and effort. The result is that the customer becomes more loyal to the enterprise, because it is simply in the customer's own interest to do so. It is more worthwhile for the customer to remain loyal than to switch. As the relationship progresses, the customer's convenience increases, and the enterprise becomes more valuable to the customer, allowing the enterprise to protect its profit margin with the customer, often while reducing the cost of serving that customer.

Learning Relationships provide the basis for a completely different arena of competition, separate and distinct from traditional, product-based competition. An

---

[8] Ibid.

[9] Adele Berndt and Annekie Brink, *Customer Relationship Management and Customer Service* (Lansdowne, South Africa: Juta and Co., 2004), p. 25.

enterprise cannot prevent its competitor from offering a product or service that is perceived to be as good as its own offering. Once a competitor offers a similar product or service, the enterprise's own offering is reduced to commodity status. But enterprises that engage in collaborative Learning Relationships with individual customers gain a distinct competitive advantage, because they know something about one customer that a competitor does not know. In a Learning Relationship, the enterprise learns about an individual customer through his transactions and interactions during the process of doing business. The customer, in turn, learns about the enterprise through his successive purchase experiences and other interactions. Thus, in addition to an increase in customer loyalty, two other benefits come from Learning Relationships:

1. *The customer learns more about his own preferences from each experience and from the firm's feedback,* and is therefore able to shop, purchase, and handle some aspect of his life more efficiently and effectively than was possible prior to this relationship.
2. *The enterprise learns more about its own strengths and weaknesses from each interaction and from the customer's feedback,* and is therefore able to market, communicate, and handle some aspects of its own tactics or strategy more efficiently and effectively than was possible prior to the relationship.[10]

Cultivating Learning Relationships depends on an enterprise's capability to elicit and manage useful information about customers. Customers, whether they are consumers or other enterprises, do not want more choices. Customers simply want exactly what they want—when, where, and how they want it.

> Customers, whether they are consumers or other enterprises, do not want more choice. Customers simply want what they want when, where, and how they want it.

And technology is now making it more and more possible for companies to give it to them, allowing enterprises to collect large amounts of data on individual customers' needs and then use that data to customize products and services for each customer—that is, to treat different customers differently.[11]

One of the implications of this shift is an imperative to consider and manage the two ways customers create value for an enterprise. We've already said that a product focus tends to make companies think more about the value of a current transaction than the long-term value of the customer who is the company's partner in that transaction. But building Learning Relationships has value only to a company that links its own growth and future success to its ability to keep and grow customers, and therefore commits to building long-term relationships with customers. This means we find stronger commitments to customer trust, employee trust, meeting community responsibilities, and otherwise thinking about long-term, sustainable strategies. Companies that are in the business of building the value of the customer base are companies that understand the importance of balancing short-term and long-term success. We talk more about that in Chapters 5 and 11.

---

[10]Katherine Lemon, Don Peppers, and Martha Rogers, Ph.D., "Managing the Customer Lifetime Value: The Role of Learning Relationships," working paper.

[11]Pine, Peppers, and Rogers, "Do You Want to Keep Your Customers Forever?"

Return on Customer: Measuring the Efficiency with Which Customers Create Value

Most business executives would agree, intellectually, that *customers* represent the surest route to business growth—getting more customers, keeping them longer, and making them more profitable. Most understand that the customer base itself is a revenue-producing asset for their company—and that the value it throws off ultimately drives the company's economic worth. Nevertheless, when companies measure their financial results, they rarely if ever take into account any changes in the value of this underlying asset, with the result that they are blind—*and financial analysts are blind*—to one of the most significant factors driving business success.

Think about your personal investments. Imagine you asked your broker to calculate your return on investment for your portfolio of stocks and bonds. She would tally the dividend and interest payments you received during the year, and then note the increases or decreases in the value of the various stocks and bonds in the portfolio. Current income plus underlying value changes. The result, when compared to the amount you began the year with, would give you this year's ROI (return on investment). But suppose she chose to ignore any changes in the underlying value of your securities, limiting her analysis solely to dividends and interest. Would you accept this as a legitimate picture of your financial results? No?

Well, this is exactly the way nearly all of today's investors assess the financial performance of the companies they invest in, because this is the only way companies report their results. They count the "dividends" from their customers and ignore any increase (or decrease) in the value of the underlying assets. But just as a portfolio of securities is made up of individual stocks and bonds that not only produce dividends and interest but also go up and down in value during the course of the year, a company is, at its roots, a portfolio of customers, who not only buy things from the firm in the current period but also go up and down in value.

Return on investment quantifies how well a firm creates value from a given investment. But what quantifies how well a company creates value from its *customers?* For this you need the metric of Return on Customer[sm] (ROC[sm]). The ROC equation has the same form as an ROI equation. ROC equals a firm's current-period cash flow from its customers plus any changes in the underlying customer equity, divided by the total customer equity at the beginning of the period.

Source: Excerpted from Don Peppers and Martha Rogers, Ph.D, *Return on Customer* (New York: Currency/Doubleday, 2008), pp. 6–7. Return on Customer will be discussed in more detail in Chapter 11.

When it comes to customers, businesses are shifting their focus from product sales transactions to **relationship equity**. Most soon recognize that they simply do not know the full extent of their profitability by customer.[12] Not all customers are equal. Some are not worth the time or financial investment of establishing Learning Relationships, nor are all customers willing to devote the effort required to sustain such a relationship. Enterprises need to decide early on which customers they want to have relationships with, which they do not, and what type of relationships to nurture. (See Chapter 5 on customer value differentiation.) But the advantages to the enterprise of growing Learning Relationships with valuable and potentially valuable customers are immense. Because much of what is sold to the customer may be customized to his precise needs, the enterprise can, for example, potentially charge a premium (as the customer may be less price-sensitive to customized products and services) and increase its profit margin.[13] The product or service is worth more to the customer because he has helped shape and mold it to his own specifications. The product or service, in essence, has become *decommoditized* and is now uniquely valuable to this particular customer.

Managing customer relationships effectively is a practice not limited to product and services. When establishing interactive Learning Relationships with valuable customers, customer-strategy enterprises remember a customer's specific needs for the basic product but also the goods, services, and communications that surround the product, such as how the customer would prefer to be invoiced or how the product should be packaged. Even an enterprise that sells a commodity-like product or service can think of it as a bundle of ancillary services, delivery times, invoicing schedules, personalized reminders and updates, and other features that are rarely commodities. The key is for the enterprise to focus on customizing to each individual customer's needs. A teenager in California had gotten a text from her wireless phone service suggesting her parents could save money if she texted "4040" in an offer to switch her to a cell phone plan that was a better fit for her and the way she actually uses the service. She was so impressed she made a point of telling us about it. And of course, she told all her friends at school—and on Twitter and Facebook. The coverage, the hardware, the central customer service, and the "brand" all remained the same. But the customer experience, based on actual usage interaction with the customer—information not available to competitors—improved the customer relationship, increased loyalty and lifetime value of the customer, and positively influenced other customers as well.

When a customer teaches an enterprise what he wants or how he wants it, the customer and the enterprise are, in essence, *collaborating* on the sale of the

---

[12]Carrie Johnson and Elizabeth Davis, with Kate van Geldern, "Beyond Sales: Driving eBusiness with Engagement," May 15, 2009, Forrester Research, Inc., www.forrester.com, accessed September 1, 2010; Jeff Sands, "Account-Based Marketing," *B to B* 91, no. 6 (2006): 11; Ian Gordon, "Best Practices: Customer Relationship Management," *Ivey Business Journal* (November/December 2002): 1–5, reprint #9B02TF08; Ian Gordon, *Relationship Marketing* (New York: John Wiley & Sons, 1998).

[13]B. Joseph Pine II, Don Peppers, and Martha Rogers, Ph.D., "Do You Want to Keep Your Customers Forever?" in James H. Gilmore, and B. Joseph Pine II, eds., *Markets of One: Creating Customer-Unique Value through Mass Customization* (Boston: Harvard Business School Publishing, 2000).

product. The more the customer teaches the enterprise, the less likely the customer will want to leave. The key is to design products, services, and communications that customers *value*, and on which a customer and a marketer will have to collaborate for the customer to receive the product, service, or benefit.

> Enterprises that build Learning Relationships clear a wider path to customer profitability than companies that focus on price-driven transactions.

Enterprises that build Learning Relationships clear a wider path to customer profitability than companies that focus on price-driven transactions. They move from a make-to-forecast business model to a make-to-order model, as Dell Computer did when it created a company that reduced inventory levels by creating each computer after it was paid for. By focusing on gathering information about individual customers and using that information to customize communications, products, and services, enterprises can more accurately predict inventory and production levels. Fewer orders may be lost because mass customization can build the products on demand and thus make available to a given customer products that cannot be stocked ad infinitum. (We will discuss customization further in Chapter 10.) Inventoryless distribution from a made-to-order business model can prevent shortages caused in distribution channels as well as reduce inventory carrying costs. The result is fewer "opportunity" losses. Furthermore, efficient mass-customization operations can ship built-to-order custom products faster than competitors that have to customize products.[14]

> Learning Relationships have less to do with creating a fondness on the part of a customer for a particular product or brand and more to do with a company's capability to remember and deliver based on prior interactions with a customer.

Learning Relationships have less to do with creating a fondness on the part of a customer for a particular product or brand and more to do with a company's capability to remember and deliver based on prior interactions with a customer. An enterprise that engages in a Learning Relationship creates a *bond of value* for the customer, a reason for an individual customer or small groups of customers with similar needs to lose interest in dealing with a competitor, provided that the enterprise continues to deliver a product and service quality at a fair price and to remember to act on the customer's preferences and tastes.[15] Learning Relationships may also be based on an inherent trust between a customer and an enterprise. For example, a customer might divulge his credit card number to an organization, which records it and remembers it for future transactions. The customer trusts that the enterprise will keep his credit card number confidential. The enterprise makes it easier and faster for him to buy, because he no longer has to repeat his credit card number each time he makes a purchase. (In the next chapter, we'll learn more about the link between attitude and behavior in relationships.)

---

[14]Fabrizio Salvador, Pablo Martin de Holan, and Frank T. Pillar, "Cracking the Code of Mass Customization," *MIT Sloan Management Review* 50, no. 3 (Spring 2009): 71–78; David M. Anderson, *Agile Product Development for Mass Customization* (New York: McGraw-Hill Professional Book Group, 1997).

[15]B. Joseph Pine II, Don Peppers, and Martha Rogers, Ph.D., "Do You Want to Keep Your Customers Forever?" *Harvard Business Review* (March–April 1995), pp. 103–114.

The Technology Revolution and the Customer Revolution

During the last century, as enterprises sought to acquire as many customers as they possibly could, the local proprietor's influence over customer purchases decreased. Store owners or managers became little more than order takers, stocking their shelves with the goods that consumers would see advertised in the local newspaper or on television and radio. Mass-media advertising became a more effective way to publicize a product and generate transactions for a wide audience. But now technology has made it possible, and therefore competitively necessary, for enterprises to behave, once again, like small-town proprietors and deal with their customers individually, one customer at a time.

Customers Have Changed Too

The technological revolution has spawned another revolution, one led by the customers themselves, who now demand products just the way they want them and flawless customer service. Enterprises are realizing that they really know little or nothing about their individual customers and so are mobilizing to capture a clearer understanding of each customer's needs. Customers, meanwhile, want to be treated less like numbers and more like the individuals they are, with distinct, individual requirements and preferences. They are actively communicating these demands back to the enterprise. Where they would once bargain with a business, they now tell managers of brand retail chains what they are prepared to pay and specify how they want products designed, styled, assembled, delivered, and maintained. When it comes to ordering, consumers want to be treated with respect. The capability of an enterprise to remember customers and their logistical information not only makes ordering easier for customers but also lets them know that they are important. Computer applications that enable options such as "one-click," or express, ordering on the Web are creating the expectation that good online providers take the time to get to know customers as individuals so they can provide this higher level of service.[16]

Initial Assessment: Where Is a Firm on the Customer-Strategy Map?

Recognizing that two families of technology have mandated the competitive approach of building customer value by building customer relationships, we can map any organization—large or small, public or private, profit or nonprofit—by

---

[16]See Sucharita Mulpuru, "The State of Retailing Online 2009: Merchandising and Web Optimization," August 14, 2009, Forrester Research, Inc., available at www.forrester.com, accessed September 1, 2010; Dave Frankland, "The Intelligent Approach to Customer Intelligence" (October 16, 2009), Forrester Research, Inc., available at www.forrester.com, accessed September 1, 2010; Peppers & Rogers Group and Institute for the Future, "Shopping Behavior in the Age of Interactivity," Focus Group Summary (Spring 2000): 12–13, available at: www.1to1.com, accessed September 1, 2010.

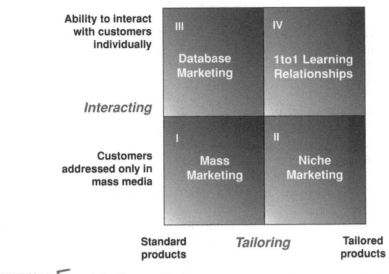

EXHIBIT 1A ⌈Enterprise Strategy Map⌉

Source: Don Peppers and Martha Rogers, Ph.D., *Enterprise One to One* (New York: Doubleday/ Currency, 1997).

the level of its capabilities in the arenas of *interacting* with customers and *tailoring* for them. A company would be rated high on the interactivity dimension if it knows the names of its individual customers and if it can send different messages to different customers and can remember the feedback from each one. A low rating would go to a company that doesn't know its customers' identities or does but continues to send the same message the same way to everybody. On the tailoring dimension, a firm would rate highly if it mass-customizes in lot sizes of one; it would rate low if it sells the same thing pretty much the same way to everybody. Based on its rating in these two dimensions, a company can be pinpointed on the Enterprise Strategy Map (see Exhibit 1A).

> *Quadrant I: Traditional Mass Marketing.* Companies that compete primarily on cost efficiencies based on economies of scale and low price. Companies in this quadrant are doomed to commoditization and price competition.
>
> *Quadrant II: Niche Marketing.* Companies that focus on target markets, or niches, and produce goods and services designed for those defined customer groups. This more strategic and targeted method of mass marketing still offers the same thing the same way to everyone, but for a small, relatively homogeneous group.
>
> *Quadrant III: Database Marketing.* Companies utilize database management to get better, more efficient use of their mailing lists and other customer information. Generally focused primarily on continuation of traditional strategies but at lower costs to serve.

(continued)

(Continued)

Quadrant IV: One-to-One Learning Relationships. Companies use data about customers to predict what each one needs next and then are able to treat different customers differently and increase mutual value with customers.

In Quadrants I through III, the focus is still primarily on the product to be sold, with an eye to finding customers for that product. In Quadrant IV, the direction of the strategy changes; the Quadrant IV company focuses on a customer and finds products for that customer.

To realize the highest possible return on the customer base, the goal of an enterprise will be to move up and to the right on the Enterprise Strategy Map.

- To move up on the Enterprise Strategy Map, an enterprise has to be able to recognize individual customers' names and addresses, to send different messages to different customers, and to remember the responses of each.
- To move to the right on the Enterprise Strategy Map, an enterprise has to be able to increase its production and logistics flexibility. The most flexible production would entail customizing and delivering individual products for individual customers. The least flexible would be mass-producing a standardized product or service for a large market. (We talk more about customization in Chapter 10.)

The customer revolution is part of the reason enterprises are committing themselves to keep and grow their most valuable customers. Today's consumers and businesses have become more sophisticated about shopping for their needs across **multiple channels**. The online channel, in particular, enables shoppers to locate the goods and services they desire quickly and at a price they are willing to pay, which forces enterprises to compete on value propositions other than lowest price.

Customer Retention and Enterprise Profitability

Enterprises strive to increase profitability without losing high-margin customers by increasing their customer retention rates or the percentage of customers who have met a specified number of repurchases over a finite period of time. A retained customer, however, is not necessarily a loyal customer. The customer may give business to a competing enterprise for many different reasons.

Royal Bank of Canada's 18 Million Loyal Customers

Organizations have accelerated their customer-focused strategies during the last few years, but managing customer relationships has been a business discipline for many years. Before the Industrial Revolution, and before mass production was born, merchants established their businesses around *keeping* customers.

Small towns typically had a general store, a local bank, and a barbershop. Each proprietor met and knew each one of his customers individually. The bank teller, for example, knew that Mr. Johnson cashed his paycheck each Friday afternoon. When Mr. Johnson came into the bank, the bank teller already had his cash ready for him in twenties and tens, just as he liked it. If Mr. Johnson unexpectedly stopped cashing his paycheck at the bank, the teller would wonder what had happened to him. In short, the bank depended on the relationship with the individual customer and how much the people who worked for the bank knew about that customer. The teller's memory in this example is akin to today's data warehouses, which can store millions of data points, transaction histories, and characteristics about customers. Personal memory enabled the teller to fulfill each customer's individual banking needs and, ultimately, to build a profitable relationship with each one. The more the teller knew about a customer, the more convenient he could make banking for that customer—and the more likely the customer would continue to use the bank.

But here's the important question 100 years later: Can an international financial services enterprise with 18 million customers[a] ever hope to deliver the same intimate customer service as a small-town bank? The attitude at Royal Bank of Canada (RBC), according to several of its executives, is "Absolutely."

Beginning in the 1990s, RBC developed superior computing and database power, along with sophisticated statistical programs, to analyze customer information and test specific actions it should take with specific customers. Only then could the bank's front-line personnel be able to deliver more effective personal contact and attention to individual customers.

To learn the most about its customers, RBC has undertaken an intense, ongoing statistical analysis of them. It is developing and refining the prototype for an algorithm to model the long-term lifetime values of its individual customers. Part of this effort includes a "client potential" model that measures how "growable" certain kinds of customers are to the bank. The bank also analyzes a customer's vulnerability to attrition and tries to flag the most vulnerable before they defect, in order to take preventive action in a focused, effective way.

To expand share of customer, Royal Bank also tries to predict statistically which additional services a customer might want to buy, and when. Royal Bank not only makes different offers to different customers, it also equips its sales and service people with detailed customer profiles. Thus, rather than providing a one-size-fits-all service, the bank's customer-contact people spend their time and energy making on-the-spot decisions based on each customer's individual situation and value. Note that this type of business practice not only benefits from individual customer interactions, it *requires* individual interactions to achieve the greatest success. In fact, RBC reports that the bank discovered it "could lift contributions and penetration rates by up to 10 percent by virtue of the contact alone."[b] (We look at Royal Bank's customer-profitability strategies more in Part Three.)

---

[a]Royal Bank of Canada, 2009 Annual Report, available at: http://www.rbc.com/investorrelations/pdf/ar_2009_e.pdf.
[b]Martha Rogers, Ph.D., "Royal Bank's 9 Million Loyal Customers," *Inside 1to1* (September 1999); available at: *www.1to1.com*, accessed September 1, 2010.

In 1990, Fred Reichheld and W. Earl Sasser analyzed the profit per customer in different service areas, categorized by the number of years that a customer had been with a particular enterprise.[17] in this groundbreaking study, they discovered that the longer a customer remains with an enterprise, the more profitable she becomes. Average profits from a first-year customer for the credit card industry was $30; for the industrial laundry industry, $144; for the industrial distribution industry, $45; and for the automobile servicing industry, $25.

Four factors contributed to the underlying profit growth:

1. *Profit derived from increased purchases.* Customers grow larger over time and need to purchase in greater quantities.
2. *Profit from reduced operating costs.* As customers become more experienced, they make fewer demands on the supplier and fewer mistakes when involved in the operational processes, thus contributing to greater productivity for the seller and for themselves.
3. *Profit from referrals to other customers.* Less needs to be spent on advertising and promotion due to word-of-mouth recommendations from satisfied customers.
4. *Profit from price premium.* New customers can benefit from introductory promotional discounts, while long-term customers are more likely to pay regular prices.

No matter what the industry, the longer an enterprise keeps a customer, the more value that customer can generate for shareholders.[18] Reichheld and Sasser found that for one auto service company, the expected profit from a fourth-year customer is more

> No matter what the industry, the longer an enterprise keeps a customer, the more value that customer can generate for shareholders.

than triple the profit that same customer generates in the first year. Other industries studied showed similar positive results (see Exhibit 1.4).

Enterprises that build stronger individual customer relationships enhance customer loyalty, as they are providing each customer with what he needs.[19] Loyalty

---

[17]Frederick F. Reichheld and W. Earl Sasser, Jr., "Zero Defections: Quality Comes to Services," *Harvard Business Review* 73 (September–October 1990): 59–75.

[18]Authors' note: This point is not without controversy. Some research has shown that in some instances—especially those where a business is very dependent on one or a very few customers, such as automotive parts makers—a long-term customer has the power to extract so many concessions that the company's margins are squeezed sometimes to the breaking point. But generally, academic research and real-world experience have demonstrated that if a company acquires the right customers, the longer those customers continue to do business, the more profitable they become—for many reasons, especially reduction in churn replacement costs, increasing value to the customer of the relationship, and positive word of mouth and social networking by a contented or delighted customer.

[19]Authors' note: Which comes first, loyalty or satisfaction? In a 2008 article, Mark Johnson, Eugene Sivadas, and Ellen Garbarino questioned the directionality of the link between satisfaction and loyalty, suggesting there is more evidence to indicate that loyalty leads to customer satisfaction rather than satisfaction (customer relationships) leading to loyalty; see "Customer Satisfaction, Perceived Risk, and Affective Commitment," *Journal of Services Marketing* 22, no. 4/5 (2008): 353–362. Also see an earlier article, which originally questioned some of our

EXHIBIT 1.4   Profit One Customer Generates over Time

INDUSTRY	Year 1	Year 2	Year 3	Year 4	Year 5
Credit Card	$30	$42	$44	$49	$55
Industrial Laundry	$144	$166	$192	$222	$256
Industrial Distribution	$45	$99	$123	$144	$168
Auto Servicing	$25	$35	$70	$88	$88

Source: Frederick F. Reichheld and W. Earl Sasser, Jr., "Zero Defections: Quality Comes to Services," *Harvard Business Review* 68:5 (September–October 1990), 106.

building requires the enterprise to emphasize the value of its products or services and to show that it is interested in building a relationship with the customer.[20] The enterprise realizes that it must build a stable customer base rather than concentrate on single sales.[21]

A customer-strategy firm will want to reduce customer defections because they result in the loss of investments the firm has made in creating and developing customer relationships. Customers are the lifeblood of any business. They are, literally, the only source of its revenue.[22] Loyal customers are more profitable because they likely buy more over time if they are satisfied. It costs less for the enterprise to serve retained customers over time because transactions with repeat customers become more routine. Loyal customers tend to refer other new customers to the enterprise, thereby creating new sources of revenue.[23] It stands to reason that if the central goal of a customer-strategy company is to increase the overall value of its customer base, then continuing its relationships with its most profitable customers will be high on its list of priorities.

On average, U.S. corporations tend to lose half their customers in five years, half their employees in four, and half their investors in less than one.[24] In his classic study on the subject, Fred Reichheld described a possible future in which the only business

---

assertions here: Ellen Garbarino and Mark Johnson, "The Different Roles of Satisfaction, Trust, and Commitment in Customer Relationships," *Journal of Marketing* 63 (April 1999): 70–87.

[20] Jill Griffin, *Customer Loyalty: How to Earn It, How to Keep It* (San Francisco, CA: Jossey-Bass, 1997).

[21] See Werner Reinartz and V. Kumar, "The Mismanagement of Customer Loyalty," *Harvard Business Review* (July 2002): 86–94, for a different view of the value of loyalty. Reinartz and Kumar's work shows that more loyal customers are not necessarily more profitable as a class, especially using their methodology of one moment in time; but we should also point out that in the case of an individual customer, the more loyalty and the greater share of customer achieved from one customer *over time*, the more valuable by definition that individual customer will become.

[22] Authors' note: Some may question the statement: "Customers are a company's only source of revenue." By definition, however, this is literally true. If a company sells products, for example, then the revenue does not come from the products; it comes from the customers who buy them. And if that same company *also* runs some ancillary businesses—say, renting out unused real estate space or spare capital—then those who make lease payments or interest payments are also customers.

[23] Phillip Kotler, *Kotler on Marketing* (New York: Free Press, 1999).

[24] Fred Reichheld, "Learning from Customer Defections," *Harvard Business Review* 74:2 (March–April 1996): 87–88.

relationships will be one-time, opportunistic transactions between virtual strangers.[25] However, he found that disloyalty could stunt corporate performance by 25 to 50 percent, sometimes more. In contrast, enterprises that concentrate on finding and keeping good customers, productive employees, and supportive investors continue to generate superior results. For this reason, the primary responsibility for customer retention or defection lies in the chief executive's office.

CRM ROI in Financial Services

Managing individual customer relationships has a profound effect on enhancing long-term customer loyalty, thereby increasing the enterprise's long-term profitability. Relationship strategies, for example, have a substantial effect on customer retention in the financial services sector. A study conducted in 2000 by Peppers & Rogers Group (with Roper Starch Worldwide) found that—looking at a group of "satisfied customers"—only 1 percent of consumers who rate their financial services provider high on relationship management say they are likely to switch away products. One-fourth of consumers (26 percent) who rate their primary financial services provider as low on relationship management attributes say they are likely to switch away one or more products during the next 12 months. The financial implications of these findings are staggering (see Exhibit 1B). Using a conservative average annual profitability per household for U.S. retail banks of $100, a reduction in attrition of 9 percent represents over $700 million in incremental profits for all U.S. households with accounts. If an individual financial institution with 20,000 customers can reduce attrition by 9 percentage points by providing excellent customer relationship management (e.g., recognizing returning customers, anticipating their needs, etc.), that institution can increase profits by $180,000. For a similar-size financial institution with an average household profitability of $500, the increase in profitability climbs to $900,000.

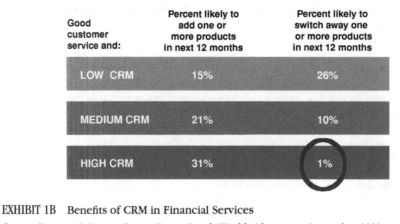

EXHIBIT 1B   Benefits of CRM in Financial Services

Source: Peppers & Rogers Group, Roper Starch Worldwide survey, September 2000.

---

[25] Reichheld, *The Loyalty Effect.*

Customer loyalty is closely associated with customer relationships and may, in certain cases, be directly related to the level of each customer's satisfaction over time.[26] According to James Barnes, satisfaction is tied to what the customer gets from dealing with a company as compared with what he has to commit to those dealings or interactions.[27] You'll read more about Dr. Barnes's views on satisfaction and relationships in the next chapter. For now, it's enough to know that the customer satisfaction issue is controversial—maybe even problematic. There are issues of relativity (Are laptop users just harder to satisfy than desktop users, or are they really less satisfied?) and skew (Is the satisfaction score the result of a bunch of people who are more or less satisfied, or a bimodal group whose members either love or hate the product?). Barnes believes that by increasing the value that the customer perceives in each interaction with the company, enterprises are more likely to increase customer satisfaction levels, leading to higher customer retention rates. When customers are retained because they enjoy the service they are receiving, they are more likely to become loyal customers. This loyalty leads to repeat buying and increased share of customer. (We will discuss more about the differences between attitudinal loyalty and behavioral loyalty, as well as ways to measure loyalty and retention, in the next chapter.)

Retaining customers is more beneficial to the enterprise for another reason: Acquiring new customers is costly. Consider the banking industry. Averaging across channels, banks can spend at least $200 to replace each customer who defects. So, if a bank has a clientele of 50,000 customers, and loses 5 percent of those customers each year, it would need to spend $500,000 or more each year simply to maintain its customer base.[28] Many Internet start-up companies, without any brand-name recognition, faced an early demise during the 2000–01 dot-com bubble bust, largely because they could not recoup the costs associated with acquiring new customers. The typical Internet "pure-play" spent an average of $82 to acquire one customer in 1999, a 95 percent increase over the $42 spent on average in 1998.[29] Much of that increase can be attributed to the dot-com companies' struggle to build brand awareness during 1999, which caused Web-based firms to increase offline advertising spending by an astounding 518 percent. Based on marketing costs related to their online business, in 1999, offline-based companies spent an average of $12 to acquire a new customer, down from $22 the previous year. Online firms spent an unsustainable 119 percent of their revenues on marketing in 1999. Even

---

[26]Authors' note: It is generally a challenge to agree on what we all mean by "customer satisfaction." Dave Power III has defined customer satisfaction as measuring the difference between what the customer expects to get and what he perceives he gets. More and more we are becoming capable of measuring what Pine and Gilmore call "customer sacrifice," which is the difference between what the customer wants exactly and what the customer settles for. B. Joseph Pine and James Gilmore, "Satisfaction, Sacrifice, Surprise: Three Small Steps Create One Giant Leap into the Experience Economy," *Strategy and Leadership* 28, no. 1 (January–February 2000): 18.

[27]James G. Barnes, *Secrets of Customer Relationship Management* (New York: McGraw-Hill, 2001).

[28]Banks' customer acquisition costs can vary wildly, between $150 and $3600, depending on the source, the product, and the channel, so $200 is a more-than-conservative figure.

[29]Boston Consulting Group and Shop.org, "The State of Online Retailing" (April 2000), available for purchase at www.shop.org/web/guest/research/store.

EXHIBIT 1.5   Customer Acquisition Costs
(Q1, 2009)

On the Web	$63
Over the phone	$122
In a branch/store	$146

Source: February 2009 Global eBusiness and
Channel Strategy Professional Online Survey, from
"2009 Cost of eBusiness Operations and Customer
Acquisition," Carrie Johnson and Elizabeth Davis
with Kate van Geldern, Forrester Research, Inc.,
available at www.forrester.com, accessed
September 1, 2010.

with the advantages of established brands, offline companies spent a still-high 36 percent.

The problem is simple arithmetic. Given the high cost of customer acquisition, a company can never realize any potential profit from most customers, especially if a customer leaves the franchise (see Exhibit 1.5). High levels of customer churn trouble all types of enterprises, not just those in the online and

> The problem is simple arithmetic. Given the high cost of customer acquisition, a company can never realize any potential profit from most customers, especially if a customer leaves the franchise.

wireless industries. The problem partly results from the way companies reward sales representatives: with scalable commissions and bonuses for acquiring the most customers. Fact is, many reps have little, if any, incentive for keeping and growing an established customer. In some cases, if a customer leaves, the sales representative can even be rewarded for bringing the same customer back again! Although it's always somebody's designated mission to get new customers, too many companies still don't have anybody responsible for making sure this or that particular customer sticks around or becomes profitable. Often a service company with high levels of churn needs to rethink not only how its reps engage in customer relationships but also how they are rewarded (or not) for nurturing those relationships and for increasing the long-term value to the enterprise of particular customers. Throughout this book, we will see that becoming a customer-value enterprise is difficult. It is a strategy that can never be handled by one particular department within the enterprise. Managing customer relationships is an ongoing process—one that requires the support and involvement of every functional area in the organization, from the upper echelons of management through production and finance, to each sales representative or contact-center operator. Indeed, customer-driven competition requires enterprises to integrate five principle business functions into their overall customer strategy:

1. *Financial custodianship of the customer base.* The customer-strategy enterprise treats the customer base as its primary *asset* and carefully manages the investment it makes in this asset, moving toward balancing the value of this asset to long-term as well as short-term success of the company.

2. *Production, logistics, and service delivery.* Enterprises must be capable of customizing their offerings to the needs and preferences of each individual customer. The Learning Relationship with a customer is useful only to the extent that interaction from the customer is actually incorporated in the way the enterprise behaves toward that customer.

3. *Marketing communications, customer service, and interaction.* Marketing communications and all forms of customer interaction and connectivity need to be combined into a unified function to ensure seamless individual customer dialogue.

4. *Sales distribution and channel management.* A difficult challenge is to transform a distribution system that was created to disseminate standardized products at uniform prices into one that delivers customized products at individualized prices. **Disintermediation** of the distribution network by leaping over the "middleman" is sometimes one solution to selling to individual customers.

5. *Organizational management strategy.* Enterprises must organize themselves internally by placing managers in charge of customers and customer relationships rather than of just products and programs.[30]

A customer-strategy enterprise seeks to create one centralized view of each customer across all business units. Every employee who interacts with a customer has to have real-time access to current information about that individual customer so that it is possible to pick up each conversation from where the last one left off. The goal is instant interactivity with the customer. This process can be achieved only through the complete and seamless integration of every enterprise business unit and process.

Summary

A customer-strategy enterprise seeks to identify what creates value for each customer and then to deliver that value to him. As other chapters in this book will demonstrate, a customer-value business strategy is a highly measurable process that can increase enterprise profitability and shareholder value. We also show that the foundation for growing a profitable customer-strategy enterprise lies in establishing stronger relationships with individual customers. Enterprises that foster relationships with individual customers pave a path to profitability. The challenge is to understand how to establish these critical relationships and how to optimize them for profits. Learning Relationships provide the framework for understanding how to build customer value.

Increasing the value of the customer base by focusing on customers individually and treating different customers differently will benefit the enterprise in many ways. But before we can delve into the intricacies of the business strategies behind this objective, and before we can review the CRM analytical tools and techniques required to carry out this strategy, we need to establish a foundation of knowledge

---

[30]Don Peppers and Martha Rogers, Ph.D., *Enterprise One to One* (New York: Doubleday Broadway Books, 1997). Also see Peppers and Rogers's *Rules to Break and Laws to Follow: How Your Business Can Beat the Crisis of Short-Termism* (Hoboken, NJ: John Wiley & Sons, 2008).

with respect to how enterprises have developed relationships with customers over the years. That is our goal for the next chapter.

Food for Thought

1. Understanding customers is not a new idea. Mass marketers have done it for years. But because they see everyone in a market as being alike—or at least everyone in a niche or a segment as being alike—they "understand" Customer A by asking 1,200 (or so) total strangers in a sample group from A's segment a few questions, then extrapolating the average results to the rest of the segment, including A. This is logical if all customers in a group are viewed as homogeneous. What will a company likely do differently in terms of understanding customers if it is able to see one customer at a time, remember what each customer tells the company, and treat different customers differently?
2. If retention is so much more profitable than acquisition, why have companies persisted for so long in spending more on getting new customers than keeping the ones they have? What would persuade them to change course?
3. How can we account for the upheaval in orientation from focusing on product profitability to focusing on customer profitability? If it's such a good idea, why didn't companies operate from the perspective of building customer value 50 years ago?
4. In the age of information (and connectivity), what will be happening to the four Ps, traditional advertising, and branding?
5. "The new interactive technologies are not enough to cement a relationship, because companies need to change their *behavior* toward a customer and not just their *communication*." Explain what this statement means. Do you agree or disagree?

Glossary

Analytical CRM   The strategic planning needed to build customer value, as well as the cultural, measurement, and organizational changes required to implement that strategy successfully.

Business model   How a company builds economic value.

Customer equity (CE)   The value to the firm of building a relationship with a customer, or the sum of the value of all current and future relationships with current and potential customers. Term can be applied to individual customers or groups of customers, or the entire customer base of a company.

Customer relationship management (CRM)   Making managerial decisions with the end goal of increasing the value of the customer base through better relationships with customers, usually on an individual basis.

Customer-strategy enterprise   An organization that builds its business model around increasing the value of the customer base. This term applies to companies that may be product oriented, operations focused, or customer intimate.

Demand chain As contrasted with the supply chain, refers to the demand from customers.

Data warehousing A process that captures, stores, and analyzes a single view of enterprise data to gain business insight for improved decision making.

Disintermediation Going directly to customers by skipping a usual distribution channel; for example, a manufacturer selling directly to consumers without a retailer.

Enterprise resource planning (ERP) The automation of a company's back-office management.

Interactive era *or* **era of connectivity** The current period in business and technological history, characterized by a dominance of interactive media rather than the one-way mass media more typical from 1910 to 1995. Also refers to a growing trend for businesses to encourage feedback from individual customers rather than relying solely on one-way messages directed at customers, and to participate with their customers in social networking.

Multiple channel An organization that sells through more than one distribution channel (e.g., the Web, a toll-free number, mail-order catalog). Can also refer to firms that interact with customers through more than one channel of communication (e.g., the Web, e-mail, fax, direct mail, phone).

Operational CRM The software installations and day-to-day procedural changes needed in a firm to build customer value.

Recognition The ability to recognize an individual customer as that customer through any shopping or buying channel, within any product purchase category, across locations or geographies, and over time. These individual data points are linked for a universally recognized, or identified, customer.

Relationship equity *See* Customer equity.

Sales force automation (SFA) Connecting the sales force to headquarters and to each other through computer portability, contact management, ordering software, and other mechanisms.

Share of customer (SOC) Each customer buys a certain amount of goods or services in various categories. If you are a vendor in one of those categories—say, cars—then the share of customer you have with any one customer is the percentage of that customer's business you get in that category. If a family owns four cars, and two of them are your brands, then you have a 50 percent share of garage for cars. But you may also be interested in your SOC for service and repairs and your share of wallet for your automotive credit card. SOC refers to the share of each customer's business you get, contrasted with market share, which is your percentage of the total sales in your category.

Social networking The ability of individuals to connect instantly with each other often and easily online in groups. For business, it's about using technology to initiate and develop relationships into connected groups (networks), usually forming around a specific goal or interest.

Switching cost The cost, in time, effort, emotion, or money, to a business customer or end-user consumer of switching to a firm's competitor.

Value of the customer base *See* Customer equity.

CHAPTER 2

The Thinking behind
Customer Relationships

Things have never been more like they are today in history.

—Dwight D. Eisenhower

So far, our discussion of customer relationships, customer experience, and customer value has shown how businesses are undergoing a vast cultural shift—transforming from the mass marketing, product-siloed thinking of the Industrial Age to the customer-based culture of the Information Age, where the primary goal is building relationships with individual customers who become measurably more valuable to the enterprise. In this new business era, managing individual customer relationships means an organization will use the knowledge gained from these relationships to improve the quality of the overall customer experience. Consequently, it is incumbent on the enterprise to understand what constitutes a relationship, how relationships are formed, and how they can be strengthened or weakened. Many different perspectives have been developed about what comprises customer relationships and how businesses can profit from them. So before we can move forward with our discussion of becoming a customer-focused enterprise, we need to explore a couple of views besides our own about relationships.

By the early 2000s, many companies acknowledged the importance of building "relationships" with customers—of improving customer experience, taking the customer's point of view, and taking steps to measure and manage customer value. In many cases, companies that had been product-oriented changed their philosophy, their culture, their metrics, and even their organizational structure to put customers at the forefront.

Why Do Companies Work at Being "Customer-Centric"?

Becoming customer-centric has not been easy, and not without controversy. Some believed that employees matter more than customers, since without great, engaged employees, an enterprise will have a hard time building strong customer relationships and building customer equity. Others continued to focus on cash flow and on making sure that strong product managers were held responsible for product promotion, distribution, and profitability. Ad agencies continued to tend "brand promise." But while all of these are important to a successful business, a growing number of firms have recognized that three things are true about a company's customers. Because of these truths, a company stands its best chance of success when it focuses on increasing customer value through outstanding customer experiences and relationships.

1. *Customers are scarce.* There are successful organizations that do not have "products," but there is no such thing as a successful firm that doesn't have "customers." And despite the fact that the world has billions of people, only so many of them will ever want a particular company's offering. That company's ability to find them, win them, get as much business from them as possible, and keep them for a long time will be the determining factor in how much it can ever grow the size of its business. There are only so many hungry people, right now, within reach of a neighborhood pizzeria, and each of those people can cook for themselves, or go to a competitor, or start a diet today and not eat at all. Customers are scarcer than products, services, new ideas, or channels. For all but those companies in real financial trouble, customers are even scarcer than capital itself. There is no secondary market for customers. They can't be borrowed at the bank and paid back with interest. Once a company's leaders realize this fact, they may make decisions differently, as we see in Part Three.

2. *Customers are the sole source of all a company's revenue.* Products don't pay a company any money, ever. Neither do brands or services, or employees, or marketing programs, or stores, or factories. Only customers generate revenue for a business—the customers the business has today and the customers it will have in the future. All the other stuff is important to a business only to the extent that it contributes to generating more revenue from customers. Thus the goal will not just be to create value from each product or channel or even the greatest return on the investment of money, but instead to make sure the company creates the greatest value from each of its customers.

3. *Customers create value in two ways.* Today, they are generating profit this quarter (or not), and—also today—the experience they are having with a particular company's product, its brand, its contact center, or any of the rest of what it is selling is also causing them to become more (or less) likely to do more business with the company in the future, to become more (or less) likely to recommend it to friends, to think kindly of it (or not) when they need something else in its category. It's interesting that nearly every company is very, very good at measuring and managing one way that customers create value: Companies know how much they spent making money from customers this quarter and what their revenue was from customers this quarter—since that's the total of the cost and revenue on the quarterly books. But many companies are content not to know the second part of this equation: They don't know, don't measure, and don't manage what is happening to underlying customer equity while the current numbers are falling into place. That means understanding a company's Return

on Customer (ROC) is as important as understanding the return on investment (ROI).[1] We talk a lot more about ROC in Chapter 11.[2] *marg in profit*

ROI answers the question: How much value does your company create for the money it uses?

ROC answers the question: How much value does your company create for the customers it uses?

If customers are scarce, if they create all the revenue for a company, and if the value they do create is measurable and manageable in the short term and the long term, as of today, then it's natural for companies to want to understand and remember what customers need and to meet those needs better than a competitor that doesn't know the same things about the customers. Customer information provides a very powerful competitive advantage. Companies want to use this information to provide a positive experience for customers and possibly to engage customers in a "relationship" that enables the company to provide better and better service.[3]

What Characterizes a Relationship?

Merriam-Webster defines *relationship* as "a state of affairs existing between those having relations or dealings."[4] Because we are talking specifically about relationships between businesses and their customers, it is important that we agree on a few of the elements that make up a genuine relationship. And while dictionary definitions are not bad as starting points, the most important issue for us to consider is how well our own definition of *relationship* helps companies succeed in the "customer dimension" of competition. So, rather than settle for a few words from a dictionary, let's list some of the distinct qualities that should characterize a relationship between an enterprise and a customer.

---

[1]Janamitra Devan, Anna Kristina Millan, and Pranav Shirke published a research finding in "Balancing Short-and Long-Term Performance," *McKinsey Quarterly,* no. 1 (2005): 31–33. They examined 266 companies and grouped them into four groups of High versus Low Short-Term versus Long-Term performance over a 20-year period. They discovered that those companies that balanced strong long- and short-term performance had higher Total Shareholder Return, lasted longer than their more mediocre competitors, enjoyed three years longer incumbency from chief executives on average, and had less volatility in stock prices. Companies with strong short-term performance but weak long-term performance enjoyed less volatile stock prices but came out poorly on other measures. The most successful companies were seen to have "instilled a long-term mind-set."

[2]Don Peppers and Martha Rogers, Ph.D., *Rules to Break and Laws to Follow: How Your Business Can Beat the Crisis of Short-Termism* (Hoboken, NJ: John Wiley & Sons, 2008). Also see Don Peppers and Martha Rogers Ph.D., *Return on Customer: Creating Maximum Value from Your Scarcest Resource* (New York: Currency/Doubleday, 2005).

[3]Peppers and Rogers, *Rules to Break and Laws to Follow: How Your Business Can Beat the Crisis of Short-Termism.*

[4]relationship: Merriam Webster Online Dictionary, January 5, 2010, www.merriam-webster.com/dictionary/relationship.

First, a relationship implies **mutuality.** In order for any "state of affairs" to be considered a relationship, both parties have to participate in and be aware of the existence of the relationship. This means that relationships must inherently be two-way in nature. This might seem like common sense. You can't have a relationship with another person if she doesn't have a relationship with you, right? But it's a very important distinction for parsing out what does and doesn't constitute relationship-building activities with customers. Can a person have a genuine relationship with a brand? Well, it doesn't happen just because the customer herself likes the brand and buys it repeatedly. A customer can have a great deal of *affection* for a brand all by herself but, by our definition, a *relationship* between the customer and the brand can be said to exist only if the brand (i.e., the enterprise behind the brand) is also aware of the individual customer's existence, creating a neodefinition with an interesting new twist for the term *brand awareness*.

Continuing Roles for Mass Media and Branding

- Communicate to nonusers who have not yet raised their hands.
- Build image and brand identity.
- Establish a brand position with nonusers to help users make a statement about their own image.

Second, relationships are driven by *interaction.* When two parties interact, they exchange information, and this information exchange is a central engine for building on the relationship. Information exchange, of course, also implies mutuality. But interactions don't have to take place by phone or in person or on the Web. An interaction takes place when a customer buys a product from the company that sells it. Every interaction adds to the total information content possible in the relationship.

This point leads to the third characteristic of a relationship: It is *iterative* in nature. That is, since both parties are interacting mutually, the interactions themselves build up a history, over time—a context. This context gives a relationship's future interactions greater and greater efficiency, because every successive interaction represents an iteration on all the previous ones that have gone before it. The more you communicate with any one person, the less you need to say the next time around to get your point across. One practical implication of the iterative nature of a customer relationship is that it generates a convenience benefit to the customer for continuing the relationship. Amazon.com remembers your book preferences, your address, and your credit card number, based on your previous interactions with it. To purchase your next book from Amazon.com, you need only find the book and click on it. If you've bought enough books already at Amazon.com, you might not even need to find the next one—the company can do a pretty good job of finding it for you. The richer the context of any customer relationship, the more difficult it will be for the customer to re-create it elsewhere, and so the more loyal the customer is likely to be. (We find that Amazon.com recommends all of the new books we write to each of us—not surprising, since they're all very relevant!)

Another characteristic of a customer relationship is that it will be driven by an *ongoing benefit* to both parties. Convenience is one type of benefit for customers, but not the only one. Participating in a relationship will involve a cost in money, time, or effort, and no customer will engage for long in any relationship if there is not enough continuing benefit to offset this cost. However, precisely because of the context of the relationship and its continuing benefit to both parties, each party in a relationship has an incentive to recover from mistakes. This is because the future value that each party expects from the continued relationship can easily outweigh the current cost of remedying an error or problem.

Characteristics of a Genuine Business Relationship

- Mutual
- Interactive
- Iterative
- Provides ongoing benefit to both parties
- Requires a change in behavior for both parties
- Unique
- Requires—and produces—trust

Relationships also require a *change in behavior* on the part of both parties—the enterprise as well as the customer—in order to continue. After all, what drives the ongoing benefit of a relationship is not only its context—its history of interactions, developed over time—but also the fact that each party's current and future actions appropriately reflect that historical context. This is an important characteristic to note separately, because companies sometimes mistakenly believe that interactions with customers need only involve routine, outbound communications, delivered the same way to every customer. But unless the enterprise's actions toward a particular customer are somehow tailored to reflect that customer's own input, there will be no ongoing benefit for the customer, and as a result the customer might not elect to continue the relationship.

Yet another characteristic of a relationship, so obvious it might not seem worth mentioning, is *uniqueness.* Every relationship is different. Relationships are constituted with individuals, not with populations. As a result, an enterprise that seeks to engage its customers in relationships must be prepared to participate in different interactions, remember different histories, and engage in different behaviors toward different customers.

Finally, the ultimate requirement and product of a successful, continuing relationship is *trust.* Trust is a quality worth a book all by itself,[5] but fundamentally what we are talking about is the commonsense proposition that if customers develop a relationship with an enterprise, they tend more and more to trust the enterprise to act in their own interest. Trust and affection and satisfaction are all related feelings on the part of a customer toward a company with which he has a relationship. They

---

[5]See Stephen M. R. Covey and Rebecca R. Merrill, *The Speed of Trust: The One Thing that Changes Everything* (New York: Free Press, 2006); Chris Brogan and Julien Smith, *Trust Agents: Using the Web to Build Influence, Improve Reputation, and Earn Trust* (Hoboken, NJ: John Wiley & Sons, 2009); and Charles H. Green, *Trust-Based Selling: Using Customer Focus and Collaboration to Build Long-Term Relationships* (New York: McGraw-Hill, 2006).

constitute the more emotional elements of a relationship; but for an enterprise to acknowledge and use these elements profitably, it must be able to reconcile its own culture and behavior with the requirement of generating and sustaining the trust of a customer. (For more on this issue, see Chapters 3 and 9.)

Fifteen years ago, business professors Jag Sheth and Atul Parvatiyar predicted that companies are "likely to undertake efforts to institutionalize the relationship with consumers—that is, to create a corporate bonding instead of a bonding between a front-line salesperson and consumer alone."[6]

In the next section, Duke University professor Julie Edell Britton offers a perspective on relationships that outlines the way relationship theorists have addressed the issue.

Thinking about Relationship Theory

Julie Edell Britton
Associate Professor, Fuqua School of Business, Duke University

> *Special thanks to Josh Rose for his contribution on this topic for the first edition of this book.*

Personal and business relationships have many similarities. In a marriage, for example, the two individuals agree to exchange only with one another as long as the balance of trade is favorable to both and greater than what can be derived from the greater market.[a] The benefits of a successful marriage include companionship, intimacy, personal growth, shared finances, and shared household responsibilities and must be perceived to provide value to both relationship members if it is to continue. Buyer-seller relationships, whether between an enterprise and an individual consumer (B2C) or between enterprises (B2B), are made up of similar components and follow a similar development process. In this section we will review these relationship components in more detail and provide a way of thinking about relationships that will help us explore the ways businesses build relationships with customers.

The process of relationship formation between individuals provides a fitting analogy to the formation process of business relationships between buyers (customers) and sellers (enterprises). Relationships between individuals are typically formed through a systematic, multistage process. While the process might vary, the main building blocks are the same: identification, establishing rapport, information gathering, initial interaction, and intensification of interaction through commitment. For the relationship to succeed, certain elements or guidelines must be followed. For example, proper identification requires a basic understanding of the type of individual one is seeking to meet. Establishing rapport

---

[6]Jagdish N. Sheth and Atul Parvatiyar, "Relationship Marketing in Consumer Markets: Antecedents and Consequences," *Journal of the Academy of Marketing Science* 23, no. 4 (1995): 265. See also Atul Parvatiyar and Jagdish N. Sheth, eds., *Handbook of Relationship Marketing* (Thousand Oaks, CA: Sage, 1999).

requires adaptation to the other party's interaction style. Information gathering has to be relevant and provide insight into the likes and needs of the other member.

Types of Buyer-Seller Exchanges

Not all buyer-seller exchanges can be characterized as relationships. Some are merely transactional. Many enterprises have only just begun to think about their customers as parties with whom they might want to have a sustained relationship (and vice versa). In organizations focused on the sales of products, each transaction was thought of as a discrete transaction with no correlation to any prior or future transactions. Thus, exchanges can be viewed as existing on a continuum between discrete transactions on one end and **relational** or collaborative exchanges on the other.

The concept of a discrete exchange involves money on the one side, an easily measured commodity on the other, and the complete absence of any relational element. It is characterized by very limited communication and narrow content. In its abstract form, it is an instantaneous exchange between anonymous parties who will very likely never interact in the future. Economically, the transaction is a zero-sum game. (See the discussion about mass marketers in Chapter 1.) The more one party receives, the less remains for the other party. As an example of a discrete transaction, imagine an out-of-town consumer passing through a town stopping to purchase five gallons of unbranded gasoline for $14 paid in cash to an independent station. This transaction is discrete. There have been no previous transactions, there is no way to know who made this one, and no future ones are anticipated.[b] As the exchange moves to the right in the continuum (see Exhibit 2A), it has the potential to become more relational. Perhaps a customer traveling across the country repeatedly purchases the same brand of gasoline. To the customer, then, these transactions are related. When she buys this brand, she expects that it will provide the same level of performance as the last tank of gasoline provided, even though the price, service, location, and other factors may vary. Whether these transactions are seen as discrete transactions to the gasoline seller or as having a connection depends on whether that seller can relate the transactions over time to this particular customer. If the customer pays for each of these transactions with her gasoline-company credit card, then the company has the potential to recognize the connection between the transactions and determine whether she is someone with whom it would like to build a relationship. At this point, the customer is visible and identifiable as a *customer*, not just a series of discrete, independent transactions.

Discrete (transactional) $\longleftarrow$ ------------------------------- $\longrightarrow$ Relational (collaborative)

EXHIBIT 2A   Transaction/Relationship Continuum

(continued)

(Continued)

Relational exchanges transpire over time with each transaction acting as a link in a chain having a history and an anticipated future. In contrast to the situation where there is no relational content in the discrete exchange, participants in relational exchanges share information and hope to improve on the quality of the exchange for both the customer and the enterprise. This often means that the nature of the deliverable becomes less obvious, necessitating deeper discussion, preplanning, and, most important, trust. Especially in uncertain environments, cooperation is required to meet the needs of both parties.

The significance of the difference between the characteristics of exchanges on either end of the continuum lies in the extent to which relational exchanges contribute to product or service differentiation that create incentives to remain in the relationship, thus creating a competitive advantage. As a relationship deepens, it becomes increasingly difficult for either party to see how other parties could provide the same degree of benefit as received by the existing relationship.

An alternative mapping of the realm of buyer-seller relationships is represented by the matrix in Exhibit 2B. Here each party's interest in developing the relationship forms a dimension. Some relationships are not symmetric; the two parties view the relationship differently. If a seller has a great deal of interest in developing a relationship but the buyer does not, we might see repeated attempts by the seller to extract information from the consumer, but the consumer failing to respond. Conversely, when the buyer has a great interest in developing a relationship with the supplier, she might contact the enterprise and provide them feedback about how they could better meet her needs, but the enterprise is uninterested in using that information to customize its offerings to her. Note that the continuum described in Exhibit 2A exists along the main diagonal of the Exhibit 2B matrix. Purely discrete exchanges exist when neither buyer nor seller is interested in developing a relationship, while strong relational exchanges exist only when both parties have a great deal of interest.

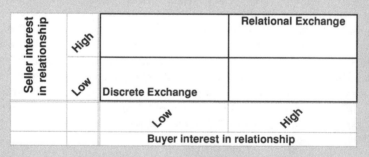

EXHIBIT 2B   Relationship Development Process

Relationship Development Process

An understanding of how relationships develop provides insight into how to improve and to maximize the benefits from the relationship. In their classic inventory of relationship development, Dwyer, Shurr, and Oh[c] suggest that B2B relationships evolve through five general phases:

1. *Awareness*. In this pre-exchange phase, the parties recognize each other as viable relationship partners. While the parties work to demonstrate their attractiveness via signaling or self-promotion, there is no interaction in this phase.

2. *Exploration*. This phase is a testing period for the relationship. Potential relationship members engage in search and trial activities in an effort to determine goal compatibility, integrity, and performance capabilities of the other. Communication takes place and is used to convey wants, issues, and priorities. Initial negotiations could signal the willingness of the potential relationship members to be flexible and work toward mutual value creation. The lack of perceived willingness to negotiate could lead to termination of the relationship development process. In similar fashion, participant fairness is also evaluated. Demonstrating commitment to achieving joint goals and fair exercise of power will provide momentum to advance the relationship. Although this phase is an important one, it is also a very fragile one. Minimal commitments or investments by the parties have been made, which allows for easy termination of the building process.

3. *Expansion*. Positive outcomes of the exploratory phase provide evidence of the other relationship member's worthiness and thus the impetus to advance to the expansion phase. This phase is characterized by an increase in the derived relationship benefits and in interdependence and risk taking. At the same time, participants are testing and reaffirming perceptions developed during the previous exploration phase.

4. *Commitment*. In this phase, relationship members have achieved a level of value and satisfaction that enables them to comfortably make a commitment to the relationship and, by doing so, significantly lower their focus on alternative relationships. Three measurable criteria denote commitments:[d]
   - *Inputs*. Both parties provide a high level of inputs to the relationship.
   - *Consistency*. Inputs quality is reliable and allows accurate prediction of future relationship outcomes.
   - *Durability*. Exchange benefits are identifiable and can be expected to continue in future exchanges.

5. *Dissolution*. Dissolution that leads to relationship disengagement can occur at any stage in the development process. In contrast to relationship development, which requires painstaking bilateral effort, dissolution can be easy and can be initiated unilaterally. Dissolution occurs when a participant evaluates the value of the relationship and determines that the cost of continuation outweighs the benefits.

Throughout the relationship development process, certain elements act as enhancing agents. *Communication,* defined as formal or informal sharing of information through two-way interchange, positively acts to strengthen the relationship. Although not specifically required, especially given recent

(continued)

(Continued)

advancements in personalized electronic communication, personal contact can lead to increased commitment and to development of customer trust.[e] (The role of trust in buyer-seller relationships is significant and will be described further later in this section.) *Cooperation,* defined as coordinated actions taken by both relationship members to achieve mutually desirable outcomes, enhances the development process by increasing the communication component, prolonging the exchange, and providing a sense of future reciprocity. While conflicts can have negative impacts on the relationship, effective *conflict resolution* can have a positive influence. Reaching mutually agreeable compromises without the use of formal procedures increases the sense of trust and commitment of the relationship members.

Finally, the Learning Relationship process,[f] in which enterprises and customers engage in a series of interactions that serve as a continuous feedback loop, allows each party to learn about the other (needs, preferences, responsiveness) while at the same time learning about itself. The Learning Relationship process can be employed at every phase of the development process just outlined. Viewing each phase as an opportunity for learning via a feedback loop allows the relationship to develop faster and to a deeper level. Exhibit 2C provides a conceptual representation of the ideas put forth in this section.

Development Enhancers:

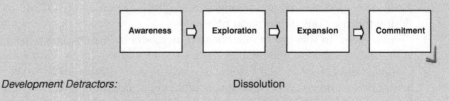

EXHIBIT 2C   Learning Relationship Process

Relationship Building Blocks

The previous section provided an overview of the relationship development process. Here we provide a more granular perspective by analyzing the six most important building blocks, or key mediating variables, that are required for relationships to form. Relational building blocks are not to be confused with relational contingencies (i.e., reasons why relationships form), such as necessity, efficiency, and stability.[g] Rather, the building blocks uniformly influence the resulting nature of the relationship, irrespective of the originating motive.

Exhibit 2D provides a representation of the building blocks as they influence relationships. The position of the individual building blocks on the discrete/relational continuum is representative of its relative importance to relationship formation. For example, "Trust" is located closest to the relational side since it is more important to the relationship-forming process than "Symmetry," which is located closest to the discrete side. The box with the curved bottom

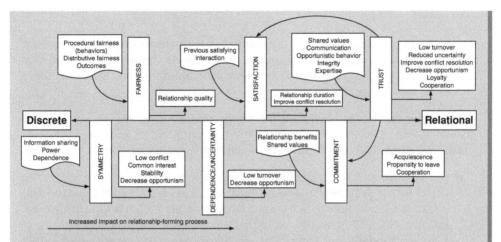

EXHIBIT 2D   Relationship-Forming Building Blocks

side preceding each building block contains the antecedents, or conditions, for the block. The rectangle that follows each block shows the aspects of the relationship it impacts.

TRUST   *Trust* is defined as one party's confidence in the other relationship member's reliability, durability, and integrity and the belief that its actions are in the best interest of and will produce positive outcomes for the trusting party. As evidenced by the abundance of literature on the importance of trust in the formation of relationships, the presence of trust is central to successful relationships.[h] As an illustration, consider the situation where a consumer pays for a one-year subscription to a magazine. The magazine has not yet been produced, and its content and quality are subjective and unknown at the time of payment. Trust that the service provider will live up to its obligation is what allows the exchange to proceed. [We discuss more about trust in the Learning Relationship process in Chapter 3.] The benefits of a relationship based on trust are significant and are described next.

- *Cooperation.* Trust serves to mitigate feelings of uncertainty and risk, thus acting to engender increased cooperation between relationship members.[i] By increasing the level of cooperation, members learn that joint efforts lead to outcomes that exceed those achieved individually.
- *Commitment.* Also a relationship building block that entails vulnerability, commitment will be formed only with trustworthy parties.[j]
- *Relationship duration.* Trust encourages relationship members to work to preserve the relationship and to resist the temptation to take short-term gains and or act opportunistically. Trust of a seller firm is positively related to the likelihood that the buyer will engage in future business, therefore contributing to increasing the duration of the relationship.[k]
- *Quality.* Trusting parties are more inclined to receive and use information from trusted partners and in turn to derive greater benefit from the

(continued)

(Continued)

information.[l] Furthermore, the existence of trust allows disputes or conflicts to be resolved in an efficient and amicable way. In the absence of trust, disputes are perceived as signals of future difficulties and usually bring about relationship termination.

Trust is clearly very beneficial and important to those seeking to establish a relationship. However, becoming a trusted party is not easy and requires concerted effort. The next factors are the main contributors to formation of trust.

- *Shared values.* Values are fundamental to the development of trust. The extent to which parties in a relationship share beliefs regarding appropriate behaviors, goals, and policies influences the ability to develop trust in one another. After all, it would be difficult to trust a party whose ideas about what is important and appropriate are inconsistent with one's own.
- *Interdependence.* Dependence on another party implies vulnerability. To reduce the associated risk, parties will seek out relationships with others who can be trusted.
- *Quality communication.* Open and frequent communication, whether formal or informal, serves to align expectations, resolve disputes, and alleviate uncertainty associated with exchanges. For communication to result in formation of trust, it must be frequent and of high quality; in other words, it must be relevant, timely, and reliable. While past positive communication leads to trust, trust—in turn—leads to better communication. To establish and maintain relationships, it is important that organizations use the information to shape appropriate responses to customer needs.[m]
- *Nonopportunistic behavior.* Behaving opportunistically is fundamental to discrete exchanges. After all, there is only one shot at maximizing benefits. However, long-term relationships based on trust require that participating parties are not solely self-serving and act to increase shared long-term benefits. John Deighton suggests that if customers lose trust in firms and believe that their data are used for purposes of exploiting them, they will keep their data private or distort the data.[n]

COMMITMENT   The second building block in the relationship formation process is commitment. *Commitment* is the belief that the importance of a relationship with another is so significant as to warrant maximum effort at maintaining it. Like trust, commitment is viewed as extremely important in the formation of customer relationships. As Morgan and Hunt state in their seminal article, "The Commitment-Trust Theory of Relationship Marketing," "The presence of relationship commitment and relationship trust is central to successful relationship marketing. . . . Commitment and trust lead directly to cooperative behaviors that are conducive to relationship marketing success."[o]

Generally, there are two different types of commitment: *calculative* and *affective*. *Calculative commitment* results from an economic analysis of the costs and benefits of making a commitment. For example, the decision to commit resources to an enterprise to develop a new technology might result from the lack of other potential relationship members in the market or from the inability to obtain the necessary services/products at a lower price outside the relationship. Calculative commitment is related negatively to trust and is based on calculated cost and benefits. It is thus not conducive to a long-term successful relationship. In contrast, *affective commitment* is based on the continuation of the relationship not just because of what its economic benefits are in the short term but because each of the parties feels an emotional or psychological attachment toward the other relationship member. Affective commitment is positively related to trust and thus supports relationship benefits much longer in duration, decreased opportunism, and the willingness to resolve conflicts in a way that is amicable to both parties.

Since commitment entails vulnerability, parties seek relationships with those who are trustworthy. Hence trust is a strong contributor to commitment. Along similar lines, communication and open exchange of information can be used to create a positive attitude toward relationship members and also can be used to reinforce the benefits of the relationship. Relationship members who demonstrate the ability to deliver superior benefits will be highly valued by others, who will gladly commit to a relationship. Finally, relationship members who are in a position of power who do not revert to coercive tactics, even when they can, will be perceived positively, thus increasing the likelihood of long-term commitment to a relationship.

SATISFACTION   The third relationship building block is satisfaction. The overall role that customer satisfaction plays in the formation of relationships is intuitive: A dissatisfied customer generally will seek to replace the supplier with an alternative, if it is available. The converse is also intuitive: Satisfied customers generally are more inclined to remain in the relationship. While it is accepted that there exists a positive relationship between customer satisfaction and customer loyalty, the relationship between customer satisfaction and the duration of the relationship is more complex.

As enterprises seek effective ways to have relationships with customers, many have turned to the traditional tool of customer satisfaction monitoring. Customer satisfaction tools have long been used to understand customer perceptions of products and services, but now they are also being used to monitor customer relationships. Mithas, Krishnan, and Fornell found that firms with customer relationship management (CRM) applications are positively associated with an improvement in customer satisfaction.[p] By contacting customers directly by telephone, enterprises can demonstrate to their customers that they are interested in them as customers and value their input. Enterprises strive to uncover the reasons for customer dissatisfaction without alienating or losing customers entirely. Automobile repair services companies, in fact, that call their customers for a customer satisfaction survey have experienced an increase in repeat business as a result.[q]

The duration of the buyer-seller relationship depends on the customer's subjective assessment of the value of a relationship that is continuously updated based on perceptions of previous experiences.[r] Customers tend to weigh prior satisfying experiences more heavily than they do new experiences. This fact

(continued)

(Continued)

is consistent with the relationship benefits of trust and commitment identified earlier, and it has some interesting managerial implications. It suggests that new customers are far more vulnerable to relationship mishaps than customers with longer satisfying relationships. Companies must focus more closely on customer satisfaction during the early stages of the relationship. Early mishaps have a higher probability of resulting in a defection than if the same problems occurred after a satisfying relationship had been more firmly established. We might think of this as the basic principle of first impressions.

Customers also weigh negative experiences, or losses, more heavily than they weigh positive experiences, or gains. Companies attempt to entice customers to stay longer by attempting to improve existing satisfaction levels. This is known as the Satisfaction Trap,[s] in which companies become preoccupied with satisfaction ratings scores at the expense of attention to relationship duration. Focusing on improving the customer experience (i.e., more gains) should not come at the expense of assuring the lack of customer mishaps. In fact, customers with longer satisfying relationships tend to evaluate recent negative encounters against previous levels of satisfaction. Thus, for longer-duration customers, emphasis should be placed on preventing negative encounters.

UNCERTAINTY AND DEPENDENCE   Two related variables that influence the relationship formation process are the degree of uncertainty in the environment and the degree to which relationship members are dependent on each other. Dependence as a contingency for relationship formation is rooted in the scarcity of resources (product, services, etc.). Relationships are formed when each relationship member has access to resources essential to the other.[t] By working together, relationship members secure better access to essential resources than working independently. Uncertainty impacts the availability of resources, thus creating the dependence. By forging relationships, parties are able to gain better control over their environment in order to reduce uncertainty. In B2B relationships, "resources" takes on a broader meaning to include access to markets, creating market entry barriers, and strategic positioning.

Relationships based on uncertainty and/or dependence tend to be less stable as they focus on current existing conditions. Changes in external conditions, availability of resources, and environmental uncertainty could modify the original parameters that once justified the formation of the relationship, such that the resulting relationship no longer provides mutual benefits. In addition, as dependence is not a strategically desirable situation, relationship members will constantly seek relationships that provide them with more favorable positioning. Thus, while dependence plays a role in long-term relationship development, it is not sufficient to maintain the relationship. An element of trust also is required for a dependence-based relationship to have a long-term orientation.[u]

FAIRNESS   The fifth relationship building block is fairness. While *relationship quality* is a somewhat subjective term, it is plausible to measure relationship quality based on the levels of trust, commitment, and ability to effectively resolve conflicts. The higher the levels of these contributors, the greater the quality of the relationship. High-quality relationships result in lower levels of conflict, greater expected continuity, and greater willingness of members to invest in the relationship and thus lead to more successful long-term relationships. Research has shown that the perception of relationship fairness also enhances relationship quality.[v]

There are two distinct types of relationship fairness: *distributive* and *procedural*. **Distributive fairness** is based on the perception of relationship rewards versus relationship burdens or obligations and is therefore more focused on relationship outcomes. **Procedural fairness** is based on the perception that procedures and processes used are fair and is therefore more focused on behaviors, independent of the outcome. Viewed in the context of a relationship, distributive fairness is influenced by a combination of elements that may or may not be under the control of the relationship members. It is entirely possible that a relationship fails not because of the actions of either the buyer or seller, but rather because of an act of nature, like a new baby, or a job transfer that necessitates a move. In contrast, procedural fairness is influenced largely by elements under the control of the relationship members, such as notifying the buyer if she is on the wrong subscription plan rather than allowing her to continue to pay a higher price than necessary. CRM activities create the potential for differential treatment of customers who interact with a firm. Reitz provides examples where airline customers do not perceive differential treatment to be unfair.[w]

Of the two types, procedural fairness has a much stronger effect on the development of trust and commitment and is therefore a stronger contributor to the development of an effective long-term relationship. Procedurally fair-exchange systems have a more enduring quality and are more likely to constitute the basis for a sustainable relationship. It is especially important that the stronger relationship member develops processes and procedures that other relationship members judge to be fair, in order to sustain the relationship in times of disagreements.

SYMMETRY   The final relationship building block to be discussed is symmetry. **Relationship symmetry** refers to the degree of equality between relationship members. It is a function of many relationship elements, including information sharing, dependence, and power. **Symmetric relationships** are more stable than asymmetric ones. This is because asymmetry undermines the balance of power and creates motivation for the stronger party to take advantage of the weaker party, especially in difficult economic conditions.[x] Commonality of interests is strongest when the relationship is symmetric. Symmetry discourages the development and expression of conflict because the relationship members have equivalent stakes in the relationship. In contrast, parties in **asymmetric relationships** are more likely to have diverging interests and greater motivation to engage in conflict; thus such relationships are more dysfunctional and less stable.[y]

Asymmetric dependence is a specific type of symmetry. Dependence describes the (lack of) options that one may have to replace the relationship member, or a measure of one party's need to maintain the relationship in order

(continued)

(Continued)

to achieve its goals. Symmetric interdependence exists when the relationship members are equally dependent on each other. As the difference in the relative dependence between the members increases, the relationship becomes more asymmetric and less stable. From the perspective of the less dependent, or stronger, member, structural impediments preventing opportunistic behavior are reduced. The more dependent member may feel vulnerable, seek to better his relationship position, and be constantly looking for a more favorable relationship.

To increase relationship quality, relationship members should seek to lower the level of asymmetry and increase the degree of interdependence. Achieving perfect symmetry in a relationship is extremely difficult and fairly rare. Reducing the degree of asymmetry or modifying the relative dependence of relationship members is a more achievable goal. The more vulnerable member can reduce dependence by developing additional relationships with others. Alternatively, the more vulnerable member can increase dependence by increasing her value to the relationship. Of the two approaches, the more dependent member should seek the latter. Striving for autonomy by seeking alternatives may reduce the level of asymmetry, but it will come at the expense of relationship benefits.[z]

Finally, it should be noted that trust and commitment can develop in asymmetric relationships, if the vulnerable party is treated fairly and with respect. While the more powerful relationship member might be tempted to act unfairly by imposing self-serving procedures, avoiding these behaviors can lead to a more lasting relationship that provides greater benefits.[aa]

---

[a]M. McCall, *Courtship as Social Exchange: Some Historical Comparisons* (New York: John Wiley & Sons, 1966).

[b]Ibid.

[c]Ibid.

[d]Ibid.

[e]K. Ruther, L. Moorman, and J. Lemmink, "Antecedents of Commitment and Trust in Customer-Supplier Relationships in High Technology Markets," *Industrial Marketing Management* 30, no. 3 (2001), 271–286.

[f]B. Joseph Pine, Don Peppers, and Martha Rogers, Ph.D., "Do You Want to Keep Your Customers Forever?" *Harvard Business Review* 73, no. 2 (March-April 1995), 103–114.

[g]C. Oliver, "Determinants of Interorganizational Relationships: Integration and Future Direction," *Academy of Management Review* 15, no. 2 (1990), 241–265.

[h]See the classic introduction by C. Moorman, R. Deshpande, and G. Zaltman, "Factors Affecting Trust in Market Research Relations," *Journal of Marketing* 57, no. 1 (1993), 81–101.

[i]B. Squire, P. D. Cousins, and S. Brown, "Cooperation and Knowledge Transfer within Buyer-Supplier Relationships: The Moderating Properties of Trust, Relationship Duration, and Supplier Performance," *British Journal of Management* 20 (2009): 461–477; T. Dagger, P. Danaher, and B. J. Gibbs, "How Often Versus How Long: The Interplay of Contact Frequency and Relationship Duration in Customer-Reported Service and Relationship Strength," *Journal of Service Research* 11 (May 2009): 371–388; R. Morgan and S. Hunt, "The Commitment-Trust Theory of Relationship Marketing," *Journal of Marketing* 58, no. 3 (1994), 20–38.

[j]Dagger, Danaher, and Gibbs, "How Often Versus How Long: The Interplay of Contact Frequency and Relationship Duration in Customer-Reported Service and Relationship Strength," *Journal of Service Research* 11 (May 2009): 371–388; R. Morgan and S. Hunt, "The Commitment-Trust Theory of Relationship Marketing," Journal of Marketing (1994).

[k]Dagger, Danaher, and Gibbs, "How Often Versus How Long"; P. Doney and J. Cannon, "An Examination of the Nature of Trust in Buyer-Seller Relationships," *Journal of Marketing* 61, no. 2 (1997), 35–51.

[l]Squire, Cousins, and Brown, "Cooperation and Knowledge Transfer within Buyer-Supplier Relationships"; Dagger, Danaher, and Gibbs, "How Often Versus How Long"; Moorman, Deshpande, and Zaltman, "Factors Affecting Trust in Market Research Relations."

[m]S. Jayachandran, S. Sharma, P. Kaufman, and P. Raman, "The Role of Relational Information Processes and Technology Use in Customer Relationship Management," *Journal of Marketing* 69, no. 4 (2005), 177–192.

[n]J. Deighton, "Privacy and Customer Management," *Customer Management* (2005).

[o]Morgan and Hunt, "The Commitment-Trust Theory of Relationship Marketing."

[p]S. Mithas, M.S. Krishnan, and C. Fornell, "Why Do Customer Relationship Management Applications Affect Customer Satisfaction?" *Journal of Marketing* 69, no. 4 (2005), 201–209.

[q]C. Gengler and P. Popkowski Leszczyc, "Using Customer Satisfaction Research for Relationship Marketing: A Direct Marketing Approach," *Journal of Direct Marketing* 11, no. 4 (1997), 36–41.

[r]Ibid.

[s]F. Reichheld, *The Loyalty Effect: The Hidden Force behind Growth, Profits, and Lasting Value* (Boston, MA: Harvard Business School Press, 1996).

[t]Squire, Cousins, and Brown, "Cooperation and Knowledge Transfer within Buyer-Supplier Relationships"; W. Keep, S. Hollander, and R. Dickinson, "Forces Impinging on Long-Term Business-to-Business Relationships in the United States: An Historical Perspective," *Journal of Marketing* 62, no. 2 (1998), 31–45.

[u]S. Ganesan, "Determinants in Long-Term Orientation in Buyer-Seller Relationships," *Journal of Marketing* 58, no. 2 (1994), 1–19.

[v]N. Kumar, L. Scheer, and J. Steenkamp, "The Effects of Supplier Fairness on Vulnerable Resellers," *Journal of Marketing Research* 32, no. 1 (1995), 54–65.

[w]B. Reitz, "Worst to Favorite: The Inside Story of Continental Airline's Business Turnaround," *Customer Management* (2005).

[x]E. Anderson and B. Weitz, "Determinants of Continuity in Conventional Industrial Channel Dyads," *Marketing Science* 8, no. 4 (1989), 310–323.

[y]Ibid.

[z]C. Lai, "The Use of Influence Strategies in Interdependent Relationship [sic]: The Moderating Role of Shared Norms and Values," *Industrial Marketing Management* 38 (May 2009): 426–432; Kumar, Scheer, and Steenkamp, "The Effects of Perceived Interdependence on Dealer Attitudes."

[aa]V. Belaya, "Measuring Asymmetrical Power Distribution in Supply Chain Networks: What Is the Appropriate Method?" *Journal of Relationship Marketing* 8 (2009): 165–193.

Customer orientation is powerful in theory but, some say, troubled in practice. In some industries, customer satisfaction rates in the United States fall while complaints, boycotts, and other consumer discontent rise. Some say there has been a decline in the fundamentals of relationship building among enterprise executives who are more concerned with increasing quarterly profits for their own sake than establishing closer ties to profitable customers. Every aspect of customer relationship management and managing customer relationships and experiences is affected by the firm's understanding of relationships. Enterprises must examine and fully comprehend the basic foundations of relationships in general, and the basic principles of the Learning Relationship in particular, before embarking on a CRM or customer experience initiative.

Views on relationships and their role in business vary, but all provide a relevant perspective to building a framework for CRM. Jim Barnes says that relationships between enterprises and their customers can exist at four different levels:[7]

1. *Intimate* relationships are characterized as personal and friendly and generally involve the disclosure of personal information. Such relationships may involve physical touch, as in the relationship between doctors and patients or hairstylists and clients.
2. *Face-to-face* customer relationships may or may not require the customer to reveal personal information. Such relationships often occur in a retail store.
3. *Distant* relationships involve less frequent interactions and might occur over the telephone, online, or through videoconferencing.
4. *No-contact* relationships rarely or never require a customer to interact with an enterprise directly. Customers typically interact with a distributor or agent, as in the case of buying a favorite brand of soda at a supermarket.

We should also acknowledge that a company may build a "relationship" with a customer that the customer has no emotional interest in. By learning from a customer, or a small group of customers with similar needs and behaviors, the company may be able to offer the right product at the right time and provide convenience to a customer who may not be emotionally attached to the product or company but does more and more business with it because it's easier to continue with the current provider than to switch. In many other cases, of course, the "relationship" is specifically enjoyed by the customer—at the extreme by the Harley-Davidson customer who tattoos the company's brand on his bicep.

We have discussed the foundation of relationship theory and the benefits of getting, keeping, and growing customers, and, so far, the discussion has included concepts that foster an often-emotional involvement between the customer and the enterprise. The Learning Relationship is a highly personal experience for the customer that ensures that it is always in the customer's self-interest to remain with the enterprise with which he first developed the relationship. We believe this may go beyond emotional attachment and beyond a customer's favoritism for any enterprise. It may or may not be derived from some sense of obligation or duty. Instead, many scholars believe that by establishing a Learning Relationship, the customer-focused enterprise increases customer retention by making loyalty more beneficial for the customer than nonloyalty.

Here we present a different view of customer relationships: Although many disagree, Jim Barnes believes relationships work only when the customer acknowledges that we are having one.

---

[7]James G. Barnes, *Secrets of Customer Relationship Management* (New York: McGraw-Hill, 2001).

Cultivating the Customer Connection: A Framework for Understanding Customer Relationships

James G. Barnes

Professor Emeritus, Faculty of Business Administration, Memorial University of Newfoundland; CEO, BMAI-Strategy

The establishment of relationships is a fundamental part of human life. Most people have many different relationships, some of which have lasted for many years, and some of which are closer or more intimate than others. When we ask people about their relationships, most often they speak of those that are most important to them, namely relationships with family, friends, neighbors, classmates, or the people with whom they work. Some of these relationships are very important to us, and we would feel a tremendous sense of loss if the people involved were no longer around. We trust them, we rely on them, and they play a central role in our lives.

What is really interesting is that people typically use very similar language when they talk about businesses with which they deal or brands that they buy regularly. Can customers establish a long-lasting relationship with a brand of ketchup, a coffee shop, or a hotel chain? I suspect the folks at Heinz, Starbucks, and Marriott would unanimously agree that they can and do. We can all think of brands that we and our families have been using for years or even for generations. We all have favorite restaurants, a regular pub or sports bar, a deli where Julie behind the counter knows exactly how thick to slice our pastrami, and a hairdresser to whom we have been going for years.

Customers Are People Too

At the end of the day, customers are people, and they bring to the role of "customer" the same set of needs and emotions that they exhibit in other facets of their daily lives. If a business is interested in establishing genuine relationships with its customers, relationships that will last for many years, then it must understand the psychology that underlies the establishment of relationships in general.

Customers do not deliberately set out to establish relationships with other people or with brands of shampoo, cologne, or beer. Relationships evolve over time, and some evolve to the point where there is an extremely strong connection with the company or brand. Relationships take time to develop and must be nurtured. But once they are established, customers feel a genuine, long-lasting sense of loyalty to the company. Most customers want to deal with businesses and use brands that they can trust and rely on, organizations with which they feel comfortable and that treat them fairly and honestly. Unless business executives understand how customers develop such relationships and what customers get from them, they will not begin to understand how to build a solid customer connection.

(continued)

(Continued)

It is only in recent years that business has begun to focus its attention on the development of customer relationships and to acknowledge that customers do indeed develop strong emotional connections to certain companies and brands. Most businesses now understand the potential long-term value of a loyal customer. It is clearly more productive for a business to encourage its customers to come back and do business with it over and over again rather than having to deal with **customer churn**, where new customers must be recruited in a constant struggle to replace those who are leaving. One of the objectives, therefore, in building customer relationships is to reduce customer turnover by increasing retention.

Retention Is Not a Relationship

But customer retention is not the same as a customer relationship. Retention, meaning that customers continue to buy from a company over time—they have been retained—is essentially a behavioral concept. There are many ways in which businesses succeed in encouraging customers to return, none of which leads to the establishment of customer relationships. Retention is behavioral loyalty; relationships imply the existence of **emotional loyalty**.

A relationship in its simplest form and as understood by customers is based on feelings and emotions. It is not behavioral, although there are behavioral outcomes of customers developing solid relationships with firms: customers go back again and again; they spend more money there; they buy more items at full price rather than waiting for the sales; and they recommend the company or brand to their friends and associates. But such behavior is the *result* of the relationship and not the relationship itself.

There is, however, a tendency in some businesses to mistake behavior for loyalty. Just because customers buy a large percentage of their items in a particular product or service category from a certain company or visit on a regular basis does not mean that they are loyal or that a relationship exists. It is possible for a company to develop a high level of "behavioral loyalty" among its customers while having relatively little emotional loyalty. For example, many customers will buy a large percentage of their groceries from a supermarket that is close to their homes. They shop there every week and they have been doing so for years. When asked why they are "loyal," customers will point to factors such as convenience of location, 24-hour opening, large parking lots, speedy checkouts, one-stop shopping, and so on. All of these reasons relate to functional factors that drive repeat buying. These customers may be described as "functionally loyal" because the factors that drive their behavior are largely functional.

Among the functionally loyal, there is a notable absence of any sense of attachment to the company. There is little or no emotional connection. If these behaviorally loyal regular shoppers were to move across town or to a new city, they would likely seek out an equally convenient supermarket for most of their grocery shopping. This form of loyalty, therefore, is extremely vulnerable; there is no relationship from the customers' perspective. As soon as they see a better deal or greater convenience elsewhere, they're gone.

Contrast this with other customers who shop regularly at the same supermarket, often driving past two or three competing supermarkets to get there. When asked why they shop where they do, they will say that they are known there, employees recognize them, they feel comfortable shopping there, they have come to know the cashiers and engage in conversation with them, or they go there with friends for coffee. There is among this group of customers evidence of *emotional* loyalty, a connection between the company and its customers, a lasting bond that is grounded not in functional factors but in genuine emotions. When these customers move to a new location, they seek out a branch of *their* supermarket.

Let's Have a Relationship with Her

Customer relationships develop over time, just as do interpersonal relationships. No company or brand can simply decide that it will establish a relationship with a particular group of customers and then go out and do it, because it is the customers themselves who will decide whether a relationship can develop. Relationships are, by definition, two-sided in nature; they must be mutually felt. We all know what happens to relationships where only one of the parties is getting any benefit. Therefore, in order to attract customers to the point where a relationship might be said to exist, a company must genuinely care about its customers. For a customer relationship strategy to work, a company must establish a focus on the customer, a commitment to genuinely understanding the customer, and a culture in which every employee believes that the customer comes first. In short, the company needs to have a customer strategy, one focused on ensuring that everything the company does is oriented toward building solid customer relationships.[a]

Think for a moment about those businesses and brands to which you and your family return again and again. You probably wouldn't do so unless you were receiving some unique form of value that you simply can't get anywhere else. You feel special when you walk through the door. The employees know you there and treat you like a friend. They engage in conversation with you and go out of their way to help you find the things you need. You trust their advice. You know you can rely on them to deliver on time and offer you quality products at a reasonable price. Actually, you may even admit that you may be paying a slightly higher price than you could get from a competing business nearby, but it is worth it to you because of the other, less tangible things that you derive from the relationship.

By thinking about the relationships that you, your friends, and family have already established with businesses, we begin to reveal some of the essential characteristics of genuine customer relationships. You don't go back to your favorite businesses only because they have the lowest price in town or because they have a frequent-shopper program. You go back primarily because of how you are treated, the quality of service provided, the people with whom you deal, and ultimately how you are made to feel.

(continued)

(Continued)

I make an important distinction between *genuine* customer relationships and those that are artificial or synthetic. Some companies, through the use of marketing tools such as frequent-shopper or frequent-flyer programs, have succeeded in creating high levels of behavioral loyalty, driven largely by the rewards that customers obtain by giving a company a large share of their business. Do such programs succeed in driving an increased share of wallet and repeat buying? Yes, in many cases they do. But such attempts to build customer relationships are not based on a strategy to create an emotional connection but rather see relationships from the perspective of the company and the benefits that it will derive from increased frequency of purchase.

At the end of the day, it is the customer who understands what a customer relationship involves. One of the difficulties that some businesses have in establishing long-lasting customer relationships stems from the fact that many simply don't understand their customers.

The Need for Insight

One of the fundamental needs that underlies the establishment of successful customer relationships is for companies to obtain the kind of insight necessary to understand what is actually a very complex concept. They must understand customers, and they must understand the nature of the genuine relationship. If we are to truly understand the emotional connection between customers and brands, then we need to understand how customers live their daily lives and where various companies and brands fit in. What role do they play? What does Heinz ketchup, or Starbucks Coffee, or Chanel No. 5 really enable a customer to do? What does The Home Depot, or State Farm, or Wells Fargo help customers accomplish?

To obtain customer insight, we must understand customers as people. We need to understand what they need to get done in their daily lives, what their goals and ambitions are, and how they define success. By knowing such things, a business can understand how it can play a role in allowing customers to accomplish the things that they want to get done and to achieve success. However, insight gathering also involves understanding the things that customers wish to avoid or that they dread happening. Understanding those things that customers do not want to happen allows a business to step in and help customers to prevent them. Understanding the complexities of consumer behavior and how customers develop lasting relationships requires deep thinking on the part of marketing practitioners.[b]

Companies that are successful in building genuine relationships with customers are rewarded well into the future. Not only do they experience lower rates of customer turnover, but their customers stay with them longer, give them a higher share of spend, buy more items at full price, reduce their tendency to shop around, and recommend the company or brand to their friends and family members. Think again about those companies and brands that you couldn't do without and how you deal with them. That's how genuinely loyal customers treat their favorite stores and brands.

A Framework for Understanding: The 5 Es of Customer Relationships

This section represents a framework that I have developed that helps me think more deeply about the concept of customer relationships and the factors that are important in allowing companies and brands to connect more closely with their customers. I've labeled it the 5 Es of Customer Relationships: environment, expectations, emotions, experience, and engagement.

CUSTOMER ENVIRONMENT   If a company is to be successful in establishing genuine relationships with a large number of its customers, it must first have a deep understanding of the *environment* in which the customer operates. We are dealing here with the notion of customer context; everything that customers do happens within a wider context. Every day, customers have things they must get done; they face challenges and opportunities. There are things that they are looking forward to and things that they dread. Companies, if they are to understand how to build relationships, must first understand what is going on in the personal and business lives of their customers: What are their goals; what are they trying to accomplish; what are they looking forward to? Only by knowing such things can a company play the role of partner or facilitator in helping its customers get those things done.

Many years ago, Harvard professor Theodore Levitt famously observed that no customer ever went out to buy a quarter-inch drill bit. What the customer needed, of course, was a quarter-inch hole. This was Levitt's insightful way of saying that all products and services are bought not for their own inherent features but for what they enable their buyers to do; people need solutions to what they are facing. More recently, Christiansen, Cook, and Hall have written about the job that we hire products to do,[c] suggesting that the customer at the supermarket this afternoon doesn't really want or need those raspberries he is buying; what he really wants is an attractive dessert to serve his guests at dinner. Every product and service the customer buys represents a means to an end; he has something that he needs to get done. It is no accident that The Home Depot adopted as its slogan "You can do it; we can help."

Even more recently, Ariely and Norton have written of "conceptual consumption," arguing that customers buy products and services not only for the outcomes they provide but even more for the feelings or emotions those products enable them to enjoy or avoid.[d] Therefore, we buy digital cameras not only to enable us to have photographs to show friends or to post on Facebook or to put up on Picasa but, more important, to enshrine memories and to facilitate sharing. Similarly, we don't buy paint merely to obtain a fresh new look in the living room but to hear the "oohs" and "aahs" of friends and neighbors.

To be able to facilitate success by enabling customers to achieve the things they need to get done, to receive the accolades of friends, or to look good in the eyes of people who are important to them, companies must understand the context in which customers are operating. Companies that succeed in helping customers achieve the praises of guests for a dessert well made or the favorable comments of visiting parents-in-law when they enter the recently

(continued)

(Continued)

decorated living room will be well on their way to establishing genuine customer relationships.

CUSTOMER EXPECTATIONS   It probably goes without saying that, in order to be successful in impressing customers, companies should set out to at least meet customer *expectations*. The company that falls short of meeting expectations can be confident that customers are already moving on to deal with one of its competitors. Meeting customer expectations is obviously of great importance, but it is not sufficient to move customers toward the establishment of genuine relationships.

Research has shown that customers have considerable difficulty verbalizing what they expect from the companies with which they deal.[e] My experience is that customer expectations are, for the most part, entirely predictable and bounded by the customer's experience in dealing with similar companies or brands. For example, if we were to ask a customer who is planning a business trip to Chicago what she expects of the airline that will be taking her there, she is likely to comment that she expects to be able to buy her ticket online, to check in from her office, to be able to check her suitcase efficiently, to have her flight depart and arrive on time, and to find her suitcase intact on the luggage carousel when she arrives.

In short, the customer expects the airline to do exactly what well-run airlines are expected to do, nothing more. The customer will be satisfied if the airline delivers on those things that she expects of it and will likely give it a 9 or even a 10 in a post-flight customer satisfaction survey if they get all of these things right. But satisfaction does not make a relationship. Satisfaction is a short-term state driven mainly by predictable, functional aspects of the company's value proposition. Other research indicates that even the most satisfied customers remain receptive to competitive offers and are prone to defect.[f] A customer relationship that has achieved only satisfaction is a vulnerable one.

> A customer relationship that has achieved only satisfaction is a vulnerable one.

What our airline customer is *not* expecting may be just as important as what she expects of the airline. She is clearly not expecting a flight attendant to retrieve the BlackBerry that she has left in the seat pocket and to bring it to her as she stands at the baggage carousel. These are the kind of events that customers don't think of when they are asked to state their expectations. Yet by delivering the BlackBerry, the flight attendant has exceeded subconscious expectations and created a state of customer delight. That episode then becomes the basis for storytelling; you know, the ones that always begin "You'll never believe what happened to me yesterday . . ."

From the company's perspective, it is as important to understand what customers are not expecting as it is to know what they are expecting. Ultimately, customers are not expecting to be surprised. Creating customer surprise, by doing the unexpected, is an important part of building genuine, emotion-based customer relationships. As Lehrer recently observed, "Nothing focuses the mind like surprise."[g] Companies should set out to surprise and delight their customers more often.

CUSTOMER EMOTIONS Relationships are essentially *emotional* constructs. When asked about their most important relationships, most people will make mention of other people with whom they are close: family members, friends, neighbors, workmates, our Saturday morning foursome, the girls on the bowling team. In other words, people generally use the word *relationships* when discussing interpersonal connections. But customers also build emotional connections with companies and brands—ultimately reaching a stage where they would miss them if they were no longer available.

In attempting to build genuine customer relationships, companies must, therefore, set out to reduce negative emotions and strengthen positive ones. It is useful, in this regard, to think about a hierarchy of emotions, ranging from relatively weak emotions to particularly strong ones. On the negative side, some fairly mild emotions are merely irritants. For example, a customer may experience confusion, annoyance, or frustration in dealing with a certain business. These feelings may not lead the customer to decide never to deal with the company again but, if left unaddressed, may lead to a situation where the customer simply walks away, or at least Twitters negatively. If a company continues to frustrate, disappoint, let down, or ignore its customers, ultimately more strongly felt negative emotions, such as anger, hatred, and disgust, will emerge and any hope of developing a long-term relationship will be lost.

However, positive customer relationships that last for years or even decades begin with some relatively weak positive emotions, such as comfort level, friendliness, and affection. Ultimately, the strongest and longest-lasting customer relationships are characterized by deep positive emotions that are regularly referred to by loyal customers, including love, pride, and respect. In research projects that I have conducted with a major telecom company and an international grocery chain, we found more than 70 percent of customers agreed with the statement, "I am proud to be a _____ customer." We regularly hear shoppers comment, "I just love shopping there."

CUSTOMER EXPERIENCE There has been a lot of attention paid in recent years to the customer *experience*, and it represents an important contribution to an expanded view of how relationships develop.[h] Simply put, a succession of positive experiences is likely, over time, to develop into a genuine relationship. However, inconsistency in the delivery of the customer experience—or, worse, a series of negative experiences—will lead to little hope of solid relationships being developed. Unfortunately, many businesses seem to take a narrow view of what customer experience entails. As a result, they fail to realize the potential that exists to create long-lasting customer relationships through delivering impressive customer experiences.

Some writers on the subject of customer experience suggest that it is something that can be orchestrated or that must involve some form of entertainment.[i]

(continued)

(Continued)

But *every* interaction with a company or brand is an experience, whether it involves face-to-face contact with employees, telephone interaction with a call center, visits to the Web site, or actual use of the product. My research suggests that companies need to think about customer experiences at four levels.

First, and this is the view of customer experience that is most often discussed in business, companies must be *easy to do business with*. This assumes that customer experience is all about access and convenience; how easy do we make it for customers to order from us, to get served in our stores, to speak with someone on the telephone? Being "easy to deal with" means returning their calls, delivering when we said we would, and generally not putting barriers in the way of good service.

Second, I believe that an important part of the customer experience involves *interaction with employees*. Many customer experiences involve meeting or talking with employees or others who represent the company or brand. This interpersonal interaction is central to the development of a positive customer relationship. Indeed, many customer relationships are based on the customer's relationship with individual employees—think travel agents, mechanics, and hairdressers. This view that the customer experience is delivered or co-created by employees suggests implications for human resources departments and is one of the main reasons why HR must be an active partner in the development of a customer relationship strategy.

Third, we must realize that the customer experience does not end when the customer makes the purchase—there is *"product in use" experience*. Many services, for example, are continuously delivered. The customer, therefore, has an ongoing relationship with banks, cable and telecom companies, Internet service providers, and others. In the case of tangible products, many are used for months if not years. The satisfaction and enjoyment that the customer obtains from "product in use" is important in determining whether a long-term relationship will develop. So, an important part of the customer experience involves delivery, helping set up the product, helping the customer obtain maximum value from it, fixing it when it breaks, and offering advice on how to use it properly. Often this seems to be forgotten by businesses. I hear, for example, from customers of auto dealers who do not receive any communication for the entire length of the four-year lease. Customers feel let down, disappointed, or abandoned as a result. Companies need to have a "keep in touch" strategy, making occasional meaningful contact with customers as they use their products and services.

Finally, businesses need to think about the customer *experiences that they can create or enhance*. This represents a proactive side of customer experience delivery. Think about the kinds of experiences that companies create by organizing workshops, inviting customers to lectures, or providing them with valuable information. Think, for example, how The Home Depot helps the "all-thumbs" father build that tree house for his son. Think also about how Avis might make my long weekend in the Napa Valley truly memorable. Think how Canon might help me get a "You took that!!??!!" reaction when my friends see the framed black-and-white photo in my living room.

CUSTOMER ENGAGEMENT   Recently, customer relationship strategists have begun to consider the importance of creating customer *engagement*.[j] This concept builds on the notion that, by involving customers more in the production and delivery of products and services, we can create a higher level of commitment. How, for example, can we get customers to become partners, to become involved in the co-creation of products and services, to become actively engaged in the delivery of desired solutions and outcomes? This is, I believe, an important part of the success that IKEA has enjoyed around the world. Not only does this much-admired company offer reasonably priced furniture of reasonable quality, but the customer puts part of himself into every item through his involvement in its assembly.

Dell allows its customers to build their own laptop computers. Customers go to The Home Depot to learn how to lay ceramic tile or to build shelves in the kids' closet. Committed customers of the Running Room train together with other novice runners for their first 10K race. In all cases, the customer puts something of herself into the creation of the value proposition by partnering with the business to get something done. An engaged and involved customer is more likely to spread positive word-of-mouth, to create communities for the business, leading to a co-dependency that eventually becomes a solid, genuine relationship.

Overview

The most successful customer relationships are those grounded in an emotional attachment. Companies must accept the fact that, if they hope to see customers coming back again and again and sing their praises to friends and family members, they must pay attention to how they make their customers feel. To really impress their customers, they will also have to invest in customer insight so they can truly understand what those customers need to get done and how they need companies and brands to help them. Customer relationship building should not be seen as the sole or even the principal responsibility of the marketing department; in fact, building customer loyalty must be accepted as the responsibility of every employee.

---

[a]J. G. Barnes, *Build Your Customer Strategy: A Guide to Creating Profitable Customer Relationships* (Hoboken, NJ: John Wiley & Sons, 2006).
[b]Gerald Zaltman and Lindsay Zaltman, *Marketing Metaphoria: What Deep Metaphors Reveal about the Minds of Consumers* (Boston: Harvard Business Press, 2008).
[c]C. M. Christensen, S. Cook, and T. Hall, "Marketing Malpractice: The Cause and the Cure," *Harvard Business Review* 83 (December 2005): 74–83; C. M. Christensen, S. D. Anthony, G. Berstell, and D. Nitterhouse, "Finding the Right Job for Your Product," *MIT Sloan Management Review* 48, no. 3 (2007): 38–47.
[d]D. Ariely and M. I. Norton, "Conceptual Consumption," *Annual Review of Psychology* 60 (2009): 475–499.
[e]V. A. Zeithaml, L. L. Berry, and A. Parasuraman, "The Nature and Determinants of Customer Expectations of Service," *Journal of the Academy of Marketing Science* 21, no. 1 (1993): 1–12.

(continued)

(*Continued*)

[f]R. L. Oliver, *Satisfaction: A Behavioral Perspective On the Customer*, 2nd ed. (Armonk, NY: M. E. Sharpe, 2009).

[g]Johan Lehrer, *How We Decide* (Boston: Houghton Mifflin Harcourt, 2009).

[h]See, for example, Christopher Meyer and Andre Schwager, "Understanding Customer Experience," *Harvard Business Review* 85, no. 2 (February 2007): 117–126.

[i]B. Joseph Pine II and James H. Gilmore, *The Experience Economy: Work Is Theatre and Every Business a Stage* (Boston: Harvard Business School Press, 1999).

[j]J. H. Fleming and J. Asplund, *Human Sigma: Managing the Employee-Customer Encounter* (New York: Gallup Press, 2007).

Customer Loyalty: Is It an Attitude? Or a Behavior?

Definitions of customer loyalty usually take one of two different directions: attitudinal or behavioral. Although each of these directions is valid, when used separately, they have different implications and lead to very different prescriptions for businesses. The most helpful way for businesses to approach the issue of improving customer loyalty is to rely on both these definitions simultaneously.

The attitudinal definition of loyalty implies that the loyalty of a customer is in the customer's state of mind. By this definition, a customer is "loyal" to a brand or a company if the customer has a positive, preferential attitude toward it. He likes the company, its products, its services, or its brands, and he therefore prefers to buy from it, rather than from the company's competitors. In purely economic terms, the attitudinal definition of customer loyalty would mean that someone who is willing to pay a premium for Brand A over Brand B, even when the products they represent are virtually equivalent, should be considered "loyal" to Brand A. But the emphasis is on "willingness" rather than on actual behavior per se. In terms of attitudes, then, increasing a customer's loyalty is virtually equivalent to increasing the customer's preference for the brand. It is closely tied to customer satisfaction, and any company wanting to increase loyalty, in attitudinal terms, will concentrate on improving its product, its image, its service, or other elements of the customer experience, relative to its competitors.

The behavioral definition of loyalty, however, relies on a customer's actual conduct, regardless of the attitudes or preferences that underlie that conduct. By this definition, a customer should be considered "loyal" to a company simply because they buy from it and then continue to buy from it. Behavioral loyalty is concerned with re-purchase activity, rather than attitudes or preferences. Thus, it is theoretically possible for a customer to be "loyal" to a brand even if they don't really like it, provided there are other reasons for repeat purchase. A discount airline with poor service standards, for instance, might have customers who are behaviorally loyal but not attitudinally loyal, if its prices are significantly lower than those of other airlines. (Some Londoners will lament that they hate RyanAir every weekend when they take it to Barcelona!) And a business-to-business firm selling complex services may rely on long-term contracts in order to ensure it is adequately compensated for high setup costs. (We once participated in a meeting with high-tech executives at their headquarters in which one of the executives joked that their primary customer loyalty tactic was probably the lawsuit.) In its most raw form, behavioral loyalty is similar to what can be described as "**functional loyalty**," in that there is no emotional content or sense of attachment to the company on the customer's part.

In the behavioral definition, customer loyalty is not the *cause* of brand preference but simply one *result* of it, and brand preference is not the only thing that might lead to behavioral loyalty. A company wanting to increase behavioral customer loyalty will focus on whatever tactics will in fact increase the amount of repurchase. These tactics can easily include improving brand preference, product quality, or customer satisfaction, but they may also include long-term legal contracts or prices so low that service is almost nonexistent.

Behavioral customer loyalty is easier to measure because it can be objectively observed, while assessing attitudinal loyalty requires more expensive and subjective polling and surveying techniques. But positive attitudes do tend to drive positive behaviors. Even if a firm observes loyal *behavior,* if the customer has no genuine *attitude* of loyalty, then the relationship will be highly vulnerable to competition. If a competitor enters the market at a comparable price, for instance, the customer once-loyal to your discount product can easily disappear.[8]

> Attitudinal loyalty without behavioral loyalty has no financial benefit for a firm, but behavioral loyalty without attitudinal loyalty is unsustainable.

The truth is, if an enterprise wants a clear and unambiguous guide to action, it needs to pay attention to both definitions of customer loyalty. Attitudinal loyalty without behavioral loyalty has no financial benefit for a firm, but behavioral loyalty without attitudinal loyalty is unsustainable. Defining loyalty purely as an attitude is not very useful, because that attitude can exist completely apart from any continuing relationship on the part of a customer, and this simply flies in the face of the common English definition of the word *loyalty.* Customer A and Customer B might have an equally loyal *attitude* toward a particular product, but what if Customer A has never even consumed that product before while Customer B has consumed it regularly in the past? Moreover, attitudinal loyalty and brand preference seem to be redundant, so why introduce a separate term at all? However, defining loyalty in purely behavioral terms is equally unsatisfactory; monopolies have behaviorally loyal customers.

A better insight into what customer loyalty really means can be gained by examining the policies companies introduce to improve it. A credit card company or mobile phone carrier, for instance, often concerns itself with reducing its "customer churn" rates. *Churn* is a colloquial term meaning "defection." These companies often can count the customers who voluntarily elect to leave their franchises every month, and it is a legitimate and time-honored business practice to try to reduce this churn rate. A company usually tackles the churn problem with both reactive and proactive tactics. Reactive tactics can include predictive modeling to identify those customers who are most likely to try to leave the franchise in the near future and then trying to intercede in advance; or actively trying to persuade churning customers not to leave at the point they announce they want to defect; or perhaps attempting to win defectors back immediately with offers of special pricing or improved services.

---

[8]Thanks to Doug Pruden (http://customerexperiencepartners.com), Esteban Kolsky (www.estebankolsky.com), Wim Rampen (http://contactcenterintelligence.wordpress.com), and Mark Ratekin (www.walkerinfo.com) for their insights provided in comments on our Strategy Speaks blog post: www.peppersandrogersgroup.com/blog/2009/10/customer-loyalty-is-it-an-atti.html.

Proactive tactics, however, can include identifying as many of the service and pricing problems that cause customers to want to leave in the first place, and trying to fix them; or perhaps designing new, customized products and services that do a better job of locking customers in for convenience reasons; or improving service friendliness and competence to increase customer affection for the brand.

A company trying to reduce its customer churn—and thereby increase its customer loyalty—shouldn't think of customer churn as a disease but as the symptom of a disease, somewhat like a fever. If a fever is severe enough, the doctor will want to treat it immediately and directly, but she also knows that the only long-term solution to reducing a fever is to cure the underlying disease causing it. If we pursue this analogy, we could visualize a lack of behavioral loyalty in our customer base as a fever that is affecting our company while the actual disease causing this fever is a lack of attitudinal loyalty.[9]

When dealing with the issue of customer loyalty, a firm should try to forge as direct a connection as possible to loyalty's actual financial results. That is, we ought to be able to "connect the dots" between whatever strategies and tactics we employ to increase our customers' loyalty and the actual economic outcomes of those actions. The customer-strategy enterprise will want to quantify the benefit of a customer's increasing loyalty, and the most direct and unambiguous metric to deploy for this task is the customer's "lifetime value," as described in Chapter 5.

Loyalty Programs

A "loyalty program" is a promotion that awards points, miles, or other benefits to a customer in exchange for the customer's doing business with the program's sponsoring company. Also known as a frequent-shopper or frequent-flyer program, loyalty programs are sometimes referred to as "frequency marketing." The distinction between behavioral and attitudinal loyalty, however, suggests an important criterion for evaluating the benefits and effects of whatever loyalty program a company implements.

Probably the most commonly found type of program is one that simply awards prizes to customers and ends right there, with little effort put into transforming the company's subsequent behavior or "treatment" of individual customers to reflect the needs or preferences revealed by the customer's own transactions. The problem is that while awards and prizes will in fact generate behavioral loyalty, by themselves they amount to little more than bribes for customer transactions—really, just a sophisticated form of price competition. The *faux* loyalty generated will have little impact on customer attitudes or intentions, as evidenced by the fact that most consumers are members of several different loyalty programs for competitive firms simultaneously.

A more effective kind of loyalty program is one that uses the information provided by a customer's rewarded behavior to fashion more relevant, personalized, or satisfying services or offers for that individual customer, thereby earning

---

[9]Thanks to Peppers & Rogers Group consultant Ozan Bayulgen for this very useful "fever" analogy, told to us on February 2, 2010.

more and more of the customer's attitudinal loyalty as well. In this kind of program the discounts and prizes given to customers are, in effect, incentives to ensure that the company can accurately track customer transactions and interactions over time, allowing it to compile a useful profile of customer needs and to tailor future offers and experiences for that customer. Tesco, the largest grocery retailer in the United Kingdom, uses the information generated by its Clubcard program to tailor each of its mailing pieces to each of its millions of Clubcard member households individually, through mass-customized printing capabilities.[a] Each mailing piece includes personally relevant offers for its addressee and represents incremental income for Tesco, based on an estimated 25 percent response rate. (In Chapter 4, we talk more about how Tesco's capability to identify individual customers contributes to its success.)

Loyalty programs have become ubiquitous marketing tools in a variety of industries, from grocery stores and airlines to credit-card and packaged-goods retailers, restaurant chains, and others. They are even used as a tool for managing and engaging employees and for encouraging healthy lifestyle habits. As these kinds of programs have proliferated, however, a few important "best practices" have emerged, which we can summarize in this way:

- *Never waste an opportunity to gain insight about a customer.* An effective loyalty program will offer a choice of services or treatments that reveal something about a customer's personal preferences. For example, if customers can identify their own prize in advance, the company can gain additional insight into what motivates particular customers. Loyalty programs in financial services, for instance, take advantage of the insights gained by identifying someone who chooses an award for lifetime achievement compared to one who chooses the largest prize for short-term behaviors. Providing points in return for completing surveys or responding to inquiries can also generate insight.
- *An effective program offers modularity, enabling participants to mix and match aspects to their own preferences.* Modular offerings are a practical way to allow for customer-driven personalization of a program without going to the extreme of full customization. Key aspects of the program, such as member qualification, can be developed with several alternatives, and customers can be offered a set of guided choices to select from. A sophisticated marketing approach would offer different sets of choices for different groups of customers based on their value—so everybody wouldn't be choosing from the same set. For example, a lower-value customer might choose from rewards alternatives that include a service upgrade, while high-value customers might have choices that include additional redemptions or alternative merchandise. In addition, modularity will allow a program to incorporate partners and cosponsors more easily.
- *Consumers value openness. They want a service or program that works with other programs.* The more open a loyalty program is, the more beneficial and attractive it will be to customers. Transferable points and rewards offer the customer the greatest flexibility in using program earnings. As a program

(continued)

(Continued)

gains confidence and customer insight, it can mature to a more and more open proposition without endangering customer loyalty, because the barrier to a customer's switching will no longer be pure economics (i.e., the value of the points earned) but convenience (having to "teach" another program about individual desires and preferences). Openness is inevitable in loyalty marketing programs, and companies must choose whether to lead the charge or to react to it.

- *A loyalty program should be managed around customers, not products.* The customer-strategy firm will align the organization of a loyalty program around certain identified sets of customers and then measure people by the positive impact they have on customer behaviors within these different groups. The marketing effort should be organized so that the customers whose behaviors are intended to be affected are the responsibility of managers whose evaluations are based on improving the numbers. This is the most direct way to make progress in each customer segment and to improve the loyalty (and lifetime values) of the individual customers in each segment.

- *Above all else: simplicity.* A program with fewer rules and restrictions is more engaging to the customer. It's better for a company to narrow its offers to those that can be delivered dependably rather than to include elements that can't be relied on. Airline programs frequently suffer, for instance, when they offer high-value redemptions that are not very readily available. Such offers often do more harm than good, by unnecessarily raising customer expectations and then not delivering. If a company can't deliver reliably on what it promises in its loyalty program, it risks undermining trust in the brand.

---

[a]"Tesco Clubcard Signs Up One Million Customers since Relaunch," *Marketing Magazine*, October 5, 2009, available at: www.marketingmagazine.co.uk/news/943397/Tesco-Clubcard-signs-one-million-customers-relaunch/, accessed September 1, 2010.

The important thing to remember about loyalty programs is that most are just a "me, too" way of reducing profit margin. Once all the major players in a space offer one, it's just a bribe for doing business with a particular restaurant, store, airline, or product consumable. In contrast, the best-practice loyalty programs are the ones that offer a reward in exchange for ongoing customer information (shopping basket data, preferred services and routes) and then *use that information* to serve a customer better than a company that does not have the information.

Summary

Our goal for this chapter has been to give the reader a grounded perspective of how Learning Relationships enable enterprises to develop more personalized and collaborative interactions with individual customers. Our next step is to begin to understand "the business sense" of building a customer-strategy enterprise. Learning Relationships, after all, result in many pragmatic and financial benefits, not only for the customer but also for the enterprise that engages in them. The objective of increasing the overall value of the customer base by getting, keeping, and growing a customer is achieved through these highly interactive relationships.

The enterprise determined to increase the value of the customer base will start with a commitment to increase customer value and then move to implement the strategic levels of the Learning Relationship. The tasks needed to make this happen are: identifying their customers individually, ranking them by their value to the company, differentiating them by their needs, interacting with each of them, and customizing some aspect of the business for each. From the enterprise's perspective, these tasks are by no means chronological or finite. We will examine each of them more carefully in the next chapters.

Food for Thought

1. Based on what we now know about the essence of relationships, is it possible for a customer to have a relationship with a commercial (or other) firm? Is it possible for a customer to have a relationship with a brand? Is it possible for a firm to have a relationship with a customer—especially a customer who is one of millions of customers? If you said no to any of these questions, what conditions would have to be met before a relationship *would* be possible?

2. James Barnes says an important ingredient to a good relationship is an emotional connection, but customer relationships have elsewhere been referred to as a "bond of value" or a "bond of convenience." What do you think? Do customers have to love a product or company in order to have a "relationship" with that enterprise? Or is a perceived benefit—especially one that grows from a vested interest—enough? How would you approach a debate on this controversy?

3. Consider the relationship enhancers and building blocks mentioned by Julie Edell Britton. For each one, think of a for-profit or a nonprofit enterprise that serves as an example.

4. Assume that there exists asymmetrical dependence between a buyer and a seller. Answer the following questions two ways: First, assume the buyer is more dependent; next, assume the seller is more dependent.[10]
   a. How do you reduce uncertainty if you are a buyer? A seller?
   b. Will there always be some transactional purchases?
   c. How is the relationship with your buyers/sellers different from the way it would be with symmetrical interdependence?

5. Pick a brand that you will always buy. What happened specifically to create this loyalty from you? Is there anything that could dissolve your loyalty or make it even stronger?[11]

Glossary

Asymmetric relationship The two parties view the relationship differently; it is more important or salient, perhaps, to one party than the other. *Asymmetric dependence* refers to a situation where one party has few alternatives but to remain

---

[10]This question was suggested by an anonymous reviewer.
[11]This question was suggested by reviewer John Westman.

in the relationship whereas *symmetric interdependence* exists when the relationship members are equally dependent on each other.

Customer churn   The rate at which customers leave and enter the franchise. High churn indicates a simultaneously high number of defecting customers and high number of new customers. Usually a symptom of low customer loyalty.

Discrete (transactional) versus relational (collaborative) relationships   *See* relational (collaborative) versus discrete (transactional).

Distributive fairness   Based on the perception of relationship rewards versus relationship burdens or obligations and, therefore, focused on relationship outcomes.

Emotional loyalty   Attitudinal loyalty, or a preference for one brand over another. Customers with attitudinal loyalty may buy another brand or shop elsewhere for practical reasons (e.g., accepting a Pepsi instead of the preferred Coke on an airplane because Coke is not available).

Functional loyalty   Behavioral loyalty, or, basically, buying the same thing over and over, or repeatedly, from a particular vendor.

Iterative   Builds on itself: A relationship is iterative because it gets smarter and smarter over time. It can pick up where it left off; it doesn't need to start all over at the beginning with each contact.

Mutuality   Refers to the two-way nature of a relationship.

Procedural fairness   Based on the perception that procedures and processes are fair and are focused on behaviors, regardless of outcome.

Relational (collaborative) versus discrete (transactional) relationships   Relational strategies take into account the lifetime costs and payoffs of the total of all projectable interactions and transactions whereas discrete or transactional approaches concentrate on the value of the current transaction. This distinction is important because, for example, a company that focuses on a relationship and the long-term value of a customer would be willing to resolve that customer's complaint about a single transaction by taking a loss on the transaction whereas the company that focuses just on the value of transactions insists on making a profit on each transaction.

PART II

IDIC Implementation Process: A Model for Managing Customer Relationships

In order for a firm to build customer value through managed relationships, the company must *identify* customers, *differentiate* them, *interact* with them, and *customize* some aspect of its behavior toward them.

CHAPTER 3

Customer Relationships: Basic Building Blocks of IDIC and Trust

The purest treasure mortal times can afford is a spotless reputation.

—William Shakespeare

In order for a firm to build customer value through managed relationships, the company must engage in a four-step process we call **IDIC** (*identifying* customers, *differentiating* them, *interacting* with them, and *customizing* for them). These steps represent the mechanics of any genuine relationship, which by definition will involve mutuality and customer-specific action. But while the IDIC process represents the *mechanics* of a relationship, generating a customer's trust should be the most important *objective* of that process. Relationships simply cannot happen except in the context of customer trust. In succeeding chapters, we take a more detailed look at each of the IDIC tasks as well as at the subject of trust itself, but for now, what's important is to get an overview of both the mechanics and the objective of relationship building.

We've seen that the customer relationship idea has many nuances. For instance, there likely will be an emotional component to most successful customer relationships (at least in consumer marketing), but it's important to recognize that the obverse of this statement is not necessarily true: because you have an emotional attachment to a company does not mean you have a relationship with that company.

We can't afford to dismiss entirely the notion that nonemotional relationships between an enterprise and its customer do, in fact, exist. For instance, you probably have no actual emotional connection with one or more banks whose credit cards you carry in your wallet. But, everyone keeps asking, does that mean you have no *relationship* with such a company, even though it communicates with you monthly, tracks your purchases, and (at least in the best cases) proactively offers you a new card configuration based on your own personal usage pattern? Yes, there might be an element of emotion involved in this relationship, but must that always be the case?

Conversely, you might have a highly emotional attachment to an enterprise, but if the enterprise itself isn't even "aware" that you exist, does this constitute anything we can call a relationship? The simple truth is that, in most cases, your relationship with a brand is analogous to your relationship with a movie star. You might love his pictures, you might follow his activities avidly in the magazines, but will he even know who you are? It can be said to be a relationship only if the movie star somehow also acknowledges it. This is because, as we said in Chapter 2, the most basic, core feature of any *relationship* is mutuality. Mutual awareness of another party is a prerequisite to establishing a relationship between two parties, whether we are talking about movie star and fan or enterprise and customer. People who are emotionally involved with a brand, not unlike the most avid fans of a rock music group, are usually engaged in one-way affection. There's nothing wrong with this at all. One-way affection for a brand has sold a lot of merchandise. But this kind of affection will be only part of a relationship if the brand is mutually involved; and in the overwhelming majority of cases, it is not.

So let's return to the basic, definitional characteristics of a relationship, as outlined at the beginning of Chapter 2, and try to derive from this list of characteristics a set of actions that an enterprise ought to take if it wants to establish relationships with its customers through deeper insights that lead to better experiences. A relationship is mutual, interactive, and iterative in nature, developing its own richer and richer context over time. A relationship must provide an ongoing benefit to each party; it must change each party's behavior toward the other party; and it will therefore be uniquely different from one set of relationship participants to the next. Finally, a successful relationship will lead each party to trust the other. In fact, the more effective and successful the relationship is, from a business-building standpoint, the more it will be characterized by a high level of trust.

Trust and Relationships Happen in Tandem

The first few relationship characteristics we've seen are simply analytic descriptions of the nature of a relationship while the last characteristic—trust—is a much richer term that could serve as a proxy for all the affection and favorable emotion that most of us associate with a successful relationship. In any case, what should be apparent from the outset is that we are talking about an enterprise engaging in customer-specific behaviors. That is, because relationships involve mutuality and uniqueness, an enterprise can easily have a wonderful relationship with one customer but no relationship at all with another. It can have a deep, very profitable relationship with one customer but a troubled, highly unprofitable relationship with another. An enterprise cannot have the same relationship with both Mary and Shirley any more than Mary can have the same relationship with both her banker and her golf instructor.

A business strategy based on managing customer relationships, then, necessarily involves treating different customers differently. A firm must be able to identify and recognize different, individual customers, and it must know what makes one customer different from another. It must be able to interact individually with any customer on the other end of a relationship, and it must somehow change its behavior to meet the specific needs of that customer, as it discovers those needs. And to build trust, it must act in the customer's best interest as well as its own.

In short, in order for an enterprise to engage in the practice of treating different customers differently, it must integrate the customer into the company and adapt its products and services to the customer's own, individual needs. But as a company begins to understand the customer, interact with him, learn from him, and provide feedback based on that learning, the customer's view of what he is buying from the company will probably also begin to change. For instance, a person may shop from L.L. Bean initially to buy a sweater. But over time, he may browse the L.L. Bean Web site or flip through the catalog to match other clothes to the sweater, or look for Christmas gift ideas, or research camping equipment. Now L.L. Bean has become more than just a place to buy sweaters; it is a source of valuable information about future purchases. Ultimately, this is likely to increase the importance of trust, as an element in the relationship. So will the no-questions-asked return policy as well as the fast, reasonably priced shipping. The more the customer trusts L.L. Bean, the more likely he will be to accept its offers and recommendations.[1]

It is customer information that gives an enterprise the capability to differentiate its customers one from another. Customer information is an economic asset, just like a piece of equipment, a factory, or a patent. It has the capability to improve an enterprise's productivity and reduce its unit costs. Individual customer information, if used properly, can yield a return for many years. And because customer information is based on an individual, not a group, it is more useful for its scope rather than its scale. When two enterprises are competing for the same individual customer's business, the company with the greatest scope of information about that customer will probably be the more effective competitor. And, because technology now makes it possible for businesses of nearly any size to keep track of individual relationships with individual customers, the scale of a company's operations may become less important as a competitive advantage. Cultivating a profitable customer relationship will depend primarily on having information about a specific customer and using it wisely. It will matter more than who has the biggest pile of customers.

> Cultivating a profitable customer relationship will depend primarily on having information about a specific customer and using it wisely. It will matter more than who has the biggest pile of customers.

Once a company begins to take a customer-specific view of its business, it will begin to think of its customers as assets that must be managed carefully, in the same way any other corporate asset should be managed. From a strictly financial perspective, this kind of strategy will tend to focus more corporate resources on satisfying the needs of those customers offering higher long-term value to the firm while limiting or reducing the resources allocated to lower-value customers. But, operationally, increasing the long-term value of a particular customer will necessitate addressing that customer's own individual needs, even to the point of tailoring—or at least mass-customizing—individual products and services for individual customers.

The technologies that allow a company to track individual customers and treat them differently have made it possible to create what is, in effect, an individual *feedback loop* for each customer. This loop ensures that a successful relationship continues to get better and better, one customer at a time. When such a relationship exists between a customer and an enterprise, many traditional marketing principles,

---

[1] See Peter Kenning, "The Influence of General Trust and Specific Trust on Buying Behaviour," *International Journal of Retail & Distribution Management* 36 (2008): 461; Ellen Garbarino and Mark Johnson, "The Different Roles of Satisfaction, Trust, and Commitment in Customer Relationships," *Journal of Marketing* 63 (April 1999): 70–87.

formerly held sacred, will simply be irrelevant, at least insofar as that particular customer is concerned. No longer must the enterprise rely on surveys of current or potential customers to determine which action is appropriate for *this* customer; nor is it necessary to plot the reach and frequency with which its advertising message is getting out, in order to determine its effectiveness with *this* customer. Instead, the customer and the enterprise are mutually engaged in a continuously improving relationship: "I know you. You tell me what makes this work for you. I do it. You tell me if I did it right. I remember that, and I do it even better for you next time."

In addition to the company–customer feedback loop involving customer satisfaction surveys, questionnaires, and even customer complaints, a company may also gain insight about customer wants, needs, or expectations by monitoring social media communications—customers interacting with customers (see Chapter 8). A company has the opportunity to learn from conversations taking place in the social networks. This is highly important for companies trying to build relationships with their customers for three main reasons:

1. Social networks have high impact on the flow and quality of information. As opposed to a belief in impersonal and generic sources, customers prefer to rely on peers and their perspectives.
2. Information within networks disseminates quickly and impacts word-of-mouth referrals and recommendations.
3. Social networks of customers also carry the implication of trust as the information becomes more personalized with experience and familiarity of the members of the social network.[2]

The secret to keeping and growing a single customer forever is this feedback loop. Creating it requires the customer's own participation and effort along with his trust in the company that's getting his information. It is the effort on the part of the customer that results in a better product or service than the customer can get anywhere else from any company that is not so far up a particular customer's learning curve. The successive interactions that characterize such a Learning Relationship ultimately result in the enterprise's capability to make its products and services highly valuable to an individual customer; indeed, the Learning Relationship, because it is unique to that customer, and because it has been formed in large part from the customer's own participation, can become *irreplaceably* valuable to that customer, ensuring the customer's long-term loyalty and value to the enterprise.

IDIC: Four Implementation Tasks for Creating and Managing Customer Relationships

Setting up and managing individual customer relationships can be broken up into four interrelated implementation tasks. These implementation tasks are based on

---

[2]See Mark Granovetter, "The Impact of Social Structure on Economic Outcomes," *Journal of Economic Perspectives* 19, no. 1 (Winter 2005): 33–50; Clara Shih, *The Facebook Era* (Boston: Pearson Education, 2009), pp. 29ff.

the unique, customer-specific, and iterative character of such relationships. We list them roughly in the sequence in which they will likely be accomplished, although, as we see later in this book, there is a great deal of overlap among these implementation tasks (e.g., an enterprise might use its Web presence primarily to attract the most valuable customers and identify them individually rather than as a customer interaction platform), and there may be good reason for accomplishing them in a different order:

> An enterprise must be able to *recognize* a customer when he comes back, in person, by phone, online, or wherever.

1. **Identify** *customers.* Relationships are possible only with individuals, not with markets, segments, or populations. Therefore, the first task in setting up a relationship is to identify, individually, the party at the other end of the relationship.

Many companies don't really know the identities of many of their customers, so for them this first step is difficult but absolutely crucial. For all companies, the "identify" task also entails organizing the enterprise's various information resources so that the company can take a customer-specific view of its business. It means ensuring that the company has a mechanism for tagging individual customers not just with a product code that identifies what's been sold but also with a customer code that identifies the party that the enterprise is doing business with—the party at the other end of the mutual relationship. An enterprise must be able to *recognize* a customer when he comes back, in person, by phone, online, or wherever. Moreover, enterprises need to "know" and remember each customer in as much detail as possible—including the habits, preferences, and other characteristics that make each customer unique. When you call the toll-free number at Cabela's, the rep knows about your last catalog order, because you've been identified.

> Customers represent different levels of value to the enterprise, and they have different needs from the enterprise. The customer's needs drive his behavior, and his behavior is what the enterprise observes in order to estimate his value.

2. **Differentiate** *customers.* Knowing how customers are different allows a company (a) to focus its resources on those customers who will bring in the most value for the enterprise, and (b) to devise and implement customer-specific strategies designed to satisfy individually different customer needs and improve each customer's experience. Customers represent different levels of value to the enterprise, and they have different needs from the enterprise. The customer's needs drive his behavior, and his behavior is what the enterprise observes in order to estimate his value. Although not a new concept, *customer grouping*—the process by which customers are clustered into categories based on a specified variable—is a critical step in understanding and profitably serving customers. Specifically, the "customer differentiation" task involves an enterprise in categorizing its customers by both their value to the firm and by what needs they have. Some call centers constantly change the order to serve based on the different values of those customers who are waiting on hold. Although it would be ideal to answer every call on the second ring, when that's not possible, it would be better to vault the customers keeping you in business

ahead of the customers of lower value. In most call centers, this reshuffling is not at all apparent to customers.

3. **Interact** *with customers.* Enterprises must improve the effectiveness of their interactions with customers. Each successive interaction with a customer should take place in the context of all previous interactions with that customer.

> A conversation with a customer should pick up where the last one left off. And a company should never ask the same question twice.

A bank may ask one question in each month's electronic statement, and next month's question may depend on last month's answer. A conversation with a customer should pick up where the last one left off. Effective customer interactions provide better insight into a customer's needs and don't waste a customer's time by asking the same question more than once, even in different parts of the organization.

3. **Customize** *treatment.* The enterprise should adapt some aspect of its behavior toward a customer, based on that individual's needs and value. To engage a customer in an ongoing Learning Relationship, an enterprise needs to adapt

> The enterprise should adapt some aspect of its behavior toward a customer, based on that individual's needs and value.

its behavior to satisfy the customer's expressed needs. Doing this might entail mass-customizing a product or tailoring some aspect of its service.[3] This customization could involve the format or timing of an invoice or how a product is packaged.

This IDIC process implementation model can also be broken into two broad categories of activities: *insight* and *action* (see Exhibit 3.1). The enterprise conducts the first two tasks, identify and differentiate, behind the scenes and out of the customer's sight; they constitute *insight*. The latter two tasks, interact and customize, are customer-facing steps that require participation on the part of the individual customer. Visible to the customer, they constitute *action*. You'll recall from Chapter 1 that "interacting" and "customizing" are the two capabilities an enterprise must have in order to engage customers in relationships and that the degree to which a firm uses each of these capabilities is an easy way to categorize the type of customer strategy it is pursuing—mass, niche, database, or one-to-one Learning Relationship. We can also think of the identify and differentiate steps as the tasks that make up "analytical customer relationship management [CRM]" or "customer insight" while interact and customize are the tasks involved in "operational CRM" or "customer experience."

Throughout the rest of this book, we refer back to this set of four implementation tasks as the *IDIC methodology.* As a model for relationship management processes, this methodology can be applied in any number of situations. For instance, it could help a company understand the steps it must take to make better use of its call center for initiating and strengthening customer relationships. Applied to a sales force, it could be used to understand the strengths and weaknesses of a new contact

---

[3]Don Peppers, Martha Rogers, Ph.D., and Bob Dorf, *The One to One Fieldbook: The Complete Toolkit for Implementing a 1to1 Marketing Program* (New York: Doubleday, 1999).

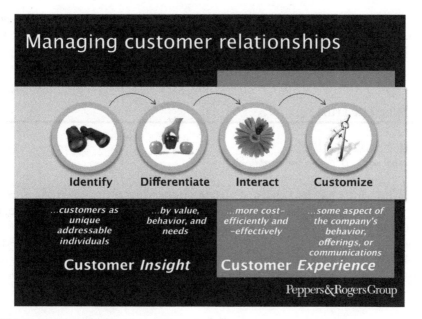

EXHIBIT 3.1   IDIC: Analysis and Action

management application or to improve a sales compensation policy. We devote specific chapters in the book to examining all the activities and processes, as well as the pitfalls and problems, associated with each of these four tasks.

How Does Trust Characterize a Learning Relationship?

But before we begin this journey, we will spend the rest of this chapter discussing in greater detail just what it means to say that trust is a quality that will characterize a good customer relationship. In an enterprise focused on customer-specific activities, any single customer's purchase transactions will take place within the context of that customer's previous transactions as well as future ones. The buyer and seller collaborate, with the buyer interacting to specify the product and the seller responding with some change in behavior appropriate for *that* buyer. In other words, the buyer and seller, in a relationship, must be willing to trust each other *far beyond the general reputation of the brand*. By extension, we can easily see that the more "relationship like" any series of purchase transactions is, the more that trust will become a central element in it.

When a company is focused on building customer equity, earning customer trust becomes an inherent goal of its decision making. It's not possible to balance the creation of long- and short-term value, to build Return on Customer, or to focus resources on building superior customer experiences unless the company understands that the lifetime values of customers are just as important as current sales and profits.

A relationship of trust is one in which both parties feel "comfortable" continuing to interact and deal with each other, whether during a purchase, an interaction, or a service transaction. Trust rarely happens instantaneously. Even if the trusted source has been recommended by another, a customer must "feel" the trust from within before he will begin to divulge personal information about himself.

The Speed of Trust

Stephen M. R. Covey
Cofounder and CEO, CoveyLink Worldwide

Simply put, trust means *confidence*. The opposite of trust—distrust—is *suspicion*. When you trust people, you have confidence in them—in their integrity and in their abilities. When you distrust people, you are suspicious of them— of their integrity, their agenda, their capabilities, or their track record. It's that simple. We have all had experiences that validate the difference between relationships that are built on trust and those that are not. These experiences clearly tell us the difference is not small; it is dramatic.

■ ■ ■

Trust is a function of two things: *character* and *competence*. Character includes your integrity, your motive, your intent with people. Competence includes your capabilities, your skills, your results, your track record. And both are vital.

With the increasing focus on ethics in our society, the character side of trust is fast becoming the price of entry in the new global economy. However, the differentiating and often ignored side of trust—competence—is equally essential. You might think a person is sincere, even honest, but you won't trust that person fully if he or she doesn't get great results. And the opposite is true. A person might have great skills and talents and a good track record, but if he or she is not honest, you're not going to trust that person either. For example, I might trust someone's character implicitly, even enough to leave him in charge of my children when I'm out of town. But I might not trust that same person in a business situation because he doesn't have the competence to handle it. On the other hand, I might trust someone in a business deal whom I would never leave with my children; not necessarily because he wasn't honest or capable, but because he wasn't the kind of caring person I would want for my children.

While it may come more naturally for us to think of trust in terms of character, it's equally important for us to think in terms of competence. Think about it: People trust people who make things happen. They give the new curriculum to their most competent instructors. They give the promising projects or sales leads to those who have delivered in the past. Recognizing the role of competence helps us identify and give language to underlying trust issues we otherwise can't put a finger on. From a line leader's perspective, the competence dimension rounds out and helps give trust its harder, more pragmatic edge.

Here's another way to look at it: The increasing concern about ethics has been good for our society. Ethics (which is part of character) is foundational to trust, but by itself is insufficient. You can have ethics without trust but you can't have trust without ethics. Trust, which encompasses ethics, is the bigger idea.

Excerpt from Stephen M. R. Covey and Rebecca R. Merrill, *The Speed of Trust: The One Thing That Changes Everything* (New York: Free Press, 2006), pp. 5, 30.

According to Covey and Merrill, "the true transformation starts with building credibility at the personal level." The best leaders are those who have made trust an explicit objective, being aware of the quantifiable costs associated with the lack of it in a company or a relationship. One of the simplest ways to look at the quantifiable costs of a so-called soft factor, such as trust, is to think about a simple transaction taking place between two parties. When the two parties in business trust each other, they can act more quickly and minimize the frictional costs of the transaction, such as spending on lawyers, contracts, or due diligence. With the increase in trust in a given relationship, not only are costs lower, but the time required to complete the transaction also goes down significantly. Covey points out that when Warren Buffett's Berkshire Hathaway acquired McLane Distribution from Wal-Mart, the $23-billion acquisition was sealed over a handshake and completed in less than a month, because both parties knew and trusted each other completely. Normally a deal like this would have required six months or more to execute and perhaps several million dollars of legal and accounting fees.[4]

The element of trust is an indispensable component of a healthy, growing relationship between a company and its customer, but it may not be an absolute requirement for every relationship. A customer may remain in a relationship with a company either because he desires the relationship or simply because he perceives no suitable alternative. It should be obvious, however, which relationship will be the stronger, from the standpoint of increasing the customer's long-term value to the enterprise.[5] The customer's own level of commitment to his relationship with a company will depend on the extent to which the relationship derives from dedication, rather than from constraint. Trust-based relationships foster dedication.[6]

Enterprises create trust-based customer relationships through the actions of their employees and partners and through company strategies and policies. There are sound ways to think about the trust-building process and the policies necessary to

---

[4]Stephen M. R. Covey and Rebecca R. Merrill, *The Speed of Trust: The One Thing that Changes Everything* (New York: Free Press, 2006), pp. 13–15.

[5]Michael Wheeler also makes the case that building a reputation for generosity pays off: "Want to Pull Ahead of the Competition?," *Negotiation* 8, no.10 (October 2005): 3–5.

[6]Kuo-Ming Chu, "The Construction Model of Customer Trust, Perceived Value and Customer Loyalty," *The Journal of American Academy of Business* 14, no. 2 (March 2009): 98–103; Nelson N. H. Liao amd Tsui-chih Wu, "The Pivotal Role of Trust in Customer Loyalty: Empirical Research on the System Integration Market in Taiwan," *Business Review* 12, no. 2 (Summer 2009): 277–283; Gregory S. Black, "Trust and Commitment: Reciprocal and Multidimensional Concepts in Distribution Relationships," *S.A.M. Advanced Management Journal* 73, no. 1 (Winter 2008): 46–55; Leonard L. Berry, *Discovering the Soul of Service* (New York: Free Press, 1999).

generate trust. In the next section, Charles Green shares his views on trust between customer and supplier by discussing what he calls the "myths" of trust.

The Trust Equation: Generating Customer Trust

Charles H. Green
CEO, Trusted Advisor Associates

It's no secret: Building customer relationships is a powerful tool for identifying high-loyalty-potential customers as well as to fine-tune products and services to elicit loyalty. And the literature of retention economics is well documented as well as intimately bound up with customer-centricity. That customer "loyalty" is immensely profitable is not in dispute by anybody not living under a rock for the past 10 years.

But the role of trust in the economic equation is rarely noticed. For one thing, research generally suggests that high levels of customer satisfaction are only mildly correlated with high levels of loyalty. But other data show that while satisfaction might not lead to loyalty, dissatisfaction clearly leads to disloyalty. It is only when high levels of customer satisfaction are encountered that we find a major upswing in customer loyalty, and hence in customer profitability. And there are some data to suggest that extremely high levels of customer satisfaction and loyalty are also examples of extremely high trust.[a]

What all this suggests, in actuality, is that the presence or absence of trust is a significant driver of economic profit.

> The presence or absence of trust is a significant driver of economic profit.

Also, the business literature is now full of books and articles linking customer loyalty directly to profit and describing the issue more or less purely in business-process terms. High profits are said to derive from high customer-retention rates because of efficiencies, such as increased familiarity with buying processes and customer-enterprise shared processes, or from price insensitivity and referrals. But viewed from just a slightly different angle, these same process improvements arise directly from the greater sense of trust that particular customers have with the enterprise they're dealing with.

There can be trust-based relationships without a one-to-one business model. And there may be companies operating customer-specific businesses that are not very successful at creating trusted relationships. (Think about the companies that call you at the dinner hour.) Clearly, however, for an enterprise to generate the kind of long-term, profitable, ongoing relationship with a customer that is the subject of this book, the customer must have some level of trust in the enterprise.

But trust is not always so easily understood, and the steps required to generate a customer's trust aren't necessarily simple. In fact, with all the emphasis on process, a number of businesses have focused more on the activities required rather than the desired outcome. As a result, several "myths" about trust ought to be exposed at the outset:

Myth 1: Intimate customer relationships require time and proximity.

Fact: Intimacy is the one trust factor that can be instantaneous; it can be conveyed by a tone of voice, by attentive listening, or by a sense of being understood. It is also not dependent on proximity; consider interactions by way of various social media; consider conversations between seatmates on transcontinental plane flights.

Myth 2: Trust takes time.

Fact: Only one component of trust requires the repetition of experiences, not time per se; that component is reliability. Other components of trust are not necessarily time-bound at all: credibility, intimacy, an assessment of the other's **self-orientation**. And even the accumulation of repeated experiences *used to* take time; now experiences can be accumulated rapidly.

Myth 3: More customized contact is better.

Fact: If I am passed from one customer service agent to another and the second agent knows my name and transaction history, I am pleased. If a cold-call direct marketer knows my name and transaction history, I am not pleased. Context and intent are everything.

Myth 4: People trust companies.

Fact: Reliability is the only trust component that people associate with enterprises. Credibility and especially intimacy and self-orientation are traits associated almost entirely with individual persons, not organizations. The movie *The Godfather* had it wrong—it *is* business, and it *is* personal.

Myth 5: People like to be asked their opinion.

Fact: People like to be *listened to*; it's not the same thing as being asked. When was the last time you filled out an in-room hotel service questionnaire?

Trust is a genuine buzzword; nearly everyone uses it, and assumes that what they mean by the word is what everyone else means by the word. In fact, it has many different meanings, hence many opportunities for misinterpretation if the word is not clearly and mutually defined.

The bulk of those meanings, however, can be captured in a simple model I call the Trust Equation. (See Exhibits 3A and 3B.)

The first two of these components—credibility and reliability—operate mainly in the rational realm. The second two—intimacy and self-orientation—are largely nonrational (*not* the same as irrational).[b]

The power of the fourth component—self-orientation—is greater than that of the other three, as evidenced by its solo position in the denominator.

(*continued*)

(Continued)

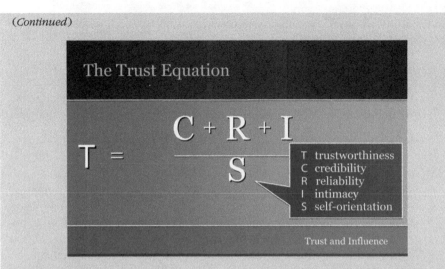

EXHIBIT 3A   The Trust Equation

A customer who perceives lack of credibility may sense empty words. If the customer senses low levels of reliability, he may say the offer is "flaky." If the customer senses low levels of intimacy, she views the enterprise as technical, or full of technicians. All these are destructive of trust, of course. But none so much as being perceived as having high levels of self-orientation, for that goes to motive—high self-orientation is equated with insincerity, a lack of caring, and deviousness, the presumption that actions are motivated not by a desire to help the customer but by a desire to get the customer's money. The perceived motive behind another's actions has a large impact on the level of trust we give to someone.

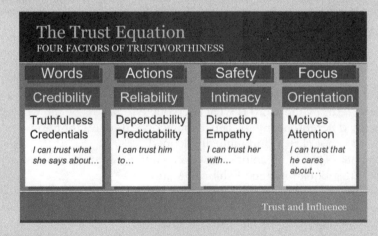

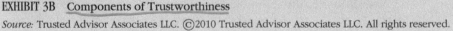

EXHIBIT 3B   Components of Trustworthiness

The Trust Equation (see Exhibit 3A) allows us to see more clearly the trust-destroying nature of many of the activities enterprises engage in when they install CRM technologies without adopting an appropriately customer-oriented business philosophy. Companies might have the best of intentions, but few technology implementations are perfect, and when little attention is paid to the enterprise's own philosophy of business, the results often can be counterproductive. Here are just a few examples:

- *False accuracy.* Errors in detailed information, such as street names, reduce credibility.
- *Presumed intimacy.* Using precise information as a lever, as in "Now that you bought green house paint, you'll probably be wanting XYZ," can feel like Big Brother is watching, which not only reduces intimacy but greatly increases perceived self-orientation.
- *Inconsistent application of CRM.* If an automated answering system asks a customer to key in an ID, don't ask her to repeat it verbally later in the call; doing so reduces perceived reliability.
- *Unintegrated application of CRM.* If you're a bank offering overdraft protection on checks written by key customers, better make sure the online banking side of the house offers the same service for online checks written; otherwise, you lower credibility and perceived reliability.
- *Treating all kinds of trust as fungible.* "I trust my dog with my life—but not with my ham sandwich." To be meaningful, we have to ask: Trust to do what? To say what? To behave how? It is one thing to trust a company to give us good information about benefits of a $10 product; it is another to trust the same company with our private finances. A CRM system that doesn't distinguish between the varying requirements of trust in different contexts is a system that is at risk of appearing emotionally tone-deaf. One pitfall is giving customized answers before being asked; a computer company's CRM system may give a sales rep 98 percent confidence that a particular product is right for a given customer, but if the rep tries to "sell" the solution before the customer feels listened to, then he or she will not buy, even if buying would be the "rational" thing to do. Jumping to conclusions before the customer feels listened to combines the two major process trust violations.

High trust leads to higher sales. Yet many selling models do not actually foster the development of high levels of trust. Some models view trust as entirely rational—a subset of rational decision making, in fact. Yet trust includes some critical, nonrational components. Some selling models view trust-based relationships as one-dimensional, moving from impersonal and distant to intimate and close. Yet trust is more complex than that.

To generate trust, the enterprise must address all four components of it in the customer's mind—credibility, reliability, intimacy, and self-orientation (i.e., the self-orientation of the seller).

(continued)

(Continued)

Credibility Enhancers

Online information is an excellent vehicle for increasing a customer's sense of credibility of the seller. This is partly because the buyer can browse at her own pace and depth. But it is also because the online buyer is free to assess credibility without any of the social interactions necessary to judge intimacy or self-orientation. You don't have to be polite when reading a Web site; nor does the Web site (usually) tell you to hurry up or slow down.

CRM can help tremendously in such credibility enhancement; Amazon.com's programs for customization by past purchases offer deep customization in a way that is seen as value-adding by customers.

Reliability Enhancers

Reliability can be enhanced in several ways. The most obvious is to be religious about delivering on promises made: don't ask the customer to input an ID number if you're going to ask him to repeat it later in the call; don't mislead customers regarding availability; and so forth. Another is to create a number of implied promises and then deliver on them. Such promises might include a call back within X minutes, a successful hand off on a service call, or a revision made to a database. Yet another is to improve familiarity; customers perceive as reliable a company that can adapt its ways to their own habits, whether in the form of mildly customized Web sites, adoption of personal terms on a phone call, or matching the formality of language to the other.

CRM can be helpful in this regard as well; anytime that the enterprise can act vis-à-vis a customer given full awareness of all previous interactions, perceived reliability is increased.

Intimacy Enhancers

Customer relationships offer big chances to either increase or destroy intimacy. Intimacy is all about security, comfort, integrity, confidentiality, and a sense of safety. Someone with detailed information about me can make me feel very good or very bad, entirely depending on how they handle that information. If they hide their knowledge of me or pretend it doesn't exist, then they run the risk of appearing like Big Brother. If, however, the information is openly acknowledged, then it can become a useful tool. Similarly, if a company flaunts customer-specific data with no apparent purpose in mind, it will appear cavalier and untrustworthy. But if it brings specific information to bear on the problem at hand ("Do you want to use the same MasterCard number you used last time?"), then it becomes highly useful.

To understand this difference, consider two different ways a customer service rep (CSR) might use customer-specific information in an interaction with the customer:

Version A
Customer: I'm calling because my computer start button won't engage; it's ticket number LFX897A.

CSR: OK, this is your fourth call on the "won't start" problem. Are you sure you did what we suggested last time?

Version B

Customer: I'm calling because my computer start button won't engage; it's ticket number LFX897A.

CSR Hmm, my records say this is your fourth call on that ticket number; is that right? You must be getting a little frustrated by now; tell me about the problem.

Both CSRs have access to tremendously powerful CRM data, but the CSR in Version A turns data into a negative by basic trust-destroying language (stating the CRM data as definitive rather than asking for confirmation; starting with solutions before going through problem definition; not using good listening or empathy). By contrast, the CSR in Version B is able to turn real-time CRM data into a true asset simply by utilizing it in a trust-sensitive context.

What this goes to show is that it isn't just having the right technologies or information available that creates trust. Instead, an enterprise hoping to build and preserve its customers' trust must worry about how customer-specific information is actually deployed, how proficiently the customer-contact people operate with it, and, above all, whether the business is prepared to acknowledge that meeting genuine customer needs is the most important overall goal: that profits are guaranteed only if they are sought not as the goal of the interaction but as its healthy by-product.

Orientation Enhancers

CRM can help increase trust; it can also serve to decrease trust. Trust itself is a major factor in customer satisfaction, customer loyalty, and firm profitability. But there is a Catch-22: You can't become trustworthy by focusing very narrowly on your own bottom line.

Self-orientation has more weight in the Trust Equation than the other three factors. And the approach that the enterprise takes to CRM will speak volumes to a customer about the enterprise's level of self-orientation. If anything, the application of CRM raises the already-high stakes on the self-orientation part of the Trust Equation.

CRM starts with customer focus. But there are two kinds of customer focus. One is focus on the customer for the sake of the enterprise. The other is focus directly on the customer's interests, with the belief that if those needs are addressed, the enterprise will also be well served.[c]

Customers easily and quickly detect the difference in these two approaches. If the research implications are right—that trusted relationships are profitable relationships—then the fastest way to kill trust is to demonstrate that you are only in it for the money, for yourself. If your customers trust you, you'll be very

(continued)

(Continued)

profitable; but if you try to become profitable by using trust as a self-serving tactic, it won't work. Enterprises actually have to care; customers can tell the difference.

There is nothing wrong, of course, with strategic customer management and customer profitability studies, and CRM data technology can be extremely helpful in doing such analysis. But an enterprise's focus is critical to establishing relationships of trust with its customers. People do not tend to trust enterprises that act clearly, consistently, and only in their own self-interests. The question is not whether CRM should be used as a profit management tool—of course it should. The larger question is whether profit is best maximized by acting directly on profit levers, or achieving profit through focus on identifying and meeting customer needs. An enterprise that embarks on CRM with purely mercenary aims such as "increase share of wallet" or "eliminate unprofitable customers" has a mind-set that is fundamentally self-oriented at the outset. The implementation runs the risk of never getting to the larger, win-win implications of CRM: to find out truly what customers need, and then to make informed decisions on the basis of that knowledge—including customer focus, deselection, and so forth.

Research on the Trust Equation has gathered data from over 12,000 respondents and has been independently validated by psychographic experts and by comparison with existing studies.[d] A few conclusions are relevant to the role of the Trust Equation and those seeking to link CRM, trust, and profitability.

- Trustworthiness strongly goes up with age; The self-ratings of older people consistently exceed those of younger people, and this is consistently true across 10-year brackets.
- Men and women are nearly identical in trustworthiness, though the way they get there differs; in particular, women score higher on the intimacy component.
- Of the six possible top-two-factor combinations (Credible/Reliable, Credible/Intimate, Credible/Self-Orientation, Reliable/Intimate, Intimate/Self-Orientation, and Reliable/Self-Orientation), the intimacy factor appears in three of the top four most-trusted combinations. The "soft" side of trust is demonstrably stronger than the "hard" side of trust (i.e., credibility and reliability).
- The last bullet point notwithstanding, the largest group of respondents rely most heavily on the credibility/reliability combination—the combination that produces the lowest trust. What is most popular is least effective.

Several lessons for relationship managers are clear: You will generate more trust by focusing on the nonrational side of things than by focusing on the "rational" side. If you view your CRM system as simply a tool for statistically manipulating behavioral data, you will probably create a CRM system that does a poor job of creating intimacy, thus creating faux relationships that appear high in self-orientation. That is a system that itself acts to lower trust.

By contrast, a relationship approach that considers the emotional impact of the system itself (data collection used in interaction with customers) has a doubly powerful set of benefits: data plus trust.

---

[a]See William T. Brooks and Tom Travisano, *You're Working Too Hard to Make the Sale!: More Than 100 Insider Tools to Sell Faster and Easier,* rev. 2nd ed. (Burr Ridge, IL: Irwin Professional Publishing, 2005); and Robert Miller, *Strategic Selling* (New York, NY: W. W. Morrow, 1985).

[b]Note from authors: Charles Green's use of the terms "rational" and "nonrational" closely parallel the more widely accepted terms "cognitive," which refers to thinking, and "affective," which refers to feeling. These terms may also be seen as reflecting the current controversy about rational versus "emotional" processes.

[c]Note from authors: We might say that a vulture is highly customer-centric and customer-focused. It's just that the purpose of the focus has nothing to do with what's good for the "customer"—and everything to do with the vulture itself.

[d]See Trusted Advisor Associates' various articles on the Trust Quotient, an online self-assessment built on the Trust Equation, including Charles H. Green, "Findings from the Trust Quotient Self-Assessment" (2010), available at: http://trustedadvisor.com/cgreen.articles/75/Findings-from-the-Trust-Quotient-Self-Assessment, accessed April 2, 2010; Sandy Styer, "Trust and the Standard Deviation" (2010), available at: http://trustedadvisor.com/trustmatters/751/Trust-and-the-Standard-Deviation, accessed April 2, 2010; and Charles H. Green, "Trust in Business: The Core Concepts" (2007), available at: http://trustedadvisor.com/cgreen.articles/38/Trust-in-Business-The-Core-Concepts#equation, accessed April 2, 2010.

> People do not tend to trust enterprises that act clearly, consistently, and only in the company's own self-interests.

Green's outline here of the types of policies and practices necessary to create a trust-building environment for customers is very helpful. One of the most important aspects of his essay is the concept he introduces regarding an enterprise's self-orientation. It is closely akin to what we call the **trusted agent**[7] concept.

Becoming the Customer's Trusted Agent

Green's formula places the enterprise's perceived level of self-interest in the denominator of the Trust Equation because he believes that the degree to which a customer is likely to trust any company is inversely proportional to the amount of "me-first" attitude shown by the company. The more it appears to a customer that the enterprise is acting in its own interest, the less willing the customer will be to trust the enterprise's suggestions and recommendations. And we know that the more a customer does trust an enterprise, the more the customer is likely to want to

---

[7]Don Peppers and Martha Rogers, Ph.D., *The One to One Manager* (New York: Doubleday, 1999); David H. Maister, Charles H. Green, and Robert M. Galford, *The Trusted Advisor* (New York: Touchstone, 2000); Charles H. Green, *Trust-Based Selling* (New York: McGraw-Hill, 2006); Covey and Merrill, *Speed of Trust.*

continue a relationship with it, increase the scope of the relationship, and recommend the company or product to others.

It follows that the most secure, most influential, most profitable type of relationship between an enterprise and a customer is one in which the customer actually trusts the enterprise to act in his own interest. In such a relationship, the customer perceives the enterprise to be his trusted agent, making recommendations and giving advice that furthers the customer's interest, even when it occasionally conflicts with the enterprise's self-interest, at least in the short term.

With technology reducing barriers between customers and a choice of companies, a seller's reputation is now a distinguishing asset—and one that is continuously available for inspection by the buyer on a variety of online review sites. Trustworthiness has become more transparent, and as a result even distant strangers can confidently conduct business when integrity has been demonstrated and documented. Trust and fairness make the wheels of commerce turn.[8]

Earning the customer's trust is one of the earliest goals in any enterprise's effort to build a long-term relationship. Only in a relationship of trust can information pass back and forth freely between buyer and seller.

> Trust is the currency of all commerce.

Moreover, in a world of increasingly commodity-like products and services, a relationship founded on trust can provide a genuinely sustainable competitive edge. Trust is the currency of all commerce.

The Age of Transparency

Dov Seidman
CEO, LRN, and author of HOW

In the olden days (before about 1995), when people wanted to buy, say, a toaster, they would pick a local store known for its good selection or good pricing of small appliances and buy the one that seemed best for the needs. If they were particularly industrious, thrifty, or enamored of the process, they might call or visit two or three stores before making their purchase, dig out back issues of consumers' testing magazines, or consult a catalog or two to compare price and features. As more businesses went online, people suddenly had the ability to shop not only within their local area, but almost anywhere. Large and trusted online retailers were added to the shopping mix, giving consumers a few more options if they wished to pursue them. Between June 2004 and March 2005, however, as e-commerce began exploding worldwide, people who bought online suddenly became more prone to visiting ten or more web sites before returning to a favored location hours or days later to make a purchase.

---

[8]Don Peppers and Martha Rogers, Ph.D., *Rules to Break & Laws to Follow: How Your Business Can Beat the Crisis of Short-Termism* (Hoboken, NJ: John Wiley & Sons, 2008).

It has been said that information is like a toddler: It goes everywhere, gets into everything, and you can't always control it.[a] Someone should have told that to David Edmondson, former CEO of RadioShack. For consumers, easy access to information about vendors has become an advantage; for those like Edmondson, who had something to hide, it has meant devastation. When he joined RadioShack in 1994, Edmondson invented a couple of lines for his resume in the form of college degrees in theology and psychology from Pacific Coast Baptist College in California that he never earned. In February 2006, after just eight months at the top of his profession, he was forced to resign. Though the school had relocated to Oklahoma and renamed itself, a reporter from the *Fort Worth Star-Telegram* tracked it down and uncovered the discrepancies. Edmondson's career, built on the foundation of these lies, lay in pieces at his feet.[b]

He's not alone, of course. The news is full of examples of the mighty who have taken the fall. Kenneth Lonchar, former CFO and Executive Vice President of Silicon Valley software storage firm Veritas (the Latin word for *truth*), got caught in 2002 claiming a false Stanford MBA.[c] University of Notre Dame head football coach George O'Leary resigned when it was revealed that he had not only lied on his resume about playing football at his alma mater, but he had also falsely claimed a master's degree.[d] Even Jeff Taylor, founder of online job-search company Monster.com, posted on his own web site an executive biography touting a phony Harvard MBA.[e]

We live in the age of transparency. In 1994, it might have been easy to get away with such shenanigans, but with the massive shift of personal records and personal profiles to databases easily accessed over the Internet, virtually everything about you can be discovered quite easily. The fact that *The New Oxford American Dictionary* lists "Google" as a verb makes this perfectly clear, as does the sample sentence it uses to illuminate its meaning: "You meet someone, swap numbers, fix a date, and then Google them through 1,346,966,000 Web pages."[f] The *Pittsburgh Post-Gazette* recently reported a Harris Interactive poll showing that 23% of people routinely search the names of business associates or colleagues on the Internet before meeting them.[g] The DontDateHimGirl.com web site allows a woman to post the name and photograph of a man she says has wronged her. As the web site's founder, Tasha C. Joseph, told *The New York Times,* "It's like a dating credit report" for women.[h] Anyone with a video camera can share with the world your worst moments by posting them on YouTube.com, a revolution that within just a couple of years of its launch has had a dramatic effect on politics, entertainment, law enforcement, music, and countless people's private lives. Political pollsters can compare your age, income, party registration, type of car you own, charities you donate to, and a glut of other readily available personal information to predict with a very high degree of accuracy how you will vote.[i]

These facts exert a profound influence on business. Before transparency allowed them to peer through the tall trees, outside observers could discern the outline of a forest, but thought little about what was growing beneath. Companies, for instance, could form a joint venture to protect themselves from

(continued)

(Continued)

the ramifications of a dubious enterprise, believing that if the unit got into trouble it would not hurt the reputation of the parent company. In a transparent world, however, when your joint venture transgresses, everybody knows who owns it. In the past, training its managers in proper conduct was sufficient to protect a company's reputation because line employees had little contact with the outside world and rarely got a company into trouble. Now any employee can say something about a company in a chat room or in a blog and the next day it might appear on DrudgeReport or The Smoking Gun. There's even a new word for it—whistleblogging—when employees create personal online journals to report company wrongdoing. The new transparency doesn't allow you to hide in the dark underbrush, to have a joint venture here, or hire an agent there. Observers can easily tell the trees from the forest.

An information society also breeds a surveillance society. People are more curious and they *look* a lot more. They look because it is suddenly easy to do so; looking costs little, requires even less effort, and pays off with everything from the best prices for goods and services to revelations of the unsavory. Around the world, viewers are glued to their television sets by "reality TV," programming that purports to give true glimpses of private lives (the United States now has a whole network dedicated to it, and the British version of *Celebrity Big Brother* touched off an international incident[j]). We've always been interested in what was happening next door, but now we can actually see it. It's like examining a drop of water under a microscope. When you first place the drop on the slide, it looks clear and pristine. But the microscope's lens reveals a hidden world. With each adjustment of the magnification you see organisms and objects that before you could only have imagined; what first appeared clear and unpolluted suddenly appears messy and complex. Microscope technology changes the way you look at water, and with your curiosity thus piqued, you can't help but wonder what worlds might exist within other familiar objects.

People look more often because the looking is easier and there has been more to find. Imagine the gratification of Heather Landy, the *Fort Worth Star-Telegram* staff writer who uncovered David Edmondson's embellished RadioShack resume. She began her investigation "into Edmondson's credentials after learning that the executive, who started two churches before making the transition to a full-time business career, [was] scheduled to go to court . . . to fight his third drunken-driving charge."[k] Corporate scandals, celebrity breakups, political corruption: Each day's news—delivered instantly via television, radio, web site, cell phone, RSS feed, and BlackBerry–exposes the transgressions of the icons of the age. Whether the media are addicted to it because they have so much bandwidth/airtime/column space to fill or we're hooked by our newfound access, in the information age, once we've gotten a taste of scandal we can't seem to get enough.

Source: Reprinted with permission of John Wiley & Sons from Dov Seidman, *How: Why How We Do Anything Means Everything. . .in Business (and in Life)* (Hoboken, NJ: John Wiley & Sons, 2007), pp. 34–37.

[a]Lev Grossman and Hannah Beech, "Google under the Gun," *Time,* February 5, 2006.
[b]Heather Landy, "RadioShack CEO Admits 'Misstatements,'" *Fort Worth Star-Telegram,* February 16, 2006.
[c] "Veritas CFO Resigns over Falsified Resume," TheStreet.com, www.thestreet.com/markets/marketfeatures/10045724.html.
[d] "Academic, Athletic Irregularities Force Resignation," ESPN, December 14, 2001.
[e] Rob Wright, "A Monster.com of a Problem," *VARBusiness,* February 13, 2003.
[f] The New Oxford American Dictionary, 2nd ed., s.v. "Google."
[g] Madlen Read, "Should I Worry about Prospective Employers 'Googling' Me?" *Pittsburgh Post-Gazette,* March 5, 2005.
[h] Lizette Alvarez, "(Name Here) Is a Liar and a Cheat," *New York Times,* February 16, 2006.
[i] Peter Wallsten and Tom Hamburger, "Two Parties Far Apart in Turnout Tactics Too," *Los Angeles Times,* November 6, 2006.
[j] "Anger over Big Brother 'Racism,'" *BBC News,* January 16, 2007.
[k] Landy, "RadioShack CEO."

Many professional relationships are based on the concept of the trusted agent. Doctors, lawyers, psychologists, and financial planners must learn a lot about a customer before they can make their individualized recommendations; and their sense of professionalism compels them to make these recommendations in the best interests of their customers. This is, in fact, one of the hallmarks of any profession—that the client's interest will be paramount. The truth is, it's in a doctor's interest to keep her patients ill, so she can continue treating and billing them. But true professionals don't act in their own self-interest; they act in the client's interest, as trusted agents.

Becoming a trusted agent involves more than simple policy decisions on a company's part, no matter how revolutionary those policies might be. A deep, cultural change in attitude at most firms will also be required.

Corporate Heresy

As a corporate policy, [being a trusted agent] is a heretical undertaking at most companies, and flies directly in the face of product-centered principles of marketing and competition. If you and I have no relationship prior to the purchase, and we have no relationship following it, then our entire interaction is centered on a single, solitary transaction. And our interests are diametrically opposed. I want to buy the most product at the lowest price from you, and you want to sell me the least product at the highest price. In a transaction-based, product-centric business model, buyer and seller are adversaries, no matter how much the seller may try not to act the part. In this kind of business model, nearly the only assurance a customer has that he

(continued)

(Continued)

can trust the product and service being sold to him is the general reputation of the brand itself. But in a one-to-one marketing model, the purchase transaction exists within the context of previous transactions and more that will follow it. Moreover, the buyer and seller collaborate, with the buyer interacting to specify the product, and the seller responding with some change in behavior appropriate for that buyer. In the customer-oriented business model, in other words, the buyer and seller must be willing to trust each other far beyond the general reputation of the brand itself.

Source: Excerpted from Don Peppers and Martha Rogers, Ph.D., *The One to One Manager* (New York: Doubleday, 1999).

Trust isn't just "nice": it's a necessity for all companies wishing to enhance the value of their business. In fact, when a customer decides not to buy, more than 50 percent of the time the primary factor is a lack of trust.[9] Additonally, the strength of a customer's relationship to the company—strongly influenced by trust—has a direct impact on a customer's intention to purchase more products/services, to recommend the company to family and friends, and to remain a customer.[10] In total, these business outcomes that are contingent on trust can either enhance or diminish a company's value.

For example, consider the case of First Direct, a division of HSBC Bank. The company was named the United Kingdom's most trusted mortgage provider and most trusted current account provider.[11] As a result, the company wins a new customer every eight seconds; and, among its new customers, more than a third (36 percent) come because of a referral.[12]

When General Robert McDermott took the helm at the USAA insurance company in 1968, he turned this stodgy, bureaucratic company into what was to become a virtual icon of great customer service and customer trust. To do so he instituted a large amount of reorganization, retraining, computer technology, and reengineering. In addition, he implemented a single, overriding company policy with respect to customer service, which he called his "Golden Rule of Customer Service." McDermott's policy, to be adhered to by all USAA employees, was: "Treat the customer the way you would want to be treated if you were the customer." And, today, the trusted agent mentality at USAA has earned it one of the most loyal and valuable customer bases in the financial services industry, now in its third generation.

---

[9]Blake Landau, "Winning True Customer Loyalty and Trust in a Recession: A Conversation with Expert Shaun Smith" (March 23, 2009). Retrieved July 23, 2009 from: www.customermanagementiq.com/podcenter.cfm?externalID=71.

[10]Luc Bondar and Thomas Lacki, Ph.D., "Connecting with Wireless Customers: The Relationship Opportunity" (2009). Retrieved July 23, 2009 from: http://loyalty.carlsonmarketing.com.

[11]"The Results—Most Trusted Companies." Retrieved July 23, 2009 from: www.moneywise .co.uk/customer-service-awards/results/most-trusted.

[12]Shaun Smith, "Winning Customer Loyalty in an Economic Crisis" (February 26, 2009). Retrieved July 22, 2009 from: www.customermanagementiq.com/article.cfm?externalID=676.

Conditions exist today that make it even more competitively important for enterprises to take on a role as trusted agent for their customers. In particular:

■ *Commoditization.* Traditional marketers have always viewed customers through the lens of "Which product are we trying to sell?" Accordingly, in the old economy, a key driver of value was the "rent" producers of products could extract—derived from restricted information flows, brand "uniqueness," and other high-friction elements. Today, the Internet and computer technology have dramatically reduced the friction that used to characterize the exchange of information. As a result, products are becoming more and more like interchangeable commodities, which thereby puts the squeeze on rents.

■ *Needs, not products.* More relevant—more rent-producing than specific products—are the surrounding services. Customers are not looking for products as much as they are searching for experiences or solutions to problems. Consequently, value propositions are shifting. Value will increasingly be produced based on what companies know about "that customer" and what they do to provide customized product/service bundles to meet that customer's needs or to solve that customer's problem.

> The focus of every twentieth-century business was its product and inventory. In the twenty-first century, a company's products are, of course, important, but a company can still exist without any products at all. Now the company must have *customers* to thrive.

To foster a trusted relationship, a customer-based enterprise ensures that it always has a customer's interest in mind. It would not hesitate, for instance, to sell a customer a competitor's product rather than send the customer away empty-handed to look for help at the competitor's door. The focus of every twentieth-century business was its product and inventory. In the twenty-first century, a company's products are, of course, important, but *a company can still exist without any products at all*. Now the company must have *customers* to thrive. A trusted agent is one that can be relied on to make the customer's interest paramount, to speak on the customer's behalf in all its dealings.

The Man with the Folding Chair

A sales manager at Siemens AG often carried a folding chair into internal meetings with sales representatives. At first, the other participants in the meeting were puzzled. "Who are you expecting to join us?" someone asked. "Shouldn't we just get some more chairs brought in here?" others suggested.

"No," the manager replied, "This is my customer's chair. I brought it into the meeting so my customer can sit right here and listen to our discussion." The simple presence of the folding chair always changed the character of the meeting. It reminded everyone of the importance of the customers

(continued)

(Continued)

and caused everyone to ask, "What would our customer say?" and "How would our customer react?" It changed the very language and focus of the conversation.

The sales manager eventually became known as "Der Mann mit dem Klappstuhl," or "the man with the folding chair." The lesson he taught was powerful: Never fail to consider the customer's perspective in every decision.

Source: Adapted from Don Peppers & Martha Rogers, Ph.D., *Rules to Break & Laws to Follow: How Your Business Can Beat the Crisis of Short-Termism* (Hoboken, NJ: John Wiley & Sons, 2008), pp. 61–62.

A trusted agent's role is to improve the customer's ability to make choices, to manage his life or business. If that means using the agent's own products or services, so much the better. But in any given situation, it might well mean not using the agent's products. An online bookstore, for example, might warn a customer that the book she just ordered does not fit her Web profile and that other people who have read and enjoyed books similar to the ones she has bought from the bookstore in the past have not liked this particular book. As of this writing, Amazon.com has a policy somewhat (but not exactly) like this in place. Click on a book, and using a one-to-five-star system, Amazon will predict your rating of it, based on your previous purchases and ratings of other books, and incorporating all the other book buyers who have tastes and preferences somewhat similar to yours. While the company displays higher ratings prominently, it doesn't show any ratings on some books—apparently the ones you might not score so highly.

The trusted agent is confident that, in the long term, its knowledge of a customer's individual needs and preferences can be *monetized* at a higher value and with greater dependability than can a product or service differentiation. The trusted agent is betting that customer relationships will give it a refuge from the assault of product and service commoditization. Instead of focusing on the profitability of a single transaction, the trusted agent focuses on the profitability of the long-term relationship with the customer. Wall Street calls it "loyalty equity," a concept that is virtually synonymous with "customer equity" and "relationship equity" (see Chapters 1, 5, 11, and 13).

How, exactly, can a trusted agent actually go about monetizing a relationship if it doesn't push its own products in a preferential way? Many possible trusted agent business models exist. The easiest to imagine is the financial counselor who recommends a variety of products and services to a customer, even though some of these might be offered by competitors. The counselor will likely get a disproportionate share of the customer's business simply because the customer trusts his judgment. Trusted agency is almost certainly the future of relationship management. A trusted agent will recommend product-service combinations based on a customer's individual needs, irrespective of the level of profit that will be made on any particular transaction and nearly irrespective of the companies that might participate in the product-service delivery. Trusted agency is a compelling, perhaps irresistible, response against the increasing commoditization of products and services.

> The right question to ask is "How can the enterprise use interactivity, databases, social networking, innovation, and personalization technologies to add value for its customers, by saving them time or money or by creating a better fitting or more appropriate offering?"

Relationships, to be effective, must be built on trust, but the problem is that most enterprises view their businesses and their enabling technologies through the "wrong end of the telescope." If an enterprise starts by asking how it can use interactivity, databases, social networking, innovation, and personalization to sell its customers more products, then failure is almost inevitable. This view of the issue is highly self-oriented and simply cannot build a significant level of customer trust. Without trust, customer relationships will not take root, and the company, in the end, will find it impossible to achieve its business goals. The right question to ask, instead, is how can the enterprise use interactivity, databases, social networking, innovation, and personalization technologies to add value for its customers, by saving them time or money or by creating a better fitting or more appropriate offering?

Relationships Require Information, but Information Comes Only with Trust

Customers will ultimately have to decide how much information they are willing to share about themselves with an enterprise. Those who are freer with their information will receive more customized and personal service but will sacrifice a level of privacy. The future of a customer-strategy business world depends on gaining the customer's trust; relationships don't exist without it. Furthermore, a customer who is willing to "collaborate" may have a higher value to a company, but "willingness to collaborate" will be possible only when a customer trusts a company to use his information fairly. Without trust, customers will not give an enterprise the information it needs in order to serve that customer better. Lose customer trust and everything is lost. If a customer wasn't sure that his insurance company was not sharing his vital information with other companies, would he even think about filling out all those forms? If a customer does not trust her bank, would she give it every single iota of financial information about her business to qualify for a loan? (Businesses give their patronage to more than one bank so they won't be unduly dependent on any single institution, but some consumers give their business to more than one bank so that no single financial institution will have complete knowledge of their finances.)

In handling customer information, mistakes sometimes do happen. In these cases, it is critical for the company to take prompt action to minimize the consequence of the error and to maximize the restoration of customer trust. An apology goes a long way in rebuilding the relationship, especially one that has three characteristics:

1. It must be truly sincere, must forthrightly acknowledge the wrongdoing, and must reiterate the importance that the company places on its trustworthiness.
2. It must accept responsibility for the mistake rather than attempting to shift the blame to another party (e.g., the company's database management vendor).

3. It must articulate what the company has learned through the incident and how it is improving its processes and procedures to ensure that the mishap is not repeated.

When these steps are taken, most customers are willing to forgive temporary bouts of incompetence, provided that goodwill is demonstrated.

The late marketing guru Fred Newell wrote that as marketers develop more and more information about the lives and lifestyles of customers, the privacy issue heats up around the world.

Privacy issues will have to be examined from fresh perspectives if we are to continue the delicate balance between the marketer's need for information and the consumer's desire to control that information. The marketing community, so anxious for a continuing flow of customer information, must work to keep the balance by sharing more positive stories of customer benefits, to balance the media focus on Big-Brotherism, and the legislators' zeal to "protect us" from ourselves.[13]

Once customers feel assured that their data are safe with the company, the next logical step is to make it comfortable for them to share more and more information. It is better to build a customer relationship gradually, one piece at a time, than to flood the relationship with massive doses of data. At every step of the collaboration, enterprises need to

> "**P**rivacy issues will have to be examined from fresh perspectives if we are to continue the delicate balance between the marketer's need for information and the consumer's desire to control that information."
> —Fred Newell

concentrate on gathering the information useful to them. To build the necessary trust for customers to share that information, enterprises often need to offer their customers something of value in return. Many offer direct, cash-oriented benefits such as discounts, coupons, or promotions. Not surprisingly, some of the most successful companies working on this kind of "information exchange" take steps to individualize the offer so that it has greater value to a particular customer.

Customers are also becoming comfortable using automatic personalization tools on the Web. Although these tools are fine for customizing Web sites, they often fall short for nurturing enterprise/customer relationships. The enterprise must work harder truly to get to know the customer. A customer is more likely to stay loyal if she has taken the time to personalize a Web site herself *and the enterprise acts on the information given*. One of the primary goals of the enterprise focused on building customer value is to use the information it gathers about a customer to customize some aspect of its product or service to suit the customer's needs. The enterprise should begin to offer the customer things relevant to him, things that the customer could never find anywhere else, not from any generic offering that doesn't have information to use about him to meet his needs better. As a result, the customer will trust the company more. Once the flow of information begins between the customer and the enterprise, it is imperative for the enterprise to enable the customer to feel

---

[13]Frederick Newell, *The New Rules of Marketing* (New York: McGraw-Hill Professional Book Group, 1997).

she controls her information. The enterprise should enable the customer to use the information to save her time and money and deliver value. All of this will fulfill the customer's expectations of trust and earn her lifetime loyalty. Using a customer's information to her advantage might involve reminding her when she is going to run out of a product she uses regularly or developing a related product or service she could use.

The irony of the ongoing privacy debate is that, provided the customer is doing business with a legitimate enterprise committed to responsible privacy protection, if the information flow to the enterprise is severed, the ultimate loser will be the consumer himself. Precise product targeting can dramatically lower marketing costs and subsequently product prices. Although some consumers have said that they want customized offerings and the advantages enterprises can give them by tracking their personal data, it is essential to guarantee that the customized benefits provided will not jeopardize their privacy. Customers need to know that the company will use that data in a limited way for services agreed on in advance. Without such trust, customization is not a benefit.

CRM Scenario: Governments Develop Learning Relationships with "Citizen-Customers"

The "citizen as customer" is an innovative concept that is becoming more of a reality in the information era. Governments are becoming more "citizen-centric." State motor vehicle departments are streamlining and customizing the task of renewing a driver's license. Municipalities now allow residents to pay parking tickets and municipal bills online. Municipalities that develop Learning Relationships with their individual citizens can benefit primarily by being able to spend taxpayer money more productively and fairly. Suppose the parks department of a small city were to distribute bar-coded cards that could be swiped each time a citizen uses a parks service, permitting easy identification, record keeping, and tracking of individual interactions. By identifying who is using the city's swimming pools, playing fields, summer camps, or senior citizens' programs, the agency can see which services are in higher demand on the part of particular citizens or types of citizens. It might then be able to save money by customizing the seasonal fliers and catalogs it mails. For those citizens who have shown an interest in park concerts, e-mail messages could notify them of upcoming events. Perhaps the department's services could even be tailored to reflect the more specific needs of the town's most interested and active citizens.

One thing that is very clear is that building a Learning Relationship between a citizen and a government will require just as much trust as does building a commercial relationship. But can a government really build this kind of trust? And would the answer to this question be different in different countries? If a government were indeed capable of providing a great deal more convenience to you, would you trust it with the information required to do so?

E-ZPass, an automated toll-collection technology designed to reduce traffic volume in several states, including New York City's bridge and tunnel tollbooths,

(continued)

(Continued)

has provided a tool for the government to use individual information to improve itself and the efficiency of its public service: the roads, bridges, and tunnels. The electronic pass automatically identifies the vehicle as it passes through the tollbooth and automatically charges the toll to the owner's credit or debit card. This both permits faster movement through the tolls and enables database tracking of an individual's whereabouts (and presumably the speed with which the car gets from one checkpoint to the next!). The New York Transit Authority has maintained that the owner's information will be protected. Becoming a genuine, citizen-focused government agency, therefore, requires much more thought and effort than a few programs such as E-ZPass. As businesses everywhere are discovering, what really ensures a customer's goodwill and loyalty is not just putting up a Web site but creating a Learning Relationship with her.

Suppose a city began to monitor traffic intersections with video surveillance to nab vehicles that run through red lights. Would you object if the city sent you a traffic ticket because it had videotaped evidence of your car involved in such a misdemeanor? What if the city decided to keep track of your vehicle's location as it passed video cameras around town? Or what if it kept records of photos of you and your passengers without your knowledge?

In the context of a government developing individual relationships with its citizen-customers, a give-and-take scenario emerges with respect to the right to privacy and the demand for personalization (see Chapter 9 for a detailed discussion on privacy). In this scenario, the citizen-customers would want a government that could personalize their experience of living and working in the city; at the same time they would want to be able to trust the government enough to protect and respect any personal information that it gathered about them. The government, in contrast, would want to collect as much information as possible about each citizen-customer to create a more personalized living experience.

It must be noted, however, that, with respect to privacy, there is a big difference between a government and an enterprise. An enterprise that collects personal information about a customer would hold it in confidence from other enterprises because its proprietary nature provides a competitive advantage. The more it knows about an individual customer that its competitor does *not* know, the better an enterprise can personalize its relationship with that customer and grow its share of that customer's business. The customer would be less likely to defect to a competitor. A government, however, would like to know all it could about its citizens *and* might find advantages in sharing information with other government agencies. One government agency, for example, might like the capability to cross-check a criminal's driver's license number with his Social Security number and all of his prior aliases. Although this would make it harder to commit a crime under such a jurisdiction, many citizen-customers would likely object to such an invasion of privacy. Indeed, a number of influential citizens objected to allowing intelligence agencies and criminal investigation agencies to share information about specific suspects in an effort to prevent future terrorist attacks—a government activity that was made legal by the Patriot Act passed post–September 11, 2001.

Summary

Trust is the currency of all commerce. The single most powerful position in any customer's mind is a position of trust. For that reason, earning the customer's trust almost

> Trust is the currency of all commerce.

always becomes one of the earliest goals in any effort to build a long-term relationship with a customer and to build shareholder value by growing customer equity. Business expert Tom Peters points out: "In our world gone mad, trust is, paradoxically, more important than ever."[14] Let's face it: In a world of increasingly commodity-like products and services, a relationship founded on trust is the only genuinely sustainable competitive edge. Without trust, you're back to square one: *price competition*. The alternative is to build trusted Learning Relationships with customers, one customer at a time, and the way to build a Learning Relationship is IDIC.

In Chapter 4, we talk in more detail about the first implementation task in the IDIC methodology: identifying customers.

Food for Thought

1. Think about the companies you do business with as a customer. Name an example of a company that identified and recognized you, one that differentiated you by need or value, one that has made interaction easy and fun, and one that has changed something about the way it does business with you now, based on what it knows about you.
2. Do you agree or disagree that a relationship must always be characterized by some level of emotional involvement? Why?
3. Now that you've read Green's essay on trust, can you think of examples of companies that have little or no self-orientation? What are the signs that a company has too much self-orientation? (Check the company's stock performance for the last 15 years.)
4. In the last few years we have seen many examples of the breakdown between company governance and stakeholder interests. Do you think these corporate scandals might have played out differently if the corporations involved had built their businesses on the basis of becoming trusted agents for their customers? Is it really possible for companies to be trusted?

Glossary

Customize   Become relevant by doing something for a customer that no competition can do that doesn't have all the information about that customer that you do.

Differentiate   Prioritize by value; understand different needs. Identify, recognize, link, remember.

---

[14]Tom Peters, at www.tompeters.com.

Identify   Recognize and remember each customer regardless of the channel by or geographic area in which the customer leaves information about himself. Be able to link information about each customer to generate a complete picture of each customer.

IDIC   Stands for Identify-Differentiate-Interact-Customize.

Interact   Generate and remember feedback.

Self-orientation   Self-interest. A company that focuses on building customer value is obviously interested in its own bottom line but believes the bottom line is best served by focusing on the needs of customers.

Trusted agent   A person or organization that makes recommendations and gives advice to a customer that furthers the customer's own interest, even when it occasionally conflicts with the enterprise's own self-interest, at least in the short term.

CHAPTER 4

Identifying Customers

It wasn't raining when Noah built the Ark.

—Howard Ruff

Before any relationship can start, both parties have to know each other's identities and be able to build a comprehensive view of the other. The goal of identifying customers refers not so much to figuring out which customers we want (that comes later) but to *recognizing* each customer *as that customer* each time we come in contact with her and then linking those different data points to develop a full picture of each particular customer. This chapter addresses the issue of "identify" for consumers as well as for business customers and defines the different elements of this "identify" task. We also address *frequency marketing* in the context of customer identification.

All enterprises use information about their customers to make smarter decisions. But for most traditional marketing decisions and actions, information is really needed only at the aggregate, or market, level. That is, any marketer needs to know the *average* demand for a particular product feature within a population of prospective customers, or the range of prices that this market population will find attractive. The enterprise then uses this information to plan its production and distribution as well as its marketing and sales activities.

But building relationships with customers necessarily involves making decisions and taking actions at the level of the *individual* customer, using customer-specific information in addition to information about the aggregate characteristics of the market population. This is because a "relationship" inherently implies some type of mutual interaction between two individual parties. We cannot have a "relationship" with a population or group but only with another individual. So the competitor trying to win with superior customer relationship strategies needs first to know the individual *identities* of the customers who make up the traditional marketer's aggregate market population. Then the enterprise will make different marketing, sales, distribution, and production decisions, and take different actions, with respect to different customers, to create better experiences and increase customer value, even within the same market or niche population.

Individual Information Requires Customer Recognition

The essence of managing customer relationships is *treating different customers differently*; therefore, the first requirement for any enterprise to engage in this type of competition is simply to "know" one customer from another. However, identifying individual customers is not an easy process, and usually not a perfect one. Not many years ago, a British utility launched a December promotion to recognize its very best customers by mailing each of them a holiday greeting card. To the astonishment of its management, nearly 25 percent of these cards were returned to the company unopened in January. Apparently, many of the firm's "most valuable customers" were actually lampposts. Until that time, this company's management had equated electric meters with customers, comfortable in the knowledge that because they tracked meters, they also tracked customers. But lampposts don't read mail or make decisions.

Most enterprises will find it difficult simply to compile a complete and accurate list of all the uniquely individual customers they serve, though some businesses and industries are more naturally able to identify their customers than others. Consider the differences among these businesses, and consider the advantage that would accrue to a company that's able to identify individual customers and recognize each one at every contact:

- *Telecommunications companies* sell many of their services directly to end-user consumers. After all, to bill a customer for her calls in any given sales period, a phone company's computers must track that customer's calling activities—numbers connected to, time spent in each connection, day of week, and time of day. But even a cell phone company will likely make some sales to prepaid customers whose identities it can't actually learn, because they buy their top-up cards in convenience stores or through distributors, and often prepaid customers want to maintain their anonymity. Such a firm may also serve a number of corporate clients whose end users are not specifically identified.
- *Retail banks* must know individual customer identities to keep track of each customer's banking activities and balances. Historically, banks have been organized along lines of business, with credit cards, checking accounts, and home equity loans processed in completely different divisions. As a result, information about whether a branch banking customer is also a credit card customer often has not been readily available to either separate division. More and more banks are recognizing the need to coordinate and integrate information across product divisions, to produce a complete relationship profile of the customer accessible to all divisions in real time.[1]
- *Consumer packaged goods* companies sell their grocery and personal care products in supermarkets, drugstores, and other retail outlets. Although their true end customers are those who walk into the stores and buy these products, there is no technically simple way for the packaged goods companies to find out who these retail consumers are or to link their individual identities with

---

[1]"Achieving Customer Centricity in Retail Banking" (2006), Tibco Software, Inc.; available at: www.tibco.com/multimedia/solution-brief-achieving-customer-centricity-in-retail-banking-tcm8-2434.pdf, accessed September 1, 2010.

their buying histories, except in some cases by using a "loyalty card" or other information-collection program. Recently, Infosys released Shopping 360, a sensor-based way for retailers and consumer packaged goods companies all to monitor and share information about what is bought off store display shelves by whom, if customers have given their individual permission.[2]

- *Insurance companies* can nearly always tell you how many policies they have written, but many cannot tell you how many customers they have or even how many households or businesses they serve. This is changing, of course, as more and more insurance companies recognize the need to base the organization and the reward structure for policy sales on customers.[3]

- *A computer equipment company* selling systems to other companies in a business-to-business environment may be able to identify the businesses it is selling to, but it is much more difficult for the firm to identify the individual *players* who actually participate in each organization's decision to buy. Yet within any business customer it is these players—decision makers, influencers, specifiers, approvers, contract authorities, purchasing agents, reviewers, end users—with whom the selling company should be developing relationships. Thus some Web-based selling and contact-management tools are now able to help keep this information in a way that's useful to the selling company.

- *Carmakers,* as well as state and local governments, have for decades recorded the current owner of each registered automobile by the vehicle identification number (VIN), visible through the front window of any car. However, even though the owner of each car can be determined, the cars belonging to each owner cannot. More recently, carmakers have begun relying on customer identification numbers, in order to tell whether two VINs are concurrently or sequentially owned by the same customer.[4]

Identifying customers, therefore, is not usually very easy, and the degree of difficulty any company faces in identifying its own customers is largely a function of its business model and its channel structure. In her book *Customers.com*, business consultant Patricia Seybold speculates that Microsoft probably has more than 100 million customers who have purchased its products through indirect channels (i.e., buying the software bundled on a computer, ordering it through a catalog, or picking it up at a store). And yet, for many years, the only end customers Microsoft knew about were the 90 enterprise accounts it maintained and the 25 million people who had sent in warranty registration cards. Then, in the late 1990s, as customers flocked to Microsoft's Web site and interacted with the company, Microsoft began identifying

---

[2]Infosys press release, "Infosys Technologies Launches Breakthrough Services for Retailers and Consumer Packaged Goods Companies," Bangalore, India (July 31, 2008); available at: www.infosys.com/newsroom/press-releases/Pages/launches-breakthrough-services-retailers. aspx, accessed September 1, 2010.

[3]Nadine Gatzert, Ines Holzmuller, and Hato Schmeiser, "Creating Customer Value in Participating Life Insurance," *working papers on Risk Management and Insurance,* no. 64, Institute of Insurance Economics, University of St. Gallen (January 2009).

[4]Richard Barrington, "Hard Lessons from CRM Experience: Six Mistakes to Avoid," VendorGuru white paper; available at www.vendorguru.com, p. 4, accessed February 2, 2010.

greater numbers of its customers and collecting specific information about them individually, including e-mail addresses and product preferences.[5]

To engage any of its customers in relationships, an enterprise needs to know these customers' identities. Thus, it must first understand the limitations, make choices, and set priorities with respect to its need to identify individual customers. How many end-customer identities are actually known to the enterprise today? How accurate are these identities? How much duplication and overlap is there in the data? What proportion of all customer identities is known? Are there ways the enterprise could uncover a larger number of customer identities? If so, which customer identities does the enterprise want to access first?

Step 1: How Much Customer Identification Does a Company Already Have?

To assess more accurately how much customer-identifying information it already has, an enterprise should:

- *Take an inventory of all of the customer data already available in any kind of electronic format.* Customer identification information might be stored in several electronic places, such as on the Web server or in the contact center database.
- *Find customer-identifying information that is "on file" but not electronically compiled.* Data about customers that has been written down but not electronically recorded should be transferred to a computer database, if it is valuable, so that it will be accessible internally and protected from loss or unnecessary duplication.

Only after it assesses its current inventory of customer-identifying information should a company launch its own programs for gathering more. Programs designed to collect customer-identifying information might include, for instance, the purchase of the data, if it is available, from various third-party database companies; the scheduling of an event to be attended by customers; or a contest, a frequency marketing program, or some other promotion that encourages customers to "raise their hands."

Real Objective of Frequency Marketing Programs

Frequency marketing is a tactic by which an enterprise rewards its customers with points, discounts, merchandise, or other incentives, in return for the customer patronizing the enterprise on a repeated basis. Often called loyalty programs (see Chapter 2), frequency marketing programs can provide indispensable tools enabling companies to identify and track customers, one customer at a time, across different operating units or divisions, through different channels, and over long periods of time. By providing the customer with an incentive for purchasing that is linked to the customer's previous purchases, the enterprise ensures that

---

[5]Patricia B. Seybold, *Customers.com: How to Create a Profitable Business Strategy for the Internet and Beyond* (New York: Random House, 1998).

she has an interest in identifying herself to the company and "raising her hand" whenever she deals with the company. The customer wants the incentive, and in order to get it, she must engage in activity that allows the enterprise to identify her and track her transactions, over time.

It is not absolutely necessary for a frequency marketing program to be linked to a customer ID system. Top Value stamps and S&H Green Stamps programs were very popular in the 1950s and 1960s. As a consumer, you might choose to shop at grocery stores or gas stations that gave away Green Stamps. You'd pay your bill and get a receipt and your stamps in exchange. Then you would go home and paste the stamps into the right places on the pages of the little paperback book you had been given. Six books would get you a toaster; 4,300 books would buy a fishing boat. These giveaways were not used to identify customers; they involved no central customer database and maintained no records of individual purchase transactions. Although a trading stamps program is technically a frequency marketing program, because customers are indeed rewarded for the frequency and volume of their purchases, such an "unlinked" program with no computer database of transaction information is practically useless when it comes to aiding a company in its effort to build customer relationships.

⌈The primary objective of a modern-day frequency marketing program should be to accumulate customer information by encouraging purchasers to identify themselves. For some companies—particularly those firms that find it difficult to identify and track customers who nevertheless engage in frequent or repeated transactions—frequency marketing programs can perform a vital part of the "identify" task, allowing a firm to link the interactions and transactions of a single customer from one event to the next. Frequent shopper programs launched by grocery chains and other retail operators are excellent examples of this kind of frequency marketing.⌋

There is an important implication here with respect to how a program creates value for the enterprise. If goods and services are simply discounted with points or prizes, and that's the entire program, then it is a *parity strategy*; once competitors match the points or the rewards, the only thing the sponsoring company will end up with are reduced profit margins. But if, say, the points are given in exchange for shopping basket data or other information about a customer that can be used to deepen the relationship, then the information derived is an investment that can generate profits as the company uses the data to build a more loyal relationship with a customer.

As a matter of practice, many companies implement such programs with the sole intention of rewarding customers for giving them more of their patronage. The risk to the enterprise of doing this is that if the frequency program is a success, competitors will eventually offer customers the same or similar rewards structures for buying from them. Over time, the program will be reduced to nothing more than a sophisticated form of price competition, as in fact did happen to the S&H Green Stamps program when other stamp programs were introduced and consumers simply kept stamps at home in separate cigar boxes.

To a customer, the incentive itself (e.g., free miles, free goods, prizes, and discounts) will often be the most immediate motive for participating. Then it is up

(continued)

(Continued)

to the enterprise to use the information to treat the customer differently. Airline frequent flyer programs tier their customers into different levels—platinum, gold, silver, and so forth—and then provide special benefits to the highest tiers, from priority check-in lines to occasional upgrades. It is the information about an individual customer's ongoing purchases and needs that enables the enterprise to tailor its behavior or customize its product or service for that particular customer. The greater the level of customization, the more loyal customers can become.

It is not always so easy to figure out how to treat different customers differently, however, even when they can be individually identified and tracked. A grocery store's frequency marketing program can return a rich detail of information about the individual shopping habits of the store's customers, but what should the store then do with this information? From a practical standpoint, the store cannot customize itself to meet the needs of individual customers. The store is destined to be the same for every customer who enters it, because it would be totally impractical to rearrange the merchandise to meet the needs of any particular customer. Nevertheless, it should be possible to use the information about the mix of products consumed by a single customer in such a way as to make highly customized offers to that customer, when those offers are communicated either by postal mail or through interactive technologies. Tesco, for instance, with well over 2,000 United Kingdom and over 2,000 additional non–United Kingdom stores,[a] is the largest supermarket chain in the United Kingdom and has a highly successful frequency marketing program that illustrates exactly what it means to make different offers to different customers (see Chapters 2 and 10).

Tesco relaunched its Clubcard program in May 2009, offering new features and enhanced rewards. Tesco boasted 16 million active Clubcard holders in the United Kingdom,[b] and its members' purchases accounted for about 80 percent of all Tesco's in-store transactions at the relaunch.

Since implementing Clubcard, in-store product turnover increased more than 51 percent behind a mere 15 percent increase in floor space. The company credits its success with the fact that it is engaged in "rifle-shot" marketing to its customer base rather than the more traditional scatter-shot approach of the mass merchant. The Clubcard program allows Tesco to link product information with each individual customer's past purchases. So, for example, based on its individual customer data, Tesco can send a Clubcard member a personalized letter with coupons aimed squarely at that particular customer's own shopping needs. This program generates an astonishing *high* redemption rate of some 90 percent! Tesco has differentiated more than 5,000 different "needs segments" among its customers and uses this insight to send out highly customized offers. All members also receive a remarkably mass-customized quarterly magazine.

Tesco originally defined eight primary "life state" customer groups, with each edition's editorial content specifically written for its target group. Counting the multiplicity of third-party advertisements, Tesco's magazines are printed and distributed in literally hundreds of thousands of combinations.

Some enterprises charge customers a membership fee to belong to a frequency marketing program. Car rental companies, for example, have in the past had programs that charge customers a separate membership fee to guarantee preferential treatment at airports; these programs tracked the customer's individual transactions as well. Customers who are willing to invest money in a continuing Learning Relationship with an enterprise become committed to the collaborative solution of a problem. And any enterprise that collaborates with its customers is more likely to be able to ask the types of questions needed to achieve a higher share of a customer's business. It is easier for the enterprise to ask questions of a customer who has agreed to enter a relationship.⌋

---

[a]See www.tescocorporate.com/plc/media/qf/ for updated information, accessed September 1, 2010.

[b]See www.marketingmagazine.co.uk/news/943397/Tesco-Clubcard-signs-one-million-customers-relaunch/ for updated information, accessed September 1, 2010.

Step 2: Get Customers to Identify Themselves

Sales contests and sponsored events are often designed for the specific purpose of gathering potential and established customer names and addresses. But to engage a customer in a genuine relationship, a company must also be able to link the customer to her own specific purchase and service transaction behavior. Analyzing past behavior is probably the single most useful method for modeling a customer's future value, as we'll see in Chapter 5, on customer differentiation, and Chapter 12, on analytics. So although a one-time contest or promotion might help a company identify customers it did not previously "know," linking the customer's identity to her actual transactions is also important.

Frequency marketing programs suit both purposes, providing not only a mechanism to identify customers, but also a means to link customers, over time, with the specific transactions they undertake. Such programs have been used for years to strengthen relationships with individual customers, but it's important to recognize that a frequency marketing program is a tactic, not a strategy. It is an important enabling step for a broader relationship strategy, because a frequency marketing program provides a company with a mechanism for identifying and tracking customers individually; but this will lead to a genuine relationship-management strategy only when the company actually uses the information it gets in this way to design different treatments for different customers.

What Does *Identify* Mean?

Given that the purpose of identifying individual customers is to facilitate the development of relationships with them individually, we are using the word *identify* in its broadest possible form. What we are really saying is that an enterprise must undertake all of these identification activities:

Identification Activities
- *Define.* Decide what information will comprise the actual customer's identity: Is it name and address? Home phone number? Account number? Householding information?

- *Collect.* Arrange to collect these customer identities. Collection mechanisms could include frequent shopper bar codes; credit card data; paper applications; Web-based interactions via Web site, blog comments, Facebook, or Twitter;[6] radio frequency identification (RFID) microchips (such as E-Z Pass and Exxon-Mobil's Speedpass); or any number of other vehicles.

- *Link.* Once a customer's identity is fixed, it must be linked to all transactions and interactions with that customer, at all points of contact, and within all the enterprise's different operating units and divisions. It is one thing, for instance, to identify the consumer who goes into a grocery store, but a frequent shopper program is usually the primary mechanism to link that shopper's activities together, so that the enterprise knows it is the same shopper, every time he comes into the store.[7] Also, if a customer shops online for a product but then contacts the company's call center to order it, the relationship-oriented enterprise wants to be able to link that customer's online interactions with her call-in order.

- *Integrate.* The customer's identity must not only be linked to all interactions and transactions; it must also be integrated into the information systems the enterprise uses to run its business. Frequent flier identities need to be integrated into the flight reservations data system. Household banking identities need to be integrated into the small business records maintained by the bank.

- *Recognize.* The customer who returns to a different part of the organization needs to be recognized as the same customer, not a different one. In other words, the customer who visits the Web site today, goes in to the store or the bank branch tomorrow, and calls the toll-free number next week needs to be recognized as the same customer, not three separate events or visitors.

- *Store.* Identifying information about individual customers must be linked, stored, and maintained in one or several electronic databases.

- *Update.* All customer data, including customer identifying data, is subject to change and must be regularly verified, updated, improved, or revised.

- *Analyze.* Customer identities must serve as the key inputs for analyzing individual customer differences (see Chapter 12).

- *Make available.* The data on customer identities maintained in an enterprise's databases must be made available to the people and functions within the enterprise that need access to it. Especially in a service organization, making individual customer-identifying information available to front-line service personnel is important. Computers help enterprises codify, aggregate, filter, and sort customer information for their own and their customers' benefit. Storing customer identification information in an accessible format is critical to the success of a customer-centered enterprise.

- *Secure.* Because individual customer identities are both competitively sensitive and threatening to individual customer privacy, it is critical to secure this information to prevent its unauthorized use.

---

[6]Michael S. Kenny and Will Yen, "Social Media: Examining Social Media Strategy and Architecture" (2009), Slalom Consulting white paper; available at www.slalom.com, accessed February 2, 2010.

[7]Other information collection tools, such as the wireless, sensor-based tracking systems mentioned earlier, could supplement or replace a frequent shopper program. Infosys press release, "Infosys Technologies Launches Breakthrough Services for Retailers and Consumer Packaged Goods Companies," Bangalore, India, July 31, 2008.

Technology is enabling enterprises to identify customers in ways never before imagined. Some enterprises still might use the old Rolodex card file system, but computer databases and sophisticated customer information databases are quickly supplanting these handwritten cards for the same reason that public libraries have abandoned their card catalog systems: because card catalog systems cost much more than their electronic counterparts and are available for search only in the physical library building. Sophisticated electronic data systems allow library patrons to search a library's holdings from anywhere and help the library cut its own costs at the same time.

Integrated computer databases don't just reduce costs. More important, they also help identify patterns that aren't possible when the data is kept in filing systems or in separate data silos. The more the company integrates data from all corners of the enterprise, even including the extended enterprise, the richer in value the customer information becomes in planning and executing customer-focused strategies.

The end customer of an enterprise is the one who consumes the product or service it provides. That said, sometimes it is more of an indirect relationship, which makes it more difficult to tag the customer and link information to her. Sometimes, a product or service might be purchased by one customer and used by another member of the household or by the recipient of a gift. And as we discuss later, sometimes an end user will be an employee of a company while it is the company's purchasing department that actually buys the product. Regardless of these intermediary relationships, however, it is the end user who is at the top of the food chain and the end user whose relationship with the enterprise is most important, because this is the person whose needs will or won't be met by the product.

Customer Identification in a B2B Setting

A business-to-business (B2B) enterprise still must identify customers, and many of the issues are the same; but there are some important differences that merit additional consideration. For instance, when selling to business customers, the B2B enterprise must consider who will be on the other side of the relationship. Will it be the purchasing manager or the executive who signs the purchase order? Will it be the financial vice president who approved the contract? Or will it be the production supervisor or line engineer who actually uses the product? The correct way for an enterprise to approach a B2B scenario is to think of each of these individuals as a part of the customer base. Each is important in his or her own way, and each one should be identified and tracked. The greatest challenge for many businesses that sell to other businesses is identifying the product's end users. Discovering who, within the corporate customer's organization, puts a product to work (i.e., who depends on the product to do her job) is often quite difficult. Some methods for identifying end users include:[8]

- If the product consumes any replenishable supplies (e.g., inks, drill bits, recording paper, chemicals), providing a convenient method for reordering these supplies is an obvious service for end users.

---

[8]Don Peppers, Martha Rogers, Ph.D., and Bob Dorf, *The One to One Fieldbook: The Complete Toolkit for Implementing a 1to1 Marketing Program* (New York: Doubleday, 1999).

■ If the product is complicated to use, requiring a detailed instruction manual or perhaps different sets of application notes or even training, one way to secure end-user identities is to offer such instructions in a simplified, individually tailored format.

■ If the product needs periodic maintenance or calibration or regular service for any reason, the enterprise can use these occasions to identify end users.

B2B firms use many strategies to get to know the various role players within the corporations they are selling to, from end users to chief financial officers—setting up personal meetings, participating at trade shows, swapping business cards, sponsoring seminars and other events, inviting people to work-related entertainment occasions, and so forth. But the single most important method for identifying the "relationships within relationships" at an enterprise customer is to provide a service or a benefit for the customer that can really be fully realized only when the players themselves reveal their identities and participate actively in the relationship. Thus, even though relationship marketing has always been a standard tool in the B2B space, today's new technologies are making it possible more than ever before to manage the actual mechanics of these individual relationships from the enterprise level. In so doing, the enterprise ensures that the relationship itself adheres to the enterprise, not just to the sales representative or other employee conducting the activity.

Customer Identification in a B2C Setting

Can we identify—and recognize again and again—*millions* of customers? In the business-to-consumer (B2C) space, the technology-driven customer relationship management (CRM) movement has only recently made it possible even to conceive of the possibility of managing individual consumer relationships. But while managing relationships within the B2C space might be a relatively new idea, mass marketers have always understood that customer information is critical and that the possible ways of identifying customers are nearly limitless.

New technologies have made it possible to identify customers without their active involvement. ExxonMobil, the gasoline retailer, dispenses RFID microchips that can be carried around on the keychain of a customer who participates in its Speedpass campaign. When the customer drives up to a gas pump, the microchip device automatically identifies the customer and charges the customer's credit card for the transaction. The customer is rewarded with a speedier exit from the gas pump (although she still must pump her own gas). The company, in turn, can identify each customer every time she buys gas at any ExxonMobil station and link that identification with every transaction.

Of course, few would deny that the Internet gave the biggest push to the customer relationship movement in the B2C arena. Not only did the World Wide Web provide tools to existing firms with which they could interact more effectively with their customers and identify an increasing number of them individually, but it also led to the creation of many new, Internet-based businesses with extremely streamlined business models based on direct, one-to-one relationships with individual customers, online.

As writer Stewart Alsop described the way Amazon.com led the way at the turn of the new century:

> *What Amazon.com has done is invent and implement a model for interacting with millions of customers, one at a time. Old-line companies can't do that—I like Nordstrom, Eddie Bauer, Starbucks, and Shell, but they have to reach out to me with mass advertising and marketing. Amazon's technology gives me exactly what I want, in an extraordinarily responsive way. The underlying technology, in fact, is revolutionizing the way companies do business on the Web.*[9]

Customer Data Revolution

> The computer has brought about "three awesome powers": the power to *record*, the power to *find*, and the power to *compare*.
>
> —Stan Rapp

Clearly, in the Information Age, an enterprise can reach and communicate with individual customers one at a time, it can observe as customers talk to each other about the company, and it can follow strategies for its customer interactions that are based on relevant, customer-specific information stored in a customer database. The computer can now store millions of customer records—not just names and addresses, but age, gender, marital status and family configuration, buying habits, history, and demographic and psychographic profiles. Individuals can be selected from this database by one, two, three, or more of their identifying characteristics. CRM expert Stan Rapp has said that the computer has brought about "three awesome powers": the power to *record*, the power to *find*, and the power to *compare*.[10]

- *The computer's power to record.* In precomputer days, there would have been no point in recording by typewriter dozens of bits of information about each customer or prospect on thousands of index cards. Without the computer, there would have been no practical way to make use of such information. As computer data storage rapidly became more economical, however, it became possible and desirable to build up and use a prospect or customer record with great detail.
- *The computer's power to find.* Selections can be made from the prospect or customer file by any field definitions or combination of field definitions.
- *The computer's power to compare.* Information on customers with one set of characteristics can be compared to customer information using a different set of characteristics. For instance, the computer can compare a list of *older people* and a list of *golfers*.

---

[9]Back in 2001, *Fortune* columnist Stewart Alsop rightly pegged Amazon.com not only as a technology company when most relegated it to the more mundane role of e-tailer but as one of the only companies that had "mastered the use of technology in serving individual customers." Stewart Alsop, "I'm Betting on Amazon," *Fortune,* April 30, 2001, 48.

[10]Stan Rapp, *The Great Marketing Turnaround* (Upper Saddle River, NJ: Prentice Hall, 1990).

For all its power, however, the truth is that when it comes to customer-oriented activities, the computer is an underutilized technology at most businesses—not because companies don't want to use it, but because most customer data are simply not fit for use in an analytical database. The development of a database of customer information requires a *data model*—the tool required to bring data complexities under control. The data model defines the structure of the database and lays out a map for how information about customers will be organized and deployed.

At present, customer data are often duplicated in multiple operational databases. Multiple instances of data usually create data quality issues (think of how many times you've gotten mail from your bank with your name misspelled or with the wrong address), and these issues need to be addressed head-on if a customer relationship program is to be successful. This raises issues of data ownership and accountability, and can become a politically charged issue in the organization. But those companies that try to implement CRM without addressing this critical issue usually fail. It has to start with a single, complete view of each customer.

What Data Do We Need When We Identify a Customer?

After it has mined its existing customer databases and developed a plan to gather new customer information, the enterprise then decides how to tag its customers' individual identities. Names are not always a sufficient customer identifier. More than one customer might have the same name, or a customer might use several different varieties of the same name—middle initial, nickname, maiden name, and so forth. To use a customer database effectively, therefore, it is usually necessary to assign unique and reliable customer numbers or identifiers to each individual customer record. It could be the customer's e-mail address, phone number, a "user name" selected by the customer, or an internally generated identifier.

In addition to transaction details, other types of data generated from internal operations can make significant contributions. Information relating to billing and account status, customer service interactions, back orders, product shipment, product returns, claims history, and internal operating costs all can significantly affect an enterprise's understanding of its customers. Directly supplied data consists of data obtained directly from customers, prospects, or suspects. It is generally captured from lead-generation questionnaires, customer surveys, warranty registrations, customer service interactions, Web site responses, or other direct interactions with individuals.

Directly supplied data consists of three obvious types:

1. **Behavioral data**, such as purchase and buying habits, clickstream data gleaned from the way a firm's website visitor clicks through the firm's website, interactions with the company, communication channels chosen, language used, product consumption, and company share of wallet

2. **Attitudinal data**, reflecting attitudes about products, such as satisfaction levels, perceived competitive positioning, desired features, and unmet needs as well as lifestyles, brand preferences, social and personal values, opinions, and the like

3. **Demographic** (i.e., "descriptive") **data**, such as age, income, education level, marital status, household composition, gender, home ownership, and so on.[11]

---

[11]Andrew R. Thomas, ed., *Direct Marketing in Action: Cutting Edge Strategies for Finding and Keeping the Best Customers* (Westport, CT: Praeger, 2007); David Shepard, *The New Direct Marketing* (New York: McGraw-Hill Professional Book Group, 1999).

In categorizing data contained in a customer database, it's important to recognize that some data—*stable data*, such as birth date or gender—will need to be gathered only once. Once verified for accuracy, these data can survive in a database over long periods and many programs. Updates of stable data should be undertaken to correct errors, but, except for errors, stable data won't need much alteration. In contrast, there are other data—*adaptive data*, such as a person's intended purchases or even her feelings about a particular political candidate— that will need constant updating. This is not a binary classification, of course. In reality, some data are *relatively* more stable or adaptive than other data.

Why Is Identification Important?

Ultimately, of course, the central purpose of collecting customer information is to enable the development of closer, more profitable relationships with individual customers. In many cases, these relationships will be facilitated by the availability to the enterprise of information that will make the customer's next transaction simpler, faster, or cheaper. Remembering a customer's logistical information, for instance, will make reordering easier for her, and therefore more likely. Remembering this type of information will also lead the customer to believe she is important to the company and that her patronage is valued.

In order to make any of this work, however, it is essential for the enterprise to establish a trusting relationship with the customer, so she feels free to share information. A vocal privacy-protection movement—perhaps more active in Europe than in North America—has been energized by the increasing role that individual information plays in ordinary commerce and the perceived threat to individual privacy that this poses. However, both practical experience and a number of academic studies have shown that the vast majority of consumers are not at all reluctant to share their individual information when there is a clear value proposition for doing so and when they trust the company. Therefore, if a company can demonstrate to the customer that individual information will be used to deliver tangible benefits (and provided the customer trusts the enterprise to hold the information reasonably confidential beyond that), then the customer is usually more than willing to allow the use of the information. Trusting relationships or not, protecting customer privacy and ensuring the safety and security of customer-specific information are critical issues in the implementation of customer strategies and will be discussed in greater detail in Chapter 9.

Integrating Data to Identify Customers

The process of identifying customers in order to engage them in relationships requires that customer-identifying information be integrated into many different aspects of an enterprise's business activities. It used to be that customer data could be collected over a period of time, and the customer database would be updated with revised profile and analytic information in batches. On weekends, perhaps, or late at night, information collected since the last update would be used to update the customer database. Increasingly, however, companies rely on Web sites and call centers to interact with customers, and this places a much greater emphasis on ensuring real-time access to customer-identifying information.

Enterprises must be able to capture customer information and organize it, aggregate it, integrate it, and disseminate it to any individual or group, throughout the enterprise, in real time. Technology is enabling enterprises to accelerate the flow of customer information at the most strategically timed moment. Enterprises strive for **zero latency**—that is, no lag time required—for the flow of information from customer, to database, to decision maker (or to a rules-based decision-making "engine"). The computer-driven processes of data mining, collaborative filtering, and predictive modeling will increasingly alter the process of forecasting how consumers behave and what they want,[12] and, as more and more real-time interactivity continues to permeate all aspects of our lives, we can expect customers to demand more and more real-time service, which means enterprises will need real-time access to customer data.

In any service context, it is critical that an enterprise's customer-facing people have ready access to customer-identifying data as well as to the records attached to particular customer identities. Making valuable customer information available to front-line, customer-facing employees, whether they work on board a passenger airliner, behind the counter at a retail bank branch, or at the call center for an automobile manufacturer, is an increasingly important task at all B2C enterprises.[13]

Borders Group uses a customer database and its Borders Rewards Program to give managers a consolidated view of its customers, including those from Borders Books, Borders Music, Waldenbooks stores, and the Borders.com Web site. With these kinds of data, Borders can discern whether customers who purchased books in its retail stores are the same ones who bought online. Borders is using data-integration technology to build the system and software to analyze the data and manage customer relationship campaigns based on the findings.[14]

Many enterprises underestimate the cost and difficulty of creating an integrated view of customer-identifying information. According to John McKean, author of *Information Masters*, testing an enterprise's competency for using customer data requires that every aspect of the enterprise's information environment affecting the efficiency of information flow be taken into account. This includes what McKean considers important, customer-facing functional areas, including direct marketing, customer service, and sales.[15] McKean divides enterprises into three distinct

---

[12]Dolores Romero Morales and Jingbo Wang, "Forecasting Cancellation Rates for Services Booking Revenue Management Using Data Mining," *European Journal of Operational Research* 202, no. 2 (April 2010): 554–562; Heung-Nam Kim et al., "Collaborative Filtering Based on Collaborative Tagging for Enhancing the Quality of Customer Recommendation," *Electronic Commerce Research and Applications* 9, no. 1 (January-February 2010): 73–83; Rodolfo Ledesma, "Predictive Modeling of Enrollment Yield for a Small Private College," *Atlantic Economic Journal* 37, no. 3 (September 2009): 323.

[13]Don Peppers, "Customer Service at a CLIP," *Inside 1to1,* June 10, 1999; available at: www.1to1.com.

[14]Borders Group press release, "Borders Group Presents Long-Term Strategic Plan to Focus on Core Domestic Superstore Business," Ann Arbor, MI, March 22, 2007; available at PR Newswire, www.prnewswire.com/news-releases/borders-group-presents-long-term-strategic-plan-to-focus-on-core-domestic-superstore-business-52175002.html, accessed September 1, 2010; Rick Whiting, "Borders Wants to Read Its Customers Like a Book," *Information Week,* August 21, 2000, p. 34.

[15]John McKean, *Information Masters* (New York: John Wiley & Sons, 1999).

categories based on their customer information competency: mass-market, transitional, and information mastery.

1. *Mass-market customer information competency.* Essentially, a firm devoting a majority of its resources to processing transactional-oriented information. This task is viewed as an obligatory encumbrance to finish transactional tasks within the firm; for example, sending out bills, invoices, accounting practices, and customer notices.
2. *Transitional customer information competency.* Still similar in many respects to the mass-market category, yet this firm has had pockets of success in increasing the level of information sophistication.
3. *The customer information master, or an "information-based competitor."* A firm that believes customer information is truly its most valuable asset and provides its only sustainable, distinct operational competency.

Professor Rashi Glazer clarifies the implications of an enterprise-wide view of the customer—what several authorities have called "one view of the truth" and others have called the "360-degree view of the customer."

Role of Smart Markets in Managing Relationships with Customers

Rashi Glazer
Professor and Co-Director of the Management of Technology Program, Walter A. Haas School of Business, University of California at Berkeley

Perhaps the most important implication of the Information Age for business is the emergence of information-intensive or *smart* markets—that is, markets defined by frequent turnovers in the general stock of knowledge or information embodied in products and services and possessed by firms and consumers. In contrast to traditional "dumb" markets—which are static, fixed, and basically information-poor—smart markets are dynamic, turbulent, and information-rich.

Smart markets are based on smart products, those product and service offerings that have intelligence or computational capability built into them and therefore can adapt or respond to changes in the environment as they interact with customers. Smart markets are also characterized by smart consumers, consumers who, from the standpoint of the firm, are continually "speaking" (i.e., they are not mute, or "dumb"); and, in so doing, educate or teach the firm about who they are and what they want. In such an environment, competition is less about who has the best products and more about which firm can spend the most time interacting with—and therefore learning from—its customers.

A major implication of information-intensive, or smart, markets is the widespread breaking down of boundaries where there once were well-defined roles or discrete categories:

(continued)

(Continued)

- Boundaries between products are breaking down (in particular, the boundary between products and services).
- Within the firm, boundaries between departments are breaking down, as no department or area has all the information necessary (and the flow of information between departments is not fast enough) to respond to customer requests before the competition does.
- Most significantly, the boundaries between the firm and the external world are breaking down: between the firm and its competitors, as firms realize they need to partner in order to put in place the infrastructure issues necessary for the sale of their own products; and, of course, between the firm and its customers, as customers participate or collaborate in the design and delivery of their own products, and as communications become more interactive and two-way—never mind the increase in interconnectivity among customers.

The organizing "tool," or asset, on which the full range of information-intensive strategies is based is the customer information file (CIF), a single virtual database that captures all relevant information about a firm's customers. The database is described as "virtual" because, while operating as if it were an integrated single source housed in one location, it may in reality comprise several isolated databases stored in separate places throughout an organization.

Although the concept of the CIF as the core corporate asset should be comfortable to marketers, it is nevertheless one that is at odds with the conventional view. Many firms may pay lip service to the notion that "our customers are our most important resource," but the typical firm's real assets are still seen to be its products or services and the facilities and operations used to support them. This is reflected in the product (or brand) management organizational structure—that is, where profit and loss responsibility is defined with respect to a set of products—that still predominates in many firms.

Within the newer framework being developed here, the firm sets as its overall objective maximizing the returns to the CIF (as the key corporate asset) and then chooses any one or several information-intensive strategies to accomplish this objective. The records are individual customers—both actual as well as potential—not segments. The data collected about customers, at least conceptually, can be organized into three categories:

1. *Customer characteristics*. Typically (although not exclusively) composed of demographic data, this is information about customers (who they are) that is independent of the firm's relationship with them.
2. *Response to firm decisions*. Perception and preference (e.g., product attribute importance weights) and other marketing-mix response data (price sensitivity, sources of information, channel shopping behavior), this is information about customers (when, where, how, and why they buy) that is based on some (perhaps limited) level of interaction between the firm and its customers.

3. *Purchase history.* Data on which products customers have purchased as well as the revenues, costs, and, thus, profits associated with these purchases, this is information that is based on the firm's actual transactions with its customers.

When a firm sets as its overall performance objective the task of maximizing returns to the CIF, notions such as profitability per sales period or market share per product are replaced with concepts such as profitability per customer (increasingly referred to as *lifetime value of customer*) and *share of customer* (the total share of a customer's purchases in a broadly defined product category, such as VISA's "share of wallet" or "share of personal consumption expenditures"). Perhaps one of the most challenging tasks facing the information-intensive service firm—and proof of the extent to which it is serious about the required transformation in perspective—is the integration of these new measures of performance into the organization's traditional accounting system.[a]

---

[a] See also Rashi Glazer's "Meta-Technologies and Innovation Leadership: Why There May Be Nothing New Under the Sun," *California Management Review* 50 (Fall 2007): 120–143; and "Winning in Smart Markets," *Sloan Management Review* 40 (Summer 1999): 59–69.

Summary

The first task to accomplish in building relationships with a customer is to *recognize* each one at every point of contact, across all products purchased or locations contacted, through every communication channel, over time. Doing this requires knowing the identity of each customer at every contact point in the organization.

Food for Thought

1. Describe and name two companies you have done business with as a customer. One of them treats you as if you are a new customer every time you show up, or at least any time you show up anywhere you haven't done business with the company before. At the other company, you are recognized as *you* every time you have any dealings with the company. What's the effect on you of these disparate approaches? How would you guess each company manages its data, given their different approaches to customers?
2. How can a company identify customers when those customers don't talk to its representatives very often, if at all—at least not individually? (Consider a pet food manufacturer that sells to retailers, not directly to consumers. Or a convenience store that operates on a cash basis. Or a fast-food chain. Or a business-to-business company that doesn't have a human sales force.)
3. What will encourage customers to "raise their hands" and agree to be identified and recognized?

Glossary

Attitudinal data   Directly supplied data that reflect attitudes about products, such as satisfaction levels, perceived competitive positioning, desired features, and unmet needs as well as lifestyles, brand preferences, social and personal values, and opinions.

Behavioral data   Directly supplied data that includes purchase and buying habits, clickstream data, interactions with the company, communication channels chosen, language used, product consumption, company share of wallet, and so on.

Demographic data   Directly supplied data that include age, income, education level, marital status, household composition, gender, home ownership, and so on.

Zero latency   No lag time required for the flow of information from customer, to database, to decision maker (or to a rules-based decision-making engine).

CHAPTER 5

Differentiating Customers:
Some Customers Are Worth
More than Others

The result of long-term relationships is better and better quality, and lower and lower costs.

—W. Edwards Deming

All value created by a business comes from customers. Without a customer or client, at some level, no business can create any shareholder value at all, and this simple fact is inherent in the very nature of a business. By definition, a business exists to create and serve customers and, in so doing, to generate economic value for its stakeholders. But some customers will create more value for a business than others will, and understanding the differences among customers, in terms of the value they each will or could create, is critical to managing individual customer relationships. In this chapter, we explore the most fundamental ideas about the value that customers represent for an enterprise, including both a customer's "actual" value and "potential" value. We show how a firm can use insights about customer value to better allocate resources and prioritize sales, marketing, and service efforts. We consider whether and under what conditions a firm should consider "firing" very low-value or even negative-value customers.

I dentifying each customer individually and linking the information about that customer to various business functions prepares the customer-strategy enterprise to engage each customer in a mutual collaboration that will grow stronger over time. The first step is to identify and recognize each customer at every touchpoint. As we saw in Chapter 4, when the "identify" task is properly executed, information about individual customers should allow a company to see each customer completely, as one customer throughout the organization. And seeing customers individually will enable the company to compare them—to *differentiate* customers, one from another. By understanding that one customer is different from another, the enterprise reaches an important step in the development of an interactive, customer-centric Learning Relationship with each customer.

The inability to see customers as being different does not mean the customers are the same in needs or value, only that the firm sees them that way. Understanding, analyzing, and profiting from individual customer differences are tasks that go to the very heart

> The inability to see customers as being different does not mean the customers are the same in needs or value, only that the firm sees them that way.

of what it means to be a customer-strategy or customer-centric enterprise—an enterprise that engages in customer-specific behaviors, in order to increase the overall value of its customer base.

Customers are different in two principal ways: Different customers have different *values to* the enterprise, and different customers have different *needs from* the enterprise. The entire value proposition between an enterprise and a customer can be captured in terms of the value the customer provides for the firm and the value the firm provides for the customer (i.e., what needs the firm can meet for the customer). All other customer differences, from demographics and psychographics, to behaviors, transactional histories, and attitudes, represent the tools and concepts marketers must use simply to get at these two most fundamental differences.

Knowing which customers are most valuable and least valuable to the enterprise will enable a company to prioritize its competitive efforts, allocating relatively more time, effort, and resources to those customers likely to yield higher returns. In effect, an enterprise's financial objectives with respect to any single customer will be defined by the value the customer is currently creating for the enterprise (her **actual value**) as well as the **potential value** the customer *could* create for the enterprise, if the firm could present the exact right offerings at the right time as needed by the customer and thus change the customer's behavior in a way that works for both the customer and the enterprise. Of course, changing a customer's behavior (which is the basic objective of all marketing activity) can be accomplished only by appealing to the customer's own personal motives, or needs. So while understanding a customer's value profile will determine a firm's financial objectives for that customer, the strategies and tactics required to achieve those objectives require an understanding of that customer's needs. It should be noted that a customer has value to the enterprise in two ways that matter to shareholders and decision makers: A customer has current value (revenue minus cost to serve) as well as long-term value *in the present* that goes up or down based on experience with the company or brand, influence from the outside, and changes in his own needs.

In this chapter, we discuss the concept of customer *valuation,* including various ways a company might rank its customers by their individual values to the enterprise. In Chapter 6, we address the issue of customer *needs.* Importantly, we return again and again throughout the book to these two issues: the different valuations and needs of different individual customers. For instance, we return to the issue of short-term and long-term customer valuation in Chapter 11, when we discuss metrics and measurements. And we come back to the issue of customer needs during our discussion of customization and mass customization in Chapter 10.

Customer Value Is a Future-Oriented Variable

Mail-order firms, credit card companies, telecommunications firms, and other marketers with direct connections to their consumer customers often try to understand their marketing universe by doing a simple form of prioritization called *decile analysis*—ranking their customers in order of their value to the company and then dividing this top-to-bottom list of customers into 10 equal portions, or deciles, with each decile comprising 10 percent of the customers. In this way, the marketer can begin to analyze the differences between those customers who populate the most valuable one or two deciles and those who populate the less valuable deciles. A credit card company may find, for instance, that 65 percent of top-decile customers are married and have two cards on the same account while only 30 percent of other, less valuable customers have these characteristics. Or a catalog company may find that a majority of customers in the bottom three or four deciles have never before bought anything by direct mail while 85 percent of those in the top two deciles have.

It would not be unusual for a decile analysis to reveal that 50 percent, or even 95 percent, of a company's profit comes from the top one or two deciles of customers. Mail-order houses and other direct marketers are more likely than other marketers to have used decile analysis in the past, largely as a means for evaluating the productivity of their mailing campaigns, but this kind of customer ranking analysis will become increasingly important as more companies begin to adopt a customer focus.[1]

But just how does a company rank-order its customers by their value in the first place? What data would the credit card company use to analyze its customers individually and then array them from top to bottom in terms of their value? And what variables would go into the mail-order firm's customer rankings? What do we mean when we talk about the value of a customer, anyway?

For our purposes, the value a customer represents to an enterprise should be thought of as the same type of value any other financial asset would represent. To say that some customers have more value for the enterprise than others is merely to acknowledge that some customers are more valuable, as assets, than others are. The primary objective of a customer-strategy enterprise should be to increase the value of its customer base, for the simple reason that customers are the source of all short-term revenue and all long-term value creation, by definition. In other words, a company should strive to increase the sum total of all the individual financial assets known as customers.

But this is not as simple as it might sound, because in the same way any other financial asset should be valued, a customer's value to the enterprise is a function of the profit the customer will generate *in the future* for the enterprise.

Let's take a specific example. Suppose a company has two business customers. Customer A generated $1,000 per month in profit for the enterprise over the last two years while Customer B generated $500 in monthly profit during the same period. Which customer is worth more to the enterprise?

Knowing only what we've been told so far, we can say it's *probable* that Customer A is worth more than Customer B, but this is not a certainty. If Customer A

---

[1]See Don Peppers and Martha Rogers, Ph.D., *The One to One Future* (New York: Doubleday, 1993).

were to generate $1,000 in profit per month in all future months while Customer B were to generate $500 per month in all future months, then certainly A is worth twice as much to the enterprise as B. But what if we know that Customer A plans to merge its operations into another firm in three months and switch to a different supplier altogether while Customer B plans to continue doing its regular volume with the company for the foreseeable future? In that case, our ranking of these two customers would be reversed, and we would consider B to be worth more than A. However, if what actually happened was that a competitor derailed A's merger while B went bankrupt and ceased all operations the following month, then our assessment would still be wrong.

By definition, a customer's value to an enterprise, as a financial asset, is a future-oriented variable. Therefore, it is a quantity that can truly be ascertained only from the customer's actual behavior *in the future*. We mortals can analyze data points from past behavior, we can interview a customer to try to understand the customer's future opportunities and intent, and we can even conclude contractual agreements with customers to guarantee performance for the contract period, but the plain truth is that, without clairvoyant powers, we can't *know* what a customer's true value is until the future actually happens.

However, until that future does happen, we can affect its outcome—at least partially—by our own actions. Suppose we were to find a revenue stream for Customer B that allowed it to continue in business rather than going bankrupt. By our own deliberate action, in this case, we would have changed B's value to our firm as a financial asset.

To think about customer valuation, therefore, we need to use two different but related concepts:

1. *Actual value* is the customer's value, given what we currently know or predict about the customer's future behavior.
2. *Potential value* is what the customer's value as an asset to the enterprise *could* represent if, through some conscious strategy on our part, we could change the customer's future behavior in some way.

Customer Lifetime Value

The "actual value" of a customer, as we defined it, is equivalent to a quantity frequently termed customer **lifetime value** (LTV). Defined precisely, a customer's LTV is the net present value of the expected future stream of financial contributions from the customer.[2] Every customer of an enterprise today will be responsible for some specific series of events in the future, each of which will have a financial impact

---

[2]It should be noted that a vigorous body of research and literature is emerging in this important field and the notes in this book should be supplemented with a review of the latest findings. Also see Don Peppers and Martha Rogers, Ph.D., *Return on Customer: Creating Maximum Value from Your Scarcest Resource* (New York: Currency/Doubleday, 2005); as well as the next resources:

Andrews, Katherine Zoe. "Optimizing Customer Value and Resource Allocation," *Insights from MSI* (Winter 2003–04): 1, 2. Offers a straightforward value analysis with attendant prioritization and treatment strategies.

on the enterprise—the purchase of a product, payment for a service, remittance of a subscription fee, a product exchange or upgrade, a warranty claim, a help-line telephone call, the referral of another customer, and so forth. Each such event will take place at a particular time in the future and will have a financial impact that has a particular value at that time. The **net present value (NPV)**, today, of each of these future value-creating events can be derived by applying a discount rate to it to factor in the time value of money as well as the likelihood of the event. LTV is,

Bell, David, John Deighton, Werner Reinartz, Roland Rust, and Gordon Swartz. "Seven Barriers to Customer Equity Management," *Journal of Service Research* 5, no. 1 (March 2002), 77–85.

Berger, Paul D., Ruth N. Bolton, Douglas Bowman, Elten Briggs, V. Kumar, A. Parasuraman, and Creed Terry. "Marketing Actions and the Value of Customer Assets: A Framework for Customer Asset Management," *Journal of Service Research* 5, no. 1 (August 2002): 39–54. Develops a framework for assessing how marketing actions affect customer LTV. Based on four critical actions: database creation, market segmentation, forecasting customer purchasing behavior, and resource allocation.

Berger, Paul D., and Nada I. Nasr. "Customer Lifetime Value: Marketing Models and Applications," *Journal of Interactive Marketing* 12, no. 1 (Winter 1998): 17–30. Presents a series of models for calculating LTV to take it beyond the traditional direct-marketing concept.

Berger, Paul, et al. "From Customer Lifetime Value to Shareholder Value: Theory, Empirical Evidence, and Issues for Future Research," *Journal of Service Research* 9, no. 2 (November 2006): 156–167.

Blattberg, Robert, Gary Getz, and Jacquelyn S. Thomas. *Customer Equity: Building and Managing Relationships as Valuable Assets.* Boston: Harvard Business School Press, 2001. Focuses on measuring so that marketers can allocate resources wisely between acquisition and retention efforts.

Bolton, Ruth N., P. K. Kannan, and Matthew D. Bramlett. "Implication of Loyalty Programs and Service Experiences for Customer Retention and Value," *Journal of the Academy of Marketing Science,* 28, no. 1 (2000): 95–108.

Bolton, Ruth N., Katherine N. Lemon, and Peter C. Verhoef. "The Theoretical Underpinnings of Customer Asset Management: A Framework and Propositions for Future Research," *Journal of the Academy of Marketing Science* 32, no. 3 (2004): 271–292. Proposes CUSAMS—customer asset management of services—and claims that CUSAMS enable service organizations to make a comprehensive assessment of the value of their customers, and to understand the influence of marketing instruments on them. Examines leading indicators of key customer behaviors reflecting the length, depth, and breadth of customer/service-organization relationship: duration, usage, and cross-buying.

Gross, Neil. "Commentary: Valuing 'Intangibles' Is a Tough Job, But It Has to Be Done," *BusinessWeek,* August 6, 2001, pp. 54–55. If companies can account for intangibles on a balance sheet when there's a merger or acquisition, why not all the time? Worries that FASB (Financial Accounting Standards Board) will never buy it because any whiff of subjectivity leads to a label of "voodoo accounting."

Gupta, Sunil. "What Is a Free Customer Worth?" *Harvard Business Review* 86, no. 11 (November 2008): 102–109.

Gupta, Sunil, and Donald R. Lehmann. "Customer Lifetime Value and Firm Valuation," *Journal of Relationship Marketing* 5, nos. 2/3 (2006): 87–110.

Gupta, Sunil, and Donald R. Lehmann. *Managing Customers as Investments: The Strategic Value of Customers in the Long Run.* Philadelphia: Wharton School Publishing, 2005. Although its focus is still primarily on investment choices surrounding marketing decisions, it is the best discussion we've seen yet of ROMI or "return on marketing investment."

in essence, the sum of the NPVs of all such future events attributed to a particular customer's actions.

One useful way to think about the different types of events and activities that different customers will be involved in is to visualize each customer as having a "**trajectory**" that carries the customer through time in a financial relationship with the enterprise. For example, a customer could begin his relationship at a particular starting point and at a particular spending level. At some point, he increases his spending, taking another product line from the company; later he also begins paying

Gupta, Sunil, Donald R. Lehmann, and Jennifer Ames Stuart. "Valuing Customers," *Journal of Marketing Research* (February 2004): 7–18. Makes the case that much of the financial value of the firm depends on assets not listed on the balance sheet—for example, brands, customers, employees, and knowledge. Demonstrates how valuing customers makes it feasible to value firms, including high-growth firms with negative earnings. Study examines Capital One, Ameritrade, E*TRADE, Amazon.com, and eBay.

Kordupleski, Ray, *Mastering Customer Value Management: The Art and Science of Creating Competitive Advantage.* Cincinnati: Pinnaflex Educational Resources, 2003.

Kumar, V., Katherine N. Lemon, and A. Parasuraman. "Managing Customers for Value: An Overview and Research Agenda," *Journal of Service Research* 9, no. 2 (November 2006): 87–94.

Lenskold, James D. *Marketing ROI: The Path to Campaign, Customer, and Corporate Profitability.* New York: McGraw-Hill, 2003.

Malthouse, Edward C., and Robert C. Blattberg. "Can We Predict Customer Lifetime Value?" *Journal of Interactive Marketing* 19, no. 1 (Winter 2005): 2–16. Argues that the feasibility of predicting the future profitability of customers depends on the probabilities and costs of misclassifying customers. Proposes that of the most valuable 20 percent of customers, 55 percent will be misclassified (and not receive special treatment), and of the bottom 80 percent, 15 percent will be misclassified (and receive special treatment), if treatment decisions are based on historical transaction data (such as RFM used by database marketers).

Mathias, Peter F., and Noel Capon. "Managing Strategic Customer Relationships as Assets: Developing Customer Relationship Capital," White paper, Columbia University, 2003. Refers to customer equity as CRC (customer relationship capital), discusses six steps for creating and acquiring the future customer wallet (using only business-to-business applications).

Mulhern, Francis J. "Customer Profitability Analysis: Measurement, Concentration, and Research Directions," *Journal of Interactive Marketing* 13, no. 1 (Winter 1999): 25–40.

Niraj, Rakesh, Mahendra Gupta, and Chakravarthi Narasimhan. "Customer Profitability in a Supply Chain," *Journal of Marketing* 65, no. 3 (July 2001): 1–16. Emphasizes the need for individual customer profitability calculations if customer lifetime values are to be determined.

Parasuraman, A. "Reflections in Gaining Competitive Advantage through Customer Value," *Journal of the Academy of Marketing Science* 25, no. 2 (1997): 154–161.

Rust, Roland T., Katherine N. Lemon, and Valerie A. Zeithaml. "Return on Marketing: Using Customer Equity to Focus Marketing Strategy," *Journal of Marketing* 68, no. 1 (Winter 2004): 109–127. Presents a strategic framework that enables competing marketing strategy options to be weighed on the basis of projected financial return. LTV factors in the frequency of category purchase, average quantity of purchase, brand-switching patterns, firm's contribution margin. Based on "what-if" evaluation and focuses on return on advertising, return on loyalty programs, return on corporate citizenship. Defines "customer equity" as the total discounted lifetime values summed over all of the firm's current and potential customers.

more for some added service. Still later he has a complaint, and it costs the company some expense to resolve it. He refers another customer to the company, and that customer then begins her own trajectory, creating a whole additional value stream. Eventually, perhaps several years or decades later, the original customer "leaves the franchise," because his children grow up, or he decides to switch to another product altogether, or he gets divorced, or retires, or dies. At this point, his relationship with the enterprise comes to an end. (We could describe a business customer's trajectory in the same way. Although a "business" may have an indefinite future potential as a customer, each of the individual potential end users, purchasing agents, influencers, and so forth eventually will quit, get promoted or transferred, or fired, retire, or die.)

Different customers will have different trajectories. In a way, the lifetime value of each customer amounts to the NPV of the financial contribution represented by that customer's trajectory through the customer base. From a customer's stream of positive contributions, including product and service purchases, an enterprise must

Rust, Roland T., Christine Moorman, and Gaurav Bhalla. "Rethinking Marketing," *Harvard Business Review* 88, no. 1 (January–February 2010): 94–101.

Rust, Roland T., Valerie A. Zeithaml, and Katherine N. Lemon. *Driving Customer Equity: How Customer Lifetime Value Is Reshaping Corporate Strategy.* New York: Free Press, 2000.

Ryals, Lynette. *Managing Customers Profitably.* Hoboken, NJ: John Wiley & Sons, 2008.

Srivastava, Rajendra K., Tasadduq A. Shervani, and Liam Fahey. "Market-Based Assets and Shareholder Value: A Framework for Analysis," *Journal of Marketing* 62 (January 1998): 2–18. Develops a conceptual framework for the marketing-finance interface and its implications for the theory and practice of marketing. Asserts that assets are based on customer relationships, channel relationships, and partner relationships, which increase shareholder value by accelerating and enhancing cash flow, reducing cash-flow volatility, and increasing residual value of cash flow.

Stahl, Heinz K., Kurt Matzler, Hans H. Hinterhuber. "Linking Customer Lifetime Value with Shareholder Value," *Industrial Marketing Management* 32, no. 4 (2003): 267–279. Emphasizes increasing importance of ability to evaluate market strategies against ability to deliver shareholder value; therefore, acquisition and maintenance of customers must result in improved cash flows and shareholder value. Argues that customers are assets and increase shareholder value by accelerating and enhancing cash flows, reducing cash flow volatility and vulnerability, and increasing residual value of the firm.

Thomas, Jacquelyn S., Werner Reinartz, and V. Kumar. "Getting the Most Out of All Your Customers," *Harvard Business Review* 82, nos. 7–8 (July–August 2004): 116–123. Builds on the Return on Marketing Investment literature by asserting that profitability of customers matters more than their raw numbers or their loyalty.

Woodall, Tony. "Conceptualising 'Value for the Customer': An Attributional, Structural, and Dispositional Analysis," *Academy of Marketing Science Review,* no. 12 (2003): 1–42. Note that "customer value" is used in literature to portray both value from supplier to customer and vice versa. This author calls the first of these two "value for the customer," or VC.

Woodruff, Robert P. "Customer Value: The Next Source of Competitive Advantage," *Journal of the Academy of Marketing Science* 25, no. 2 (1997): 139–153.

Zeithaml, Valerie A. "Service Quality, Profitability, and the Economic Worth of Customers: What We Know and What We Need to Learn," *Journal of the Academy of Marketing Science* 28, no. 1 (2000): 67–85.

This sampling cannot serve as an exhaustive review of this important body of literature, since it is developing faster than a textbook or reference book can keep up with. Rather, this list serves as an introduction and basis for understanding and evaluating the ongoing work by others.

deduct the expenses associated with that customer, including the cost of maintaining a relationship. For instance, relationships usually require some amount of individual communication, via phone, mail, e-mail, or face-to-face meetings. These costs, along with any others that apply to a specific individual customer, will reduce the customer's LTV. It sometimes happens that the costs associated with a customer actually outweigh the customer's positive contributions altogether, in which case the customer's LTV is **below zero.**

We are using the term *contribution*, as opposed to *profit*, deliberately, because the value of a particular customer is equivalent to the marginal contribution of that customer, when he is added to the business in which the enterprise is already engaged. Suppose we add up all the positive and negative cash flows an enterprise will generate over the next few years, and the total is $X. But then Customer A's trajectory of financial transactions is removed from the enterprise, and the positive and negative cash flows will only amount to a lesser total of $Y. The customer's marginal contribution is equal to $X - Y$. The NPV of those various contributions by Customer A is the customer's LTV. There are additional "contributions" a customer can make, not all of them monetary. Aside from the obvious word-of-mouth given by a customer, a nonprofit organization looks to volunteer work or other participation.

In practice, of course, it is not possible for an enterprise to know what any particular customer's future contributions will actually be, and if we want to be able to make current decisions based on this future-oriented number, then we will have to estimate it in some way. Traditionally, the most reliable predictor of a customer's future behavior has been thought to be that customer's past behavior. We are usually quite justified in making the commonsense assumption that a customer who has generated $1,000 of profit each month for the last two years will continue to generate that profit level for some period of time in the future, even though we simultaneously acknowledge that any number of forces can appear that will change this simplistic trend at any moment. Various computational techniques can be used to model the probable trajectories of particular types of customers more precisely and to project these expected trajectories into the future. Some companies have customer databases that allow highly sophisticated modeling and analysis. Such analysis can sometimes be used to give an enterprise advance warning when a credit card customer, or a cell phone customer, or a Web site subscriber, is about to defect to a competitor. A whole class of statistical analysis tools, frequently termed *predictive analytic*, is designed to help businesses sift through the historic records of certain types of customers, in order to model the likely behaviors of other, similar customers in the future.

According to the late CRM consultant Frederick Newell, LTV models have a number of uses. They can help an enterprise determine how much it can afford to spend to acquire a new customer or perhaps a certain type of new customer. They can help a firm decide just how much it would be worth to retain an existing customer. With a model that predicts higher values for certain types of customers, an enterprise can target its customer acquisition efforts in order to concentrate on attracting higher-value customers. And, of course, the LTV measurement represents a more economically correct way to evaluate marketing investments compared to simply counting immediate sales.[3]

---

[3]Frederick Newell, *The New Rules of Marketing* (New York: McGraw-Hill, 1997). Also see Rajkumar Venkatesan, V. Kumar, and Timothy Bohling, "Optimal Customer Relationship

Although sophisticated modeling methods help to quantify LTV, many variables cannot be easily quantified, such as the assistance a customer might give an enterprise in designing a new product, or the value derived from the customer's referral of another customer, or the customer's willingness to advocate for the product or company on a social networking Web site. Any model that attempts to calculate individual customer LTVs should employ some or all of these data, quantified and weighted appropriately:

- Repeat customer purchases
- Greater profit and/or lower cost (per sale) from repeat customers than from initial customers (converting prospects)
- Indirect benefits from customers, such as referrals (Imagine that you are a book author and Oprah Winfrey bought and likes your book!)
- Willingness to collaborate—the customer's level of comfort and trust with the company and participation in data exchange that results in the opportunity for better customer experience (sometimes called relationship strength)
- Customers' stated willingness to do business in the future rather than switch suppliers
- Customer records
- Transaction records (summary and detail)
- Products and product costs
- Cost to serve/support
- Marketing and transaction costs (including acquisition costs)
- Response rates to marketing/advertising efforts[4]
- Company- or industry-specific information

The objective of LTV modeling is to use these and other data points to create a historically quantifiable representation of the customer and to compare that customer's history with other customers. Based on this analysis, the enterprise forecasts the customer's future trajectory with the enterprise, including how much he or she will spend, and over what period.

For our purposes, it is sufficient to know that:

- The actual value of a customer is the value of the customer as a financial asset, which is equivalent to the customer's lifetime value—the NPV of future cash flows associated with that customer. (This is the current value, assuming business as usual.)
- LTV is a quantity that no enterprise can ever calculate precisely, no matter how sophisticated its predictive analytics programs and statistical models are.

Using Bayesian Decision Theory: An Application for Customer Selection," *Journal of Marketing Research* 34, no. 4 (November 2007): 579–594; V. Kumar et al., "Managing Retailer Profitability—One Customer at a Time!" *Journal of Retailing* 82, no. 4 (2006): 277–294; and Peter S. Fader et al., "'Counting Your Customers the Easy Way: An Alternative to the Pareto/NBD Model," *Marketing Science* 24, no. 2 (Spring 2005): 275–284.
[4]Jack Schmid and Alan Weber, *Desktop Database Marketing* (Chicago: NTC/Contemporary Publishing Group, 1998).

- Nevertheless, even though it can never be precisely known,[5] LTV is a real financial number, and every enterprise has an interest in understanding and positively affecting its customers' LTVs to the extent possible, and—as we shall see in Chapter 13—to hold members of the organization responsible for exactly that.

As difficult as LTV and actual value may be to model, *potential* value is an even more elusive quantity, involving not just guesses regarding a customer's most likely future behavior but guesses regarding the customer's options for future behavior.

Still, potential value isn't impossible to estimate, especially if the analysis begins with a set of customers who have already been assigned actual values or LTVs. Probably the most straightforward way to estimate a customer's potential value is to look at the range of LTVs for similar customers and then to make the arbitrary assumption that in an ideal world it should at least be possible to turn lower-LTV customers into higher-LTV customers. In the consumer business, this means examining the LTVs for customers who are perhaps at the same income level, or have the same family size, or live in the same neighborhoods. For business-to-business (B2B) customers, it would mean comparing the LTVs of corporate customers in the same vertical industries, with the same sales levels, or profit, or employment levels, and so forth and better decisions.

The problem at many companies is that a customer's "value to the firm" is confused with the customer's current profitability. Often, measuring customer profitability at all, even in the short term, is an achievement for a firm. But when a customer's LTV is taken into account, the results will be more revealing, and estimating potential values will yield still more insight.

Recognizing the Hidden Potential Value in Customers

Pelin Turunc
Consultant, Peppers & Rogers Group, Europe

Differentiating or grouping customers in terms of various characteristics such as value, needs, and behavioral trends has proven to be an effective and widely accepted marketing practice among a variety of industries across the world. The most widely used segmentation method, pursued by the vast majority of companies focused on a customer strategy, involves differentiating customers by value and then designing different strategies for different value segments—launching aggressive retention strategies for high-value customers, for instance. Even though it is a popular strategy, many companies still succumb to a costly pitfall, related to just how a customer's value is assessed. Far too frequently, companies take into account only the narrow viewpoint of the customer's current "actual value," largely based on historical behavior patterns, (this phrase

---

[5]For that matter, some of the deeply ingrained and generally accepted—indeed, revered—financial measures more or less in use universally are themselves not perfect measures.

actually only applies to "actual value") while overlooking the immense potential of many customers to generate even more value than they have in the past or to generate value not directly indicated by transactional records or the historical picture.

It is understandable, of course, that a firm's marketing analysts may be reluctant to forecast future behaviors for a customer when they haven't already observed and modeled those behaviors in the customer's transactional history. In addition, analysts may hesitate to try to quantify the results of customer behaviors that are not directly associated with purchasing and service costs. However, leading companies know that success often comes from taking account of individual customers' potential values, not just their actual values. (Remember that both current value and actual value are "future" oriented, but, while a customer's *current* value is the estimated net present value of future financial contributions currently expected, based on what is known now, a customer's *potential* represents the increased value that could be realized if the customer were to behave differently, presumably based on the firm's behavior.)

Consider, for instance, the idea that today's customer might actually increase his or her patronage with a firm considerably, based solely on the fact that, as time goes on, the customer matures into an older and more productive person. Royal Bank of Canada (RBC)[a] was one of the first banks to look carefully and analytically at the youth segment as a promising group of retail banking customers when most banks were overlooking this segment due to their low current (actual) value. RBC recognized the high potential value of young college students, many of whom would become highly paid professionals in the future. The bank gained a competitive advantage by reaching out to and building loyalty in this segment early on. In a similar way, certain groups of customers who are in a temporary financial slump, or even in bankruptcy, could have the potential to be promising and high-value customers in the future. A bank that identifies such customers (differentiating them from other customers who are bankrupt now and likely to remain in financial distress for the long term) and reaches out to them at this difficult stage in their lives is certain to win these customers' loyalty and trust.

In telecommunications, some companies find hidden word-of-mouth power in the ranks of their currently low-value "public sector employees" segment. For example, when Sprint offered attractive rates and group discounts to this public sector group, the word-of-mouth impact resulted in increased new customer acquisitions, increasing each company's profitability and market share.[b] A close look at the needs of the customers was of course an enabling step in this strategy, where the telecommunications company was able to find the rate, payment, or discount benefits that best suited the needs and payment behavior of this customer group. The benefits could easily have been missed, however, had this company looked solely at these customers' historically based actual values.

Taking into account the "customer influence" factor in modeling lifetime value is even more critical in some industries where a small number of customers exert a disproportionate share of influence on others' buying decisions, such as in the pharmaceuticals industry. The primary customers here, at least in most

(continued)

(Continued)

countries, are physicians, and some physicians almost always stand out for the amount of influence they have on the medical practices of other physicians. Identifying and trying to quantify the value of such "key opinion leaders" (KOLs) is a high priority for pharmaceutical companies, such as Abbott Labs, Bristol-Myers Squibb, and Biogen Idec.[c] KOLs usually are viewed by their peers as experts in specific therapeutic areas, and as such they exert immense influence over other doctors when it comes to the types of medications to be prescribed and the kinds of medical treatments to be administered in these therapeutic areas. Even though some KOLs may have low actual values themselves, in terms of the prescriptions they write in their own medical practice, their influence is disproportionately valuable. Some pharmaceutical companies (e.g., Roche[d]) even try to identify rising KOL stars, who are for the most part relatively less well-known professionals who show signs of future success and influence. The companies then invite these rising stars to participate in medical education and other activities, hoping to build long-lasting relationships.

One industry in which potential value can be an important differentiator is the airline business. Because of their widely used frequent-flyer programs, airlines usually have a fairly good handle on the transactional histories of their most frequent travelers who are, for the most part, business flyers. But even if a business traveler flies 50,000 miles a year on an airline, the airline has no way of knowing, from its own transactional records, whether that traveler is flying another 50,000 miles on a competitive carrier. So, in trying to estimate the potential value of an airline customer, it is critical to look at external data sources (and, in some cases, simply to *ask* a customer in order to get share-of-customer information) when such sources are available and perhaps to tap into the data available from distributor partners, such as travel agencies or credit card firms. Lifestyle changes can also create shifts in the potential value of a customer and should be taken into account. Southwest Airlines, for example, identified and sent relevant offers to some currently low-value customers who moved to another country as expatriates, and these customers proved to have high potential value as evidenced by their future travels on holidays to their home country.

In addition to overlooking customers with high potential value, some companies make wrong and unprofitable investments in customers who seem to be high in value now but in fact have a low or sometimes negative potential value. In the retailer category, Best Buy[e] successfully differentiated its customers to deliver exceptional treatment to identified high-potential customers while paring some of their less valuable customers from their mailing lists and tightening up their return policies to prevent abuse. In this way, Best Buy avoided unnecessary time and monetary investment on customers with low potential values. Filene's Basement Discount Stores[f] represents a more extreme example. When Filene's Basement realized that some of its customers who appeared to be high-value customers with high sales volumes were actually serial returners (often returning clothing after using it once), it banned some of them from its stores altogether, preventing losses from this group who proved to be Below Zero over the long term.

Another company that avoided unnecessary investment in low-potential-value customers is Capital One Bank, which recognized its low potential value customers and adjusted its reactive retention strategy to deemphasize them. (After all, why should the company go out of its way to retain a low-value customer?) One variable that can reduce the potential value of a financial services customer is financial risk. Understanding the likelihood that a customer will need to be charged off in the future is an important function for any credit-granting institution. Capital One, while giving incentives and positive offers to its high-value customers who want to close their accounts in order to save them, encouraged the high-risk customers (i.e., low-potential-value customers) to close their accounts with the bank. This policy helps to minimize future financial losses to the bank, improving overall profitability.

Assessing customer value as a combination of current and potential value is no longer a choice if a firm wants to remain truly competitive. Estimating a customer's potential value is certainly more complex than simply trying to forecast actual value, or LTV, and requires a deeper look into factors such as needs, lifestyle phases, and behavioral trends. But making a genuine attempt to do so will likely prove quite beneficial.

---

[a]V.G. Narayanan and Lisa Brem, "Case Study: Customer Profitability and Customer Relationship Management at RBC Financial Group (abridged)," *Journal of Interactive Marketing* 16, no. 3 (Summer 2002): 76.

[b]Advisory Opinion No. 05-1, "Conditions under which a State Employee May Accept a Discount on Goods or Services"; Sprint PCS ("Sprint") provides wireless telephone services for OTDA and other state agencies through a contract approved by the State Office of General Services (2004), available at: www.nyintegrity.org/advisory/ethc/05-01.htm, accessed September 1, 2010. Sprint PCS company Web site and Nextel company Web site indicate 15 percent for government employees, available at: www.nextel.com/en/solutions/federal_govt.shtml.

[c]Rachel Farrow, "Forging Key Opinion Leader Relationships: Developing the Next Generation," *TVF Communications* (July 2008); available at: www.tvfcommunications.com/publications.aspx, accessed September 1, 2010.

[d]Ibid.

[e]Rajiv Lal, Carin-Isabel Knoop, and Irina Tarsis, "Best Buy Co., Inc.: Customer-Centricity," *Harvard Business School Cases*, April 1, 2006, p. 1.

[f]Scott Wilkerson, "Marketers Must Understand Customer Value to Make Segmentation Pay," Hawkpartners Group, *Alert! Magazine*, September 10, 2009, available at: www.hawkpartners.com/perspectives/articles/alert-mag-October-2009.pdf, accessed September 1, 2010.

Growing Share of Customer

With respect to its relationship with a customer, the goal of any customer-strategy enterprise should be to positively alter the customer's financial trajectory, increasing the customer's overall value to the enterprise. The challenge, however, is to know how much the enterprise really can alter that trajectory— how much increase in the customer's value an enterprise can actually generate.

Unrealized potential value is a term used to denote the amount by which the enterprise could increase the value of a particular customer if it applied a strategy for doing so. It's a very straightforward concept, really, because the unrealized potential of a customer is simply the difference between the customer's potential value and actual value. It represents the potential *additional* business a customer is capable of doing with the enterprise, much of which may never materialize. As an enterprise realizes more and more of a customer's potential value, however, it can be said to have a greater and greater share of that customer's business. (Indeed, if we divide a customer's actual value by the customer's potential value, the quotient should give us "share of customer.")

Increasing share of customer[6] is an important goal for a customer-strategy enterprise and can be accomplished by increasing the amount of business a customer does, over and above what was otherwise expected (i.e., by applying a strategy to favorably affect the customer's trajectory). This is often referred to as "share of wallet." For example, a bank might have a relationship with a customer who has a checking account, an auto loan, and a certificate of deposit. The customer provides a regular profit to the bank each month, generated by transaction fees and the investment spread between the bank's own investment and borrowing rates, compared to the lending and savings rates it offers the customer. The net present value of this income stream over the customer's likely future tenure is the customer's LTV. This LTV amount is equivalent to the present value of the financial benefits the bank would lose in the future, if the customer were to defect to another financial services organization today.

But suppose that, in addition to the accounts the customer now maintains at the bank, he also has a home mortgage at a competitive institution. This loan represents unrealized potential value for the bank, while it represents actual value to the bank's competitor. The expected profit from that loan is one aspect of the customer's potential value to the bank, which may devise a strategy to win the customer's mortgage loan business away from its competitor.

Or suppose this customer owns a home computer and modem but doesn't participate in the bank's online banking service. If he were to do more of his banking online, however, the cost of handling his transactions would decline, his likelihood of defection would decline, and his value to the bank would increase. Thus, the increased profit the bank could realize if the customer banked online represents another aspect of the customer's potential value to the bank.

Or perhaps the customer is a night student attempting to qualify for a more financially rewarding career. If the bank could help him achieve this objective, he would earn more money and do more banking, and his value to the bank would increase. All these possibilities represent real opportunities for a bank to capture some of a customer's unrealized potential value.

---

[6] *Share of customer* (SOC) refers to the percentage of total business conducted by a customer with a particular enterprise, in the product and service arena offered by that enterprise. For example, if a voter contributes a total of $1,000 in the 2020 presidential primaries to several candidates, the candidate who gets a $400 contribution would have a 40 percent SOC with that voter. If a Christmas shopper buys most of his presents at Toys "R" Us, generating December purchases there of $800, as compared to a combined total of all other shopping of $400, then Toys "R" Us would have an SOC of $800 of a total $1,200 in holiday shopping, or SOC = 67 percent. See Chapter 1 for a complete discussion of share of customer.

Assessing a Customer's Potential Value

In trying to assess a particular customer's potential value, some of the questions you want to answer include:

- How much of the customer's business currently goes to your competition, but might be pried away with the right approach or relationship?
- How much more of a customer's business could you capture if you modify your treatment of him?
- How many more product lines might the customer buy from you? What other services or products could you sell the customer if you had the products available?
- What additional value would you capture if you could prevent the customer's defection?
- The customer has needs you know about. How can you identify the needs you don't yet know about?
- How much could you reduce the cost of serving this customer, while maintaining his satisfaction?
- How much could this customer be worth in terms of referrals and other non-monetary contributions?

Your opportunity for organic growth is directly related to the unrealized potential values of your current and future customers. But that is just your perspective. From the customer's perspective, potential value has to do with [the customer's] *need.* This is important:

The outside limit of any customer's value is defined by the customer's need, not by your current product or service offering.

Source: Excerpted from Don Peppers and Martha Rogers, Ph.D., *Return on Customer* (New York: Currency/Doubleday, 2005), p. 82.

Different Customers Have Different Values

Increasing a customer's value encompasses the central mission of an enterprise: to *get, keep,* and *grow* its customers. When it understands the value of individual customers relative to other customers, an enterprise can allocate its resources more effectively, because it is quite likely that a small proportion of its **most valuable customers (MVCs)** will account for a large proportion of the enterprise's profitability. This is an important principle of customer differentiation, and at its core is what is known as the Pareto principle, which asserts that 80 percent of any enterprise's business comes from just 20 percent of its customers.[7] The Pareto principle implies

---

[7]Philip Kotler, *Marketing Management: Analysis, Planning Implementation, and Control,* 13th ed. (Upper Saddle River, NJ: Pearson Prentice Hall, 2009). For application in attributing

that a mail-order company ordering its customers into deciles by value is likely to find that the top two deciles of customers account for 80 percent of the business the company is doing. Obviously, the percentages can vary widely among different businesses, and one company might find that the top 20 percent of its customers do 95 percent of its business while another company finds that the top 20 percent of its customers do only 40 percent of its business. But in virtually every business, some customers are worth more than others. When the distribution of customer values is highly concentrated within just a small portion of the customer base, we say that the **value skew** of the customer base is steep.

Pareto Principle and Power-Law Distributions

When it comes to analyzing how customer values are distributed, the 80-20 Pareto principle does not result in a "normal" distribution, like a bell curve. (See Exhibit 5A.) The Pareto principle is a special case of what mathematicians call a power-law distribution, or a log-normal distribution. The key to understanding how a power law differs from a bell curve is to recognize that power laws go on and on with the same kind of distribution. (for this reason, we say that power-law distributions are "scale-free.")

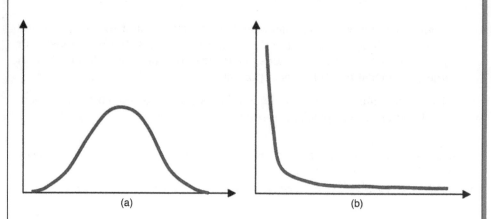

(a)   (b)

EXHIBIT 5A   (a) Bell Curve or Normal Distribution and (b) Power-Law or Log- Normal Distribution

For instance, if customer lifetime values are distributed according to the 80-20 Pareto principle, so that the top 20 percent of customers account for 80 percent of the total value, then the 20 percent of *that* top 20 percent of customers will account for 80 percent of *that* 80 percent of value. In other words, just 4 percent of customers (20 percent of 20 percent) will account for 64 percent

---

value to different customer segments, see V. Kumar and Danish Shah, "Expanding the Role of Marketing: From Customer Equity to Market Capitalization," *Journal of Marketing* 73 (November 2009), p. 121; and Peter S. Fader et al., "'Counting Your Customers' The Easy Way: An Alternative to the Pareto/NBD Model," *Marketing Science* 24 (2) (Spring 2005), pp. 275–284.

of a company's total lifetime values (80 percent of 80 percent). Multiply it again and you'll find that fewer than 1 percent of customers will account for more than 50 percent all customer lifetime value, and so forth.

It's important to remember that all such distributions are still inherently random, and no random distribution of discrete quantities (e.g., individual customer lifetime values) will ever conform precisely to a particular mathematical formula. But it's easy to be confused by the Pareto principle, because it represents a power law, while many of the natural phenomena we observe in everyday life are distributed according to the more intuitively understandable bell curve. Human height, for instance, is distributed according to a bell curve, while wealth is distributed according to a power law. If you walk down a crowded city street and catalog the different heights of the people you encounter, chances are you'll see an occasional 6 foot 6 person or maybe even someone who is nearly 7 feet tall, but the odds of finding someone much taller than 7 feet 6 inches are vanishingly small. (You'll also see one or two adults who are under 5 feet tall and maybe even an occasional person less than 4 feet 6 inches.)

Wealth, however, has no natural upper limit and is distributed according to a power law. Let's suppose human height were distributed the same way personal wealth is distributed, with the average "height" of wealth being about 6 feet. If that were the case, then when you walked down the street you'd run into a few people in the 5- to 7-foot range, but many of the people you meet would actually be shorter than 3 feet tall, and the vast majority of *them* be only a few inches high! Every block or so, however, you'd encounter a couple of people 20 feet tall, and you'd likely see a 100-foot-tall person or even a 500-foot-tall person once in a great while. The longer you walk, the more likely you'll see someone even taller than the last giant you encountered. If you happened to run into the two tallest people in the United States, Bill Gates and Warren Buffett, they would each tower over the city, their heads more than a mile in the sky. Now, that would be a power-law distribution.

Power-law distributions characterize many kinds of measurable quantities that are based on networks, including the increasing proliferation of Internet-enabled social networks. As technology improves and continues to connect customers more and more closely together, power-law distributions can be expected to characterize things like the number of comments accumulated by different blogs, or the number of viewers of different YouTube videos, or the number of Twitter followers acquired by various users. As we read in Chapter 8, this is an important and more or less universal characteristic of social networks.

While LTV is the variable an enterprise wants to know, often a financial or statistical model is too difficult or costly to create. Instead, the enterprise may find some *proxy variable* to be nearly as useful. A proxy variable is a number, other than LTV, that can be used to rank customers in rough order of LTV, or as close to that order as possible, given the information and analytics available. A proxy variable should be easy to measure, but it obviously will not provide the same degree of accuracy when it comes to quantifying a customer's actual value or ranking customers relative to each other.

For instance, many direct marketers use a proxy variable called RFM, for *recency, frequency,* and *monetary value* to rank-order their customers in terms of their value. The RFM model is based on individual customer purchase histories and incorporates three separate but quantified components:

1. *Recency.* Date of this customer's most recent transaction
2. *Frequency.* How often this customer has bought in the past
3. *Monetary value.* How much this customer has spent in the most recent specified period

An airline, by contrast, might use a customer's frequent-flier mileage as a proxy variable to differentiate one customer's value from another's. The mileage total for the last year, or the last two years, or some other period, will be a good indicator of the customer's value, but it won't be entirely accurate. For instance, it won't tell the airline whether the customer usually flies in first class or in coach, and it won't tell whether the customer always purchases the least expensive seat, frequently chooses to stay over on Saturdays, and takes advantage of various other pricing complexities and loopholes in order to guarantee always obtaining the lowest fare.

A proxy variable is, in effect, a representation of a customer's value to the enterprise rather than a quantification of it. Nevertheless, proxy variables can be efficient tools for helping an enterprise rank its customers based on value, and with this ranking the company still can apply different strategies to different customers, based on their *relative* worth. Sophisticated LTV models can be expensive and time-consuming to create. If an enterprise is to explore and benefit from customer valuation principles, proxy variables that allow initial rank-ordering of customers by value are a good starting point.

The goal of value differentiation is not a *historical* understanding but a *predictive* plan of action. RFM and other, similar, proxy-variable methods show that while differentiating among customers can be mathematically complex, it is still fundamentally a simple principle.

> The goal of value differentiation is not a *historical* understanding, but a *predictive plan of action.*

Customer Value Categories

Every customer has an actual value and a potential value. By visualizing the customer base in terms of how customers are distributed across actual and potential values, marketing managers can categorize customers into different value profiles, based on the type of financial goal the enterprise wants to achieve with each customer. For instance, one of a company's goals for a customer with a high unrealized potential value would be to grow its share of customer (in order to realize some of this value), while one of the goals for a customer with low actual value and low potential value would be to minimize servicing costs. By thinking of individual customers both in terms of each one's actual value (i.e., current LTV) and its unrealized potential values (i.e., growth potential), a company could array its customers roughly as shown in Exhibit 5.1.

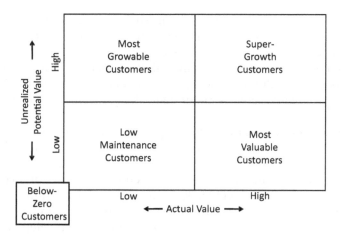

EXHIBIT 5.1   Customer Value Matrix

⌈Five different categories of customers are shown on this diagram, and an enterprise should have different strategic goals for each one:

1. **Most valuable customers (MVCs).** In the lower right quadrant of Exhibit 5.1, MVCs are the customers who have the highest actual value to the enterprise. This could be for any or all of a number of different reasons: They do the highest volume of business, yield the highest margins, stay more loyal, cost less to serve, and/or refer the most additional customers. MVCs are also customers with whom the company probably has the greatest share of customer. These may or may not be the traditional "heavy users" of a product; the MVC may, for example, fly a lot less often but always pays full fare for first-class tickets. The primary financial objective an enterprise will have for its MVCs is *retention,* because these are the customers likely giving the company the bulk of its profitability to begin with. In the airline business, these are the "platinum flyers" in the frequent-flyer program. In order to retain these customers' patronage, an airline will give out bonus miles, offer special check-in lines, provide club benefits, and so forth. For a pharmaceutical company marketing prescription drugs to physicians, however, the most valuable customers may be those particular physicians who have the most *influence* over other physicians. (See "Customer Referral Value")

2. **Most growable customers (MGCs).** In the upper left quadrant of Exhibit 5.1, MGCs are customers who have little actual value to the enterprise but significant growth potential. Here, of course, the enterprise's financial objective is to realize some of that potential value. As a practical matter, these customers are often large-volume or high-profit customers who simply patronize a different company. MGCs are often, in fact, the MVCs of the enterprise's competitors. So the company's objective will be to change the dynamics in some way so as to achieve a higher share of each of these customers' business. (Don't forget, however, that the reverse is also true: Your own MVCs are your competitors' MGCs.)

3. **Low-maintenance customers.** In the lower left quadrant are customers who have little current value to the enterprise and little growth potential. But they are still worth something (i.e., they are still profitable, at some level), and there

are almost certainly a whole lot of them. The enterprise's financial objective for low-maintenance customers should be to streamline the services provided them and to drive more and more interactions into more cost-efficient, automated channels. For a retail bank, for instance, these are the vast bulk of middle-market customers whose value will increase substantially if they can be convinced to use the bank's online services rather than taking the time and attention of tellers at the branch.

4. **Super-growth customers.** In the upper right quadrant of Exhibit 5.1, many enterprises will have just a few customers who have substantial actual value *and also* a significant amount of untapped growth potential. This is more likely to be true for B2B firms than for consumer-marketing companies. If a company sells to corporate customers, it will likely have a few very large firms in its customer base that are giant, immense firms that already give the company a substantial amount of business. That is, they are likely already high-value customers, but they are so immense that they could still give the enterprise much more business. No matter what size B2B firm an enterprise is, if it sells to Microsoft, or Intel, or Nissan, or GE, or other corporate customers with similarly large financial profiles, chances are these customers are super-growth customers. The business objective here is not just to retain the business already achieved but to mine the account for more. There is one caveat, however: Sometimes super-growth customers, who obviously know that they represent immense opportunity for the companies they buy from, use their customer relationships to drive very hard bargains, squeezing margins down as they push volumes up. They can be merciless, because they know they are highly valuable to the firms they choose to buy from. (See "Dealing with Tough Customers.")

5. **Below-zeros (BZs).** With very low or negative actual and potential values, BZs are customers who, no matter what effort a company makes, are still likely to generate less revenue than cost to serve. No matter what the firm does, no matter what strategy it follows, a BZ customer is highly unlikely ever to show a positive net value to the enterprise. Nearly every company has at least a few of these customers. For a telecommunications company, a BZ might be customer who moves often and leaves the last month or two unpaid at each address. For a retail bank, a BZ might be a customer who has little on deposit with the bank, but tends to use the teller window often. (Some banks in the United States estimate that as many as 40 to 50 percent of their retail customers are, in fact, BZs.) For a B2B firm, there can be a razor-thin difference between a super-growth customer and a BZ, because some giant business clients can threaten to drive margins down so low that they no longer cover the cost of servicing the account. The enterprise's strategy for a BZ should be to create incentives either to convert the customer's trajectory into a breakeven or profitable one (e.g., by imposing service charges for services previously given away for free) or to encourage politely the BZ to become someone else's unprofitable customer.

This categorization of customers by their value profiles is fairly arbitrary, because it presumes customers can be split into just a few tight groups, based on actual and potential value. But whether the enterprise uses the MVC-MGC-BZ typology or not, what should be clear is that the enterprise should have different financial objectives for different customers, based on its assessment of the kind of value each customer is or is not creating for it already and what kind of value is possible.

Customer Referral Value

Obviously, some customers will refer new customers to an enterprise more frequently than others will, and this represents real value "created" by the referring customers. In most situations, a customer who comes into the enterprise's franchise because of another customer's referral is likely to be more satisfied with the service he or she receives, more loyal, and often significantly more valuable to the business than a customer who comes in through normal marketing or sales channels. This is only logical, because a friend's recommendation is a highly trustworthy vote of confidence.

An enterprise should try to track customer referrals by individual customer, of course. For one thing, the enterprise needs to consider the fact of a referral in a customer's transactional records, because referred customers as well as referring customers may tend to have different patterns of behavior and trajectories. In addition, the enterprise probably should thank the referring customer or provide other positive feedback that encourages additional referrals (although explicit monetary rewards are tricky here, as we discuss soon).

Fred Reichheld's Net Promoter Score (NPS) is a compact metric designed to quantify the strength of a company's word-of-mouth reputation among existing customers. Leading Bain consultant Reichheld suggests a business survey of its customers to ask how willing they would be to recommend the business or product to a friend or colleague, on a scale of 1 to 10. The NPS is then calculated by subtracting the percentage of "detractors," who rate the likelihood anywhere from 1 to 6, from the percentage of "promoters," who rate it 9 or 10. With research from Bain and Satmetrix, Reichheld claims that the resulting metric is positively correlated not only with customer loyalty but with a company's growth prospects and its general financial performance. Reichheld also argues strongly that if a customer is willing to refer another customer, then he must be relatively more satisfied (and therefore more likely to remain loyal and valuable) himself as well.[a] As a very simple number based on a single question, NPS doesn't offer a lot of diagnostic benefit—that is, by itself, it isn't likely to say much about *why* a customer is or is not willing to recommend, but it has to be admired for its simplicity and practicality as well as its intuitive logic.

Significantly, calculating NPS requires subtracting detractors from promoters, which is an excellent idea, because customer dissatisfaction has been found to be a much better predictor of defection than customer satisfaction is of loyalty. Despite this fact, most companies that do track their customer satisfaction scores don't bother trying to track dissatisfaction scores. This is a big mistake, because when customers talk about a company with other customers, it isn't always positive. And negative word of mouth can be an insidious, destructive force all by itself, with a real effect on the financial value of the firm. (More about this in Chapter 8, when we discuss social media.)

At least one study more recent than Reichheld's original NPS argument suggests that a customer's actual referral value—that is, the true financial value of a customer's referrals to an enterprise—is not well correlated with the value created by the customer's own spending. In other words, although a customer

(*continued*)

(*Continued*)

may refer others to a business, this doesn't necessarily mean that the customer herself spends much more than other customers. In a 2007 *Harvard Business Review* article, "How Valuable Is Word of Mouth?" the authors developed a comprehensive model for calculating the value of referrals, taking into account the likelihood that a referred customer might have become a customer anyway, even without the referral. They then applied their model to a sample set of customers taken from two different actual firms—one telecom company and one financial services firm. What they found was that the value created by customer referrals (CRVs) is a very significant component of overall customer lifetime values.[b]

So, for instance, a decile analysis of customer spending values (CSV) and customer referral values (CRV) for the telecom company's customers would look like Exhibit 5B.

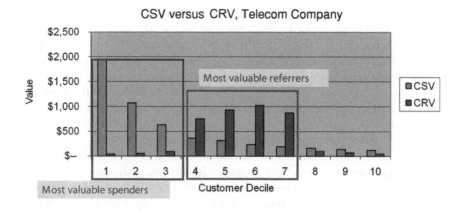

EXHIBIT 5B   Decile Analysis of Customer Spending Values (CSV) and Customer Referral Values (CRV)

Rewarding customers with monetary incentives for referring other customers can be helpful sometimes in encouraging more referrals. This is the basis for the classic direct marketing strategy colloquially known as member-get-a-member and is a common feature even today of many airline frequent-flyer programs. Then there was the classic "Friends and Family" program launched by MCI, which was a remarkable success in the long-distance business in the 1990s. Name 10 friends or family members you make long-distance calls to, and if they become MCI customers, then everyone in your "circle" of friends and family will get a 10 percent discount off their calls to one another. More recently Sprint PCS has made it a practice to give any customer who refers another customer a service credit of $20, while Scottrade, the online brokerage firm, provides a few free stock trades to both referring and referred customers.[c] But the very best and likely most valuable referrals will come without requiring any monetary incentive. If a customer is very happy with a company's product or service, then she is much more likely to see referring her friend to the company as doing the friend a favor. If, however, a financial incentive is offered, then (the customer might think) how confident can the company be in the quality of its product?

A highly successful online banking service in the United Kingdom, for instance, had a reputation for extremely good customer service. By its own analysis, this bank had customer satisfaction levels and "willingness to recommend" levels far above its nearest bricks-and-mortar banking competitors. Moreover, the bank had grown substantially in the past through customer recommendations. Citing Market & Opinion Research International, the firm's own Web site claimed it was "the UK's most recommended bank."[d]

However, after a few years in business, it had apparently begun to wear out its welcome among many of its most loyal customers. One customer, for instance, reported that while he used to recommend the bank to his friends regularly, he had stopped doing so. Why? Because lately the bank had been sending him repeated, irrelevant solicitations by mail. A 12-year customer of the bank, he "never borrows," but he and his wife now get about one solicitation a week for mortgages or loans. "I still bank there. It's a good bank," he says. "But I used to recommend [this bank] all the time to friends and others. I just thought I was doing a good turn for my friends by recommending it to them. But now they're more like all the other banks out there—just trying to hustle me for more business. So I haven't recommended them recently to anyone. Also, I know several other customers who feel the same way."[d] And this may be one reason why this bank now pays its customers £25 for each new customer recommended to it. Put another way: The bank's current lower customer experience levels required it to pay a fee for recommendations it formerly got for free.

---

[a]Fred Reichheld, The *Ultimate Question: Driving Good Profits and True Growth* (Boston: Harvard Business Press, 2006).
[b]The authors defined customer lifetime values in terms of spending only, but we will call this "customer spending value," while in our definition of "lifetime value" customer referrals are already included.
[c]V. Kumar, "How Valuable Is Word of Mouth?" *Harvard Business Review* 85, no. 10 (October 2007): 139–146.
[d]Customer interview, November 12, 2003.

One large B2B company performed a value analysis of its customer base and arrayed its customers by actual value and unrealized potential value, creating the scattergram shown in Exhibit 5.2. Each of the dots in the exhibit represents a different business customer. The customers in this graph that occupy the long spike out to the right represent this company's MVCs. Clearly, these are the customers giving the company the most business, and few of them have much unrealized potential value, because the company is getting the bulk of each one's patronage in its category. Down in the lower left of the graph we can find a few customers who have less than zero actual value; these (of course) are this company's BZ customers.

The tall spike up the left-hand side of the scattergram represents this company's MGCs. These are the customers who don't give the firm much of their

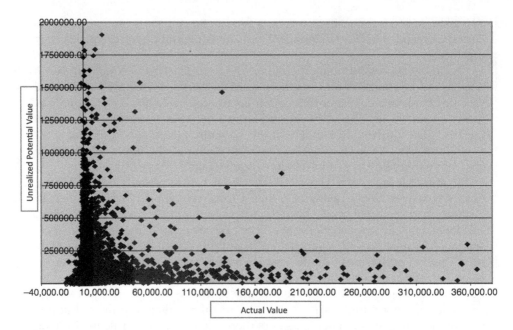

EXHIBIT 5.2   National Accounts' Actual versus Unrealized Potential Value

business right now but clearly have a great deal of business to give it, if they could be convinced to do so. You might note that the horizontal-vertical scales on this scattergram are not the same—that is, the vertical spike, if drawn to the same scale as the horizontal one, would soar up the page much farther than the illustration allows. And most of the customers in this vertical spike are the company's *competitor's* MVCs.

Is It Fair to "Fire" Unprofitable Customers?

As a company gets better at predicting actual and strategic value, it will become clear that just as 20 percent or so of its customers will likely account for the lion's share of the firm's profitability, another relatively small group of customers is likely to account for the lion's share of service costs and transaction losses. It is not uncommon for a retail bank, for instance, to do a customer valuation analysis and learn that 110 percent of its profit comes from just the top 30 percent or so of its customers while the vast bulk of customers are either break-even or unprofitable for it, when considered individually. Other businesses have similar problems, although retail banking is probably one of the most extreme examples.

Because of traditional marketing's heavy emphasis on customer acquisition, for many companies, it would be anathema even to suggest it, but the plain truth is that in many cases, a company will simply be more profitable if it were to *get rid* of some customers—provided, of course, that the customers it rids itself of are the ones who create losses without profit and who will likely continue to do so in the future.

Before leaping to the conclusion that this is unfair to customers, consider that it is the profitable customers who are, in effect, subsidizing the unprofitable ones. So "firing" unprofitable customers is not at all a hostile activity but one designed to make the overall value proposition fairer for all. Nevertheless, there are some important ground rules to follow when reducing the number of BZ customers at a company:

- However a company defines the value of a customer, the analysis must apply the same way to everyone. The company engaging in careful customer value differentiation does not care about skin color or gender, religion or political views. It cares only about each customer's actual and potential value, and it acts accordingly. This may disadvantage some customers who have long ago abandoned loyalty in favor of coupon clipping or other price shopping but will appropriately reward the customers who are keeping the business in business.

- Some companies, such as utilities or telecommunications firms (or banks, in some countries), have enjoyed monopoly or near-monopoly status in the past through regulatory directive. Even if they are no longer government-sanctioned monopolies, as the established incumbents these firms are likely to continue to have universal service mandates that require them to serve any and all customers. Such firms still may choose to define value or customer profitability in a more sophisticated way than simple revenue minus cost of service. The telephone company that provides basic service to Aunt Matilda in a rural area cannot hope to make a "profit" on her, in the strictest financial sense, but rather than classifying her as a BZ customer, it should consider her part of the company's mission to serve the community. Moreover, accomplishing this mission probably will be related to the company's regulatory situation, and foreswearing such a customer might violate a legal requirement. For such a company, the real BZ customers would be those who move every few months and leave the final bill unpaid, requiring extra collection efforts; or who often cause mishaps with neighborhood lines; or who frequently change carriers or otherwise create excessive paperwork. These customers can be omitted from promotional mailing lists and other spending efforts. It's okay to stop spending money trying to get a customer to generate a greater loss for the firm.

- Most important: Nothing about customer differentiation means treating anybody badly, ever. The enterprise that treats different customers differently will be required to maintain a consistently high "floor" of service that is the result of a fundamental recognition that customers are a twenty-first-century firm's most valuable asset, and—by definition—the firm's only source of revenue.

Nothing about customer differentiation means treating anybody badly. Ever.

Dealing with Tough Customers

Sometimes, because of the structure of an enterprise's own industry or its distribution network, or simply because of the type of market it has to deal with, it will have to cope with very powerful customers—customers who have a great deal of negotiating leverage in their relationship with the vendors they buy from. Customers like these, while they may represent super-growth customers when considered in one light, are large enough that they can also demand and get highly favorable terms, in the form of lower prices, better service, priority delivery, and so forth. Occasionally such customers are so powerful that they may all but require an enterprise to lose money just to serve them. But extremely large customers also have prestigious names and are difficult for any company to resist.

In retailing, the giant mega-stores and category killers, such as Wal-Mart and Toys "R" Us, are very tough customers. In the high-tech field, companies that manufacture components in mature markets, such as microchips, must sell to tough customers like Dell and Hewlett-Packard. In the automotive category, almost all of the manufacturers are large, difficult to deal with, and obsessively concerned with price.

It's important for a company to keep its perspective when serving "oppressive but necessary customers."[a] In the first place, a firm can make rational decisions with respect to such relationships only if it understands its customers' actual and potential values across the entire enterprise. But in addition, management at the enterprise should keep in mind that it really is a power struggle, so their firm must somehow develop more power for itself in the relationship. (Ironically, given all our discussion about "trust," a tough customer will very likely trust the enterprise, but the enterprise will need to step carefully when dealing with this customer.) The goal, however, is to serve the customer's best interests, and the enterprise won't be able to do this if it has to give up on the relationship entirely because it has become too one-sided.

One former senior executive at Company X, a Fortune 100 technology firm, says that "[Company X] was always looked upon as the must-win account for every supplier—and we knew that well. So we routinely adopted very tough positions and made stringent demands." According to this executive, the company's "typical behavior" with respect to suppliers was to "work closely with that company, study them, and try to extract as much of the process and knowledge as possible, then fire the supplier and do it ourselves. Overall, being self-sufficient was always a key objective. A few companies managed to avoid this ultimate fate by continually innovating faster than we [at Company X] could absorb; so they maintained the ability to deliver new value each year."

This is not unethical behavior on the part of a customer—far from it. It's the policy that many large and powerful buyers follow, especially in highly competitive environments or during periods of rapid and potentially disruptive innovation. The problem, when selling to such a customer, is that it will be very difficult to increase profitability or even to maintain it. It will be nearly impossible to establish any kind of loyalty or to protect margins—but that is in fact the purpose behind the customer's behavior in the first place. When dealing with suppliers, this kind of customer *wants* to use its power to hammer its costs down; and powerful firms have powerful hammers.

Sometimes an enterprise can maintain loyalty and protect its margins with tough customers by perpetually innovating new products or services, staying ahead of the customers themselves. Magna International sells automobile parts to all the world's giant auto companies. Automotive companies are renowned for their tight-fistedness, their tough price negotiations, and their buying power. This is a brutal environment for a seller, but Magna is an innovative firm. With 238 manufacturing operations and 79 product-development, engineering, and sales centers employing 72,525 people around the world,[b] Magna is a large company—but it is still at a disadvantage when it comes to selling to most of its gigantic customers.

Magna set up its Magna Steyr operation specifically to cater to the most important, unmet needs of these auto giants.[c] As the auto business has matured, it has seen increased fluctuations in demand for particular models. The car companies themselves are often unable to cope with these demands, and a "hot" model might be sold out for months at a time. Rather than selling auto parts at arm's length, the Magna Steyr division brings together all the capabilities required to manufacture cars, from parts to engineering, design, and production. For example, when demand for the new Mercedes M-Class SUV exceeded the capabilities of Mercedes' Tuscaloosa assembly line in late 1998, Magna Steyr was producing additional M-Class vehicles for Daimler-Chrysler on its own assembly line in Graz, Austria, within just nine months. This kind of service can help a firm protect its margins even with the toughest customers. And as a strategic asset, Magna Steyr's capabilities provide the company with a sustainable competitive advantage over its own competitors.

Sometimes an enterprise can deal effectively with tough customers by devising some service or offering that is customized to each customer's own needs, or that is available only because of the enterprise's own, larger breadth of experience or knowledge of the marketplace. In the commercial explosives business, Orica is a global company serving a large number of mining companies and quarry operators.[d] Quarry operators want their blasts to break rocks up into pieces of optimal size. An ineffective blast might leave the rock in chunks too large to be processed in an economically viable way. But as many as 20 different variables have to be considered when calibrating an explosive blast, and each quarry's ability to experiment with these parameters is limited. Because of its size, and the many different mines and quarries Orica deals with, the company can collect a great deal of information from around the world, cataloging input parameters and blast results for a wide variety of situations. As a result, Orica has developed a sound understanding of blasting techniques and now offers to take charge of the entire blasting process for a customer, selling a service contract for broken rocks of a specific size. This service has two advantages for Orica's customers.

1. They minimize the risk of poorly executed blasts. With an Orica contract, a customer, together with Orica, basically establish a "floor price" for correctly broken-up rock.

(continued)

(*Continued*)

2. Many of a customer's fixed costs, such as equipment for drilling and employees to manage the process, now become variable costs, which makes it that much easier for the company to manage each separate blasting project for its own customers. What makes this service useful to customers is the fact that Orica is uniquely positioned to compile information on blast techniques and parameters in a wide variety of situations. Any single one of its customers would have a great deal of difficulty duplicating this expertise.

Four principle tactics can be used to improve and maintain the value of even the toughest customers, and each of these tactics involves increasing the enterprise's relative power, uniqueness, or indispensability in the relationship:

1. *Customization of services or products.* An enterprise can build high-end, customized services around the more commodity-like products or services it sells, which creates switching costs that increase a customer's willingness to remain loyal, rather than bidding out the contract at every opportunity. Ideally, the enterprise will lock the customer into a Learning Relationship, but most tough customers will be wary of allowing such relationships to develop. The trick here is for the company to ensure that whatever high-end services are developed can be duplicated only by its competitors with great effort, even if they are instructed in advance (and they almost certainly will be by this tough customer!). This was Orica's strategy in offering "broken rock of a certain size" to customers rather than simply selling them explosives.

2. *Perpetual, cost-efficient innovation.* To the extent that an enterprise can stay ahead of its tough customer with innovative product or service ideas, it will always have something to sell. The organizational mission must center on being nimbler, more creative, and cost-efficient—all at the same time. But the value such a firm is really bringing to the customer here is innovation, not the products themselves. Many tough customers will do their best to absorb a seller's innovation in order to do it themselves or perhaps even to disseminate it to the seller's own competitors, in order to maintain vigorous competition and low prices. In either case, the customers' motive is to regain their negotiating power in dealing with the seller. So perpetual innovation is just that—perpetual. If a company can keep the wheels spinning fast enough, and provided that it doesn't lose control of costs, it can safely deal with very tough buyers. This is the strategy behind Magna Steyr's relationship with auto company customers.

3. *Personal relationships within the customer organization.* In the end, businesses have no brains, and they make no decisions. Only the people within a business make decisions, and people are both rational and emotional by nature. Therefore, the individuals within the enterprise need to have personal relationships with the individuals within the customer's organization. In the high-tech or automotive arena, this might mean developing

relationships with the engineers within a customer's organization who are responsible for designing the company's components into the final product. In the retailing business, it could mean developing relationships with the regional merchandising managers who get promoted based on the success of the programs the enterprise helps organize for them.

4. *Appeals directly to end users.* A highly desirable brand or a completely unique product in heavy demand by the customer's own customers will pull a seller's products through the customer's own organization more easily. The "Intel Inside" advertising campaign is designed to create pull-through for Intel. When Mattel offers Toys "R" Us an exclusive arrangement for particular configurations, or products with brand names such as "Barbie" or "Transformers" or "Harry Potter," it is making itself indispensable to this very tough customer. Similarly, any sort of information system or added service that saves time or effort for the end user can also be expected to put pressure on a tough customer. Dell's Web pages for enterprise customers not only save money for the customers but also give Dell a direct, one-to-one relationship with the executives who actually have the Dell computers on their desks.

Management should never forget, however, that selling to a tough customer is a deliberate decision, and it's possible sometimes that this decision will be made for the wrong reason. There are almost always choices to be made when thinking about the types of customers to serve, but often companies focus on the very large, most visible and "strategic" customers (i.e., tough customers), in the erroneous belief that simply because of their size they will be the most profitable. But, according to the ex-technology executive from Company X:

> *Overall, I don't think that we at [Company X] are all that different from most category-dominant companies. These guys know they're good and can get away with demanding just about anything. What many suppliers discover sooner or later is that despite the outward allure of serving a company like ours, once you actually win the business, the long-term payoff can be too painful to harvest. It was not unusual for a supplier to "fire" us as a customer by politely declining to bid on the next program.*

---

[a]Thanks to Bob Langer, Tom Spitale, Vernon Tirey, Steve Skinner, and Lorenz Esguerra for their perspectives on the issues in this section on "tough customers." The term *oppressive-but-necessary customers* is from Tom Spitale.

[b]Available at: www.magna.com/magna/en/media/facts/default.aspx; accessed March 2010.

[c]For more about Magna, see Mark Vandenbosch and Niraj Dawar, "Beyond Better Products: Capturing Value in Customer Interactions," *MIT Sloan Management Review* 43, no. 4 (Summer 2002): 35–42.

[d]See www.oricaminingservices.com, accessed March 29, 2010.

Managing the Mix of Customers

One way to think about the process of managing customer relationships is that the enterprise is attempting to improve its situation not just by adding as many new customers as possible to the customer base but also by managing the mix of customers it deals with. It wants to add to the number of MVCs, create more profitability from its MGCs, and minimize its BZs. An enterprise in this situation could choose either to emphasize adding new customers to its customer base or (instead or in addition) to increase the values of the customers in its customer base. So imagine if an enterprise were to plot the distribution of its customer values on a chart, as in Exhibit 5.3, with actual values of customers shown across the bottom axis and the number of customers shown up the vertical axis.

Curve 1 on Exhibit 5.3 shows the enterprise's current mix of customers, with just a few BZs and MVCs and the bulk of customers lying in between these two extremes. By applying a customer-acquisition marketing strategy the enterprise will end up acquiring more and more customers, but these customers are likely to show the same mix of valuations as in its current customer base, as shown by Curve 2. Market share will likely improve, but the mix of customers will almost certainly remain the same. In fact, a customer acquisition strategy often results in a degraded **mix of customer values**, when an enterprise focuses on the number of customers acquired (as happens at many companies) without respect to their values. Almost by definition, low-value customers are easier to acquire than high-value customers. If the only variable being measured by the firm's management is the number of customers acquired, then average customer values will almost certainly decline rather than remain the same.

If, however, the enterprise employs a customer-centric strategy, it will not be trying to acquire just *any* customers; instead, it will be focusing its customer acquisition efforts on acquiring higher-value customers. Moreover, it will focus a lot of its effort on improving the value of its existing customers, and moving them up in value individually. The result of a such a strategy is shown as Curve 3 in Exhibit 5.3. An

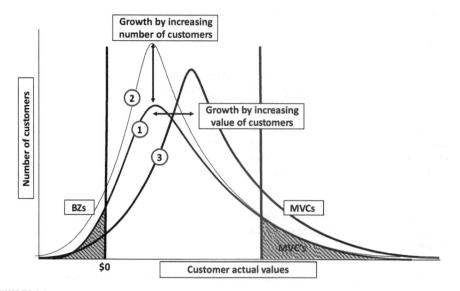

EXHIBIT 5.3   Managing the Mix of Customers

enterprise that launches a successful CRM effort will end up shifting the customer mix itself, moving the entire customer base into a higher set of values.

Creating a valuable customer base requires understanding the distribution of customer relationship values and investing in acquisition, development, and retention accordingly.[8] By taking the time to understand the value profile of a customer relative to other customers, enterprises can begin to allocate resources intentionally to ensure that the most valuable customers remain loyal. The future of an enterprise, therefore, depends on how effectively it acquires profitable new customers, develops the profitability of existing customers, and retains existing profitable relationships.[9] Customers will want to spend money with a business that serves them well, and that is nearly always a company that knows them well and uses that knowledge to build relationships in which customers perceive great value and benefit.[10]

Certainly one of the most important benefits of ranking customers by value is that the enterprise can more rationally allocate its resources and marketing efforts, focusing more on high-value and high-growth customers and less on low-value customers. Moreover, the enterprise will likely find it less attractive, as a marketing tactic, to acquire strangers as "customers"—some of whom will never be worth anything to the company.

Janet LeBlanc, named a 1to1 Customer Champion in 2008 by 1to1 Media, tells the story about how Canada Post differentiated its customers by value and, in the process, increased top-line revenue and cut costs to serve as well.

Canada Post: Using Value to Differentiate Customer Relationships

Janet LeBlanc
Principal, Janet LeBlanc & Associates
Former Director, Customer Value Management, Canada Post

Canada Post is a major contributor to the Canadian economy, generating almost $5.5 billion in gross domestic product and $9 billion in labor income. With a 150-year history of serving Canadian consumers and businesses, Canada Post is the country's leading delivery organization, serving 32 million consumers through 6,700 post offices across the country. Every day, it delivers 40 million

(continued)

---

[8]Michael Lewis, "Customer Acquisitions Promotions and Customer Asset Value," *Journal of Marketing Research* 43 (May 2006): 195–203; Roland T. Rust, Katherine N. Lemon, and Valarie A. Zeithaml, "Return on Marketing: Using Customer Equity to Focus Marketing Strategy," *Journal of Marketing* 68 (January 2004): 109–127; Paul Cole and Robert E. Wayland, *Customer Connections* (Cambridge, MA: Harvard Business School Press, 1997).

[9]Yichen Lin, Jr Jung Lyu, Hwan-Yann Su, and Yulan Hsing, "A Feasibility Study of the Customer Relationship Management Application on Small and Medium Enterprises," *Journal of Scientific and Technological Studies* 41, no. 1 (2007): 54; Katherine N. Lemon, Roland T. Rust, and Valarie Zeithaml, *Driving Customer Equity* (New York: Free Press, 2000).

[10]Bob Evans, "A Question of Customer Loyalty," *InformationWeek,* Issue 793, July 3, 2000, 52.

(Continued)

messages to over 14 million addresses as of 2010—a number that increases by 240,000 annually. A key driver of the Canadian economy, Canada Post's size and scale make it a formidable presence on the Canadian landscape, recognized as one of Canada's top 10 brands—one that Canadians trust.

Canada Post is in the business of connecting Canadians. Its 72,000 employees work around the clock to process 11 billion pieces of mail, parcels, and messages each year to every corner of our vast country. Focusing on these daily operational requirements had led Canada Post to be inward looking—cultivating an "inside-out" culture where the needs of the company were put before the customer experience. Furthermore, Canada Post had traditionally and successfully operated in an environment with very little competition. However, with emerging communication technologies and multinational courier companies, the world has become much smaller and competition for business more fierce.

Canada Post faces intense competition in all its lines of business. The exclusive privilege of collecting and delivering the mail is becoming irrelevant as businesses, which generate 90 percent of Canada Post revenues, see in electronic communications a means to significantly reduce their costs of reaching customers. The erosion of transaction mail (bills, invoices, notices, statements) is a phenomenon that Canada Post and all postal administrations around the world are coping with.

To meet these challenges, Canada Post embarked on a major transformational change with the vision to become a more modern postal service. Over the last decade, these changes have included the implementation of an enterprise resource planning system, improved process performance, development of new technologies, and, most recently, the investment in new plants and equipment. These upgrades have and will continue to positively impact its ability to serve and create value for customers.

Company executives realized that if it was to be successful in the future, it needed to turn its focus outward, building customer relationships and making customer growth a priority by building flexibility into its business and responding more quickly to evolving needs.

Canada Post embarked on a journey to bring customers to the forefront of its business. In a little more than three years, Canada Post defined what customers value most, measured and tracked weekly performance in the marketplace, and identified customer-value metrics and competitive benchmarks to maximize customer value and drive cultural change across the organization. Today, its award-winning Customer Value Management program guides business strategy, helps focus redesign efforts, and shapes employee incentives and rewards.

Canada Post wanted its Customer Value Management program to be more than just research. It needed it to be a data-driven functional model used across all lines of business to help the organization prioritize its efforts and focus resources on those customers who yield the highest value. The company needed to shift its view from market development to customer development with the goal of revenue protection and growth.

But how do you focus on individual customer development when you are mandated to provide universal service to all Canadians? And what tools can you use to rank customers according to their true value to the organization and their potential value?

The Customer Value Management program became an important tool to understand a customer's current strength and to influence a customer's future behavior in order to impact unrealized potential.

Canada Post surveys more than 25,000 customers each year to measure the end-to-end customer experience, including its products' features and benefits; how the product was delivered; and the service customers received from any one of its seven channels, including contact with a telephone service agent or its Web site, through face-to-face interaction with a sales representative, or interaction with a letter carrier or delivery person. Each customer is asked to evaluate the overall experience based on his perception of quality, the overall perceived value received, and the likelihood of recommending Canada Post to a friend or colleague. These three questions comprise its Customer Value Index. Those customers who rated Canada Post a top two box rating of 9 or 10 on a 10-point scale for all three questions were viewed as loyal to the organization and were calculated as part of its Customer Value Index.

This Customer Value Index is used as a proxy variable to assess the strength of the relationship customers have with Canada Post and the potential value they could bring to the organization. Using the Customer Value Index rating, Canada Post classifies customers into a loyalty classification (see Exhibit 5C). Those customers who rated Canada Post a 9 or 10 on all three Customer Value Index questions are ranked as loyal; conversely, customers who rated Canada Post a 6 or below are considered "at risk." Customers with variable ratings are classified as either positive or hesitant.

EXHIBIT 5C Canada Post's Customer Value Index and Loyalty Classification

Loyalty Classification	Range	Rating	Description
Loyal	Top Two Box	9–10	Customers rated Canada Post a 9 or 10 on all three questions.
Positive	Top Four Box Mixed Answer	7–10	Customers rated Canada Post a 7 to 10 on all three questions. Does not include loyalty group.
Hesitant	Mixed Answer	1–10	Customers gave a mix of ratings on the questions ranging from 1 to 10.
At Risk	Bottom Six Box	1–6	Customers rated Canada Post a 1 to 6 on all three questions.

Detailed linkage analysis revealed a strong link, making it clear that loyal and positive customers contributed more revenue to Canada Post than those who were classified as hesitant or at risk. This finding was an important discovery as it helped to direct the resources and activities of the organization's

(continued)

(Continued)

sales, marketing, and operations teams toward areas of opportunity and growth or potential risk.

Canada Post used this value and loyalty classification plan to guide the account development strategies of its sales and marketing teams. Sales strategies for customers classified as loyal and positive were focused on cross-sell and up-sell opportunities. Customer retention plans were put in place to meet the needs of customers identified as hesitant or at risk.

A closed-loop process was also created to feed sales representatives with the Customer Value Index rating and overall evaluation of the experience for each of their customers who completed a survey. Sales representatives were alerted to a new Customer Value Index rating from their customers when received, indicating those areas of opportunity and potential risk. Sales managers and sale representatives were trained to review the findings and initiate a business review with their customers to understand the required action plans and initiatives. The business objective was to strengthen the relationship to grow and protect the business.

As difficult as relationships are to strengthen, they are remarkably easy to lose. Customers who identified themselves as "at risk" by rating Canada Post a 6 or below on its three Customer Value Index questions were highly likely to defect or erode their business. A detailed analysis revealed that customers who were identified as "at risk" defected within a year and took not only one line of business revenue with them but all of their Canada Post revenue. In fact, for one line of business, more than 50 percent of customers who identified themselves as "at risk" or "hesitant" defected.

All customers were grouped into one of four categories based on current Canada Post revenue: "growth," "lost," "eroding," or "new." By using the Customer Value Index as its proxy variable, Canada Post could validate whether customers who classified themselves as loyal or positive were in fact spending more with Canada Post and had growing revenue. The results showed that for one line of business, almost 75 percent of customers who were classified in the category of "growth" were rated as loyal or positive to Canada Post. This finding was important for Canada Post because it validated the measurement proxy within its Customer Value Management program as a significant indicator of the strength of the relationship that customers had with the company.

This structured approach to managing the customer relationship has been extremely valuable to Canada Post. Many companies use loyalty data to monitor relationship health, but few consistently act on the data in order to solve identified customer problems to ensure retention. By integrating the process of using customer data to pinpoint strengths and opportunities throughout the company, Canada Post instituted an ongoing customer management strategy focused on revenue growth and retention.

When Canada Post launched its Customer Value Management program in 2003, it wanted customer value to influence strategic planning and to incorporate customer data into the annual business planning process and the identification of process improvement initiatives. The Customer Value Management program identifies the critical elements essential to making progress from the customers' perspective, directs scarce resources, and creates alignment across the organization for those areas that matter most to customers. Its successful implementation is a major achievement, moving Canada Post closer to its goal of becoming a world-class provider of physical and electronic delivery services.

Summary

For an enterprise to engage its customers in relationships, it must be prepared to treat different customers differently. Before designing its relationship-building strategy, the firm must understand the nature of its customers' differences, one from another. From Chapter 5, we know that the value of a customer is a function of the future business the customer does with the enterprise, and that different customers have different values. Knowing which customers are more valuable allows an enterprise to allocate its relationship-building efforts to concentrate first on those customers that will yield the best financial return. However, because the future patronage of any customer is not something that can actually be known in the present, making decisions with respect to customer valuation necessarily involves approximation and subjectivity. Companies with large numbers of customers whose transactions are electronically tracked in a detailed way might be able to use statistical modeling techniques to make reasonably accurate forecasts of the future business that particular types of customers will likely do with the firm, but for the vast majority of enterprises, no such scientific models are readily available. Instead, companies that rank their customers by value usually do so by using a mix of judgment and proxy variables—at least at first.

As this chapter has shown, the enterprise that defines, quantifies, and ranks the value of its individual customers takes great strides toward becoming a business truly based on growing customer value. By relying on a taxonomy of customer types based on their value profile—including not just actual values but unrealized potential values as well—the enterprise can create a useful model for how it would like to alter the trajectories of individual customers. Not only can it devote a greater portion of its internal resources to serving its most valuable customers, but it also can set more rational financial objectives for each customer, based on that customer's value profile.

Setting financial objectives is only a part of the job, however. To achieve those objectives for each customer, no matter what they are, the enterprise will have to alter the customer's trajectory. It will have to change the customer's behavior; that is, it will need to get a customer to do something (or not do something) that he or she was not otherwise going to do. To do this in the most efficient way possible, the enterprise needs to be able to appeal directly to the customer's motivations. It must communicate to the customer in a way that the customer is going to understand. It must, in a word, understand the customer's own perspective and needs.

In Chapter 6, we explore how the enterprise can differentiate its customers based not just on their value profiles, but on their individual needs as well.

Later in the book, we talk about how to manage the value of the enterprise based on the rate of change of the lifetime value of customers. You'll see a lot more about

Return on Customer in Chapter 11. Ultimately, of course, the value the customer has to the enterprise is a direct result of the value the enterprise has to the customer.

Food for Thought

1. Why is it not enough to consider average customer value?
2. How often should actual value be calculated? Potential value? Why?
3. Search the Web for a company that has successfully "fired" customers in the past. What policies are successful, and what policies are likely to create mistrust?
4. What are likely to be the best measures of actual and potential value for each of the listed customer bases? How would you confirm that your answer is right? Would the company likely be best served by proxy or statistical/financial value analysis?
   - Customers for a B2B electronics components distributor
   - Customers for a dry cleaner
   - Customers for an automobile manufacturer; for an automobile dealer
   - Customers for a chemical supply company
   - Customers for a discount department store
   - Customers for a large regional supermarket chain
   - Customers for a long-haul trucking company
   - Customers for Disney World; for Six Flags; for Club Med
   - Customers for CNN; for HBO (Caution: They're different. CNN sells viewers to advertisers while HBO sells programming to viewers.)
   - "Customers" for a political campaign; for the American Cancer Society; for NPR (formerly National Public Radio); for Habitat for Humanity
5. For each of the companies listed in #4, what's the next step? How does a company use the information about customer value to make managerial decisions?

Glossary

Actual value   The net present value of the future financial contributions attributable to a customer, behaving as we expect her to behave—knowing what we know now, and with no different actions on our part.

Below zero (BZ)   The below-zero customer will, no matter what strategy or effort is applied toward him, always cost the company and its best customers more than he contributes.

Lifetime value (LTV)   Synonymous with "actual value." The net present value of the future financial contributions attributable to a customer, behaving as we expect her to behave—knowing what we know now, and with no different actions on our part.

Low-maintenance customers   Customers with low actual values and low unrealized potential values. They are not very profitable for the enterprise individually, nor do they have much growth potential individually. But there are probably a lot of them.

Mix of customer values   For a particular company, the mix refers to the percentage of most valuable customers versus most growable customers versus below-zero customers.

Most growable customers (MGCs)   Customers with high unrealized potential values. These are the customers who have the most growth potential: growth that can be realized through cross-selling, through keeping customers for a longer period, or perhaps by changing their behavior and getting them to operate in a way that costs the enterprise less money.

Most valuable customers (MVCs)   Customers with high actual values but not a lot of unrealized growth potential. These are the customers who do the most business, yield the highest margins, are most willing to collaborate, and tend to be the most loyal.

NPV   Net Present Value

Potential value   The net present value of the future financial contributions that *could* be attributed to a customer, if through conscious action we succeed in changing the customer's behavior.

Super-growth customers   Customers with high actual value and high unrealized potential value as well.

Trajectory   The path of the customer's financial relationship through time with the enterprise.

Unrealized potential value   The difference between a customer's potential value and a customer's actual value (i.e., the customer's lifetime value).

Value skew   The distribution of lifetime values by customer ranges from high to low. For some companies, this distribution shows that it takes a fairly large percentage of customers to account for the bulk of the company's total worth. Such a company would have a shallow value skew. Another company, at which a tiny percentage of customers accounts for a very large part of the company's total value, can be described as having a steep value skew.

CHAPTER 6

Differentiating Customers
by Their Needs

I don't know the key to success, but the key to failure is trying to please everybody.

—Bill Cosby

All value for a business is created by customers, but the reason any single customer creates value for a business is to meet that particular customer's own individual **needs.** While it's important to recognize that different customers will create different amounts of value for the enterprise (i.e., some customers are worth more than other customers, a subject we explored in Chapter 5), it's even more important to understand how customers differ in terms of their individual needs, and this is the topic we will tackle in this chapter. Individual customer valuation methods are fairly well established as an important stepping-stone for managing the customer-strategy enterprise. Academics and business professionals alike spend much time and energy testing the effectiveness of alternative methods and models. But differentiating customers based on their needs is still a relatively new idea, not as widely practiced by companies—not even by those professing to take a customer-centric approach to business. At its heart, needs differentiation of customers involves using feedback from an identifiable, individual customer to predict that customer's needs better than any competitor can who doesn't have that feedback. In addition to categorizing customers by their value profiles (see Chapter 5), it is vital to categorize customers based on their individually expressed needs, when they are similar. This is the only practical way to set up criteria for treating different customers differently.

Having a good knowledge of customers' value is certainly important, but to use customer relationship management (CRM) tools and customer strategies to increase a customer's value, the business must be able to see things from the customer's perspective, with the realization that there are many different types of customers whose perspective must be individually understood. Value differentiation by itself will not give a company this perspective. Think about it: Customers don't usually know or care what their value is to a business. Customers simply want to have their problem solved, and every customer has his own slightly different twist on how the process should be handled, even if more than one customer wants a problem solved a particular way. The key to building a customer's value is understanding how *this* customer wants it solved. So one key to building profitable relationships is developing an understanding of how customers are different in terms of their needs and how such needs-based differences relate to different customer values, both actual and potential. What behavior changes on the customer's part can be accomplished by meeting those needs? What are the triggers that will allow the firm to actualize some of that unrealized potential value?

In this chapter, we consider the different needs of different customers and the role that customer needs to play in an enterprise's relationship-building effort. In most situations, it makes sense to differentiate customers first by their value and then by their needs.[1] In this way, the relationship-building process, which can be expensive, will begin with the company's higher-value customers, for whom the investment is more likely to be worthwhile. (An important exception to this general rule, however, applies to treating different customers differently on the World Wide Web. On the Web, the incremental costs of automated interaction are near zero, so it makes little difference whether an enterprise differentiates just its top customers by their needs or all its customers.)

Definitions

Before going too much further, let's pause to define the important terms relevant to this discussion.

Needs

When we refer to customer needs, we are using the term in its most generic sense. That is, what a customer needs from an enterprise is, by our definition, what she wants, what she prefers, or what she would like. In this sense, we do not distinguish a customer's needs from her wants. For that matter, we do not distinguish needs from preferences, wishes, desires, or whims. Each of these terms might imply some nuance of need—perhaps the intensity of the need or the permanence of it—but to simplify our discussion, we will refer to them all as "needs."

It is what a customer needs from an enterprise that is the driving force behind the customer's behavior. Needs represent the "why" (and often, the "how") behind a customer's actions. How customers want to buy may be as important as why they want to buy. The presumption has been that frequent purchasers use the

---

[1] In the view of some, differentiating by value first, then needs, may appear to focus first on the company's needs, then those of the customers; but another way to look at this order of strategic imperatives is to think about how a company that used to treat every customer's needs as equally important will now focus more on the needs of those customers who contribute the most to the success of the firm and therefore will put the needs of some customers ahead of the needs of other customers, thus allocating resources best for the most valuable customers.

product differently from irregular purchasers, but it may be that they alternatively or additionally like the available channel better. For that matter, it may be that they like the communications channel better. The point is that needs are not just about product usage but about an *expanded need set* (which we discuss fully in Chapter 10) or the combination of product, cross-buy product and services opportunities, delivery channels, communication style and channels, invoicing methods, and so on.

In a relationship, what the enterprise most wants is to influence customer behavior in a way that is financially beneficial to the enterprise; therefore, understanding the customer's basic need is critical. It could be said that while the amount the customer pays the enterprise is a component of the customer's value to the enterprise, the need that the enterprise satisfies represents the enterprise's value to the customer. Needs and value are, essentially, both sides of the value proposition between enterprise and customer—what the customer can do for the enterprise and what the enterprise can do for the customer.

Customers

Now that we have defined both customer value and customer needs, we should pause for a reminder of the definition of *customer* before continuing with our discussion. In Chapter 1, we defined what we mean by *customer*. On the surface, the definition should be obvious. A customer is one who "gives his custom" to a store or business; someone who patronizes a business is the business's customer. However, the overwhelming majority of enterprises serve multiple types of customers, and these different types of customers have different characteristics in terms of their value and their individual needs.

A brand-name clothing manufacturer, for instance, has two sets of customers: the end-user consumers who wear the clothes and the retailers that buy the clothes from the manufacturer and sell them to consumers. As a customer base, clothing consumers do not have as steep a value skew as, say, a hotel's customer base, even though some consumers might buy new clothes every week. (In other words, the discrepancy in value between the very most valuable consumers and the average will generally be smaller for a particular clothing merchant.) But all consumers of the clothing manufacturer do want different combinations of sizes, colors, and styles. So even though clothing consumers may not be highly differentiated in terms of their value, they are highly differentiated in terms of their needs. Retailer customers also have very different needs: Some need more help with marketing, or with advertising co-op dollars, or with displays. Different retailers will have very different requirements for invoice format and timing or for shipping and delivery. They may need different palletization or precoded price tags. Interestingly, retailers will also vary widely in their values to the clothing manufacturer—with much more value skew than consumers will show. Some large department store chains will sell far more stock than can a local mom-and-pop clothing shop. Thus retailer customers display high levels of differentiation in terms of both their needs and their value.

For the clothing manufacturer, if the enterprise expresses an interest in improving its relationships with its customers, the question to answer is: Which customers?

And this is, in fact, the type of structure in which most enterprises operate. They won't all sell products to retailers, but the vast majority of businesses do have distribution partners of some kind—retailers, dealers, brokers, representatives, value-added resellers, and so forth. Moreover, a business that sells to other businesses, whether these business customers are a part of a distribution chain or not, really is selling to the *people* within those businesses, people of varying levels of influence and authority. Putting in place a relationship program involving business customers will necessarily entail dealing with purchasing agents, approvers, influencers, decision makers, and possibly end users within the business customer's organization, and each of these people will have quite different motivations in choosing to buy.

The logical first step for any enterprise embarking on a relationship-building program, therefore, is to decide which sets of customers to focus on. A relationship-building strategy aimed at end-user consumers can (and in most cases, should) involve some or all of the intermediaries in the value chain in some way. However, it is a perfectly legitimate goal to seek stronger and deeper relationships with a particular set of intermediaries. The basic objective of relationship building with any set of customers is to increase the value of the customer base; thus, it's important to understand from the beginning exactly which customer base is going to be measured and evaluated. Then, when focusing on that customer base, the enterprise must be able to map out its customers in terms of their different values and needs.

It is easy to confuse a customer's needs with a product's **benefits.** Companies create products and services with benefits that are specifically designed to satisfy customer needs, *but the benefits themselves are not equivalent to needs.* In traditional marketing discipline, a product's benefits are the advan-

> Companies create products and services with benefits that are specifically designed to satisfy customer needs, *but the benefits themselves are not equivalent to needs.*

tages that customers get from using the product, based on its features and **attributes**. But features, attributes, and benefits are all based on the product rather than on the customer. Needs, in contrast, are based on the customer, not the product. Two different customers might use the same product, based on the same features and attributes, to satisfy very different needs.

When it focuses on the customer's need, the enterprise will find it easier to increase its share of customer, because ultimately it will seek to solve a greater and greater portion of the customer's problem—that is, to meet a larger and larger share of the customer's need. And because the customer's need is not directly related to the product, meeting the need might, in fact, lead an enterprise to develop or procure other products and services for the customer that are totally unrelated to the original product but closely related to the customer's need. That's why focusing on customer needs rather than on product features often will reveal that different customers purchase the same product in order to satisfy very different individual needs.[2]

---

[2] A large body of academic research, as well as trade articles and professional work, has been published on the topics of benefits, attributes, and needs as well as the findings about the different reasons two customers with the same transaction history are motivated to buy the same products.

Demographics Do Not Reveal Needs

Thirty years ago, a groundbreaking marketing article asked: "Are Grace Slick and Tricia Nixon Cox the same person?" Grace Slick, lead singer for the rock group Jefferson Starship, and Tricia Nixon Cox, the preppy daughter of Richard Nixon who married Dwight Eisenhower's grandson, were demographically indistinguishable. They were both urban, working women, college graduates, age 25 to 35, at similar income levels, household of three, including one child.

What made this question startling in the early 1970s was that it undermined the validity of the traditional demographic tools that marketers had been using for decades to segment consumers into distinct, identifiable groups. With demographic statistics, mass marketers thought they could distinguish a quiz show's audience from, say, a news program's. Then marketers could compare these audiences with the demographics of soap buyers, tire purchasers, or beer drinkers. The more effectively a marketer could define her own customers and target prospects, differentiating this group from all the other consumers who were not her target, the more efficiently she could get her message across. She could buy media that would reach a higher proportion of her own target audience.

But demographics could not explain the distinctly nondemographic differences between Grace Slick and Tricia Nixon Cox. So, as computer capabilities and speeds grew, marketers began to collect additional information to distinguish consumers, not by their age and gender, but by their attitudes toward themselves, their families and society, their beliefs, their values, their behaviors, and their lifestyles.

Source: Excerpted from Don Peppers and Martha Rogers, Ph.D., *The One to One Future* (1993), in reference to John O'Toole, "Are Grace Slick and Tricia Nixon Cox the Same Person?" *Journal of Advertising* 2 (1973): 32–34.

Differentiating Customers by Need: An Illustration

Consider a company that manufactures interlocking toy blocks for children, such as LEGO Lego® or MEGA Bloks®, and suppose this firm goes to market with a set of blocks suitable for constructing a spaceship. Three seven-year-old children playing with this set of blocks might all have different needs for it. One child might use the blocks to play a make-believe role, perhaps assembling a spaceship and then pretending to be an astronaut on a mission to Mars. Another child might enjoy simply following the directions, meticulously assembling the same spaceship in exact detail, according to the instructions. Once the ship is built, however, the child would be less interested in it. A third child might use the block set meant to construct a spaceship to build something entirely different, drawn from his own vivid imagination. This child simply wouldn't enjoy putting together a toy according to someone else's diagram.

Each of these three children may enjoy playing with the same set of blocks, but each is doing so to satisfy a different set of needs. Moreover, it is the child's need

EXHIBIT 6.1   Product Attributes versus Benefits

Product Attribute	Product Benefit
Toys in fantasy configurations	Recognizable make-believe situations
Colorful, unusual shapes that easily interlock	Large variety of interesting combinations
Meticulously preplanned, logically detailed instructions	Complex directions that are nevertheless easy to follow

that, *if known to the marketer*, provides the key to increasing the child's value as a customer. If the toy manufacturer actually knew each child's individual needs, and if it had the capability to deal with each child individually, by treating each one differently, it could easily increase its share of each child's toy-and-entertainment consumption. For example, for the "actors," it might offer costumes and other props, along with storybooks and videos or DVDs, to assist the children in their imaginative role-playing activities. For the "engineers," it might offer blueprints for additional toys to be assembled using the spaceship set; or it might offer more complex diagrams for multiset connections. And for the more creative types, the "artists," the company might provide pieces in unusual colors or shapes, or perhaps supplemental sets of parts that have not been planned into any diagrams at all.

We can use this example to compare and contrast the different roles of product attributes and benefits versus customer needs. Exhibit 6.1 shows that each product attribute yields a particular benefit that consumers of the product can enjoy.

It should be easy to see that each product attribute can be easily linked to a particular type of benefit. And the benefits will appeal differently to different customers, but each benefit springs directly from each attribute. If, instead, we were to map out the *types of customers* who buy this product, based on the needs of these end users as just outlined, we could then list the additional products and services that each type of customer might want, based on what that customer needs from this and other products. If we just looked at our actor, artist, or engineer end-user customers to see which needs they wanted to address, then our table would look like Exhibit 6.2.

This is only a hypothetical example, of course, and we could easily come up with several additional types of customers, based on the needs they are satisfying with these construction blocks. For instance, there might be some girls who want the spaceship set of blocks because they are really interested in rockets, outer space, and other things astronautical. Or there might be some boys who want the set because

EXHIBIT 6.2   Beyond Benefits: Customer Needs

Customer Need	Additional Products and Services
Actor: Role-playing, pretending, fantasizing	Costumes, videos, storybook, toys
Artist: Creating, making stuff up, doing things differently	Colors and paints, unique add-ons, nonsequitur parts
Engineer: Solving problems, completing puzzles	More diagrams, problems, logical extensions

they are collectors of these kinds of building-block toys, and they want to add this to a large set of other, similar toys. Or there might be others who like to use this kind of toy to invite friends over to work together on the assembly. Any single child might, in fact, have any combination of these needs that she wishes to satisfy, either at different times or in combination.

The point is, by *taking the customer's own perspective, the customer's point of view*—by concentrating on understanding each different customer's needs—the enterprise will more easily be able to influence customer behavior, and changing the future behavior of a customer by becoming more valuable to him is the key to realizing additional value from that customer.

Scenario: Financial Services

A large B2B financial services organization faced both increasing competition and product commoditization.[a] The customers of this firm are channel members—the brokers and financial advisors (FAs) who sell stocks and bonds and other financial instruments to consumer clients from their own business. The enterprise sought to increase loyalty and reduce the effects of cost cutting among these channel-member customers by meeting their individual needs, one customer at a time. Research, based on interviews with the enterprise's sales staff and customers, uncovered several key customer needs.

Five needs-based portfolios were identified and given nicknames—High-Potential Newbies, Marketing Machines, Active Growers, Transitional Players, and Cruise Controls—in a research project that combined customer needs information with customer valuation. As a result, the enterprise determined its customers' needs while at the same time uncovering which high-value customers posed the greatest defection risk. This led to the development of a defection reduction strategy to retain those customers. For customers not at risk of defection, the organization developed interaction strategies to begin meeting their needs immediately.

As it builds relationships with these customers over time, the financial services enterprise will seek to increase customer knowledge and to act on the individual needs of its customers. In the process, both the enterprise and its customers will benefit. For the enterprise, an interaction strategy for each FA, based on the individual FA's needs and value, will provide clear direction and focus for the sales force. As more needs are uncovered, the firm will be able to offer more products and services. Ultimately, defection will be reduced, which should substantially reduce marketing and sales costs.

For the customers themselves, the relationship-building program should improve the relevance and usefulness of incoming information from the enterprise. This will enable individual FAs to run their own businesses faster, more efficiently, and in a way that is likely to please their own clients more.

[a]Thanks to Jennifer Monahan, Nichole Clark, Laura Cococcia, Bill Pink, Valerie Popeck, and Sophie Vlessing for the ideas here.

Understanding Customer Behaviors and Needs

Kerem Can Özkısacık, Ph.D.
Manager, Middle East, Peppers & Rogers Group

Understanding the differences in customer behaviors, and the needs underlying these behaviors, is critical for all stages in a company: from product development to financial consolidation, from production planning to strategic planning or marketing budgeting. All decisions and activities made by customers in order to evaluate, purchase, use, and dispose of any goods or services offered by a company are subject to being captured in the transactional record and are subject to behavioral analysis.

A customer's need is what she wants, prefers, or wishes while her behavior is what she does or how she acts in order to satisfy this need. In other words, "needs" are the "why" of a customer's actions, and "behaviors" are the "what." Behaviors can be observed directly, and from behaviors an enterprise can often infer things about a customer's needs. This hierarchy or logical ordering in these two notions, that customer needs drive customer behaviors, is a critical pillar for the relationship-marketing practitioner.

All companies want to understand why and how customers make their buying decisions. Factors that affect this process are analytically assessed and examined, then reexamined. Clearly segmenting customers by their needs and behaviors will allow an enterprise to identify and describe different categories of customers and ensure that its marketing efforts are effective for each of these groups.

Characterizing Customers by Their Needs and Behaviors

Companies now have comprehensive systems and processes to capture and store customer data covering almost every aspect of a customer's relationship with a firm. Descriptive characteristics like gender, age, and income, along with transactional data such as interactions, purchases, and payments, and usage-related measures such as service requests—all this information can be captured and stored by the enterprise. The information companies store on individual customers is usually referred to as customer profiles.

Now let's consider a customer database in a bank environment where there has been a significant information technology (IT) investment. The department in charge of business intelligence can describe the same customer in two different ways, providing two different profiles:

1. Customer is married, is European, has two children, lives in an upscale neighborhood, and is a member of a frequent-flyer program.
2. Customer visited the online banking site once a week over the last six months, always visiting the site at least once in the first three days of each month; has a tenure of more than two years; uses investment tools; checks

her statement and balance regularly; pays her credit debts promptly and has a clear credit history; and has increased her assets under management by 5 percent in the last three months.

The first profile is demographic. It is a set of characteristics that are less dynamic compared to the second profile. These data probably are stored by other companies doing business with this customer as well, and perhaps even by the bank's own competitors. The second profile is behavior-based, and involves a record derived from what the customer is actually doing or has done in the past with this bank. Details of her behavior are dynamic and only available inside the bank's database, thus providing the bank with an opportunity for competitive advantage—if the bank uses the information to serve this customer better than other firms that do not have the specific customer information.

Both profiles are important in their own ways. For someone preparing an advertising campaign, creating a marketing strategy, or deciding on content for a piece of marketing communication, the first profile is very useful, because it defines the customer (or the market) at a macro level and provides clues to editorial direction. If someone in the bank's marketing department just wanted to describe this customer to someone else, this is the profile they would probably use. The second type of profile, however, is about action and behavior, and is certainly more relevant than the demographic profile for any executive at the bank who really wants to know what customers are doing. Will this customer visit again? Will she buy again? What is the risk she will default on her credit, or cost the bank money? These are the questions an executive tries to answer by looking at behavioral records.

But let's now assume that the business intelligence department can produce a third profile on this customer as well:

3. The customer the future of her family and her children very carefully, and this is her primary motivation while using the bank's products and services. She is comfortable with technology and enjoys engaging with the bank online rather than having to visit branches, because she is always pressed for time.

This new profile actually defines *why* this particular customer uses the banking services she uses. It shows why she prefers online services and why she has accumulated an investment account. Moreover, while different customers will have different needs, many of these needs will be shared by others. Needs describe the root causes behind a customer's actions, whether those actions include choosing to work with another bank or staying loyal to this bank and subscribing to a new service.

It's important to get the sequence right also. Needs are not based on a customer's value or behavior. Rather, a customer's needs drive her behavior, and her behavior is what generates her value to the business. The needs just described are not generic, true-for-everybody statements, such as "I want to

(*continued*)

(*Continued*)

have cheaper products with higher quality." They are very specific needs, valid only for some portion of the bank's customers.

> Behaviors are the customers' footprints on a company.

Behaviors are the customers' footprints on a company. They represent the evidence of customers trying to meet their needs, and this evidence is likely to be accumulated in different company systems over different periods of time.

Needs May Not Be Rational, but Everybody Has Them

In his groundbreaking book, *Predictably Irrational,*[a] Dan Ariely makes the case that humans are irrational in what they want and what they do, but—oddly enough—in completely predictable ways. Some of the research he cites draws from lab work on rats and other animals. In one of the most telling studies, mice were offered a food pellet instantly if they pressed a green button. If, instead, they pressed a purple button, they could get *10* pellets, but they had to wait 10 whole seconds, which must seem like forever in mice time. If they pressed the purple button, and—while they were waiting for the big reward—had a chance to press the green button, they could not stop themselves and just had to press the green button—even after they figured out that pressing the green button stopped the delivery of the 10 pellets from the purple button. They learned that if they could not (and therefore did not) press the green button, but they had already pressed the purple button, they did in fact get their 10 pellets after a delay.

What did they do about this situation? Enter the red button, which, as it turns out, makes it impossible to press the green button. So the mice learned to press the purple button, then immediately press the red button, then press the green button all they wanted, but since pressing the red button had turned off the green button, the mice still got to collect the big win of 10 pellets.[b]

And this is just lab rats, managing to balance their own short- and long-term goals. Can companies do as well? And can we understand that the same customer wrestles with multiple kinds of needs at the same time?

This customer needs thing: It's complicated.

---

[a]Dan *Ariely, Predictably Irrational: The Hidden Forces That Shape Our Decisions* (New York: HarperCollins, 2008).

[b]Paraphrased from a story told by Dan Ariely in a keynote address to the Duke University Fuqua School of Business Marketing Club annual conference, January 27, 2010.

Why Doesn't Every Company Already Differentiate Its Customers by Needs?

It is reasonable to ask, if the logic outlined is so compelling, why toy manufacturers and other firms aren't already attempting to differentiate customers by needs. But keep in mind that the hurdles to doing so are sizable. For one thing, most toy manufacturers sell their products through retailers and have little or no direct contact with the end users of their products. In order to make contact with consumers, a manufacturer will have to either launch a program in cooperation with its retailing partners or figure out how to go around those retailers altogether—a course of action likely to arouse considerable resentment among the retailers themselves. So the majority of a manufacturer's end-user consumers are destined to remain unknown to the enterprise. Moreover, even if it had its customers' identities, the manufacturer still would have to find some means of interacting with the customers individually and of processing their feedback, in order to learn their genuine needs. Then it would have to be able to translate those needs into different actions, requiring a mechanism for actually offering and delivering different products and services to different consumers.

These obstacles make it very difficult for toy manufacturers simply to leap into a relationship-building program with toy consumers at the very end of the value chain. That said, the manufacturer does not have to launch such a program for all consumers at once. Rather, it could start by identifying its most avid fans, its highest-volume, most valuable consumer customers. Perhaps it could devise a strategy for treating each of those highly valuable customers to individually different products and services, in a way that wouldn't undermine retailer relationships. A Web site designed to attract and entertain such consumers could play this kind of role, and the toymaker could take advantage of social networking connectivity as well. Although the toy manufacturer still would encourage other shoppers to buy its products in stores, perhaps it could begin to offer more specialized sets and pieces directly to catalog and Web purchasers. If it had a system for doing this, launching a program designed to make different types of offers to different types of end-user consumers—based on their individual needs— would be much simpler and would, for practical reasons, start that process with customers of high value.

Indeed, the primary reason so many firms are now attempting to engage their customers in relationships is that the new tools of information technology—not just the World Wide Web in general and social networking sites in particular, but customer databases, sales force automation, marketing and customer analytics applications, and the like—are making this type of activity ever more cost-efficient and practical. But for an enterprise engaged in relationship building, the "hot button," in terms of generating increased patronage from the customer, is the customer's need.

Categorizing Customers by Their Needs

In the end, behavior change on the part of the customer is what customer-based strategies are all about. To capture any part of a customer's unrealized potential value requires us to induce a change in the customer's behavior; we want the customer to buy from an additional product line, or take the financing package as well as the product, or interact on the less expensive Web site rather than through the call center, and so forth. This is why understanding customer needs is so critical to success. The customer is master of his own behavior, and that behavior will change only if our strategy can appeal persuasively to his needs. Being able to see the situation from *the customer's point of view* is key to any successful customer-based strategy.

But in order to take action, at some point, different customers must be categorized into different groups, based on their needs. Clearly, it would be too costly for most firms to treat every single customer with a custom-designed set of product features or services. Instead, using information technology, the customer-focused enterprise categorizes customers into finer and finer groups, based on what is known about each customer, and then matches each group with an appropriately mass-customized product-and-service offering. (More about mass customization and the actual mechanics of the process in Chapter 10.)

One big problem is the complexity of describing and categorizing customers by their needs. There are as many dimensions and nuances to customer needs as there are analysts to imagine them. For consumers, there are deeply held beliefs, psychological predispositions, life stages, moods, ambitions, and the like. For business customers, there are business strategy differences, financial reporting horizons, collegial or hierarchical decision-making styles, and other corporate differences—not to mention the individual motivations of the players within the customer organizations, including decision makers, approvers, specifiers, reviewers, and others involved in shaping the company's behavior.

Marketing has always relied on appealing to different customers in different ways. Market segmentation is a highly developed, sophisticated discipline, but it is based primarily on products and the appeal of product benefits rather than on customers and their broader set of needs considered in a holistic fashion for each individual customer. To address customers as *different types of customers*, rather than as recipients of a product's different benefits, the customer-based enterprise must think beyond market segmentation per se. Rather than grouping customers into *segments* based on the product's appeal, the customer-based enterprise places customers into *portfolios* based primarily on type of need.

⌐A **market segment** is made up of customers with a similar attribute. A **customer portfolio** is made up of similar customers.⌐ The market segmentation approach is based on appealing to the segment's attribute while the customer portfolio approach is based on meeting each customer's broader need, based on the customer's own worldview. If segments and portfolios were made up of toys, then red fire trucks might be in a segment of toys that included red checkers sets, red dolly makeup lipsticks, and red blocks. But red fire trucks would be in a portfolio of toys that included ambulances, fireboats, police cars, and maybe medical helicopters, along with fire hats and axes, stuffed Dalmatians, and ladders. A market segment might be composed of women, over age 45, with household incomes in excess of $50,000. A portfolio of customers might be made up of women who value friendships and like to entertain.

In Chapter 13, we discuss customer management, including the grouping of customers into portfolios. There is a continuing role for traditional market segmentation, even in a highly evolved customer-strategy enterprise, because understanding how a product's benefits match up with the attributes of different customers continues to be an important marketing activity. But as the enterprise gains greater and greater insight into the actual motivations of particular categories of customers, it will find that managing relationships cannot be accomplished in segment categories, because any single customer can easily be found in more than one segment. Instead, when they take the customer's perspective, the managers at a customer-strategy enterprise will learn that they must meet the complex, *multiple needs* of each customer, as an individual. And doing this will require cate-gorizing customers according to their own, broader needs rather than according to how they react to the product's individually con-sidered attributes and benefits. Each cus-tomer can appear in only one portfolio.

> A single customer can be found in more than one customer "segment" but in only one customer "portfolio."

Understanding Needs

Understanding different customers' different needs is critical to any serious relationship-building program. Some of the characteristics of customer needs should be given careful consideration:

- *Customer needs can be situational in nature.* Not only will two different consumers often buy the same product to satisfy different needs, but a cus-tomer's needs might change from event to event, and it's important to recognize when this occurs. An airline might think it has two customer types—business travelers and leisure travelers—but in reality this typology refers to events, not customers. Even the most frequent business traveler will occasionally be traveling for leisure, perhaps with a spouse or family instead of the usual solo travel, and in that event she will need different services from the airline than she needs when she travels on business.
- *Customer needs are dynamic and can change over time as well.* People are changeable creatures; our lives evolve from one stage to another, we move from place to place, we change our minds. Moreover, certain types of people change their minds more often than others, tending to be less predictable. That said, the fact that a certain type of customer is not predictable is a customer characteristic itself, which can be used to help guide an enterprise's treatment of *that* customer. Marriage, new babies, and retirement typically lead to profound changes in needs for most people.
- *Customers have different intensities of needs and different need profiles.* Even when two customers have a similar need, one customer will have that need intensely while the other may feel the need but less intensely and perhaps in a different profile, combined with other needs. One homemaker is committed to running a very "green" kitchen while another wants to take care of the environment where it makes sense, but also has the need to save time as much as possible and may use paper plates so she doesn't have to spend so much time washing dishes.
- *Customer needs often correlate with customer value.* Although it is not always true, more often than not a high-value customer is likely to have certain types of needs in common with other high-value customers. Similarly, a below-zero

customer's needs are more likely than not to be similar to other below-zero customers' needs. A business that can correlate customer value with customer needs is generally in a good situation, because by satisfying certain types of needs, it can do a more efficient job of winning the long-term loyalty of higher-value customers.

- *The most fundamental human needs are psychological.* When dealing with human beings as customers (as opposed to companies or organizations), understanding the psychological differences among people can provide useful guidance for treating different customers differently.
- *Some needs are shared by other customers while some needs are uniquely individual.* When an online bookstore makes an automated book recommendation to an individual customer, this recommendation is based on the fact that other customers who have bought similar books as this customer has bought in the past have also bought the book being recommended now. There are hundreds of thousands of books a person could buy at an online bookstore, but people who buy similar books do so because they share similar needs. A retailer with a good database of past customer purchases can use "community knowledge," purchases, and traits found in common among disparate customers, to infer which products the members of a particular community of customers might find more appealing. Software for sorting through groups of customers to find commonalities is called *collaborative filtering* (more about these concepts later in this chapter). However, if a florist remembers a customer's wedding anniversary or a relative's birthday and sends the customer a reminder, the florist is very likely to get a great deal more business, simply by remembering these unique dates for each customer. But any single customer's wedding anniversary has very little to do with any other customer's anniversary date. In both the bookstore's and the florist's case, individual customer needs are being met, but some needs are unique and personal while some are tastes or preferences that are shared by other customers, as well (see Exhibit 6.3).
- *There is no single best way to differentiate customers by their needs.* As difficult as it is to predict and quantify a customer's value to the enterprise, at least the

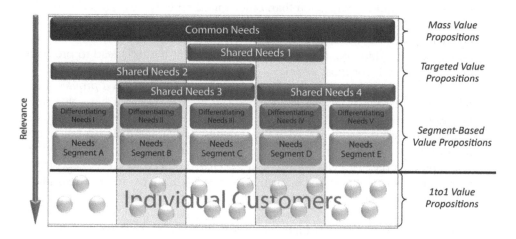

EXHIBIT 6.3   Common and Shared Needs of Customers

final result will be measured in economic terms. Value ranking, in other words, is done in one dimension: the financial dimension.[3] But when an enterprise sets out to differentiate its customers by their needs, it is embarking on a creative expedition, with no fixed dimension of reference. There are as many ways to differentiate customers by their needs as there are creative ways to understand the deepest human motivations. The value of any particular type of needs-based differentiation is to be found solely in its usefulness for affecting the different behaviors of different customers.

■ *Even in business-to-business (B2B) settings, a firm's customers are not really another "company," with a clearly defined, homogeneous set of needs.* Instead, customers are a combination of purchasing agents, who need low prices; end users, who need benefits and attributes; the managers of the end users, who need those end users to be productive; and so on.

Community Knowledge

In the competition for a customer, the successful enterprise is the one with the most knowledge about an individual customer's needs. In a successful Learning Relationship, the enterprise acts in the customer's own individual interest as a result of taking the customer's point of view. What if the customer were to maintain her own list of specifications and purchases? If the record of a customer's consumption of groceries were maintained on her own computer rather than on a supermarket's computer, this would undercut the competitive advantage that customization gives to an enterprise. Each week a whole cadre of supermarkets could simply "bid" on the customer's list of grocery needs, reducing the level of competition once again to the lowest price. The customer-strategy enterprise can avoid this vulnerability, as it has devised a way to treat an individual customer based on the knowledge of that customer's transactions as well as on the transactions of many other customers who have similarities to her. This is known as *community* knowledge.

Community knowledge comes from the accumulation of information about a whole community of customer tastes and preferences. It is the body of knowledge that an enterprise acquires with respect to customers who have similar tastes and needs, enabling the firm actually to *anticipate* what an individual customer needs, even before the customer knows he needs it. The *collaborative filtering* software that sorts through customers for similarities is essentially a matching engine, allowing a company to serve up products or services to a particular customer based on what other customers with similar tastes or preferences have preferred in this particular product or service.

---

[3]And the financial dimension is not limited to for-profits: For nonprofit organizations, the financial dimension might include maximizing funds from outside sources or maintaining fiscal stability. See Michael Martello, John G. Watson, and Michael J. Fischer, "Implementing a Balanced Scorecard in a Not-for-Profit Organization," *Journal of Business and Economics Research* 6, no. 9 (September 2008): 68. For nonprofits, "customer" or member, or donor, or volunteer value may include proxies for financial value such as willingness to participate, compliance rates, voting record, donations of time and volunteerism, and so forth.

Technology has accelerated the rate at which enterprises can apply community knowledge to better understand individual customers. This tool can help not just the individual consumers of a company like an online bookstore, but also B2B customers. The idea of community knowledge has a direct lineage from one of the most important values any B2B business can bring its own business customers: education about what other customers with similar needs are doing—in the aggregate, of course, never individually. Firms know that they must teach their customers as well as be taught by them. An enterprise brings insight to a customer based on its dealings with a large number of that customer's own competitors. Community knowledge can yield immense benefits to many businesses, but especially to those businesses that have:

- *Cost-efficient, interactive connections with customers as a matter of routine,* such as online businesses, banks and financial institutions, retail stores, and B2B marketers, all of which communicate and interact with their customers directly and on a regular basis.
- *Customers who are highly differentiated by their needs,* including businesses that sell news and information, movies and other entertainment, books, fashion, automobiles, computers, groceries, hotel stays, and healthcare, among other things.

Marketing expert Fred Wiersema[4] has said that there are three characteristics of market leadership: bringing out the product's full benefits, improving the customer's usage process, and breaking completely new ground with the customer. Any one of these types of customer education can come from the knowledge an enterprise acquires by serving other customers. An enterprise with a large number of customers can use community knowledge to *lead* a customer to a product or service that the enterprise knows the customer is likely to need, even though the customer may be totally unaware of this need. It might be as simple as choosing a hotel in a city the customer has never visited, but it could also apply to pursuing an appropriate investment and savings strategy, even though the customer may not have thought of it yet.

Pharmaceutical Industry Example

Consider, for example, a pharmaceutical company. Traditionally, this firm has not engaged in much relationship building with its end-user consumers (i.e., the patients for whom its drugs are prescribed). Rather, the firm has always considered its primary customers to be the prescribing physicians and other related healthcare professionals, along with pharmacies, employers, some government entities, and healthcare organizations. But now, faced with the cost-efficient, powerfully interactive technology of the World Wide Web, this pharmaceutical company wants to

---

[4]Fred Wiersema, *Customer Intimacy: Pick Your Partners, Shape Your Culture, Win Together* (Middleboro, MA: Country Press, 1996). Also see Wiersema's *The New Market Leaders: Who's Winning and How in the Battle for Customers* (New York: Touchstone, 2001), pp. 63–64.

begin to establish genuine, one-to-one relationships with at least some of the more valuable consumers of its products. The company sells medicine for diabetes, which can be kept in check through constant vigilance, but, as is the case with many such diseases, *compliance* is a problem. Patients often simply fail to keep up the medical treatment or fail to monitor their own condition properly. The company knows that patients want help in understanding and dealing with the disease, so it sets up a Web site to serve as a resource for information and support. The benefits for the pharmaceutical company and for the patient are straightforward: A better-informed and supported patient is likely to exhibit better compliance, which will both keep the patient healthier and sell more of the pharmaceutical company's drugs.

Knowing that different consumers will need different types of support and assistance, the pharmaceutical enterprise undertakes to design a patient-centric Web site. To do so, it conducts a research survey of patients, and discovers that a patient's attitude toward keeping the disease in check will drive her individual needs for using the Web site. Newly diagnosed patients for the most part simply want any and all information related to their disease. They need to be able to select content relevant to their own problems. However, as patients come to grips with their sickness, their attitudes toward the disease tend to fall into one of three primary categories. For this pharmaceutical company, working with a set of diabetic patients, the needs groupings tend to look like this:

- *Individualists*. This type of patient relies on herself to make educated decisions on how to manage her disease. Individualists could be directed to online clinical support, and they could opt for customized electronic newsletters or for online health-tracking tools.
- *Abdicators*. This patient's attitude toward the disease is one of resignation and detachment. She basically decides that she will "just have to live with the conditions of her disease," so she ends up depending on the help given by a significant other. The site directs abdicators to various caregiver resources and provides planning information related to nutrition and meals.
- *Connectors*. This type of patient welcomes as much information and support as she can get from others to help her make educated decisions about how to manage her disease. The site directs connectors to online chat rooms and electronic bulletin boards where they can meet and converse with other patients. It has an "e-buddy" feature that pairs her up with a patient similar to herself.

For the pharmaceutical company to design a Web site that is truly customer-focused, it should try to figure out, for each returning visitor, what the particular mind-set of that visitor is, and then serve up the best features and benefits for that particular type of patient. The easier the enterprise can make it for different patients to find the support and assistance they need, individually, the more valuable those patients will become for the enterprise.

At this juncture, however, it is important once again to separate our thinking about the features and benefits of the Web site (i.e., the product, in this case) from the actual psychological needs and predispositions of the Web site visitors themselves. Any one of the visitors might in fact use any of the Web site's many features on any particular visit. That means each of the Web site's benefits will probably overlap several different types of customers, with different types of needs. But the customers themselves do not overlap—they are unique individuals, each with her own unique psychology and motivation. It is only our categorization of these unique and different customers into needs-based groups that might give us the illusion that they are the same. They may be similar in their needs, but at a deeper level, they are still uniquely individual, and this will be true no matter how many additional categories, or portfolios, we create. We simply categorize customers in order to better comprehend their differences by making generalizations about them.[5]

Healthcare Firms Care for and about Patient Needs

As much as any industry, healthcare could benefit from applying principles that address individual patients' needs and values. In addition, relationships with donors and volunteers, medical staff, and suppliers would benefit from one-to-one Learning Relationships. But there are special challenges in this field.

Similar to any manufacturing enterprise, a health maintenance organization (HMO) can rank its patients by their value to the HMO. Interestingly, for an HMO, its most valuable patients are those it never hears from—those in good health.[a] However, the HMO does not want this group of customers to switch to another healthcare provider; it wants this set of valuable customers to use preventive healthcare procedures and to engage in a dialogue with its representatives so that they can understand each of its customers' personal medical-related needs. The goal of a healthcare provider, therefore, could be to create an ongoing, interactive relationship with the customer-patient, a relationship that does not revolve around what happens between admission to the institution and discharge but rather between discharge and admission. That's why many HMOs are engaged in building relationships by establishing contact with patients *before* an illness sets in, by inviting them to participate in reduced rates on exercise equipment, classes on smoking cessation, nutrition, and so on. These programs are win-win: They can contribute to the health and well-being of the patient or HMO member, and they help the HMO reduce costs through improved health of its patients.

Gary Adamson, who served as past president of Medimetrix/Unison Marketing in Denver, Colorado, said the power of healthcare integration lies in creating the ability to do things differently for each customer, not to do more of the same for all customers.[b] One of Medimetrix's clients, Community Hospitals in Indianapolis, Indiana, for example, implemented "Patient-Focused Medicine," a

---

[5]The fact is, the pharmaceutical industry faces a challenge shared with other companies in other industries: the need to stay ahead of the proliferation of readily available information Web sites that already offer some level of personalization. For example, WebMD offers a Symptom Checker that helps patients understand what their medical symptoms could mean (http://symptoms.webmd.com/) as well as a Diet and Weight Loss Tool that provides a personalized diet assessment and access to a calorie calculator, a "Food-o-Meter," and a "Fit-o-Meter" (www.webmd.com/diet/healthy-eating-fitness-services).

CRM initiative aimed at four constituent groups: patients, physicians, employees, and payers. The hospital has found that most medical practitioners customize the "care *for* you" component of healthcare by individually diagnosing and treating medical disorders. But Community also individualizes the "care *about* you" component—the part that makes most patients at most hospitals feel like one in a herd of cattle.

The hospital encourages thoughtful, high-level "service" by its doctors and nursing staff because it wants to show patients that they are being cared for; but the hospital also recognizes that random acts of kindness by a dedicated staff are not the same as customizing healthcare, which works only if the patient's special needs are remembered and continued at the next shift and between visits.

The opportunity—and the challenge—for customization lies in caring *about* an individual patient's needs. That means treating different patients differently in a cost-efficient and well-planned way. Healthcare, by its very nature, is among the most personal of any industry. Personal information provided to a doctor, hospital, pharmacy, or insurance company can be valuable to the organization but is highly private to the customer-patient. Healthcare personalization, of course, has existed for a long time, and certainly since the time when doctors made house calls and local druggists remembered each of their customers' medical histories. The vast majority of healthcare services could benefit from a shift in focus from event treatment to patient relationships, for the good of the healthcare organization as well as the patient—perhaps starting with an integrated billing system that makes sense to patients and their caregivers.

Some companies in the healthcare industry already see personalization as a strategic advantage in a crowded marketplace. By adding Web-based services for its customers, Oxford Health Care, which offers health insurance in New York, New Jersey, and Connecticut, has provided the same level of personalized service a customer would get from a telephone call. Not only does the My Oxford program, a subsection of its Web site, allow customers to access their coverage plans and process claims, but Oxford Health Care has also fully invested in efficient, remote patient access services. Its Lifeline medical alert system connects patients with their Personal Response Associate at the push of a button; these associates can access personal information, contact the individual, and send appropriate help. Similarly, telemonitoring devices can gather vital signs and other health information daily from patients at home and transmit this information via phone line to Oxford HealthCare, where a nurse reviews it and responds according to parameters set by the patient's physician.[c]

While reducing its cost to service "customers," Oxford serves each customer better. But personalized online services go far beyond customized content or a listing of available healthcare products or services. The real opportunity lies in building a Learning Relationship between the healthcare provider and the customer. A drugstore, for example, might know a customer buys the same over-the-counter remedy every month. But if the same drugstore detects that the customer is suddenly buying the product every week, it could personalize its service by asking her whether she is having a health problem and how it could assist her with personal information or other types of medication. Already the

(continued)

(Continued)

pharmacy is the last resort for many patients to help spot possible drug interactions for prescription and over-the-counter drugs prescribed and recommended by a variety of different physicians. Using information to serve the customer better helps the drugstore create a long-lasting bond with this customer.

For instance, Medco, formerly part of Merck and a pharmacy benefits management company of Merck & Co., has created a sophisticated information system that links patients, pharmacists, and physicians, helping to ensure the appropriate use of medication for each individual based on his health profile. Merck-Medco customers are issued a pharmacy card that enables the company to identify customers when they fill and refill a prescription. But the company goes the extra step and shows that it not only cares for its customers but cares about them too. When a customer suddenly stops refilling a prescription, a Medco representative will likely contact him to see if he has forgotten to refill the prescription or if his health status has changed.

Personalization also lets healthcare providers focus their sales efforts on their most valuable customers. For example, Florida Hospital, which serves 1 million patients a year, provides a concierge service for patients that can track and automatically schedule routine appointments such as well-check visits and flu shots as well as referrals to specialists to help a patient avoid the usual three or four phone calls it takes to get the right person. Even in the hospital, patients can have an interactive experience with bedside kiosks, where they can access medical records and the Internet, purchase vitamins or medical supplies with a card swipe, or leave messages for physicians. "We're really looking to bring value through coordination of care that is for the whole person," says Des Cummings, executive vice president of Florida Hospital. "We're looking at a whole person system for health and healing; caring for a person throughout their life."[d]

---

[a]Jaeun Shin and S. Moon, "HMO Plans, Self-Selection, and Utilization of Health Care Services," *Applied Economics* 39 (2007): 2769–2784.
[b]Don Peppers, Martha Rogers, Ph.D., and Bob Dorf, *The One to One Fieldbook* (New York: Doubleday, 1999).
[c]Available at www.oxfordhealthcare.net, accessed April 27, 2010.
[d]Marji McClure, "Florida Hospital Prescribes a Personalization Cure," *1to1 Magazine's Weekly Digest*, August 16, 2004, available at: www.1to1media.com/view.aspx? DocID=28465, accessed September 1, 2010.

Using Needs Differentiation to Build Customer Value

The scenarios of the toy manufacturer and the pharmaceutical company show how each had to be aware of its respective individual customer's needs so it could act on them. Once a particular customer's needs are known, the company is better able to put itself in the place of the customer and can offer the treatment that is best for that customer. Each company gets the information about customer needs primarily by interacting. Therefore, an open dialogue between the customer and the enterprise is critical for needs differentiation. Moreover, customer needs are complex and intricate enough that the more a customer interacts with an enterprise, the more learning an enterprise will gain about the particular preferences, desires, wants, and whims of that customer. Provided that the enterprise has the capability required to act on this more and more detailed customer insight, by treating the customer differently, it will be able to create a rich and enduring Learning Relationship.

A successful Learning Relationship with a customer is founded on changes in the enterprise's behavior toward the customer based on the use of more in-depth knowledge about that particular customer. Knowing the individual customer's needs is essential to nurturing the Learning Relationship. As the firm learns more about a customer, it compiles a gold mine of data that should, within the bounds of privacy protection, be made available to all those at the enterprise who interact with the customer. Kraft, for example, empowers its salespeople with the data they need to make intelligent recommendations to a retailer. (The retailer is Kraft's most direct customer, and the retailer sells Kraft products to end-user consumers, who can also be considered Kraft's customers.) Kraft has assembled a centralized information system that integrates data from three internal database sources. One database contains information about the individual stores that track purchases of consumers by category and price. Another database contains consumer demographics and buying-habit information at food stores nationwide. A third database, purchased from an outside vendor, has geodemographic data aligned by zip code.

> Information is the raw material that is transformed into knowledge through its organization, analysis, and understanding. This knowledge then must be applied and managed in ways that best support investment decisions and resource deployment.

But truly to get to know a consumer through interactions directly with her, enterprises must do more than gather and analyze aggregated quantitative information. Accumulating information is only a first step in creating the knowledge needed to pursue a customer-centered strategy successfully. Information is the raw material that is transformed into knowledge through its organization, analysis, and understanding. This knowledge then must be applied and managed in ways that best support investment decisions and resource deployment.

Customer knowledge management is the effective leverage of information and experience in the acquisition, development, and retention of a profitable customer. Gathering superior customer knowledge without codifying and leveraging it across the enterprise results in missed opportunities.[6]

---

[6]Paul M. Cole, *Customer Connections* (Cambridge, MA: Harvard Business School Press, 1997). See also Andrew L. S. Goh, "Adoption of Customer Relationship Management (CRM) Solutions as an Effective Knowledge Management (KM) Tool: A Systems Value Diagnostic," *Journal of Knowledge Management Practice [online]* (February 2005), available at: http://www.tlainc.com/articl80.htm, accessed September 1, 2010; and Yichen Lin, Jr Jung Lyu, Hwan-Yann Su, and Yulan Hsing, "A Feasibility Study of the Customer Relationship Management Application on Small and Medium Enterprises," *Journal of Scientific and Technological Studies* 41, no. 1 (2007): 53–63.

Scenario: Universities Differentiate Students' Needs

Like more enterprises around the world, universities are building Learning Relationships with individual students as well as with the corporate concerns that are already providing much of the funding for tuition and research.

Higher education has a variety of different customers. Students, parents, employers, government, states, and donors are just some examples. Instead of measuring the success of a university by the number of students it enrolls, or even the cutoff point for admission, a customer-focused university gauges its success by the projected increase or decrease in a particular student's expected future value. The university no longer focuses just on acquiring more students but on retaining existing learners and growing the business each gives the institution.

Interestingly, the fastest-growing sector of global higher education (and every university's market is indeed global) is the for-profit university, which enrolls one-third of students worldwide. According to Sir John Daniel, a university administrator who has worked in Canada and the United Kingdom, a for-profit university offers three benefits to its students: efficiency, a focus on teaching students based on market demand rather than conducting research, and a focus on ensuring that its students succeed.[a]

Whether for-profit or public, academic universities want to attract and retain the most valuable customers and most growable customers (i.e., highly qualified, tuition-paying students) and to reap the most benefit from them, not just over their four years of study but over their many years as alumni as well. In order to integrate the typically siloed information on recruitment, retention, and development, higher-education spending on CRM will have seen a doubling from 2007 to 2012, reflecting universities' increasing value of the 360-degree view of their customers.[b]

Acknowledging both actual and potential value of students and alumni is just as important. Higher levels of financial contribution coming from alumni are associated with higher income, but, most important, the degree of satisfaction with one's undergraduate/graduate experience. Moreover, in many universities, each newly graduating class leaves behind a "Class Gift" that varies in expense and type. Some classes raise thousands of dollars to donate toward scholarships and loan funds; others raise money to help renovate university buildings that otherwise would have been left untouched. Retaining strong relationships with alumni is seen as beneficial not only for financial purposes; they also play other critical roles for the academic university—returning to teach, counseling graduate students, or serving on advisory boards to the university.

As more universities consider their options for achieving those goals, attention often turns to alumni as the answer. Institutions of higher learning have understood that prolonging relationships with alumni can improve the accuracy of the fundraising list, which in turn improves fundraising response rates and donor lifetime value. The number of schools that are implementing strategies for those purposes is increasing.

Because it is now possible to keep track of relationships with individual students, the size of a university is becoming a less potent competitive advantage.

A university of any size has the opportunity to use information about each student to secure more of that individual's participation. Notwithstanding the "brand" or status value of a handful of high-status Ivy League and top-ranked higher education institutions, securing and keeping the participation of more students will likely depend on who has and uses the most information about a specific student, not on who has the most students.

To compete, the customer-focused university has to integrate its entire range of business functions around satisfying the individual needs of each individual student. The school's organizational structure itself will have to be altered, and it must embrace significant change, affecting virtually every department, division, administrator, and employee. Once it has migrated to a customer-strategy model, the university will be able to generate unprecedented levels of participant loyalty by offering an unprecedented level of customization and relationship building.

Student-customer valuation will require measures of success based on individual student results, not just product or program measures. Rather than seeing whether enough students enrolled in a particular course to justify its existence, for instance, the institution will also predict whether a particular student is valuable enough to justify a certain level of expenditure.

The customer-focused university will be able to calculate share of student on an individual, participant-by-participant basis, with the goal of capturing a greater share of dollars, time, and other investment in learning. The customer-focused university builds a Learning Relationship with each student by interacting over time and continuing to increase its level of relevance to each student by understanding her motivation. Although participation in the university should be motivation enough, the customer-focused university will understand whether a student is, for example, taking a course because of interest in the material, admiration for the professor, a need to be respected, a desire to make business contacts, as part of a degree program, career participation, or some other reason. Remembering what each student wants and finding ways to make the collaboration effort valuable to the participant leads to mass-customizing the offering, the response, the dialogue process, the level of recognition, the opportunity for active participation, and so on.

The implications of more cost-efficient electronic interaction for higher education are immense. Many universities are pioneers in adopting a customer strategy to develop Learning Relationships with each of their students. Western Governor's University in Salt Lake City, Utah, is creating independent measurements of "output"—their graduates. In addition to traditional assessment of learning outcomes, such as those required by the Association to Advance Collegiate Schools of Business (AACSB)—measuring the university's quality by the number of doctorates on the faculty or books in the library—the school also is rating the academic performance of its students against an objective measure of the student's overall accomplishment. The nation's first online competency-based university, Western Governor's University received the United States Distance Learning Association's 2008 International Distance Learning Awards in two categories: the 21st Century Award for Best Practices in Distance Learning and Outstanding Leadership by an Individual in the Field of Distance Learning.[c]

(continued)

(Continued)

Franklin University, an independent nonprofit institution serving 11,000 students in Columbus, Ohio, created a new position, Student Services Associate (SSA), designed to be the "customer manager" for its students. Each of the university's 25 SSAs is evaluated and paid based on how many of his or her students make it to graduation. Every SSA interaction with a student is captured on the computer so that anyone interacting with the student can view his or her complete profile and history. In addition, to better meet the needs of busy students, the university became part of a Community College Alliance and now offers 24 undergraduate majors and 2 graduate programs entirely on-line. For Franklin, customer-focused strategies—led originally by past-university president Paul Otte and now by current president Dr. David R. Decker—have translated directly into revenue increases and greater share of student. In the mid-1990s, 60 percent of students were freshmen and sophomores; now 60 percent are juniors and seniors, another 10 to 12 percent are continuing on to graduate school, and surveys indicate higher levels of student satisfaction.[d]

Students at the University of Phoenix (UP), Arizona, are often underwhelmed at its physical facilities, but they enthusiastically participate in the school's accredited programs in business, nursing, and education because they can get the learning they want and need on their own terms, according to their own schedules. UP draws "working students" who do not want to put their lives on hold to earn their degrees, so their courses last only five or six weeks and can be started virtually anytime.[e] Similarly, Boston University, whose online Bachelor of Liberal Studies degree ranks first among online teaching institutions, is reaching out to this working student population, aiming to provide a high-quality but flexible degree program that can fit in busy adult schedules.[f]

According to Arthur Levine, the president and professor of Teachers College, Columbia University, current demographic shifts will push colleges to choose a target audience to meet the various needs in the market. The fastest-growing student segment in the United States—women over the age of 25 who are attending part time and working—want the cost-effective, à la carte educational experience and don't want to pay for a giant athletic facility they are not using. Simultaneously, the traditional 18- to 22-year olds who attend full time and live on campus (or nearby) want the widest possible course offerings and food options and expect student activities 24 hours a day. It is indeed not easy to serve a population of two opposite poles, those who want the bare minimum and the other half who want everything. So colleges face a challenge to decide whom they will serve and how, coming up with the ideal solution of reconsidering their mission and being able to accommodate different expectations under the same roof.[g]

To draw alumni in and keep the relationships going, academic institutions are building peer-to-peer communities on their Web sites that foster involvement and camaraderie. Free services include a lifelong university-branded e-mail address, searchable alumni directories, and customizable Web pages. For some institutions, the central focus of their Web community is the alumni database; others take a portal approach, using diverse content as the core property. Most universities hope that alumni will set the school's Web portal as their default Web browser home page.

---

[a]Sir John Daniel, "The Fastest Growing Sector of Higher Education," convocation speech, University Canada West, November 22, 2008, available at: www.col.org/RESOURCES/SPEECHES/2008PRESENTATIONS/Pages/2008-11-22.aspx, accessed September 1, 2010.

[b]Christopher Musico, "Making CRM Mandatory for University Administration," Customer Relationship Management 12, no. 8 (2008): 20.

[c]"USDLA Recognizes Western Governors University with Two Major Distance Learning Awards," press release, April 23, 2008, available at: www.wgu.edu/about_WGU/usdla_awards_4-23-08, accessed September 1, 2010.

[d]2009–2010 Franklin University Academic Bulletin, available at www.franklin.edu.

[e]Available at http://university.phoenix.edu/, accessed April 29, 2010.

[f]"2009 Rankings of Online Colleges and Online Universities," Guide to Online Schools, available at: www.guidetoonlineschools.com/online-colleges, accessed April 29, 2010.

[g]Karla Hignite, "Insights: Arthur Levine's Call for Clarity," *Business Officer* (May 2006), available at: www.nacubo.org/Business_Officer_Magazine/Magazine_Archives/May_2006/Arthur_Levines_Call_for_Clarity.html, accessed April 29, 2010.

Summary

We have now discussed the necessity of knowing who the customer is (identifying) and knowing how the customer is different individually (valuation and needs). Getting this information implies that the enterprise will need to interact with each customer to understand each one better. Once the enterprise has ranked customers by their value to the enterprise and differentiated them based on their needs, it conducts an ongoing, collaborative dialogue with each customer. This interaction helps the enterprise to learn more about the customer, as the customer provides feedback about her needs. The enterprise can then use the customer's feedback to modify its service and products to meet her needs (i.e., to "customize" some aspect of the customer's treatment to the needs of that particular customer).

The "identify" and "differentiate" steps in the Identify-Differentiate-Interact-Customize (IDIC) taxonomy for developing and managing customer relationships can be accomplished by an enterprise largely with no actual participation by the customer. That is, a customer won't necessarily have to know or involve herself in the process that the enterprise uses to identify her, as a customer, or to rank her by value, or even to evaluate her needs, as a customer. These first two steps—"identify" and "differentiate"—can be thought of as the "customer insight" phase of relationship management. However, the third step—"interact"—requires the customer's participation. Interaction and customization can only really take place with the customer's direct involvement. These latter two steps could be thought of as managing the "customer experience," based on the insight developed.

Interacting with customers, the third step in the IDIC taxonomy, is our next point of discussion.

Food for Thought

1. Why has more progress been made on customer value differentiation than on customer needs differentiation?
2. If it could only do one, is it more likely that a customer-oriented company would rank all of its customers differentiated by value or differentiate all of its customers by need?
3. Is it possible to meet individual needs? Is it feasible? Describe three examples where doing this has been profitable.
4. For each of the listed product categories, name a branded example, then hypothesize about how you might categorize customers by their different needs, in the same way our sample toy company and pharmaceutical company did. Unless noted for you, you can choose whether the brand is business to consumer (B2C) or B2B:
   - Automobiles (consumer)
   - Automobiles (B2B, i.e., fleet usage)
   - Air transportation
   - Cosmetics
   - Computer software (B2B)
   - Pet food
   - Refrigerators
   - Pneumatic valves
   - Hotel rooms

Glossary

Attributes   Physical features of the product.

Benefits   Advantages that customers get from using the product. Not to be confused with *needs,* as different customers will get different advantages from the same product.

Customer portfolio   A group of similar customers. The customer-focused enterprise will design different treatments for different portfolios of customers.

Market segment   A group of customers who share a common attribute. Product benefits are targeted to the market segments thought most likely to desire the benefit.

Needs   What a customer needs from an enterprise is, by our definition, synonymous with what she wants, prefers, or would like. In this sense, we do not distinguish a customer's needs from her wants. For that matter, we do not distinguish needs from preferences, wishes, desires, or whims. Each of these terms might imply some nuance of need—perhaps the intensity of the need or the permanence of it—but in each case we are still talking, generically, about the customer's needs.

CHAPTER 7

Interacting with Customers: Customer Collaboration Strategy

Most conversations are simply monologues delivered in the presence of witnesses.

—Margaret Millar

So far, we have discussed the ways an enterprise can identify and differentiate customers. Both of these efforts help the enterprise prepare to treat different customers differently. But, essentially, both "identify" and "differentiate" are analytical tasks. They are at the heart of the efforts, working behind the scenes to gather information about a customer, to rank him by his value to the company and to differentiate his needs accordingly. These tasks aren't really visible to a customer. In this chapter, we introduce a part of the Interact-Differentiate-Interact-Customize (IDIC) implementation methodology that gets the customer directly involved: *interaction*. We will see different viewpoints on the broad and growing emphasis on interaction with customers. But even as the discussion touches on the general and the particular, the main reason for interaction remains the same: to get more information directly from a customer in order to serve him in a way no competitor can who doesn't have the information.

Managing individual customer relationships is a difficult, ongoing process that evolves as the customer and the enterprise deepen their awareness of and involvement with each other. To reach this new plateau of intimacy, the enterprise must get as close to the customer as it can. It must be able to understand the customer in ways that no competitor does. The only viable method of getting to know an individual, to understand him, and to get information about him is to interact with him—one to one.

In Chapter 2, we began to define a relationship, and provided a foundation for relationship theory. We listed several important characteristics in our definition of the term *relationship*; but one of the most fundamental of these characteristics is interaction. A relationship, by its very definition, is characterized by two-way communication between the two parties to the relationship.

Interacting with customers acquires a new importance for a customer-strategy enterprise—an enterprise aimed at creating and cultivating relationships with individual customers. The enterprise is no longer merely talking *to* a customer during a transaction and then waiting (or hoping) the customer will return again to buy. For the customer-strategy enterprise, interacting *with* individual customers becomes a mutually beneficial experience. The enterprise learns about the customer so it can understand his value to the enterprise and his individual needs. But in a relationship the customer learns, too—about becoming a more proficient consumer or purchasing agent for a business. The interaction, in essence, is now a *collaboration* in which the enterprise and the customer work together to make this transaction, and each successive one, more beneficial for both. The focus shifts from a one-way message or a one-time sale to a continuous, iterative process, which de facto moves both customer and enterprise from a transactional approach to a relationship approach. The goal of the process is to be more and more satisfying for the customer, as the enterprise's Learning Relationship with that customer improves. The result of this collaboration, if it is to be successful, is that both the customer and the enterprise will benefit and want to continue to work together. This is no longer about generating messages about your organization. This is about *generating feedback,* creating a collaborative feedback loop with each customer by treating her in a way that the customer herself has specified during the interaction.

Interacting with an individual customer enables an enterprise to become both an expert on its business and an expert on each of its customers. It comes to know more and more about a customer so that eventually it can predict what the customer will need next and where and how he will want it. Like a good servant of a previous century, the enterprise becomes indispensable.

> This is no longer about generating messages about your organization. This is about *generating feedback.*

Customer-strategy enterprises ensure that each customer gets exactly what he needs, no matter what, and this priority should extend from the front line all the way to upper management. Years ago, Southwest Airlines created a high-level position to coordinate all proactive customer communications—from the information sent to front-line representatives when flights are delayed, to personally sending letters and vouchers to customers thus inconvenienced. All the while, when the inevitable delay does occur, Southwest flight attendants and even pilots walk the aisles to update passengers and answer questions, conveying genuine concern in the moment. For a company to be truly customer-centric, interaction must happen at all levels, so as many employees as possible know what it feels like to be a customer.[1]

In this chapter, we show how a customer-strategy enterprise interacts with its customers in order to generate and use individual feedback from each customer to strengthen and deepen its relationship with that customer. This two-way communication can best be referred to as a dialogue, which serves to inform the relationship.

Dialogue Requirements

An enterprise should meet six criteria before it can be considered engaged in a genuine dialogue with an individual customer:

---

[1]"25 Companies Where Customers Come First," *BusinessWeek,* March 2, 2007; available at MSN Money, http://articles.moneycentral.msn.com/News/25CompaniesWhereCustomersComeFirst .aspx, accessed September 1, 2010.

1. *Parties at both ends have been clearly identified.* The enterprise knows who the customer is, if he has shopped there before, what he has bought, and other characteristics about him. The customer, too, knows which enterprise he's doing business with.

2. *All parties in the dialogue must be able to participate in it.* Each party should have the means to communicate with the other. Until the arrival of cost-efficient interactive technologies, and especially the World Wide Web, most marketing-oriented interactions with customers were prohibitively costly.

3. *All parties to a dialogue must want to participate in it.* The subject of a dialogue must be of interest to the customer as well as to the enterprise.

4. *Dialogues can be controlled by anyone in the exchange.* A dialogue involves mutuality, and as a mutual exchange of information and points of view, it might go in any direction that either party chooses for it. This is in contrast to, say, advertising, which is under the complete control of the advertiser. Companies that engage their customers in dialogues, in other words, must be prepared for many different outcomes.

5. *A dialogue with an individual customer will change an enterprise's behavior toward that individual and change that individual's behavior toward the enterprise.* An enterprise should begin to engage in a dialogue with a customer only if it can alter its future course of action in some way as a result of the dialogue.

6. *A dialogue should pick up where it last left off.* This is what gives a relationship its "context" and what can cement the customer's loyalty. If prior communication between the enterprise and the customer has occurred, it should continue seamlessly, as if it had never ended.[2]

Implicit and Explicit Bargains

Conducting a dialogue with a customer is having an exchange of thoughts; it's a form of mental collaboration. It might mean handling a customer inquiry or gathering background information on the customer. But that is only the beginning. Many customers are simply not willing to converse with enterprises. And rare is the customer who admits that she enjoys receiving an unsolicited sales pitch or telemarketing phone call. For an enterprise to engage a customer in a productive, mutually beneficial dialogue, it must conduct interesting conversations with an individual customer, on his terms, learning a little at a time, instead of trying to sell more products every time it converses with him.

If the customer-strategy enterprise is to remain a dependable collaborator with its customers, then it must not adopt a *self-oriented* attitude (see Chapter 2, "Thinking about Relationship Theory" and "CRM: The Customer's View," both of which emphasize the importance to the enterprise of *not* being self-oriented in its approach to customer relationships). Instead of sales-oriented commercials and interruptive, product-oriented marketing messages, the customer-strategy enterprise will use interactive technologies to provide something of value to the customer. By providing this value, the enterprise is inviting the customer to begin and sustain a dialogue.

---

[2]Don Peppers and Martha Rogers, Ph.D., *Enterprise One to One* (New York: Doubleday, 1997).

The resulting feedback increases the scope of the customer relationship, which is critical to increasing the enterprise's share of that customer's business.

To understand how radical this idea is, think about television. When advertisers sponsor a television program, they are in effect making an implicit bargain with viewers: "Watch our ad and see the show for free." During television's early decades, these implicit bargains made a lot of sense, because viewers had only a few other channels to choose from and no remote control to make it easy to change the channel. In the early days, everybody watched commercials.

But today's television viewer lives in a vastly different environment. Not only are there hundreds of channels from which to choose, but people are also watching television more selectively, with instant—and constant—control. Audiences have the power to tune out commercials at their will or even to block out the advertisements altogether. And video delivered via broadband connections through the Web soon likely will overwhelm the traditional broadcast model entirely, as more and more consumers will be downloading full-length movies and television programs the way they currently download YouTube videos and then wirelessly pushing them to their large-screen television monitors for viewing. These technological trends are inevitable, driven not just by innovation but by intense consumer demand for choice and immediacy. The problem for marketers, therefore, is that, because the broadcast television medium is **nonaddressable** and *noninteractive*,[3] there is no real way to tie the particular consumer who watches the television show back to the ad or to know whether she saw it in the first place. There is also no real incentive, usually, for the consumer even to watch the ad.

However, interactive communications technologies are two-way and individually **addressable**. Because of these attributes, interactive media equip marketers with the tools to make "explicit" bargains rather than "implicit" ones with their consumers. They can interact, one to one, directly with their individual media customers. An **explicit bargain** is, in effect, a "deal" that an enterprise makes with an individual to secure the individual's time, attention, or feedback. Dialogue and interaction have such important roles to play, in terms of improving and enhancing a relationship, that often it is useful for an enterprise actually to "compensate" customers, in the form of discounts, rebates, or free services, in exchange for the customer participating in a dialogue.

The interactive world is chock full of examples of explicit bargains. Hundreds of Web site operators around the globe, from Hotmail to Yahoo!, offer free e-mail to customers who are agreeable to receiving advertising messages or facilitating the delivery of ad messages to others. Some of the ads are highly targeted, and even based on the content of the e-mail messages themselves. For example, if a Google Gmail user writes a personal message to a friend discussing, say, a trip to the Bahamas, Google will likely show banner ads on the e-mail page that promote air travel, vacation packages, or hotels. Marketers routinely buy "keywords" from search engines like Google, Yahoo!, Bing, and others, so that when a consumer uses one of these engines to search for, say, "flat screen televisions," the marketer's own ad will appear prominently within the search results. It is standard practice for a Web site operator

---

[3]Customers who are individually addressable can be sent individually different messages. Mass media are characterized by nonaddressability, since mass media send the same message to everyone simultaneously.

to require a visitor to register, providing personal identifying data and preferences, in return for gaining access to the site's more detailed information or automated tools.

Do Consumers Really Want One-to-One Marketing?

A *New York Times* article[a] raised serious issues about the viability of one-to-one marketing. Citing a survey of consumer attitudes commissioned by professors at the University of Pennsylvania and the University of California, Berkeley, the article reported that a clear majority of Americans (66 percent) reject the whole idea of tailored ads and personalized news, even without being told how their own interests are being tracked online.

But this survey is deeply flawed, and its authors' conclusions are biased (they're professors, they should know better!). This would be an irrelevant non-issue, not worth our time and trouble (or yours), except for the possibility that a survey like this could inflame public opinion enough to encourage some sort of ham-handed government regulation of online advertising and marketing. Other bloggers are already worried about this.

The survey was conducted by telephone. A thousand adult Americans were interviewed, and each interview began with three basic questions, asked in a random rotation:

1. Please tell me whether or not you want the Web sites you visit to show you ads that are tailored to your interests.
2. Please tell me whether or not you want the Web sites you visit to give you discounts that are tailored to your interests.
3. Please tell me whether or not you want the Web sites you visit to show you news that is tailored to your interests.

The problems with this survey should be obvious: First, people really don't like advertising and marketing messages in general. (Is that a surprise to anyone?) Of course they don't want tailored advertising, but they don't want untailored advertising either. Consumers are, in general, suspicious of marketers' motives and hostile to being "sold" things. But that doesn't mean they reject personalization. They reject all the loud, interruptive messaging out there, ceaselessly clamoring for their attention span.

Second, these questions present no alternative. If the authors are going to conclude that consumers prefer not to have tailored ads, they have to say what they prefer instead. The only way to understand consumer preference is to compare consumers' desire for one thing relative to their desire for something else. That's part of the very definition of the word *preference*. However, doing that would have required a question such as:

> Please tell me whether you would prefer the Web sites you visit to show you ads tailored to your interests or, instead, to charge you a small fee for viewing the Web sites.

(continued)

(Continued)

And of course we all know what the answer to that question would be. You don't need a survey to demonstrate it, because the history of the Web already makes it very clear that free, ad-supported content will triumph over paid content at least 90 percent of the time.

But third, any rookie market researcher can tell you that consumers who are asked generalized questions like this often have difficulty visualizing the actual situation. The right way to have asked this question would have been to demonstrate it to the consumer directly. For instance, prior to asking these questions, what if the interviewer had first asked:

Please tell me whether you prefer diet drinks or nondiet drinks.

And then they could ask:

Please tell me whether you would prefer the Web sites you visit to show you ads for diet drinks or for nondiet drinks? (Pick one.)

There is still, however, a very important lesson to be drawn from this survey: the fact that consumers don't see any benefit to tailoring is an indictment of most of us marketers, because we have done such a lame job of tailoring our messages and making them genuinely relevant to our customers. It is not surprising that ordinary consumers would have difficulty visualizing personalized advertising messages, because even today, with all the computer power and interactive technologies available to marketers, most consumers have very rarely witnessed personalized ads that are genuinely relevant!

Source: Based on blog post by Don Peppers, "Do Consumers Really Want One-to-One Marketing?" October 21, 2009, available at: www.1to1media.com/weblog/2009/10/do_consumers_really_want_one-t.html#more, accessed September 1, 2010.
[a]Stephanie Clifford, "Two-Thirds of Americans Object to Online Tracking," *New York Times*, September 29, 2009, available at: www.nytimes.com/2009/09/30/business/media/30adco.html?_r=3&partner=rss&emc=rss, accessed September 1, 2010.

Explicit bargains with consumers are certainly not confined to the Web either. More than one mobile phone company has been launched based on the idea of offering free voice minutes and text messaging in return for accepting advertising messages and responding to marketing offers.

In an interactive medium, an advertiser can secure a consumer's actual permission and agreement, individually. By making personal preference information a part of this bargain, the service can also ensure that the ads or promotions delivered to a particular subscriber are more personally relevant, in effect increasing the value of the interaction to the marketer by increasing its relevance to the consumer. Explicit bargains like this are good examples of what author Seth Godin calls "permission marketing" (a concept we discuss in more detail in Chapter 9) in which a customer has agreed, or given permission, to receive personalized messages.

Two-Way, Addressable Media: A Sampling

In contrast to the one-way media that characterized mass marketing, the future of customer relationships will be interactive. Not "I talk, you listen" but "You talk, I listen," and vice versa, and "We all talk, and everybody can listen in." Likewise, more and more media are "addressable." That means I can send a particular message to a particular individual at a known "address," whether that address is a geographic address on a street, or an e-mail address, or Facebook account, or telephone number, or text address, or a combination of these and other new interactive, addressable media available every day.

- *World Wide Web.* The Web has become one of the most effective media to engage a customer in an individual interaction. An enterprise's Web site is a highly customizable platform for collaborating with customers and learning about their individual needs effectively and inexpensively. (We talk more about the Web as a venue for customization in Chapter 10.)
- *Social media.* While technically just one aspect of the World Wide Web, the Web sites and online services that have been constructed to allow people simply to create content for other people and to share conversations and comments with others who have similar or intersecting interests—sites such as Facebook, YouTube, Flickr, and LinkedIn—represent a major change in how consumers acquire information and interact with their environments. The social media phenomenon is complex and rich enough all by itself to require a customer-strategy enterprise to plan deliberate strategies for dealing with social media, in an effort to build and strengthen its customer relationships.
- *Wireless.* The increasing proliferation of wireless technology is promising to "unhook" people from the network of cables and wires that used to connect them to the ground, freeing them not just to surf the Web using their iPhones, BlackBerries, and other smart phones but to connect their devices wirelessly to the Internet in coffeeshops, hamburger outlets, universities, airliners, and even many major cities, where ubiquitous WiFi technology has been installed for everybody. It is becoming clear that in the twenty-first century, not just in developed countries but across the whole world, people are going to be connected to the network and able to interact electronically with companies and other people more often than they will be offline. (Indeed, the very term *online* has now been rendered an archaic usage, much like "dialing" a phone number. Both terms will mystify our grandchildren as much as the word *typewriter* will.)
- *Voicemail.* Enterprises have established voicemail systems for their customers that enable them to phone in a question or comment and leave a message. Voicemail has many different potential dialogue applications.
- *E-mail.* Enterprises are using e-mail to write personalized messages to customers about their latest product offerings, sales promotions, customer inquiries, and many other important topics (we discuss more about e-mail later in this chapter).

(continued)

(Continued)

- *Texting (SMS—Short Message Service) and instant messaging (IM).* Texting from a mobile phone and using the instant messaging feature of various e-mail and online services is another mechanism for quick, highly efficient interactions. Although it's a more common business practice outside the United States, marketers can incorporate text-back codes to encourage customers to interact with them wherever they are, at any time—because everyone always has their mobile phone with them. Always.

- *Fax.* Fax machines are a highly interactive medium. The customer can fax an order to the enterprise. Or the enterprise can use a fax-on-demand service to enable customers to request product or service information via their fax machines. The enterprise also can fax customized catalogs, product information sheets, newsletters, and other documents to the customer on request. Fax also makes it easy to reach those who do not have online capability.

- *Digital video recorders.* The digital recording device, such as TiVo and others like it, has revolutionized television by enabling audiences to create highly personalized TV-viewing experiences. **Digital video recorders (DVRs)** are also changing television advertising. Instead of bombarding viewers with commercials that are not relevant, advertisers now have the opportunity to personalize their messages. Knowing the viewers' demographics and viewing preferences, advertisers will be better able to match their ads to the right people.

- *Interactive voice response.* Now a feature at most call centers, **interactive voice response (IVR)** software provides instructions for callers to "push one to check your current balance, push two to transfer funds," and so forth. One frequent problem with IVRs is that companies tend to use them more to reduce their costs than to improve their service, with the result that customers often are frustrated if the choice they want is not offered or if it becomes difficult to contact a "live" human.

- *More new media every week.* No print listing can keep up with the myriad of ways popular and esoteric that people of different generations and technical expertise will use and adapt to connect with each other and the companies they do business with.

Technology of Interaction Requires Integrating across the Entire Enterprise

Most business-to-business (B2B) companies already have active sales forces engaged in some form of relationship building with the accounts they serve, but new technologies allow them to automate a sales force to better ensure that customer interactions are coordinated among different players within an account and that the records of these interactions are captured electronically. For a business-to-consumer (B2C) company, however, interactive technologies enable it to create a consumer-accessible Web site, and to coordinate the interactions that take place on this

Web site with the interactions that take place at the call center and at the point of sale and at any other point of contact with the customer. The universal question for such an enterprise, wrestling with how to use these technologies, is: What is the right communication or offer for *this* particular customer, interacting with us at this time, using this technology?

The point is that the arrival of cost-efficient interactive technologies has pretty much forced companies in all industries, all over the world, to take a step back and reconsider their business processes entirely. To deal with interactivity, they must create new processes that are oriented around the coordination of all these newly possible customer interactions. And they must ensure that the interactions themselves not only run efficiently but are effective at building more solid, profitable relationships with customers.

Don Schultz, Stanley Tannenbaum, and Robert Lauterborn's classic book, *The New Marketing Paradigm: Integrated Marketing Communications*,[4] documented the problems that occur whenever a single customer ends up seeing a mishmash of uncoordinated advertising commercials, direct-mail campaigns, invoices, and policy documents, and made the case for consistent marketing communications across the entire enterprise. Today, sophisticated interactive technologies enable enterprises to ensure that their customer-contact personnel can remember an individual customer and his preferences. A company can use software that creates an "ecosystem" of data about its customers and cull information from all of the touchpoints where it interacts with customers—call centers, Web sites, e-mail, and other places. If the enterprise can better understand its customers, it can better serve them by providing individually tailored offers or promotions and more insightful customer service.[5] The result is that integrating the enterprise's marketing communications is no longer a cutting-edge strategy but a must-have standard.

For this reason, the enterprise has to integrate all of its customer-directed communication channels so that it can accurately identify each customer no matter how an individual customer or a customer company contacts the enterprise. If a customer called two weeks ago to order a product and then sent an e-mail yesterday to inquire about his order status, the enterprise should be able to provide an accurate response for the customer quickly and efficiently. The company should remember more about the customer with each successive interaction. More important, as we said before, it should never have to ask a customer the same question more than once, because it has a 360-degree view of the customer, and "remembers" the customer's feedback across the organization. The more the enterprise remembers about a customer, the more unrewarding it becomes to the customer to defect. The customer-strategy enterprise ensures that its interactive, broadcast, and print messages are not just *laterally* coordinated across various media, such as television, print, sales promotion, e-mail, and direct mail, but that its communications with every customer are *longitudinally* coordinated, over the life of that individual customer's relationship with the firm.

---

[4]Don E. Schultz, Stanley I. Tannenbaum, and Robert F. Lauterborn, *The New Marketing Paradigm: Integrated Marketing Communications* (New York: McGraw-Hill, 1996).

[5]Jim Ericson, "25 Top Information Managers: 2010; Movers, Shakers, and Game Changers Who Are Making Information Work for Business," *Information Management* 20, no. 2 (April 2010): 10; Kim Cross, "Captain Connected," *Business 2.0,* April 17, 2001, p. 31.

Providing any kind of dialogue tool to customers enables the enterprise to secure deeper, more profitable, and less competitively vulnerable relationships with each of them. The deeper each relationship becomes, and the more it is based on dialogue, the less regimented that relationship will be. The customer may want to expand the dialogue on his own volition because he knows that each time he speaks to the enterprise, it will listen. Today, what most enterprises fail at is not the mechanics of interacting but the *strategy* of it—the substance and direction of customer interaction itself.

Companies that employ such integration of customer data and coordination of customer interaction develop reputations as highly competent, service-oriented firms with excellent customer loyalty. Dell Computer

> Today, what most enterprises fail at is not the mechanics of interacting but the *strategy* of it—the substance and direction of customer interaction itself.

has used direct mail, e-mail, personal contact by sales representatives, and special access to what amounts to intranet Web sites for large Dell accounts to stay connected with those customers.[6] JetBlue's reputation for service[7] has been burnished by its extremely good online interaction efficiency and the seamless connections that customers experience among the airline's reservations, ticketing, baggage tracking, and flight operations systems. Best Buy can use interactive connections to help customers analyze product features, track deliveries, and even solve technical problems by getting help from any one of several thousand company employees linked through Twitter into what the company calls its Twelp Force.[8]

Over time, a customer who interacts with a competent customer-strategy enterprise will come to feel that he is "known" by the enterprise. When he makes contact with the enterprise, that part of the organization—whether it is a call rep or a service counter or any other part of the firm—should have immediate access to his customer information, such as previous shipment dates, status of returns or credits, payment information, and details about the last discussion. A customer does not necessarily want to receive *more* information from the enterprise; rather he wants to receive better, more focused information—information that is relevant to him, individually.

Integrating the interactions with a customer across an entire enterprise requires the enterprise to develop a solid understanding of all the points at which a customer "touches" the firm. Stated another way, the customer-strategy enterprise needs to be able to see itself through the eyes of its customers, recognizing that those customers will be experiencing the enterprise in a variety of different situations, through

---

[6]John Wheeler and Mark Krueger, "Electrifying Customer Relationships," *Customer Relationship Management [online]* September 1999, available at: www.destinationcrm.com/Articles/Older-Articles/The-Edge/E-Lectrifying-Customer-Relationships-48441.aspx, accessed September 1, 2010.

[7]JetBlue provides an excellent example of how day-in and day-out investment in long-term customer equity and trust pays off on a bad day. After apologizing for stranding passengers on planes for hours, JetBlue still faced blogosphere resentment. Their own best customers came to the rescue, encouraging everyone else to come back to the airline.

[8]Robin Wauters, "Best Buy Goes All Twitter Crazy with @Twelpforce," *TechCrunch,* July 21, 2009; available at: http://techcrunch.com/2009/07/21/best-buy-goes-all-twitter-crazy-with-twelpforce/, accessed September 1, 2010.

different media, dealing with different systems, and using different technologies. Mapping out these touchpoints is one of the first tasks many customer-strategy enterprises choose to undertake, and one comprehensive process for accomplishing the task is outlined in the next section by Mounir Ariss, a managing partner at Peppers & Rogers Group.

Touchpoint Mapping

Mounir Ariss
Managing Partner, Middle East, Peppers & Rogers Group

Our goal is to help client companies do a better job of managing the experiences their customers have, by using customer insight to fashion better, more convenient, and more personalized relationships with these customers individually. A customer's experience with a brand or an enterprise can be thought of as occurring in three different dimensions:

- *Physical*. Pertaining to the design of physical locations such as stores, sales and service offices, bank branches, and so forth, the physical dimension includes not just the location itself but factors such as the availability of parking space, pedestrian accessibility, interior design, and even the smoothness of flow of customers within the premises.
- *Emotional*. Harder to pin down, but highly important to the customer experience, the emotional dimension is related to the culture of the customer-facing employees and their behaviors when interacting with a customer. More than once we've seen companies go through comprehensive **business process reengineering (BPR)** and automation and then fail when it comes to dealing with their customers due to a culture that is just not customer oriented. Culture-change programs, while challenging, can achieve results. The key is to create awareness and desire for change while enabling employees, measuring them, and providing constant feedback. A culture-change program could be as basic as training contact center employees on the 10 things never to say to a customer or on how to deal with difficult customers. Measurements feedback mechanisms could then be set up using mystery shopper programs.
- *Logical*. The "logical" issues at a company include the firm's business processes, information flows, and technology components. This is often the first dimension of the customer experience addressed by enterprises trying to become more customer-centric. Understanding (and then modifying) its business processes is an important step any company must take in order to begin managing customer relationships in a more directed, beneficial way. And this is the dimension covered by a **Customer Experience and Interaction Touchmap**.[a]

(continued)

(Continued)

Within the IDIC framework, "identify" and "differentiate" are purely internal steps to a company. They could be done without the customer knowing about them. However, "interact" and "customize," as the names indicate, are external steps where a company is actually managing the customer's experience. Over the years, different companies have introduced tools to try to document the customer experience, diagnose gaps, and redesign it.

The Touchmap is a graphical depiction of the interactions a company has with each segment of its customers across each of the available channels. Its purpose is to take an outside-in view of customer interactions instead of the traditional inside-out view typically taken in BPR work. This approach is usually an eye-opener for organizations, and very often it is one of the rare times the customer perspective is actually brought to the attention of senior executives and explicitly considered in designing some interactions. For instance, more than once we have asked executives with a financial services client to go through the process of opening an account and then applying for a credit card at the enterprise where they themselves are employed. Many find just completing the application forms highly frustrating; some are amazed at how their customer-facing employees lack the information needed and even at the interpersonal skills required to deal with customers. Sources of frustration include not just the sheer volume of information being requested in an application form but also the fact that much of the requested information is already stored in the bank's own systems, even though it is demanded from the customer anew, multiple times, in different application forms.

One useful way to think about this is to generate both a "Current State" Touchmap, to depict all the enterprise's current interactions with customers and identify gap areas, and a "Future State" Touchmap, to depict the desired customer interactions—interactions that will be customized based on the needs and values of individual customers. Ideally, these Future State interactions should be a tool for a company to deliver on its brand promise and build customer value.

In addition to representing customer interactions from the customer's own perspective, a Touchmap links these interactions with the enterprise's internal processes, systems, and high-level information flows. This allows a company easily to identify organizational silos and broken processes, insufficient or nonexistent information sharing, poor system integration, and the general lack of cooperation among departments found at many companies. In our experience, most firms are already aware of many of the issues highlighted in a Current State Touchmap, but they probably never saw all of them illustrated at once, nor were they cognizant of how intricately these flaws and problems are related to each other and how seriously they inhibit a good customer experience.

Current State Touchmap

Preparing a Current State Touchmap for a company consists of several steps, all designed to ensure that the customer's perspective is taken into consideration. In our consulting practice, we architect the process to meet the needs of the particular client and industry being served (telecom, e.g., has different issues from banking or government services), but in general, these tasks need to be accomplished to render a satisfactory and useful Touchmap:

- *Recognition of different types of customers.* Taking the customer's point of view necessarily involves recognizing that different customers will have very different perspectives. The basic premise of CRM is "treating different customers differently," so a Touchmap must accurately represent any customer-based differentiation within the same interaction. For a Current State Touchmap, these variations could be based, at least initially, on broadly defined segments—individual customers and business customers, for instance. Depending on the level of sophistication of a company, the Future State Touchmap could include variations based on a more granular segmentation or actual portfolio building. For example, most valuable customers (MVCs) could benefit from a totally different complaint-management process. Therefore, before starting a Touchmapping exercise, a company needs to identify its current customer groups and decide whether the current portfolio grouping or segmentation strategy will be sufficient for the customization of future interactions.
- *Analysis of the customer life cycle.* Broadly, a customer's life cycle can be broken down into four principle parts: (1) awareness of a need, (2) decision to buy or contract with an enterprise to meet that need, (3) use of the product or service bought, and (4) support for the product and the ongoing relationship.
- *High-level customer interviews.* Customer interviews should allow us to identify a more granular breakdown of these four life-cycle steps and also will allow an enterprise to develop a better understanding of what the customer goes through, even before first interacting with the company. For example, how, where, and in what context did the customer become aware of a certain need? Was the customer talking to a friend? Did the customer have a promotion or a salary raise? Is the customer going through a change in life stage? What were the customer's general perceptions about the company's offering before starting to interact with the company? Did those perceptions change after the customer started interacting with the company or after buying a product or service? These customer interviews should be set up with a small sample of customers from each of the preidentified customer groups—typically 5 to 10 customers representing each group are sufficient for this stage.
- *Customer satisfaction surveys.* When available, satisfaction surveys can add some intelligence to the analysis of customer life cycle. A comprehensive survey, in fact, could minimize the need for and sometimes even replace customer interviews.
- *Graphical illustration of customer life cycle.* By linking customer feedback and comments from surveys and interviews to each stage of the life cycle, an initial diagnostic can be rendered, and a number of potential "quick wins" can almost always be identified—inadequate coordination of marketing materials or inaccurate transfer of information from the Web site,

(continued)

(Continued)

and so forth. After first illustrating a **customer life cycle** with each of its identified stages highlighted, we can then use callout boxes to document actual customer comments and color-code them (bad, neutral, and good) to pinpoint problematic areas visually. Often some of the underlying problems a company is facing in its customer interactions will be obvious from a color pattern that emerges. For example, if the early stages of a customer life cycle are in green, middle stages in yellow, and late stages in red, the company is probably performing really well in its marketing and sales functions but the high expectations it is setting for its products or services are not then being met. A more random distribution of good, neutral, and bad comments could be an indicator of inconsistencies in employee training, culture, and performance.

- *Voice of customer.* More detailed interviews with customers are now called for, in order to get at the actual details of what different customers go through at different states of the life cycle when interacting with the enterprise.
- *Voice of employee.* Detailed interviews of employees, emphasizing various business process owners, will allow the enterprise to link the customer's perspective with the company's own internal processes. Gaps between the two indicate potential improvement opportunities.
- *Analysis of high-level information flows.* It is important to identify **critical data elements (CDEs)** that facilitate decision making and process execution. During employee interviews with process owners, information should be compiled about which CDEs are captured or missing, updated consistently or out of date, disseminated effectively or stored in silos, utilized to generate customer insight or stored but not effectively used. Graphically, customer data that are not being captured in any system are highlighted with a "STOP" sign on the Current State Touchmap. Data being captured but not disseminated are highlighted with a "DEAD END" sign.
- *Review of high-level technology components in use.* Each of the processes illustrated in the Touchmap should be linked to supporting technology, when available. Once the technology components are identified and plotted at the center of the Touchmap, each of the processes can then be linked with the appropriate technology. The result will look something like a business process map for the enterprise, but rather than starting with business processes and mapping their effects, the Touchmap will start with customer interactions and map them in toward the business processes.

Future State Touchmap

The Future State Touchmap (see Exhibit 7A) should be drawn to depict how a redesigned set of customer interactions will function, once all improvement opportunities have been applied. Typical BPR work focuses on reducing the time it takes to complete an interaction or a process, and reducing the cost of completing it. BPR usually involves introducing quality controls to ensure time and cost efficiencies are achieved. The Future State Touchmap is designed to achieve these goals, but also to do a more complete and accurate job of taking the enterprise's customer strategy into consideration. Therefore, when putting a Future State Touchmap together, it's vital to incorporate a variety of "best practices" in managing customer relationships and experiences.

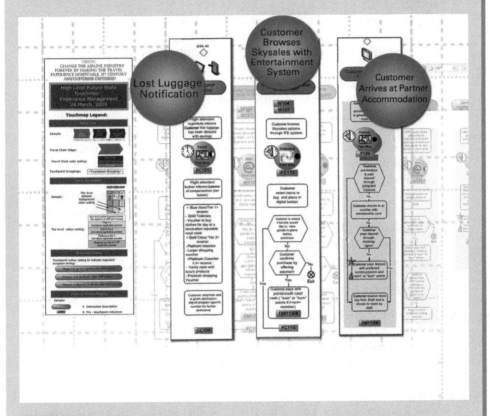

EXHIBIT 7A   Future State Touchmap

While there are a large number of such best practices for relationship management (many of them covered in different chapters of this book), some examples would include:

- *Treat different customers differently.* Doing this usually will mean that different business processes have to be designed for the same type of interaction when it is applied to different customers or different customer groups. As a "best practice," the first level of differentiation in business processes should be by customer value—for instance, treating MVCs to a more personalized service level based on their preferences. Working with one of the main telecommunication operators in the Middle East, for instance, we introduced four value tiers and designed different sales and service

(continued)

(Continued)

models for each of the tiers. Customers in the lower value tiers were driven toward remote self-service channels, but the high-value tiers were offered preferential treatments at all channels, assigned to the head of the queue at the contact center, receiving shorter complaint resolution times and shorter product installation times, and so forth.

- *Unique customer identification at all touchpoints to identify customers.* As just one example, many interactive voice response (IVR) systems in call centers request customers to enter their identification (ID) and personal ID number (PIN) before being directed to an agent. Then, when the customer finally talks to a human voice, often the first question the agent asks the customer is to repeat this identifying information.
- *"Drip irrigation" techniques for collecting customer information.* Rather than long application forms that request excessive information and often turn customers off, future-state interactions should focus on collecting less information at the beginning of a relationship with a customer but then enriching that information over time, as the relationship progresses.
- *Never ask for the same information twice.* Many companies request the same information from a customer over and over again. The future-state design would eliminate such occurrences to the extent possible, so the burden of repeating information falls on the company, not the customer.

Why Is a Touchmap Important?

The Customer Experience and Interaction Touchmap is a visual tool illustrating a strong link among customer groups, customer interactions, delivery channels, business processes, information flows, and technology components. It provides a holistic picture of how a company interacts with customers and sheds light on some of the burning issues affecting customer satisfaction, loyalty, retention, and growth.

Many companies are not fully aware of the services they offer and the multitude of channels they actually use. Others don't have a standard definition of what a service is. For one of our recent clients, the number of different "customer services" reported to senior management varied between 12 and 200. This large variation was due to the fact that the company did not have a standard definition of what a service is. In addition, several departments in the company were allowed to offer services with no central coordination whatsoever. Through a Touchmapping project, this client was able to introduce standards in service definition, development, and deployment.

In a recent public sector project, we worked with a government in the Europe, Middle East, and Asia region to develop a full inventory of the services that each government department provides. As a part of this project, we introduced a standard way of defining government services. Two Touchmaps were produced, one covering citizen "customers" and the other covering business "customers." The Touchmaps covered over 2,000 government services and resulted in a multiyear effort to enhance public service delivery in that country.

The Touchmap has also proven to be a versatile tool for a variety of other purposes related to managing customer relationships. Some of the uses we have seen over the past 15 years are:

- *Technology implementation tracking.* Some of the companies we have worked with have used monthly updates of the Touchmap to highlight their progress in CRM implementation and automation of business processes.
- *Employee induction and training.* Other companies have used a Touchmap to provide high-level training and orientation to employees, allowing them to better understand and visualize what the company does in general and how their jobs or tasks affect customers and the rest of the organization.
- *Employee performance tracking.* Some companies have added traffic light indicators next to each of the interactions illustrated on the Touchmap and linked quarterly customer satisfaction survey results to each of these indicators.
- *Executive sponsorship.* The visual display of complex information brought the topic closer to senior executives and helped secure more support and sponsorship for customer issues.
- *Elimination of redundancies and other opportunities for efficiencies.* Often a company realizes that different parts of the company each have the same good idea and each one has reinvented the wheel in trying to build customer relationships. A Touchmap contributes to a central repository for customer learning and methodology.
- *Revealing data gaps and silos.* A Touchmap exposes needs for particular data to be collected and to share data between and among parts of the organization to build a single view of the customer across the organization, without burdening the customer by asking for the same information more than once.

In summary, a Touchmap is an illustration of all interactions that happen between a company and its customers, based on the customer segments and depicted from the customer's perspective. Its primary benefit is to enable the enterprise to maximize customer value by treating different customers differently.

---

[a]Based on 1to1[SM] Touchmap work conducted by Peppers & Rogers Group.

Customer Dialogue: A Unique and Valuable Asset

Interaction with a customer, whether it is facilitated by electronic technologies or not, requires the customer to participate actively. Interaction also has a direct impact on the customer, whose awareness of the interaction is an indispensable part of the process. Since interaction is visible to customers, interacting customers gain an impression of an enterprise interested in their feedback. It is a vital part of the customer experience with the brand or the enterprise. The overarching objective on the part of the enterprise should be to establish a dialogue with each customer that will generate customer insight—insight the enterprise can turn into a valuable business asset, because no other enterprise will be able to generate that insight without first engaging the customer in a similar dialogue.

This is one of the key benefits of the Learning Relationship we've been discussing, and it is based on the fact that different customers want and need different things. This means we also should expect different customers to prefer different *interaction methods*. One customer prefers mail to phone; another likes a combination of e-mail and regular mail; still another only visits social networking sites, such as Facebook. The level of personalization that the Web affords to a customer also should be available in more traditional "customer-facing" venues. Retail sales executives in the store, for instance, should have access to the same knowledge base of customer information and previous interactions and transactions with the enterprise as a **customer service representative (CSR)** at corporate headquarters or **customer interaction centers**. Enterprises must be able to identify which channels each of their customers prefer and then decide how they will support seamless interactions. Those enterprises that fail to provide these interaction capabilities can lose sales and compromise relationships.[9]

The goal for the customer-strategy enterprise is not just to understand a *market* through a *sample* but also to understand each *individual* in the population through *dialogue*. The dialogue information that is of most interest to the enterprise falls into two general categories:

> The goal is not understanding a *market* through a *sample* but to understand each *individual* in the population through *dialogue*.

1. *Customer needs.* The best method for discovering what a customer wants is to interact with him directly. Each time he buys, the enterprise discovers more and more about how he likes to shop and what he prefers to buy. Interactions are important not only because the customer is investing in the relationship with the enterprise, but also because the enterprise learns substantive information about the customer that a competitor may not know. Interaction gives the enterprise valuable information about a customer that a competitor cannot act on.

2. *Potential value.* With every customer interaction, customers help the enterprise estimate more accurately their trajectory and their actual value to the enterprise. Getting a handle on a customer's potential value, however, is often problematic. Through dialogue, a customer might reveal more specific plans or intentions regarding how much money she will spend with the enterprise or how long she will use its products and services. Insight into a customer's potential value could include, among other things, advance word of an upcoming project or pending purchase; information with respect to the competitors a customer also deals with; or referrals to other customers that could be profitably solicited by the enterprise. This type of information is not usually available from a customer's buying history or transactional records and can be obtained *only* through direct interaction and dialogue with the customer.

---

[9]Patricia Warrington, "Multi-Channel Retailing and Customer Satisfaction: Implications for e-CRM," *International Journal of E-Business Research* 3, no. 2 (April–June 2007): 57–70; Todd Wagner, "Multichannel Customer Interaction," Accenture white paper, 1999.

Customizing Online Communication

Tom Spitale
Principal, Impact Planning Group

"Nice product. Bad price. Let me go check the competition's site." Every chief executive in the world has felt the double-edged sword of online commerce. On one hand, the Internet boosts performance as the enterprise interacts with customers, suppliers, or channels at low costs. However, it has lowered the cost of entry for every competitor in the world. The Internet often is seen as the weapon of competitive choice for those only interested in competing on low price.

Executives at one healthcare insurer found a unique approach for using their Web site to block competition. The standard question in their industry is: How do we retain healthy customers who care very little about the features and benefits of our insurance policies? Your best customer, in this case, may be a 24-year-old man who runs three miles a day—and this dude is not likely to care much about insurance. If you run a health insurance company, you desperately want to hold on to such healthy customers, because the profit you derive from them will enable you to pay medical expenses for other insurance members who fall ill.

Lose enough healthy consumers and your entire company gets sick. A competitor with a lower price—even if it has a lousy offering—is likely to steal healthy customers away.

The executive team at this insurer decided to use its Web site to wrap a new layer of value around its core product of health insurance: customized health-related information. The company realized this was the best way to become relevant to its desired audience of physically fit consumers: Add communications and services that appeal to their healthy lifestyle, and customize the offers so they are relevant. Its Web site was the perfect vehicle, because while the firm couldn't hire an army of customer relationship experts to offer personal communications to members, it could use dynamic content generation online to mass-customize the message.

To understand which services would be most appealing, the company cataloged wide-ranging content, including media publications tangentially related to health, and came up with innovative ideas. Fitness runners and weight lifters got unique information; cosmetics and baseball game information were added to the mix—all "expanding the need set"[a] of healthy consumers who previously didn't care. This approach gave healthy customers reason to remain loyal ("My health insurer understands my preferences and provides personally relevant advice") *and* reduced benefit costs by providing information that helped those with problems get better.

The lesson: Your Web site can block competitors by surrounding your core offering with a layer of personalized information and value. How would any company duplicate this insurer's online communication customization in a

(continued)

(Continued)

different industry? Utilizing needs-based segmentation or portfolio-building in Web site design is key.

Needs-based segmentation (see Chapter 6) recognizes that different sets of customers have different needs. Filtering out content that is not relevant to each segment—and pointing people quickly to the most relevant content to them—is a valuable differentiator in a time-starved world.

This filtering can be done in a sophisticated fashion or very simply. Amazon.com has invested heavily in its Personal Recommendations strategy. In essence, it is creating a one-to-one relationship with each of its customers based on their individual ratings of books, and—wherever customers are willing to write a review—allowing customers to listen in on each other's comments as well as benefit from ratings and usage. Many customers prefer to see comments from other people, even strangers, before they buy a product.

But what about a B2B company with a limited budget? A boutique strategy consulting firm with less than $5 million in annual revenues is using this concept in a much more straightforward, yet profitable, way. This firm recognizes that its customers approach strategic planning in different ways. For example, some companies enjoy rigor and discipline in their planning processes while others prefer to maintain some "entrepreneurial freedom" in their strategic planning.

The consulting company created a "front door" to its Web site that asks visitors to identify themselves based on one of four types of companies, according to their strategic planning profile. These four types of companies are really "needs-based segments" of firms. Once a visitor has chosen a profile, the Web site content is parsed to create a pathway to more relevant content. For example, the more entrepreneurial segment won't see information on creating entire planning processes. Instead, they will be given information on "quick hit," single-topic issues and see case studies about how other entrepreneurial companies are improving their strategic planning within a very fluid culture. The process-oriented segment will see still different content, offering free webinars on how to build strategic planning road maps or downloadable white papers on how to standardize planning presentations. They can read case studies on how process-oriented companies drive standardization throughout their organizations.

This is different from simply setting up different sections of a Web site with different types of offerings. Visit some B2B Web sites; very few, if any, will have a front door that customizes your pathway through the site.

And yet the financial return on site from this kind of interactive content customization is very high. Amazon.com is doing quite well, despite the fact that it doesn't require a purchase in order to provide you with recommendations.

And there are other benefits as well. High percentages of new visitors to the Web site of the consulting firm just profiled reach out to the company through live channels to discuss doing business. A typical quote during that first live conversation? "You listen better than your competitors." Do you think it has something to do with customized interactions on the Web site?

---

[a]Read more about the "expanded need set" in Chapter 10.

Because most customers will not sit still for extensive questioning at any given touchpoint, the successful customer-oriented enterprise will learn to use *each* interaction, whether initiated by the customer or the firm, to learn one more incremental thing that will help in growing share of customer (SOC) (see Chapter 1) with *that* customer. This is the concept we call **drip irrigation dialogue**. USAA Insurance in San Antonio, Texas, calls it "smart dialogue." As the basis for intelligent interaction, USAA uses business rules within its customer data management effort to a make a customer's immediate history available to its CSRs as soon as a customer calls. The CSRs also see a box on their computer screens that state the next question USAA needs to have answered about a customer in order to serve him better. This is not a question USAA is asking every customer who calls this month; it is the next question for *this customer*.

> Golden Questions are designed to reveal important information about a customer while requiring the least possible effort from the customer.

In many cases, an enterprise will use **Golden Questions** to understand its customers and thus achieve needs and value differentiation quickly and effectively (see Chapters 5 and 6). Golden Questions are designed to reveal important information about a customer while requiring the least possible effort from the customer. Designing a Golden Question almost always requires a good deal of imagination and creative judgment, but the question's effectiveness is predetermined by statistically correlating the answers with actual customer characteristics or behavior, using predictive modeling. In general, an enterprise should avoid most product-focused questions, except in situations in which the customer is trying to specify a product or service, prior to purchase. Instead, the most productive type of customer interaction is that which reveals information about an individual customer's underlying need or potential value. To better understand how product-focused questions differ from Golden Questions, examine the hypothetical chart in Exhibit 7.1.

Not All Interactions Qualify as "Dialogue"

Many interactions with customers are simply not welcomed by the customer. In fact, a large portion of customer-initiated interactions with businesses occur because something has gone wrong with a product or service, and the customer needs to contact the enterprise to try to get things put right. It can be frustrating in the extreme for a customer to try to navigate through a complex IVR in order to get a problem resolved. One of the best books on managing contact-center interactions with customers is *The Best Service Is No Service: How to Liberate Your Customers From Customer Service, Keep Them Happy, and Control Costs*.[10] Author Bill Price is the former vice president of Global Customer Service at Amazon.com, certainly a sterling example of a highly competent customer-strategy enterprise, and coauthor David Jaffe is a consultant in Australia focused on helping companies manage their

---

[10]Bill Price and David Jaffe, *The Best Service Is No Service: How to Liberate Your Customers from Customer Service, Keep Them Happy, and Control Costs* (San Francisco: Jossey-Bass, 2008).

ORGANIZATION GOAL	PRODUCT-FOCUSED QUESTIONS	UNDERLYING NEED OR MOTIVATION OF HIGH-GROWTH CUSTOMES	GOLDEN QUESTION
My company produces premium pet food. I want to get my message to consumers likely to buy a lot of expensive dog food. I am looking for MVCs.	"Did you buy a lot of dog food last year?" "Do you spend more than $20 a week on dog supplies?"	*I'm a customer, and I really love my pet. I'd do almost anything for him.*	"Do you buy your pet a holiday gift?"
Mv retail chain sells women's clothing, and I want to find out who is likely to shop at my store and spend a lot of money.	"Did you spend more than $1,000 last year on women's clothing?" "Do you shop for clothes at least once a month?"	*I'm a woman, and my personal appearance is very important to me.*	"Is it okay to wear jeans when you go to the movies, or do you prefer something dressier?"
My brokerage firm offers many products. We want to find the existing clients most likely to consolidate their assets with us, to increase total assets under management.	"Do you have more than two investment accounts?" "Do you have more than $500,000 in liquid assets?"	*Retirement is important to me, but I have other interests as well—such as investing for my son's college education and using some "fun money" to play the market.*	"Have you ever used your savings to play a hot stock?"

EXHIBIT 7.1   Development of Golden Questions

customer experiences. In this excerpt from *The Best Service Is No Service,* the authors consider all the ways customers can be simply annoyed at the necessity of contacting the companies they buy from and interacting with them.

When the Best Contact Is No Contact

Let's consider how often some organizations force us to make contact with them:

- A leading cable TV company requires three contacts for each new connection—why not just one contact?
- Some mobile phone companies handle as many as ten to twelve contacts per subscriber per year, whereas others have only three to four. Why do we need to call mobile providers so often? Shouldn't we just be making calls and paying bills, preferably online?
- A water utility was averaging two contacts for each fault call. The first call should have been enough to fix the problem. The subsequent calls asked,

"Why isn't it fixed yet?" or "When are you coming to fix it?"—not good enough.

- A leading self-service bank averaged one contact per customer per year and nearly two for each new customer. Don't we sign up for self-service applications like Internet banking so that we don't have to call? Other banks have half this contact rate, so clearly something is broken.
- A leading insurance company was averaging more than two contacts per claim. The first contact makes sense, setting the claim in motion, but why were the subsequent contacts needed?
- "Customers reported making an average of 3.5 contacts in an attempt to resolve their most serious customer-service problem in the past year."[a] Why isn't this 1.0 contact or, perish the thought, zero contacts because nothing needs to be resolved in the first place?

We should make it clear that we are not talking about such interactions as placing orders, making payments, or using self-service solutions, such as checking balances, that the customers chose to use. Instead, we are talking about having to call or take the time to write or visit a branch to get something done or to get something fixed. In some industries, these contact rates are much worse: Every contact with a technical support area of an Internet provider or computer manufacturer is a sign that something is broken. Ideally, customers should never need to make these contacts.

---

[a]Spencer, "Cases of 'Customer Rage' Mount as Bad Service Prompts Venting," *Wall Street Journal*, September 17, 2003, p. D4.
Source: Reprinted with permission from Bill Price and David Jaffe, *The Best Service Is No Service: How to Liberate Your Customers from Customer Service, Keep Them Happy, and Control Costs* (San Francisco, CA: Jossey-Bass, 2008), p. 7.

Tapping into feedback from customers is an immensely powerful tactic for improving a company's sales and marketing success. But customers will share information only with companies they trust not to abuse it. (See Chapter 9 for more on privacy issues.) Here are some ways to earn this trust, encouraging customers to participate more productively, improving both the cost efficiency and the effectiveness of customer interactions:

- *Use a flexible opt-in policy.* Many opt-in policies are all-or-nothing propositions, in which customers must elect either to receive a flood of communications from the firm, or none at all. A flexible opt-in policy will allow customers to indicate their preferences with regard to communication formats, channels, and even timing. To the extent possible, give customers a choice of how much communication to receive from you, or when, or under what conditions.
- *Make an explicit bargain.* Customers have been used to getting news and entertainment for free, in exchange for being exposed to ads or other commercial messages. As customers gain more power to zap commercials, eliminate

pop-ups, and avoid unwanted calls, SMS messages, and e-mail they consider to be spam, marketers who want to talk to customers may need to make an explicit offer, something like this: Watch the last episode of your favorite weekly show on ABC.com and, when you do, we'll post commercial messages from sponsors for your viewing three times during the show, and you'll need to click your way through it to show us you see it. Or pay $4.00 to download the show and watch it without commercials.

■ *Tread cautiously with targeted Web ads.* Even though targeted online ads are popular with marketers, research has shown that consumers are especially wary of sharing information when targeted Web ads are the result. This doesn't mean don't do it, but it does mean don't pile on. In any case, for behavioral targeting to succeed, an enterprise must have the customer's informed consent.

■ *Make it clear and simple.* Have a clear, readable privacy policy for your customers to review. Procter & Gamble (P&G) provides a splendid example. Instead of posting a lengthy document written in legalese, P&G presents a one-page, easy-to-understand set of highlights outlining the policy, with links to more detailed information. By contrast, Sears Holding Company, in its online offer to consumers to join the "My Sears Holding Community," has a scroll box outlining the privacy policy that holds just 10 lines of text but requires you to read 54 boxfuls to get through the whole policy. Buried far into the policy is a provision that lets the firm install software on your computer that "monitors all of the Internet behavior that occurs on the computer."[11]

■ *Create a culture based on customer trust.* Emphasize the importance of privacy protection to everyone who handles personally identifiable customer information, from the chief executive officer to contact center workers. Line employees provide the customer experiences that matter, and employees determine whether your privacy policy becomes business practice or just a piece of paper. If your business culture is built around acting in the interest of customers at all times, then it will be second nature at your company to protect customers from irritating or superfluous uses of their personal information—things most consumers will regard as privacy breaches, whether they formally "agreed" to the data use or not.

■ *Remember: You're responsible for your partners too.* It should go without saying that whatever privacy protection you promise your customers, it has to be something your own sales and channel partners—as well as your suppliers and other vendors—have also agreed to, contractually. Anyone in your "ecosystem" who might handle your own customers' personally identifiable information and feedback will have the capacity to ruin your own reputation. Take care not to let that happen!

If an enterprise wants to conduct dialogues with customers, it must remember that the customers themselves must want to engage in these dialogues. Simply contacting a customer, or having the customer contact the enterprise, does not constitute dialogue, and will likely convey no marketing benefit to the enterprise.

---

[11]Hal Abelson, Ken Leueen, and Harry Lewis, *Blown to Bits: Your Life, Liberty, and Happiness After the Digital Explosion* (Reading, MA: Addison-Wesley, 2008), p. 67.

Is the Contact Center a Cost Center, a Profit Center, or an Equity-Building Center?

Judi Hand
President and General Manager, Direct Alliance

We have all become very familiar with "call centers." With all the technology that permeates our homes and our lives, undoubtedly we have all had to call an 800 number. This experience typically has been associated with long, confusing interactive voice response (IVR) menus, a single way of communicating, agents with poor English skills, and a frustrating lack of resolution. In a quest to lower support costs, companies have sacrificed the customer experience. A vicious cycle has emerged, driven by the focus on single metrics such as cost per call. Although companies may think they are lowering the cost to serve by focusing on this metric, the reality is that overall costs increase in the face of repeat calls, rework, and—most damaging to shareholder value—customer churn.

Enlightened companies are realizing they can turn this vicious cycle into a virtuous one. A virtuous cycle looks at the entire customer experience and focuses on metrics such as cost to serve and cost to retain. It starts with mapping out **integrated touch plans** for every customer segment, all the way down to segments of one. An integrated touch plan is the conversation that you want to have with a customer over their life cycle. It defines the key messages that you want to send with each and every interaction. It cuts across multiple channels of communication from voice, to chat, to SMS and online communities.

This is changing the very nature of call centers and transforming them into *customer interaction centers*. A customer interaction center handles all calls, regardless of type, for a certain customer segment or customer portfolio. Although there still may be an IVR, it is simplified with only a few choices. The interaction center associate is cross-trained to handle many different questions, issues, and tasks. This cross-training includes the ability to turn service calls into sales opportunities.

An integrated customer experience such as this typically involves multiple legacy systems. But desktop tools are available that help simplify the job of bringing together information about a customer. For example, a "single sign-on," which allows the associate to sign in once and have access to all applications necessary to do the job, can lower average handle times (AHT) by up to 10 percent. Another tool would be a "desktop wrapper," which picks up information that is required multiple times, such as a serial number or a telephone number. This "wrapper" will prepopulate all the applications that require it so that the associate does not have to spend time reentering the same information over and over again. It also results in lower AHTs. The result is an overall lower cost to serve, lower cost to acquire, and lower cost to retain. A major global consumer electronics company has implemented this customer experience strategy. It combined sales, care, and technical support functions into one integrated

(continued)

(Continued)

organization. It offers both voice and chat support. The center is "virtual" to take advantage of the "right shore" for the work. Within six months of launch, this center has driven down the cost to serve, increased revenue per call, and increased customer satisfaction.

Technology is also playing a major role in the transformation of customer support. Today's young adults have grown up in a wireless, borderless world. Most would rather instant message their "chat" with a service associate than talk. It is imperative that any customer experience strategy offer this option. Best-in-class providers have associates handling up to four chats at once, thus driving strong cost savings.

Another emerging trend is the use of blogs and forums for customer support. According to Gartner, "By 2012, 65 percent of support conversations will happen outside of your enterprise."[a] It is imperative that companies integrate traditional CRM channels with these new social CRM communities. One way to do this is to create a certified knowledge base. This base will capture all the information being shared across these interactions so that all associates have the benefit of the most up-to-date knowledge about a given topic. For example, I posed a question on a blog about accidentally running my son's iPodTouch through the washing machine. I wanted to know if there was anything that I could do to save it. The blog community suggested that I immediately submerge the device in uncooked rice and leave it there for 48 hours. The rice would absorb the liquid and—with any luck—save the device. This is not the kind of information that you can predict needing, so you can't really train support associates to deliver it, but it is important that they are aware of the advice being offered through crowd service if customers who call in ask about it. A certified knowledge base can assure this.

In summary, the industry is moving away from point solutions that address only a small part of the total customer experience, to integrated multichannel solutions. These solutions offer customers the choice of how they want to communicate, on their terms, and help a firm remember all the previous "conversations" with a customer.[b] The measures of success move from productivity measures to bottom line business outcomes.

---

[a]K. Collins, "CRM 'hype' continues, but maturity and adoption of enabling technologies vary widely," September 8, 2008, accessed March 9, 2009, available at: http://blog.gartner.com/blog/crm.php.
[b]Based on what Don Peppers and Martha Rogers call a "Learning Relationship."

Cost Efficiency and Effectiveness of Customer Interaction

Regardless of how automated they are, every interaction with a customer does cost something, if only in terms of the customer's own time and attention, and some interactions cost more than others. The cost of customer interaction can be minimized partly by reducing or eliminating the interactions that the customer does not want. But ranking customers by their value also allows a company to manage the customer interaction process more cost efficiently. A highly valuable customer is more apt to be worth a personal phone call from a manager while a not-so-valuable customer's interaction might be handled more efficiently on the Web site. An enterprise requires a manageable and cost-efficient way to solicit, receive, and process the interactions with its customers. It will need to categorize customer inquiries and responses in some effective way so it can customize its interactions for each customer.

Customer-strategy enterprises concentrate not just on the *efficiency* of the communication channel used for interactions with the customer but also on the *effectiveness* of the customer dialogue itself. Measuring efficiency might include tracking the percent of inbound customer inquiries satisfactorily answered by the enterprise's Web site FAQ section, or monitoring how long customers stay on hold with the customer service department before they disconnect. Measuring effectiveness might include tracking **first-call resolution**, or the ratio of complaints handled or problems resolved on the first call. Critical to the success of any dialogue, however, is that each successive interaction with the individual customer be seen as part of a seamless, flowing stream of discussion. Whether the conversation yesterday took place via mail, phone, the Web, or any other communication channel, the next conversation with the customer must pick up where the last one left off.

For decades now, technology has been dramatically reducing the expenses required for a business to interact with a wide range of customers. Enterprises can now streamline and automate what was once a highly manual process of customer interaction. Different interactive mechanisms can yield widely different information-exchange capabilities, such as speed trackability, tangibility (the ability to hold it or refer back to it later), and personalization. Interacting regularly with a customer via a Web site is usually highly cost-efficient, and can be customer-driven, yielding a rich amount of information. Postal mail is not as practical for dialogue, because it involves a lengthy cycle time, although it can prove effective for delivering more detailed information to the customer, who can keep the hard copy to read later—hard copy that might include glossy photos or diagrams harder to render online. Telephone interaction has the advantages of real-time conversation, but neither phone nor face-to-face interaction facilitates easy tracking of the content of these conversations, and the enterprise trying to employ voice interactions to strengthen its customer relationships must be sure the employees responsible for the interactions are diligently and accurately capturing the key elements of customer dialogues (although scripted phone calls can aid in this effort).

⌐Complaining Customers: Hidden Assets?⌐

Customers generally contact an enterprise of their own volition for only three reasons: to get information, to obtain a product or service, or to make a suggestion or a complaint. Despite the fact that technology should make it easier for customers to contact companies, the Technical Assistance Research Program (TARP) found that customer complaints are declining; not because there are fewer problems but likely because, unfortunately, customers have been trained to expect problems as part of the cost of doing business.[12] But sometimes a complaint can provide an opportunity for real dialogue.

Thus, one way to view a complainer is to see him as a customer with a current "negative" value that can be turned into positive value. In other words, a complainer has extremely high potential value. If the complaint is not resolved, there is a high likelihood that the complaining customer will cease buying, and will probably talk to a number of other people about his dissatisfaction, causing the loss of additional business. The customer-oriented enterprise, focused on increasing the value of its customer base, will see a customer complaint as an opportunity to convert the customer's immense potential value into actual value, for three reasons:

1. *Complaints are a "relationship adjustment opportunity."* The customer who calls with a complaint enables the enterprise to understand why their relationship is troubled. The enterprise then can determine ways to fix the relationship.
2. *Complaints enable the enterprise to expand its scope of knowledge about the customer.* By hearing a customer's complaint, the enterprise can learn more about the customer's needs and strive to increase the value of the customer.
3. *Complaints provide data points about the enterprise's products and services.* By listening to a customer's complaint, the enterprise can better understand how to modify and correct its generalized offerings, based on the feedback.

To a customer-centered enterprise, complaining customers have a collaborative upside, represented by a high potential value. In fact, they might have the highest potential value: Research from TARP has shown that the most loyal customers are the ones most likely to take the time to complain to a company in the first place. It has also found that customers who are satisfied with the solution to a problem often exhibit even greater loyalty than do customers who did not experience a problem at all.[13]

> To a customer-centered enterprise, complaining customers have a collaborative upside, represented by a high potential value.

Because the handling of complaints has so much potential upside, a one-to-one enterprise will not avoid complaints but instead will seek them out. An effort to "discover complaints"—to seek out as many opportunities for customer dialogue as possible—becomes part of dialogue management. **Complaint discovery** contacts typically ask two questions:

> Customers who are satisfied with the solution to a problem often exhibit even greater loyalty than do customers who did not experience a problem at all.

1. Is there anything more we can do for you?
2. Is there anything we can do better?

At one European book club,[14] for example, customer service representatives have called new members during their first month and ask one simple question:

---

[12]Janelle Barlow and Claus Moller, *A Complaint Is a Gift: Recovering Customer Loyalty When Things Go Wrong*, 2nd ed. (San Francisco: Berrett-Koehler, 2008), p. 74.
[13]Ibid., pp. 104–105.
[14]DirectGroup, Bertelsmann AG; available at: www.bertelsmann.com (accessed April 2010).

"Is there anything we can do better?" No sales pitch or special promotion has been discussed. The results of this customer satisfaction initiative speak volumes to its effectiveness in retaining customers: nearly an 8-percent increase in sales per member, and 6 percent fewer drop-offs after the first year of membership, among those contacted.

By complaining, a customer is initiating a dialogue with an enterprise and making himself available for collaboration. The enterprise focused on building customer value will view complaining customers as an asset—a business opportunity—to turn the complainers into loyal customers. That is why enterprises need to make it easy for a customer to complain when he needs to.

TRG's i-Sky unit is a telephone and Internet service firm specializing in dialogue management for enterprise customers that want to do more than simply feed messages to their clients. Complaint discovery is one of the key activities i-Sky performs for its customers. An automobile dealer might retain i-Sky to telephone new car owners a week after they purchase its vehicles. The i-Sky representative would ask the customer if he is happy with his new car, and send any newly discovered complaints directly to the automobile dealer for handling. i-Sky also attempts to uncover any unspoken concerns a customer might have but was reluctant to tell the enterprise directly. In essence, the company attempts to initiate a dialogue with the customer to gather information about his needs, using his complaint and feedback as the opportunity to enhance his relationship with the brand (i-Sky's client), converting him to a satisfied and loyal customer.

For their part, most customers see complaint discovery as a highly friendly and service-oriented action on the part of a firm. In one survey commissioned by an auto dealer, i-Sky discovered that for the vast majority of the 6,500 automobile owners included in the survey, the very act of asking for their opinions made them into happier and more loyal (i.e., more valuable) customers. Customers who received a phone call simply asking about their opinion tended to become more satisfied with the automobile dealer than those who did not receive a call.

Summary

At this point, we've shown with this chapter the importance of customer interaction in the Learning Relationship. The enterprise that creates a sustaining dialogue with each customer can learn more about that customer and begin to develop ways to add value that spring from learning about that customer and consequently to create a product/service bundle that he is most interested in owning or using. And, like drip irrigation, which never overwhelms or parches, a sustained dialogue helps a company get smarter and serves the customer better than sporadic random sample surveys. The customer-based enterprise engages in a collaborative dialogue with each customer in that customer's preferred channel of communication—whether it is the customer interaction center, e-mail, the phone, wireless, the Web, or snail mail.

The development of social media, however, has revolutionized a company's capacity to interact with its customers—and its customers' capacity to broadcast their experiences with a company, both good and bad. In the next chapter, we discuss how these different communication channels can help facilitate customer interaction and relationships with customers in general.

Food for Thought

1. TiVo and other digital recording devices collect very specific data about household television viewing. These services make it possible to know which programs are recorded and watched (and when and how many times), which programs are recorded and never watched, and which programs are transferred to DVD or other electronic format. The services also know when a particular part of a program is watched more than once (a sports play, or a favorite cartoon, or movie scene, or commercial). What are the implications of that knowledge for dialogue? For privacy? For the business collecting the data (i.e., data or a cable company)? How might TiVo or a cable company use this information to increase the value it offers to advertisers and marketers? What would a marketer have to do differently to make the most of this information? How can DVR companies protect their own customers' privacy?

2. What problems might occur if an enterprise participates in customer dialogues but its own information and data systems are not integrated well? Do you remember any personal experience in dealing with a company or brand that could not find the right records or information during your interaction with it? How did this make you feel about the company? Did you feel the company was less competent? Less trustworthy?

3. What are some of the explicit bargains companies have made with you in your role as a customer to get some of your time, attention, or information?

4. How does the European book club mentioned in the discussion of complaint discovery actually *know* that it's the calling program that led to 6 percent fewer drop-offs and 8 percent more sales per member? Might it not have been the book selection that year? Or the economy?

5. When you plan to buy a product and want to investigate its benefits and drawbacks, whose advice do you seek? Do you think the advertiser will tell you about the drawbacks, or just the benefits? If you are trying to evaluate the product by researching it online, do you have more confidence in it if the seller makes other customers' reviews available? What if you read a negative comment? Might you still buy the product?

Glossary

Addressable   Refers to media that can send and customize messages individually.

Business process reengineering (BPR)   Focuses on reducing the time it takes to complete an interaction or a process and on reducing the cost of completing it. BPR usually involves introducing quality controls to ensure time and cost efficiencies are achieved.

Complaint discovery   An outbound interaction with a customer, on the part of a marketer, to elicit honest feedback and uncover any problems with a product or service in the process.

Critical data elements (CDEs)   High-level information flows that facilitate decision making and process execution.

Customer Experience and Interaction Touchmap   A graphical depiction of the interactions a company has with each segment of its customers across each of the available channels. Its purpose is to take an outside-in view of the customer interactions, instead of the traditional inside-out view typically taken in business process reengineering work. Current State Touchmaps depict all the enterprise's current interactions with customers and identify gap areas; Future State Touchmaps depict the desired customer interactions that will be customized based on the needs and values of individual customers.

Customer interaction center   Where all calls are handled, regardless of type, for a certain customer segment or customer portfolio.

Customer life cycle   The "trajectory" a customer follows, from the customer's first awareness of a need, to his or her decision to buy or contract with a company to meet that need, to use the product or service, to support it with an ongoing relationship, perhaps recommending it to others, and to end that relationship for whatever reason. The term *customer life cycle* does not refer to the customer's actual lifetime or chronological age but rather to the time during which the product is in some way relevant to the customer.

Customer service representative (CSR)   A person who answers or makes calls in a call center (also called a customer interaction center or contact center, since it may include online chat or other interaction methods).

Digital video recorder (DVR)   A digital recording device (such as TiVo) that uses a hard disk drive to record television shows just like a videocassette recorder (VCR), but with interfaces (such as an on-screen program guide) that are regularly downloaded to the device.

Drip irrigation dialogue   An enterprise's sustained, incremental dialogue that uses each interaction, whether initiated by the customer or by the firm, to learn one more incremental thing that will help in growing share of customer with that customer.

Explicit bargain   One-to-one organizations give something of value to a customer in exchange for that customer's time and attention, and perhaps for information about that customer as well. An example: discounts on prices bought at a store where a customer shows his membership card.

First-call resolution (FCR)   When customer complaints are resolved at their first interaction with a company, whether it is through telephone, e-mail, or any other method of interaction. The measurable benchmark for customer service.

Golden Questions   Questions designed to reveal important information about a customer while requiring the least possible effort from the customer, in order to differentiate customer needs and potential value. The most productive Golden Questions will be customer need–based rather than product–based.

Implicit bargain   Advertisers have in the past bought ads that pay for the cost of producing the media that consumers want—television programming, newspaper copy, magazine stories, music on the radio, and so on. The implied "deal" was that consumers would listen to the ads in exchange for getting the media content free.

Integrated touch plan   In customer interaction centers, an integrated touch plan defines the key messages a company wants to send with every interaction throughout a customer's life cycle and across multiple channels of communication.

Interactive Voice Response (IVR)   Now a feature at most call centers, IVR software provides instructions for callers to "push '1' to check your current balance, push '2' to transfer funds," and so forth.

Nonaddressable   Refers to media that cannot send and/or customize messages individually.

CHAPTER 8

Customer Insight, Dialogue, and Social Media

It's a rare person who wants to hear what he doesn't want to hear.

—Dick Cavett

⌐Although the strategy of customer relationships must precede the successful implementation of customer-relationship technology, it was the technology that mandated that enterprises map out their path down the road we've been following in the preceding chapters.⌐Customers have always been able to interact with a company, but mainly on the company's terms—through mail, if a customer could get the name of a person to send a letter to; through phone, if a customer could get the right phone number; and maybe through salespeople, if the customer were important enough to warrant a personal sales call and if the salesperson was authorized to provide service to the customer's satisfaction. That was pretty much it. Today, the customer rules. And savvy customers are leveraging social networking tools to get what they want, when they want it, more than ever before.⌐But **social media** also allows new possibilities for dialogue and collaboration between customers and enterprises that can benefit both parties.⌐This chapter addresses how a customer-centric company can recognize and reap the positive impact on customer value these technologies potentially provide.

So far we have been talking about interaction and dialogue as if the only thing of importance to a marketer is the dialogue that can take place between an enterprise and a customer. But customers are human beings, and humans prefer conversing with other humans much more than with brands or businesses. Humans are social animals, and the same Web-based technologies that have made it possible for businesses to interact directly with their customers have also made it possible for humans to interact socially with other humans anywhere on the planet. Moreover, the capabilities inherent in computers, mobile phones, and the Internet make it possible for individual consumers to produce vast quantities of their own content, from blogs and written comments, to pictures, podcasts, and videos. People can now create their own content and then upload it to the network for others to see on a wide array of hosting Web sites, from Facebook and Flickr, to YouTube and

Yahoo!. They can choose to make the content available only for select friends or associates, or for a variety of categories of other users, or for everyone.

The "social media revolution" that has occurred as a result of these new technological capabilities may actually dwarf the Industrial Revolution in its ultimate impact on the human race, eventually making possible an entirely new, noneconomic production system based not just on money and exchanges of value, but on social ties, trust, generosity, status, and informal "normative" mores. Complex works and projects, from **open source** software, such as the Linux operating system or the Mozilla family of Web browsers, to detailed and evolving documents such as the user-generated reference work Wikipedia, provide small previews of how this new production system might function and flourish.

But this is a topic for another book. What we are concerned with here is how these rapidly flourishing social ties among people, mediated by a proliferating assortment of software and interactive technologies loosely termed social media, are likely to alter an enterprise's ability to interact with its customers and prospects and to create and manage profitable, mutually beneficial relationships with them.

The Dollars and Sense of Social Media

A colleague of ours was angry about the way Orbitz handled a service issue, so she tweeted about it. She also sent a complaint via the company's Web site customer support page. Orbitz responded to her Twitter posts via e-mail and resolved the issue. But in response to our friend's e-mail sent via the "contact us" form on the Web site, the company only sent a generic "we're reviewing your inquiry" e-mail.

This is just one of the many examples of customer interaction via social channels benefiting customers. The question is, does it benefit the company as well? It does, and here are a few examples:

- Barnes & Noble's retail sales of specific books increase when customers discuss those books in its online community.
- User-generated content on Hewlett-Packard's online community site helps improve the company's search engine optimization. In one case, Hewlett-Packard went from not appearing at all on the first results page of a specific keyword search to dominating that first page.
- Candy bar Wispa (a product of Cadbury Schweppes) was given a second chance thanks to Facebook groups reminiscing about the chocolate sweet. About 14,000 customers banded together and collectively demanded that their nostalgia be returned to store shelves.
- Tibco Software's customer community enables customers to help each other solve technical issues (that's what **"crowd service"** is). Every time that happens, a customer gets the help he needs but the company also saves about $1,000 on a support call. The savings gained more than covers the cost of hosting an online community. "We can show tangible value from our social media strategy," says Ram Menon, executive vice president of worldwide marketing for Tibco.

According to a 1to1 Media study on marketing spending, respondent companies increased their recent spending on reaching customers in new ways.

- 69 percent increased spending on social media
- 68 percent increased spending on e-mail
- 50 percent increased spending on search

The hard-dollar benefits include:

- Increased buzz around a brand, product, or service online. Not only increases awareness but also has the potential to increase sales across channels.
- Improved search results from customer conversations about an organization and its products that happen on a company's online community, blog, customer forum, and the like. Potentially drives more traffic to a company's Web site.
- More influence from customer recommendations given on social networks and in online communities than referrals in the offline world. Can lead to more deal closings—in some cases, with less selling required on the part of the company.
- Deeper insight into customers' uncensored preferences, needs, and behaviors is invaluable. Potentially leads to improvements in such areas as service delivery, product features, and pricing. Also can lead to better customer experience, increased sales, and greater customer engagement.
- Customers helping other customers online. Crowd service can reduce costs to serve by deflecting calls and e-mails from the contact center, and may result in better service results for customers as well.

Although some executives are still searching for the best way to measure the return on investment of what many call Social CRM, the bottom-line benefits are clear. That doesn't mean it's easy. Start with the end in mind: Determine your ultimate goal or set of objectives for social media interactions. Then create a strategy to get you there that includes measureable results. As Barnes & Noble, Hewlett-Packard, and Tibco can attest, it's a journey worth taking.

Source: Excerpted and adapted from Don Peppers and Martha Rogers, Ph.D., "The Dollars and Sense of Social Media," in The Social Customer's e-book, *The Social Contract: Customers, Companies, Communities, and Conversations in the Age of the Collaborative Relationship* (2010), available at: http://thesocialcustomer.com/submitform/tscebook030810/?utm_source=socap&utm_medium=multi&utm_campaign=contract_ebook&reference=smt_socap, accessed September 1, 2010.

Social media can be employed by an enterprise in a number of ways, but we should highlight four that are highly important for an enterprise trying to build stronger customer relationships:

1. Engaging and activating the enterprise's most enthusiastic supporters to "spread the word" about the brand

2. Empowering customers to defend the enterprise's brand in times of stress, and help it recover from missteps or disasters
3. Listening in on customer conversations that involve the enterprise and/or its competitors
4. Enlisting the enterprise's own customers (and, sometimes, other volunteers) to help provide service for other customers

Engaging Enthusiastic Supporters

If a company or brand has some proportion of avid supporters, hobbyists, enthusiasts, or just very loyal fans within its customer base, then using social media to draw these highly enthusiastic customers out and cater to their needs can be a highly rewarding relationship-building strategy. Lego, for instance, the well-known Danish toy manufacturer, certainly has its share of enthusiastic users. The company embraced social media early on and has been reaping the rewards through innovative product ideas and a growing population of enthusiastic customers. Several online groups, such as the Lego Certified Professionals and the First Lego League, focus their efforts on running local community events and then sharing their experiences online—inspiring current fans and drawing new ones. Other online groups have produced insightful product ideas, such as the Lego Ambassadors' Forum, a group of selected Lego fans who communicate daily with the company on various topics; and most recently, Lego Click, a forum that aims to capture "light-bulb moments" relevant to toys and Lego's market. Lego Click is a hub-and-spoke venue where users can contribute content from a variety of social media sources: Twitter, YouTube, Flickr, and more.[1] The best news? All this is done by the customers themselves, which the company gladly helps facilitate.

Zappos, the online shoe store, is another company using social media to reach out and energize avid customers. With an employee culture already centered on "making personal and emotional connections," the company was well positioned from its beginning to lead the way in using social media forums such as Twitter, blogging, and Facebook. Most Zappos employees have Twitter accounts (and its CEO Tony Hsieh, tweets often). It should be no surprise that most people who are even aware of the Zappos brand today initially heard of the firm by word of mouth. Employees' tweets at Zappos aren't so much about the company's products as they are about getting to know the people themselves—capitalizing on the commonsense fact that when people feel connected to others as individuals, they are more likely to trust them and want to do business with them. This is not a marketing scheme but transparent and authentic relationship building that clearly benefits both customers and employees. As Hsieh said to an interviewer:

> *Brand building today is so different than from what it was 50 years ago. Fifty years ago you could get a few marketing people in a small room and decide, "This is what our brand will be," and then spend a lot of money on TV advertising—and*

---

[1]"Social Media Helps Lego Connect with Users," Ericsson Telecom Report, February 23, 2009; available at: www.ericsson.com/ericsson/corpinfo/publications/telecomreport/archive/2009/social-media/article1.shtml, accessed September 1, 2010; Matt Rhodes, "Social Media Case Study: LEGO CLICK," *Fresh Networks*, January 21, 2010; available at: www.freshnetworks.com/blog/2010/01/social-media-case-study-lego-click/, accessed September 1, 2010.

that was your brand. If you as a consumer only had your neighbors to talk to, you had to believe what the TV was telling you. Today anyone, whether it is an employee or a customer, if they have a good or bad experience with your company they can blog about it or Twitter about it and it can be seen by millions of people. It's what they say now that is your brand.[2]

Cosmetics company Sephora is another example. This enterprise has been able to become even more customer-centric while maintaining a high return on social media by knowing which media outlet was best suited to meet their customers' needs. Sephora continues to invest in print catalogs, knowing that for some, the Web or the phone can't reproduce the glossy photo. But in addition, it pays attention to technology and uses it carefully to make it ever more convenient for customers. Sephora's custom mobile application, for instance, allows customers to view product reviews on their mobile device—making quick work of assessing the dozens of moisturizers displayed on a store wall. One result is that Sephora now has a massive fan base that fuels these reviews: 437,000 fans on Facebook and 53,000 Twitter followers—fans who love talking about beauty and passing along information about great products.[3]

Empowering Customers to Defend the Brand

On Wednesday, February 14, 2007, just prior to the President's Day holiday weekend, a snow-and-ice storm hit New York City, crippling operations at several airlines. The degree to which it incapacitated JetBlue, however, was of a different order of magnitude altogether. A low-fare new entrant that had previously earned high marks among passengers for efficient service and friendly, capable employees, JetBlue had to cancel more than 1,000 flights over the course of a few days. Angry mobs formed at several of its gates. Passengers were stuck on one plane for a full 10 hours without taking off (and then interviewed about their experience on every network news program). In the aftermath of the crisis, previously loyal customers publicly bemoaned what an awful company JetBlue had suddenly become, and congresspeople began beating the drum about customers' rights. This nightmare would be enough to make the average CEO want to curl up and hide.

Instead, JetBlue's founder and then-CEO David Neeleman responded quickly and with sincere atonement, hitting every media outlet he could, taking responsibility for the problem, discussing its causes openly and honestly, and issuing apologies not just to all the inconvenienced flyers but to his airline's own crew members as well. He sent apology e-mails to every customer affected and also to the members of the airline's True Blue loyalty program who weren't even flying that weekend. The company posted Neeleman's video apology on its Web site, and the video was soon circulated and posted on YouTube and a variety of other sites, all over the Web.

---

[2]Soren Gordhamer and Paul Zelizer, "The New Social Engagement: A Visit to Zappos," *Mashable: The Social Media Guide*, 2009; available at: http://mashable.com/2009/04/26/zappos/, accessed September 1, 2010; Samir Balwani, "Presenting: 10 of the Smartest Big Brands in Social Media," *Mashable: The Social Media Guide*, 2009, available at: http://mashable.com/2009/02/06/social-media-smartest-brands/, accessed September 1, 2010.

[3]Ellen Davis, "Sephora Exec Discusses the ROI of Social Media," National Retail Federation: Retail's BIG Blog, February 26, 2010; available at: http://blog.nrf.com/2010/02/26/sephora-exec-discusses-the-roi-of-social-media/, accessed September 1, 2010.

In addition, the airline announced a Customer Bill of Rights, promising specific compensation payments for delayed and inconvenienced customers in the future, including travel vouchers worth at least $25 for passengers experiencing a ground delay of more than 30 minutes once they arrive at their destination airports (ranging up to full round-trip refund vouchers for arrival ground delays of more than three hours) and vouchers worth at least $100 if ground delays of more than three hours occur on departure. In media interviews, Neeleman said the airline would make its Bill of Rights for customers retroactive and send the appropriate travel vouchers to all passengers already inconvenienced by the previous weekend's operational catastrophe, which he estimated would cost the company $30 million or more, in total. Even after Neeleman's extensive apologies and new policy announcements, however, many customers continued to rail against the airline in a blogosphere thick with customer outrage. Blog sites such as Church of the Customer seethed with resentment at JetBlue for this unmitigated service disaster.

But just when it looked as if no one, anywhere, would step up to JetBlue's defense, someone did. Who? The company's most frequent flyers. These were the folks who, month in and month out, had been treated decently in the past by JetBlue—actually, a good deal more decently than other airlines were treating them. These customers knew that JetBlue's intentions were good, and they trusted in the airline's ability to make it better next time. They believed the company's apology, applauded the remedial steps, and came to the blogs themselves to join the discussion and defend the young airline's reputation.

In their book *Authenticity*,[4] Jim Gilmore and Joe Pine suggest that JetBlue was able to recapture its reputation with its Customer Bill of Rights primarily because such a Bill of Rights fit "authentically" into the character of the JetBlue brand. It was, in fact, exactly the kind of thing you would expect from an airline like JetBlue, which had built its reputation on being fair, open, and honest with customers. Its "authentic" reputation was already one of trustworthiness.[5]

Listening to Customers

Social media are two-way media, and in most cases the interactions and dialogues on social media sites have been initiated and are largely conducted by private individuals, not by company representatives or officials. This means the conversations are objective, frank, and highly informative. They can serve as an excellent resource for understanding what a brand's own customers are thinking about the brand. Yes, "listening" has never been part of most mass marketers' primary skill set, but forward-thinking companies are now realizing what an invaluable resource these social media conversations actually provide. In the next contribution, consultant Becky Carroll outlines some of the dos and don'ts of social media listening.

---

[4]James H. Gilmore and B. Joseph Pine II, *Authenticity: What Consumers Really Want* (Boston: Harvard Business School Press, 2007).

[5]This section was excerpted from Don Peppers and Martha Rogers, Ph.D., *Rules to Break & Laws to Follow* (Hoboken, NJ: John Wiley & Sons, 2008), pp. 151–153. (Also see notes in Chapter 7.)

The Importance of Listening and Social Media

Becky Carroll
Founder, Petra Consulting Group/Customers Rock!
Instructor of Social Media, University of California, San Diego

One of the keys to being successful in the use of social media for marketing is not how we talk to customers; rather, it is how we *listen* to the ongoing conversations taking place online. Active listening is critical to the creation of the appropriate social media interaction plans. When we skip listening, our customer interactions via social media begin to sound like traditional, one-way broadcast messages; and in this space, such messages will simply be tuned out.

Think of a Cocktail Party

How we interact with customers via social media can be seen as analogous to attending a cocktail party. Upon entering a room, it would be considered rude for you to walk up to a group of people already conversing and start talking about yourself. Unfortunately, however, this is exactly how many firms use social media. If an enterprise sees social media as just another communication channel, it is likely to use the same mass-messaging and marketing "spin" that infuses the company's direct mail campaigns, its Web site, and its advertising. These messages talk *at* people, not *with* people, and are rarely tuned to the needs and concerns of the individual customers being addressed. Definitely rude behavior at a cocktail party, and not appropriate for social media either. Social media is *social*, and requires social activities—conversation, not pronouncements.

If you are a savvy partygoer and you approach a group of people at the cocktail party who are already conversing, you don't say a word. Instead, you spend a few minutes listening to see what's being discussed and to get the proper context. Then, after introducing yourself briefly, you may begin to engage in the conversation by sharing your viewpoint or something relevant and interesting to the other party guests. Or you may enter the discussion by asking a question related to the topic at hand. Either way, you are *engaging* the other partygoers in a meaningful dialogue. Nontransactional conversations like this are the foundation for using social media to build stronger customer relationships. The familiarity created by a series of social media interactions tends to build better relationships than any series of advertisements could.

How to Listen and What to Listen For

There are two things to listen for in social media: brand and customer. Both are important when determining the optimal methods for interacting with customers (inside and outside of social media), but in different ways. And keep in mind that listening, as we describe the process here, doesn't occur just once; it needs to occur continuously, over months and years.

(continued)

(Continued)

BRAND MONITORING An enterprise should always listen for social media conversations that mention the firm's brand names or areas of specialization. It should also monitor the social media space for any mentions of executives' names as well as the names of competitors. When monitoring brand social media conversations, these are the questions the enterprise should be trying to answer:

- *Who* is talking about the brand? Do we need to respond? Are they influencers, potential stakeholders, clients, or most valuable customers? Who else do they influence? The monitoring effort should track those who start conversations, along with those who add to conversations; over time it will become apparent that some customers can be enlisted as evangelists, whether they are major influencers, stakeholders, or simply effective conversationalists. (Note: A customer's value to the enterprise is certainly related to his or her level of social media influence, so one goal of tracking the people who are conversing about the brand is to have a better idea of who they are and where the most valuable customers are participating.)
- *What* are people saying? Are they praising or condemning? Are they demanding a response? Are they trying to encourage others to act (either negatively or positively)? Understanding how influence takes place will help shape future conversations.
- *Where* are they talking? Are they conversing on the enterprise's own sites or social media properties, or are they having discussions in different forums and communities? Understanding where conversations are occurring will help determine the best places to interact with customers, which often can be in their own "territory."

An enterprise can use many software and subscription tools to listen to the social media conversation or the chatter taking place online. A company should monitor customer conversations through these online tools at least weekly, and possibly daily, tracking the trends on an ongoing basis. It should track the issues that generate most of the chatter and continue to monitor these issues over time. It should also be alert for mentions of key terms and determine quickly whether a response is needed. If someone mentions the brand, or some other relevant term being followed, the enterprise may want to consider leaving a response or comment in the conversation, if appropriate. Quick responses to potentially negative comments can help put out fires and preempt additional inflammatory statements from other frustrated customers.

CUSTOMER MONITORING Listening for customer insight goes beyond simple observation of what customers are saying via social media sites. Listening pays attention to what customers are saying between the lines, leading to insight about customer behaviors and, ultimately, individual customer needs. This takes place in social media as customers' voice their opinions and insights, along with *unsolicited* feedback (i.e., highly valuable, spontaneous feedback not related to the enterprise's own consumer research). When monitoring customers, here are the questions the enterprise should be trying to answer:

- What are the pain points being highlighted by customers? Are they legitimate concerns? Are they directed toward the company at large, or is something being said about a particular situation or individual? When monitoring these comments, the enterprise should never dismiss customer rants, just because they are emotionally charged. *All* critical comments—100 percent of them—should be checked out to ensure no underlying issue exists. Even when a customer gets the facts wrong, the perspective or impression still can be valuable. Complaints picked up in social media can also help point out potential unmet customer needs.
- What is the emotion or sentiment being shared, either negative or positive? Uncovering emotions will help reveal how customers feel about the brand, product, or service (or about related and/or competitive brands). Emotions can lead to better understanding of important and influential customer needs.
- What information is being shared about the various customer experience touchpoints? This information can help to supplement customer experience Touchmap details.

Dig into any pain points quickly, efficiently, and without emotion. Once any problems at all are voiced in a social media setting, even if they are relatively minor by nature, they can easily turn into a rant by some other customer (or customers) with a similar experience. As with all human interactions, people engaged in social media interactions easily succumb to the confirmation bias, latching on to every shred of evidence that proves their own view and ignoring conflicting viewpoints. So when a complaint is aired, apologize directly and immediately to the customer for their dissatisfaction, get the customer service team involved where appropriate, and learn from the discussion. Social media can alert a company to a potential product or service issue faster than any other channel. This allows the organization to alert contact centers, mobilize resources behind the scenes, and proactively employ social media to alert other customers to a problem in advance.

The insight gained from listening in on social media conversations among customers can easily be used to refine the enterprise's understanding of its customer needs groupings. In fact, a company may find out just as much (or more) about particular needs-based types of customers through their verbatim language on their favorite social media site (be it a consumer-focused or business-focused site) as can be obtained from costly research surveys and interviews. After all, the conversations started by customers in the social media context are likely to be much more genuine than the responses elicited by even the most carefully designed research questionnaire. Nevertheless, it's also important for the company to supplement what it learns via social media with additional primary research. Social media is likely to provide great insights, but sometimes it represents only a subset of your customer base.

(continued)

(Continued)

Now more than ever, it's critical for customer-centric companies to move beyond organizational silos to listen to their customers across the entire experience, and social media channels offer a superb opportunity for doing this. Social media interactions involving proactive brand and customer listening can serve as a very effective tool for strengthening and deepening a company's customer relationships.

Enlisting Customers to Help Other Customers

The widespread success of open source projects makes it obvious that people have an urge to contribute to benefit others, even when they get no monetary benefit from doing so. They contribute for the satisfaction of accomplishment, for the fulfillment of creating something, and for the personal pride of authorship that goes with this fulfillment. As it turns out, the urge that people have to create content can be harnessed by an enterprise, if it is careful, and if it provides the right tools and structure. Rather than straightforward self-service, the result is something that could be called *crowd service.*[6]

According to one *New York Times* article that chronicles the rise of this kind customer service and describes it in terms of what will help a company help its customers, the result might be the same as if a company were willing to pay for the service for those customers:

Here's the job description: You spend a few hours a day, up to 20 a week, at your computer, supplying answers online to customer questions about technical matters like how to set up an Internet home network or how to program a new high-definition television.

Justin McMurry of Keller, Tex., volunteers up to 20 hours a week in Verizon's community forums, helping the company's Internet, TV and phone customers.

The pay: $0.

A shabby form of exploitation? Not to Justin McMurry, who spends about that amount of time helping customers of Verizon's high-speed fiber optic Internet, television and telephone service, which the company is gradually rolling out across the country.

Mr. McMurry is part of an emerging corps of Web-savvy helpers that large corporations, start-up companies, and venture capitalists are betting will transform the field of customer service.

Such enthusiasts are known as lead users, or super-users, and their role in contributing innovations to product development and improvement—often selflessly—has been closely researched in recent years. There have been case studies of early skateboarders and mountain bikers and their pioneering tweaks

---

[6]As far as we can tell, CustomerThink's Bob Thompson was first to use the term "crowd service," a particularly descriptive and appealing label, analogous to "crowd sourcing."

to their gear, for example, and of the programmers who were behind open-source software like the Linux operating system. These unpaid contributors, it seems, are motivated mainly by a payoff in enjoyment and respect among their peers.[7]

Crowd service is an extremely potent economic force and probably best epitomizes the power that social media interactions have for revolutionizing how businesses will operate in the not-too-distant, even more socially interactive future.[8] Nor is Verizon alone in applying these ideas. Lithium has more than 100 clients for its service, including such name-brand companies as Best Buy, AT&T, Nintendo, and Linksys. Natalie Petouhoff, formerly social media analyst with Forrester Research, Inc., has documented how a number of enterprises turn their own customers into ardent, capable workers dispensing customer service to other customers—for no monetary benefit whatsoever.

Crowd Service: Customers Helping Other Customers

Natalie L. Petouhoff
Digital Strategist, Digital Communications Group, Weber-Shandwick

In 2009, Forrester found that 44 percent of U.S. online adults are "persuaders"—those who tell others about products that interest them. They're brand-motivated, open to ads, and highly active in social applications.[a] And in those conversations, these persuaders are not just affecting a few people, they are affecting millions, often in the time frame of a nanosecond, through social media vehicles as diverse as Facebook, MySpace, LinkedIn, blogs, third-party community Web sites, and perhaps even your own company's Web site. Using these new technologies, anybody can post information about anything at any time, including views about your own company's products and services. No matter where they choose to converse, engage, or persuade, customers increasingly have a free voice in the affairs of your company. What's disconcerting for many companies is that they can't control this voice. Many are finding it difficult to get used to the fact that their customers, their employees, and their suppliers are talking about them through unregulated social media. But companies do have a choice. They can choose to abstain from this conversation and allow anything to be said about them, without their knowledge or participation. Or they can choose to join the conversation and try to help customers get what they want—including honest opinions and advice, objective service and support, and informed assistance for solving problems they encounter.

(continued)

---

[7]Steve Lohr, "Customer Service? Ask a Volunteer," *New York Times*, April 25, 2009; available at: www.nytimes.com/2009/04/26/business/26unbox.html?_r=2&scp=1&sq=Justin percent20McMurry&st=cse, accessed September 1, 2010.

[8]Verizon's platform for facilitating crowd service is provided by Lithium Technologies, but other software companies offering similar capabilities include Jive Software, HelpStream, and Telligent.

(*Continued*)

One of the most thrilling and interesting developments in how companies have come to rely on social media is in the area of customer service. In the old days, customer service had to answer all customer questions directly. A company's customer service department might do this over the phone, or sometimes via e-mail, and of course contact-center capabilities often now include chat and cobrowsing technologies. Naturally, companies *want* their customers not to have to call in at all, and we are all familiar with the concept of "self-service" when it comes to fixing problems—whether they are problems with a credit card account, or a computer printer, or a trip to Spain, or a vacuum cleaner. The customer goes to the company's Web site and expects to find the solution to the problem in the frequently asked question (FAQ) section or perhaps in a downloadable user's manual. If the problem is one that many other customers frequently encounter, the company might even have chosen to highlight some guidelines right on the site. But today's customer doesn't want to read the whole 100-page manual, they want the one paragraph out of the manual that answers their question. The key is providing advanced knowledge management capabilities, but most companies don't distinguish between the types of search or realize the need to use natural language processing to help identify the context of the question and its resulting answer.

Often companies see self-service as a way to minimize their own service costs and, if it's done right, customers like self-service for the same reason they like automated teller machines (ATMs) more than standing in line at a bank branch during bankers' hours to get cash: because they are in control. But especially for very complicated or technical problems, or for issues that require some degree of personal judgment or experience, self-service often just doesn't work very well, leaving a customer unsatisfied and a service problem unsolved. And then it means that your investments in self-service go up in smoke, because when self-service doesn't work, customers call and are angry and desperate for help. This leaves you wide open to having customers comment about how lousy your service is. Especially if you hide your 1-800 number, and the customer who can't find the answer online is also deterred from calling you.

Today, however, using the tools of social media, a company can solve a customer's complex or difficult problem by harnessing the insight and expertise of thousands, or even millions, of other customers. Rather than self-service, some pundits are calling this "crowd service." This is a transformation in who is solving what. Instead of asking the company to solve a problem with its own product or service, customers are asking other customers to help them solve their problem. At first, this might seem a little risky to many companies. (What if customer 1 gives customer 2 the wrong information? Who is liable?) Inherent in the very idea of crowd service is the notion that the company itself will be giving up some degree of control over its own service processes, but experience to date shows that this is actually much less of a problem than most executives would think.

Myfico.com is a site where consumers who no longer have good credit can register, buy products, and work toward improving their credit. What myfico.com found, though, was that because it was a government-regulated business, its call center agents could not provide answers to customers' many questions. What myfico.com couldn't do was provide advice on what products to buy and what process to follow to improve a customer's credit scores, even though it sold products on its Web site specifically designed to do that. Faced with a dilemma, the customer service folks at myfico.com turned to social media.

What exactly did they do? They created an online community (via a Lithium Technologies platform). What myfico.com did not know was if anyone would join a community to talk about messed-up credit scores. It's generally not the type of thing that you want to admit. So as the brave souls at myfico.com designed their community, they did the single most important thing: They invited super-users (experts in the field of consumer credit) to join the community. As myfico.com launched, it had a nagging doubt about whether anyone would actually step forward to join. It also did the second most important thing one has to do in social media initiatives: It marketed and advertised the community. It sent out e-mails to all those customers who had bought something from myfico.com.

How does this story turn out? With 850,000 unique registered users, myfico.com is one of the most interactive and vibrant communities online. What myfico.com realized was that if it could draw, engage, and keep super-users in its community site, those super-users would answer the questions that agents couldn't. How did they get around the legal aspects? Specific guidelines around community policies.

The third thing myfico.com did right was to deploy a community platform technology that allows customers (users) to rate the answers super-users provided. So when 10,000 people say "Yes, this answer was useful and solved my issue," you can have confidence that the answer has been tested and found to be accurate and helpful. (Of course, the community platform you use also has to be "game" proof, meaning that there are controls that won't allow one or several customers to vote for a solution more than once. This way, a Superuser can't game the system to increase their followership or apparent expertise.)

You might be wondering what the business results are with this community, right? What myfico.com found was that sales increased by 61 percent for those in the community! Why? Simply because customers were getting straight answers from people who had used myfico.com and felt they benefited from the company. What better marketing avenue could you ever wish for?

Are other companies' results similar? In many cases, yes. Consider iRobot, for instance. Executives at iRobot, a manufacturer of consumer robot vacuums (e.g., the Roomba) knew that top-notch technical and customer support was critical to the brand's success and revenue growth. But its customer support technologies were not integrated into a seamless customer experience, nor had the company considered employing social media as a part of its customer care efforts. The global technical support director at iRobot led an effort to revamp customer service, incorporating a social media initiative to allow existing iRobot customers to help other customers. The company's management embraced the idea immediately, realizing the power of using social media to improve its

(continued)

(Continued)

customer service. And with the actionable voice of the customer data it began collecting, the company transformed not only its service process but the way the whole organization worked together. The results? Customer-focused business decisions by integrated multidisciplinary teams working together to solve customers' issues, develop new products, create fanatical customer experiences, increase customer retention and revenue, and reduce costs for customer service, marketing, and engineering.

What about a company that decides to build its own communities (as opposed to contracting with an outside vendor, such as Lithium Technologies, which helped both myfico.com and iRobot)? Although it's not recommended unless software is one of your core competencies, Intuit has shown it can be done. Intuit began more than 25 years ago with a mission to revolutionize people's lives by solving their important problems. The company wanted to make so profound an impact for each customer that people would not be able to imagine going back to the old ways. The company's flagship products are Quicken, QuickBooks, and TurboTax. In 2007, with the acquisition of Digital Insight, Intuit also began creating the next generation of online banking, and today the company helps banks and credit unions offer easier and simpler online financial services to their customers.

To continue to transform the way people manage their money and their small businesses, Intuit has embraced social technologies and social media. Kira Wampler, director of social media interactions for Intuit's SmallBusiness United.com, is not a traditional marketer and was quick to realize that rather than using social media simply to push content to its constituents, Intuit needed to tap customers' feedback and incorporate it into the way it handled the service task. When Wampler ventured into the social sphere to monitor and listen to customers, she said what impressed her was the passion with which customers were talking about Intuit's products. But she also found that sometimes this passion did not have a positive sentiment. Rather than simply monitoring for negative comments and then turning them over to someone else for handling, Wampler began responding directly to customers. She apologized. She began by soliciting what Peppers and Rogers call "complaint discovery" and asked, "What would be better if . . . ?" And she didn't stop there; she went back into the company and actually made the changes that customers were looking for. Once she did that, she tweeted the changes or posted them on the e-review sites. As customers realized that there was someone behind the brand who actually cared, jaws began to drop. Intuit was not some big monolithic monster that didn't pay attention. Instead, customers saw the heart that all Intuit employees put into their work.

As a result, in the first few months of Wampler's care, sentiment in the cloud went up by 30 percent. Wampler had proven that even just one brave soul showing she cared made a difference. Over the next five years, Intuit was able to drive better and better online customer sentiment and awareness for its consumer and small business offerings, and increased marketing campaign effectiveness. It also systematically integrated Voice of the Customer data into its product development process, improving customer support while lowering support costs.

One important key to social media is what I call the 1-9-90 rule, which describes how to visualize the ratio of contributions different participants will make in an online social community. In most communities, about 1 percent of the population post, about 9 percent respond to posts, and 90 percent just read the posts. To return to the cocktail party analogy often used to characterize the dynamics of social media, at a party you have several different types of people in the crowd. There are some who are interested in others and interested in sharing, and aren't shy about doing so. They are driven by a need to contribute. Some other guests, as they come in the door, spot those gregarious folks who have a crowd around them. Although they aren't the type to lead the crowd themselves, they enjoy hanging with the 1 percent who do, and they're good at responding to or riffing off what the crowd leaders are saying. And then there is the rest of the party, and you could think of them as the audience. They come to the party to be entertained, to rub shoulders with and to listen to the 1- and 9-percenters. This is not only the way a party comes together; it's the makeup of a healthy online community as well.

Two things are important to understand about the 1-9-90 dynamic.

1. If you want a vibrant online social community, you have to invite the people who will drive the conversation. So you must ask yourself: Have you invited this 1 percent? That is, have you publicized the community in venues where these 1 percenters can be found, and will your community be attractive for them? You may also need a community manager to help others participate in the conversation.
2. Just as important, you must realize that for 90 percent of your community's population, "engagement" might not involve actual "participation." Don't mistake lack of actual conversational input as lack of interest. These people still read, they consider, they think...and they *use* the information you have in the community to make decisions, to make recommendations, to solve their own problems, and so forth. I have worked with companies that, when they see just 10 percent of registered users posting or responding, wonder if the effort was really worth it. But you have to remember, if someone comes to a party and just hangs out, never even opening his mouth, he still must be enjoying it in some way. Otherwise, why would he come to the party at all?

Sometimes, of course, when you venture down the social business path, you have to show upper management some results. Good community management software will help you monitor the health of your community and discern what is and is not working, providing reports that include various community metrics, benchmarking, and influencer reporting along with analysis on how to maximize your investment. Lithium's software, for instance, will compare your community's performance to the attributes of other communities, drawn from a data pool with more than a decade's worth of data. In addition to an analysis

(continued)

(Continued)

of your overall community, you can also get a handle on how successfully you are cultivating your super-users. You'll have quarterly community success checkpoints to compare to previous periods, allowing you to measure and refine your community strategy as you accumulate experience.

Using Facebook to Its Fullest

What if you can't afford an online community? Maybe you opt for a Facebook fan page. But if you do this, you need to consider adding a software tool that transforms fan discussions into actionable content that ripples throughout the organization: product development, relationship marketing, brand management, and public relations. Customer interactions, conversations, and relationships are what transform customer relationship management (CRM) into social CRM. Companies such as Get Satisfaction and others like it have adapted their successful conversational and peer-to-peer support model specifically for Facebook, allowing brands to engage social customers directly. This kind of software collects and organizes all social knowledge (questions, feedback, concerns, and praise) found inside Facebook into a central platform that can be shared and leveraged across all customer-facing channels to help a company become more customer-centric.[b]

And Then There Is Twitter

Although opinions have varied on whether Twitter has any real use or sustainability, much less as an application for enterprise businesses, as of this writing over 100 companies are actively using this microblogging tool to improve their customer service, and whether Twitter itself persists or is replaced by similar networks, our research shows that customers are turning to Twitter over traditional contact-center channels because they find that:

1. Their complaint via traditional channels has fallen through the cracks.
2. They are not being heard or taken seriously.
3. The digital ecosystem affords Twitter agents more flexibility to be objective and empathetic than agents are allowed to be in more traditional customer service channels.
4. They get immediate resolution to issues that require cross-departmental solutions.
5. They avoid the call center, where customers could feel that they end up with the raw end of the deal.
6. The crowd can participate in solving a customer's issues, providing better answers.

One great example of a company putting Twitter to productive customer service use is Carphone Warehouse (CPW), Europe's leading independent retailer of mobile phones and services, operating more than 2,400 stores in nine countries.[c] CPW observed a range of issues in the content it monitored on Twitter—complaints, such as negative in-store customer experiences, customer service requests, links to posts on third-party sites like ComplaintCommunity.com, and links to complaints on Facebook. Particularly worrying were links to third-party anti-CPW Facebook groups. What CPW wanted was to participate in the crowd, learn from its customers' reported experiences and conversations with other customers, and then use this insight to improve its services and product offerings.

One of the things that CPW learned by using Twitter is that unhappy customers will post comments in their own blog and tweet about it to their followers, including a link to the blog post that goes out to the world, in effect pushing their own blogged complaint out to a much wider audience of other customers and potential customers. Using RSS feeds, CPW began picking up these kinds of tweets and trying to turn them around within an hour. Using the Direct Message function in Twitter, CPW would contact the customer and ask him to e-mail CPW with his contact information and more details about the problem. Not only could CPW resolve a customer's issue directly, they could also detect when a problem tended to occur more frequently, showing up on many posts in the Twitter cloud. Using this crowd-sourced knowledge, it could update missing information on CPW's Web site, alert CPW's channel operations department with respect to the misunderstanding in the CPW store, amend details on the order confirmation e-mail, and notify contact centers and headquarters about which credit/debit cards can be used online and in CPW stores.

CPW found that social media provide a certain immediacy when dealing with customer issues. So the company uses Twitter to deal with first-line customer queries about handset setup, repair queries, stock availability, and delivery issues. When it tweets out an answer, it knows that many others (sometimes hundreds of people) will see it and benefit from it. Every time CPW points a customer in the right direction via Twitter, it educates thousands of others as well. For example, when customers want to know whether a certain town has a CPW store, CPW tweets them a link to the store locator. In one case, a European was on a train in the United States. The customer sent a tweet to CPW asking how to remove a SIM card from his iPhone, and CPW tweeted the customer a solution within minutes. (In the "Twitterverse," geographic boundaries are no longer a barrier to service!)

Customers frequently comment or complain about companies on third-party sites, and CPW uses RSS feeds to carefully monitor many of these sites. At Complaint Community, for instance, a customer posted the message:

I have just been into Carphone Warehouse to collect a Bluetooth earpiece for a work colleague. When I arrived at the store, I saw the Motorola Communications set for her model advertised in the shop at £29.99. When they scanned it at the register, the price came up as £59.99 . . . I have looked at the Carphone Warehouse site and still cannot find details on who to contact to rectify my complaint and hope that Complaint Community can help me.

(continued)

(Continued)

Within hours, a CPW customer service employee e-mailed the customer directly, to ask if he could help and resolve the situation:

> *Hi. . . . I work for Carphone Warehouse. I am the Online Help Manager for them. Thank you for your open and honest feedback. In the first instance, let me apologise for the experience you have had. I am currently looking into it based on the details you have provided and will be back in touch shortly. If you wish to contact me directly in the meantime, please feel free to do so by e-mail.*

After replying directly to this e-mail, the customer immediately went back to Complaint Community and posted a positive message about the help he had received:

> *I have been contacted by a helpful customer services manager . . . from Carphone Warehouse . . . I must say I am incredibly impressed, as I didn't expect this level of excellent customer service from such a huge organization.*

One thing very important to remember about social media is that once customer complaints are "in the cloud" (i.e., sent out on Twitter or posted on a Web site), they become part of a permanent record. They will always be searchable, so getting customers to update their original complaint will help a company regain positive brand sentiment. In this CPW case and others similar to it, not only will a customer get the help they need, but hundreds of other customers will likely be witness to it.

---

[a]Josh Bernoff (with Cynthia N. Pflaum, Emily Bowen, and Angie Polanco), "Persuasive Consumers Are Socially Connected," Forrester Research, Inc., February 17, 2009, available at: www.forrester.com, accessed September 1, 2010.

[b]Get Satisfaction launched March 10, 2010, under the leadership of CEO Wendy Lea. Get Satisfaction provides a "Crowd Service" tab on a brand's fan page, where customers can begin four different types of wall discussions: Ask a Question, Share an Idea, Report a Problem, or Give Praise. When customers post a question, the Get Satisfaction search engine finds similar threads to give consumers instant answers to commonly asked questions. Customers can respond to any thread (i.e., voice a similar problem, suggest a remedy, emerge as an advocate in response to another's complaint, or offer a new twist to a product suggestion). Community members can also make their experience heard by simply clicking "me too." Representatives of the brand can also participate, to offer response and establish themselves as a brand that "listens." By inviting this type of community participation inside of a community platform like Facebook, a company can get real-time market feedback, generate new product and service ideas, and encourage peer-to-peer support and advocacy.

[c]Natalie Petouhoff, "How Carphone Warehouse Uses Twitter and Social Media to Transform Customer Service," Forrester Research, Inc., January 26, 2010, available at: www.forrester.com, accessed September 1, 2010.

Dr. Petouhoff's mention of the 1-9-90 rule and of super-users (the 1- percenters) is worth thinking carefully about whenever an enterprise begins to participate in social networks of any kind. Social networks are known to follow a "power law" distribution of influence, rather like the classic 80-20 distribution of customer value known as the Pareto principle (see Chapter 5). Influence within a network—or value within a customer base—is not something that can be arrayed along a more traditional bell-curve distribution. Rather, in networks of customers, employees, constituents, or influencers, we are almost always likely to find that a relatively small number of super-users have a disproportionate influence over the network.

This means is that in order to participate in social media with any real success, an enterprise has to recruit to its team of super-users themselves. In most corporate social network situations, this should be done by providing the trappings and symbols of status—designations such as "gold" or "platinum" supporter, for instance. Status and recognition of super-users can best be facilitated in an enterprise's social networking platform by allowing readers and responders to rate the contributions of different participants, and then the platform ranks them, for all to see.

It is this noneconomic aspect of social media, characterized by a power-law distribution of influence and importance, that offers the possibility of transforming our entire economic system, over time. In a seminal work on the economics and justice of a more networked information society, *The Wealth of Networks: How Social Production Transforms Markets and Freedom*, Yochai Benkler suggests that two different kinds of rewards have always motivated human behavior: the quest for economic standing and the quest for social standing. According to Benkler:

> *These rewards are understood as instrumental and, in this regard, are highly amenable to economics. Both economic and social aspects represent "standing"— that is, a relational measure expressed in terms of one's capacity to mobilize resources. Some resources can be mobilized by money. Social relations can mobilize others. For a wide range of reasons—institutional, cultural, and possibly technological—some resources are more readily capable of being mobilized by social relations than by money. If you want to get your nephew a job at a law firm in the United States today, a friendly relationship with the firm's hiring partner is more likely to help than passing on an envelope full of cash. If this theory of social capital is correct, then sometimes you should be willing to trade off financial rewards for social capital.*[9]

If Benkler's model is indeed correct, when an enterprise goes to the trouble of creating a social media community of customers serving other customers, social rewards will be much more beneficial to motivate super-users than economic rewards. Economic rewards (from free products to cash payments) may in fact erode the effectiveness of the network entirely.

Age of Transparency

If there is one all-pervasive requirement for social media effectiveness, by people and companies alike, it is the need for honesty, straightforwardness, and transparency.

---

[9]Yochai Benkler, *The Wealth of Networks: How Social Production Transforms Markets and Freedom* (New Haven, CT: Yale University Press, 2006), pp. 95–96.

On one level, these values are driven by people themselves, because no one will tolerate deception and dissembling for long in any ordinary social relationship. Trustworthiness is probably the most important element when it comes to social relations among people, and if companies wish to engage in the same kinds of social relations as people do, then trustworthiness will be required of them as well.

It may be shameful to reflect on, but traditional mass marketing does not really require trustworthiness at all. It merely requires believability. Marketing and public relations (PR) messages are carefully crafted to be as appealing as possible, and the "spin" put on a tagline or a press release is an important marketing asset. Inherent in the whole idea of spin is the fact that there is a genuine reality—presumably known to the marketer or the author of the spin—while a separate, *created* reality is meant to be conveyed by the spin. Because they aren't stupid, and they know that sellers have a vested interest in persuading them to part with their money, customers have learned to maintain a healthy skepticism about advertising claims, in general. Consumer research bears this fact out. One report found that 14 percent of consumers say they trust advertisements while 78 percent trust the opinions of their peers, and more than half trust total strangers whose opinions they find online. There is nothing evil here, and no one can really blame a marketer for wanting to put a brand or a story in the best possible light. The only reason such deception was tolerated in the past, however, was that it was beyond anyone's capacity to detect, and even when the deception was detected, it was beyond anyone's capacity to spread the news. But no longer. Spin is out, transparency is in, and the fact that this higher ethical standard is being applied today by more and more consumers in a wider and wider variety of marketing and selling situations owes much to the social media revolution and to the kind of word-of-mouth recommendations and experience sharing that goes on among consumers now, electronically.

In September 2006, Wal-Mart set up a blog entitled "Wal-Marting Across America," which featured two intrepid recreational vehicle (RV) owners, known only as Jim and Laura, driving from Wal-Mart to Wal-Mart across the United States, visiting stores to buy things and interviewing a whole stream of ever-upbeat Wal-Mart employees, and then posting their insights on the blog. Other bloggers, however, suspected that Jim and Laura were fictitious, and not "real" people driving their RV across the country. Soon it was revealed that the two bloggers were actually paid contract writers for Wal-Mart and that they had been hired by Edelman Public Relations, the company's PR firm, to create a series of glowing articles. This ignited a firestorm of protest from others in the blogosphere, and Richard Edelman himself apologized on his own blog for having created the idea.[10]

Enterprises wanting to engage their consumers via social media need to be highly cognizant of the requirement for straightforward transparency in all social media communications. If a company creates a blog for communicating with customers and others, it has to pay close attention to the authenticity and sincerity of its postings. Spin and marketing language are just not close enough to transparency

---

[10]Pallavi Gogoi, "Wal-Mart vs. the Blogosphere: Fallout from the Retailer's Blog Scandal May End Up Hitting PR Firm Edelman," MSNBC citing *Newsweek* article, October 16, 2006, cited at: www.msnbc.msn.com/id/15319926/, accessed September 1, 2010.

for the blogosphere. A blog can be an incredibly powerful and persuasive tool for an enterprise, but only if it is used in a trustworthy and honest way.

In his manual for companies engaging their customers in social media, *The New Influencers*, Paul Gillin argues:

> *The premium on transparency may be the single greatest cultural shift that businesses will face as they engage with social media. The move from messages to conversations will tax many marketers and swamp some. The emerging culture of transparency and openness in social media is a story taking shape, but it's clear that companies that choose to participate will need to speak to their communities in very different ways.*[11]

> The move from messages to conversations will tax many marketers and swamp some.

Wal-Mart eventually came back to the blogosphere with a series of honest, employee-written blogs—conversational postings from real people about real issues, treated personally. Many of the employees who author various blog posts for Wal-Mart will write about their own kids' baseball teams in one posting, and the next day their posting will give the "straight skinny" on the best deals at their particular Wal-Mart store that day. Occasionally, a Wal-Mart blogger will even advise readers what products aren't such good deals. Most companies that have figured out how to infuse their social media activities with honesty, transparency, and authenticity have come at it from the same direction. Several thousand employees at Microsoft, for example, write occasional blog posts about their work, their company's products, and their lives in general. At most companies that have well-respected blogs that attract communities of customers, the blog-writing process itself is only loosely supervised as to content. Rules are applied to ensure quality writing and honest opinions, and to avoid legal issues and other potential dangers, but within these rules, forward-thinking enterprises allow their employees to create their own content.

As a result of social media, the word gets out, and it can't be stifled. Secrets—particularly dirty, nasty, deceptive secrets—are quickly exposed for what they are (see "Social Media: Power to the People!" later in the chapter for a great story of how one major media company was laid low by the power of the blogosphere). "Word of mouth" spreads faster than ever through social media, as customers share their experiences and impressions with each other. Good products are easier to find by checking out customer reviews, and bad products die quicker deaths, as people communicate with each other more and more prolifically. Sacha Baron Cohen's 2009 movie *Bruno*, for example, was apparently awful, at least in the eyes of those who paid to go see it the night it was released. In an event remarkable for its speed and severity, box office receipts fell 40 percent within 24 hours of the movie's release, as opening-night viewers texted and tweeted it into oblivion, interacting with their friends through what is now a vast social media infrastructure. According to *L.A. Times* film critic John Horn, this rapid a death for a bad movie was unprecedented.

---

[11]Paul Gillin, *The New Influencers: A Marketer's Guide to the New Social Media* (Sanger, CA: Quill Driver Books, 2007), p. 14.

"Even if they had a turkey, [studios] used to get two weeks of business before the stink really caught up to the film," according to Horn. "Now they have 12 hours."[12]

Most people are familiar with the kinds of product reviews that usually can be obtained online for a variety of purchases. Surprisingly, however, a majority of companies, at least as of this writing, do not host those kinds of reviews on their own Web sites. That

> **B**efore customers connected, advertising ruled. Now that customers talk to each other, it's the customer experience that counts.

is, only a small minority of marketers allow their customers to post honest reviews of the products and services that they sell, for the benefit of other customers. Research shows that when an enterprise allows honest reviews on its own Web site, its closing ratios increase—that is, the percentage of shoppers who go ahead and make purchases improves. So it is puzzling that more companies aren't already hosting product reviews. The truth is, because of technology, companies soon won't have the choice *not* to "host" reviews, anyway. Google's "Sidewiki" product allows Sidewiki members to post their comments directly "on" any Web site they visit, and those comments can then be read by any other Sidewiki members. When Sidewiki was first introduced, there was some controversy about it, with Web site publishers arguing that their own right to publish what they want online was being overridden by Google; the truth is, however, that the publishers have no right to limit what one Sidewiki member says to other Sidewiki members about anything, including their own products. Regardless of whether it is Google or Yahoo! or Bing or someone else, the technology is readily available, and the consumer demand for this kind of service is irresistible, because humans want to talk to other humans. And when they talk about products, they won't be talking about the spin on the tagline or brand promise. They'll be talking about their own customer experience with the product. Before customers connected, advertising ruled. Now that customers talk to each other, it's the customer experience that counts.

Social Media: Power to the People!

Yochai Benkler
Jack N. and Lillian R. Berkman Professor of Entrepreneurial Legal Studies, Harvard Law School; Faculty Co-Director, Berkman Center for Internet and Society, Harvard University

> Sinclair [Broadcasting Group], which owns major television stations in a number of what were considered the most competitive and important states in the 2004 election—including Ohio, Florida, Wisconsin, and Iowa— informed its staff and stations that it planned to preempt the normal schedule of its 62 stations to air a documentary called *Stolen Honor: The Wounds That Never Heal*, as a news program, a week and a half before the elections.

---

[12]NPR (formerly National Public Radio), "Summer at the Movies, and the Livin' Ain't Easy," *All Things Considered*, hosted by Robert Siegel and Madeleine Brand, July 17, 2009; transcript available at: www.npr.org/templates/transcript/transcript.php?storyId=106742097, accessed September 1, 2010.

The documentary was reported to be a strident attack on Democratic candidate John Kerry's Vietnam War service. One reporter in Sinclair's Washington bureau, who objected to the program and described it as "blatant political propaganda," was promptly fired. . . . The story of Sinclair's plans broke on Saturday, October 9, 2004, in the *Los Angeles Times*. . . . By Tuesday, October 12, the Democratic National Committee announced that it was filing a complaint with the Federal Elections Commission (FEC), while 17 Democratic senators wrote a letter to the chairman of the Federal Communications Commission (FCC), demanding that the commission investigate whether Sinclair was abusing the public trust in the airwaves. Neither the FEC nor the FCC, however, acted or intervened throughout the episode.

Alongside these standard avenues of response in the traditional public sphere of commercial mass media, their regulators, and established parties, a very different kind of response was brewing on the Net, in the blogosphere. On the morning of October 9, 2004, the *Los Angeles Times* story was blogged on a number of political blogs—Josh Marshall on talkingpointsmemo.com, Chris Bowers on MyDD.com, and Markos Moulitsas on dailyKos.com. By midday that Saturday, October 9, two efforts aimed at organizing opposition to Sinclair were posted in the dailyKos and MyDD. A "boycott-Sinclair" site was set up by one individual, and was pointed to by these blogs. Chris Bowers on MyDD provided a complete list of Sinclair stations and urged people to call the stations and threaten to picket and boycott. By Sunday, October 10, the dailyKos posted a list of national advertisers with Sinclair, urging readers to call them. On Monday, October 11, MyDD linked to that list, while another blog, theleftcoaster.com, posted a variety of action agenda items, from picketing affiliates of Sinclair to suggesting that readers oppose Sinclair license renewals, providing a link to the FCC site explaining the basic renewal process and listing public-interest organizations to work with. That same day, another individual, Nick Davis, started a Web site, BoycottSBG.com, on which he posted the basic idea that a concerted boycott of local advertisers was the way to go, while another site, stopsinclair.org, began pushing for a petition. . . . By 5:00 A.M. on the dawn of Tuesday, October 12, however, TalkingPoints began pointing toward Davis's database on BoycottSBG.com. By 10:00 that morning, Marshall posted on TalkingPoints a letter from an anonymous reader, which began by saying: "I've worked in the media business for 30 years and I guarantee you that sales is what these local TV stations are all about. They don't care about license renewal or overwhelming public outrage. They care about sales only, so only local advertisers can affect their decisions." This reader then outlined a plan for how to watch and list all local advertisers, and then write to the sales managers—not general managers—of the local stations and tell them which advertisers you are going to call, and then call those. By 1:00 P.M. Marshall posted a story of his own experience with this strategy. He used Davis's database to identify an Ohio affiliate's local advertisers. He tried to call the sales manager of the station, but could not get through.

(continued)

(Continued)

He then called the advertisers. The post is a "how to" instruction manual, including admonitions to remember that the advertisers know nothing of this, the story must be explained, and accusatory tones avoided, and so on. Marshall then began to post letters from readers who explained with whom they had talked—a particular sales manager, for example—and who were then referred to national headquarters. He continued to emphasize that advertisers were the right addressees. By 5:00 P.M. that same Tuesday, Marshall was reporting more readers writing in about experiences, and continued to steer his readers to sites that helped them to identify their local affiliate's sales manager and their advertisers.

By the morning of Wednesday, October 13, the boycott database already included eight hundred advertisers, and was providing sample letters for users to send to advertisers. Later that day, BoycottSBG reported that some participants in the boycott had received reply e-mails telling them that their unsolicited e-mail constituted illegal spam. Davis explained that the CAN-SPAM Act, the relevant federal statute, applied only to commercial spam, and pointed users to a law firm site that provided an overview of CAN-SPAM.

By October 14, the boycott effort was clearly bearing fruit. Davis reported that Sinclair affiliates were threatening advertisers who cancelled advertisements with legal action, and called for volunteer lawyers to help respond. Within a brief period, he collected more than a dozen volunteers to help the advertisers. Later that day, another blogger at grassrootsnation.com had set up a utility that allowed users to send an e-mail to all advertisers in the BoycottSBG database. By the morning of Friday, October 15, Davis was reporting more than fifty advertisers pulling ads, and three or four mainstream media reports had picked up the boycott story and reported on it. That day, an analyst at Lehman Brothers issued a research report that downgraded the expected twelve-month outlook for the price of Sinclair stock, citing concerns about loss of advertiser revenue and risk of tighter regulation. Mainstream news reports over the weekend and the following week systematically placed that report in context of local advertisers pulling their ads from Sinclair. On Monday, October 18, the company's stock price dropped by 8 percent (while the S&P [Standard & Poor's index] 500 rose by about half a percent). The following morning, the stock dropped a further 6 percent, before beginning to climb back, as Sinclair announced that it would not show *Stolen Honor*, but would provide a balanced program with only portions of the documentary and one that would include arguments on the other side.

Source: Excerpted from Yochai Benkler, *The Wealth of Networks: How Social Production Transforms Markets and Freedom* (New Haven, CT: Yale University Press, 2006), pp. 220–223.

Summary

In this chapter, we have outlined how a forward-thinking enterprise can best employ the tools and capabilities of social media to engage with customers. Our goal here has been to discuss the principles, since the technology will continue to change rapidly. Without question, social media has exponentially increased opportunities for companies to interact with their customers and develop Learning Relationships at rates previously impossible. But at the same time, successful marketing today requires a much higher standard of trustworthiness and transparency.

Enterprises, however, cannot simply interact with individual customers and expect them to remain loyal. The Learning Relationship must mature even further. The enterprise needs to address another task in the Identify-Differentiate-Interact-Customize process by *customizing* the relationship with each customer—by modifying how it behaves with her, how it communicates with her, and how it manufactures products or provides services for her. A relationship can't exist without customization; without a change in behavior that results from feedback, the best a company can do is give the appearance of a relationship. But how can customization be done effectively and efficiently? We take a closer look at that issue in Chapter 10, after we consider the privacy issue that inevitably arises when we address customer interaction and data.

Food for Thought

1. You've been appointed as the new chief marketing officer (CMO) for a large packaged-goods company. Your CEO has decided that your company will be the premier "relationship" company in your industry.
   - What could that mean?
   - How will you execute that?
   - What will you use as data collection tools?
   - What role will interactivity play in your plans?
     What role will e-mail play? Mobile devices? Social networking platforms? Be as specific as you can.
2. Now imagine you work for a large automotive company and answer all the questions in number 1. Are your answers different? Why or why not?
3. Now answer the questions in number 1 for:
   - A natural gas company
   - A retail shoe chain
   - A company that makes pneumatic valves for construction
   - The U.S. Navy
   - Other kinds of organizations (you decide)

Glossary

Crowd service   Customers helping other customers solve problems online.

Open source   Products (software, etc) created by unpaid individuals, usually in collaboration with others online, typically distributed for free.

Social media   Interactive services and Web sites that allow users to create their own content and share their own views for others to consume. Blogs and microblogs (e.g., Twitter) are a form of social media, because users "publish" their opinions or views for everyone. Facebook, LinkedIn, and MySpace are examples of social media that facilitate making contact, interacting with, and following others. YouTube and Flickr are examples of social media that allow users to share creative work with others. Even Wikipedia represents a form of social media, as users collaborate interactively to publish more and more accurate encyclopedia entries.

CHAPTER **9**

Privacy and Customer Feedback

Being good is good business.

—Anita Roddick

> Getting customer information is easy. You can buy it from the government, from list brokers, from competitors even. But getting customer information *from* customers is *not* easy, as we've seen in the last two chapters. Yet it's absolutely necessary, because the only real competitive advantage an enterprise can have derives from the information it gathers from a customer, which enables it to do something for him that no one else can. Competitors without a customer's personal information are at a disadvantage. That is the one compelling reason an enterprise must interact with its customers and reward them for revealing their personal information. It is also the main reason why an enterprise should never misuse the information it owns about a customer or violate a customer's trust—because a customer is the most valuable asset the firm has, and the ability to get a customer to share information depends so much on the comfort level a customer has with giving that information to an enterprise.

Interestingly, for the first time since we all became aware of privacy as an issue, enterprises and customers share a common interest: protecting and securing the customer's information. At least that's true of customers who are thinking about the implications of their far-flung data and of enterprises that are building their value through strategies designed to build the value of the customer base.

In this chapter, we first look at some general privacy issues and how they are being addressed. We next examine the distinct issues raised by data held and exchanged online.

Every day, millions of people provide personally identifiable information about themselves to data collection experts. As a result, an average U.S. consumer is buffeted by thousands of marketing messages every day[1]—far too many to hit any consumer's consciousness. How many do *you* remember from yesterday? Consumers

---

[1]The number now circulating (on the level of urban legend) is 5,000 marketing messages daily. At the least, Forrester predicts an average of 9,000 marketing messages sent annually to the primary inbox by 2014. Shar VanBoskirk, "U.S. Interactive Marketing Forecast,

sometimes unknowingly divulge their personal data during commercial transactions, financial arrangements, and survey responses. And the Web has escalated the privacy debate to new heights. Never before has technology enabled companies to acquire information about customers so easily. Watchdog privacy advocates and government regulators are mobilizing against the threat to a consumer's right to privacy.

Consider these points:

- Privacy policies of individual companies vary tremendously, as does compliance with these policies (largely self-generated and self-enforced).
- Privacy preferences vary tremendously among individuals and across nations and cultures.
- Hundreds of new privacy laws have been introduced worldwide in the past 10 years.
- Courts around the world are awarding significant damages to consumers and Internet users over claims of privacy violation.
- New technologies that support data collection, Internet monitoring, online surveillance, data mining, automatic mailing, personal searching, phishing, identity spoofing, and identity theft (now a billion-dollar industry)[2] are rolling out into the electronic marketplace every month.
- Personalized, customized products and services over the Internet—most of which require users to provide more personal information than they have ever given to companies before—are growing.[3]

And yet, in the twenty-first century, we realize that customer data are among the most valuable assets an enterprise can have, because the personal information about a particular customer that no other enterprise has is a unique asset that can provide an insurmountable competitive advantage in dealing with that single customer. For a customer-based enterprise to be successful in this century, it needs to protect that information—to hold it sacred. Privacy and personalization are inextricably interwoven.

> In the twenty-first century, we realize that customer data are among the most valuable assets an enterprise can have, because the personal information about a particular customer that no other enterprise has is a unique asset that can provide an insurmountable competitive advantage in dealing with that single customer. For a customer-based enterprise to be successful in this century, it needs to protect that information—to hold it sacred.

Customers who feel like they could lose control over their own information are not likely to become willing participants in a dialogue. Privacy should not be taken lightly by the customer-based enterprise.

For the enterprise interested in increasing its share of each customer's business, there has to be a balance between getting enough information from customers to help them do business with the firm while respecting their right to lead a private life. The dilemma for the customer-strategy firm is how to remain sensitive to privacy

---

2009–2014," Forrester Research, Inc., July 6, 2009, p. 19; available at: www.forrester.com, accessed September 1, 2010.

[2] Gary Garner, "ID Theft Billion-Dollar Industry, Says Federal Trade Commission," *Mississippi Business Journal,* July 21–27, 2008, p. 35.

[3] Charles Jennings and Lori Fena, *The Hundredth Window* (New York: Free Press, 2000).

while improving the business to suit each customer's individual needs. This is in stark contrast to a product-selling company, which likely views privacy simply as a roadblock on the road to profitability.

The privacy debate continues as the interactive and interconnected era matures. Despite the ongoing controversy over a person's legal right to privacy, customers find it difficult to quantify the damage they incur when their privacy has been violated. It is difficult to place a monetary value on the abuse of personal information, unlike other crimes, such as a car theft. For that matter, what does it cost when someone's credit card number is exposed to a third party who does not use it?

Our society subscribes to two antithetical beliefs simultaneously: that people should have the right to remain inconspicuous to others but also have the right to learn the identity of someone else when we need to. For instance, a consumer might want anonymity when shopping, especially online. But the same person might support a system that reveals the identity of computer hackers or those who plant e-viruses. To ponder further, our society requires the display of license plate numbers, for public revelation of each automobile owner. Should we also have "license plates" for Internet users so it would be easy to track them down when they commit an offense, such as identity theft or launching a virus maliciously?

Two events since the beginning of the century have shaped our opinion of privacy, at least in the Western world:

1. The terrorist attacks in the United States on September 11, 2001, called into question the wisdom of ironclad privacy protection and the anonymizing technologies available online.
2. The increased capabilities of social media and their surge in popularity, especially among younger consumers (see Chapter 8), have significantly increased the volume and detail of personal information many people make available online.

A 2008 study by the American Consumer Institute's (ACI) Center for Citizen Research found that online users' concern about privacy issues is continuing to rise: 74 percent were "very concerned" about identity theft, and 61 percent reported "great concern" about their privacy due to online tracking programs.[4] In contrast, a Forrester study conducted that same year found that only 35 percent of 18- to 28-year-olds are concerned with sharing information online.[5] Ironically, although most Americans do seem to think privacy is fairly important, a lot of U.S. popular culture has been inspired by snooping: So-called reality television programs, such as *Survivor, Wife Swap,* and *Extreme Makeover: Home Edition,* have enabled viewers to peer into the private lives of ordinary *other* people. It has become a cultural norm to be flies on the walls of a stranger's personal conversations when his cell phone

---

[4]"Consumer Concern Rises about Online Threats, ACI Survey Shows," American Consumer Institute's Center for Citizen Research, September 29, 2008; available at: www.theamerican consumer.org/2008/09/29/consumer-concern-rises-about-online-threats-aci-survey-shows/, accessed September 1, 2010.

[5]Dave Frankland, "Consumer Privacy Is a Ticking Time Bomb for Customer Intelligence Executives," Forrester Research, Inc., October 29, 2009; available at: www.forrester.com, accessed September 1, 2010.

rings while riding a bus or a plane. Voyeurism seems to be more in vogue, so long as no one is snooping on *me*. But the increasing popularity and use of social media has led to what might also be an epidemic of exhibitionism (discussed later in this chapter), at least among the younger generation. It's possible that kids who were born after 2000 will simply not get the idea of privacy, since they will have been raised in a world of increasing transparency.

Privacy concerns have long existed in traditional shopping methods, not just the Web. Walk into a supermarket or department store and the customer is often asked to hand over a loyalty card in exchange for a purchase coupon. But what if he buys something in a retail store, and simply uses a standard bank credit card? In such a case, the store has very little way of tracing the information about that shopping transaction and may have difficulty linking it to a particular customer, unless the customer is having the merchandise delivered. (It should be noted that the credit card company will have a complete record of that transactional information, for that customer, store to store.) Nordstrom Inc. has found a way to gather information from nearly all in-store purchases, regardless of payment type. Its store personnel ask customers for permission to affix a bar code to the back of a customer's own (non-Nordstrom) credit card, giving the store the capability to track its customers' purchases made with other credit cards.

Profiling of a customer's personal data is standard protocol in the direct-mail industry and has been for nearly a century. Traditionally, this has meant that catalog retailers and credit card companies have collected names and addresses for their own use and have sold or rented those lists to other direct marketers. Phone a catalog merchant, and the buying process involves divulging an address and phone number. For that matter, call L.L. Bean or many other catalog companies, and the customer service representative might even be able to identify the customer before he states his name, thanks to the caller identification (ID) technology integrated into the company's call center. Interactive voice response systems, when programmed with metadata detailing the kind of calls individual customers have made in the past, can ensure that the most valuable customers end up at the top of the queue to speak directly with a customer service representative.[6]

Remembering a customer and his logistical information makes it easier for him to order and also leads him to believe he is important to the enterprise. The Internet offers the greatest opportunity to date for gathering personal customer information, as long as a mutually valuable relationship between provider and consumer is honored. Over time, data collected about Web-site visitors empower companies with a keen ability to identify their most valuable customers and deploy relevant marketing campaigns—as long as the information customers enter is true, that is.[7] But, in general, customers themselves are recognizing the convenience of being known by the Web sites they visit: A 2006 Ponemon Institute survey found only

[6]Patrick Barnard, "Call Center Efficiency through Improved Customer Categorization," TMCnet, December 31, 2009; available at: www.tmcnet.com/channels/call-center-solutions/articles/71846-call-center-efficiency-through-improved-customer-categorization.htm, accessed September 1, 2010.

[7]Amit Poddar, Jill Mosteller, and Pam Scholder Ellen, "Consumers' Rules of Engagement in Online Information Exchanges," *Journal of Consumer Affairs* 43, no. 3: 419–448, Capturing Visitor Feedback," CyberDialogue, March 1997.

8 percent of people "very frequently" delete cookies (down from 14 percent in 2004) and 24 percent "never" delete them. Further clarifying that convenience is outweighing past privacy concerns, 63 percent said marketers should understand their interest before advertising to them, and 55 percent said that Web ads that suit their needs improve or greatly improve their online experience.[8]

However, even questionable security is a deal breaker for most customers. Sixty-three percent of respondents to a National Cyber Security Alliance and Symantec poll did not complete a Web site purchase due to security concerns—with the majority of those choosing not to purchase "simply not sure" about whether the site was secure. As important as convenience may be, more than 75 percent of respondents said they would be just as likely to make a purchase from a Web site if it required additional steps to verify their identity.[9] Clearly, customers want both maximum convenience and maximum (identity) security, creating a very precise tightrope for customer-centered businesses to walk.

> Managing customer relationships in the interactive age requires enterprises to collect information about customers in a "virtuous cycle" in which they can deliver additional value to individual customers.

Enterprises gather information about their customers and create loyalty programs to build lasting relationships. But with increasingly complex product choices, many sophisticated customers enjoy comparing and contrasting products to find the best price and most efficient service—and want both the information and the privacy to make a decision on their own terms, without being pressured too soon to make a purchase. The goal, therefore, is for the enterprise to find out as much information *about* a customer and use it *for* that customer to make the buying experience more valuable to that customer in various ways. Managing customer relationships in the interactive age requires enterprises to collect information about customers in a "virtuous cycle" in which they can deliver additional value to individual customers. Once the customer begins receiving personalized attention and customized products, he is motivated to divulge more information about himself.

For instance, a recent Forrester report, which concluded that few consumers perceive a value exchange for sharing personal data, did find that some consumers surveyed are "willing" or "extremely willing" to share personal information in exchange for:

- Receiving product samples—34 percent
- Gaining entry in a sweepstakes or contest—22 percent
- Receiving better products or services—20 percent
- Receiving ads and offers relevant to their wants and needs—18 percent
- Finding/meeting people with similar interests—9 percent[10]

---

[8]Kelly Shermach, "Growing Acceptance of Cookies," *Sales and Marketing Management* 158, no. 7 (2006): 20.

[9]"Americans' Online Shopping Decisions Affected by Security Concerns, Poll Finds," *PR Newswire* 17 (November 2009), *Academic OneFile*, accessed 8 March 2010.

[10]Dave Frankland, "Consumer Privacy Is a Ticking Time Bomb for Customer Intelligence Executives," Forrester Research, Inc., October 29, 2009.

Although the preponderance of evidence shows that consumers do like the customized offerings and other advantages companies can give them by tracking their data, it is essential to guarantee that the customized benefits provided will not jeopardize their privacy. Customers must know that the company will use that data in a limited way for services agreed on in advance. Without such trust, customization is not a benefit. Once earned, trust in an enterprise enhances customer loyalty. But enterprises need to address customer concerns about privacy, to offer guarantees, and stick to them. Those enterprises that gain the customer's trust first often will have the first-mover advantage. (We talk more about privacy pledges later in this chapter.)

Some believe that a customer might be more trusting of an enterprise and would provide the personal information that can foster a mutually beneficial relationship if the enterprise simply first asks the customer his permission to do so. The relationship in which a customer has agreed to receive personalized messages and customized products forms the basis of *permission marketing*, an idea from author Seth Godin.

Permission Marketing

Seth Godin
Blogger and Author

Two hundred years ago, natural resources and raw materials were scarce. People needed land to grow food, metal to turn into pots, and silicates and other natural elements to make windows for houses. Tycoons who cornered the market in these and other resources made a fortune. By making a market in a scarce resource, you can make a profit.

With the birth of the Industrial Revolution, and the growth of our consumer economy, the resource scarcity shifted from raw materials to finished goods. Factories were at capacity. The great industrialists, like Carnegie and Ford, earned their millions by providing what the economy demanded. Marketers could call the shots, because other options were scarce.

Once factories caught up with demand, marketers developed brands that consumers would desire and pay a premium to own. People were willing to walk a mile for a Camel, and knew things go better with Coke. When brands were new and impressive, owning the right brand was vital.

But in today's free market there are plenty of factories, plenty of brands, and way too many choices. With just a little effort and a little savings we can get almost anything we want. You can find a TV set in every house in this country. People throw away their broken microwave ovens instead of having them repaired.

This surplus situation, or abundance of goods, is especially clear when it comes to information and services. Making another copy of a software program or printing another CD costs almost nothing. Bookstores compete to offer 50,000, 100,000, or even 1 million different books—each for less than $25. There's a huge surplus of intellectual property and services out there.

Imagine a tropical island populated by people with simple needs and plenty of resources. You won't find a bustling economy there. That's because you need two things in order to have an economy: people who want things, and a scarcity of things they want. Without scarcity, there's no basis for an economy.

When there's an abundance of any commodity, the value of that commodity plummets. If a commodity can be produced at will and costs little or nothing to create, it's not likely to be scarce, either. That's the situation with information and services today. They're abundant and cheap. Information on the Web, for example, is plentiful and free.

There is one critical resource, though, that is in chronically short supply. Bill Gates has no more than you do. And even Warren Buffett can't buy more. That scarce resource is *time*. And in light of today's information glut, that means there's a vast shortage of *attention*.

The combined shortage of time and attention is unique in today's information age. Consumers are now willing to pay handsomely to save time, while marketers are eager to pay bundles to get attention.

> Consumers are now willing to pay handsomely to save time, while marketers are eager to pay bundles to get attention.

Interruption Marketing is the enemy of anyone trying to save time. By constantly interrupting what we are doing at any given moment, the marketer who interrupts us not only tends to fail at selling his product, but wastes our most coveted commodity, time. In the long run, therefore, Interruption Marketing is doomed as a mass-marketing tool. The cost to the consumer is just too high.

The alternative is Permission Marketing, which offers the consumer an opportunity to *volunteer* to be marketed to. By talking only to volunteers, Permission Marketing guarantees that consumers pay more attention to the marketing message. It allows marketers to tell their story calmly and succinctly, without fear of being interrupted by competitors or Interruption Marketers. It serves both consumers and marketers in a symbiotic exchange.

Permission Marketing encourages consumers to participate in a long-term, interactive marketing campaign in which they are rewarded in some way for paying attention to increasingly relevant messages. Imagine your marketing message being read by 70 percent of the prospects you send it to (not 5 percent or even 1 percent). Then imagine that more than 35 percent responded. That's what happens when you interact with your prospects one at a time, with individual messages, exchanged with their permission over time.

Permission marketing is anticipated, personal, relevant.

Anticipated. *People look forward to hearing from you.*
Personal. *The messages are directly related to the individual.*
Relevant. *The marketing is about something the prospect is interested in.*

(continued)

(Continued)

I know what you're thinking. There's a catch. If you have to personalize every customer message, that's prohibitive. If you're still thinking within the framework of traditional marketing, you're right. But in today's information age, working with customers individually is not as difficult as it sounds. Permission Marketing takes the cost of interrupting the consumer and spreads it out, over not one message, but dozens of messages. And this leverage leads to substantial competitive advantages and profits. While your competition continues to interrupt strangers with mediocre results, your Permission Marketing campaign is turning strangers into friends and friends into customers.

The easiest way to contrast the Interruption Marketer with the Permission Marketer is with an analogy about getting married. It also serves to exemplify how sending multiple individualized messages over time works better than a single message, no matter how impressive that single message is.

Two Ways to Get Married

The Interruption Marketer buys an extremely expensive suit. New shoes. Fashionable accessories. Then, working with the best database and marketing strategies, selects the demographically ideal singles bar.

Walking into the singles bar, the Interruption Marketer marches up to the nearest person and proposes marriage. If turned down, the Interruption Marketer repeats the process on every person in the bar.

If the Interruption Marketer comes up empty-handed after spending the entire evening proposing, it is obvious that the blame should be placed on the suit and the shoes. The tailor is fired. The strategy expert who picked the bar is fired. And the Interruption Marketer tries again at a different singles bar.

If this sounds familiar, it should. It's the way most large marketers look at the world. They hire an agency. They build fancy ads. They "research" the ideal place to run the ads. They interrupt people and hope that one in a hundred will go ahead and buy something. Then, when they fail, they fire their agency!

The other way to get married is a lot more fun, a lot more rational, and a lot more successful. It's called dating.

A Permission Marketer goes on a date. If it goes well, the two of them go on another date. And then another. Until, after 10 or 12 dates, both sides can really communicate with each other about their needs and desires. After 20 dates they meet each other's families. Finally, after three or four months of dating, the Permission Marketer proposes marriage.

Permission Marketing is just like dating. It turns strangers into friends and friends into lifetime customers. Many of the rules of dating apply, and so do many of the benefits.

Five Steps to Dating Your Customer

Every interaction must offer the prospective customer an incentive for volunteering. In the vernacular of dating, that means you have to offer something that makes it interesting enough to go out on a first date. A first date, after all, represents a big investment in time, money, and ego. So there had better be reason enough to volunteer.

Without a selfish reason to continue dating, your new potential customer (and your new potential date) will refuse you a second chance. If you don't provide a benefit to the consumer for paying attention, your offer will suffer the same fate as every other ad campaign that's vying for their attention. It will be ignored.

The incentive you offer to the customer can range from information, to entertainment, to a sweepstakes, to outright payment for the prospect's attention. But the incentive must be overt, obvious, and clearly delivered.

This is the most obvious difference between Permission Marketing and Interruption Marketing. Interruption Marketers spend all their time interrupting strangers, in an almost pitiful attempt to bolster popularity and capture attention. Permission Marketers spend as little time and money talking to strangers as they can. Instead they move as quickly as they can to turn strangers into prospects who choose to "opt in" to a series of communication.

Second, using the attention offered by the consumer, the marketer offers a curriculum over time, teaching the consumer about the product or service he has to offer. The Permission Marketer knows that the first date is an opportunity to sell the other person on a second date. Every step along the way has to be interesting, useful, and relevant.

Since the prospect has agreed to pay attention, it's much easier to teach him about your product. Instead of filling each ensuing message with entertainment designed to attract attention or with sizzle designed to attract the attention of strangers, the Permission Marketer is able to focus on product benefits—specific, focused ways this product will help that prospect. Without question, this ability to talk freely over time is the most powerful element of this marketing approach.

The third step involves reinforcing the incentive. Over time, an incentive wears out. Just as your date may tire of even the finest restaurant, the prospective customer may show fatigue with the same repeated incentive. The Permission Marketer must work to reinforce the incentive, to be sure that the attention continues. This is surprisingly easy. Because this is a two-way dialogue, not a narcissistic monologue, the marketer can adjust the incentives being offered and fine-tune them for *each* prospect. Along with reinforcing the incentive, the fourth step is to increase the level of permission the marketer receives from the potential customer. Now I won't go into detail on what step of the dating process this corresponds to, but in marketing terms, the goal is to motivate the consumer to give more and more permission over time. Permission to gather more data about the customer's personal life, or hobbies, or interests. Permission to offer a new category of product for the customer's consideration. Permission to provide a product sample. The range of permission you can obtain from a customer is very wide and limited only by its relevance to the customer.

(continued)

(Continued)

The goal is to motivate the consumer to give more and more permission over time. Permission to gather more data about the customer's personal life, or hobbies, or interests. Permission to offer a new category of product for the customer's consideration. Permission to provide a product sample. The range of permission you can obtain from a customer is very wide and limited only by its relevance to the customer.

Over time, the marketer uses the permission he's obtained to change consumer behavior—that is, get them to say "I do." That's how you turn permission into profits. After permission is granted, that's how it becomes a truly significant asset for the marketer. Now you can live happily ever after by repeating the aforementioned process while selling your customer more and more products. In other words, the fifth and final step is to leverage your permission into a profitable situation for both of you. Remember, you have access to the most valuable thing a customer can offer—attention.

Permission Marketing Is an Old Concept with New Relevance

Permission Marketing isn't as glamorous as hiring Steven Spielberg to direct a commercial starring a bevy of supermodels. It isn't as easy as running an ad a few more times. It isn't as cheap as building a Web site and hoping that people find it on a search engine. In fact, it's hard work. And it costs money to invest in what it takes to get a customer's permission.

Worst of all, Permission Marketing requires patience. Permission Marketing campaigns grow over time—the opposite of what most marketers look for these days. And Permission Marketing requires a leap of faith. Even a bad interruption campaign gets some results right away, while a permission campaign requires infrastructure and a belief in the durability of the permission concept before it blossoms with success.

But unlike Interruption Marketing, Permission Marketing is a measurable process. It evolves over time for every company that uses it. It becomes an increasingly valuable asset. The more you commit to Permission Marketing campaigns, the better they work over time. And these fast-moving, leveragable processes are the key to success in our cluttered age.

So if Permission Marketing is so effective, and the ideas behind it are not really new, why was the concept not used with effectiveness years ago?

Permission Marketing has been around forever (or at least as long as dating), but it takes advantage of new technology better than any other forms of marketing. The Internet is the greatest direct mail medium of all time, and the low cost of frequent interaction makes it ideal for Permission Marketing.

Originally, the Internet captured the attention of Interruption Marketers. They rushed in, spent billions of dollars applying their Interruption Marketing techniques, and discovered almost total failure. Permission Marketing is the tool that unlocks the power of the Internet. The leverage it brings to this new medium, combined with the pervasive clutter that infects the Internet and virtually every other medium, makes Permission Marketing the most powerful trend in marketing for the next decade.

As new forms of media develop and clutter becomes ever more intense, it's the asset of permission that will generate profits for marketers.

Source: Excerpted from Seth Godin, *Permission Marketing* (New York: Simon & Schuster, 1999). Adapted April 16, 2010.

Trust, as discussed in Chapter 2, is always critical. Customers are dubious of unfamiliar enterprises that have not been recommended to them. Some customers won't buy anything online until they've seen other customers' reviews and comments, even though those other customers are total strangers.

Although we talk about privacy as if it were a single topic, it is really an umbrella term, and if you ask customers what bothers them about privacy, you will get several answers.

- The most common is a concern about criminal activity—misuse of stolen credit card numbers, usurpation of identity. This concern nearly always comes back to the issue of data security.
- Distinct from the first point is a concern about others knowing things about them they would rather not have "out there" as common knowledge.
- Another issue is the idea that they would rather not be bothered if they don't want to be: spam is driving them crazy, and marketing calls at dinner are a nuisance.

Meanwhile, if you ask enterprise executives what the term *privacy* means to *them,* and they're honest with you, you may find that *privacy* is a risk of fines on each breached record and a potential minefield for public relations. To the lawyers, it may be about regulation compliance and litigation avoidance. But to those in the organization whose mission is to build the value of the customer base, *privacy* is what customers think it is, and it's also:

- Getting information from customers who are comfortable giving it.
- Using the information to build mutual value with each customer.
- Protecting customer data as a valuable competitive asset (through data security, protective processes, and customer-focused culture).
- Communicating data protection to customers.

Relationships require trust, and privacy is one of its underpinnings.

Moreover, as each organization moves to globalize its operations, its leaders will need to be aware of and comply with the many legal requirements of the nations in which it serves customers, and they will need to respect the individual cultures of these countries. Enterprises will also need to protect the accuracy, transmission, and accessibility of their customer records. In the next few sections, we examine how enterprises protect the precious customer data they collect. We also peer into the many differences between privacy rules in the United States and Europe.

Individual Privacy and Data Protection

Larry A. Ponemon, Ph.D.
Chairman, The Ponemon Institute

Businesses and governments have a responsibility to maintain the security and integrity of personal data that they process. The competitive pressure to profit from data collected about a customer by analyzing it for the purposes of personalization and customization collides with privacy concerns. Advocates believe it can help customers save time and effort and supply them with better targeted offers and improved customer service. When users provide personally identifiable information during a transaction, they are looking for assurance that their personal data will not be misused. Although the data can be traced to a computer, most data collected are anonymous. It is when a user provides personally identifiable information by filling out a form or volunteering personal information during a transaction that the concerns of potential abuse grow stronger. Other areas of particular concern include linking personally identifiable profiles with more extensive demographic or credit card information or connecting and reselling information from disparate data sources.

Chief Privacy Officers Protect Customer Privacy—Ours or Theirs?

Some enterprises, recognizing the new importance of the spectrum of privacy issues, particularly if their business faces global trading issues, have created the full-time position of Chief Privacy Officer instead of assigning this responsibility to existing positions, such as the Chief Information Officer or the Chief Technology Officer. Corporate icons such as American Express, Citigroup, Prudential Insurance, and AT&T have hired privacy officers who in many cases report directly to the chairman or the CEO. At the Internet Advertising Bureau's Privacy Forum, Rich LeFurgy, Internet Advertising Bureau chairman and general partner, Walden VC, explained, "At the center of all business models is consumers. Protecting their PII (personally identifiable information) is the key to the future."

The responsibilities of the chief privacy officers (CPOs) (often undertaken by the Chief Information Officer) include addressing the following:

- How does the company ensure that consumers will be notified about what information is collected?
- How can the company protect personal data from unauthorized use?

- How does a company provide consumers access to their personal information and the ability to change it?
- How does a company have guidelines for the use of personal information?
- Does it have a complete data-flow map showing the flow of information?
- What procedures ensure consumers are notified of changes in privacy policies?
- Is notification enough? Or is awareness required?
- What procedures exist to ensure business partners use personal information according to policy?
- Is compliance enough? Or is establishing trust required?
- How often does the company train employees on fair information and privacy practices?

As enterprises continue to globalize their operations, they need to be sensitive to, and in compliance with, the legal requirements and cultural sensitivities of the individuals with whom they do business. In addition, they need to protect adequately the accuracy, integrity, transmission, and accessibility of their electronic records and, in some nations, paper records. Regulatory compliance is not achieved without cost to the organization; and, where regulation exists, it must be complied with. However, beyond reducing the risk of regulatory noncompliance, the benefits of good privacy practice include:

- *Reduction of cost* by eliminating the collection and management of unnecessary information.
- *Reduction of the risks* associated with inaccurate or out-of-date information.
- *Improvement in consumer and employee trust* and confidence in the use and security of personal data.

Ultimately, the business concerns about issues surrounding privacy fall into two categories:

1. *Individual privacy.* On an international level, the United Nations Declaration of Human Rights and the European Convention on Human Rights recognize privacy as a fundamental human right. Many nations have constitutional provisions, legislation, or court decisions that define the individual's right to privacy as the right to be left alone—to be free from unwarranted intrusion.
2. *Data protection.* Businesses and governments have a responsibility to maintain the security and integrity of the data that they process. For businesses, this primarily means information gathered about individual customers and employees that is collected in the course of completing business transactions.

Today, consumer privacy concerns have been heightened by the technological changes surrounding the Internet. Technological improvements also put

(continued)

(Continued)

new pressures on businesses. Online companies that are under intense pressure to differentiate themselves are motivated to enhance value by outfitting their sites with increased personalization, requiring more granular customer data. Consumers express concern that inaccurate information can be used against them or affect them in the future, that personal information will be disclosed to third parties without their knowledge and consent, and that the security that surrounds their data is lacking. Identity theft provides just one example of how real these concerns are.

A comprehensive approach to data protection and privacy compliance identifies and resolves the issues while noncompliance creates unnecessary risks. By identifying the elements of current regulatory and self-regulatory approaches to privacy, it is possible to derive a set of common elements that can serve as a starting point for an organization's global privacy compliance initiatives. Such a framework should include the following key elements.[a]

- *Notice*. The enterprise provides data subjects with clear and prominent notice of who is collecting their personal information, the intended use of the information, and its intended disclosure.
- *Choice*. The enterprise offers data subjects choices as to how their personal identifying information will be used beyond the use for which it was provided; choices would encompass both internal secondary uses such as marketing back to data subjects, and external secondary uses such as disclosing data to other entities.
- *Access*. The company enables data subjects to obtain appropriate access to information that it holds and to correct or amend that information where necessary.
- *Data security*. The enterprise takes reasonable precautions to protect data from loss, misuse, alteration, or destruction and ensure that those to whom data is transferred have adequate privacy protection.
- *Data integrity*. The firm keeps only personal data relevant for the purpose for which it has been gathered, consistent with the elements of notice and choice.
- *Onward transfer*. The firm transfers data only as consistent with the elements of notice, choice, and security.
- *Enforcement*. The company ensures compliance with key privacy elements and provides recourse for individuals, such as complaint and dispute procedures, verification of ongoing compliance, and obligation to remedy problems arising from noncompliance.

Source: Adapted from Larry Ponemon, Ph.D., "Individual Privacy and Data Protection," in Don Peppers and Martha Rogers, Ph.D., *Managing Customer Relationships: A Strategic Framework* (Hoboken, NJ: John Wiley & Sons, 2004), pp. 228–232.
[a]Wylie Wong, "Sun Switches Gears on Security," CNET News, July 25, 2002.

Privacy in Europe Is a Different World

The privacy debate in Europe is just as fierce as in the United States, although the rules about privacy are starkly different in Europe. In the United States, an individual's habits and behavior may be examined by an employer, a retail merchant, and by companies on the Web. This information is then used to target the customer for marketing purposes or is resold to other companies. By contrast, in most European countries, it is illegal to monitor an individual under any of these circumstances and use the information to target the customer. The ground rules for privacy for members of the European Union (EU) are laid down in the **European Union Data Protection Directive**, originally adopted in 1995, which applies to electronic and paper filing systems, including financial services. The directive requires EU member states to amend national legislation to guarantee individuals certain rights to protect their privacy and to control the contents of electronic databases that contain personal information. The data covered by the directive are information about an individual that somehow identify the individual by name or otherwise. Each European nation's government implements the directive in its own way.

Under the directive, information about consumers must be collected for specific, legitimate purposes and stored in individually identifiable form. Those collecting the data must tell the consumer who ultimately will have access to the information. The rules are stricter for companies that want to use data in direct marketing or to transfer the data for other companies to use in direct marketing. The consumer must be explicitly informed of these plans and given the chance to object. U.S. and European principles on privacy share a key similarity. The Data Protection Directive and U.S. privacy laws attempt to protect human rights. However, both do little to check the growth of government databases or information-collection powers. In his white paper, "Privacy and Human Rights: Comparing the United States to Europe," Solveig Singleton writes:

> *The view that uses of information for marketing in the private sector themselves violate human rights is a peculiar one. Why should a business not be free to record and use facts about transactions, about real people and real events, to develop products and to identify people who might have an interest in its products? Once a consumer enters into a transaction with another entity, this entity has as much of a right to use the information about the transaction as the consumer. Why would it violate someone's rights to use information about him to sell him something? This is a far cry from torturing him or seizing his home.*[11]

Europeans do not allow the sharing of personal information between enterprises; this area is not yet regulated by the U.S. government.[12] In contrast to the United States, where more of a free market approach is taken to many things, including

---

[11]Solveig Singleton, "Privacy and Human Rights: Comparing the United States to Europe," *CATO*, December 1, 1999; available at: www.cato.org/pubs/wtpapers/991201paper.html, accessed September 1, 2010.

[12]Jeff Langenderfer and Anthony D. Miyazaki, "Privacy in the Information Economy," *Journal of Consumer Affairs* 43, no. 3 (Fall 2009): 380–390.

customer privacy protection, the European Privacy Directive prohibits enterprises from transferring electronic records of personal information—including names, addresses, and personal profiles—across borders. It is at least partly intended to reduce trade barriers within the EU by standardizing how various companies treat individual information in different countries. If European nations must follow the same standards about privacy protection, then trade between nations can occur more freely. Personal data on EU citizens may be transferred only to countries outside the 15-nation block that are deemed to provide "adequate protection" for the data. But the rising use of social networking sites worldwide is putting the European Privacy Directive to the test. A strict reading implies those that who "tag" their friends in Facebook, upload videos to YouTube, or post other personal material to social networking sites without consent are breaking the law.[13]

European Organization for Economic Cooperation and Development Privacy Guidelines

1. Data must be collected using lawful and fair means and, where possible, with the consent of the subject.
2. Data must be accurate, complete, and up-to-date to ensure quality is adequate for use.
3. Purposes of data usage should be specified prior to collection and should not be subsequently extended.
4. Personal data should not be disclosed without legal cause or the consent of the data subject.
5. Data should be protected by reasonable security safeguards.
6. The existence and nature of personal data should be discoverable.
7. Data should be available to the subject to enable the correction of inaccurate information.

Source: Partial list excerpted from "OECD Guidelines on the Protection of Privacy and Transborder Flows of Personal Data," available at: www.oecd.org, accessed September 1, 2010.

Data protection negotiations between the United States and the EU reached a pivotal point in July 2000, when the European Commission declared that the Safe Harbor arrangement put in place by the U.S. government to protect personal data transmitted in the course of Internet commerce must meet EU standards. The Safe Harbor agreement states that if U.S. enterprises agree to a certain set of minimal

---

[13]J. Trevor Hughes, "Greetings!" *Inside 1to1 Privacy Newsletter*, March 31, 2010, published by Peppers & Rogers Group and the International Association of Privacy Professionals; available at: www.privacyassociation.org/publications/2010_03_31_greetings/, accessed September 1, 2010; "Regulations Probe 'Tagging,' Consent," International Association of Privacy Professionals Daily Dashboard, March 24, 2010; available at: www.privacyassociation.org/publications/2010_03_24_regulators_probe_tagging_consent/, accessed September 1, 2010.

privacy standards when doing business in Europe, they will be free from litigation. It was aimed at heading off the possibility that data transfers to the United States might be blocked following the enactment of the EU's Data Protection Directive. Under Safe Harbor, U.S. companies can voluntarily adhere to a set of data protection principles recognized by the commission as providing adequate protection and thus meeting the requirements of the directive regarding transfer of data out of the EU.

The Safe Harbor standards, however, are not as rigorous as what Europeans have set for themselves. As part of the agreement, the U.S. Federal Trade Commission (FTC) and U.S. judicial system will be authorized to impose sanctions on companies that violate data privacy rules. The U.S. Commerce Department will keep tabs on self-regulating companies, which will have to apply annually for membership in the department's register. Although participation in the U.S. Safe Harbor scheme is optional, its rules are binding on U.S. companies that decide to join, and they are enforced by the FTC.

The Privacy Directive serves an important purpose within Europe, by synchronizing these various government policies, to make it easier for any company to do business across the continent. However, some U.S. enterprises are criticizing it as little more than a nontariff trade barrier, designed primarily to ensure that any new, pan-European customer service infrastructures are staffed by employees working within the boundaries of the EU itself.

Where it exists, a regulatory approach such as the Privacy Directive may or may not be effective at curbing the abuse of individual consumer privacy. But it could potentially curb Europe's economic growth prospects and threaten consumers' own interests as well. Managing relationships in the interactive age depends on the collection and use of individual customer information. As enterprises become increasingly global, it is vital that this information be accessible to sales, marketing, and customer care professionals worldwide. It is the only way to provide seamless, personal service—based on a unified view of the customer—across borders. Call centers or Web sites in Ireland might serve consumers in the United States or Argentina as well as in France or Italy.

The potential impact of the directive, if enforced as written, is extreme. Sweden's privacy agency told American Airlines in 1999 that it could not transmit information about Swedish passengers to its U.S.–based Sabre system. This, in effect, would have prevented the airline from individualizing its service offering to its Swedish customers. Under the directive, it is even conceivable that a person could be arrested for saving business card data to his laptop and trying to cross the border with it.

No matter where in the world it conducts business, the customer-strategy enterprise tries to remain sensitive to how privacy rules are enforced and respected. Critical, too, is that the enterprise show to the world that it respects each customer's right to privacy through the publication of and adherence to its own written privacy pledge.

Privacy Pledges Build Enterprise Trust

If the enterprise is to establish a long-term relationship with a customer based on individual information, it will recognize that customer data are its most valuable asset, will secure and protect that data, and will share the policy for that protection in writing with its customers, partners, and vendors, in the form of a privacy pledge. That pledge will permeate its own culture and be part of its employees' DNA. The privacy pledge will spell out:

- The kind of information generally needed from customers
- Any benefits customers will enjoy from the enterprise's use of this individual information
- Any events that might precipitate a notification to the customer by the enterprise
- An individual's options for directing the enterprise not to use or disclose certain kinds of information

Enterprises sometimes jeopardize their relationships with customers by engaging in unethical moves that compromise customer privacy for short-term marketing gain. That's why enforcing a **privacy policy** is reassuring to many customers. Fortunately, according to a survey done by the Retail Industry Leaders Association and Retail Systems Research, 72 percent of top retailers understand that customers are concerned about privacy and that their personal information must be protected.[14] But being careful with customer data is not enough for the enterprise. Such a company must also get agreements in writing with all its vendors and partners that confirm they too will comply with enterprise privacy standards. A midwestern bank committed to protecting its customers' information learned that a printing company that produced checks for the bank's customers had been copying the names and addresses of customers, routinely printed in the upper left corner of the checks, and reselling that information to list brokers. These list sellers in turn were selling the information to insurance agencies, garden supply companies, competitive financial services institutions, and others.

As the privacy debate rages, customers are, more and more, aware of whether they are given a chance either to **opt in** (proactively elect to receive future communications from the enterprise) or **opt out** (tacitly choose to receive them by inaction, unless they actively opt out). Consumer groups tend to favor opt-in as a better protection for consumers, whereas industry groups point to very low participation levels and, ironically, fewer targeted messaging efforts, and therefore tend to favor opt-out. Frequently, however, this opt-in or opt-out choice is an all-or-nothing toggle switch. To treat customers in a more one-to-one fashion, best practice today is to offer choices to the customer, with respect not just to the types of information he may choose to receive, but also as to the frequency with which he is contacted with this information.

What greater assets do any company, online or off, have to dangle in front of other companies than the private data of thousands, or even millions, of customers? Do the rules change when a company is bought out or goes bankrupt? What happens to a company's privacy pledge when there no longer is a company? And what guarantee is there that the new owner of your data will honor the same privacy standards as the former owner?

---

[14]"According to RILA Survey: Protecting Customer Data Is a Top Priority for Retailers," *PRNewswire,* March 1, 2010, available at: www.prnewswire.com, accessed September 1, 2010.

There is a simple, universal solution: The global business community needs to prevent such abuses, and preferably without government intervention. In this Information Age, technologies are cropping up to help the process. Software enables online users to control how sites collect, control, use, and share their personal information. With privacy pledges under scrutiny, more enterprises are adopting and publicizing them. Nonetheless, many enterprises still do not state their policies, and others never share user data with third parties.

What constitutes a good privacy protection policy? For starters, it should explain to customers what kinds of information the company needs from them, how the information will be used, and how it will *not* be used. It should also explain the benefits a customer would gain by sharing personal information. Enterprises need to promote their privacy policies beyond the Web site and corporate promotional collateral, including it in direct-mail pieces, invoices, and other company mailings. A privacy policy will reinforce the foundation on which each customer relationship is built. Trust is an essential part of any Learning Relationship, and a privacy policy helps build that trust.

Building a trusted relationship goes far beyond simply writing a privacy policy and posting it on the Web site. Unless the enterprise is careful as to how it uses sensitive customer information, the opportunity for forming Learning Relationships may disappear. It is important to recognize, however, that some individuals do not want companies to know which Web sites they visit or anything about their personal information. In the headlong rush of enterprises to use the latest databases, data-mining techniques, neural nets, and Internet-based information collection systems, some have neglected or overlooked this important issue. Moreover, a customer's willingness to collaborate with an enterprise by interacting with the firm could be one important measure of the customer's value to the enterprise.

It is important to explain the motives for wanting to create a relationship with a customer. Enterprises need to describe to customers how they will benefit by exchanging personal information with them. Once customers have read the privacy pledge and understand that their personal information will not be sold or shared irresponsibly, they simply want to know how providing their personal data will affect customer service. Beyond the security or convenience of the actual transaction, what assurance does a customer have that his personal information will not be misused or abused? After all, most customers have experienced the irritation of "getting on a list" and, as a consequence, received unsolicited direct mail and outbound telemarketing calls. Ironically, if a customer does not provide information to an enterprise about what he likes to buy, the likelihood is that he will receive more junk mail or direct-mail pieces that promote products and services of little interest to him and his needs. Clearly, this question has yet to be definitively resolved.[15]

These and many other privacy-related questions may never be fully settled. But the customer-based enterprise has to monitor changing privacy issues closely.

---

[15]Amit Poddar, Jill Mosteller, and Pam Scholder Ellen, "Consumers' Rules of Engagement in Online Information Exchanges," *Journal of Consumer Affairs* 43, no. 3 (2009): 419–448; Dan Seligman, "Too Much of a Good Thing?" *Forbes,* February 23, 1998, pp. 64–65; James W. Peltier and John A. Schribrowsky, "The Use of Need-Based Segmentation for Developing Segment-Specific Direct Marketing Strategies," *Journal of Direct Marketing* 11, issue 4 (Autumn 1997): 53–62; Rob Yoegel, "Fulfillment on the Net," *Target Marketing* 19, no. 7 (July 1996): 30–31.

Intensifying the privacy debate is the way customer information is being collected and used on the Internet. The Web has created a powerful medium to collect and analyze customer data. But how can enterprises afford customers the same privacy protection online as they do in the "real world"? And how sensitive are customers to divulging personal information on the Web?

Ten Points to Consider in Developing a Company's Privacy Pledge

Every enterprise that maintains a Web site or collects personal information about its customers needs to establish an explicit privacy protection policy. The enterprise might call it a Privacy Pledge or a Privacy Bill of Rights, but it needs to consider covering these 10 key points:

1. Itemize the kind of information it collects about individual customers.
2. Specify how personal information will be used by the company. If its policy is to use this kind of information only within the company on a need-to-know basis, and not to make it accessible to unauthorized employees at any time, the enterprise needs to explain this policy explicitly.
3. Make whatever commitments it can make with respect to how individual customer information will *never* be used (e.g., personal information is never sold or rented to others, or never used to change prices or insurance premiums, etc.).
4. State the benefits an individual customer can expect as a result of its use of his information (faster or preferential service, reduced costs, etc.).
5. List a customer's options for directing the enterprise not to use or disclose certain kinds of information.
6. State how a customer can change or update personal information it has collected. For example, can the consumer access his profile or account information online or modify it?
7. Identify events that might precipitate a notification to the customer by the enterprise. If, for instance, a court subpoenas your customer records, will you notify any customers whose information was subpoenaed?
8. Assign a corporate executive as the "data steward," charged with overall responsibility for assuring the adherence to company information and privacy policies.
9. Specify the situations in which it accepts or denies liability for damages incurred through the collection and use of customer data, such as through credit card fraud or misuse.
10. Provide specific procedures allowing a customer to order the company to stop collecting data about him, or to purge his information files at the company.

Source: From Don Peppers, Martha Rogers, Ph.D., and Bob Dorf, *The One to One Fieldbook* (New York: Doubleday, 1999), 99–100.

The bottom line is that the information that technology provides about your customers, and the increasingly cost-efficient tools you have to interact directly with customers and to facilitate them interacting with each other, should be used to build more trust. It really won't matter what your formal privacy protection policy is, or how well you comply with whatever anti-spam regulations are enforced, if you don't see the problem through the right end of the telescope—that is, from the customer's perspective. Fail to take this point of view and you are still going to be undermining your customers' trust.[16]

Submitting Data Online

For many consumers who buy online, the protection of their personal information is a valid concern. To the selling enterprise, however, information is like currency—it enables them to identify customers and customize their offerings based on that information.

By personalizing their products and services for online customers, enterprises stand to enhance their revenue. More than half of frequent online shoppers are more likely to make a purchase on a Web site that offers personalization features.[17] Still, online users believe that Web sites should be accountable for explaining to them how their information will be used, as more and more consumers feel out of control regarding their personal information.[18] According to a Pew Internet & American Life survey on cloud computing:

- 90 percent of users would be "very concerned" if the company storing their data sold it to another company.
- 80 percent would be "very concerned" if companies used their data for marketing purposes.
- 68 percent would be "very concerned" if service providers analyzed their information and then displayed ads to them based on their actions.[19]

Web site personalization requires consumers to submit information about themselves, such as their names, zip codes, interests, and even credit card numbers. Consumers personalize the online sites they visit to enhance their online experiences, but many do not want to have their information shared among Web sites without their knowledge.

Personalization online helps customers to access the specific content and products they are looking for while giving the enterprise access to their browsing habits. For many enterprises, the objective of personalization on the Web is to increase

---

[16]Don Peppers and Martha Rogers, Ph.D., *Rules to Break and Laws to Follow: How Your Business Can Beat the Crisis of Short-Termism* (Hoboken, NJ: John Wiley & Sons, 2008), p. 91.
[17]ChoiceStream press release, "Annual ChoiceStream Survey Finds Personalized Ads Attract High-Value Customers," January 13, 2009, Cambridge, MA; available at: www.choice stream.com/news/pressrelease.asp?id=84, accessed September 1, 2010.
[18]Ponemon Institute, "2008 Most Trusted Companies for Privacy: Study of U.S. Consumer Perceptions," December 2008; available at: www.ponemon.org/research-studies-white-papers.
[19]Pew Research Institute, "Use of Cloud Computing Applications and Services," Pew Internet & American Life Project report (2008); available at: www.pewinternet.org/Reports/2008/Use-of-Cloud-Computing-Applications-and-Services.aspx?r=1, accessed September 1, 2010.

customer loyalty through return visits. Privacy advocates claim that the instances of abuse of consumer data are a sign of how Internet marketers are overstepping their boundaries. The marketers, in turn, argue that data gathering is merely a non-threatening way of fine-tuning marketing for the convenience of consumers. A firm will have to accomplish two things to break down the mistrust barrier between the customer and the online merchant:

1. *Offer assurances of confidentiality*. Customers want to know whether their personal data will be sold or used beyond simply information gathering.
2. *Build Learning Relationships on trust*. Enterprises will need to develop individual, personalized relationships with their customers to promote trust and enhance loyalty.

As privacy-protection advocates in Australia, the United States, and Europe continue to fuel the debate that it is wrong for companies to abuse personal information about their customers on the Web, enterprises will need to take a balanced view, not second-guess what their customers "really" want. The customer-strategy enterprise will strive to protect an individual's privacy online but also weigh the real benefits of personalization against its real costs, as we see in the following excerpt, from Blown to Bits, by Abelson, Ledeen, and Lewis.

Blown to Bits

Hal Abelson
Class of 1922 Professor of Electrical Engineering and Computer Science, Massachusetts Institute of Technology, and IEEE Fellow

Ken Ledeen
Chairman and Chief Executive Officer, Nevo Technologies, Inc.

Harry Lewis
Gordon McKay Professor of Computer Science, Harvard University

Why can't we just keep our personal information to ourselves? Why do so many other people have it in the first place, so that there is an opportunity for it to go astray, and an incentive for creative crooks to try to steal it?

We lose control of our personal information because of things we do to ourselves, and things others do to us. Of things we do to be ahead of the curve, and things we do because everyone else is doing them. Of things we do to save money, and things we do to save time. Of things we do to be safe from our enemies, and things we do because we feel invulnerable. Our loss of privacy is a problem, but there is no one answer to it, because there is no one reason why it is happening. It is a messy problem, and we first have to think about it one piece at a time.

We give away information about ourselves—voluntarily leave visible footprints of our daily lives—because we judge, perhaps without thinking about it very much, that the benefits outweigh the costs. To be sure, the benefits are many.

Saving Time

For commuters who use toll roads or bridges, the risk-reward calculation is not even close. Time is money, and time spent waiting in a car is also anxiety and frustration. If there is an option to get a toll booth transponder, many commuters will get one, even if the device costs a few dollars up front. Cruising past the cars waiting to pay with dollar bills is not just a relief; it actually brings the driver a certain satisfied glow.

The transponder, which the driver attaches to the windshield from inside the car, is a radio frequency identification (RFID), powered with a battery so identifying information can be sent to the sensor several feet away as the driver whizzes past. The sensor can be mounted in a constricted travel lane, where a toll booth for a human toll taker might have been. Or it can be mounted on a boom above traffic, so the driver doesn't even need to change lanes or slow down

And what is the possible harm? Of course, the state is recording the fact that the car has passed the sensor; that is how the proper account balance can be debited to pay the toll. When the balance gets too low, the driver's credit card may get billed automatically to replenish the balance. All that only makes the system better—no fumbling for change or doing anything else to pay for your travels.

The monthly bill—for the Massachusetts Fast Lane, for example—shows where and when you got on the highway—when, accurate to the second. It also shows where you got off and how far you went. Informing you of the mileage is another useful service, because Massachusetts drivers can get a refund on certain fuel taxes, if the fuel was used on the state toll road. Of course, you do not need a Ph.D. to figure out that the state also knows when you got off the road, to the second, and that with one subtraction and one division, its computers could figure out if you were speeding. Technically, in fact, it would be trivial for the state to print the appropriate speeding fine at the bottom of the statement, and to bill your credit card for that amount at the same time as it was charging for tolls. That would be taking convenience a bit too far, and no state does it, yet.

What does happen right now, however, is that toll transponder records are introduced into divorce and child custody cases. You've never been within five miles of that lady's house? Really? Why have you gotten off the highway at the exit near it so many times? You say you can be the better custodial parent for your children, but the facts suggest otherwise. As one lawyer put it, "When a guy says, 'Oh, I'm home every day at five and I have dinner with my kids every single night; you subpoena his E-ZPass and you find out he's crossing that bridge every night at 8:30. Oops!" These records can be subpoenaed, and have been, hundreds of times, in family law cases. They have also been used in

(continued)

(Continued)

employment cases, to prove that the car of a worker who said he was working was actually far from the workplace.

How Sites Know Who You Are

1. *You tell them.* Log in to Gmail, Amazon, or eBay, and you are letting them know exactly who you are.
2. *They've left cookies on one of your previous visits.* A **cookie** is a small text file stored on your local hard drive that contains information that a particular web site wants to have available during your current session (like your shopping cart), or from one session to the next. Cookies give sites persistent information for tracking and personalization. Your browser has a command for showing cookies; you may be surprised how many web sites have left them!
3. *They have your IP address.* The web server has to know where you are so that it can ship its web pages to you. Your IP address is a number like 66.82.9.88 that located your computer in the Internet. . . . That address may change from one day to the next. But in a residential setting, your Internet Service Provider (your *ISP*—typically your phone or cable company) knows who was assigned each IP address at any time. Those records are often subpoenaed in court cases.

If you are curious about who is using a particular IP address, you can check the American Registry of Internet Numbers (www.arin.net). Services such as whatismyip.org and ipchicken.com also allow you to check your own IP address. And www.whois.net allows you to check who owns a domain name such as Harvard.com—which turns out to be the Harvard Bookstore, a privately owned bookstore right across the street from the university. Unfortunately, that information won't reveal who is sending you spam, since spammers routinely forge the source of email they send you.

Source: Excerpted with permission from Hal Abelson, Ken Ledeen, and Harry Lewis, *Blown to Bits: Your Life, Liberty, and Happiness After the Digital Explosion* (Reading, MA: Addison-Wesley Professional, 2008), p. 40.

It's Just Fun to Be Exposed

Sometimes, there can be no explanation for our willing surrender of our privacy except that we take joy in the very act of exposing ourselves to public view. Exhibitionism is not a new phenomenon. Its practice today, as in the past, tends to be in the province of the young and the drunk, and those wishing to pretend they are one or the other. That correlation is by no means perfect, however. A university president had to apologize when an image of her threatening a Hispanic male with a stick leaked out from her MySpace page, with a caption indicating that she had to "beat off the Mexicans because they are constantly flirting with my daughter."

And there is a continuum of outrageousness. The less wild of the party photo postings blend seamlessly with the more personal of the blogs, where the bloggers are chatting mostly about their personal feelings. Here there is not exuberance, but some simpler urge for human connectedness. That passion, too, is not new. What *is* new is that a photo or video or diary entry, once posted, is visible to the entire world, and that there is no taking it back. Bits don't fade and they don't yellow. Bits are forever. And we don't know how to live with that.

For example, a blog selected with no great design begins:

> *This is the personal website of Sarah McAuley. . . . I think sharing my life with strangers is odd and narcissistic, which of course is why I'm addicted to it and have been doing it for several years now. Need more? You can read the "About Me" section, drop me an email, or, you know, just read the drivel that I pour out on an almost-daily basis.*

Because You Can't Live Any Other Way

Finally, we give up data about ourselves because we don't have the time, patience, or single-mindedness about privacy that would be required to live our daily lives in another way. In the United States, the number of credit, debit, and bank cards is in the billions. Every time one is used, an electronic handshake records a few bits of information about who is using it, when, where, and for what. It is now virtually unheard of for people to make large purchases of ordinary consumer goods with cash. Personal checks are going the way of cassette tape drives, rendered irrelevant by newer technologies. Even if you could pay cash for everything you buy, the tax authorities would have you in their databases anyway. There even have been proposals to put RFIDs (radio frequency identifications) in currency notes, so that the movement of cash could be tracked.

Only sects such as the Amish still live without electricity. It will soon be almost that unusual to live without Internet connectivity, with all the fingerprints it leaves of your daily searches and logins and downloads. Even the old dumb TV is rapidly disappearing in favor of digital communications. Digital TV will bring the advantages of video on demand—no more trips to rent movies or waits for them to arrive in the mail—at a price: Your television service provider will record what movies you have ordered. It will be so attractive to be able to watch what we want when we want to watch it, that we won't miss either the inconvenience or the anonymity of the days when all the TV stations washed your house with their airwaves. You couldn't pick the broadcast times, but at least no one knew which waves you were grabbing out of the air.

Source: Excerpted with permission from Hal Abelson, Ken Ledeen, and Harry Lewis, *Blown to Bits: Your Life, Liberty, and Happiness After the Digital Explosion* (Reading, MA: Addison-Wesley Professional, 2008), pp. 36–37, 40–42.

So much changed about the U.S. national attitude toward privacy on September 11, 2001. With the terrorist attacks on New York and Washington, D.C., U.S. national security was threatened as it had never been before. But on a more personal level, U.S. citizens felt that their individual safety was in jeopardy. The threat of additional terrorist attacks led to a heightened state of security at many public places, including airports, sporting events, and bridges and tunnels.

Universal ID

One solution offered after September 11, 2001, was the creation of a Universal ID card for each citizen to carry. The card could contain an electronic thumbprint of the cardholder so the person could be easily identified if questioned. This concept is akin to automobile license plates, which automatically expose the owner of the vehicle to the police, who simply need to check the plate number against their database. Would citizens be opposed to carrying a card that revealed personal information to anyone who swipes their cards? What about an embedded RFID chip?

In the immediate aftermath of September 11, the civil rights of private citizens became a public issue. How much could the government encroach on a person's right to privacy in the shadow of terrorism? How much was okay if it made us all safer? What if it only made us *feel* safer? Could the government begin to check the backgrounds and personal information of anyone it deemed to be a suspicious terrorist?

As you read Esther Dyson's classic contribution, Privacy on the Net, think about what the world will be like in a few years. What would happen if enterprises and the government became adept at combining personal information about individuals from different sources? What would it mean for people who participate in society and those who do not (such as the Amish)?

Privacy on the Net

Esther Dyson
Chairman, EDventure Holdings

By 1997, consumer privacy had become a big issue in the United States. A number of trends had been combined. More data was being collected, online and off. Direct marketers, telemarketers, and assorted shady people were invading people's privacy, and press coverage highlighted this issue. The Federal Trade Commission held hearings on consumer privacy, saying in effect: "Tell us the problems and propose some solutions, or we'll have to regulate."

There were also several bills pending in Congress, likely to change form over time: the Consumer Internet Privacy Protection Act of 1997 (Rep. Bruce

Vento, D-MN); the Children's Privacy Protection and Parental Empowerment Act (Rep. Bob Franks, R-NJ); and the Communications Privacy and Consumer Empowerment Act (Rep. Ed Markey, D-MA).

With some justification, many people, both potential users and potential government regulators, perceived the Net as a scary, unregulated place. The Net makes it even easier for lots of people, not just well-capitalized mass marketers or obsessive creeps, to get at information and use it for undesirable and even dangerous ends.

Beyond Web Sites, beyond Labels

These issues of privacy didn't begin with the Internet, and they can't be resolved by controlling what happens on any, or even all, individual Web sites. The problems arise when information travels among Web sites—or away from them to places where people and companies assemble databases of information gleaned from many Web sites and from non-Web mailing lists, directories, news reports, listings . . . and other databases. A lot of this information has traditionally been available to people willing to go to a lot of trouble, visiting county document vaults, calling companies posing as a prospective employer or old boyfriend, or spending several hundred dollars to get an investigator's license. It has also been available on a random basis to criminals in jail doing data-entry work, bored clerks at the IRS, and various other untrustworthy people in trusted positions.

Many companies, notably TRW, Equifax, metromail, and some credit card providers, manage huge amounts of such data and trade it among themselves. Yes, it makes the economy more efficient and keeps revenues up and costs down. But not all of the companies who manage the information are especially honorable—nor are all of their employees.

The growing presence of the Web increases the ease of both collecting such data and assembling it. The interconnectedness of the Net makes safeguarding privacy an increasing challenge. People are rightly concerned about the combination of data from different sources: Web behavior, buying habits, travel history, income data. Often, facts are innocuous until they're combined with other facts.

The user wants a seamless experience as he explores the Web, but he wants to appear as a discrete entity to each place he visits, with a legitimate identity revealed as appropriate—a credit rating, an employment record, a bank account, or a medical history. Indeed, a person's identity gets plastered all over the Net in little fragments—no problem. But then someone in particular—anyone from a benign marketer only after the customer's business, to an employer, a stalker, or a blackmailer—can start collecting those fragments. One version of the problem is when the data are incorrect (and the user is the last to know); another version is when they are true.

In response, the marketplace and the government are setting up systems to foster privacy. As a society, we can't totally guarantee everyone's privacy. But

(continued)

(Continued)

we can create a situation where people can choose the lever of privacy they want according to trade-offs they determine for themselves, and provide them with a means of recourse when promises are breached. When that happens, I believe, people will feel more comfortable on the Net overall and no longer fear the visibility it fosters.

Two Kinds of Information

There are two broad classes of information about yourself that you create on the Net: one kind that you generate when you engage in a one-to-one transaction with someone, and another kind that you generate when you do something in "public"—post an opinion, send out a message to several people, or supply information on your own Web site.

The "one-to-one" data is created by a variety of individual exchanges and transactions—anything from visiting a Web site to buying a racy book, revealing personal data in order to win a prize, or stating your income on Barron's site for investors. In principle such information is private—but not in practice. Here's one tale of woe from Russell Smith, a privacy activist who testified at the Federal Trade Commission hearings:

> . . . *my every move on the Internet could potentially be tracked. For instance, I recently did a search of newsgroups via the DejaNews service. In my search I was searching on my username "russ-smith." The search turned up an entry in some type of an adult newsgroup. When I clicked on the message it turns out it had nothing to do with me. However, the banner ad I received was for an adult site from a widely used banner network called The Link Exchange. Does my profile now include this information? Is my search criterion ("russ-smith") also associated with this information? Do they have my name and address since I have purchased products (and entered personal information) at other sites with these banner ads? Is it being sold? How can I find out? Can I expunge it?*

Flawed Solutions

The solutions most often presented in response to this situation generally miss the point. We don't need new government regulation that stops the free flow of information voluntarily given, outlaws cookies, and makes customization difficult (except perhaps where children and coercion are concerned).

Nor do we need a Direct Market*ed* Association—a force equal in power to the Direct Marketing Association but aligned with someone's vision of consumers' interests. After all, consumers don't all have the same interests; what they really need is choice.

Instead, we need the kinds of policies that the Liberty Alliance is fostering, which would allow users more control over the kind of data that gets passed from vendor to vendor. An even more user-focused initiative is Ping Identity, based in Denver.

Tools for Customer Empowerment

Much as I hate the term, what I'm talking about here is customer "empowerment," not "self-regulation"—transforming passive customers into active customers who can monitor vendor practices for themselves. That implies some kind of broad movement to give customers the tools to do so, but the actual enforcement and use of the tools should be decentralized into users' hands.

The reason to avoid government regulation is not that government oversight is always bad; government courts and other enforcement mechanisms are a necessary backup to systems such as **TRUSTe** and Liberty Alliance. It's simply that front-line customer enforcement is likely to be more flexible and more responsive to actual conditions than government regulation. A decentralized system scales up nicely and crosses borders with ease. Customer enforcement will give users greater choice, while at the same time giving them confidence that they can trust the medium. People can pick data-control practices that suit them, rather than be forced to operate in a one-rule-fits-all environment. The overriding rule should be that providers must disclose—label—themselves clearly and honestly. And then they must do what they promise.

The goal is not to regulate cyberspace, nor to solve all problems concerning privacy (or content) online, but rather to carve out enough clean, well-lighted territory so that the dark parts of the Net lose their power to scare people away. In the end, most people will prefer to live in safe neighborhoods, while potential predators will find few victims other than their own kind.

In practice, privacy protection is more than data or technology. How can we achieve it without making the world into a sterile place where everyone is anonymous? Most customers actually like to be treated as known individuals by marketers that they in turn know and trust. The rhetoric promises a global village, not a global city. Real privacy—which is respect for people rather than mere absence of data—depends on human judgment and common sense.

> Real privacy—which is respect for people rather than mere absence of data—depends on human judgment and common sense.

What Would Deep Blue Be Like with Hormones?

Let's try a thought experiment. Imagine that you have lived your entire life on the Net, isolated from the physical world. You know a lot of people intimately: You've heard their ideas; you've argued with them; you've watched them mature, get angry, trade jokes, do business, make and lose friends. You have made and lost friends yourself. These people are real to you; you want their respect; you ask them for advice. And you are real to them. You and they take your Net presence for granted—all the things you have ever

(continued)

(Continued)

posted, all the data about you, all the Net chatter about you. But you have never seen them.

Now suppose you meet these people in real, physical, terrestrial life. They're fat or thin; blond or dark; young or old; white or African American or Asian; male or female. There's more! Each person has these little peculiarities—a scar, asymmetrical eyebrows, a particular style of dress or pattern of speech, and so on. None of them is any big deal; they're merely expressions of each person's identity. (Yes, some people do hate their nose, undergo cosmetic surgery, or have an obsession with their own hair, but few people wear a mask.)

None of these features is any big secret, and most are familiar (if not explicitly so) to that person's friends and even acquaintances. Others—for example, presidents and movie stars—are known to the world. Some are genetically determined; some are shaped by the person; some are an artifact of culture (such as a woman's shaved legs).

But how about you? You would probably at first be very sensitive about your *own* physical being. You would feel vulnerable and exposed as you joined the physical world. All these people can see how you look, judge your hairstyle, criticize your weight or your taste in shirts....Should you shave? Should you wear your trousers rolled?

But after a while you would probably relax, just as you have already in the real world since being an awkward teenager. People know how you dress and how you look, and most of them now are accustomed to it. Meanwhile, you're accustomed to the face you present to the world. You may be taken aback to see your profile or, worse, the back of your head in a mirror. But on the whole, you're probably relaxed about your physical existence because it has come to seem normal.

That same thing happens with your Net persona.

The New Privacy

As people feel more secure in general on the Net, they will become accustomed to seeing their words recorded and replayed. They will no longer feel uncomfortable being on display, since everyone around them is on display too. In the same way, feelings of physical exposure tend to depend on fashion and custom as well as innate sensibility. Thirty years ago the sight of a woman's navel was shocking except by the pool; now it's routine. One hundred years ago, a nanny told my grandmother she was a "shameless hussy" for taking off her shoes at the beach.

Everyone has personal preferences for privacy, but they are influenced by the surrounding culture and by the surrounding economy. It's hard to fulfill

> a desire for privacy if you're living in a one-room apartment with the rest of your eight-person extended family. If you travel or mingle with people from other cultures, you will notice that Americans expect a lot more "personal space" than most people.
>
> Nowadays, people reveal much more about themselves—for better or worse—than they used to. It's inevitable that people will simply become more comfortable with the fact that more information is known about them on the Net. The challenge is not to keep everything secret, but to limit misuse of such information. That implies trust, and more information about how the information is used. At the same time, we may all become more tolerant if everyone's flaws are more visible.
>
> *Source:* Adapted from Esther Dyson, *Release 2.0: A Design for Living in the Digital Age* (New York: Bantam Doubleday Dell Broadway Books, 1997).

There's no easy, immediate answer to what is always a best practice in privacy. The capabilities to get and share data about individuals become cheaper and easier daily. Smart cards can carry not only your retinal scan and fingerprints with you everywhere but your entire medical record.[20] And Intellicheck already enables bars to swipe your driver's license to ascertain your legal age (and then, in many states, to also suddenly "know" your Social Security number, gender, weight, address, etc.).

The real commercial questions are these:

- What do we need to "know" to serve a customer better and make him more valuable to us?
- What information do we really need to "know" that?
- Once we get that information, how do we balance distribution at the front lines with the need to protect a customer's privacy?
- What are the limits in how we will share or distribute data?
- How will we protect and secure the data?

Summary

The fluid collaboration between enterprise and customer is ceaseless throughout the life of the relationship. But for the relationship to flourish, customers sometimes will have to reveal personal information about themselves to the enterprise. The enterprise, in turn, will have to promise to keep this private information private. Indeed, privacy—the customer's right to it, and the enterprise's protection of it—has become an important, and controversial, subject of the Information Age.

---

[20]From Smart Card Alliance, "Smart Card Standards"; available at: www.smartcardalliance. org/pages/smart-cards-intro-standards, accessed September 1, 2010.

Food for Thought

1. Who owns a customer's information?
   - Who should profit from it?
   - How would that work?
2. Is anonymity the best solution to privacy?
3. What is the difference between *privacy* and *data security*, and how should that difference affect the way we use customer data?
4. Compare the situation of Big Business versus Big Brother having detailed information about you.

Glossary

Cookie A small text file stored on your local hard drive that contains information that a particular Web site wants to have available during your current session (like your shopping cart), or from one session to the next. Cookies give sites persistent information for tracking and personalization.

European Union Data Protection Directive Requires EU member states to amend national legislation to guarantee individuals certain rights to protect their privacy and to control the contents of electronic databases that contain personal information. Information about consumers must be collected for specific, legitimate purposes and stored in individually identifiable form. Those collecting the data must tell the consumer, who will ultimately have access to the information, and companies wanting to use data in direct marketing must explicitly inform consumers of these plans and give them a chance to object.

Opt in When customers proactively elect to receive future communications from an enterprise.

Opt out When customers proactively elect *not* to receive future communications from an enterprise.

Privacy policy A written document detailing how a company will share (or not share) data collected from its customers. Ideally it should explain to customers, in simple language, what kinds of information the company needs from them, how the information will be used, how it will *not* be used, and the benefits a customer would gain by sharing personal information.

TRUSTe An organization that endorses each customer's control of his own information and offers a publishable mark to groups and companies that meet TRUSTe's requirements for privacy protection.

CHAPTER 10

The Payoff of IDIC: Using Mass Customization to Build Learning Relationships

On average, each American household has about 300 branded products—food items, cleaning goods, over-the-counter-remedies, grooming products. Yet there are 30,000 stock-keeping units (SKUs) in the average supermarket. That means that each shopper sifts through 100 times as many products she doesn't want as she does finding the ones she buys. But the truth is that "choice" is not the same as getting things our way. Most of the time, in fact, especially for routine purchases, people don't want more choice. They just want what they want. They want to satisfy their need, and choosing from a large assortment of alternatives is the only way they can accomplish this. **Customization**, however, involves producing a single product, or delivering a single service, to satisfy a single customer's need without requiring the customer to go to the trouble of having to choose from a wide variety of other products or services. This is the payoff of the Learning Relationship—to the customer and to the company. This chapter shows how the customer-based enterprise should use what it learns about each customer to customize and/or personalize some aspect of its offering for that customer, in order to increase its share of that customer's business. The whole point is to know more about a customer than the competition does and then to deliver something in a way the competition cannot.

Treating different customers differently could be prohibitively expensive, if every interaction and transaction had to be individually crafted as a tailored offering for a single customer. Fortunately, information technology can be used to improve and streamline the manufacturing and service delivery processes, so that an enterprise can deliver individually different products or services to different individual customers cost efficiently. This technique is called **mass customization**.

For the past 100 years, enterprises have standardized their products and services to take advantage of economies of scale. They have standardized the product and their messages about the product, and they have standardized its distribution. In the process, they have also standardized the customer. Even sophisticated segmentation strategies aggregate customers into groups a marketer defines as being alike, so the communication and the offer made to all customers in a "segment" can be standardized. By contrast, the customer-strategy enterprise, spurred by the rising power and declining cost of information processing, interactivity, and customization technologies, identifies each of its Most Valuable Customers

> For the past 100 years, enterprises have standardized their products and services to take advantage of economies of scale. They have standardized the product and their messages about the product, and they have standardized its distribution. In the process, they also have *standardized the customer*.

(MVCs), remembers everything it learns about each one, and acts on that learning in all its dealings with that customer.

Mass customization can be defined as the mass production of goods and services in lot sizes of one. Stan Davis, who first coined the term in his groundbreaking book *Future Perfect*, says the term implies delivering "customized goods on a mass basis."[1] The principles of mass customization are not limited to physically produced goods; they can also be applied to the customization of services and communication. For some customers, being treated individually with personalized services and communication may be an even more important dimension than being treated to uniquely tailored products made possible by individualized production.[2]

How Can Customization Be Profitable?

The mechanics of mass customization are simple in theory. A mass customizer does not really *customize* anything at all—at least not from scratch. What a mass customizer actually does is not customization but *configuration.* The mass customizer preproduces dozens, or hundreds, of "modules" for a product and/or its related services, delivery options, payment plans, and the like. Then, based on an individual customer's needs, the company puts different modules together to yield thousands, or even millions, of possible product configurations.[3] When an enterprise embraces mass customization and determines how to modularize its offerings, it must thoroughly understand all of the component elements its products or services can be combined with, connected to, reduced from, or built onto. By determining the related products or services it could offer to customers, either by producing them itself or by forming alliances with other firms, the enterprise takes a critical step in the mass customization process (see Exhibit 10.1).

Consider how a credit card company might go about mass-customizing its credit card. Perhaps the company is capable of offering 10 different interest rates, 5 different

---

[1] Stanley M. Davis, *Future Perfect* (Reading, MA: Addison-Wesley, 1987).
[2] Amit Poddar, Jill Mosteller, and Pam Scholder Ellen, "Consumers' Rules of Engagement in Online Information Exchanges," *Journal of Consumer Affairs* 43, no. 3 (2009): 419–448; Ian Gordon, *Relationship Marketing* (New York: John Wiley & Sons, 1998).
[3] P. T. Xu, "Integrated Vehicle Configuration System—Connecting the Domains of Mass Customization," *Computers in Industry* 61, no. 1 (January 2010): 44–52; Don Peppers, Martha Rogers, Ph.D., and Bob Dorf, *The One to One Fieldbook* (New York: Doubleday Broadway Books, 1999).

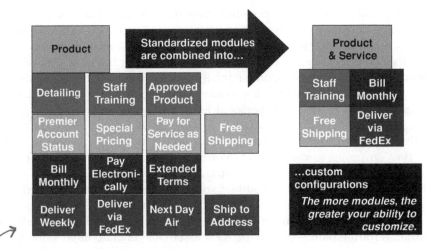

[EXHIBIT 10.1   **How Mass Customization Works: Example]**

annual fee schedules, and 4 different physical card designs. Altogether, in other words, the credit card company can make 19 different modules of the product. But these modules fit together to make a total of $10 \times 5 \times 4$, or 200 different credit card configurations. This is the basic principle of mass customization, and it applies to manufacturing in the same way. A window manufacturer, for instance, could offer 5 different sash types, 10 windowpane styles, 3 grades of insulation, and 12 frames. That would be 30 modules that could configure a total of 1,800 different windows, many of which would never be requested but any of which *could* be configured on demand.

The biggest obstacle to mass-customizing a manufactured product, as opposed to a delivered service, is simply ensuring that different parts actually work with one another and can be fit together easily. But if a product's components can be put together in a standardized way, or *modularized,* then the process of mass customization actually can reduce a company's all-in costs, when compared to traditional mass production. [Using **modularization**, building to order is inherently more efficient than building to forecast, because the enterprise need not take ownership of the parts any earlier than it needs them, and often the final product itself isn't even built—or the parts even ordered—until the product has already been paid for by a customer.]Mass customization can significantly reduce speculative manufacturing as well as inventory costs, and these two benefits are often enough to more than offset the cost of producing digitally combinable components. Indeed, cost reduction is one of the principle reasons manufacturing companies consider mass-customization technologies in the first place.[4]

---

[4]Mass-customized products: Ron Manwiller, "Cost-Effective Customization," *Ceramic Industry* 159, no. 7 (August 2009): 21–22; Mila D'Antonio, "Profiles in Leadership," *1to1 Magazine,* January 3, 2003, p. 34. Mass-customized clothing: Mila D'Antonio, "MyShape Sees Double Digit Growth Using Personalized Recommendations," *1to1 Magazine,* December 4, 2008; available at: www.1to1media.com/view.aspx?docid=31277, accessed September 1, 2010; Martha

Analogous cost reductions are possible when mass-customizing a delivered service. By giving a customer exactly what she wants—and especially if the enterprise remembers this preference for the next interaction—the entire transaction can be streamlined, made not only more convenient for the customer but more cost-efficient for the firm. In Australia, the St. George Bank automated teller machines (ATMs) will remember your "usual" transaction, if you have one. When you put your card into a St. George ATM and enter your personal identification number (PIN) code, the first menu item will offer you your usual cash withdrawal amount and receipt preference. This means the first question for returning customers will not be "What language do you prefer to use?" or "Do you want to (a) check your balance, (b) withdraw funds, (c) make a deposit, (d) transfer funds between accounts, or (e) other?" but instead will be "Would you like your usual $250.00 cash deducted from your checking account—yes or no?" Remembering a customer's "usual" not only provides faster and more convenient service for him, but it also yields more efficient asset utilization for the bank—that is, the ATM asset will generate more value to the bank when customers use it faster, because more customers will be able to use the same machine in any given time period.

Mass customization of products offers similar advantages. For instance, Dell's well-known mass-customization model, the first in the computer industry, provided the company with tremendous cost advantages when it came to managing its production. As one observer noted, "Dell Computers maintains no inventory. The production schedule is provided to all vendors a couple of days before production and allows the suppliers to provide just-in-time and just-in-sequence inventory. In this system, marketing and purchasing have to partner to ensure quick deliveries as well as develop better long term forecasts."[5]

Demand Chain and Supply Chain

When a firm remembers a customer's specification and uses this memory to deliver a product or service to that specification later (i.e., customization), the customer has a clear incentive to stay loyal. The more complex the product or service is, and the more "customization" that can be embedded in the company's treatment of the customer, the more likely the customer will be to remain loyal, even in the face of pricing pressure. However, to create such a Learning Relationship, the enterprise must be capable not only of *remembering* the customer's information but also of *acting* on it. It must be able to integrate its back-end production or service-delivery operations, **supply chain**, with its front-end sales, marketing, or customer service operations, **demand chain**.

Rogers, "Custom Clothing Sets One to One Retail Examples," *Inside 1to1,* June 16, 2003, available at: www.1to1media.com/View.aspx?docid=27182, accessed September 1, 2010; Mila D'Antonio, "Is Custom Apparel Finally Taking Off?" *1to1 Magazine,* March 1, 2003, available at: www.1to1media.com/View.aspx?docid=26147, accessed September 1, 2010.

[5]Jagdish N. Sheth, "Why Integrating Purchasing with Marketing Is Both Inevitable and Beneficial," *Industrial Marketing Management* 38, no. 8 (November 2009): 865–871.

For this reason, managing individual customer relationships effectively requires that an enterprise's demand-chain activities be coordinated with, if not integrated into, its supply-chain activities. Good customer relationships on top of a weak supply chain merely provide customers with a clearer view of the mediocrity of a company's underlying logistical capabilities, undermining a customer's trust in the enterprise by calling the company's competence into question.[a] Customer experience management that is not effectively tied to supply-chain management (SCM) results in:

- *Underdelivering*. Front-office strategies and processes will increase customer interactions—and customer expectations. If the back office can't deliver on what the front office promises, then "hollow customer relationship management (CRM)" will result, and customer satisfaction will decrease.
- *Overdelivering*. Customer strategies and processes that don't provide "cost transparency" into SCM information may result in delivering products or services that are unprofitable for the firm. Even while customers may be satisfied that their individual needs are being met, the firm loses money on every transaction, and such overdelivery is clearly not sustainable.
- *Lost share-of-customer opportunities*. Without integration, the supply chain can't capitalize on the information about customer needs that customer insight uncovers in order to form new supplier partnerships that intelligently and profitably increase the scope of a firm's offerings.

Because implementing CRM technologies and adopting customer strategies require supply-chain activities to be coordinated with and integrated into demand-chain activities, it is clear that managing customer relationships should no longer be thought of as a purely "customer-facing" set of business processes. When an enterprise truly succeeds in its customer-specific initiatives, that critical business practice will impact virtually all the firm's processes, with customer-specific insight and action permeating the supply chain, the product-development cycle, the financial systems, service delivery, and even the firm's organizational structure.

Once an enterprise truly embraces "building customer value" as a business practice, it will find itself compelled to drive every activity, every process, and every strategy around the customer. Everything that the firm *does*—every action it takes—eventually will revolve around the customer. Moreover, this process integration will extend even beyond the enterprise itself, allowing customers to serve themselves (and each other, using crowd service) in increasingly sophisticated and detailed ways and enabling channel members to configure, order, install, and service products according to the individual requirements or preferences of particular customers. Customized treatment of individual customers requires robust yet flexible processes that join demand chain and supply chain together.

---

[a]Ginger Conlon, "Supply Chain and the Customer Experience," Think Customers: The 1to1 Blog, January 16, 2009; available at: www.1to1media.com/weblog/2009/01/supply_chain_and_the_customer.html#more, accessed September 1, 2010.

Not All Customization Is Equal

Management advisor Joe Pine literally wrote the book on mass customization.[6] He and his partner, James H. Gilmore, have chronicled a business evolution—from creating standardized value through mass production to creating customer-unique value through mass customization. Pine and Gilmore have hypothesized four distinct approaches to mass customization:

1. *Adaptive customization* offers a standard, but customizable, product that is designed so that customers can alter it themselves. One lingerie company makes a slip that a customer can cut off in a finished way to make the slip the length she wants.

2. *Cosmetic customization* presents a standard product differently to different customers. Catalog company Lillian Vernon encourages buyers to personalize backpacks and sleeping bags with a child's name.

3. *Collaborative customization* conducts a dialogue with individual customers to help them articulate their needs, identify the offering that fulfills those needs, and then make customized products for them. Ross Controls, a Michigan-based manufacturer of pneumatic valves and other air control systems used in heavy industrial processes in such industries as automobile, aluminum, steel, and forestry, learns about its customers' business needs so it can collaborate with them on precisely tailored designs.

4. *Transparent customization* provides each customer with a customized product or service without necessarily telling her about the customization itself. This is what the Ritz-Carlton does, when it configures a guest's stay based on the preferences the guest expressed during previous visits to the hotel chain. The guest who gets a hypoallergenic pillow in her room may not even be aware that this is customized service; she may think this is how all guests are treated.[7]

Notice that *adaptive* and *cosmetic* customizers offer customers a better way to get what they want, compared to a mere standardizer; but also notice that these customizers *have no memory* of the **personalization** they do offer, thereby requiring customers to begin the specification process again with the next order. And that next transaction will depend entirely on the customer for its initiation. Therefore, adaptive and cosmetic customization offer no real sustainable competitive advantage against a competitor offering the same thing.

In contrast, notice that *collaborative* and *transparent* customizers maintain a distinct competitive advantage because they *remember* what a customer wants and can therefore better predict what she will want next time—reducing her need to make a choice. In many instances, the company takes a proactive role in offering to the customer what she's most likely to want next. The customer is able to get from a

---

[6]B. Joseph Pine II, *Mass Customization* (Cambridge, MA: Harvard Business Press, 1993).

[7]For more on the four types of mass customization, see James H. Gilmore and B. Joseph Pine II, "The Four Faces of Mass Customization," *Harvard Business Review* 75, no. 1 (January–February 1997).

┌ EXHIBIT 10.2   Supply Chain versus Demand Chain ┐

Mass Production	Mass Customization
Supply chain management	Demand chain management
Economies of scale	Economies of scope
Make to forecast	Make to order
Speculative shipping costs	Goods presold before shipping
Inventory carrying costs	Just-in-time inventory

collaborative or a transparent customizer something she can't get elsewhere—even from a competitor that offers the exact same thing—unless she goes to the trouble (and risk) of starting all over in a new Learning Relationship.

Gilmore and Pine say that many companies resist mass-customizing their offerings and instead "manage the supply chain" by placing more and more variety into their distribution channels and leaving it to buyers to fend for themselves. Manufacturers maintain large inventories of finished goods, and service providers maintain excess personnel and provisions to meet potential demands.

> The customer is able to get from a collaborative or a transparent customizer something she can't get elsewhere—even from a competitor that offers the exact same thing—unless she goes to the trouble (and risk) of starting all over in a new Learning Relationship.

These practices add costs and complexity to operations. Customers then must sort through numerous alternatives to find the one that most closely approximates what they want. In many situations, a majority of buyers never do find an exact match for their own personal tastes; instead they settle for the one that seems to be the best fit overall, considering both the positives and the negatives. Gilmore and Pine call this **customer sacrifice**—it's also known as the **satisfaction gap**—the difference between what customers want and what they're willing to settle for (see Chapter 1). Producing greater variety in anticipation of potential, yet uncertain, demand often represents a last-ditch attempt to preserve the mass-production mind-set in the face of rapidly fragmenting markets, say Gilmore and Pine.[8]

An enterprise focused on building customer value, by contrast, brings information about an individual customer's needs directly into its operations in order to achieve efficient, on-demand production or provisioning. This effectively turns the old supply chain into the back end of a *demand chain*.[9] In this process, the firm diminishes the importance of product *price* in favor of *relationship value* (see Exhibit 10.2).

SPAR is the brand name for a chain of more than 12,000 grocery stores and outlets operating in 33 countries and generating some €27 billion in worldwide

---

[8]James H. Gilmore and B. Joseph Pine II, *The Experience Economy* (Cambridge, MA: Harvard Business School Press, 1999); Pine, *Mass Customization*.
[9]Per Hilletofth, "Demand Chain Management: A Swedish Industrial Case Study," *Industrial Management & Data Systems* 109, no. 9 (2009): 1179–1196.

sales annually.[10] The company refers to itself as a kind of "soft" franchise operation, because most of its stores carrying its brand name are owned and operated independently. SPAR is the wholesaler for the stores in the chain, providing most—but not all—of the products sold by the member stores. SPAR's customers are the store operators themselves, and the company performs many services for them, in addition to wholesaling. For some storeowners, SPAR does the books and minds the payroll, for instance.

One of SPAR's innovations worth a closer look has been implemented in Austria, a relatively strong market for the firm, where it has an 18 percent share.[11] In 2003, SPAR Austria implemented a system that preconfigures its wholesale deliveries to a store in the same order in which the items are shelved in that store. So, as the stock clerk rolls the trolley down the aisle at her store she can effortlessly find the next items for the store's shelves, simplifying the process and saving considerable time and cost for the storeowner. Importantly, the ease with which SPAR Austria's products can be placed on a store's shelves provides an incentive for the storeowner to rely as much as possible on SPAR rather than going to the trouble of dealing with an additional supplier. Even if for a few items the other supplier might offer a more advantageous price, getting *goods onto shelves* costs less with SPAR.

Of course, each store's configuration is different, so SPAR's preconfiguration requires the firm to maintain an up-to-date record of each store's individual configuration. But it must also *act* on that information cost efficiently by changing the actual product delivery configuration for each store. Until this program was launched, the configuration of grocery products as they leave SPAR's own warehouses was not something that would have been considered a "customer-facing" activity. Mass-customizing those configurations, however, so as to treat different customers differently is very definitely a customer-facing action and perfectly illustrates how difficult CRM makes it to draw a line between supply-chain and demand-chain activities. It has allowed SPAR to shift the core of its business from the price-driven "grocery-goods supplier" to a unique collaborative supplier of "goods stocked on your shelves," which has a very different value. This is the heart of the payoff of mass customization: Collaboration leads to a new definition of the business a company is in, and this new business model defies commoditization, even when somebody else tries to do the same thing the same way.[12]

Mass customizers can adjust to changes in markets and technology easily, as they can rapidly shift their production, creating new products to accommodate changing environments. Fewer customer orders will be lost because mass customization always can, within overall capacity limits, build the products in demand. This contrasts again with mass-production factories, each of which has its own capacity limitations—limitations that usually cannot be offset by excess capacity elsewhere in the company. Distribution based on lower inventory levels at a build-to-order

---

[10]Figures as of 2008, available at: www.spar-int.com/, accessed April 2010.

[11]Available at: www.spar-int.com/, accessed April 2010.

[12]This idea of rethinking the industry and business a company is in was well described by W. Chan Kim and Renee Mauborgne in their book, *Blue Ocean Strategy: How to Create Uncontested Market Space and Make the Competition Irrelevant* (Boston: Harvard Business School Press, 2005).

factory can prevent shortages caused in distribution channels. The result is fewer opportunity losses.[13]

Because customized products can be ordered with only the options customers want, customers will not be forced to buy a "bundled" option package to get the one option they really want. Even at a premium price, customers may still save money by avoiding unwanted options.

The mass-customizing enterprise is driven by observing and remembering individual customer requests and by comparing them to what other customers have requested. The success of mass customization as a relationship-building tool stems from the fact that a customer can participate in the actual design and development of her own product. As a result of her own collaborative effort, the customer is much more likely to be satisfied with the overall performance of the product and to find it costly to start over with a competitor, even when that competitor can do the same thing the same way.

Mass Customization: Some Examples

Examples of mass customization abound in business today, both in business-to-consumer (B2C) and in business-to-business (B2B) settings:

- Lenscrafters can mass-customize eyeglass lenses in about an hour while the customer waits. (Customers don't just buy lenses off the rack!) The Miki Corporation, a Japanese eyewear firm, has taken eyeglasses a step further. With its Mikissimes Design System, available at several of its stores around the world, a person not only specifies the lens prescription but also can design the actual frame and tailor its shape and lenses to any one of thousands of configurations.[a]
- Mattel Inc. has used the Internet to allow children to create the doll of their dreams by selecting the hair, skin color, and clothing of their choice. The My Twinn doll company goes a step further. Customers input the doll's desired features, which are then assembled from a fixed assortment of parts. Once the customer receives her customized doll, My Twinn continues to sell clothing and accessories to fit the growing-girl customer as the doll "grows up" with its human twin.[b]
- Mercury Asset Management has taken mass customization in the print arena to a whole new level. To better serve its customers, Mercury, owned by the Merrill Lynch Group, released its first mass-customized magazine, *The*

(continued)

---

[13]David M. Anderson, *Agile Product Development for Mass Customization* (New York: McGraw-Hill Professional Book Group, 1997). Also see H. Agbedo, "A Note on Parts Inventory and Mass Customization for a Two-Stage JIT Supply Chain with Zero-One Type of Bills of Materials," *Journal of the Operational Research Society* 60, no. 9 (September 2009): 1286–1291, for more on the realities of material management in the electronics and automobile industries, which have found mass customization most profitable.

(*Continued*)

Mercury Investor's Guide. The 46-page, twice-yearly magazine mixes common pages with personalized pages in 7,700 versions.

- Shoe manufacturer Nike, Inc. and Apple have collaborated to provide customers the ultimate personalized workout. A special sensor can be inserted into a pair of Nike+ shoes that allows an iPod or iPhone to track workout time, distance, pace, and calories burned. The iPod or iPhone remembers each workout, so you can choose your own customized workout complete with personalized playlist. The Nike+ iPod can also be plugged into compatible gym equipment to track gym workouts, allowing customers to sync their workout data at nikeplus.com and track their progress over time.[c]

- Rodgers Instruments, a manufacturer of digital pipe organs, has found that mass customization provides not only greater value for clients but greater efficiency in production. Clients can customize almost 1,000 features, from control labels, to the number of keyboards, and pay only about 3 percent more than the standard model.[d]

- MyShape's online stores help women find clothing to match their body shapes with "sizeless dressing"—making mass customization as personal as it gets. MyShape has developed a patented algorithm that, when customers input their specific measurements and style preferences, displays individualized clothing recommendations in their Personal Shops and provides "freedom from the fitting room."[e]

- International Truck & Engine Corp. has used mass customization to learn more about its customers. It has introduced a custom truck configurator on the company Web site, where prospective customers can create hundreds of different designs—providing important information about customers in an industry where the manufacturer has little contact with the buyer. Customers still need to buy from the dealer, but now even the dealer can know more about its customers' preferences before they buy: serious Web site inquiries are sent to the dealer closest to the prospective client for direct follow-up.[f]

- Tesco, the celebrated relationship builder based in the United Kingdom that sells household products, mass-customizes its quarterly newsletter to its millions of Clubcard members using mass-customization software and printing techniques. Each member's mailing is pulled together based on individual shopping-basket data, and the company claims a 25 percent response rate from the mailings, resulting in significant incremental sales.[g]

[a]Paris Miki Holdings, Inc. Company Profile (2009); available at: www.paris-miki.com/about/pdf/miki_profile_english.pdf.

[b]Laurie J. Flynn, "Built to Order," *Knowledge Management* (January 1999). Also see: www.mytwinn.comwww.mytwinn.com, accessed April 2010.

[c]See www.apple.com/ipod/nike, accessed September 1, 2010.

[d]Elizabeth Glagowski, "Rodgers Instruments Makes Beautiful (Personalized) Music," *1to1 Magazine's Weekly Digest,* November 3, 2008; available at: www.1to1media.com/view.aspx?DocID=31196, accessed September 1, 2010.

[e]Mila D'Antonio, "MyShape Sees Double Digit Growth Using Personalized Recommendations," *1to1 Magazine,* December 4, 2008; available at: www.1to1media.com/view.

aspx?docid=31277, accessed September 1, 2010. Also see: www.myshape.com, accessed September 1, 2010. Our content editor, Amanda Rooker, tried this in March 2010 and reported that she can vouch that "it works amazingly well—it really did seem to pull everything I would have pulled off the rack and put it right in front of me; and it guaranteed it would fit. It even takes budget into consideration by listing all the prices up front."
[f]Kevin Zimmerman, "Rockin' Your Rig," *1to1 Magazine's Weekly Digest*, May 12, 2008; available at: www.1to1media.com/view.aspx?DocID=30854, accessed September 1, 2010. Since the mid-1990s, Harley-Davidson has been encouraging bikers to design their own motorcycles using their online Customizer program, where they can create a custom design and take it to a dealer to build it; available at https://customizer.harley-davidson.com/GMA_customizer.jsp?locale=en_US&bmlocale=en_US&locale=en_US&bmLocale=en_US, accessed April 2010.
[g]From a presentation by Andrew Mann, who heads the Clubcard program for Tesco, at the Gartner CRM Symposium, London, 2007.

Technology Accelerates Mass Customization

No matter how much value an enterprise adds, it is the value a customer adds for herself that makes a product or service worth a higher price. As the demand for personalized and customized products grows, more enterprises are offering build-to-order services to enable customers to configure products to their own needs—and improvements in technology have made it possible. Technology is enabling enterprises to meet their customers' demands through mass production, but in ways that offer people their own choice of products that are personalized and made to measure.[14] The Web, for instance, has become an ideal tool for mass customization, precisely because *anything that can be digitized can be customized*. The Web permits consumers to submit their specifications online directly to the manufacturer or sales executive.

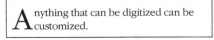

> Anything that can be digitized can be customized.

Capital One Financial Corp. developed a successful mass-customization model that changed the credit card industry.[15] The company is best known for gathering and analyzing consumer and customer data. Technology enables Capital One to observe and evaluate customer preferences and behavior and to do so dynamically, by market segment. The company can forecast trends and strategically shift its focus away from commoditized products, such as

---

[14]For example, best-in-class presenters at the 2010 MIT Smart Customization Seminar included toy companies (Build-A-Bear Workshop and LEGO Group), luxury brands (Louis Vuitton), apparel manufacturers (Archetype's indiDenim and indiTailored), and cereal makers (mymuesli), to name a few. See documentation of MIT's Smart Customization Seminar at http://scg.mit.edu/events/scg-events/84-the-mit-smart-customization-seminar-2010, accessed October 26, 2010.)
[15]Capital One, of course, mass-customizes products that take the form of digitized information and, in that sense, has an easier challenge than, say, an industrial manufacturer. But the same principles apply to both: modularization, closing the feedback loop, improvement through increased service levels at decreased cost to serve, and so forth.

balance transfer cards, before the market is
saturated with offers from competitors. Capital One planned for the obsolescence of balance transfer cards and plotted a course to
move the credit card company into mass cus-

> **I**t is the value a customer adds for her-
> self that makes a product or service
> worth a higher price.

tomization. This strategy enabled the firm to leverage its information resources to
identify customers with low-limit, high-fee potential and to send these customers the
marketing materials about products that would likely interest them, such as secured
cards for people with poor credit. Using a database that contains the histories of all
consumer interactions with Capital One has enabled the firm to customize its credit
card offerings. Capital One's CardLab also allows customers to add a personalized
image to their card for free—well worth it, considering that it can increase use per
card by 15 to 20 percent.[16]

Redefining the Business: Tesco

Tesco, the U.K. retail grocery chain ... is a great example of a company that
has used its powerful brand name to gain permission to sell a wide variety of
products and services to customers. (See elsewhere.) Both in its physical stores
and through its relationships with online consumers, Tesco has succeeded in
categories far removed from "grocery retailing."

Renowned for its frequent-shopper program, Tesco has been interacting
with customers at the point of sale and tracking those interactions since 1995.
When a customer presents her card to ensure she gets whatever discounts she's
entitled to, the company can her current shopping visit with all her previous
shopping, compiling a comprehensive transaction history, and assembling a
"picture" of the customer, based on the things she's bought. The customer might
fit neatly into one of several lifestyle segments that Tesco has created as a way of
categorizing its different customers by their grocery needs—from "convenience"
to "finer foods" to "cost conscious."

Tesco didn't start by trying to design the largest database it could, but instead focused on designing the smallest store of data that would give it useful
information. Using this data, Tesco customizes its discounts and other offers to
the individual needs of each customer. Ten million customers each quarter are
mailed some four million variations of coupon offers, based on each individual
customer's history and profile. The program generates £100 million of incremental sales annually for the retailer.

At the individual store level, Tesco's data can show the firm which products
must be priced at or below competitors' prices, which products have fewer
price-sensitive customers, which products need to be "everyday low price" to be

---

[16]Adam Elgar, "Card Personalization Can Generate 'Top of Wallet' Use in Tough Economy,"
CardLine 9, no. 15 (April 2009): 37; Judith Trotsky, "Future Bankers of the Year: Capital One
Financial Corp.'s Richard Fairbank & Nigel Morris," *FutureBanker* (December 1998): 106.

successful, and which have different levels of price elasticity for different types of customers. This kind of data gives Tesco the insight necessary to generate store-specific prices whenever it chooses.

In 2000, Tesco began offering online grocery shopping coupled with home delivery, and now 500,000 Tesco customers, accounting for about 10 percent of the company's overall sales, shop regularly online. Moreover, nearly 40 percent of Tesco's customers have given the company their e-mail addresses, which makes e-mail communications one of the most cost effective—and important—channels available to the firm. Tesco's ongoing, interactive relationships with its customers are buttressed by the trust that it constantly seeks to earn.

Today, based on (1) the strength of its brand and (2) its increasingly detailed relationships with its individual customers, the company now sells nearly any type of product or service that a regular consumer might consider ordering from a well-known, reputable brand name like Tesco. On Tesco's Web site you can buy books, computer games, CDs and DVDs, consumer electronics products, flowers, and wine; you can take out a loan or a mortgage, procure a credit card, open a savings or retirement account, or book a trip; you can buy insurance for your car, your life, your home, your pet, or your vacation; you can arrange for low-cost gas or electricity services, Internet access service, and mobile or home telephone service; in addition to all this, you can get advice on health and diet issues, babies, families, or Christmas gift ideas.

More than ten years after launching its relationship program, Tesco's brand now stands for a great deal more than "groceries." It is a brand that consumers have come to trust, based on the company's own culture. In a trusting relationship, the customer is more willing to consult the brand with respect to additional products and services that may appear to be outside the scope of the brand's original offering.

Over just the last few years, by using technology to expand its relationships with customers under the shelter of a powerful brand, Tesco has *dramatically* increased its growth potential, and as a result its publicly traded share price has grown commensurately. . . .

It was insight into customer needs, at the customer-specific level, that gave Tesco the knowledge to carry out this expansion of its business, and it was a powerful brand, built on customer trust, that enabled them to do it.

Source: From Don Peppers and Martha Rogers, *Return on Customer: A Revolutionary Way to Measure and Strengthen Your Business* (New York: Currency/Doubleday, 2005), pp. 50–52.

Customizing products and services can yield a competitive advantage if the enterprise deploys the correct design interface and remembers its customers' unique specifications and interactions. By linking an individual customer's interactions with previous knowledge of that customer, and then using that learning to drive the production process, the enterprise takes an integrative approach to competition—one customer at a time.

Customization of Standardized Products and Services

When the executives of a company believe they can sell only standardized products, sometimes those executives bemoan their inability to participate fully in the strategic payback of the customer relationship revolution.

> It's important to realize that even companies that cannot customize a product *per se* still can customize what they offer to individual customers and thus build Learning Relationships.

It's important to realize that even companies that cannot customize a product *per se* still can customize what they offer to individual customers and thus build Learning Relationships. A company may, for example, be able to change the product, add features, or combine it with other products. It may be able to sell standardized product, but provide various services that enable a customer to receive personalized attention before and after she buys the product, and make it possible for her collaboration with the firm to benefit her. The company that truly cannot mass-customize its products can look for service and communication opportunities to build in mass customization that makes the customer's investment in the relationship pay off—for both the customer and the company. There are many customization options beyond the physical product itself, and many ways an enterprise can modify how it behaves toward an individual customer, other than customizing a physical product. These include:

- Configuration of the product or services surrounding it
- Bundling of multiple products or services
- Packaging
- Delivery and logistics
- Ancillary services (repair, calibration, finance, etc.)
- Training
- Service enhancements
- Invoicing
- Payment terms
- Preauthorization

The key, for any enterprise trying to plan ways to tailor its products and services for individual customers, is to visualize the "product" in its broadest possible sense—not simply as a product but as an object that provides a service, solves a problem, or meets a need. One widely cited *Harvard Business Review* article from 2005 suggested, for instance, that we should try to think of products as being "hired" by customers to do a "job."[17] This is exactly what we mean when we talk about visualizing the broadest possible definition of the service a product provides, or the problem it solves, for a customer. And this is where a strict adherence to the

---

[17]Clayton M. Christensen, Scott Cook, and Taddy Hall, "Marketing Malpractice: The Cause and the Cure," *Harvard Business Review* 83, no. 12 (December 2005): 74–83.

CORE	PRODUCT-SERVICE	ENHANCED NEED SET
• Configuration • Size, fit, style • Features • Timing, frequency	• Billing, invoicing, cost control • Packaging, palletization • Logistics, delivery • Promotion, communication • Service operations	• Related products and services • Strategic alliances • Collaborative opportunities • Value streams

EXHIBIT 10.3   Enhanced Need Set

discipline of differentiating customers by their *needs* will pay off. What a customer needs and what she buys are often two different things. But if an enterprise has a full understanding of the customer's own need, then that enterprise can often devise a customized set of services or products that will meet that need. Meeting the customer's need is the service being performed by the enterprise, and the product itself is the means for delivering that service, or for doing that "job."

This product-as-service idea can be thought of in terms of three successively complex levels in the set of needs a customer is trying to meet (see Exhibit 10.3):

1. The *core product* itself includes its physical nature, if it is an actual product, or its component services and executional elements, if the core product is actually a service. Customizing the core product could include:
   - Product configuration
   - Features or capabilities
   - Fit and size
   - Color, design, style
   - Timing or frequency
2. The *product-service bundle* includes the services and features that surround the core product. Customization of the product-service bundle could include:
   - Invoicing, billing, and cost control (i.e., helping the customer manage or control costs)
   - Additional services
   - Packaging and palletization of the products
   - Promotion and marketing communication
   - Help lines and product support
3. The **enhanced need set** includes product or service features that could meet related customer needs, enhancing or expanding the customer's original set of needs. Activities undertaken to customize an enhanced need set could include:
   - Offering related products or services
   - Forming strategic alliances with other firms serving the interests of the same customers

- Providing the customer with opportunities to collaborate in product or service design
- Offering **value streams** of services or benefits following the actual sale of a product or service (more on value streams later in the chapter)[18]

As the definition of the customer's need is broadened, and as the need set is expanded, the definition of the product itself will become more complex. With a more complex product, the enterprise can make customization more beneficial. At each successive level of product complexity, the enterprise has another opportunity to remember *something* that later will make a difference to a specific individual customer. Remember, when a customer base is characterized by customers with dramatically different needs, remembering an individual customer's own personal needs or preferences will be highly beneficial to the customer. The more different the customers are in terms of their needs, the more benefit each customer will see in engaging in a Learning Relationship.

Thus, when customers have more uniform needs, as is particularly true of companies selling commodity-like products and services, the customer-strategy enterprise should try to expand the need set. Customers then will be seen as more diverse in the way they individually define their needs. The enterprise should assess which products and services it now offers that can cement the loyalty and improve the margin on its customers, even if the firm's competitors offer the same products and services at the same price, customized in the same way. Simply improving the quality of a product or service, while advantageous in the short term, will not necessarily yield a competitive benefit over the long term. A customer-strategy enterprise instead tries to improve a product's quality by customizing some aspect of it to suit the different needs of an individual customer in order to build a collaborative Learning Relationship with that customer. If the firm is selling a commodity-like product, what it actually customizes might not be the core product but the bundle of services surrounding the product or a configuration of additional products and services designed to meet an expanded definition of the customer's need.

One of the easiest ways for a B2B enterprise to customize its product-service bundle, for example, is to remember how and when *each customer* wants to be invoiced. A credit card company with corporate cards, a phone company, or any other firm that sells a high-transaction product or service to other businesses might consider offering some customers the opportunity to tailor the invoices to weekly totals rather than monthly ones. Or a firm could provide the invoices on a quarterly summary basis, or even offer to allow the customer itself to specify which time periods to invoice at one time. Some banks are already offering some personalization capabilities for formatting of monthly statement options. Enterprises that already offer customized products can benefit by customizing these ancillary services even further.

In addition to the services and operations that naturally accompany a core product, most products and services can easily be associated with a customer's

---

[18]Don Peppers and Martha Rogers, Ph.D., *Enterprise One to One* (New York: Doubleday Broadway Books, 1996).

other, related needs. When a customer buys a car from a car dealer, for instance, she will likely need automobile insurance, loan financing, a good mechanic, and, possibly, a carwash subscription. Catering to an enhanced need set means providing extra services to meet the customer's broadest possible set of needs.

Some hotels, such as Hotel La Fontana in Bogotá, Colombia, cater to the international business traveler. If a guest has a trip to Bogotá planned, the hotel will set up her appointments in advance for her. All the guest need do is tell the hotel the names and phone numbers of the people she will meet. The deeper an enterprise can penetrate a particular customer's needs, the more likely that enterprise will be able to cement a Learning Relationship with the customer, earning the customer's loyalty not simply out of gratitude but because it is more convenient for that customer to remain loyal. As long as he is certain his own interests are being protected, the customer will trust the enterprise with a greater and greater share of her business.

Value Streams

Some enterprises believe they have nothing to offer their end-user customers to entice them to want relationships. A firm that produces a single product, infrequently purchased, is in this kind of situation. One strategy for a one-product company would be to create a "stream of value" behind the actual product sale. Here's the choice: Find another customer for the product you sell, and then another and another, to generate more and more transactions; or find a related stream of products and services you could offer in order to get a greater share of customer from each of the customers you've already acquired.

> Here's the choice: Find another customer for the product you sell, and then another and another, to generate more and more transactions. Or find a related stream of products and services you could offer in order to get a greater share of customer from each of the customers you've already acquired.

Usually a value stream relies on some type of follow-on service, after the product sale, but it could also be an interaction designed to generate income later from customer referrals. The home builder who, in order to satisfy customers and generate more referrals, calls her customer the week before the one-year warranty expires and offers to inspect the home for any persisting problems is creating a value stream behind the sale of the home. The simple fact is that most people who build a home won't build another any time soon. But having received this kind of service, they will likely tell their friends about their positive experience, and the builder could generate a much higher level of referral service.

We could cite other examples. A furniture retailer could create a different kind of value stream behind its infrequently sold products, selling a sofa with a free upholstery cleaning, to be scheduled by the customer one year after the initial purchase. That way, when it comes time to schedule the cleaning appointment, the retailer would be reestablishing contact with the customer, to the customer's own benefit. At that point, the retailer could generate more revenue from the customer in any number of ways—selling a longer-term subscription to furniture cleaning, or selling items of furniture to go with the original purchase, and so forth. A clothing store could offer a dry cleaning or repair service for the clothing it sells. Customers who buy their suits from the store and pay an extra fee could have all of their dry cleaning, pressing, laundering, tailoring, and sewing done for the first two or three years, perhaps.

> Value streams eventually lead to supplemental revenue streams for the enterprise. A customer is willing to pay for the ancillary product or service because it is valuable to *her*. But, meanwhile, the enterprise will be strengthening its ongoing relationship by exchanging information with the customer, as the value stream is delivered.

Note that in each of these hypothetical cases, the enterprise increases the revenue generated from each customer by expanding the needs set, and builds an interactive Learning Relationship at the same time. The value stream approach has been used to encourage warranty card registration, particularly by software vendors whose products are bundled into the original equipment manufacturer's personal computer hardware. Those who mail in the registration (or who connect to register online) could receive 90 days' free advice and help in putting the software to work. Value streams eventually lead to supplemental revenue streams for the enterprise. A customer is willing to pay for the ancillary product or service because it is valuable to *her*. But, meanwhile, the enterprise will be strengthening its ongoing relationship by exchanging information with the customer, as the value stream is delivered.

Bentley Systems Creates Value Streams

What is the best way for an organization to remain actively involved with each of its customers—even when those customers may be years away from making another purchase? This is a key question for companies in some types of business, and it is a question likely to be faced especially by B2B organizations.

Bentley Systems faced just such a dilemma: It already owned a huge share of its market, so a strategy focused primarily on market development would not deliver the kind of results sought by the company's management. Instead, Bentley turned to a strategy that emphasized account development, launching an entirely new, subscription-based service to meet the needs of its clients.

One of the world's leading providers of software for the engineering, construction, and operation (E/C/O) market, Bentley Systems Incorporated has annual revenues topping $450 million. The company's primary products consist of architectural and engineering design software applications that it sells for a workstation environment. The typical Bentley customer buys a three-year software solutions contract worth $1 million, and might take as long as 18 months to close the deal. At any given moment, Bentley might have dozens of such deals in the works, all in various stages of development. Once a deal has been inked, it might be four or five years before the customer is ready for another purchase of similar magnitude. If nothing else, this makes it exceptionally difficult to project revenue very far into the future, as all of next year's revenue has to come from new customer sales or winbacks.

Many B2B organizations don't have a strategy or system in place to take advantage of the quiet intervals between sales. It's not that they're unaware of these intervals. More likely they've been trained or acculturated to see them as lost time, as dead zones in the purchase cycle. Sometimes these quiet times represent opportunities simply to deploy their customer acquisition resources elsewhere.

Or perhaps they're looking at the problem backward. Most enterprises believe it's important to know the purchase cycles of their customers: If you know the moment when your customer is ready to buy, you will be in a better position to sell your customer something—at that moment.

This type of reasoning works if you're in a business where you get to see your customers relatively often. Some B2C businesses—such as supermarkets, drug stores, and other retailers—can count on seeing their customers at least once or twice a week. But organizations that sell products such as boats, cars, refrigerators, manufacturing tools, real estate property, or high-end business equipment have customers who purchase much less frequently. If you have customers who buy from you only every few years, how can you establish and cultivate customer relationships?

There are two basic ways to address this type of challenge: You could sell or give away a range of additional services related to your product—cleaning, adjusting, calibrating, refilling, repairing it under a warranty's terms, configuring other products and services to go with your product, and so forth; or you could alter your business model to "subscribe" customers to your product, rather than selling it to them. In either case, you're talking about trying to create a value stream to supplement or replace a sales pattern marked by infrequent spurts of purchasing activity, enabling you to maintain and strengthen relationships with your clients over a longer period of time.

Greg Bentley is the one who spearheaded the company's evolution beyond product sales. His choice was to wrap a wide array of ancillary services and perks into a single, all-encompassing subscription plan called SELECT.

SELECT provides subscribing customers with literally dozens of benefits, such as 24/7 technical support, discounts on Bentley products, free platform swaps, and free software upgrades. SELECT customers are allowed concurrent licensing of their Bentley software, which essentially means the licenses are transferable from moment to moment within the company. This benefits the customers by giving them greater flexibility to redeploy expensive software applications among their users. And it benefits Bentley by expanding usage and creating demand for more software products.

The beauty of SELECT is that it functions as both a dependable income stream and a robust customer retention tool. When a customer signs up for the subscription plan, Bentley can bank on that customer's loyalty. For the duration, Bentley has a window of opportunity to sell more products to a customer who already has declared her allegiance.

The important idea here is that it is not only possible but also essential to create a practical system for bridging the gap between infrequent sales, if you plan to build your business success around customer relationships. SELECT

(continued)

(Continued)

is an example of a system designed to bridge this gap. It helps Bentley stay involved with its customers; it makes it easier for Bentley to cross-sell a variety of its products; and it allows Bentley to focus on growing the firm's share of customers instead of just its share of market.

In the final analysis, the most enduring legacy of SELECT may be how it fundamentally changed the way Bentley Systems measures success and allocates resources for the future. Under the old model, Bentley set annual goals for increasing its sales revenue, and it measured its own performance against these goals. This essentially kept the company locked into a customer acquisition mode, no matter how many innovative programs or initiatives it designed to break free. The launch of SELECT, and its rapid acceptance by customers, liberated Bentley to measure its performance with a refreshingly simple set of metrics tied to customer development.

Bentley has found it advantageous to move "up the food chain" to deliver more comprehensive service packages to its clients. For now, SELECT can be used to provide seamless document management, including filing, archiving, and transmittal to involved third parties. And the right way for Bentley to gain the most leverage out of SELECT is for the company to reorient its thinking about the nature of its customer base to begin with. With SELECT, rather than selling products to customers, Bentley is *subscribing* customers to an ongoing stream of products and services. Running a subscription business is very different from running a product transaction business.

In addition, many of Bentley's customers almost certainly want to develop their own value streams of services to transcend the periodic projects they do for their own clients. SELECT provides Bentley with an ideal opportunity to begin helping them in this task.

SELECT is a program that should be configured in such a way as to allow an architectural firm to go into not just the "project" business of designing and constructing a building, but into the "long-term management" business of taking care of the building, maintaining it, and upgrading it even after it has been built. Because Bentley's program can provide continual, updated documentation of a project's design, it can also help the architectural firm do a lot more than just creative work. A building is a complex system of pipes, wires, ducts, heating and cooling elements, and lighting treatments, not to mention the surrounding landscaping, lawn maintenance, irrigation and gardening care, as well as driveway and parking lot construction and maintenance. The more of this comprehensive system that SELECT can accommodate, the more Bentley's clients will rely on it to drive their own profitability.

When Bentley looks for additional ways to strengthen its relationships with its customers, the company might want to consider services that aren't tied directly to SELECT. It's not hard to imagine Bentley helping its customer firms with the preparation and financing of the bid they render for a project. Or instituting training classes for a client's engineers or architects—not just in the use of Bentley's software, but in the nuances of design. Or hosting Web sites and other IT infrastructure for a client, allowing the client to manage its own far-flung collection of independent architects and engineers more efficiently. See

Exhibit 10A for a comparison between Bentley's old "product" business model and the new "relationship" business model.

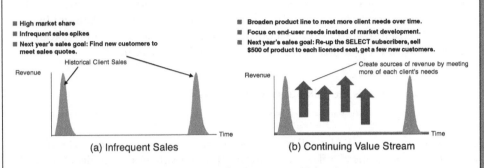

Source: Adapted from *One to One B2B*, by Don Peppers and Martha Rogers, Ph.D. (New York: Doubleday Books), 2001. Updated April 20, 2010, Bentley Systems, Inc. Company Record, available at: www.hoovers.com, accessed September 1, 2010; and Bentley Systems' SELECTservices Web site, available at: http://selectservices.bentley.com/en-US/, accessed September 1, 2010.

Mass customization, as we defined the term near the beginning of this chapter, involves creating a product by digitally combining a number of different modules representing premanufactured or preconfigured product and service components. The business processes that result in a product or service being rendered for a customer in a certain way can also be thought of, metaphorically anyway, as "modules" of the enterprise's overall behavior toward a customer. The instructions that an enterprise follows in configuring different processes for different customers are **business rules** that allow the company to ensure that its own behavior is delivered in what amounts to a mass-customized way—that is, tailored, as a matter of routine, to each situation. As Bruce Kasanoff explains in the next section, monitoring how the business rules operate at an enterprise is an important task, especially for any customer-strategy enterprise.

Who Will Write the New Business Rules for Personalization?

Bruce Kasanoff
President, Now Possible

Business rules are the instructions that tell software—or people—how to operate. They are a reusable set of instructions that enable an organization to operate in a consistent yet flexible way. Ronald Ross, cofounder of the

(continued)

(Continued)

consulting firm Business Rule Solutions, LLC, says, "Business rules are literally the encoded knowledge of your business operations." "Upgrade platinum flyers to first class before gold flyers" is a business rule. So is "Most valuable customers are those who order at least $1,500 of merchandise in a year."

> "Personalization is the killer app for business rules."

"Personalization is the killer app for business rules," says Ross. He argues that because business rules drive most of the leading personalization and e-commerce applications, companies now have a compelling reason to invest the time and effort in documenting the way they want to do business.

Instructions that Live Outside of Programming Languages

Business rules are not new; what is new is that today many rules are being created and changed via interfaces accessible to nontechnical business managers. Rules used to live deep within programming that was difficult and time-consuming to change. The resulting inflexibility of systems resulted in equally inflexible companies. By "externalizing" some business rules, enterprises are seeking to be more adaptable and efficient as they get closer to their customers, to deliver personalized and customized service. Not every rule should be accessible to business managers, who lack the technical training—or the inclination—to manage systems reliably and securely, but more and more, are accessible to nontechnical managers as the technology makes it possible.

Dealing with inflexible companies can be maddening for customers. Take a bank, for example, that requires a loan application for every customer, regardless of the customer's net assets or history with the bank. You can almost hear the assistant manager saying, "The system won't let me process your application without a completed application." She's right; that requirement is probably buried deep within the bank's programming, where it would take years to change.

The business rules approach makes it possible for such requirements to be contained in a far more accessible location. Thus, the bank could create a rule that would accommodate special circumstances. The rule might say: "If the customer has a clean credit report, the loan is secured, and the customer agrees to keep at least 20 percent of the loan's value in cash in her account, then waive the application requirement."

Transferring Knowledge from Your Head

It is difficult to transfer the knowledge of each employee—and of the organization as a whole—into a set of effective rules, and the very fact that it is so difficult is one reason business rules are so valuable. Think about the best salesperson you have ever met. Now imagine being able to capture what makes him so talented and imbue an automated system with those qualities. That is one promise of business rules, but the challenge is to translate his approach into a manageable number of repeatable principles. In this example, you might start with rules such as these:

- Listen to the customer's needs before you present any products, services, or offers.
- Present offers specific to the customer's stated needs before you show other special offers.
- Show the blue items first, because this customer has shown a preference for blue, then yellow, then gray.

Stew Leonard's is a Connecticut-based "dairy store" that is world-renowned for staying close to its customers and generating immense sales. In a largely nonautomated setting, the store has captured its principles in a set of rules that produce extraordinary service and a highly effective merchandising system.

One of those rules is that if an item is not properly marked for price, the customer gets it for free. I experienced this firsthand while buying an eight-pound piece of filet mignon for a holiday celebration. When a price didn't come up on the register, the cashier gave it to me for free. I began to protest—the meat was worth at least $50—but she explained that because the company did so much volume, it was cheaper to give the meat away than to hold up the checkout line. And, besides, Stew Leonard's has "The customer is always right" carved in stone at the front of the store.

Ken Molay, director of product marketing at Blaze Software (now part of Brokat), explained that business rules can also be used to balance the needs of a customer with those of the enterprise: "The goal of personalization is not just to give a customer whatever he needs, but rather to keep him happy while also ensuring that the company profits from delivering the service."

> "The goal of personalization is not just to give a customer whatever he needs, but rather to keep him happy while also ensuring that the company profits from delivering the service."

New Rules, New Skills

It is not hard to create a simple business rule, such as "Send a thank-you e-mail to every customer who places an order." It is difficult, however, to create and manage a full complement of rules; yet this is exactly what is required when the goal is to treat different customers differently.[a] As rules multiply, the odds increase that they will cancel each other out or cause unexpected results. This is especially problematic when multiple business units target the same customers. What if 10 units create rules that specify what happens when a new prospect

(continued)

(Continued)

visits the firm's Web site? Does the prospect get 10 different offers, all seemingly oblivious to each other, or does one take precedence?[b]

> It is not hard to create a simple business rule, such as "Send a thank-you e-mail to every customer who places an order." It is difficult, however, to create and manage a full complement of rules; yet this is exactly what is required when the goal is to treat different customers differently.

When Rich Lloyd, senior manager of online relationship marketing for Dell Home Systems, noted that theory is often much different from practice and that personalization rules are no different, he said, "Rules get written through trial and error, by testing and retesting. We start with some sort of hypothesis, and then we work hard to isolate the confusing noise from what's really working." For example, Lloyd's team might have tried an approach in which the division sent an e-mail promoting printers to everyone who purchased a laptop but not a printer in the past 10 months. But they don't look at the result of that promotion in isolation; they track results over 3 months to determine whether the e-mail reduces the response to other promotional messages sent to the same group of customers. The question to ask, says Lloyd, is "Am I better off with this additional rule in place or not?"

One of the first challenges for these pioneers is to develop rules for inter-acting with individual customers. Although personalization and customization[c] have become hot topics in recent years, many enterprises have only recently identified their customers, or begun efforts to do so. Until the rise of the Web, any firm that sold through a distribution channel had long been disconnected from its end users. Even enterprises that deal directly with customers have often engaged in monologues ("Buy this; it works") rather than true dialogues ("What works for you?").

The solution is customer portfolio management—putting one person or team in charge of making a customer or group of customers more valuable to the firm and then giving the customer manager exclusive access and final authority to each customer as well as ultimate responsibility for the value of the customer. (You'll read more about this in Chapter 13.)

Who "Owns" the Customer Relationship?

In a typical company, Product Manager A wants the Web site to send an of-fer for his product to every new site visitor. But Product Manager B wants to send an offer for her product. No one can document the correct processes, because no one agrees on them. Thus, the increasing use of business rules to drive the automation of customer interactions will accelerate the pressure on enterprises to shift from product management to customer management orga-nizational structures. If one division "owns" a certain group of customers, then it is clear who is responsible for managing the rules that apply to those individuals. The process of creating and managing rules highlights the limitations of product management structures. These organizations were logical when the toughest challenge an enterprise faced was creating and selling high-quality products. But today the toughest challenge is managing relationships, often in real time. If divisions are competing internally, they make decisions that aren't in the customer's interest.

Alan Crowther has observed, "Organizational barriers mean that personalization objectives are often compromised to individual business objectives. Even though it may make sense to personalize a site so that certain products or services are not highlighted, a business unit may have the clout to demand it." Of course, the real loser is the company that remains burdened by an organizational structure that is illogical in today's era of real-time interactions. Most customers are starved for time and increasingly unwilling to tolerate treatment that doesn't make sense to them. The bottom line: Creating rules for e-commerce and personalization is much easier when one person or business unit has clear ownership of a portfolio of customers.

Even with such clarity, large enterprises are still, well, large. So business rules need to be created using a common vocabulary. Ron Ross explains: "You must be able to trace who is using what terms in what context; you need to be able to trace the impact across the business environment." While business rules can theoretically be created using everyday language, each term must be used with more precision and consistency than we use in normal conversation.

Another issue in large businesses is traceability: being able to follow the impact of certain rules across the entire business environment. "You need to know what task each rule relates to," says Ross, "and you also want to be able to trace rules to the parties that have a stake in a particular rule. When it comes time to change the rule, you must know whom to call." This is a good application for the Customer Interaction and Experience Touchmap described in Chapter 7.

What to Expect

The more you study the use of business rules to drive personalization, the more obvious it becomes that the approach has tremendous potential but is still in its infancy. While there are no tried-and-true best practices, it is possible to offer some conclusions about what will likely work best.

- *Minimize the number of enterprise-wide rules.* Only about 2 to 3 percent of all business rules are "core rules" that impact the entire enterprise and specify qualities that give the firm its identity and differentiating qualities, Ross says. These rules usually existed long before the advent of automated systems. Here is an example that used to apply at Domino's Pizza: All pizzas are delivered within 30 minutes or the pizza is free. This rule drove the company and its marketing messages, but it eventually was changed

(continued)

(Continued)

after communities began to question whether the pressure on drivers to deliver so quickly was resulting in serious traffic accidents. Note that rules such as this need to include two portions: the rule itself and what happens if the rule is violated.

- *Use the simplest approach possible.* The more complex an approach, the more likely it is to fail. The question to ask is: What are the simplest changes that will have the most powerful positive impacts on customer relationships? One practice to consider is that all databases containing customer information have at least one field with a common, firm-wide format, enabling the firm to link individual customer data from one unit to the next when necessary. Sometimes this approach can be simpler than building a data warehouse or requiring all business units to conform to more restrictive data conventions.
- *Combine business rules with other approaches.* Matching business rules with specialized data mining, domain-specific algorithms, and other applications will generate better results, Crowther says. Ontologies provide a consistent, logical model for accommodating multiple data sources and goals. Done right, they provide a flexible system for understanding and managing interactions with individual customers.
- *Maintain a separate rule base.* A rule base is essentially a database for rules. By separating business logic from specific applications, rules can be shared by numerous applications. This approach speeds development and increases flexibility. As the number of rules grows, it becomes increasingly important to be able to test in advance what impact the addition of new rules will have. This task is easier when all the rules are stored in a common location and format.

Source: Adapted from Bruce Kasanoff, *Making It Personal* (New York: Perseus, 2001).

[a]Alan Crowther, quoted in Bruce Kasanoff, *Making It Personal* (New York: Perseus, 2001). Rules have the potential to produce outcomes that are undesirable or even illegal. Crowther warns, "Enterprises have to be careful that rules do not result in certain content that is accessible only to certain people based on inappropriate data. For example, a financial services site that uses location to determine which people see loan officers might generate outcomes that could be considered redlining. While no one may pursue this explicitly, algorithms that augment business rules can make this happen inadvertently." Colleen McClintock, product manager at iLog Software, admits that there is a political aspect to the creation of business rules. "Rules can support the interests of the organization writing the policies," she said.

[b]Authors' note about the difference between personalization and customization: Many companies and writers in this field use these terms interchangeably, and that's probably okay. But generally, when there is a distinction, it's usually as given in the glossary. Perhaps it's helpful to think of personalization as Pine and Gilmore's "adaptive" and "cosmetic" customization whereas what we refer to as customization is more along the lines of "collaborative" and "transparent" customization.

Culture Rules

Mass customization makes a lot of intuitive sense, but aren't there still some situations that won't be covered by an enterprise's business rules? What happens when a customer presents some problem or need for which there is no valid, preconfigured set of solutions that can be rendered in a cost-efficient way?

An enterprise can automate the contact report a sales rep has to file, but no computer can look into a client's eye and judge whether to push for the sale or ask another question first. And no enterprise can write a business rule that requires employees to delight customers. The employees themselves have to want to do that. An enterprise's secret sauce is its *culture*—the unwritten rules and unspoken traditions that define how employees actually approach their jobs. This is what guides employees when there is no policy—no applicable business rules. It's what they do when no one's looking.

Abraham Lincoln was once asked the secret of General Ulysses S. Grant's success during a particularly difficult Civil War campaign. Always ready with an anecdote, Lincoln told the reporter it reminded him of a story about the great "automaton" chess player that had astonished Europeans nearly a century before. Popularly known as the Mechanical Turk, it had been constructed to resemble a mechanical man, dressed in a costume like a Turk, seated behind a wooden cabinet, and apparently capable of playing chess. It had defeated many human players, but after one celebrated competitor suffered two embarrassing defeats at the hands of the machine, he angrily wrenched off the cabinetry to peer inside and then rose up to exclaim, "Hey! There's a person in there!" That, said Lincoln, was the secret of Grant's success.

It is also the final, underlying secret of any business enterprise's success when it comes to satisfying customers and ensuring they continue to create value. There has to be a person in there somewhere. No matter how well the business rules are architected, and no matter how many "modules" of product or service delivery are available to drive the mass-customization effort, human judgment always will have to be accommodated in the enterprise's customer-facing processes. It's impossible to serve customers well without it, and generally the more important decisions are the ones that require the most judgment. For a customer, the most vital problem or difficult issue often involves some type of crisis situation—a situation that is likely to be unusual or at least one that hasn't already been anticipated by the enterprise. This means that almost by definition, any issue of utmost importance to a customer is likely to be something that falls through the cracks if an enterprise is operating entirely by predocumented processes and procedures. The enterprise won't be able to specify it in advance. There has to be a person in there, capable of making the right judgment call.

As a result, nowhere does an enterprise's corporate culture play a more important role than in dealing with customers, because doing this often requires conceptual-age, nonroutine skills such as empathy, creativity, and sensitivity.[19] Many companies try to cut costs by outsourcing and automating their more routine customer service tasks. Most find out the hard way that it's a big mistake to outsource judgment calls. Nor is it the best idea to hardwire all a company's policies and processes entirely into "the system," leaving no room for flexible responses to unanticipated situations.

---

[19]Daniel H. Pink, *A Whole New Mind* (New York: Riverhead, 2005).

Not long ago a friend of ours went online to book family trips on two different airlines for successive weekends. The first trip was on a well-established carrier with a great service reputation, but it is heavily unionized and often hemmed in by its own bureaucracy. It was a complicated itinerary involving coordinating with some other people, so our friend first booked her family's outbound trip, then did some more calling to make sure the return flight was coordinated with others before booking it too. But guess what? When she booked the return flight, she realized that a round trip would cost less than either of the one-way trips just purchased. So she called the reservations office directly now, having been defeated by the online experience, and—you guessed it—"No, sorry, no can do." Basically, she was told, she had bought the tickets online and a deal was a deal, that's that. Then the agent even said something to the effect that "Yes, I know it's unfair, but I am powerless to make the change; the system just won't let me."

Fast forward to the following weekend, and our friend was on the way to a different weekend destination with her family, this time on a new entrant carrier, one of the price competitors. You book your seat, and it's a great low price but absolutely nonrefundable. The family ran into a traffic snarl and arrived at the airport way too late for the flight. Our friend found herself thinking that this was going to be a very expensive weekend for not going anywhere at all. But when the family got to the counter, an agent said something like "Sorry you missed your flight, but why don't you just take a room at the airport hotel tonight and I'll put you all on the 7 a.m. flight tomorrow morning? Tell you what, I'm also going to waive the $50 rebooking fee, and I'll call your destination hotel, see if they can resell your rooms for tonight, maybe save you some money."

Here are two different companies with two different ways to handle exceptional customer service situations. Although it's important to do a competent job using efficient processes, good service cannot spring solely from processes or rules or systems. The important process for winning customer loyalty is *customization*, which has been the subject of this chapter. We need to remember that *mass* customization is simply a process for customizing more cost efficiently. However, it is in the exceptions to the rules, the unusual and problematic situations, that a company has to rely on individual people to make wise decisions. If an enterprise has the wrong employee culture, for whatever reason, good systems and processes actually might magnify this problem. Instead, particularly in the service sector, the enterprise wants front-line employees who are not only *empowered* to make decisions and take action (as the first airline's employee was not) but also *motivated* to make those decisions in a way that is in the long-term interest of the firm (i.e., in a way that customers feel they have been treated fairly).[20]

The payoff for enterprises that engage in customization is twofold. In most cases, by employing automation and business rules to mass-customize its products or the delivery of its services, the enterprise actually can reduce its unit production costs, on an all-in basis, essentially because it will only make those goods that customers will have already bought. More important, however, customization will enable the enterprise to engage in a *collaborative* Learning Relationship with each customer.

---

[20]Excerpted and adapted from Don Peppers and Martha Rogers, *Rules to Break and Laws to Follow: How Your Business Can Beat the Crisis of Short-Termism* (Hoboken, NJ: John Wiley & Sons, 2008), pp. 113–115.

Summary

Instead of expecting a customer to use what *she* knows about a company to figure out what she should buy, the customer-focused enterprise uses what *it* knows about the customer to figure out what she needs. In the process, such an enterprise increases the number of transactions it gets from a customer, makes it progressively easier for that customer to come back to that enterprise for purchases and service, and likely increases the profit per transaction.

Our story of managing customer relationships in the interactive era now takes a turning point. We have laid the foundation of relationship theory and provided a comprehensive examination of each of the four tasks of the IDIC methodology: Identify-Differentiate-Interact-Customize. We have shown the importance of Learning Relationships and the sensitive issues related to privacy protection. We have peeked at the technical tools that help to accelerate the relationship management process and reinforced how technology does not, and should not, manage customer relationships alone.

With Part Three (beginning with Chapter 11), we begin to look at what it means to manage the customer relationship process. We discuss the challenges an enterprise faces in measuring and maintaining a customer-based initiative and look at the quantifiable metrics associated with managing customer experiences and Return on Customer. We delve into the science of customer analytics as a method to predict each customer's behavior and anticipate his needs so he will be treated the way he wants and remain a customer. Finally, we show how transforming into an enterprise that grows through building customer value requires a number of different infrastructure changes that will need to be addressed by managers who fully understand and support the underlying concepts we have been discussing so far—and so much more that we have yet to discuss.

Food for Thought

1. How will Lego practice mass customization? To think about mass customization for Legos, consider:
   - Who are the customer types for Lego? (Think retailers, B2B.) Who are the MVCs? The MGCs? The BZs? (See Chapter 5.)
   - What are customers buying when they buy Legos? (It's not "toy building bricks.")
   - If customers buy packages of Legos to resell, what else do they need? What is their expanded need set?
   - What is the opportunity to lock customers into a Learning Relationship and build share of customer for Lego?
   - Is there any opportunity, ever, at all, for Lego to build Learning Relationships with any end user? How and why?
2. If customization is such a good idea, why don't we see more of it in the marketplace right this minute?
3. Name half a dozen examples of mass customization or expanded needs sets in the enterprises where you do business.

Glossary

Adaptive customization   Offering a standard but customizable product that is designed so that customers can alter it themselves.

Business rules   The instructions that an enterprise follows in configuring different processes for different customers, allowing the company to mass-customize its interactions with its customers.

Collaborative customization   Conducting a dialogue with individual customers to help them articulate their needs, identifying the offering that fulfills those needs, and then making customized products for them.

Cosmetic customization   Presenting a standard product differently to different customers.

Customer sacrifice   See *Satisfaction gap*.

Customization   Most often, *customization* and *mass customization* refer to the modularized building of an offering to a customer based on that customer's individual feedback, thus serving as the basis of a Learning Relationship.

Demand chain   A company's front-end sales, marketing, or customer service operations.

Enhanced need set   The capability of a company to think of a product it sells as a suite of product plus service plus communication as well as the next product and service the need for the original product implies. The sale of a faucet implies the need for the installation of that faucet, and maybe an entire bathroom upgrade and strong nesting instinct.

Mass customization   See *Customization*.

Modularization   Configuring a product's components to put them together in a standardized way, in order to facilitate the process of mass customization and reduce company costs.

Personalization   Refers to a superficial ability to put a customer's name on something—to insert a name into a message, for example, or to monogram a set of sheets.

Satisfaction gap   The difference between what customers want and what they're willing to settle for.

Supply chain   A company's back-end production or service-delivery operations.

Transparent customization   Providing each customer with a customized product or service without necessarily telling him about the customization itself.

Value stream   A compilation of related products and services a company could offer to an existing customer in order to get a greater share of customer from each customer already acquired.

Measuring and Managing to Build Customer Value

Customer relationships cannot be installed; they must be adopted. And building customer value requires process, organization, technology, and culture management. It's a shift in strategy after 100 years dominated by mass marketing, so it can't happen overnight. The management of customer relationships to build the value of the customer base is a journey, not a destination.

PART III

Measuring and Managing
to Build Customer Value

CHAPTER 11

Optimizing around the Customer:
Measuring the Success of
Customer-Based Initiatives

We've long felt that the only value of stock forecasters is to make fortune tellers look good. Even now, Charlie [Munger] and I continue to believe that short-term market forecasts are poison and should be kept locked up in a safe place, away from children and also from grown-ups who behave in the market like children.

—Warren Buffett

Traditional marketing measures such as response rates, cost per 1,000, gross ratings points, and awareness levels help a company understand how successful a campaign has been or how successful or efficient a particular message is, on average, in reaching a target market. But when using interactive technologies and dealing with customers one at a time, the key task most marketers face is how to optimize the enterprise's behavior around individual customers rather than products. Optimizing the enterprise around a customer is the problem confronted whenever a firm is trying to decide how to design a Web site, how to define objectives and scripts for a contact center, or how to frame the selling strategy for a face-to-face meeting with a customer. The question being asked in these situations isn't, What's the best overall message for this particular product, when talking to everyone? but What's the best message for this particular customer, during this particular interaction? As we learned in the chapters on Identify-Differentiate-Interact-Customize (Chapters 3–10), the customer-centric competitor hopes that by optimizing the enterprise's behavior around a particular customer during a particular interaction or event, the firm will be able to maximize the value created by that customer, including not just the short-term, current-period value created by immediate product sales or costs generated, but also the long-term value created by changes in the customer's predisposition toward the brand.

Customers create long-term value because they have memories.[1] Each customer's decision whether to buy from a business today will be based at least partly on his memory of any past experience he's had with the firm, or perhaps on his impressions of it based on his friend's past experience. The important thing is that every time a customer has an experience with any business, his intention or likelihood of buying from that business in the future is liable to change. Nice experience? Likely to buy more later. Might even talk about the brand with a friend. Bad experience? Likely not to buy much in the future. Also might criticize the brand to a friend.

Although this is not a textbook on accounting or economics, nevertheless it's important to remember that the actual economic value of any business enterprise can be measured in terms of the discounted net present value of the future stream of cash flow that the enterprise is expected to generate. So when a customer's likelihood of buying in the future changes, or when her likelihood of sharing her experience with a friend changes, the company's likely future cash flow also changes—which means that the company's actual economic value goes up or down as a result of the customer's changing frame of mind. This is the long-term component of the value that customers create.

For the overwhelming majority of companies, this kind of value creation (or, sometimes, value destruction) is not captured in the financial statements. Note, however, that the customer experience driving an increase or decrease in the enterprise's value occurs in the present. Although the firm may not realize the cash effect for days or weeks or months, the value itself is created or destroyed today, with the customer's current experience. Moreover, this is happening whether marketers at the enterprise think about it or not and whether they try to measure it or not. Even though the financial systems of most firms don't recognize the long-term value constantly being created or destroyed by the individual current experiences of their customers, the financial metric that we introduced in Chapter 5, customer **lifetime value** (LTV), is specifically designed to capture it. To reprise the concept, a customer's LTV is defined as the net present value of the future stream of cash flow attributable to that customer. It therefore directly represents the long-term financial benefit of a customer's continuing patronage. When the customer becomes more predisposed to buy from the enterprise, her LTV will increase. When the customer becomes less enamored with the enterprise's brand, her LTV will decrease. As a result, the increases and decreases in a customer's LTV can be thought of as the direct, dollars-and-cents quantifications of the long-term value created or destroyed in particular customer interactions.

However, there is a certain tension between encouraging customers to create value in the short term (through immediate sales) and encouraging them to create value in the long term (through changes in the customer's predisposition). Focusing on either task can undermine the other. If a firm markets too aggressively in order to build up current sales, it will almost certainly damage a customer's long-term value—maybe by cannibalizing sales it would have made in the future anyway, or perhaps by irritating the customer into not wanting to receive further

---

[1] This chapter is based in large part on Peppers and Rogers's books *Rules to Break & Laws to Follow: How Your Business Can Beat the Crisis of Short-Termism* (Hoboken, NJ: John Wiley & Sons, 2007) and *Return on Customer: Creating Maximum Value from Your Scarcest Resource* (New York: Currency/Doubleday, 2005).

communications or not even wanting to do more business. But by the same token, if a company smothers a customer in great service in order to maximize the future business he does with the firm—well, great service isn't free either, and the funds required today to provide this service reduce whatever short-term value the customer might create. Therefore, companies have to strike a balance, because they need to create both short- and long-term value.

Unfortunately, for most businesses, the temptation to maximize the short term is nearly irresistible. Publicly held companies may have the excuse of investor pressures, but even nonpublic companies will succumb to the short-term temptation if they allow themselves to forget about the way customers really create value. An endemic problem among businesses is the fact that the traditional measures of financial success drive short-term thinking and actions, and these measures just do not account for all the ways customers actually can create shareholder value. Reconciling the conflict between current profit and long-term value is one of the most serious difficulties facing business today. Failing to take a properly balanced approach not only penalizes good management practices but also undermines corporate ethics by encouraging managers to "steal" from the future to fund the present. Often companies end up destroying value unintentionally—or worse, they know they are destroying value but feel they have no real choice about it. At the extreme, a firm might even resort to overpromising or tricking customers out of their money, in order to maximize short-term profit. Of course, doing this almost certainly hampers future sales and destroys long-term value by eroding the trust that customers have in the firm.

Balancing between such extremes in order to maximize overall value creation is not a new or revolutionary idea. As early as 1996, in an innovative and forward-thinking *Harvard Business Review* article, Bob Blattberg and John Deighton suggested that a firm should apply "the **customer equity** test" to balance marketing expenditures between customer acquisition and customer retention efforts. They even proposed a mathematical model for fitting exponential curves to find the optimum levels of acquisition and retention spending, based on executives' answers to some level-setting questions.[2] And the very concept of "brand equity," which was a widely used metaphor during the heyday of mass advertising, was based on the idea that a brand's value could be built up over time, with appropriate messaging, and that this store of value could become a genuine asset for driving competitive success.[3]

A 2003 white paper from Peter Mathias and Noel Capon of Columbia Business School considers the implications of managing customers for three "quite different outcomes: maximizing revenue in the near term, maximizing profitability in the short to intermediate term, and optimizing the asset value of customer relationships—customer relationship capital—over the long term."[4] The paper

---

[2]Robert C. Blattberg and John Deighton, "Manage Marketing by the Customer Equity Test," *Harvard Business Review* 74, no. 4 (July-August 1996): 136–144.

[3]Roland T. Rust, Valerie A. Zeithaml, and Katherine N. Lemon, *Driving Customer Equity: How Customer Lifetime Value Is Reshaping Corporate Strategy* (New York: Free Press, 2000).

[4]Peter F. Mathias and Noel Capon, "Managing Strategic Customer Relationships as Assets: Developing Customer Relationship Capital," *Velocity, Strategic Account Management Association* 5 (Q1, 2003): 45–49.

suggests that salespeople traditionally have been held accountable for short-term revenues, but as more organizations have come to emphasize key account management over the last decade, the metric of success has shifted perceptibly from customer revenue to customer profitability. To be successful in the future, say the authors, a firm will have to "take the long view" and "maximize the net present value (NPV) of future profit streams from these customers."

Determining the appropriate measurements to be used in quantifying the results of a company's marketing efforts has always been a particularly elusive task, and to many it seems to have been made doubly difficult by the complexity of customer-specific marketing initiatives that new interactive technologies make possible. The very culture at many firms is intertwined with more traditional measures of success—or what we might call *legacy metrics*: quarterly product sales; cost of goods sold; number of new customers acquired; earnings before interest, taxes, depreciation, and amortization (EBITDA); return on investment (ROI); return on equity (ROE)—the tried and true. It shouldn't be surprising that companies often find it challenging to supplement such legacy metrics with updated measurements designed around capturing the values that individual customers create, one customer at a time.

It is precisely because customers create both long- and short-term value that the customer-centric competitor will be well served to think of individual customers as being similar to financial assets—assets that are generating some cash flow now and are likely to continue generating cash flow for some time into the future. Each customer, in other words, represents a bundle of likely future cash flows—costs and revenues tied to that particular customer's most likely future behavior.

The asset value of a customer is the customer's LTV. Consumer marketing firms with databases of transactional and other customer records can use statistical modeling techniques to forecast their customers' future behaviors and then calculate the LTVs represented by those behaviors. This is not an exact science, however, and no matter how sophisticated the computer modeling becomes, it will never be completely accurate, for the simple reason that predicting the future never can be completely accurate. (For that matter, the accepted calculations of the "tried and true" have limitations in accuracy too. See Chapter 5.) However, many would argue that using predictive models to forecast future customer behavior is not substantively different from, and not inherently any less accurate than, using similar statistical models to forecast future economic variables, such as the supply and market demand for a particular product or service. In any case, the basic principle that a customer's asset value should be thought of in terms of the future cash flows he represents is very useful, especially when we consider how this asset value goes up and down on a daily basis with the customer's current experience.

The problem is that while LTV is a known and accepted concept in marketing circles, few marketers and even fewer finance people fully appreciate its real implications. Customers have memories and free will, so (unless we're talking about the utilities monopoly) the treatment they receive from an enterprise *today* has a significant impact on the value they can be expected to yield for that enterprise not only today but also in the future. If a customer can be thought of as a financial asset, then *changes* in the value of this asset—changes in the customer's LTV—are important. When a customer's opinion of a firm improves or deteriorates, based on her experience with the firm today, her LTV goes up or down, and the amount of this increase or decrease in LTV is real economic value that has been created or destroyed as a result of the customer's experience in the present. In this light, changes in the LTV of a customer are every bit as important, financially, as the current-period sales or costs attributable to that customer and captured on financial statements.

Consider this analogy: Suppose a business has some physical asset, perhaps a warehouse full of spare parts. Then suddenly the asset is rendered worthless by a disaster. Suppose a hurricane wipes out the warehouse, and the firm isn't insured for the loss. If that were to happen, generally accepted accounting principles (GAAP) would require the firm to write down the value of that asset, and this quarter's income would be reduced by the amount of the write-down. Now think again about the customer's asset value. Suppose, instead of a hurricane wiping out a warehouse full of spare parts, there is instead some kind of customer service snafu, with the result that a very valuable customer becomes angry and upset with the firm. Because of this, his LTV plummets to zero (or even below zero, because he might communicate his bad feelings about the firm to his friends!). Didn't the company's value decrease when that happened? Surely, its future cash flow will decline if that customer's opinion is not turned around again, right? Of course, the accounting treatment for this kind of "customer" event is quite different from that prescribed for the destruction of a physical asset carried on the balance sheet—but for now, we won't focus on the accounting issues but on the simple reality of the economic loss to a company represented by an unresolved customer complaint.

The fact that a customer's asset value (or LTV) will increase or decrease with his current experience, because he'll remember that experience later, means that a customer-centric enterprise has to account for the value it is creating from customers in a different way than the way a product-centric enterprise accounts for the value created by its products. Products don't have memories, while customers do. Note that how a company treats parts and supplies today will not affect the future cost of these supplies, or the profit to be earned from the products created with them. But how a company treats customers today will definitely affect the future profits likely to be generated by those customers.

Today's accounting courses don't often acknowledge customers as significant financial assets. But in the nonaccounting real world, customers are the *only* genuine value-creating assets any business has. As we said in Chapter 1, the only reason a business exists at all is to create and serve customers. Customers create, on the most basic level, virtually 100 percent of any enterprise's value. Customers define a business as a business. And it ought to be clear to the most casual observer that a customer's experience with a company, its products, or its brands has an economic impact that goes beyond the current financial period. Any company that spends advertising money to improve its brand image is explicitly acknowledging this fact. Such a firm is investing money based on the assumption that customer intentions have a financial value. If it can affect those future intentions today, then it hopes to see the cash effect tomorrow.

Some companies—especially those that have grown up in the interactive age—have so internalized this view of the customer as a value-producing financial asset that it affects their whole philosophy of business. Amazon's Jeff Bezos says his firm would rather spend on free shipping, lower prices, and service enhancements than on advertising. "If you do build a great experience, customers will tell each other about that," he says.]

Customer Equity

Products, brands, stores, bank branches, patents, information technology systems, marketing promotions and campaigns—even the best employees—cannot pay money to any organization. Only customers—by definition—generate revenue. And if customers are the only genuine source of value creation for a business, then all the customers an enterprise has must be responsible for creating 100 percent of that enterprise's shareholder value. This is the basic idea behind the concept of "customer equity." If we sum all the LTVs of an enterprise's current and future customers, then we have calculated the actual economic value of that enterprise as a going concern.[5] Thus, if all of a company's cash flows come from its customers, then the sum of all current and future customers' LTVs is the same thing as the economic value of the firm (i.e., the NPV of the firm's future cash flows). Take away a profit-generating customer, and the value of a firm declines. Improve the cash flow expected from a customer, and the firm's value increases.

The term *customer equity* can describe the effectiveness of customer strategies and implementation because it is primarily determined by the total value of the enterprise's customer relationships. For a customer-centric competitor, a company's customer equity can be thought of as the principal corporate asset being tended. One of the hazards of short-term thinking (i.e., of marketing efforts designed to produce current-period sales without much attention being paid to customer LTV) is that even a highly profitable firm may find that it is not "banking" enough customer equity to sustain its future financial success.

Not long ago Dell got into financial trouble, as its earnings failed to keep up with expectations. For years, thanks to its groundbreaking direct-to-consumer business model, the company had been the only major personal computer manufacturer making any money, with profit margins a full 10 points higher than most of its rivals. But according to *BusinessWeek*, "Rather than use that cushion to develop fresh capabilities, Dell gave its admirers on Wall Street and the media what they want: the highest possible [short-term] earnings."[6] The result was that Dell failed to maintain its

---

[5]However, the way in which a firm adds lifetime values together to get the customer equity of a group of customers will depend on the actual LTV calculation being used. If a firm uses a "fully allocated" cash flow figure, incorporating all fixed and variable operating costs, then LTVs can simply be arithmetically summed to get customer equity. Often, however, it can be more useful to use marginal contribution when calculating LTV, in which case unallocated costs would have to be added back in to customer equity, as individual LTVs are rolled up into larger and larger groups of customers. This may sound like a complex accounting problem, but the truth is it's just ensuring that costs and revenues are neither omitted nor double-counted when summing customer LTVs to derive customer equity.

[6]Nanette Byrnes and Peter Burrows, "Where Dell Went Wrong: In a Too-Common Mistake, It Clung Narrowly to Its Founding Strategy Instead of Developing Future Sources of Growth," *BusinessWeek*, February 19, 2007, pp. 62–63.

profitability and in 2007, the original chief executive officer (CEO), Michael Dell, had to be brought back to take over again and try to restore the company to its former luster. Then, within just a few months, the company announced it would have to restate four years of earnings results because "unidentified senior executives and other employees manipulated company accounts to hit quarterly performance goals."[7]

Dell certainly wasn't the first business to suffer because it tried to maximize quarterly earnings and profit, and it won't be the last. U.S. automakers succumbed to a similar problem when they failed to plan for how newly available Japanese imports might alter consumers' tastes in cars. Consumer electronics manufacturers in the United States made the same mistake with respect to their Pacific Rim competitors. Retailers that ignored the significance of Wal-Mart's new business model have yet to catch up. Most semiconductor manufacturers failed to embrace very large-scale integration (VLSI) chip technology when it replaced transistors, and their business was taken over by new entrants like Intel and Hitachi. In industry after industry, companies focused exclusively on current sales and profit falter primarily *because* they are focused exclusively on current sales and profit.

> In industry after industry, companies focused exclusively on current sales and profit falter primarily *because* they are focused exclusively on current sales and profit.

Many executives recognize that their company's obsession with short-term results is fundamentally destructive but feel powerless to do anything about it. Others feel equally strongly that if they just focus relentlessly on immediate sales and profit, then the long term will be okay. But this is a false assumption, because the investment community's obsession with short-term performance is irrational and destructive. According to William Donaldson, former chairman of the Securities and Exchange Commission, "With all the attention paid to quarterly performance, managers are taking their eyes off of long-term strategic goals."[8] And we don't have to look any further than the financial meltdown and Great Recession of 2008–09 to see the consequences of rampant, unchecked short-termism.

Customer-centric firms, because they deal more carefully with the issue of customer value creation, are naturally more oriented to balancing long- and short-term goals. Indeed, the very idea of using a customer-centric program to improve, say, customer satisfaction and loyalty is based entirely on generating future profits as a result of providing good service currently.

An article in *Fortune* magazine[9] pointed out that many customer-centric firms concentrate on raising their "returns on specific customer segment," and that this results in a "re-rating" of a company's profits/earnings ratio, as Wall Street "decides that the company can sustain [its] profit growth for years into the future." Best Buy, for instance, launched a "customer centricity" effort that is worth a quick summary. Among other things, Best Buy trained its store-level employees to recognize and

---

[7]Ibid.
[8]Joseph McCafferty, "The Long View," *CFO* magazine, May 1, 2007, pp. 48–52.
[9]Larry Selden and Geoffrey Colvin, "Five Rules for Finding the Next Dell," *Fortune*, July 12, 2004, p. 102.

think about the different needs of five different types of highly valuable customers and encouraged all store personnel to be proactive in their efforts to satisfy them.[10]

After a successful pilot project involving 32 stores, the company began rolling its customer-centricity initiative out to an additional 110 stores, leading Best Buy to forecast an earnings increase for the following year in the 15 to 20 percent range.[11] A UBS analyst's report praising Best Buy's initiative suggested that it should provide the firm with "stronger financial results" as the company refines and improves its program; a "better defense against competitors" in the category; and "less cyclical results," as more stable relationships with high-value customers counteract shifts in general consumer spending and demand for consumer electronics.[12] The analyst's report also noted that employee empowerment was crucial to the success of the program: "Best Buy empowers its store level employees, those individuals closest to its customers, to tweak merchandising, store signage, store layout, etc., to best appeal to [particular customers]."[13]

For example, the UBS report said, a Pasadena store employee explained how store-level associates had suggested a reconfiguration of the store to better appeal to suburban moms, moving small appliances down onto a low rack along the store's main walkway rather than leaving them stocked on higher shelves among the major appliances. According to the report, "sales of small appliances skyrocketed to well into double-digit gains from moderately negative." The report continued: "The employees in the appliance department's . . . next plan was to create displays that showcase items such as refrigerators, stoves, and washers and dryers in home-like settings along the perimeter of the appliance department [and] to develop a child play area . . . so that customers have a way to entertain their kids."[14]

Best Buy's customer-centricity initiative is based on seeing its business from the customer's perspective, understanding customer needs, and then taking the initiative to meet those needs. Inherent in this initiative is the belief that how customers are treated today will have a significant impact on their value to the company tomorrow. The reason Wall Street analysts liked the initiative is that it has shown remarkable power when it comes to driving the company's financial results. The company says the stores included in the pilot project saw gains in comparable-store sales more than twice as good as other U.S. Best Buy stores and a gross profit rate higher by about 0.5 percent of revenue.

According to Brad Anderson, vice chairman and CEO of Best Buy, customer centricity is now viewed as a core competency that the company wants to develop, and not "an end in itself." Commenting on the firm's quarterly results, Anderson said: "The beauty of our customer centricity work is how it enhances our operational

---

[10]"Best Buy Accelerates Customer Centricity Transformation; Insights Gained from 32 Lab Stores Fuel Decision to Launch Customer Centricity at up to 110 Additional U.S. Bust Buy Store During Fiscal 2005," *Business Wire*, Minneapolis, MN, May 3, 2004, p. 2.

[11]"Best Buy Second-Quarter Earnings per Share from Continuing Operations Increase 10 percent to 46 Cents, After Charges of 7 Cents; Robust Revenue Growth Drove Results," *Business Wire*, Minneapolis, MN, September 15, 2004.

[12]Gary Balter and Brian Nagel, "Best Buy Co., Inc.; Best Buy Shaping Up to Become One of Retail's Great Companies," UBS Investment Research, May 5, 2004.

[13]Ibid., p. 3.

[14]Ibid., p. 4.

excellence, our ability to turn talent into performance, and our strength in building brands. We believe that if we succeed in linking those capabilities, we will clearly differentiate Best Buy from our competitors."[15] Key to Best Buy's financial success, in other words, is its ability to see things from the customer's perspective. At least that seems to be the CEO's view, as well as Wall Street's. One result, obviously, is that the firm's customer equity has been substantially increased, and therefore its value as a business has increased.

Another customer equity success story is that of Verizon Wireless, the mobile phone company. During the four-year period from the end of 2001 through the end of 2005, this firm, which was at the time a joint venture between Verizon and Vodafone, dramatically increased its customer equity. According to publicly reported figures, the company earned $21 billion in operating income in those four years while growing its customer base from 29.4 million handsets in use to 51.3 million. During the same period, Verizon Wireless reduced its monthly customer churn rate on postpaid retail (contract) customers from 2.6 percent to 1.1 percent.

A back-of-the-envelope calculation[16] would show that Verizon Wireless's customer equity grew by around $20 billion during this period. In other words, Verizon Wireless actually created nearly twice as much shareholder value as was reflected in its income statements during these four years. About half of this increase in customer equity was attributable to the new customers acquired; the other half came from the increased average LTV of all its customers due to the dramatic reduction in customer churn during the period. (Significantly, Verizon Wireless relied on some highly sophisticated predictive analytics to anticipate and reduce customer churn; we return to this case briefly in Chapter 12.)

The truth is, Verizon Wireless's four-year surge in value creation was probably a one-time event for the company, because the more customer churn has been reduced, the harder and costlier it becomes to reduce it further. But other wireless firms throughout the world face opportunities every bit as rich as this, and for the most part they have failed to take advantage of them. In fact, if anything, there is strong evidence that many mobile telecom companies are running in the opposite direction, chipping away at their customer equity as they compete fiercely to acquire new customers at any cost—even when it means acquiring customers with lower and lower LTVs at higher and higher acquisition costs.

What Is the Value Today of a Customer You Don't Yet Have?

If customer equity includes the value not just of current customers but also of prospective customers, then prospects must have some value to a firm. A current customer has a lifetime value, but how can a prospective customer have a LTV,

(continued)

---

[15]"Best Buy Second-Quarter Earnings Per Share From Continuing Operations Increase 10% To 46 Cents, After Charges of 7 Cents; Robust Revenue Growth Drove Results," *Business Wire*, Minneapolis, MN, Sept. 15, 2004.
[16]Peppers and Rogers, *Rules to Break and Laws to Follow*, p. 263.

(*Continued*)

even though a firm isn't doing any business with him and may in fact *never* do business with him?

As strange as it may sound, the fact is that an enterprise's prospect does have an LTV for the enterprise today—even if it doesn't really know whether a genuine customer relationship will ever materialize. As long as there is some probability that the prospect will become a customer, then the prospect has an expected value to the firm today.

Very simply put, the LTV of a prospective customer is equal to her LTV if she were to become a customer, multiplied by her *likelihood* of becoming a customer.

To take one highly simplified example of customer equity calculation, suppose we expect a 4 percent conversion rate from our whole prospect pool each year. If we have, say, a 20 percent market share and we lose 16 percent of current customers each year, then a 4 percent annual acquisition rate from noncustomers exactly offsets that attrition rate (20 percent × 16 percent = 80 percent × 4 percent). In other words, our hypothetical business is in a steady state, neither growing nor shrinking, but simply acquiring new customers at a rate that exactly replaces defecting ones.

Now let's suppose new customers added from our prospect pool have an average LTV of $100 when they come into the franchise (after accounting for the attrition rate once they become customers), and we'll use a discount rate of 20 percent when valuing future cash flows.

Thus, 4 percent of our prospects will come in next year, and when they do come in, each will have an LTV of $100. Using a 20 percent discount rate means that this year's discounted value of each of those LTVs that are added next year is only $80 (80 percent × $100). The following year's crop of converted prospects have a discounted LTV this year of $64 (80 percent × 80 percent × $100), and so forth. Each individual prospect's current value today is a probability-weighted calculation, based on the fact that there is a 4 percent likelihood the prospect will come into the franchise in any given year.[a]

Year 1 $100 × 80% × 4% = $3.20
Year 2 $100 × 64% × 4% = $2.56   (20% net reduction)
Year 3 $100 × 51.2% × 4% = $2.05   (20% net reduction)
Year 4   etc.

Now, to calculate the total current value of a prospective customer (i.e., the NPV of the probabilistic cash flows each year), we must add together all these probability-weighted LTVs for all future years. These numbers ($3.20, $2.56, $2.05, etc.) comprise an infinite series. Ordinary high-school math (See? We *knew* it would come in handy!) shows that the sum of this series can be calculated in this way:

Average LTV per prospect $3.20 ÷ 20% = $16.00

In this example, if our total market consists of 1 million customers and prospects, then our total customer equity is approximately $33 million, because we have 200,000 current customers (20 percent market share) times $100 LTV each ($20 million), and we also have 800,000 prospective customers, each with a $16 LTV ($12.8 million).

Note that because prospects have probability-weighted LTVs, we can generate a higher **Return on Customer** (ROC) (see "Return on Customer," p. 321) not just by targeting our customer acquisition campaigns at higher-LTV prospects, but also by taking actions to increase the *likelihood* of particular prospects becoming customers. If our business-to-business (B2B) firm conducts a free seminar for prospective customers, for instance, the prospects who elect to attend have almost certainly increased their likelihood of becoming customers. If our consumer-marketing firm offers free samples to prospective customers, the ones who respond to the offer are more likely to become customers. Because we need to know whether it makes sense to run a seminar for prospects or to give samples away, we must consider the current value of these customers we don't yet have. Increasing the value of prospective customers is a legitimate and time-honored business activity.

But what about when a prospect becomes a customer? In our example, a customer has an LTV of $100, so when we convert a prospect to a customer, doesn't that mean we've increased our customer equity by $100?

No. If the prospect was already worth $16 to us, then the net increase in value to our firm in making that prospect into a customer was only $84. Think of it in terms of a new customer being activated at a $100 LTV, at the same time that a prospect is being "deactivated" with a $16 LTV. Another way to think about it is that the prospect had a probability-weighted LTV, and the probability changed. When he became a customer, the probability of his becoming a customer increased to 100 percent from what it used to be, which was 16 percent (16 percent is the weighted average of a 4 percent annual probability, discounted at 20 percent per year, forever).

Technically, each prospective customer has an "actual value" to our firm of $16, and an additional "unrealized potential value" of $84. We could easily think of a prospective customer as a customer with a great deal of growth potential—a customer with whom we so far have a 0 percent share of customer. So our mission, as a business, is to realize some of that potential, by changing the customer's otherwise expected future behavior.

---

[a]Purists note: The exact calculation would adjust the 4 percent probability down slightly each year, because the probability of a prospect becoming a customer in Year 2 is 4 percent times the 96 percent probability that he didn't already become a customer in Year 1, and so on.

Customer Loyalty and Customer Equity

The Verizon Wireless discussion clearly illustrates the fact that customer loyalty is likely to play a large part in any enterprise's effort to maximize the value its customers create. Executives frequently cite the problem of improving customer loyalty as one of the key reasons for embarking on a customer-centric initiative to begin with. This

EXHIBIT 11.1   Effect of Increasing Customer Value on Acquisition Cost, Margin, and Retention

	Customer Equity ($b)	Percent increase in Customer Value for a 10 percent improvement in:		
	Base Case	Acquisition Cost	Margin	Retention
Amazon	2.54	0.51%	10.51%	28.34%
Ameritrade	1.45	1.19%	11.19%	30.18%
eBay	2.11	1.42%	11.42%	30.80%
E*TRADE	1.89	1.11%	11.11%	29.96%

Source: Sunil Gupta and Donald Lehmann, *Managing Customers as Investments: The Strategic Value of Customers in the Long Run*, Wharton School Publishing, 2005.

is because for many businesses, even small increases in average customer loyalty can have quite significant effects on their financial results in the long term. But because customer loyalty doesn't create nearly so much short-term value as it does long-term value, the most useful way to analyze the impact of an improvement in customer loyalty is usually to examine its impact on a firm's underlying customer equity.

This was exactly the approach taken by Sunil Gupta and Donald Lehmann.[17] Gupta and his colleagues examined the financial reports of five different publicly held companies—Ameritrade, Amazon, Capital One, eBay, and E*TRADE—in order to try to estimate each company's customer equity. Then they calculated the impact on each firm's customer equity of changes in different marketing variables, including the average cost of new customer acquisition, the average profit margin, and the average customer retention rate, or loyalty.

What they found was quite remarkable, as shown in Exhibit 11.1, which compares four of the five companies:

- If the cost of new customer acquisition is reduced by 10 percent, customer equity values of these firms will increase by between about 0.5 and 1.5 percent.
- If product margins are raised by 10 percent, the customer equity levels of the firms will go up by roughly the same 10 percent.
- But if customer loyalty is increased 10 percent, then the customer equity levels of the firms improve by roughly 30 percent.

A 10 percent boost in customer loyalty for these companies, in other words, increases their overall value, as companies, by about 30 percent! No wonder customer loyalty is such a hot topic.

Gupta and his colleagues had to use publicly reported financial data, and they limited themselves to analyzing five companies with fairly straightforward and easily modeled business structures. Each of the firms sells directly to end-user customers, for instance, so there were no complicated channel or distributor relationships to consider, and each has a high concentration of repeat customers who do business

---

[17]Sunil Gupta and Donald Lehmann, *Managing Customers as Investments: The Strategic Value of Customers in the Long Run* (Philadelphia: Wharton School Publishing, 2005).

frequently. But the implications of this study still should be applicable even to more complex businesses with more complicated business models.

In any business, customer retention may or may not be the most appropriate variable to try to evaluate. Customer values can change in many ways. Customer attrition or retention is like an on-off switch, but in most categories, customers should be thought of more in terms of volume dials. Increasing the amount of business your customer does, or at least avoiding a reduction in the business she does, could be a much more useful objective in many cases. A survey of the behaviors of more than 1,000 U.S. households across a variety of industries concludes that while reducing defection definitely represents an opportunity for most businesses, there is far more financial leverage in simply increasing the amount of business done by customers, or avoiding *reductions* in the volume of business done.[18]

Moreover, customer loyalty itself is not always easy to define. If a consumer who considers himself loyal to a particular retail brand of gasoline is to stop at a different brand's filling station because it is more convenient at a given time, has he become less loyal than he was? When a business that buys all its office furniture from a particular contractor decides to put the next set of furniture purchases out to bid, is that "defection"?

Most companies end up creating a practical definition of retention for their customers that includes two features.[19] Unless the customer has a single, subscriber-like relationship with a company and clearly "leaves," retention is rarely considered an all-or-nothing variable. Thus, at an initial level, retention tends to be defined progressively—from "downgrading" behavior, to "inactive" status, to "no longer a customer." For some firms, a downgrading pattern itself is an indicator of increased risk of loss. A cable customer with premium channels and many pay-per-views each month may downgrade to just basic cable, or even to local broadcast only, until he completely defects to satellite.

At a second level, any definition of retention must also recognize the multiple relationships that a customer may have with a firm in terms of products that span business units. Customers who terminate a relationship in one area—paying off a home mortgage with a bank, for instance—may or may not retain a strong and active relationship in other areas, such as retail banking, investments, and credit. And marketers can't come to grips with this phenomenon at all unless they take an enterprise-wide view of each customer, across all business units and channels.

Although any lost customer is a real loss, understanding the nature of the loss will help to manage the costs of trying to reactivate customers or even to win them back. At the base level, it's important to distinguish between customer attrition and customer defection. Attrition almost always results from a circumstance outside the

---

[18]Scott Neslin, Sunil Gupta, Wagner Kamakura, Junxiang Lu, and Charlotte Mason, "Defection Detection: Improving Predictive Accuracy of Customer Churn Models," *Journal of Marketing Research* 43, no. 2 (May 2006): 204–211. This project was funded by the Teradata CRM Center at Duke University. For the survey of U.S. households, see Stephanie Coyles and Timothy C. Gokey, "Customer Retention Is Not Enough," *Journal of Consumer Marketing* 22, issue 2/3, 101–105.
[19]Thanks to Linda Vytlacil, formerly at Carlson Marketing Group and now with Sam's Club, for this discussion of how to think about customer retention, attrition, and defection.

direct control of a business—an elite business traveler retires, an office supplies buyer declares bankruptcy, a retail customer moves to another territory. Defection, by contrast, is a customer loss that might have been mitigated, because the customer is clearly choosing to move part or all of her business to the competition (e.g., a landline customer choosing to drop her service in order to go "only mobile," or a video-renting family deciding to use an online movie service, etc.). By distinguishing defection from attrition, we can isolate the drivers of each behavior and invest where we are likely to earn the highest Return on Customer.[20]

There is also the question of tenure. In any population of customers, the most likely to defect will be the first to do so. Thus, the longer any particular group of customers has remained "in the franchise," the less likely any of them are to defect in any given time period. Stated another way, the average annual retention rate among any population of customers will tend to increase with time.[21] When we talk in general about "improving retention," we have to be quite careful, because the least loyal customers are always the newest ones. The easiest way for almost any enterprise to improve its *average* retention is simply to stop acquiring new customers altogether! Again, resolving this problem requires a metric that can balance immediate profits and costs against the long-term value being created or destroyed.

In the final analysis, regardless of whatever behavior change a company can effect in its customer base—whether it is an increase in purchasing or a reduced likelihood of attrition—all of the financial results are captured in the LTV and customer equity numbers. The only question is how accurately the LTV equations have been constructed and modeled.

Forecasting customers' future behaviors and estimating the financial impact will never be simple, but with the customer analytics and statistical tools now available, it's not exactly rocket science anymore either. Some straightforward factors contribute to increases or decreases in an enterprise's customer equity, some of which we've already mentioned:

- Acquire more customers.
- Acquire customers who are more valuable to begin with (i.e., acquire customers likely to have higher LTVs).
- Increase profit per customer.
- Reduce servicing costs per customer.
- Sell customers additional products or services.
- Increase the propensity of customers to refer other customers.
- Reduce the rate of customer attrition.

---

[20]We often hear about "replacing" a customer who has defected. But this idea has a fallacy. A company can never truly replace a customer it wanted to keep. If it acquires another customer, it could have had *two*.

[21]You'll find a more thorough discussion of customer "vintages" in Don Peppers and Martha Rogers, *Enterprise 1to1: Tools for Competing in the Interactive Age* (New York: Currency/Doubleday, 1997), pp. 365–366.

Many of these factors can be measured currently, even though their primary effect is to alter how customers buy in the future. These are some of the **leading indicators** of LTV change, and we return to this topic later in this chapter.

But first, we need to answer a bigger question. If customer-centric companies concentrate on maximizing the value that their customers create, and these customers create value both in the long and the short term, is there a single, overall metric that would help an enterprise gauge the efficiency with which its customers are creating value?

Return on Customer

If customers are a scarce productive resource—imposing a constraint on a company's growth—then it would make sense for executives to track how efficiently they use this scarce productive resource to create value. When an enterprise wants to track the efficiency with which it deploys capital to create more value, it uses some metric such as return on investment. Return on Customer[SM] (ROC[SM])[22] is a metric directly analogous to ROI (and thus usually is pronounced are-oh-see) and specifically designed to track how well an enterprise is using customers to create value.[23] ROC can provide a company with financial bifocals—a single lens through which it can see its earnings from customers clearly, whether these earnings are up close and immediate or in the more distant long term.

To understand the ROC metric, start with a simple analogy. Imagine that last year you bought a stock for $100, and during the year you received a dividend payment of $5, while the stock price climbed to $110 by the end of the year. Your total ROI for the year would have been 15 percent. You put up $100 initially, and the total new value created amounted to 15 percent of that initial investment. If, however, the stock price had fallen $10 during the year, from $100 down to $90, then your total ROI would have been a negative 5 percent, and even though you received a $5 dividend, you would have suffered a net loss overall.

Now apply that thinking to customers. Suppose you begin the year with a customer who has an estimated LTV of $100, and during the year you make a profit from the customer of $5. By the end of the year, let's suppose your predictive modeling calculation shows that the customer's LTV has increased to $110. In that case, your ROC for the year would be 15 percent. But if this measurement of the economic performance of a particular customer will capture not just the sales you generate from the customer during the year but also the change, if any, in the customer's value to your business—LTV, that is, or the value of his likely future purchases, recommendations to friends, and so forth, as modeled in your customer database.

To understand why ROC is important, go back to the stock purchase for a minute, and imagine that the only information you have is how much the dividend

---

[22] Return on Customer[SM] and ROC[SM] are registered service marks of Peppers & Rogers Group.
[23] Don Peppers and Martha Rogers, "Return on Customer: A Core Metric of Value Creation," *Customer Strategist* 2, no. 1 (March 2010): 30–39.

is. You can't see whether the value of the underlying stock is increasing or not. In that case, even though the actual value of the stock will be going up and down all the time, you really can't say how well your investment is doing. So far as you're concerned, as long as the dividend continues or increases, you seem to be doing just fine, but the truth is that without also knowing how the underlying stock price is changing, it's impossible to say whether you're really creating value or not. If you had a stockbroker who wouldn't tell you, you'd fire that stockbroker.

The fact is that many companies are content to measure, carefully and sometimes with maniacal precision, their current sales from customers, without ever noticing, or measuring, or demanding to know how much the customer equity lying underneath the current numbers has gone up or down. But because customers are a scarce resource for businesses, when a company doesn't try to measure how much of that resource is being used up to create its current numbers, it is getting an incomplete picture of its financial performance.

Return on Customer = Total Shareholder Return

Total Shareholder Return is a precisely defined investment term, and refers to the overall return a shareholder earns from owning a company's stock over some period of time.[a] According to one financial authority:

Total Shareholder Return (TSR) represents the change in capital value of a listed/quoted company over a period (typically one year or longer), plus dividends, expressed as a plus or minus percentage of the opening value.[b]

This definition is based on what a shareholder's actual cash flow would be if he were to buy the stock at the beginning of the period and sell it at the end. The shareholder gets cash dividends during the period, and by the end of the period there may also have been some up-or-down change in the capital value of the stock itself. In a perfect world (economically speaking, that is), a publicly traded firm's market-driven "capital value" would equal its discounted cash flow (DCF) value, corrected for the effects of its capital structure. But there's of course no way to prove or disprove this because no one really knows what any company's discounted cash flow is going to be in the future. Nevertheless, it's widely accepted that the market price of a public company's stock at any point in time should generally reflect the marginal investor's best guess as to the company's discounted future cash flow.

To understand the "ROC = TSR" argument, start with the premise that all value created by any company's business operation[c] must come from its customers at some point. If the discounted cash flow value of an operating business is created entirely by customers, then its discounted cash flow is composed of a whole lot of individual LTVs. All the firm's current and future customer LTVs added together (i.e., its customer equity) will therefore equal its total discounted cash flow. As a result:

Return on Customer (ROC) equals a company's current-period cash flow, plus the change in its discounted cash flow value during the period, expressed as a percentage of its beginning discounted cash flow value.

In other words, ROC is simply a different route to prospective Total Shareholder Return—a method that breaks the economic value of a business into smaller and smaller customer-specific units, all the way down to specific, individual customers. ROC calculations don't rely on changes in share price, but if a firm's shares are publicly traded then stock price can still provide an important additional reference point for validating the firm's total customer equity.

A final note about shareholder return: The formal definition of TSR may refer only to publicly traded companies, but *all* companies have "shareholders." Whether shareholder return is calculated in order to flesh out a Securities and Exchange Commission filing or just to decide how much everybody gets paid this year, and whether shareholder meetings take place on the 68th floor, or at the investment company's office, or around the kitchen table, shareholder return is the most fundamental metric of value creation for any kind of business.

Both shareholder return and ROC apply to every company that needs a bookkeeper.

Source: Adapted from Don Peppers and Martha Rogers, Ph.D., *Return on Customer: Creating Maximum Value from Your Scarcest Resource* (New York: Currency/Doubleday, 2005), pp. 15–16.

[a]When we talk about "shareholder return," we're really talking about the rate at which an enterprise is creating value for its owners.

[b]The definition of TSR came from Value-Based Management.net, at: www.valuebased management.net/methods_tsr.html, accessed March 27, 2010.

[c]In considering a firm's "business operation" we are purposely disregarding capital structure and thinking only of the firm's actual business as a business.

A firm can calculate ROC for a particular customer, if it has reliable information about that customer's LTV, change in LTV, and profit for the period, or it can calculate ROC for a particular group or segment of customers, as well. If the firm calculates its ROC with respect to its total customer equity, the result will be mathematically the same as its total shareholder return (TSR) during the period (see "Return on Customer = Total Shareholder Return," p. 322). Remember that a firm's customer equity is virtually the same thing as the value the firm as an operating business. Therefore, ROC equals TSR.

> Return on Customer = Total Shareholder Return

Suppose we try to estimate ROC and use it to begin tunneling a path through the mountain of a company's financial performance while at the same time the company's accountants try to estimate the firm's TSR (based on its discounted cash flow value as a going concern), and begin tunneling toward us from the opposite side of the mountain. The mathematics suggest that we should meet at roughly the same place in the middle. And because of the ROC = TSR connection, a company can be truly happy with its ROC only if it exceeds its cost of capital, because only then is the firm actually creating value, overall, for its shareholders. (Obviously, if an investment doesn't earn a return greater than a firm's cost of capital, the firm is better off not making the investment at all. Whenever a firm creates net new shareholder value, this is because its total shareholder return has exceeded its cost of capital by at least a tiny margin for some period of time.)

Therefore, when a firm's ROC for some marketing initiative is less than its cost of capital, whether it is calculating ROC for the whole company or for some smaller subset of customers and prospects, it would be better off not undertaking the initiative. No value is created for a business when TSR is lower than the cost of capital, and because ROC = TSR, no value is created for a firm when ROC is less than the cost of capital either. Even though a firm may be showing a current-period profit from some set of customers, if its ROC for those customers is less than its cost of capital, then it isn't benefiting its shareholders, because not enough customer equity is being generated.

Many companies that show little growth or hard-fought, tepid earnings are actually not creating net new shareholder value at all but simply harvesting the customer LTVs they already have "in the bank." If an enterprise wants to grow and continue to grow, it has to ensure that every sales, service, and marketing initiative will yield an ROC greater than its cost of capital. That way, even as it is realizing earnings in the current period, it will also be building enough new customer equity to support future earnings.

Analyzing a company's ROC at the enterprise level can help clarify its financial prospects in ways that traditional financial statements aren't likely to reveal. To help you visualize this, Exhibit 11.2 shows an array of five different hypothetical companies divided into three categories, depending on whether each company is creating value, destroying it, or merely harvesting it.

EXHIBIT 11.2 Are You Creating, Harvesting, or Destroying Value?

	Company 1	Company 2	Company 3	Company 4	Company 5
Customer equity at beginning of year	$1,000	$1,000	$1,000	$1,000	$1,000
Customer equity at end of year	$1,200	$1,200	$1,020	$950	$900
Change in customer equity during the year	$200	$200	$0	(–$50)	(–$100)
Profit during the year	$50	(–$50)	$30	$50	$50
Total customer value created	$250	$150	$50	$0	–$50
Return on Customer	25%	15%	5%	0%	–5%
	Value Creators		**Value Harvesters**		**Value Destroyer**

We are indebted to the insights of Taylor Duersch and other members of Carlson Marketing's Decision Sciences team, now a part of Groupe Aeroplan, for helping us to clarify the role that customer equity plays in future earnings.

Companies 1 and 2 in this exhibit are **value creators**. For these two companies, the combination of short- and long-term value created by their customers is occurring at a rate that is almost certainly higher than their cost of capital. In each case they are ending their year with higher customer equity than they started with, so they can expect to grow their earnings in future years as well. Although it's clear each company is creating net new value for its shareholders, in Company 2's case, this net new value is being created despite the fact that the firm's current profits are actually negative.

Companies 3 and 4, however, are what we would call **value harvesters.** They are simply treading the financial water by harvesting customer profits that already have been "put in the bank" in the form of customer equity. Their ROC is not negative, but it is clearly below their cost of capital. Although each is earning a current profit, neither one is replenishing its customer equity enough, so it's unlikely that either of these companies will be able to achieve much growth in future years. They may continue to report lukewarm, increasingly difficult profits for the time being, but sooner or later, their customer equity will no longer be sufficient to sustain a profit at all. Technically, they may not be destroying shareholder value yet, but if these firms were people, they would be living off their savings.

As a **value destroyer**, Company 5 is in the worst situation of all, with ROC below zero. True, the company has scraped out a profit this year, but this profit was achieved only by stealing even more from the future. One can imagine a car manufacturer offering the deepest-ever discounts in order to prop up the fourth quarter's numbers, in the process saddling itself with a saturated market and customers trained to wait for more discounts, creating a much more difficult problem when it comes to making next year's numbers. Company 5 is on the skids, whether this is revealed in its current financial statements or not. It may be reporting a profit to shareholders. But shareholders who dig deeper will see that this firm doesn't have the operating and financial strength necessary to sustain this level of earnings for long. What this firm is really doing is "eating itself" and reporting the meal as a profit.

From the figures in Exhibit 11.2, it should be clear what kind of company represents the best value for an investor, although to a large extent savvy investors will have already discounted each firm's stock price to reflect its growth prospects. Nevertheless, if a firm succeeds in converting itself from one class to another—say, from value harvester to value creator—this will likely have a major impact on its economic value as an operating business. As investors uncover this information, the firm's stock will almost certainly be revalued in a significant way.

The Verizon Wireless situation we discussed earlier in this chapter resembles Company 1's situation in the exhibit. The firm produced good earnings while simultaneously accumulating even more customer equity. We calculated Verizon Wireless's ROC in each of those four years, and it averaged a whopping 68 percent annually. Stated differently, each year during the period we analyzed, Verizon Wireless created enough total new value to equal about two-thirds of its value as an operating company at the beginning of that year.

Yes, such a high ROC for four years running represents a remarkable spurt of value creation, but the way to think about it is that each year Verizon Wireless was revaluing its entire customer base, steadily improving the overall value of its business. Its success in customer retention was building up the company's customer equity account to a level that could support even higher earnings.

Tracking customer LTV allows a firm to calculate ROC in a variety of situations, sometimes in order to decide what the best course of action is and sometimes simply to avoid self-defeating business decisions that generate unanticipated (or unmeasured) costs. At many firms, for example, customer acquisition programs are evaluated simply on the basis of the quantity of new customers acquired rather than on their quality (i.e., their expected LTVs and growth potential). Profit optimization programs often look at cost savings without considering customer retention issues. And retention programs designed to reduce churn might do so by maintaining marginally profitable customers or even unprofitable ones.

These are, in fact, the self-defeating criteria by which many telecom companies evaluate their own actions. Because they don't track changes in customer LTVs, they have no real understanding of the overall value they are creating or not creating with their everyday tactical decisions. For the most part, many telecommunications firms seem to have an indiscriminate hunger simply to win any new customers they can and to avoid losing their current ones, no matter what the LTV economics are in either situation. These firms are making decisions designed to maximize their current-period earnings, and it's possible that they actually are doing so. The problem, however, is that this undermines their companies' long-term viability. They actually may be destroying more value than they are creating.

According to one group of industry experts,[24] many if not most telecom firms have seen the average LTV within their customer bases decline quite significantly in recent years:

> Some [telecom companies], for example, have tried to reduce churn by offering discount plans and other incentives—but ended up retaining customers they would have been better off losing and making formerly marginal customers unprofitable. Others have tried to contain the surge in unpaid bills by tightening credit limits on new applicants but are now turning away many customers who would have been profitable.

In essence, according to this authority, here's one example of a whole industry full of companies that are strip-mining their base of customers and prospects in order to feed their current-period results. As they continue with these policies, it becomes harder and harder to pump up the current period, while at the same time the customer environment is becoming increasingly polluted with uneconomic offers and unprofitable programs. It is anyone's guess as to whether telecom firms are actually *willing* to sacrifice the future in their increasingly desperate effort to prop up the present, or they simply are *unaware* of what they are really doing, because they don't have the right customer-centric metrics in place.

---

[24]Adam Braff, William J. Passmore, and Michael Simpson, "Going the Distance with Telecom Customers," *McKinsey Quarterly* 4 (2003): 83–93.

Measuring, Analyzing, and Utilizing Return on Customer

Onder Oguzhan
Analytics Subject Matter Expert, Peppers & Rogers Group

Return on Customer is a metric designed to measure the efficiency with which value is created from the available customers (in contrast to measuring the efficiency with which capital creates value, i.e., return on investment). ROC analysis requires a comprehensive analytical study incorporating various foundation analytical models including an integrated segmentation study with multiple dimensions, a related attrition (churn) study, and a detailed LTV analysis. By customer segmentation, we mean categorizing customers with specific similarities (value to the enterprise, needs from the enterprise, or observable behaviors based on data from each customer). This allows us to understand the customer base both qualitatively and quantitatively, so that each customer can be recognized correctly and completely.

Customer churn modeling is the process of determining the customers at most risk of leaving and deciding which ones of these customers are most worth retaining, if it can be done. LTV modeling is the process of measuring the NPV of future cash flows attributed to a customer relationship. Using customer LTV as a marketing metric allows a marketer to place greater emphasis on customer service and long-term customer satisfaction in evaluating future actions rather than relying on short-term sales alone.

Combining these foundational analytical models, we calculate ROC, and the result incorporates not just the return generated by a customer in the current period but also any positive or negative changes in the customer's LTV during the period. Thus, the most intriguing quality of the ROC metric is that it balances the effect of short-term results with long-term ones. At the enterprise level:

$$ROC = \frac{P^{(t)} + \left(CE^{(t)} - CE^{(t-1)}\right)}{CE^{(t-1)}}$$

where:

$P^{(t)}$ = company cash flow in period t

$CE^{(t)}$ = customer equity in period t

Type of Data to Be Used in Analytical Models

ROC analysis requires a good understanding of customer behavior and hence requires good handling of customer data. Maturity of internal data collection and storage processes along with a data-sharing organizational culture are critical in establishing the basis for proper ROC study and consistency of results. Some of the critical customer information we would like to have access to include: demographic customer information, customer revenue, customer transactions,

(continued)

(Continued)

customer channel usage, customer complaints, claims, customer life stage, so-phisticated cost allocation methodologies, and so forth.

Calculating ROC (Bottom-to-Top Approach)

Calculating ROC requires models addressing acquisition, retention, and growth for calculating parameters and quantifying relations that enable LTV and cus-tomer equity estimations.

The ROC calculation has two major steps:

1. Measure the marketing activities and analyze their effect on customer ac-quisition, retention, and growth, which all form the basis for analyzing the value of a particular customer or customer group.
2. Estimate customer LTV and total equity of all customers at a certain time point.

Analytical studies, such as customer segmentation, profiling, churn model-ing, propensity modeling, response modeling, and cost analysis, will provide the behavioral traits of one customer at a certain time, based on what we know now:

$$\boldsymbol{\theta}^{(t)} = \left\{ \theta_1^{(t)}, \theta_2^{(t)}, \ldots, \theta_r^{(t)} \right\}$$

where:

θ_1: Probability to repeat purchase
θ_2: Likelihood to churn
θ_2: Probability to respond to an offer
θ_3: Probability to increase revenue
θ_4: Potential growth
θ_5: Lifestyle/Life stage phase
θ_6: Acquisition cost
θ_7: Price/Margin

Although the technological advances in recent years and increasing speed of computing tools make the statistical modeling effort relatively easier, most of the work still involves ensuring that the right attributes are collected accurately, reflecting relevant customer behaviors and appropriate values within the model. Making these decisions often involves a great deal of judgment and sometimes creativity as well.

Customers' behaviors drive their values, so customer value is a function of whatever behavioral traits we can measure and estimate:

$$\hat{\pi}_k^{(t)} = f^{(t)}\left(\boldsymbol{\theta}^{(t)}\right)$$
$$\hat{\pi}_k^{(t)} = \left\{ \hat{\pi}_k^{(t+1)}, \hat{\pi}_k^{(t+2)}, \ldots, \right\}$$

Note: Occasionally we may need to use proxies to track these behavioral traits when we don't have sufficient and reliable data.

Customer LTV is the sum of these value points over the entire length of the customer's relationship with the enterprise (or some other acceptable time frame within that business or industry), discounted back to time *t*.

$$CLV_k^{(t)} = \sum_{s=t+1}^{n} \hat{\pi}_k^s d^s$$

Note: Use of discount rate can change the valuation, and desired discount rate depends on company's actual assessment of cost of capital (i.e., preference of future cash vs. current cash).

Customer equity at a certain time *t* is the sum of all firm's customers' LTV:

$$CE^{(t)} = \sum_k CLV_k^{(t)}$$

Finally, ROC is the sum of the short-term value in time *t* and change in customer equity from *t*−1 to *t* divided by total customer equity of the firm at time *t*−1:

$$ROC = \frac{P^{(t)} + (CE^{(t)} - CE^{(t-1)})}{CE^{(t-1)}}$$
$$P^{(t)} = \sum_k \pi_k^{(t)}$$

Conceptually, if we consider that total customer equity is equal to total value that a company can generate from its customers over its lifetime (or over some foreseeable, appropriately long term), then customer equity can be assumed to be roughly equal to total enterprise value. And if we assume that the company is an investment that can be sold or reinvested in each period, ROC can be approximated to the sum of:

(ROI) Return generated by total enterprise in the short term = $P^{(t)}/CE^{(t-1)}$

and

Change in underlying enterprise value = $\dfrac{\left(CE^{(t)} - CE^{(t-1)}\right)}{CE^{(t-1)}}$

To make ROC a part of daily decision making, results of the models should be converted into customer actions and dashboards. Using analytical models and data-mining/reporting tools, multiple dashboards and a combination or intersection of multiple actions can be designed to best serve customers included in that particular study.

(continued)

(Continued)

ROC is a decision support tool for executives and can be used to evaluate total enterprise efficiency in creating and sustaining customer equity while generating short-term returns. The power of ROC in balancing these two occasionally conflicting actions makes this metric helpful for evaluating a company's performance and making the right executive decisions. At the enterprise level, under strong pressure by Wall Street to hit short-term targets, ROC can give an approximation for how company valuation changes over time while still incorporating the effect of short-term results. ROC gives the ability to measure, quantify, and communicate the impact of these investments on customer equity and allows executives and analysts to speak the same language. Additionally, the bottom-up approach that we utilize in calculating ROC gives enough flexibility for dissecting data in multiple dimensions and therefore provides the ability to look at the ROC performance of divisions, business units, customer segments, or marketing programs. With ROC embedded in the performance management process, executives can encourage department-level decisions based not only on short-term profit but also on long-term customer equity.

Constantly updating the ROC model and feeding results back to it enables the evaluation of alternative investments in light of ROC and running multiple scenario analyses. For example, an information technology investment requiring $2 million and resulting in $2.7 million in short-term cost savings would be very attractive to any executive. But wouldn't this project be prioritized higher if we could calculate that the investment would also help build 30 percent of customer equity over the next 24 months?

At the most granular level, ROC can be linked to a particular customer for in-depth insight, making it a great tool for customer service departments in the form of real-time customer dashboards. In these dashboards, agents can observe ROC at the customer level: in churn scores, the current microsegment the customer is assigned to, next-best product offers, claim resolution priorities, rules, actions, and so forth. Equipped with these real-time monitors, customer service agents can diligently treat different customers differently, satisfying the most critical requirement for improving customer equity and thus ROC.

Equally, sales organizations can use ROC to track customer-level or group-level performance of sales account executives. Using dynamically updated customer dashboards visible to these executives and their managers, planning, target setting, and incentive management activities can incorporate ROC into the equation. In doing so, companies can maintain sufficient pressure on their sales organizations to deliver results in the short term while sustaining customer equity, customer trust, and the long-term viability of the company. For example, a sales division of an insurance company can be penalized or rewarded based not only on how many new policies it brings in during the current period but on how the overall customer portfolio value changes within the same period.

Leading Indicators of LTV Change

Once a firm is practiced enough in analyzing LTVs to begin monitoring how changes in LTV are caused, it can begin to apply the ROC metric to manage its marketing initiatives and its overall business more productively, focusing on the most important factors in improving its customers' LTVs. If customer loyalty is the dominant factor in an enterprise's customer equity calculation, then improving customer loyalty will be key to success. If profit on value-added service is the dominant variable, then services should be emphasized. Making the right business decision will depend on the current performance of a firm's LTV parameters and on the effort required to influence the improvement of these parameters. Improving on a metric where performance is already high is generally more difficult (and costly) than focusing on an area with more room for improvement. Once Verizon Wireless has reduced its monthly churn from 2.6 percent to 1.1 percent, for instance, it will not be possible to duplicate that reduction, and the firm likely will have to find other ways to increase its customer equity if it wants to sustain such a high ROC.

ROC requires an enterprise to predict future customer behavior changes using currently available information. In essence, a company's analytics program must identify and track the leading indicators of LTV changes. The question is, what data are available today to forecast up or down movements in a customer's LTV?

The predictive modeling process involves two basic steps.

The first step involves devising an equation for LTV that includes whatever transactional records or other data are available on customers' actual past spending (and other measurable behaviors, such as visits to the Web site, trackable referrals, complaints, etc.) must be devised. It's best if there are several years' worth of transactions, but often a company will have to make some assumptions based on business judgment or sampling. Such records might include, for instance, each customer's purchases every year, the margin on those purchases, and the number of years the customer has done business with the firm. Essentially, the company is using the computer to go back through historical customer records and make the actual calculations of LTV for as many individual customers as possible.

The second step is to identify the most predictive currently available variables with respect to the LTVs calculated in the first step. If we start by calculating LTVs for individual customers using historical records, we then comb back through all the information we have about those individual customers in order to pick out correlations and relationships with their individual LTVs. The data to be used should include purchase transactions to the extent possible but might also include complaint and service records, demographic (B2C) or firmographic (B2B) information, needs-based research, or even information on customer attitudes—essentially, any information at all that can be obtained in a customer-specific form, with respect to the customers whose LTVs already are calculated.

In the end, the objective is to generate a second equation for LTV, but this will be an equation that uses currently available data to predict an individual customer's LTV rather than using transaction data to calculate it retrospectively, as is the case for RFM (recency, frequency, and monetary value), which often is used by database marketers. One large consumer service business devised a predictive model for LTV based on 10 years of customer transaction records. The company first ran a statistical analysis to see what independent variables most affected a customer's likelihood of returning, because likelihood of returning seemed to be the most important single factor in determining LTV. Using the findings from this analysis, the company created an equation for predicting the future revenue from each customer. This formula was not limited to transactional records but included "outside" variables as well, such as the general level of consumer confidence in the economy at large. Each customer's future contribution was estimated by applying historical margin to his or her predicted future revenue.[25] As one of their executives explained:

> *For a very high level summary of the LTV calculation, we ran a regression to see what independent variables affect a [customer's] likelihood of returning. We then used the coefficients of the successful variables to create a formula for predicting future revenue for each [customer]. At least one of these was external—something like consumer confidence. Finally we applied the historical contribution of each [customer] to get to future contribution. Our LTV calculation contains only future expected contribution. We applied the formula to historical customer data to get LTV from previous years.*

In the end, in addition to demographic data, the company's LTV model used such variables as the first type of service purchased, the average rate paid, and how recently the last service was purchased.

The variables driving any firm's LTV model can be thought of as the leading indicators of LTV change. The model won't ever be perfect, because predictions never are. There always will be problems having to do with the availability of data, analytical issues, and other obstacles. But reliability will improve with experience, as a firm learns to collect, monitor, and weight the information more and more accurately. The leading indicators of LTV change fall into four general categories:[26]

1. *Lifetime value drivers.* These are the elements of the LTV equation itself—the actual components that determine how much value the customer creates for the company, over time.
2. *Lifestyle changes.* When a customer takes a new job, or gets pregnant, or retires, or gets married or divorced—when his or her lifestyle or personal situation undergoes a substantial change, the LTV may also be affected.
3. *Behavioral cues.* The number of contacts initiated, the services or products contracted, the number of complaints or comments submitted, and payments made or not made are all examples of behavioral cues.
4. *Customer attitudes.* These include such things as satisfaction level, willingness to recommend your company or products, and likelihood of buying from you again. A customer's attitudes have a strong influence on his or her future behavior.

---

[25]The information from the large consumer service business is proprietary but was documented for us in an e-mail from a colleague sent to the authors in May 2004, including the executive statement we've been allowed to share.

[26]See footnote 2 in Chapter 5 for a more complete review of customer lifetime valuation.

Lifetime Value Drivers

Academicians as well as businesses are paying more and more attention to the issue of customer loyalty, LTVs, and customer equity.[27] But loyalty isn't the only thing that goes into an LTV model. Cross-selling rate, share of customer, and even influence on other customers can legitimately be considered to be economic drivers of a customer LTV model, with different degrees of importance, based on the business model at issue.

With today's emphasis on social networks and customer word of mouth (see the discussion in Chapter 8), the degree to which any one customer might serve as a reference for an enterprise's brand with other customers is increasingly important, and another example of an LTV driver. One academic study published in *Harvard Business Review* examined the value of word-of-mouth referrals generated by customers for both a financial services firm and a telecommunications firm.[28] What the study's authors found was that typically less than half the customers who report that they plan to refer a customer to a firm actually do so, and after that, only a small fraction of customers who are referred to a business actually become profitable customers in their own right. Therefore, the study's authors contend, it is vital to understand the dynamics of customer word of mouth as a part of calculating LTV, because while referrals can be highly valuable, they are not so easy to track and measure. (This is the same study that compared customer spending value with customer referral value, and we discussed that aspect of it in Chapter 5.)

Lifestyles Changes

Demographic information and vital statistics can be useful tools to help model a customer's LTV. A big advantage of using these kinds of data is that often they can be obtained from third-party databases, independent of a company's own transactional and other records. Because these data are available independently, often a firm can use demographic and other data to predict the LTVs of *prospective* customers with whom it may have had little or no past contact, by comparing them demographically to similar current customers. (However, many databases don't contain an individual customer's demographic information; instead they use a combination of census data and overlaid projections based on address or zip code.)

A lot of demographic information won't change much in the short term and won't be much help in predicting LTV changes. It's highly unlikely, for example, that a

---

[27] We've already discussed the elements of a lifetime value equation in great detail, but there is an increasing level of academic interest in this issue. Some of this discussion and research has been driven by an effort to explain the Internet stock bubble at the turn of the new century. For example, one study of business-to-consumer Internet companies found that a Web site's reach and "stickiness" (i.e., visitor retention) were closely correlated with genuine market value, as evidenced by the fact that those dot-com firms whose Web sites had relatively less reach and stickiness tended to lose a great deal more of their value when the bubble burst. Elizabeth Demers and Baruch Lev, "A Rude Awakening: Internet Shakeout in 2000," *Review of Accounting Studies* 6 (2001): 331–359.

[28] V. Kumar, J. Andrew Petersen, and Robert P. Leone, "How Valuable Is Word of Mouth?" *Harvard Business Review* 85, no. 10 (October 2007): 139–146.

person's race or gender will change (although it's not unlikely that a firm often has to revise incorrectly keyed data entries for these kinds of items).[29] The demographic information that will change, however, is the kind of data we generally associate with a person's lifestyle or personal situation. Categorizing customers by their lifestyles is one of the most frequently found elements of any customer management program. It's logical to think that a customer's LTV will change with his or her age, albeit gradually. But more sudden changes in a person's lifestyle are even more important, such as professional or career moves, household address changes, and changes in marital status, children added to the household, education level, or health.

For some businesses, lifestyle changes are extremely important indicators of LTV. Getting married, moving, or getting divorced, for instance, precipitates all sorts of buying activity, from appliances to cars. It's important for a business to have some mechanism to learn about customers' lifestyle changes, whether through an online profile update or perhaps special offers for special occasions.

Business customers, too, go through stages and "lifestyle changes." When a business becomes less profitable or more profitable, its buying behavior likely will change. When a privately held business goes public, or when a company acquires another firm, its behavior will change. Pharmaceutical companies, for example, watch for changes in the professional lifestyles of the physicians who write prescriptions, such as taking in new partners or employees, adopting new medical practices, relocating offices, or acquiring new medical technologies. Similar changes occur within clinics and hospitals. Technology firms watch for lifestyle changes among companies that are heavy technology users, including changes in the size or makeup of a firm's internal information technology staff, and increased (or decreased) interest in outsourcing or offshoring.

Behavioral Cues

Suppose a business has a satisfied consumer customer spending $100 a month, with an estimated LTV of $10,000. Now suppose this customer calls in to complain about a faulty product or an episode of bad service. The call center rep handles the complaint professionally. As a result, the customer not only remains satisfied but actually writes a complimentary letter to the firm and tweets to friends and followers. It is highly likely that this customer's LTV will have increased dramatically with that transaction. The transaction created actual value for the company right then, even though the firm hadn't yet collected any cash as a result of the customer's increased propensity to buy or to recommend it to friends. In point of fact, the firm actually might have incurred a current-period cost to satisfy the complaint.

---

[29]Gartner Research notes that "high costs are associated with owning data, and Gartner believes that having bad data can increase these costs by a factor of 10 when one considers the costs arising from bad business decisions and poor CRM based on such data." See S. Nelson, R. Singhai, W. Janowski, and N. Frey, "Customer Data Quality and Integration: The Foundation of Successful CRM," Gartner Research, *Strategic Analysis Report* R-14-7181, November 26, 2001. We also saw Don Hinman and Bob Wallach's. "High Cholesterol Databases—Is Your Data Quality Slowly Killing Your Business?" Webcast presented on December 18, 2003, AMA Marketing Effectiveness Online Seminar Series.

But that kind of transaction is a very big and obvious behavioral cue. There are many other such cues, not always as big and obvious, but just as predictive. In a business like telecom, or financial services, or retail, an abundance of behavioral cues exists within the billions of data points in many companies' customer transaction databases. A credit card customer begins to use her card less (or more). A mobile phone user signs up for a different plan. A customer buys a second product upgrade in just two months. A frequent business traveler begins flying in fully paid first-class seats or changes her address away from the airline's hub city. Behavioral cues apply equally well to B2B firms selling to corporate clients. Such firms may detect an increase in the number or quality of the people at the customer company who are involved in the business, or an early contract renewal, or a reduction in the service agreements in force at a customer's business site. Perhaps one client agrees to a more comprehensive service contract while another puts part of the business out for bid.

Behavioral cues always have been important to high-volume financial services businesses, primarily as an aid to managing credit risk. A credit card firm is likely to review its database of cardholder transactions closely in order to spot any anomalies that might indicate either that a card has been stolen or that a cardholder is getting into debt over his head. You might remember a call from your credit card company when you first used it in another country, or when you bought that larger-than-usual piece of jewelry, or when you ordered some expensive products online. Typically, the card company will call the cardholder just to verify that he or she is really the one engaging in these unprecedented activities and to reassure itself that the card is still actually in the holder's possession and hasn't been lost or stolen.

Behavioral cues are not hard to identify, and some of them can be easily understood at first glance:

- When a husband and wife each carry a credit card using the same account, the couple is much less vulnerable to competitive offers from other cards than either would have been as an individual cardholder.
- When a new customer buys a car on the recommendation of a friend, he is more likely to be satisfied for a longer period, and to consume additional branded services from the automobile company, such as financing and warranty extensions.
- Retail consumer-electronics customers who sign up for an e-mail newsletter have a significantly higher probability of returning for additional purchases.

Obviously, a business should track transactions involving purchase and consideration, but it should also remember that not all interactions involve purchases. In addition to purchasing events, an enterprise should keep track of Web pages visited, sales calls received, surveys completed, and call center inquiries, for instance. It's not necessarily the wisest policy to pester customers themselves for data, but it's always smart to capture whatever interactions and transactions occur naturally during the course of business. The more transactional data points a firm has with respect to its customers, the more opportunity it will have for using the data to deduce the future behavior of particular customers or groups of customers within its customer and prospect base.

Remember the large consumer service business we mentioned earlier? The company's LTV model was useful as far as it went, but executives lamented that it would have been far more useful had the company been able to access additional records. They would have liked to account for each customer's supplementary spending, because this is a key element of the company's profit. But their systems couldn't make the connection. The company also sent out a regular satisfaction survey to recent customers, and although it used the results to improve its overall service, these data might have proven even more useful in predicting individual LTVs—not to mention improving a particular customer's value by meeting the needs she indicated in the satisfaction survey, perhaps generating additional business as a result.

At one of Canada's largest banks, customer portfolio managers are evaluated and rewarded in a way that mandates their continued interest in building short-term revenue as well as long-term customer equity. If you were the portfolio manager for a group of customers (who likely don't know of your existence), you'd be the gatekeeper for communications from the bank to each of those customers. It would be your job to figure out how to eliminate roadblocks to doing more business with each of those customers, and—by taking the customers' point of view based on analysis and insight—to maximize the value created by each of those customers. At the end of the quarter, you would be rewarded based on two measurements:

1. How much profit did the bank make on your portfolio of customers this quarter?
2. As of this quarter, what is the three-year projected value of the customers in your portfolio?

This two-part compensation model guarantees that you will not be tempted to do anything that will make money in the short term but jeopardize long-term customer equity—no hidden fees, no service cuts valued by customers, nothing that will cut the long-term number. Unless both numbers are good, you still won't get a bonus.

Customer Attitudes

Other leading indicators of lifetime value change come not from observable customer behaviors but from attitudes—moods and points of view that can be accurately assessed only via surveys or fielded market research. Attitudes are important, however, because they influence behavior, so to the extent a firm tracks such attitudes, it should be able to make informed judgments about changes in its customer equity.[30] Although it's certainly not a linear relationship, in general, a customer who

---

[30]Customer attitudes, like other "soft" (nonfinancial) measures, have proven to be the epicenter of a controversy. On one side are those who believe that customer attitudes, brand value, employee turnover, and other nonfinancial measures will prove to be clear predictors of future performance, and on the other side are those who maintain that a lot of what we believe, such as "customer satisfaction adds value" and "reduced employee turnover reduces costs," is simply folklore. See Allan Hansen, "Nonfinancial Performance Measures, Externalities, and Target Setting: A Comparative Case Study of Resolutions through Planning," *Management*

is highly satisfied with a firm's product or service is more likely to remain loyal to that firm, more likely to refer other customers to it, and more likely to buy additional products or services from it than is a customer who is not highly satisfied.[31] At its core, Fred Reichheld's Net Promoter Score, discussed in Chapter 5, is based on the idea that a customer's willingness to recommend a product to a friend or colleague is directly correlated with the customer's own satisfaction with the product and with the future sales the product will generate from that customer. Some authorities have achieved moderate success in correlating customer satisfaction levels with market value.[32] According to the University of Michigan's National Quality Research Center, for instance, increasing a company's customer satisfaction by 1 percent correlates with a 3 percent increase in market capitalization.[33] Just as important, any decrease in customer satisfaction or willingness to recommend the company would almost certainly indicate a decline in a company's value.

The degree to which a firm is perceived to pay attention to its customers also affects customer attitudes and willingness to do business with it in the future. One study, jointly led by Roper Starch Worldwide and Peppers & Rogers Group, showed that among bank customers who rated their banks as providing good customer service, an ability to treat a customer as a distinct individual (such as providing a personal contact, sending only relevant messages, and anticipating the customer's needs) made a significant difference in that customer's future intentions. Twenty-six percent of those who rated their banks high on customer service but low on such "relationship capabilities" stated that they were likely to switch away at least one product in the next year. By contrast, among those who rated their banks high on customer service *and* relationship capabilities, just 1 percent stated any intention to switch products.[34] This astounding contrast is a strong endorsement for a customer

---

Accounting Research 21, no. 1 (March 2010): 17–39; and Robert Bruce, "Non Financial Measures Just Don't Add Up," *Financial Times*, March 29, 2004, p. 10.

[31] But measuring customer satisfaction is not as straightforward as it might sound. Although we know "customer satisfaction" has ardent supporters for lots of good reasons, in our minds, the greatest criterion for its value as a metric is whether it is a good predictor of future customer value. The same is true for Net Promoter Score.

[32] See Christopher Ittner and David Larcker, "Are Non-Financial Measures Leading Indicators of Financial Performance? An Analysis of Customer Satisfaction," *Journal of Accounting Research*. 36 (1998): 1–36. Also see Ellen Garbarino and Mark S. Johnson, "The Different Roles of Satisfaction, Trust and Commitment in Customer Relationships," *Journal of Marketing* 63 (April 1999): 70–87. These researchers found that for low-relational customers, satisfaction is a better predictor of future behavior, but for high-relational customers, trust and commitment are more important.

[33] The National Quality Research Center finding was cited by Viren Doshi and Richard Verity, "No-Frills CRM," in Booz Allen Hamilton's *Resilience Report*, found in *Strategy & Business* (Fall 2004): 8–10.

[34] For more about the Roper Starch and Peppers & Rogers Group study, see "Customer Relationship Management in Financial Services: A National Perspective," Roper Starch Worldwide, CNO-385, September, 2000. For an in-depth description of the research, see Jonathan Brookner and Julien Beresford, "One to One in Retail Financial Services: New Strategies for Creating Value Through Customer Relationships," Peppers & Rogers Group and LOMA (Life Office Management Association, Inc.), 2001.

relationship's benefits in retaining customers, at least when it comes to retail banking, and we've seen similar findings in the telecommunications industry.[35]

The key to ensuring that customer attitudes serve as a useful tool in tracking real-time LTV changes is to identify the correlations between a customer's current attitude—or change in attitude—and his or her actual behavior in the future (observable behaviors such as new purchases, repurchase, referrals, complaints and interactions, service calls, etc.). Measuring a customer's *change* in attitude would be particularly helpful for businesses that don't have the advantage of a sizable volume of customer transactions.

One survey tool that measures customer attitudes, RSx, uses data from customers, employees, and distribution channel partners to assess the *strength of their relationship* with the company and then correlates various elements of that relationship with particular customer behaviors or stated intentions, such as their intent to buy from the company again, to calculate financial outcomes. Designed by Carlson Marketing Group (now a unit of Aeroplan) with the assistance of Professor Robert M. Morgan of the University of Alabama, the RSx (relationship strength) framework also helps organizations identify important drivers of stronger relationships.

RSx was applied to one retailer's situation, for example, and showed that customers who had a strong relationship with the company (defined in terms of trust, commitment, and mutual benefit and alignment) delivered 48 percent more sales than customers who had a "medium" or "low" relationship with the company. The retailer found that strong relationships were driven by customers' perceptions of the store's personal service, convenience, shared values, and communication. (These customer "perceptions" are what we would call "attitudes" and were all measured based on surveys administered to individual customers.) For the retailer, the RSx model showed that strong relationships with customers resulted in:

- 34 percent higher stated intent to purchase.
- 50 percent higher positive word of mouth.
- 16 percent greater share of wallet.

These outcomes, in turn, enabled the retailer to quantify the projected impact of its relationship-building efforts on business outcomes.[36]

---

[35]In one article, David Myron notes that "bundling two services usually reduces customer churn by 25 percent. Bundling a third product reduces it by an additional 13 percent, and a fourth product reduces churn by an additional 6 percent." "Telecoms Focus on Services, Not Price, to Reduce Churn," *Customer Relationship Management* (May 2004): 18. Susana Schwartz reported that "in fact, Yankee Group finds that tying two services together causes churn to fall by one-quarter; tying three causes it to fall another eighth; and adding a forth leads to churn rates falling an additional sixteenth" in her article "The Race to Bundle Voice, Data and Video," *Billing World and OSS Today* (June 2004): 20–26. And Michelle L. Hankins asserts that "churn costs the telecom industry $10 billion a year. On average it costs a provider $60 to retain a customer but $350 to $400 to acquire a new one" and that "every time you cross-sell a service to a customer, you decrease churn by one-third," in her article "Carriers Struggle to Control Churn," *Billing World and OSS Today* (January 2003): 36–40.

[36]RSx is a proprietary framework for measuring relationship strength, developed by Dr. Thomas D. Lacki, Linda Vytlacil, and Jeffrey M. Weiner of Carlson Marketing Group in close

Stats and the Single Customer

To maximize ROC, an enterprise has to gain some practice in using LTV as a tool and in tracking changes in LTV over time. It can never be known exactly how much an investment in acquisition will yield, or how to measure retention precisely over an extended period, or how much additional business actually will be stimulated by a particular offer. Yet from empirical observations an analyst eventually will be able to deduce how LTV is likely to be influenced by various drivers and by the attitudes of customers. The big challenge will be to fashion the company's strategies not just to maximize this quarter's sales or "new customers added" but rather to maximize the rate at which the enterprise is creating overall economic value, in the long term as well as the short term.

Of course, statistical analysis has its limits. In a group of a million consumers, a statistical model can predict aggregate behavior, such as a likely response rate or attrition rate, with reasonable accuracy. Such models can detect behavior patterns that tend to indicate some future actions, such as defection, providing the manager with an ability to intervene. They can also be used as benchmarks. But reduce the size of the overall group being analyzed, and the stability of these statistical calculations begins to break down. At the level of the individual customer, even the most sophisticated statistical models are subject to a great deal of randomness and noise.

However, once a company does drill all the way down to the level of an individual customer, it can make direct, one-to-one contact, and this kind of interaction will always trump statistical models. If a firm has really good, up-to-date, reliable data about an individual customer, and if those data are based on direct interaction with the customer, then it should be able to predict the customer's behavior much more precisely than it could if the customer were simply one customer within some statistical cluster. For this reason, direct interaction with customers will provide an enterprise with the most useful and reliable leading indicators of those customers' future behavior.

For a company serving just a few hundred B2B customers, statistical models are rarely as useful as the objective judgments of the sales and account managers closest to the customers. These judgments, too, are just educated forecasts, but they can be made more reliable and accurate by adhering to a standardized set of criteria. Has a contract been proposed? Is there a standing purchase order? Do we provide the back-end maintenance as well as product installation? Is the relationship characterized by partnership and collaboration? Can this customer refer other customers to us? Have they done so in the past? Judgments made on the basis of such objective but nonquantitative criteria are critical to making educated decisions about customer LTVs. They help get a firm as close as possible, as objectively as possible, to understanding the actual values of individual customers.

collaboration with Dr. Robert M. Morgan at the University of Alabama. The reported results were generated by a series of three pilot studies conducted by Carlson Marketing Group between May 2000 and October 2001.

Maximize Long-Term Value and Hit Short-Term Targets

Yücel Ersöz
Partner, Peppers & Rogers Group, Middle East

The latest dashboard report on the CEO's desk at Bank ABC is brilliant. It says performance of his bank has been nothing short of stellar in the latest period. The bank is a large one in its market, and has not been scarred very badly by the financial sector troubles plaguing many smaller banks. Moreover, an aggressive strategy involving both branch expansion and advertising to attract the customers of some of the banks perceived as riskier has apparently paid off handsomely, with deposits and net income both up 15 percent for the period. Market share, in terms of assets under management, is up 2 percent over all. Board members are happy, shareholders are happy, the executive team is happy. And why shouldn't they all be happy? The bank's financial performance this period was stellar, as indicated on its most recent income statement (see Exhibit 11A).

EXHIBIT 11A   Income Statement of Bank ABC

	Bank ABC	
Bank ABC Financials	Last Period	This Period
Checking deposits	€170,000	€195,500
Savings deposits	€350,000	€402,500
Total deposit volume	€520,000	€598,000
Market selling rate	6.50%	6.50%
Earnings on total deposits	€33,800	€38,870
Interest paid, checking	0.50%	0.50%
Funding cost, checking	€850	€978
Interest paid, savings	4.50%	4.50%
Funding cost, savings	€15,750	€18,113
Total funding cost	€16,600	€19,090
Gross profit on deposits	€17,200	€19,780
Gross expenses	€15,288	€17,582
Net profit for bank	€1,913	€2,198
Year over year growth		**15%**

As festivities continue, however, an insidious truth is lurking beneath the surface. ABC is actually destroying shareholder value and nobody is aware of it. Its financial results emphasize product lines, and while product lines can all be profitable, it is not products that create value. Customers create all value, and the first task for Bank ABC in interpreting its own financial statement should have been to try to understand its financial results in terms of which customers accounted for which parts of it. A relatively simple and inexpensive market survey at the bank would have revealed three principle types of retail customer, at the end of the current period:

- *"Loyalists," who have always done business with Bank ABC,*
- *"Shoppers," who shop around fairly regularly, and*
- *"New Acquisitions," brought in with the advertising, who have chosen to flee to Bank ABC in the wake of the financial crisis.*

Profile details of each group are shown in Exhibit 11B.

EXHIBIT 11B   Three Types of Customer at Bank ABC

Loyalists	Shoppers	New Acquisitions
Total number: 12 million	Total number: 7 million	Total number: 1.5 million
Average age: 45	Average age: 35	Average age: 55
Bank ABC is their only bank in deposits. They may be working with other banks in other products.	They work with multiple banks and are frequently exploring alternatives, shopping for the best deals.	They work with multiple banks.
They go to branches often. Use of alternative channels is relatively low.	They are heavy users of Internet banking.	Very few of them use alternative channels.
Their price sensitivity is low.	Switching from bank to bank is easy, even for individual products, because they rely so heavily on the Internet.	They are likely to switch to smaller banks offering higher rates, once the financial crisis abates.
Loyal customers, they do not indicate any churn intentions.	Many of these customers are always hunting for the best rates.	Their main reason for coming to Bank ABC is its financial soundness, in the wake of the financial crisis.
Average churn rate: 5% p.a.	**Average churn rate: 20% p.a.**	**Average churn rate: 20% p.a.**

Survey data such as this would have allowed Bank ABC executives to better allocate costs among these three different groups of customers, and also to calculate average lifetime values, as well as each type of customer's expected length of tenure at the bank (that is, the average duration of each type of customer's patronage at Bank ABC). But even before considering the potentially serious implications of significantly higher churn rates among two types of customers, the current-period income statement for the bank could have been broken into three distinct parts based on these three customer groups. Loyalists and New Acquisitions, for instance, are responsible for a disproportionate share of branch expenses because they use branches much more frequently. And advertising costs should be allocated mostly to the "New Acquisitions" group. A revised financial statement of the bank's results, this time with revenues and

(continued)

(Continued)

costs allocated more appropriately to the three customer groups that make up the bank's customer base, is shown in Exhibit 11C.

EXHIBIT 11C   Bank ABC's Income by Customer Group

Allocated Financials (000)	Loyalists	Shoppers	New Acquisitions
# of customers (000)	12,000	7,000	1,500
Checking deposits	€127,500	€34,000	€34,000
Savings deposits	€262,500	€70,000	€70,000
Total deposit volume	€390,000	€104,000	€104,000
Deposits per customer	€32,500	€14,857	€69,333
Gross profit on deposits	€12,900	€3,440	€3,440
Allocated expenses:			
Branch expenses	€7,222	€1,317	€2,545
Call center expenses	€1,734	€885	€574
Retention concessions	€-	€46	€46
Advertising	€160	€129	€2,400
Other	€342	€91	€91
Total allocated expenses	€9,458	€2,468	€5,656
Net allocated profit	**€3,442**	**€972**	**€(2,216)**
Profit per customer	€286.83	€138.86	€(1,477.33)
Profit per cust w/o advert	€300.17	€157.29	€122.67

It should be obvious now that the acquisition campaign has not actually been quite as successful as had been assumed. It turns out that New Acquisitions, as customers, are not very profitable, consuming an inordinate amount of call center and branch expense. Compared to Shoppers, who are several times more numerous than New Acquisitions, yet have the same total level of checking and savings deposits and yield the same total gross profit as a group, the expenses required to handle New Acquisitions are much higher. Even after eliminating the cost of advertising (on the assumption that once customers have been acquired, the job of advertising has been done), the bank's expenses required for handling all the New Acquisitions are still about a third higher than for handling all the Shoppers, and on a per-customer basis the difference is quite acute. The per-customer profit figures are also revealing. It's lucky for the bank that Loyalists, at this juncture anyway, are the most numerous customers, because profit per Loyalist is by far the highest, whether advertising is counted or not.

There is, however, an even more important issue to be raised with respect to Bank ABC's financial condition, and this has to do with whether it is paying enough attention to its long-term prospects, and the quality of its customer equity. A short-term focus can easily undermine the long-term value of a bank. This should not be a surprising revelation, in the wake of the financial industry crisis of 2008 and 2009. Numerous pundits and gurus have discussed the perils of focusing on short-term results. Nevertheless, stock exchanges around the world are ruthlessly critical of banks failing to hit end-of-year targets. Being a bank executive is a thorny task these days: On the one hand, countless newspaper articles are lambasting your focus on end-of-period results and deprecating the recklessness of your peers in managing their risks. On the other hand, analysts continue to judge bank performance by the numbers in the quarterly financial reports. Everybody acknowledges a need to strike a balance between short-term and long-term results, but nobody can agree how to do it.

It is important for every bank to understand that its customer activities create value both in the short term, by delivering current-period profits (or losses), and in the long term, by creating (or destroying) customer equity. Return on Customer[SM], the metric first proposed by Don Peppers and Martha Rogers in their 2005 book *Return on Customer: Creating Maximum Value from Your Scarcest Resource*, is a straightforward performance metric combining these two objectives. But regardless of whether this metric is formally calculated, the most important issue for a bank is to monitor the lifetime values of its customers over time, and the most direct and useful way to do this is simply to drill down on its business by individual customer, or by customer segment.

Exhibit 11D is a sobering set of numbers that uses the churn rates of these various customer groups, along with their profitability-per-customer numbers (after advertising expense has been removed), to derive average customer lifetime values for the three different types of customers. In addition, some possible strategies for improving each group's profitability, over time, are evaluated, in order to see how much leverage there might be for the bank to improve LTV. Shoppers and New Acquisitions each are expected to churn at a rate of about 20 percent per year, which means their average tenure will only be about 3 years, compared to about 13 years for Loyalists. In other words, the number of Loyalists the bank starts with in Year 1 will be cut by 50 percent around year 13, while Shoppers and New Acquisitions will both be half gone in just 3 years (hardly seems worth the effort, right?). To derive customer lifetime values, we simply assumed that each customer would go on earning the same profit, year after year, provided that they remained a customer. Then we reduced this profit each year by the customer's churn rate (to account for the likelihood that this profit would no longer be coming in at all), and we applied a rather generous financial discount rate for net present value calculations of 10 percent. (A discount rate as high as 20 percent would be applicable to many businesses, but this is a large bank with little actual financial risk).

EXHIBIT 11D   Customer Lifetime Value of Different Groups for Bank ABC

Per-Customer LTV	Loyalists	Shoppers	New Acquisitions
Churn rate	5%	20%	20%
Half-life of expected customer tenure	13 years	3 years	3 years
Avg Customer 20-year LTV, w/o advertising	€1,980	€561	€437
Value of increasing cross-selling by 10%	€325	€87	€87
Value of reducing churn by 5%	N/A	€105	€82

(continued)

(Continued)

What Exhibit 11D shows is that the Loyalists, per customer, have four to five times more long-term value (customer LTV) than either of the other types of customers. Moreover, even if a marketing effort to improve cross-selling by 10 percent is successful, this effort will still increase customer LTVs by less than 20 percent each.

Perhaps of more immediate interest to the bank would be the fact that in the New Acquisitions group, the loss *per customer* in the current period is over €1400, because of the heavy one-time advertising burden, so there is just no way at all that the firm can ever pay itself back for that average loss, given these customers' tepid lifetime values. In other words, the customer-acquisition campaign might have succeeded in adding customers, but because of the extremely short duration of these customers' tenures, and the consequently low lifetime values they exhibit, it was still a dismal failure as a marketing campaign. In the end it chewed up a not-inconsequential amount of Bank ABC's shareholder value.

The executive team was very happy about the acquisition of this new group of customers, but they should have been feeling exactly the opposite. They should have been using the available information to question their decision to spend so much for so little actual economic benefit. Had Bank ABC's executives been fully aware of their bank's financial situation, doubtless their end-of-year party would not have been so cheerful.

The Bank ABC story makes it clear where priorities of the bank should be. So why do companies have such a hard time following the right path? The insurmountable barrier is the target-setting mechanism followed by most, if not all, banks. They invariably set their targets in terms of products: Sell this many credit cards, extend that many new mortgage loans, book that many new deposits into current accounts, and so forth. By focusing only on the profitability of products, campaigns, or channels, they fail to recognize how different customers may have different effects on the financial results. And because they didn't look very carefully at their customers, they missed the fact that some of these customers would be doing very little (if any) benefit for the bank within just a few years.

Trying to change completely the way targets are set is likely to be a quixotic attempt for many banks. When everybody in the stock market is holding his breath to see end-of-year growth on deposit volumes, it can be challenging to convince executives to evaluate these traditionally important figures in the context of the equally important ideas of customer equity and Return on Customer. If Bank ABC were to organize its thinking, its data, and its analysis on a customer-by-customer basis, consider the steps they might take in the next planning and budgeting cycle:

1. *Investigate customer growth opportunities*
    a. *Look for product volume asymmetries in the Loyalist group, i.e., high deposit volume with low credit card volume.*
    b. *Identify cross-sell opportunities by data mining effort. In other words, find products for customers in a way that benefits those customers.*

    c. *Uncover primary motivators for the Loyalist group to accept cross-sell offers in different product categories by a market survey. In other words, differentiate Most Valuable Customers by needs and behaviors, and communicate with those customers accordingly.*

    d. *Use needs and behavior differentiation strategies to design relevant offers and messaging for customers, in a timely way—in order to identify possible value propositions and customer growth strategies.*

    e. *Test value propositions and strategies.*

    f. *Calculate expected ROC in each case, considering the likelihood of acceptance of cross-sell offers, cost of extending these offers, and resulting changes in cash flow from customers in this group.*

2. *Investigate retention priorities*

    a. *Investigate what might be needed to entice Shoppers to remain with the bank, perhaps with a survey and some qualitative research.*

    b. *Calculate the cost of retention offers needed to address their issues.*

    c. *Identify the value proposition alternatives as well as retention strategies.*

    d. *Calculate expected churn rate decrease for each value proposition and strategy alternative.*

    e. *Test value propositions and strategies.*

    f. *Estimate expected ROC in each case considering possible reduction in churn rate, cost of reducing churn by meeting the needs of this group, and resulting change in cash flow streams from customers in this group.*

3. *Act on acquisition priorities*

    a. *Survey customers who do not currently do business with the bank.*

    b. *Identify conditions to churn to this bank and expected customer lifetime values if they can be acquired.*

    c. *Calculate cost of meeting their conditions, i.e., cost of acquisition.*

    d. *Identify different value propositions and strategies that will cater to different customer groups who do not currently work with the bank.*

    e. *Test value propositions and strategies.*

    f. *Calculate expected Return on Customer in each case, considering cost of acquisition and cash flow streams expected from acquired customers.*

    g. *Emphasize a cessation in acquisition of high-cost, low-profitability customers.*

4. *Finalize plans and budget by optimizing acquisition, retention, and growth around ROC*

    a. *Trade off growth/retention/acquisition priorities based on Return on Customer values expected from different value propositions and strategies.*

    b. *Set priorities and allocate budget by selecting value propositions and strategies that will yield highest Return on Customer. This will define exactly what the bank will be doing in growth/retention/acquisition.*

    c. *Finalize product-based targets and budget by considering:*

(continued)

(Continued)

   i. Cross-sell targets to Loyalists and associated expense budget.
   ii. Impact of reduced churn rate of Shoppers on product targets and associated retention budget.
   iii. Product volume to be brought in by New Acquisitions and associated acquisition budget.

Bank ABC will not necessarily meet all conditions demanded by all three groups. The process described above not only sets priorities for the bank in terms of how much to spend for growth/retention/acquisition, but it also helps to define how to spend the money by identifying the value propositions and strategies that need to be adopted. We should also remember that every group is likely to have subgroups and sub-subgroups. A bank with millions of retail customers should not settle for just three basic customer "types." But at Bank ABC, if they don't even analyze their business with a very few, basic groups of different kinds of customers, they will probably never be able to manage their business effectively. And, when the end comes, they are likely to be completely unaware. They might even have been celebrating just the previous year!

Source: Adapted from Yücel Ersöz, "Maximize Long-Term Value and Hit Short-Term Targets," *Customer Strategist* 2, no. 1 (March 2010): 40–44.

Summary

The metrics associated with managing customer relationships can provide invaluable insight in to the profitability potential of the enterprise's customer base and the viability of the enterprise's new customer-strategy business processes. The customer-based enterprise does, however, have to concern itself with other measurements and analyzing other pieces of information that are more specific to growing the overall value of each customer. Treating different customers differently can entail a detailed analysis of each customer to determine how the enterprise can alter his trajectory with the enterprise. Often this analysis can help turn customer information into knowledge the enterprise can use to help customers meet their needs.

The triggers, or predictors, of individual customer action and opportunity usually cannot be seen without detailed analysis. This is the increasingly complex and far-from-intuitive science of *customer-based analytics*, and having this discipline well represented on an enterprise-wide cross-functional team is critical. Sophisticated statistical models powered by technology can uncover some remarkable and highly predictive patterns. The ability to "mine data" is so valuable that its precise manifestations can be proprietary within certain companies. In the next chapter, we uncover some of these scientific applications of analytics within the customer-strategy enterprise.

Food for Thought

1. Let's imagine you are the customer portfolio manager of a wireless phone company. How should you be evaluated at the end of the quarter? Straight sales

from your customers? Net sales (sales minus cost to serve)? Customer satisfaction? Would it make sense for you to be evaluated on a combination of how much your company made from your customers this quarter and also—as of this quarter—what the two-year projected value of your customer base is? Five-year projected value? Why?

2. If a company rewards employees based on a combination of current and future values of customers, how might that change decision making?
3. Should the value of customers a company doesn't yet have be calculated and taken into account in the present quarter? Why or why not?
4. How is retention different from Share of Customer (SOC) as a measure and how would it be used differently? Why are both important?

Glossary

Customer equity   The sum of all the LTVs of an enterprise's current and future customers, or the total value of the enterprise's customer relationships. A customer-centric company would view customer equity as its principal corporate asset.

Leading indicators   The variables driving any firm's LTV model, which tend to fall into four general categories: LTV drivers, lifestyle changes, behavioral cues, and customer attitudes.

Lifetime value (LTV)   The net present value of the future stream of cash flow attributable to that customer. LTV directly represents the long-term financial benefit of a customer's continuing patronage.

Lifetime value drivers   The elements of the LTV equation—the actual components that determine how much value the customer creates for the company over time.

Return on Customer (ROC)   A metric directly analogous to return on investment (ROI), specifically designed to track how well an enterprise is using customers to create value. ROC equals a company's current-period cash flow (from customers) plus the change in customer equity during the period, divided by the customer equity at the beginning of the period. ROC is pronounced are-oh-see.

Total shareholder return   Represents the change in capital value of a listed/quoted company over a period (typically one year or longer), plus dividends, expressed as a plus-or-minus percentage of the opening value.

Value creators   Companies with increasing customer equity over time. The combination of short- and long-term value created by their customers occurs at a rate that is higher than their cost of capital.

Value destroyers   Companies with ROC below zero, regardless of current profitability.

Value harvesters   Companies whose ROC is below their cost of capital (but not yet negative), so that they are using up customer profits that have already been "put in the bank" in the form of customer equity. These companies may earn a current profit, but because they are not replenishing their customer equity enough, their future growth potential is limited.

CHAPTER 12

Using Customer Analytics to Build the Success of the Customer-Strategy Enterprise

Progress might have been all right once but it has gone on too long.

—Ogden Nash

To the customer-centric enterprise, data about individual customers are like gold nuggets that, if collected and used effectively, can increase the value of the customer base significantly. **Data mining** is a frequently used term for the process of extracting useful nuggets of information from a vast database of customer information; but as the relationship revolution has taken hold, the data-mining process itself has also undergone an important transformation. In the pre-interactive age, data-mining techniques were used to uncover information about the types of customers to whom particular offers should be made, answering the question: Who is the next most likely customer to buy this product? Today, the question asked by companies engaged in managing ongoing, interactive relationships with individual customers is: What is the next most likely product that this particular customer will want to buy? As we saw in the last chapter, rather than optimizing around each product, the customer-strategy enterprise needs to optimize around the customer.

In truth, both product optimization and customer optimization have roles to play in any competitive enterprise's efforts to get, keep, and grow customers. But in the interactive age, much more so than in the past, individual customer information drives the central engine of competition. Without reliable insights into the value and needs of individual customers, the customer-based enterprise will be completely rudderless.

In this chapter, we look at **customer analytics**—the way we think of data mining now—and learn about the fundamental issues facing customer-strategy companies when they are working with and using large amounts of customer data.

E xperts define the term *data mining* largely in terms of its usefulness in uncovering hidden trends or yielding previously unknown insight about the nature of a firm's customers. SAS Institute defines data mining as "an iterative process of creating predictive and descriptive models, by uncovering previously unknown trends and patterns in vast amounts of data from across the enterprise, in order to support decision making."[1] Michael J. A. Berry and Gordon S. Linoff, who have written several books on the subject, define data mining as "the process of exploration and analysis, by automatic or semiautomatic means, of large quantities of data in order to discover meaningful patterns and rules," and, for the customer-centric company, founded on the belief "that business actions should be based on learning, that informed decisions are better than uninformed decisions, and that measuring results is beneficial to the business."[2] Ronald Swift, Teradata vice president of cross industry business solutions, says data mining is "the process of extracting and presenting new knowledge, previously undetectable, selected from databases for actionable decisions."[3] And Jill Dyché, partner and cofounder of Baseline Consulting, says data mining is "a type of advanced analysis used to determine certain patterns within data ... most often associated with predictive analysis based on historical detail, and the generation of models for further analysis and query."[4]

Rather than limit ourselves to the term *data mining*, however, we prefer the term *customer analytics*. Although data mining and customer analytics are not really different things, the analogy to mining itself implies a batch process, with the enterprise searching out nuggets of information and then putting them to use. The reality, however, in the interactive age, is that businesses need to have continuously developing, real-time insights into the nature of their individual customers, not only so that the right marketing campaign can be created and launched, but also so the customer can be given the appropriate offer in real time (**real-time analytics**), while she is on the phone, shopping at the Web site, or standing at the checkout counter.

Customer analytics, therefore, offers the missing link to understanding customers: prediction.[5] Prediction helps enterprises use the value of customer information to optimize each interaction with each customer.

> Customer analytics enables the enterprise to classify, estimate, predict, cluster, and more accurately describe data about customers, using mathematical models and algorithms that ultimately simplify how it views its customer base and how it behaves toward individual customers.

---

[1] Available at: www.sas.com/technologies/analytics/datamining/index.html, accessed September 1, 2010.

[2] Michael J.A. Berry and Gordon S. Linoff, *Mastering Data Mining* (New York: John Wiley & Sons, Inc., 2000); Berry and Linoff, *Data Mining Techniques for Marketing, Sales, and Customer Relationship Management* (Indianapolis: John Wiley & Sons, 2004), p. 3.

[3] Ronald S. Swift, *Accelerating Customer Relationships* (Upper Saddle River, NJ: Prentice Hall, 2001).

[4] Jill Dyché and Evan Levy, *Customer Data Integration: Reaching a Single Version of the Truth* (Hoboken, NJ: John Wiley & Sons, 2006), p. 275. See also Jill Dyché, *e-Data: Turning Data into Information with Data Warehousing* (Reading, MA: Addison-Wesley, 2000).

[5] Deborah L. Vence, "Astute Analytics," *Marketing News* 41, no. 20 (December 2007): 34; Robert Nisbet, John Elder, and Gary Miner, *Handbook of Statistical Analysis and Data Mining Applications* (Salt Lake City, UT: Academic Press, 2009).

Today, leading companies integrate the most relevant elements of their data-mining algorithms into their actual touchpoint applications. If a customer behaves a certain way, then the mathematical algorithm can analyze that behavior and instantly access the most relevant offer for that customer, taking into account everything the enterprise knows or is able to predict about each customer, in *real time*. Customer analytics enables the enterprise to classify, estimate, predict, cluster, and more accurately describe data about customers, using mathematical models and algorithms that ultimately simplify how it views its customer base and how it behaves toward individual customers.

The dilemma facing many companies that amass huge customer databases today is simply how to make sense of the data. Analytical software has become a critical component of the customer-strategy enterprise, and those who can operate such software are in great demand. The mathematical data models that analytical software can produce are inherently simplifications of the "real world"—they represent how customers have behaved before and will likely behave again. They enable a company to view correlations within large sets of customer data and within and among various parts of its business. By analyzing historic information and applying it to current customer data, these mathematical models and algorithms can predict future events, with varying degrees of accuracy, based not just on the amount of data collected but also on the power of the analysis applied to the data. Using customer analytics, an enterprise can sometimes predict whether a customer will buy a certain product or will defect to a competitor.

Verizon Wireless Uses Analytics to Predict and Reduce Churn

Verizon Wireless, a joint venture between Verizon and Vodafone, dramatically increased its customer equity during the four-year period from the end of 2001 through the end of 2005 (see Chapter 11). It accomplished this feat with a mix of excellent customer acquisition tactics and superb retention improvement—dramatically reducing the monthly churn rate on retail contract customers from 2.6 percent to 1.1 percent.

And how did Verizon actually accomplish this dramatic surge in value creation? Through a sophisticated use of customer analytics. First, Verizon developed a "predictive churn model" (PCM) to identify as far in advance as possible those particular customers who might be about to leave the franchise soon. The models also matched these likely churners with specific, relevant, and timely offers—different offers being more or less relevant for different types of customers, with different calling patterns, demographics, and other characteristics. In addition, Verizon generated a "predictive takers model" (PTM)— that is, a model of the types of customers most likely to *accept* its offer and remain in the franchise. By combining its use of PCM with PTM, Verizon was able to cull the relatively large number of customers who were identified as having a high propensity to leave into a much smaller group of customers who would be more likely to accept Verizon's offer and remain loyal.

(continued)

(Continued)

Simultaneously, analytics helped predict the right kind of plan for other subscribers, based on each customer's individual call usage pattern. Many customers who were not on the optimum plan were then contacted and offered a more relevant plan; retention went up within this larger, already more loyal population as well.

Importantly, one of the factors Verizon's management credits for making this analytics program a success is the fact that the effort was fashioned by a multidisciplinary team, with representatives from several different, non–information technology (IT) departments.

Business benefits accruing to Verizon Wireless from its use of customer analytics include not just the very significant long-term revenue increase due to more loyal customers but immediately reduced marketing costs as well. For instance, the company's direct-mail budget for "churner mailing" was reduced by 60 percent because of the highly targeted nature of its analytics-driven marketing campaigns.

Sources: Don Peppers and Martha Rogers, Ph.D., *Rules to Break and Laws to Follow: How Your Business Can Beat the Crisis of Short-Termism* (Hoboken, NJ: John Wiley & Sons, 2008), p. 84; Christophe Giraud-Carrier, "Success Stories in Data/Text Mining," Brigham Young University, available at: https://facwiki.cs.byu.edu/DML/index.php/Data_Mining_Resources, accessed September 1, 2010.

Companies produce large amounts of data through a wide array of customer-related business processes, including order entry, billing, reservations, complaint handling, product specification, Web interactions, and sales calls. The data often are fed into a data warehouse, where much of it lies hidden in "data tombs," forgotten about for years. Often even when a firm has the customer analytics resources necessary to unleash the value of its data, it soon discovers that much of its information is "dirty" (expired, irrelevant, nonsequential, or nonsensible) and needs to be "cleaned" (eliminated, updated, correlated, and refined). As customer analytics tools and technology become more affordable and easier to use, however, enterprises are starting to feel competitive pressure to improve their capabilities in this area.[6] The

---

[6]See Hugh J. Watson, "Bridging the IT/Business Culture Chasm," *Business Intelligence Journal* 14, no. 1 (2009): 4–7; Matthew Shanahan, "Moving Target: Understanding Customer Demand," *Information Today* 27, no. 2 (February 2010): 21; Detlev Zwick and Janice Denegri Knott, "Manufacturing Customers: The Database as New Means of Production," *Journal of Consumer Culture* 9 (2009): 221–248; Hugh J. Watson, Dale L. Goodhue, and Barbara H. Wixom, "The Benefits of Data Warehousing: Why Some Organizations Realize Exceptional Payoffs," *Information and Management* 39 (2002): 491–502; and Hugh J. Watson, David A. Annino, Barbara H. Wixom, K. Liddell Avery, and Mathew Rutherford, "Current Practices in Data Warehousing," *Information Systems Management* (Winter 2001): 47–55.

various activities involved in readying customer data for analysis, and the **analysis process** itself, include:

- *Classification*, or assigning instances to a group, then using the data to learn the pattern of traits that identify the group to which each instance belongs.
- *Estimation*, for determining a value for some unknown continuous variable, such as credit card balance or income.
- *Regression*, which uses existing values to forecast what continuous values are likely to be.
- *Prediction*, or using historical data to build a model to forecast future behavior.
- *Clustering*, which maps customers within the database into groups based on their similarities. (See more about clustering in the following section.)

CRM in the Cloud

As open source computing and social media have both evolved, newer and more robust tools for managing customer relationships have become available. First-generation, enterprise customer relationship management (CRM) systems brimmed with functionality but were often costly and time consuming to implement, and sometimes difficult to update and maintain as well. Second-generation solutions improved cost of ownership by moving to a hosted software-as-a-service (SaaS) delivery model—without sacrificing features—but this still kept companies locked into proprietary platforms. Now, as social and open source computing technology becomes more capable, businesses can manage more and more of the CRM task "in the cloud," so to speak. This can reduce the complexity and costs of maintaining robust customer relationships while increasing their ability to mine customer insights that lead to competitive advantage.

Customer Management Evolves, and So Do the Tools

The art of managing customer relationships has evolved dramatically over the past 20 years, thanks in large part to the fragmentation of media and, more recently, the shift in control from company to customer. The traditional sales and marketing funnel, in which prospects are led from awareness to consideration to purchase in an orderly, linear fashion, has been scrambled beyond recognition. It's no longer a big bureaucracy talking to peons who can't talk back. Companies are no longer in charge. They're influential participants, but participants nevertheless.

This level playing field has been groomed primarily by social media, which has democratized the creation and sharing of information. Social media has made trust-based relationships more important. There are two elements of that relationship: customers have to believe companies have their interests at heart, and companies have to be competent enough to execute and fulfill the obligation.

(continued)

(Continued)

As the traditional vendor/customer relationship has evolved, so has the technology to support the relationship. This evolution of CRM software can be tracked through three main stages:

1. *Enterprise CRM.* Popularized during the 1990s, enterprise applications for CRM were based on client/server computing and represented a quantum leap in functionality over simple spreadsheet and contact-management applications. Unfortunately, the complexity of these applications also made them costly to implement and maintain. In some instances, adoption rates lagged because end users were forced to adapt to processes dictated more by software design than by business needs. The sometimes rigid requirements for data entry and workflow resulted in slow buy-in among users, particularly the marketing and sales people who stood to benefit the most from the use of the tools. (In one widely publicized survey, some 80 percent of salespeople reported that their own firm's CRM solution didn't work.) Although this resistance to process change was a significant barrier to many CRM implementations, the perceived benefits of improving customer account management—from increased satisfaction and loyalty, to more cross-selling opportunities—made CRM systems a must-have for many large organizations.

2. *SaaS CRM.* CRM vendors began taking their first steps into the cloud in the early 2000s, offering hosted, SaaS solutions that took the implementation burden off the shoulders of the corporate IT group—and brought the benefits of robust CRM to small and medium-size businesses. These offerings were more scalable than their predecessors, allowing companies to add seats or functionality as needed (hence the term *on demand*). IT overhead was reduced, since hosting was outsourced to the software provider. (The Gartner Group estimates that businesses have seen project savings between 25 and 40 percent after deploying CRM applications through SaaS and that 30 percent of new customer service and support application investments will be through the SaaS model by 2012.[a]) Maintenance improved as well, with vendor updates more seamlessly integrated into the subscription-based offerings. Although the deployment model improved significantly, however, the development model retained many of the characteristics of CRM enterprise solutions. SaaS solutions were still largely proprietary and entirely controlled by the vendor, resulting in limited customization capabilities on the front end and limited integration possibilities on the back end. Nevertheless, SaaS represented a significant step forward in the evolution of customer management and is part of a broader movement that shows no signs of slowing down. SaaS solutions accounted for 18 percent of the overall CRM market in 2008—with that revenue percentage reaching 33 percent in some CRM subsegments, according to Gartner.

3. *CRM in the cloud.* This step in CRM's technological evolution is slowly coming into focus. By combining SaaS with the commercial open source development model, an "open cloud" CRM solution can be created that proponents say reduces investment risk significantly. Portable across platforms

and partners, interoperable with other open source data and applications, and more customizable by end users, an open cloud CRM solution also allows customers themselves to participate in the environment rather than simply serving as targets or leads. In effect, this turns the focus of CRM away from the "M"—management—and more toward the "R"—relationship. Twitter, blogs, wikis, YouTube, and RSS feeds all become tools in the CRM toolbox. But here's a key point: IT no longer owns the toolbox.

One could argue that "CRM in the cloud" is not even CRM anymore. It's a self-service model in which the customers themselves are taking over.

Cloud computing has the potential to provide key customer insights. Access to a broader set of data residing in cloud environments, including social networks, gives companies more insight into how best to reach customers at any point in the customer life cycle, from awareness, to consideration, to repurchase. This will enable rapid redeployment of sales and marketing resources to activities that have the most impact.

A company can't change customer behavior if its customer managers don't know anything about what the customer needs or is doing with the product. Overwhelmingly, companies organize their data around who their most valuable customers are. That's looking at it from the wrong end. In best practices, companies organize the data around customer needs as well as customer values.

This is where the open cloud can have a significant impact, because it enables companies to track more than just transactions. There's a seemingly endless cache of unstructured data wafting around the Web, and the companies that can capture it, analyze it, and act on it are the ones that will carve out competitive advantage.

The goal is to see the situation faced by each customer through that customer's own eyes. The open cloud may provide an important lens to bring that view into focus.

Source: Adapted from Peppers & Rogers Group and Sugar CRM white paper, "Getting Social: The Open Road to 'CRM 3.0,'" 2009; available at: www.1to1media.com/view.aspx?docid=31736, accessed September 1, 2010.

[a] "Gartner Says that 30 Percent of New Customer Service and Support Application Investments Will Be through the SaaS Model by 2012" (November 2008); available at: www.gartner.com/it/page.jsp?id=808112, accessed September 1, 2010.

Customer analytics is especially useful for consumer marketing companies that collect transactional data through call centers, Web sites, or electronic points of sale. Banks, credit card companies, telecommunications firms, retailers, and even airlines adopted customer analytics as a vital part of their business operations earlier than other companies. These kinds of companies tend to generate large volumes of customer-specific information in the natural course of operating their businesses, often resulting in vast data warehouses, containing terabytes of data.

Royal Bank of Canada has been focused on customer relationships in its retail banking business for well over a decade and a half now and became a "best practice" case study in this area years ago. One of the secrets of the bank's success is the fact that it constantly monitors the behavioral cues in its customer database in order to optimize current income results against likely changes in lifetime value for individual customers. It has a great deal of data, but it must also do the right analysis, in order to spot the cues. For instance, until recently the bank's "Behavioural Based Modeling" system calculated the effects its various products and services had on customer lifetime values by using customer-specific revenues, but using the average (i.e., non–customer-specific) cost-to-serve figure. The problem is that banking customers don't all cost the same to serve. Different customers incur different costs. One customer might prefer dealing with the bank online, for instance, while another might prefer the more expensive teller window. Customers will generate different levels of credit risk, processing charges, and other expenses. After upgrading their software, Royal Bank of Canada began tracking customer-specific costs as well as revenues. The result was that the accuracy of its lifetime value figures improved immensely, with more than 75 percent of its consumer customers moving two or more deciles in rank as a result.

In evaluating its actions for different customers, Royal Bank of Canada optimizes "overall efficiencies," a term the bank uses to include both current income and lifetime value (LTV) changes in the calculation. One example of a policy change based on maximizing overall efficiencies has to do with "courtesy overdraft limits." This product is now provided for the vast majority of consumer customers rather than just its heavy-hitters. Each customer's overdraft limit is set based on that particular customer's overall relationship with the bank. Anyone who has been a customer for at least 90 days, has a low-risk credit score, and has made at least one deposit in the last month will have some level of overdraft protection. Not only does this enhance each customer's experience with the bank, but it actually increases the bank's efficiency during the check-clearing process, reducing the number of write-offs and allowing account managers to focus on sales activities. (It also reduces the number and cost of contact center calls handling irate customers who want their overdraft fees reversed.)

Overall, since 1997, the bank has increased the profitability of its average client by 13 percent and increased the number of high-value clients by 20 percent.[7]

Customer analytics contributes to better sales productivity and lower marketing costs in many different ways:

- By making it possible to send more relevant information and offers, analytics helps to improve shopper-to-buyer conversion rates.
- Instead of offering one product to many customers, analytics makes it possible to offer specific and more targeted cross-sell and upsell opportunities, which can result in measurably increased sales.
- By taking steps to keep customers longer, analytics can help increase customer lifetime value, profitability, and Return on Customer.

---

[7]Don Peppers and Martha Rogers, Ph.D., *Return on Customer: Creating Maximum Value From Your Scarcest Resource* (New York: Currency/Doubleday, 2005), p. 97.

- Companies use analytics to improve operational effectiveness through smarter, more relevant (and therefore, usually, faster and less costly) customer service.
- Analytics can be used to reduce the interaction time and effort, making information exchange or transactions easier, faster and, therefore, more likely.
- Analytics improves the customer's perception of the level of service as a result of relevant messaging during an interaction.
- Analytics makes improved service levels for best customers possible.[8]

For example, Coach, the global designer and retailer of accessories and gifts, has successfully used insight gleaned from customer analytics to deliver exceptional customer experiences with maximum cost effectiveness. Because the Coach mission statement is "treating customers as guests in their own home," the customer's in-store experience is key. Predictive analytics have allowed Coach not only to predict how many sales it will generate and identify its top 1 to 2 percent of customers but to predict when those customers will most likely come into the store. Coach incorporates weather forecasts and traffic patterns into its data analysis, ensuring that its staff will be ready when the best customers are most likely to visit rather than needlessly allocating staff resources when they're not.[9]

Those who use customer analytics, therefore, are trying to create an unobstructed view of the customer, allowing the enterprise, essentially, to see things from the customer's own perspective. By delving into a customer's history, analytical programs can help the enterprise customize the way it serves or manufactures a product for a customer to suit that customer's individual needs. In essence, customer analytics helps the enterprise to transform its customer data into critical business decisions about individual customers. Customer analytics software can reveal hidden trends about a customer and compare her behavior to other customers' behavior.[10] In addition, customer analytics can play an important role in customer acquisition, by helping the enterprise decide how to handle different prospects differently and by predicting which ones are more likely to become the most valuable customers.[11]

In 2001, Tesco, the U.K. retailer with the highly successful Clubcard frequent shopper program, bought a 53 percent stake in Dunn Humby, its data-mining

[8]William M. Saubert, "Using Customer Analytics to Improve Customer Retention," *Bank Accounting & Finance* 22, no. 3 (April-May 2009): 33–38; Brendan B. Read, "Why Performance Analytics Is Important," *Customer Interaction Solutions* 27, no. 2 (July 2008): 24–25; Kevin Cavanaugh, "Achieving Intelligent Interactions with Analytical CRM," *DM Review* 11, no. 5 (May 2001): 44–47.

[9]"How Coach Uses Data to Live Up to its Brand," 1to1 Case Study: Customer Initiatives in Action; available at: www.1to1media.com/downloads/Casestudy_Coach101507.pdf, accessed May 6, 2010.

[10]Matthew Shanahan, "Moving Target: Understanding Customer Demand," *Information Today* 27, no. 2 (February 2010): 21; Angela Karr, "Analytics: The Next Wave of CRM," *Customer Interface* 14, no. 5 (May 2001): 44.

[11]William M. Saubert, "Using Customer Analytics to Improve Customer Retention," *Bank Accounting & Finance* 22, no. 3 (April-May 2009): 33–38; Thomas J. Siragusa, "Implementing Data Mining for Better CRM," *Customer Interaction Solutions* 19, no. 11 (May 2001): 38.

partner. In 2006, it raised its stake to 84 percent. Tesco knows that its customer data is its most valuable asset. Dunn Humby and Tesco became partners in 1995, when Tesco was launching its Clubcard initiative, and since then the firm has helped Tesco evaluate and act on what it learns from its Clubcard customers, managing massive data sets and enabling Tesco to increase the value of its customer base.[12]

Tesco and other astute customer-strategy enterprises have learned that customer data have a dollar value associated with them, and the more accurate the information, the better the enterprise can compete. Customer analytics can provide *metadata*—information about information—spotting characteristics and trends that enhance customer retention and profitability. Furthermore, customer analytics can be a technique for examining the profitability of specific products that individual customers purchase. As the late Fred Newell pointed out in *Loyalty.com*, analytics helps profile customers so that characteristics of loyal customers can be identified to predict which prospects will become new customers. Data mining can manage customer relationships by determining characteristics of customers who have left for a competitor so that the enterprise can act to retain customers who are at risk of leaving. Moreover, analytics helps an enterprise learn the mix of products to which a group of customers is attracted so it can learn what the customers value. "With this knowledge," Newell writes, "we can mine the customer file for similar customers to offer suggestions they are likely to value. Without data and its being analyzed to develop information and knowledge about the way things are happening in the real world, all we have are opinions. Every expert we have talked to gives the same answer: 'Data mining is knowledge discovery.'"[13] Customer analytics is not a technology—it is a *business process*.

The next level of analytics might be applying financial characteristics to the data analysis, in order to yield a more accurate view of the actual economic consequences

> Customer analytics is not a technology–it is a *business process.*

of particular customer actions. For instance, an enterprise might know that a promotion should go to customers fitting a certain profile, but it probably will have more difficulty correlating the cost of the promotion with its likely outcome, at least on a customer-specific basis. In the next epoch of customer analytics, the mathematical algorithms will look across a range of promotions and associated costs to determine which tactics will generate the most profit, ideally taking into consideration the current return as well as the long-term effect on equity simultaneously. Ultimately, customer analytics will generate a revolution in how marketing decisions are made, driving companies increasingly toward solutions based on highly detailed marketing simulations.

In the end, however, the reason for analyzing all of these data is simply to develop a deeper relationship with each customer, in an effort to increase the overall value of the customer base—or, as Judy Bayer and Ronald Swift of NCR Teradata point out, to "optimize" the enterprise's customer relationships.

---

[12] Elizabeth Rigby, "Eyes in the Till," *Financial Times* (London), November 11, 2006, p. 16; Martha Rogers, Ph.D., "It's Aces High for Tesco and Dunn Humby," *Inside 1to1,* August 6, 2001; available at: www.1to1media.com/view.aspx?DocID=18843, accessed September 1, 2010.

[13] Frederick Newell, *Loyalty.com* (New York: McGraw-Hill Professional Book Group, 2000).

Optimizing Customer Relationships with Advanced Analytics

Judy Bayer
CRM Practice Partner, NCR Teradata

Ronald S. Swift
Vice President, Cross Industry Business Solutions, NCR Teradata

Customer interaction and transaction data enter a company's database system from thousands of customer contact touchpoints, through many selling and service channels—in continuous waves. A critical challenge any business faces is that of leveraging this dynamic tidal wave of customer information to gain the vital insight that can help optimize a customer relationship. It has been said that the market value of a company is a direct reflection of the value of its customer relationships. This is certainly true in a time when information—or intelligence—is the primary source of economic value. When analytical intelligence is applied systematically to optimize customer relationships, enterprises can expect improved customer equity and enhanced business performance. Here we provide a brief overview of the subject of advanced customer analytics, which concerns the methodologies that experts use to make the most of the knowledge of a company's current and future customers to create intelligence for better business decisions and optimal customer relationships.

Advanced customer analytics involves tracking and evaluating data and examining highly complex patterns and trends. It builds and expands on traditional data mining by applying statistical and reporting techniques and tools to information culled from customer contacts. And, with the help of advanced CRM technology tools, analytical intelligence can be created and applied within days, minutes, or even seconds of a customer interaction. Referred to as *real-time analytics* and enabled by advanced analytical CRM software applications, these powerful applications systematically accelerate analytic processes to incredible speeds.

Managers and business analysts use customer analytics to:

- Rank customers by business value.
- Model customer behavior to predict an individual's migration into a spectrum of value groups.
- Simulate and predict customer buying behavior based on a variety of promotion strategies.
- Perform a marketing influencers analysis to identify which customers can be influenced in their value migration, then communicate to them in ways that move them in the right direction.
- Learn what proportion of customers purchase goods or services through single and multiple channels—and know how valuable they are.
- Learn which products or services sell best through certain channels.
- Learn what impact new channels will have on current business.

(continued)

(*Continued*)

- Determine which channels would be most effective for specific customer groups.
- Build usable data on community learning.
- Predict which customers will switch or begin sharing business across channels.
- Make assessments of each customer's affinity to a message, product, or service.
- Learn how frequently to contact each customer—and which channel is best for specific messages.
- Perform detailed market-basket analysis, product-structure analysis, cross-product correlation analysis, multiple campaign response models, customer growth models, churn and attrition models, and customer lifetime value models to spot revenue and profit opportunities.

Armed with reports generated by advanced customer analytics, enterprises can more accurately predict customer behavior, forecast buying trends, identify opportunities, and ferret out the reasons for their failures and successes with customer strategies, programs, and value-building efforts. Customer analytics include segmentation studies, customer migration analysis, lifetime value (LTV) modeling, cross-sell/upsell analysis, new customer models, customer **contact optimization**, merchandising analysis, customer attrition and churn models, credit risk scoring—and a lot more.

For example, one of the practical problems facing marketers is that customer values are typically changing; they are rarely constant. Many marketers promote to customers based on differentiating their current value to the business, but with advanced customer analytics, a company will be able to predict whether a particular customer's potential value to the enterprise is moving up or down, and how quickly the movement is occurring. A company could then take action to affect this customer movement positively. Customer migration analysis can help a firm better communicate and market to its customers in ways that move them up the value chain.

Contact optimization is another problem that must be addressed with customer analytics. Given that different customers have different needs for information and different sensitivities to various offers, how can the enterprise optimize its contact strategy so as to yield the highest possible increase in value for each particular customer? Contact optimization is actually the polar opposite of today's typical marketing practices, which apparently are focused on "contact bombardment"—showering the largest possible number of prospects or customers with messages, even when those messages are often irrelevant or ill-timed. For instance, is a zero-percent financing offer on a new car always relevant to every consumer? What if a person had just bought a new car a few days prior to receiving the offer? Would he be thrilled that other customers were now able to take advantage of the financing benefit?

Some of the questions to be answered in a comprehensive analysis of customer data might include:

- What does it mean for individual messages and sales offers to be "relevant"?
- How many contacts should each of your customers receive from you—taking into account both inbound (customer-initiated) and outbound (company-initiated) contacts?
- What should be the timing of your communications with your customer?
- How should the budget be allocated across customers to make optimum use of corporate resources?
- Which products or services, which messages through which channel, are most effective in driving customer value?

One of the most important principles of customer-focused analytics is basing the analyses and models on a complete view of each customer that connects data about each customer across product silos, divisional borders, and even international regions—over time. Jim Goodnight, founder of SAS Institute, makes this important point—and several other points as well—in the next section.

Holistic Customer View Is Essential for Managing Customer-Centric Strategies

Jim Goodnight
CEO and Cofounder, SAS Institute

When developing customer-centric strategies, the basic challenge is fairly straightforward and can be expressed in a handful of crucial questions:

- How do you manage a customer-centric strategy in an extended enterprise with multiple lines of business?
- How do you convert an assortment of inward-facing processes into an outward-facing strategy that delivers consistently great experiences to your customers?
- How do you optimize this strategy to ensure profitability over time?

The answers to all these questions depend on your ability to generate accurate, relevant measurements of customer value. It is absolutely critical that you know *what* to measure and know *how* to measure. It is equally critical that you possess the capability to analyze your measurements and glean actionable intelligence from them. And, of course, you need the capability to adjust business processes based on the knowledge that you acquire from your analytics.

Moreover, you need an enterprise-wide view of your customers. This is especially important for companies that have grown through a series of mergers and acquisitions. Today it is fairly common for a single brand to represent multiple lines of business and for a single enterprise to encompass multiple brands.

(*continued*)

(Continued)

The modern global enterprise is often a tangle of sub-enterprises operating in dozens or even hundreds of markets. Given this level of complexity, it is not surprising that traditional marketing techniques are being replaced with newer strategies built around customer intelligence and customer knowledge.

Some companies have traded the standard "4 Ps" of marketing (product, pricing, placement, and promotion) for a business process we may refer to as the "3 Is of marketing." The *3 Is* represent a holistic solution for *managing multichannel customer experiences*. In this model, equal attention is paid to deepening customer *insight*, choreographing customer *interaction*, and continuously *improving* marketing performance.

Unlike the *4 Ps*, which focus primarily on gaining market share and boosting revenue, the *3 Is* are configured to drive profits, optimize investment of resources, and continuously improve results. And unlike the *4 Ps*, the *3 Is* require robust analytic capabilities. You can't make the *3 Is* work with hunches or back-of-the-envelope calculations—you need real computing power and access to mountains of data.

Customer-centric strategies require the capability to "see" customer activity across multiple channels and business units. Like a chemist working in a lab to analyze an unknown molecule, your goal is making customer behavior "visible" across the enterprise.

Only by making customer behavior visible can you achieve the summits of modern enterprise marketing—cross-brand loyalty, continuously increasing levels of customer equity, and measurable Return on Customer.

But these feats cannot be accomplished without enterprise-level technologies. Since enterprise technologies require significant investments of resources, you will have to build a strong business case for moving ahead.

Fortunately, a growing number of companies are demonstrating the value of an enterprise-wide approach to customer centricity. Let's look briefly at three companies whose efforts have earned them leadership roles in the development of customer-centric strategy. Each company uses sophisticated analytics to extract valuable customer intelligence from the mountains of customer data it collects and then uses that customer intelligence to create tangible business benefits and more profitable customer relationships.

Scotiabank

With 7 million customers in Canada and 20-plus million accounts across various business lines, Scotiabank is one of Canada's five largest financial institutions. The bank runs about 30 separate marketing campaigns per month to acquire new customers for its many product offerings, which include mortgages, mutual funds, credit cards, and deposit accounts.

"Every month we select approximately 500,000 leads from our pool of about 5 million eligible customers," says Vic Moschitto, director and head of decision support and management for Canadian banking at Scotiabank. "Using a combination of our predictive models and our optimization software, we identify the best product for each customer at that point in time."

Part of Moschitto's job is making sure that Scotiabank's customers are not bombarded with marketing messages that are not relevant to their needs. But an even larger challenge is making sure that customers get the right product or service offers at the right time, over the right channel.

Moschitto employs a highly scientific approach to develop and execute marketing campaigns. Not all 500,000 customers receive the same offer. Some might receive an offer for a new credit card, and some might receive an offer for a GIC (a deposit investment security sold by Canadian banks), while others might receive an offer for a fairly routine banking service. The point is that nobody receives an offer by chance—it's all done by the numbers, based on a host of variables including the expected profit generated by the offer, the customer's likelihood of responding positively, and the projected volume of inbound calls to the bank's call centers.

"It's a very structured process. There are a significant number of inputs and a significant number of stakeholders. You have business lines and channel partners involved in the process, and you have the campaign team and the modeling team. So there are a fair number of moving parts," says Moschitto.

There's even a control group. "We hold out a proportion and set them off as a no-contact control group, which we then measure against our result," says Moschitto.

The net result of this diligent approach is higher returns on marketing dollars spent, improved campaign response rates, and higher profits for the bank's business lines.

Says Moschitto:

We're basically trying to be relevant to the customer while at the same time delivering value to the bank. We do that by focusing on what our models indicate will be something that the customer wants rather than saying "We need to send as many leads as possible to make our numbers." And we're also trying to avoid the nuisance factor. We're contacting 500,000 customers per month, which works out to 6 million customers per year. In the old days, every campaign was its own little island. Now we can see the results of each one, and we can apply what we've learned to improve the results of future campaigns.

Optimizing future campaigns using knowledge acquired from past campaigns is a hallmark of "learning organizations." Scotiabank qualifies as a learning organization because it has the capabilities, the desire, and the expertise to convert the customer data it collects into customer intelligence, and then it applies that customer intelligence routinely to optimize its marketing operations.

In many instances, Moschitto's team helps the bank avoid potentially costly mistakes before they happen.

"Sometimes a business line comes in with an objective around growing their account base or retaining a certain group of accounts, and they make an assumption about which channel or which offer will deliver the best results," says Moschitto.

(continued)

(Continued)

A crucial part of Moschitto's job is testing those assumptions.

We set up a controlled environment where we can see the results of one channel compared to another channel and get measurements that are statistically reliable. For example, if we're trying to test the effectiveness of the call center relative to the branch network, we'll make sure when we design our experiment that the same type of customers are in both channels and that both channels have similar quantities of leads. If we're testing an offer, then we make sure that the only thing that changes is the offer.

After a campaign is launched, it is measured at regular intervals, usually monthly. Some response windows last 90 days while others only last one month. Rigorous measurement enables the bank to see which campaigns are working and which are not.

Sometimes the results yield pleasant surprises. When the bank launched a program to make follow-up "thank-you" calls to new customers, skeptics warned that it would be an unnecessary expense. But the bank's habit of measuring all customer-facing activities soon revealed that the follow-up courtesy calls were actually generating new business. Faced with the numbers, the skeptics retreated.

"Five or six years ago, you would have had a discussion around the interpretation of results. Now everyone pretty much agrees on the validity of our approach," says Moschitto.

Measurement and analysis have become part of the corporate culture. "Every campaign now is measured," says Moschitto. "It's become a discipline."

From a purely business perspective, measurement and analysis add value to every campaign run by the bank. In addition to producing a financial result, each campaign generates incremental learning that can be leveraged to optimize the next campaign.

"I like to think that we're constantly learning and trying to apply what we've learned about our customers in the past to help us do a better job of serving them in the future," says Moschitto.

Cabela's

With $2.3 billion in sales, Cabela's is the largest direct marketer, and a leading specialty retailer, of hunting, fishing, camping, and related outdoor merchandise. Cabela's combines a vast historic database, advanced analytical techniques, and powerful technology to provide optimal shopping experiences for its customers across three distinct channels: catalog, retail store, and Internet. The result has been impressive growth for several years despite a turbulent economy.

"We leverage data to predict the future in terms of product demand and customer need across all three of our channels," says Corey Bergstrom, director of marketing research and analytics for Cabela's. "The insight we create from the data has strategic value for the company."

Cabela's applies insights generated from its advanced analytics to optimize the frequency and content of the catalogs it sends through the regular mail. It also uses analytics to enhance its e-mail campaigns. It uses analytics to evaluate product assortment in its existing retail stores and to shape decisions about the size and location of its future retail stores.

Says Bergstrom:

> *We are a multichannel company and we have lots of information about our customers. We utilize our predictive analytics to help us figure out where we should put the store, what that store size should be, and which product line should be in that store. We can do that because we have detailed information about the history of the customers in the area. Retail is all about location, location, location. We're really using our analytics to make sure that we put our stores in locations where they will be successful.*

But it doesn't end there. Cabela's analytics team stays involved long after the site has been selected. "We provide lots of support. We help determine how big to build the store. Then we provide recommendations for which products will sell the best in that area. Then we work with the in-store merchants to help them find the best assortment of products that match the needs of the store's customers," says Bergstrom.

For Cabela's, the ability to create a unified view of customer activity across multiple channels is critical to success. As a result, the analytics team has evolved from a marketing support group into an enterprise strategy group.

"And we're only scratching the surface. We have multiple data points we haven't leveraged yet. We slice and dice data from every channel. Our goal is putting more of that information into the hands of the people dealing directly with customers," says Bergstrom.

Farmers Insurance

The third-largest personal lines insurer in the United States, Farmers Insurance Group sells mostly through a network of exclusive agents. But like many companies, Farmers has developed by a combination of organic growth and acquisitions. Farmers also recently purchased a direct-to-consumer carrier, adding another layer of potential complexity to its marketing efforts.

Murli Buluswar is vice president of insight and innovation at Farmers, and part of his role is optimizing strategy through science-driven insights. Through a variety of efforts, his team is engaged in shaping Farmers' pricing and distribution strategy.

Says Buluswar:

> *When I started here more than three years ago, our vision was simply to improve decision making through analytics. My team partnered with our call-center folks, our claims organization, and our marketing organization. Over time, we evolved from a back-end support function to more of a forward-looking strategy team. Now in addition to crunching numbers, we also help our internal partners gain more knowledge about their business and make better decisions based on data-driven insight.*

(continued)

(Continued)

For example, the analytics team helped the call center understand the drivers of call volume and see where there might be opportunities to mitigate volume and drive down costs. Then the team figured out which metrics actually were driving incremental customer satisfaction related to retention and helped the call center think through all the various implications of improving service levels.

The analytics team also helped Farmers change the way it measures the performance of its marketing campaigns. In the past, Farmers judged the success of its direct-mail campaigns by the number of those who responded and the number of sales completed. Farmers now factors customer LTV into its measurement, which creates a different perspective. This adjustment resulted in a 14 percent improvement in the company's internal rate of return on direct-mail campaigns.

Because the insurance industry is highly regulated, insurers generally are prohibited from following a basic rule of one-to-one marketing: *Treat different customers differently.* But that doesn't prevent them from taking steps to optimize the performance of their agents in the field.

By long-standing industry tradition, agent performance is measured by the number of policies sold and in force. A more customer-centric practice would involve predicting future revenue streams from customers and calculating the impact of those revenue streams on incremental profitability.

So Buluswar's team applied its skills to analyzing the performance of the company's agents. For example, the team noticed that for every 100 new customers acquired, there was a huge gap in LTV between the top 5 percent and the bottom 5 percent. Based on the analysis, the team surmised agents who used a more consultative approach to selling generally seemed to acquire more high-value customers than agents who focused mostly on the transactional aspects of selling.

The findings were shared with the agents, who benefited from the knowledge. The company, in turn, hopes to benefit from improved agent performance. "We show the agents how the customer lifetime value metric impacts their P&L [profit and loss]. That knowledge can help them make better decisions," says Buluswar. "We are leveraging customer analytics to help the agents drive more value."

Promoting a comprehensive customer-centric strategy across an enterprise is not a job undertaken lightly. Buluswar knows that the process will take time, and he has adopted an incremental approach. The goal is enabling customer-centric practices to be applied at every level of customer engagement, starting with brand awareness and ending in retention.

Buluswar explains:

We are asking ourselves, "What is the best way to adapt our branding, direct mail, agency location, and behavior to attract and retain higher lifetime value customers?" Part of the answer to this question involves taking a holistic, customer-level view toward growth, not just a policy or a product view. This customer-centric view enables us to live up to our brand promise.

Multiple Channels, Multiple Challenges

These brief examples show clearly that developing and executing an enterprise-wide customer-centric strategy requires hard work, intense focus, specific analytic skills, and the commitment of resources in order to overcome the specific challenges of understanding customer behaviors across brands and channels, understanding customer profitability and potential, creating meaningful segmentation, and creating relevant communications.

But the business benefits are undeniable: higher revenues and profits from sales, reduced marketing and customer acquisition costs, deeper and more profitable customer relationships, higher levels of customer satisfaction and engagement, greater "share of wallet," higher levels of retention, and greater efficiencies in at virtually every level of customer interaction.

Quite clearly, this isn't your father's marketing strategy. A quick look at the difference between the stakeholders in a traditional siloed marketing scenario and the stakeholders in a customer-centric enterprise marketing scenario shows the difference (see Exhibit 12A):

Old Stakeholders	New Stakeholders
Direct-Mail Marketing	...OLD plus...
E-mail Marketing	Web Marketing
Telemarketing	Interactive Marketing
	Finance
Program Managers	Business Development
Advertising	Merchandising
	Investor Relations
	Retail Marketing
	Partnership Marketing
	Customer Service
	Public Relations
	Human Resources
	Operations
↑	↑
Tactical Marketing	**Strategic Enterprises**

EXHIBIT 12A Maturing from Tactics to Strategy Aligns and Improves Enterprise Decision Making

In the new model, demographic segmentation is replaced by personas, and the reductive practice of finding "look-alikes" is replaced by the global strategy of finding and creating influencers. It's a brave new world indeed.

The new model for building profitable customer relationships looks like Exhibit 12B.

- Deeper customer insight can be generated through a series of steps including data integration, customer profiling and analysis, channel analytics, predictive modeling, credit scoring, and customer value management.

(continued)

(Continued)

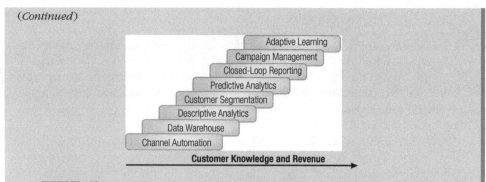

EXHIBIT 12B   Customer Knowledge and Revenue Increase with Technological
Capabilities

- Customer interactions can be "choreographed" instead of managed, with outbound campaigns, message personalization, trigger-driven behavior monitoring, optimization, and interactive marketing.
- Marketing performance can be improved continuously with newer software tools designed specifically for campaign performance reporting, marketing performance management, and marketing mix optimization.

To be sure, managing an enterprise customer-centric strategy is a complex task. But it is both doable and necessary in a global economy where news— good and bad—travels at the speed of your Internet connection. The more complete a picture you have of your customers, the faster and more effectively you'll be able to react when your customers change their preferences—which they most certainly will. Then the race will be won by the companies that know the most about their customers and can apply that knowledge to keep and grow them.

Here's an example of a company that uses customer insight to increase profitability.

Boosting Profits by Upselling in Firebrand Real Estate Developers

Yücel Ersöz
Partner, Peppers & Rogers Group, Middle East

Firebrand Real Estate Developers (FRED)[a] is a residential real estate development company specializing in the development of a broad range of properties from mass housing to ultra-luxurious residences.

FRED's business model includes:

- *Land acquisition.* FRED either purchases the land or makes a revenue-sharing agreement where the landowner gets a percentage of revenues generated in return for the land.

- *Project development.* Sales and design teams of FRED define the main features of the development (i.e., size and types of units, amenities, construction quality) and provide a design brief to the architect who completes the design.
- *Presales and construction.* FRED begins selling the units as construction begins. Buyers of units have a variety of financing options. They can either get mortgage loans from a variety of banks or use facilities provided by the financing arm of FRED.
- *Options selection.* About halfway through the construction period, FRED invites buyers to select finishing materials and optional features they would like to see in their future home.
- *Delivery.* FRED delivers the units within the time frame defined in the contract made with the buyer when presales take place. If the buyer has not completed installment payments, the title deed is granted with liens in favor of whoever provided financing to the buyer—either the bank or FRED's financing arm.
- *Completion of sales.* Units that have not been sold at the end of the construction period become the property of FRED (and landowner, if a revenue-sharing agreement had been made) to be sold later or rented. At this stage, prices are usually higher than in presales period.

Groundbreaking to delivery of units typically takes 24 to 30 months. Most buyers choose payment plans that take 10 to 30 years to complete all installments. Therefore, in many cases, title deeds are granted with liens. Approximately 85 percent of all buyers use mortgage loans provided by banks, whereas the remaining prefer loans offered by FRED's financing arm. FRED typically selects two to three banks as financing partners on its projects to provide a seamless financing process for its customers. FRED also negotiates on behalf of prospective buyers the fees and commissions—the hidden costs of mortgage loans—to be charged by banks to mortgage loan users.

If a bank loan is used, FRED gets the full payment at presale. From then on, the buyer makes installment payments directly to the bank. If the purchase is financed by FRED, the customer makes installment payments to FRED. In this case, the customer can refinance later on with a bank loan and fully pay her debt to FRED.

The Challenge

There are several important considerations in FRED's business model:

- The higher the percentage of units sold during the presales period, the better. Preselling units means financing the construction with buyers' money.
- Competition between developers for the very little vacant land that remains in the city is stiff. Like all its competitors, FRED makes most of its profit by selling options.
- FRED can sell only predefined packages of options. Otherwise, the complexity of construction outweighs the benefits of selling options.

(continued)

(Continued)

- To make a higher profit margin on options packages, FRED must:
  - Not have too many different types of packages, which will confuse the buyer and make decision making much harder.
  - Provide packages that fit a broad range of tastes.
  - Foresee how many of which package will be sold to negotiate better prices with suppliers.

Obviously, customer intelligence is a key component of FRED's business model: It will be able to make a handsome profit only if it can foresee which customers of which project will be interested in what types of packages.

What do options packages look like? Typically, options packages are produced by variations of the most critical unit components. These components are what makes a unit attractive to the buyer's eye. As one might expect, invisible features, such as concrete quality, roof insulation, and so on, hardly make a difference. What makes the difference are the finishes. Therefore, options packages typically include variations of:

- Flooring material and quality in living room and bedrooms.
- Tile design, quality, and size in bathrooms and kitchen.
- Design and quality of kitchen cabinets and materials used in countertops.
- White goods and home electronics that are provided in the unit.
- Materials used in custom-built, walk-in cabinets.

Almost an infinite number of variations are conceivable, but, as noted, only a limited number of predefined packages can be offered. Usually the number of packages is limited to three to four. It is a major challenge for FRED to define just the right packages so that every buyer will want to purchase one. Each unit sold without an options package is a failure for FRED because it makes almost no profit and a failure for the buyer because he will have to deal with lots of decisions and finish work after receiving the unit, which is a process almost no homebuyer looks forward to.

The Solution

To solve the business problem, FRED turned to customer intelligence. To be able to define the options packages for a broad range of projects it was developing, the company started with reviewing what it already knew about customers. Profiling home buyers started with identifying the dimensions of a customer profile for this specific market.

FRED determined that any home buyer in the market could be profiled by the these dimensions:

- *Purchase reasons.* Surveys indicated that each buyer falls into one of the these categories:
  - Investing in a property
  - Moving to a larger home
  - Buying a first home

- *Payment plans.* Based on payment data in previous projects, FRED determined that these dimensions defined payment preferences of buyers.
  - Down payment percentage
  - Payback period length
  - Interest rate mechanism preferred
- *Sociodemographics.* Surveys conducted by FRED indicated that out of the many different dimensions that can be used to define the sociodemographic profile of a customer, the dimensions that mattered were:
  - Marital status
  - Age of parents
  - Age of children
  - Income level
- *Unit price and size.* Based on options packages preferred in previous projects, FRED determined that the price and size of the apartment purchased were also important in forecasting buyer behavior. Specifically, these dimensions were important:
  - Size of the apartment
  - Per square meter price of the apartment

Using these profiling dimensions, data from previous projects, and data obtained from market surveys, FRED segmented its customers. The result of the study indicated five distinct customer types (see Exhibit 12C).

EXHIBIT 12C   Customer Segments in the Market where FRED Competes

	Investors	Young Families—Medium Income	Young Families—High Income	Young Families—Low Income	Space Seekers	Luxury Seekers
Purchase Reason						
Investing in a property	Investing in a property					
Moving to a larger apartment			Moving to a larger apartment		Moving to a larger apartment	Moving to a larger apartment
Buying a first home		Buying a first home	Buying a first home	Buying a first home	Buying a first home	Buying a first home
Payment Plans						
Down payment percentage	10%–15%	20%–30%	20%–50%	10%–15%	20%–30%	20%–30%
Payback period length	20–30 years	5–10 years	5–10 years	20–30 years	5–10 years	5–10 years
Interest rate mechanism preferred	Variable rate	Fixed rate	Fixed rate	Fixed rate	Fixed rate	Fixed rate
Sociodemographics						
Marital status	Mixed	Married	Married	Married	Married	Mixed
Age of parents	45 and +	30–45	30–45	30–45	45 and +	45 and +
Age of kids	Late teens and +	None or early years	None or early years	None or early years	Late teens and +	Mixed
Income level	US$ 250,000 and +	US$ 125,000–250,000	US$ 250,000 and +	US$ 50,000–125,000	US$ 125,000–250,000	US$ 500,000 and +
Unit Price and Size						
Unit price of apartment	US$ 1000–1500	US$ 2500–3500	US$ 3000–5000	US$ 1000–1500	US$ 1500–2500	US$ 5000 and +
Size of the apartment	50–90 sqm	80–110 sqm	120 sqm–250 sqm	80–110 sqm	120 sqm–250 sqm	200 sqm and +

(continued)

(Continued)

- The next challenge for FRED was to match options package preferences with segments. Data from previous projects would be used to this end. Nevertheless, because each development project is unique, FRED needed a way of standardizing the options package properties to be able to compare one project with another. Understanding customer behavior, particularly as it relates to options package decisions, helped solve the puzzle. By studying survey data FRED figured out that other than investors, all segments purchased the most expensive home for which they could afford to pay monthly installments within their payment terms.
- When it came to options packages, these segments were thrifty. Total price of the package was viewed in complete isolation from the price paid for the apartment.
- Although investors calculated the percentage of their total cost represented by options package, for other segments, cost of options package was correlated with income rather than price of the apartment.

Applying the Solution in the Next Project

Once all pieces of the puzzle fell into place, FRED was ready to apply the customer intelligence generated on a project. The first test run was on a $270 million residential development project, the largest FRED had ever undertaken. Target yield, or the discount rate which equalized discounted cashflow of the project to zero, was 15 percent. FRED achieved 17 percent, despite cost overruns and a more-sluggish-than-expected market with a slower sales rate, thanks to the margin contribution of options packages.

How did FRED succeed in transforming customer intelligence into dollars and improved return on investment? By sticking with the basics.

EXHIBIT 12D   Unit Distribution and Revenue Expectations in FRED's New Project

Type of units	Size of units (sqm)	Number of units	Sellable area (sqm)	Average unit price (US$/sqm)	Average price per unit (US$)	Expected revenue (US$)
1 BR + 1 LR	60	240	14,400	3,000	180,000	43,200,000
2 BR + 1 LR	90	240	21,600	2,700	243,000	58,320,000
3 BR + 1 LR	110	160	17,600	2,500	275,000	44,000,000
4 BR + 1 LR	140	160	22,400	2,400	336,000	53,760,000
5 BR + 1 LR	170	120	20,400	2,300	391,000	46,920,000
5 BR + 2 LR	230	50	11,500	2,300	529,000	26,450,000
TOTAL	970	units				
	272,650,000	in revenues				
BR:	Bedroom					
LR:	Living room					

As outlined in Exhibit 12D, the project primarily targeted three customer segments: young families of medium and high income, and space seekers. The old real estate maxim of "location, location, location" applied in this case to eliminate luxury seekers, since the location of this project was not a place where they would seek to reside.

At this time, FRED had an idea as to what kinds of options packages could be suitable for this unit mix and pricing, but management could be sure only after seeing the profile of buyers. Actualized sales figures are provided in Exhibit 12E.

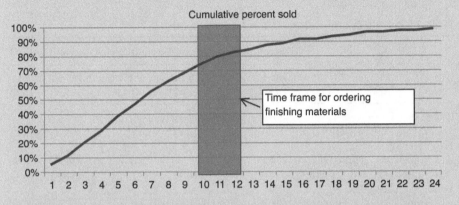

EXHIBIT 12E Cumulative Percentage Units Sold by Month in FRED's New Project

Options packages had to be designed, suggested to buyers, and ordering of finishing materials completed by the twelfth month to finish the project on time. Based on the profile of buyers, FRED had to design the right combinations of options packages, try to sell every buyer an options package, and forecast what prospective buyers of unsold units could demand ahead of time so as to be able to order just the right amount of materials.

Figuring that two months should be enough to complete sales of options packages, FRED designed the packages by the end of the tenth month, when 70 percent of the units had been sold. By looking at the buyer profile until that time and matching it customer preferences data, FRED was able to design the packages in a very short amount of time. FRED designed four types of packages, summarized in Exhibit 12F.

EXHIBIT 12F Options Packages FRED Offered to Customers

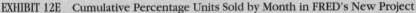

Type of unit	Size of unit (sqm)	Average price of unit (US$)	Price of options package (US$) Package 1: Home Basics	Package 2: Standard	Package 3: Deluxe	Package 4: Imperial
1 BR + 1 LR	60	180,000	7,500	9,000		
2 BR + 1 LR	90	243,000	10,500	13,200		
3 BR + 1 LR	110	275,000	12,600	15,900	17,400	22,500
4 BR + 1 LR	140	336,000	15,900	19,200	21,300	27,900
5 BR + 1 LR	170	391,000	18,600	22,500	25,200	32,100
5 BR + 2 LR	230	529,000	24,300	28,200	30,600	40,500

(continued)

(Continued)

When options packages were offered to customers, distribution of sales across segments (summarized in Exhibit 12G) helped FRED forecast with more accuracy total options revenues by the end of the project. Based on buyer behavior in past projects, FRED was to able to produce an options package purchase probabilities outline (see Exhibit 12H) to forecast total options package revenues.

EXHIBIT 12G   FRED's New Project Units Sales by Month 10

	Distribution of sales across segments at end of month 10					
	1 BR + 1 LR	2 BR + 1 LR	3 BR + 1 LR	4 BR + 1 LR	5 BR + 1 LR	5 BR + 2 LR
Investors	86%	66%	19%			
Young Families—Medium Income	14%	34%	72%		9%	
Young Families—High Income				25%	25%	57%
Young Families—Low Income						
Space Seekers			8%	75%	66%	43%
TOTAL	100%	100%	100%	100%	100%	100%

EXHIBIT 12H   Options Package Purchase Probabilities in FRED's New Project

	Expected options package sales					
	1 BR + 1 LR	2 BR + 1 LR	3 BR + 1 LR	4 BR + 1 LR	5 BR + 1 LR	5 BR + 2 LR
Package 1: Home Basics	64%	57%	35%	0%	3%	0%
Package 2: Standard	23%	27%	34%	22%	24%	26%
Package 3: Deluxe	1%	3%	10%	32%	31%	36%
Package 4: Imperial	0%	0%	3%	26%	23%	21%
TOTAL	89%	87%	82%	81%	81%	83%

By month 10, FRED expected a total options revenue of $12.7 million. In reality, it exceeded this target by roughly 12 percent. By the end of month 24, when 99 percent of units had been sold, FRED generated an options revenue of $14.3 million.

Conclusion

FRED was able to increase its revenues from the project by 4.7 percent by selling options packages. More important, because of the much higher profitability of options packages, net project profit increased by 11 percent. In doing this, FRED created value not only for its own shareholders but also for its customers. By providing options packages that closely fit customer needs, FRED was able to relieve the customers' burden of selecting and completing the finishing work themselves. Surveys reveal that completion of finishing work after delivery of apartments is the least favorable part of buying a new home for the majority of buyers. Just as important, this is the most common source of problems between contractors and tenants during the move-in period. Without customer analytics, FRED would have been unlikely to create the same value for both its shareholders and its customers and still be able to complete the project on time with top-quality finishing work.

---

[a]Not the company's real name.

Another example by Yucel Ersöz illustrates how data mining can be elevated to insight and prediction of customer behavior.

Looking for the Right Time to Sell a Mortgage Loan

Yücel Ersöz
Partner, Peppers & Rogers Group, Middle East

In emerging markets, the sources of revenue are changing. Lower interest rates, the diminishing crowding-out effect of government debt in the race for funds, and enhanced consumer confidence are encouraging savers to become borrowers. As a result, retail bankers are finding out that they have to look for ways to make money by finding products for their customers such as loans in the form of mortgages, credit cards, auto loans, and the like. This business model has a completely different set of requirements from that of the old days, when retail banking was all about collecting money from savers and selling it to debt-laden government. Instead, retail bankers must be at the right place at the right time to sell the next loan to the consumer.

Best Savings Bank (BSB)[a] embraced this challenge by changing the way it looks at customer data. Instead of a black-box approach in data mining to determine prospective customers for mortgage loans, the bank started with the basics of consumer behavior in the market where it was competing. In other words, instead of finding customers for products, it looked at how it could find products for customers.

Exhibits 12I and 12J provide the basic characteristics of consumer groups who would qualify for a mortgage loan.

Surveys indicate that different consumer segments opt for different payback periods on their mortgage loans. Although segments A and B prefer short-term (5- to 10-year) payback periods, segments B and C prefer medium-term

(continued)

(*Continued*)

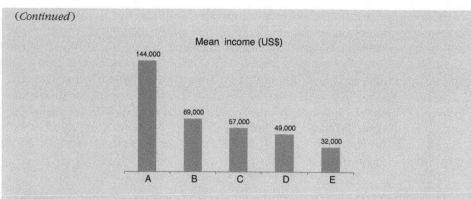

EXHIBIT 12I   Consumer Segments by Average Income

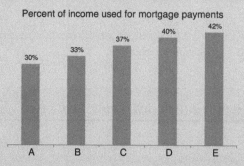

EXHIBIT 12J   Percentage of Disposable Income Used for Mortgage Payments across Segments

EXHIBIT 12K   Maximum Home Price per Customer Segment

Income level	Mean income ($)	Maximum monthly payment	Maximum price that can be afforded			
			5-year loan	10-year loan	20-year loan	30-year loan
A	144,000	3,600	202,298	313,652	408,687	437,103
B	69,000	1,898	106,628	165,321	215,412	230,390
C	57,000	1,758	98,761	153,123	199,519	213,391
D	49,000	1,633	91,783	142,305	185,423	198,315
E	32,000	1,120	62,937	97,581	127,147	135,988

(10- to 20-year) periods, and segments D and E usually prefer long-term (20- to 30-year) periods. Exhibit 12K shows home prices these different segments can afford.

The Challenge

Although BSB had extensive customer data, bank executives believed that pitching the mortgage loan offer to customers at just the right time (i.e., when the customer is actually thinking of buying a new home) would prove to be a diffi-cult task. They decided to identify the pieces of data that would tell them when different types of customers would likely consider buying a new home.

In the market where BSB operates, home buyers are required to make a down payment that equals 20 percent of the value of the home with their own funds. Banks are allowed to fund only up to 80 percent of the home value to cushion against a fall in prices. Because the bank knew which income group would go for which kind of housing, the first task was to figure out a reasonable estimate of household income, a figure that was not readily available in the bank's data systems.

To estimate this figure, the customer analytics team combined the data available in the systems and to survey results in a smart way. The amount of savings customers had in BSB and their credit card charges with BSB cards were readily available. What was missing was an estimate of total savings and total credit card expenses in all banks—in other words, the customer's Share of Customer (or share of wallet). These data came from market research surveys. Next, the analytics team needed to link these clues with monthly income es-timates. Market research surveys indicated that 70 percent of all expenditures of segments under consideration took place by credit card charges. By adding the average rate at which these segments increased their deposits—a proxy for their monthly savings rate—the team was able to produce the income estimates provided in Exhibit 12L, which illustrates results for five sample customers.

EXHIBIT 12L Annual Income Estimates for Five Sample Customers Computed by Analytics Team (All Currency Figures in USD [$])

Customer	Savings account balance	Savings flow rate per month	Monthly credit card charge	BSB Share of Customer for credit card expenses	BSB Share of Customer for savings	Customer's estimated annual income
X	12,425	1,100	1,237	50%	100%	55,611
Y	27,325	1,750	2,249	75%	100%	72,406
Z	23,345	1,000	4,362	100%	100%	86,777
T	27,896	2,450	6,747	100%	100%	145,063
U	43,233	3,750	8,765	100%	100%	195,257

In Exhibit 12L, the savings flow rate is the average monthly increase of de-posits of the customer in the bank and share of savings and share of credit card expenses are the estimated share of wallet of BSB in these product categories.

It was obvious to the customer analytics team that customers like X, Y, Z, T, and U were saving for a specific purpose. Market research revealed that in the long term, customers with demographic profiles and savings amounts similar to these actually were saving to buy a new home or for their children's college education. Typically these customers were age 35 to 45, had $15,000 to $40,000

(continued)

(Continued)

in savings accounts, and saved at a rate of $1,000 to $4,000 per month. This information helped the team pinpoint the target group.

Finally, by making use of the public information and previous mortgage loan records, the customer analytics team was able to identify which customers would be eligible to consider buying a new home, provided that their current rate of savings continued at this pace. Exhibit 12M summarizes the results.

EXHIBIT 12M   Optimum Timing for Offering a Mortgage Product to Selected Customers

Values in US($)

Customer	Estimated annual income	Expected home value	Required down payment	Estimated savings	Months to eligibility
X	55,611	225,073	45,015	12,425	30
Y	72,406	226,045	45,209	27,325	10
Z	86,777	239,413	47,883	23,345	25
T	145,063	259,879	51,976	27,896	10
U	195,257	349,802	69,960	43,233	7

This insight not only provided a way to retain customers but also helped BSB manage customers with a much longer horizon in mind. In the market where BSB operates, significant customer churn takes place as savers withdraw all their savings from a bank and finance their new home with a different bank that was at the right place at the right time. It is much harder to get the customer back once he has been lost as a result of this churn.

As a result of this initiative, BSB has been able to reduce customer churn to other banks with mortgage products by 25 percent and improved its sales conversion rate in mortgage offers by 33 percent.

Conclusion

As banks in emerging markets learn to adapt to the changing landscape in retail banking, customer analytics techniques similar to the one discussed here will guide them in charting unknown territories. Banks that are intent on deriving customer insight and acting on it to survive this challenge will find doing so much simpler than they may have expected. Complicated data analyses usually are not required to extract customer value if one knows where to look.

---

[a]Not the company's real name.

Summary

We have now covered two critical parts of customer-based enterprise "measurement": We have examined some of the ways an enterprise can measure the success of its customer value–building initiatives, and we have explored how advanced customer analytics can help predict how a customer will behave in a relationship, how a firm can positively influence that relationship behavior, and how much it's worth to the enterprise to do so. Analytics affect the "customer" issues for the company, but understanding how value is created for today and tomorrow affect decisions for the chief financial officer; the chief information officer; human resources recruiting, training, evaluation, and compensation; product development; the chief executive review and board decisions; appraisal of merger-and-acquisition opportunities; and even public reporting of competitive advantage.

> I f we can measure it, we can manage it.

If we can measure it, we can manage it. That's why the next chapters are about how to manage an organization to build the value of the customer base. Making the transition to a customer-strategy enterprise requires a careful examination of the way the company is structured and a rethinking of many business processes. Chapter 13 focuses on two key themes: What does a relationship-building enterprise, based strategically on growing customer equity, look like? What are the organizational and transitional requirements to become a customer-based enterprise? Next we take a closer look.

Food for Thought

1. From the customer's perspective, which is better: to buy through one channel or through several channels? The obvious answer is to have multiple channels available—order from the Web, make returns at the store, check on delivery by phone—and have all of those contact points able to pick up where the last one left off. But is there any advantage—to the customer—of using only one channel? Why does research show that customers who use more than one channel are more likely to be more valuable to a firm than those who use only one?

2. Often the challenge in using predictive models boils down to a misunderstanding of the nature of cause and effect. Although statistical analysis might reveal that two observable events tend to happen at similar times, it does not necessarily mean that one event "causes" the other. What is more important: to understand *what* will happen next or *why* it will happen?

3. Customer analytics can be used for improving retention rates. How?

Glossary

Analysis process   Includes classification, estimation, regression, prediction, and clustering.

Contact optimization   The capability of a company to send and request information for each customer in the way that is preferred by each customer. When contacts are optimized, a customer hears from and responds to a company on her own timetable, about topics that are most relevant to her.

Customer analytics   Enables the enterprise to classify, estimate, predict, cluster, and more accurately describe data about customers, using mathematical models and algorithms that ultimately simplify how it views its customer base and how it behaves toward individual customers.

Data mining   The process of exploration and analysis, by automatic or semiautomatic means, of large quantities of data in order to discover meaningful patterns and rules, according to Berry and Linoff.[14]

Real-time analytics   Instant updates to the customer database that allow services in multiple geographies, communication channels, or product lines to respond to customer needs without waiting for customary weekly or overnight updates.

---

[14]Michael J.A. Berry and Gordon S. Linoff, *Mastering Data Mining* (New York: John Wiley & Sons, 2000.

CHAPTER 13

Organizing and Managing the Profitable Customer-Strategy Enterprise: Part 1

Work is of two kinds: first, altering the position of matter at or near the earth's surface relative to other matter; second, telling other people to do so.

—Bertrand Russell

Throughout this book, we have described the customer-strategy enterprise by defining the principles of creating a customer-strategy business. In this and the next chapter, we will focus on how a firm establishes itself as an enterprise focused on building the value of the customer base and how it can make the transition from product management to managing for customer equity. What does a customer-value-building enterprise look like? How does a company develop the organization, skills, and capabilities needed to execute customer-oriented programs? How does the enterprise create the culture that supports these principles? How will it integrate the pieces of the organization that have traditionally been managed as separate silos (or "chimneys" or "smokestacks")? To begin our discussion, this chapter examines how the customer-strategy enterprise is different from the traditional organization.

If we can measure it, we can manage it. Now that we have become better at the metrics of customer valuation and equity, can we hold someone responsible for increasing the value of customers and keeping them longer? Most companies have brand managers, product managers, store managers, plant managers, finance managers, customer interaction center managers, Web masters, regional sales managers, branch managers, and/or merchandise managers. But with the exception of high-end personal and business services, only a few companies have customer relationship managers. Now that technology drives a dimension of competition based on keeping and growing customers, the questions to ask are:

Customer strategy (handwritten annotation)

- Who will be responsible for the enterprise's relationship with each customer? For keeping and growing each customer? For building the short-term revenues and long-term equity and value of each customer?
- What authority will that customer manager need to have in order to change how the enterprise treats "her" customers, individually?
- By what criteria and metrics will success be measured, reported, and used for compensation?

In this chapter, we ask the questions: How will executives at the enterprise develop management skills to increase the value of the customer base? How will our information about customers—and our goal to build the value of the customer base—inform every business decision we make all day, every day?

We have shown that in the customer-strategy enterprise, the goal is to maximize the value of the customer base by retaining profitable customers and growing them into bigger customers; by eliminating unprofitable customers or converting them into profitable relationships; and by acquiring new customers selectively, based on their likelihood of developing into high-value customers. The overriding strategy for achieving

> Now that technology drives a dimension of competition based on keeping and growing customers, the questions to ask are:
>
> - Who will be responsible for the enterprise's relationship with each customer? For keeping and growing each customer? For building the short-term revenues and long-term equity and value of each customer?
> - What authority will that customer manager have to change how the enterprise treats "her" customers, individually?
> - By what criteria and metrics will success be measured, reported, and used for compensation?

this set of objectives is to develop Learning Relationships, built on trust, with individual customers, in the process customizing the mix of products, prices, services, and/or communications for each individual customer, wherever practical.

It should be apparent that the new enterprise must be organized around its customers rather than just its products. Success requires that the entire organization reengineer its processes to focus on the customer.[1] In this chapter, we examine the basics of management at a customer-strategy enterprise. Our goal is to understand the capabilities necessary to create and manage a successful customer-strategy company. We draw a picture of what the organizational chart looks like and explain how to make the transition, overcome obstacles, and build momentum. We also have a look at the role of employees in the customer-strategy enterprise.

---

[1]Gary E. Hawkins, *Building the Customer Specific Retail Enterprise* (New York: Breezy Heights Publishing, 1999).

Capabilities That Yield a Relationship Advantage

George S. Day
Geoffrey T. Boisi Professor and Co-Director of the Mack Center for Technological Innovation
The Wharton School, University of Pennsylvania

A relational advantage can be gained in a variety of ways, depending on the market. Sometimes it is through customer intimacy and personalization; in other cases, customer collaboration or a best total solution is important. Two examples demonstrate the possibilities:

1. Rolls-Royce, the global market leader for commercial jet engines, powered half of the wide-bodied passenger jets built in 2008. It overcame formidable competitors, such as General Electric and Pratt & Whitney, with an engine design that was more costly to make but can be customized to a far wider range of aircraft designs than that of its rivals. But beyond supplying an excellent product, Rolls-Royce introduced an after-sale support option that addressed customers' concerns about engine maintenance costs. Rolls-Royce's airline customers don't actually buy the engines. Instead, as part of the "Power by the Hour" program, customers pay a fee based on the number of hours flown, which saves them money. Performance-based contracts align customer and supplier incentives—removing repair fees makes it in the supplier's interest to keep the engine operating. The supplier also benefits from information flows enabling product improvement. Relationships are tightened because Rolls-Royce maintains the engine and replaces it when it breaks down. Every function of each engine is continuously monitored while it is in the air to get an early warning of a service need. This means fewer emergency repairs. As the Rolls-Royce chief operating officer noted, "You could only get closer to the customer by being in the plane."

2. Fidelity Investments repositioned itself with a strategy of providing affluent investors with credible advice and investment solutions tailored to their customer's own situation and delivered with exceptional service on his own terms. Doing this required careful identification of customer segments to nurture, the formation of dedicated service models and offerings for each segment, and personalized education and guidance appropriate to the profit potential of each segment. High-net-worth customers with more than $2 million in investments with Fidelity got their own account representatives, while investors with less than $100,000 would be served through the Internet and a pool of account reps. Fidelity's move was precipitated by losing customers to Chuck Schwab's OneSource product, launched in 1992. Fidelity chief executive Edward Johnson correctly sensed the customer behavior shift from product centered to relationship centered.

(continued)

(Continued)

Characteristics of Relationship Leaders

Relationship leaders have several things in common.

1. Their relationships with their best customers are unusually tight, so there is mutual trust based on shared understanding and mutual commitments. These leaders are experts at their customers' businesses (or lives, in the case of consumers).
2. They have broadened their offering far beyond their core product to include customer information and training, complementary products, support services, and financing as required. They compete on scope rather than scale.
3. Their customers think they are getting an offering that has been tailored to their needs. It may be fully customized or simply personalized. This is not the one-size-fits-all approach of price value leaders.

These common features conceal huge differences in how relational value is delivered in different markets. Customer relationship management (CRM) approaches are used by firms like Fidelity Investments that serve mass markets with millions of customers. Comprehensive solution management approaches are applied by firms like Rolls-Royce when complex systems are sold to a small number of very valuable customers. Of course, there are many markets that use some of each approach.

The essence of CRM is customizing products and services for each particular customer. More precisely, it is a cross-functional process involving a continuing dialogue with customers, managing across all customer touchpoints, and offering personalized treatment of the most valuable customers.

Only since the 1990s have information technologies harnessed to the Internet made it possible to have dialogues with customers and gain a coherent and comprehensive view of each customer, including their profitability. But CRM is more than database management, data mining, call centers, and sales-force automation. This strategy will not deliver superior value unless it is woven into every function, including supply-chain management and channel coordination.

Comprehensive Solution Management

Solutions are bundles of products and related services that create value greater than the sum of their parts. To offer a real solution, and not just a repackaging of existing products and services, four criteria must be met:

1. Each solution is co-created with customers.
2. It is therefore tailored to each customer.
3. The relationship between customer and supplier is unusually intimate.
4. Suppliers accept some of the risk through performance-based or risk-based contracts.

The aim of CRM best practices is to form a one-to-one learning relationship. Co-creating a real solution requires relationships that are much deeper and wider, with social and information connections across many levels and functions of each partner organization. This is feasible only with high-value, long-term customers who warrant sizable investments of time and energy and also are willing to make a reciprocal commitment.

Customers who are partners can gain from such intimate relationships in several ways:

- Their costs are lowered when the supplier takes over activities that are shared with other customers or can otherwise be combined to achieve greater scale.
- They may see benefits from superior performance through preferred access to the latest technology.
- Their risks may be reduced by sharing them with the supplier.

As an example, Asea Brown Boveri (ABB) has been able to prevail in the volatile market for drilling pipe for ocean-based drilling rigs by absorbing its customers' risk that pipe deliveries stalled in transit or customs will shut down their rig. For certain key customers, ABB offers guaranteed delivery to the rig and charges only the actual cost of delivery. ABB can do this because it has had long experience in operating in more than 100 countries and a deep understanding of importation requirements.

A comprehensive solution is also much more than a bundle that enables one-stop shopping or even an option such as tailoring a personal computer to suit a customer's desired configuration. Thinking in terms of bundles of products and service we offer is an unfortunate inside-out approach that focuses on the question: How can we sell more? True solutions come from the outside in to solve a customer's problem by applying superior resources and expertise. It takes deep insights into customer needs that come from "living together" and the ability to use these insights to provide a better overall result. Not every customer will commit to such a deep relationship or even pay for a solution. Some may even ask for a discount because they are getting all their requirements from one source. (One strategy for managing these customers is to divert them to a lower-cost intermediary.)

Gaining a Relationship Advantage

Understanding the role and functioning of the customer-relating capability requires an enterprise to distinguish between the resources that are the source of its competitive advantage and the consequent positional advantages and performance outcomes, as shown in Exhibit 13A. This is a cyclical process that relies on consistency and alignment of the elements to achieve advantage and continuous reinvestment and learning to sustain the advantage.

Sources of advantage are the resources the firm deploys, comprising the assets such as databases and systems that are firm specific, factors of production that are readily available, and the capabilities that enable these resources to be deployed advantageously.

The diagnosis of an individual capability—such as the customer-relating capability—requires that the scope be disaggregated down to a level where

(continued)

(Continued)

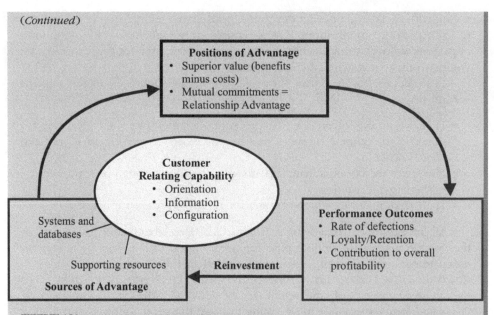

EXHIBIT 13A   Achieving a Relationship Advantage

the skills and execution of the capability are competitively superior. Broad generalizations, such as consumer marketing skills, will not suffice, when the distinctive capability may lie only in demand stimulation through image-based advertising, and the other ingredients such as pricing or channel linking may be merely average.

Although disaggregation is necessary, it may also be misleading if it doesn't consider two factors:

1. Each capability is nested within a complex network with many direct and indirect links to other resources.
2. Strategic themes prioritize, orchestrate, and direct the collective resources toward the delivery of superior customer value.

Sometimes the valuable resource is an adroit combination of capabilities, none of which are superior alone but, when combined, makes a better package. Then competitive superiority is due to (1) the weighted-average effect—the business does not rank first on any asset or capability but is better on average than any of the rivals; (2) the firm's system-integration capability, so the capabilities are mutually reinforcing; or (3) the superior clarity and focus of the strategic thrust that mobilizes the resources.

Positions of Advantage

What we see in the market—from the vantage point of the customer or competitor—is positional superiority achieved with superior capability. This requires the reliable provision of superior value to customers on the attributes they judge important when they make a choice. Whether there is a relational advantage per se depends on the customer's judgments that having a close relationship with a supplier confers benefits that exceed the costs. Typical benefits include time savings, technical assistance, assurance of performance, access to latest developments (e.g., in software and technology), superior responsiveness to service requests or problems, and a superior fit to the customer's needs because of personalized solutions. Of course, the customer must feel these benefits outweigh any costs due to loss of flexibility and the restricted ability to play one supplier against another.

The strongest positional advantages are gained when customers are willing to make mutual commitments. These can range from information exchanges, to cross-firm coordination of interdependent activities such as new product development, to multiple social linkages that engender trust and facilitate sharing of information, and possibly to relation-specific investments such as online Electronic Data Interchange (EDI) connections or the adoption of common interface standards. A firm that is better able to forge such close relations with high-value customers in a market has secured a strong positional advantage.

Performance Outcomes

We would expect a relationship advantage to be rewarded with lower rates of defection (churn), greater loyalty and retention, and higher profit margins than the competitors. However, the linkage from positional advantage to performance outcome has proven troublesome to understand because of confounding effects, and a relationship advantage is no exception. Customers buy a complete package of benefits, so it may be difficult to untangle the contribution made by the relationship itself. In addition, the construct of loyalty is itself difficult to study. Much attention has focused on proxy measures, such as satisfaction, which have a complex, asymmetric relationship to loyalty. Whereas loyal customers are likely to be satisfied, all satisfied customers will not be loyal. Loyalty is gained with a combination of performance superiority that ensures high satisfaction, plus trust and mutual commitments.

Orientation toward Relationships

A relationship orientation is embedded within the overall culture and establishes what is appropriate and inappropriate behavior for the enterprise. It signals the importance of customer relationships and the willingness of the organization to treat different customers differently. As part of the culture, it includes relevant *values* that are often deeply embedded as tacit assumptions. The more accessible outcroppings of the culture are behavioral *norms*, the shared *mental models* used to make sense out of complex realities, and the *behaviors* that people exhibit as they make choices about how to spend their time.

To better understand how a relationship orientation is likely to be manifested, we undertook extensive interviews with knowledgeable managers and

(continued)

(Continued)

consultants, perused the voluminous professional literature, and abstracted from detailed case studies. From the information gathered, we derived these indicators of a superior orientation:

- Customer retention is a priority shared throughout the organization.
- There is a willingness to treat different customers differently and a commitment to act quickly on information from these customers (complaints, queries, and changes in requirements).
- All employees exhibit an appreciation of customer lifetime value (LTV).
- Employees have considerable freedom to take action to satisfy customers without having to take time to get approval. Their judgment on what action to take is shaped not just by business rules (an important function) but also by simple observation of what other employees have done, stories about initiatives that have been recognized, and basic training programs that provide role-playing opportunities.

Provided that an organization has a suitable relationship orientation, tracking and using customer information will become a critical success factor. (Without the relationship orientation, customer information is not as useful.) Success depends on how well the firm can elicit and manage the sharing of customer information and then convert that information into knowledge to be used to change how the organization collectively behaves toward the customer. Competitive advantage in the use of customer information means outperforming rivals on each of five steps:

1. *Capturing customer information* (capacity of customer databases to reveal individual customer histories, connections, requirements, expectations, and purchasing activity, as well as the overall rate of customer defections)
2. *Collating* (having information from all customer touchpoints in one place)
3. *Retrieving* (remembering customer information and obtaining it when needed)
4. *Utilizing* (ability to differentiate among customers as to their importance, long-run potential, and anticipated needs)
5. *Sharing* (mechanisms for learning and sharing the resulting lessons throughout the organization)

Managing customer data effectively is extremely difficult, for three reasons.

1. The sheer scale of most customer databases and the rapid rate at which information about customers goes out of date and degrades the quality of the database make managing data difficult. Even so, most databases are inherently incomplete because they contain the record of the customer interactions with only one company and cannot provide a full picture of all purchasing activity.
2. These databases are usually part of larger customer support systems that provide information to customers in response to their queries, complaints,

and service requests. Front-line staff members need accurate and immediate answers to increasingly complex questions while varying their response in light of previous interactions. The potential for conflicts between these two requirements is considerable.

3. At the point where the information actually must be put to use effectively throughout the organization, it will have become knowledge that is partly tacit, highly contextual, and goes beyond the surface-level, explicit contents of the database. This fact makes it difficult to communicate and share the knowledge with others. The deeply held knowledge of customer contact and service people, acquired through problem solving and trial-and-error learning, is especially difficult for the rest of the organization to access. Thus it is all the more critical for the organization to begin with a strong relationship orientation.

The deeply held knowledge of customer contact and service people, acquired through problem solving and trial-and-error learning, is especially difficult for the rest of the organization to access. Thus it is all the more critical for the organization to begin with a strong relationship orientation.

For an enterprise with a relationship-oriented culture and a reasonably robust system of information sharing and utilization, success will depend on the degree to which the organization can be configured in these ways:

- There is a general consensus about goals and means for achieving a relationship advantage.
- The organization is designed around customers rather than around products or functions. This design could include structural variants, such as customer teams and customer managers to oversee the **customer portfolio**.
- The performance measures, incentives, and coordinating mechanisms emphasize customer retention.
- The aspects of the configuration are aligned with a compelling customer value proposition that recognizes customer differences and puts customer retention at the center of strategy.
- Enabling processes exist within the resource base so that the organization is able to personalize or mass-customize communications, products, and services.
- Resources are allocated to initiatives that give a high priority to database development and other activities that support the overall strategic thrust.

Dr. George Day at Wharton talks about the specific capabilities that make it possible to operate a company that builds valuable relationships with customers that result in current revenue and lasting customer equity. Notice that he has told us here that relationships require as fundamental requirements great products, great employees, and great services. This echoes our discussion of trust as the fundamental requirement of relationships. Trust means doing things right (that's what Dr. Day told us about) and doing the right thing. In the next section, Dr. Marijo Puleo outlines the importance of accepting and delivering change within the organization if the focus is to be on what customers need and creating value for them rather than just on efficient internal processes.

Becoming a Customer-Strategy Organization

Marijo Puleo, Ph.D.
Managing Partner, Make Change Positive
Adjunct Faculty, Peppers & Rogers Group

You walk into the headquarters of a corporation a few minutes early for a job interview. In doing research, you kept coming across articles that talked about the values of this company and its strong performance. As you walk into the lobby, you expect to see artwork and pictures of company products as you saw in the other offices of the companies you interviewed with. Instead, you see a beautiful and elegant sign that says "We make a difference in the lives of our customers and our employees." You look around and see 15 pictures of customers and employees, and you immediately connect with them—who they are, what they want in life, and how they live. A few are using the company's products in the photos, but most are not. It is as if a moment of each of their everyday lives was captured for this tribute.

You start to approach the receptionist, who has made eye contact and is smiling broadly. Instead, a well-dressed woman standing next to the desk calls your name. You look surprised and say, "Yes, that's me." She says, "Great! We have been expecting you. I'm Linda from human resources, and the team is waiting upstairs." As you walk through the halls, the customer tribute continues. You see framed photos and letters from customers. You quickly glance at the photos of families and see words like "delight," "surprised," "broken," "taken care of," "recommend you," "know me," and "made a difference." You also see charts titled "Customer Scorecards" and "Employee Scorecards" filled with bars and lines, generally all pointing in an upward direction. You notice that the marketing, sales, and customer service teams are located together, and many people are talking in the hallways, with a few groups reviewing the charts.

As you walk by a meeting room, it looks like some information technology people are discussing a project. You overhear one person say, "Let's review the customer requirements." What did he say? Not the department requirements, the *customer* requirements. You finally arrive at the conference room, where four (you hope future) team members and the hiring manager are waiting. They all smile, introduce themselves, and shake your hand, letting you know whom you will be meeting with throughout the day. The manager asks you how your trip into the office was and if you need anything to make you feel more comfortable. You get the sense already that they are genuinely interested in you being at your best. You are almost embarrassed at how warm and inviting this whole experience is, and it makes you even more motivated to work here. Already you can feel that customers and employees are important to everything they do here.

Sound far-fetched? Some companies do operate in this way and perform well across all levels of measurement.[a] Increasingly, organizations are becoming more and more complex, and it is easy to lose the voice of the customer and the employee in the daily mix of e-mails, meetings, and tasks. There are more requirements, more communication channels, more technologies, and customers are becoming more complex to understand and serve. How do these companies do this? Every human being wants to be understood and to connect meaningfully with others. This can happen in an ad hoc way, but it is a purposeful activity to consistently deepen relationships with customers and connect with employees.

To increase customer equity, an organization needs to pay careful attention to aligning its vision, values, culture, resources, organizational priorities, and measurements. This alignment begins with three critical elements: (1) a compelling vision, (2) defined by leadership that (3) defines and shapes a customer-centric culture. If all three are firmly in place, the rest of the alignment (resources, projects, organization alignment, etc.) can cascade from there. Richard Barrett states:

> *The leader and the leadership team choose the values of the organization and actively live them. They reinforce the values by constantly referring to them and make them part of every organizational system and process. They sustain a high performing culture by regularly mapping the culture and the individual performance of every executive and manager.[b]*

Once the alignment around vision, leadership, and culture is under way, the enterprise needs to adopt an infrastructure that can support all of the business-related processes and functions that characterize a customer-focused model. Large financial investments can be made in information technology, employee training and hiring, communication systems, and other areas related to the transformation, but purchasing and installing tools and technologies will be pointless without adapting the enterprise and its employees to using them properly and enthusiastically. The majority of customer-strategy "failures" didn't crash and burn because of software integration problems or employee software training. Most customer efforts fail because the company never learns to *manage* the enterprise in light of new company capabilities or to *align* those resources, priorities, and capabilities with CRM.

To complete the transition, international organization design expert Jay Galbraith outlines changes that need to be made to become truly customer-centric. The degree to which an organization can incorporate these elements determines the degree of customer centricity, according to Galbraith.

- *Strategy.* The overall commitment to develop solutions that will solve the customer's need and focus on the most profitable, loyal customers or portfolios.
- *Structure.* The organizational concept that incorporates customer segments, customer teams, and customer profit-and-loss (P&L).
- *People.* Includes several elements:

(continued)

(Continued)

- *Personnel approach*. The power base resides with the people who know the most about the customer and are rewarded accordingly.
- *Mental model*. Rather than thinking "How many uses for this product?" (divergent thinking), convergent thinking asks: "What combination of products is best for this customer?"
- *Sales bias*. The bias should be on the side of the buyer in the transaction; the company should advocate for the customer.
- *Culture*. Company culture should be a relationship culture, which searches for more customer needs to satisfy.
- *Process*. The information flow incorporates customer relationship management and solution development.
- *Rewards*. The measures that influence motivation, including customer satisfaction, share of customer, lifetime value, and customer equity.[c]

Once an enterprise commits to adopting a customer-centric model, it needs to rethink the product-centric customs and processes it has relied on for years. Traditionally, enterprises develop their technologies, support, and infrastructure to manufacture products or services and deliver those products or services to the customer in the most cost-efficient way. In turn, the technology and information captured in the systems drive business processes that influence employee behavior and how these employees interact with customers.

This may not appear too much of a change—just put the customer in the middle instead of products. Most enterprises, in fact, will say that this shift is not a big departure from the way they've always done business, because they have already designed their products or services for particular customer segments. However, in those companies, the internal processes and metrics are designed to increase share of market around defined customer segments. For example, metrics around cost of delivery, cost to manufacture, commissions, and so forth abound in a typical enterprise. Many enterprises understand the cost to process and pay an invoice, but they do not understand the value of a customer beyond a total revenue measure. Some enterprises have a "sense" of which customers are valuable, but they lack the facts and figures of customer value differentiation to justify a particular level of service and continue to engage in product-centric business and culture.

It is difficult for employees in an enterprise to make this transition because truly adopting a customer-focused strategy can challenge many of their deeply held values and beliefs about how business is done and how success is defined. One of the most challenging aspects of this new strategy is the amount of coordination and trust that needs to be developed between departments and functions. Managing customer relationships can be an unorthodox way of doing business for them, and it requires many unique skills, such as negotiation and understanding a broader view of the enterprise. Furthermore, the treatment of employees sets the tone for how customers are treated. Employees who cannot develop consensus internally are challenged to deliver to customers.

Frequently, the enterprise also must encourage its customers to change how they operate, a critical step often ignored in the overall process. Everything begins and ends with the customer. The customer-centric enterprise depends on customer participation, even when customers are unaware of their involvement. Ranjay Gulati describes a situation at Best Buy, where the customer teams were watching video surveillance footage of customers leaving the store without making a purchase. An operations team would ask, "How many customers left without buying anything?" But the customer-centric question to ask is, "Why didn't these customers buy anything? What did they come in looking for and did not find?"

The answer was found by thinking in the customers' shoes. The data had already shown that women purchase 55 percent of consumer electronics and influence about 75 percent of purchases. Many current and potential customers were busy mothers who were looking for solutions. The salespeople loved to talk about the technical aspects of products (e.g., the number of pixels and memory capacity of a camera). The conversation works well for someone who is interested in the technical details and latest features. However, the busy mom wasn't interested in technical specifications; she wanted a camera that made it easy to take pretty good digital pictures of her kids and e-mail them to family members.

Best Buy realized that its stores were geared to appeal to male consumers and were turning off female customers. It worked with merchandising, store layout, and salespeople to reengineer a new store format and train employees to be more consultative and aware of customer needs. It empowered employees to make proposals to test changes in policies, procedures, layouts, and merchandising.

If Best Buy had not cascaded the change and alignment throughout the entire system, it could have created a system of competing commitments and generated a degree of dysfunction and entropy. Despite a few pockets of internal resistance, Best Buy was able to implement the solution through most of the organization, and the company is committed to completing the rollout of the new store format. It is, in essence, continuing to refine and continuously improve the elements mentioned earlier. The early results showed that stores with the new customer-centric operations with customer segment treatments used were performing 9 percentage points better than the traditional product-centric operations, according to Gulati.[d]

In a truly customer-centric organization, customer input defines how employees will interact with customers, in turn creating processes, developing new roles, and effecting change in the basic "how" of new product and service creation. Change in the entire organization and the voice of the customer are present in every department, division, and tangibly present all throughout the business.

Leadership in a Customer-Strategy Organization

Transforming to a customer-centric organization requires solid leadership in addition to a vision and culture to support the transition. It has been demonstrated many times that the culture of an organization is determined

(continued)

(Continued)

by its leaders, and an organization can "evolve" only to the level of maturity that the leaders possess.[e] This principle has large implications for organizations that are transforming to customer centricity, because this transformation *specifically* and *absolutely* requires that leaders and employees lift their focus from their own role, department, and results to the broader view of the customer and the organization. Simply put, this customer-focused transformation requires a level of maturity that some leaders and organizations are not able to achieve without concerted focus on the leadership development and the culture.

The good news is that these can be measured and assessed to determine the organization's readiness to take on this culture and leadership shift. Several researchers have been documenting seven stages of development that are remarkably similar, even though their roots are from different sources. The four stages relevant to our discussion are shown in Exhibit (13B).

EXHIBIT 13B   Stages of Development for Leaders (progression is from Expert to Strategist) and Organizations (progression is from Self-Esteem to External Cohesion)

Transformations of Leadership[*]	Levels of Consciousness in the Development of the Organization[†]
Strategist: Generates organizational and personal change. Highly collaborative; weaves visions with pragmatic, timely initiatives; challenges existing assumptions.	**External Cohesion:** Collaboration, environmental awareness, community involvement, employee fulfillment, coaching/mentoring.
Individualist/[Pluralist]: Operates in unconventional ways. Ignores rules he/she regards as irrelevant.	**Internal Cohesion:** Shared values, vision, commitment, integrity, trust, passion, creativity, openness, transparency.
Achiever: Meets strategic goals. Promotes teamwork; juggles managerial duties and responds to market demands to achieve goals.	**Transformation:** Accountability, adaptability, empowerment, delegation, teamwork, innovation, goals orientation, personal growth.
Expert: Rules by logic and expertise. Uses hard data to gain consensus and buy-in.	**Self-Esteem:** Systems, processes, quality, best practices, pride in performance.

[*]David Rooke and William R. Torbert, "Seven Transformations of Leadership," *Harvard Business Review* 83, no. 4 (April 2005): pp. 66–76.
[†]Richard Barrett, *Building a Values-Driven Organization: A Whole Systems Approach to Cultural Transformation* (Burlington, MA: Elsevier, 2006).

Roger Martin discovered a most interesting attribute in 50 leaders with exemplary records of success. Writes Martin:

> *I have found that most of them share a somewhat unusual trait: They have the predisposition and the capacity to hold in their heads two opposing ideas at once. And then, without panicking or simply settling for one alternative or the other, they're able to creatively resolve the tension between those two ideas by generating a new one that contains elements of the others but is superior to both. This process of consideration and synthesis can be termed integrative thinking.[f]*

This skill first appears at the Individualist/Pluralist stage[g] and is very prevalent in the thinking of Strategists.

These findings have profound implications for an organization migrating to customer centricity because this transformation requires that leaders are able to think creatively, apply integrative thinking, and bring together many differing points of view in pursuit of a customer mind-set. At the Transformation level, the required culture and disciplines are in place to build a foundation for customer centricity; most notably, these are empowerment, teamwork, and innovation. It appears that this is the lowest level of maturity required to truly make the migration to customer centricity.

If we move to the next level of organizational maturity, Internal Cohesion, the organization is able to perform at a higher level because shared values are embedded across the organization. All leaders and departments share a passion for learning about and serving customers at a level that their competitors cannot. It is also at this level of leadership that we start to see the emergence of Level 5 Leaders described by business author Jim Collins.[h] They are fully able to embrace the vision, complexity, and values required to lead an organization to excellence. Strategists are very rare (they are estimated to be about 5 percent of the population). These leaders are memorable and inspiring.

My experience suggests that most leaders are at the Achiever stage, and research estimates that about 30 percent of leaders are found in this stage. Achievers primarily focus on delivering results, maximizing effectiveness (versus efficiency), the achievement of goals, and successfully working within systems.[i] They are effective at leading teams and fostering teamwork and are important to the overall success of an organization. Most can create effective relationships within the organization to build consensus and understanding with a customer mind-set.

Some leaders center at the Individualist/Pluralist stage and are able to look beyond the project to what is fully required to sustain the organization focus on the customer for the longer term. They are not likely to paint a compelling vision, but they easily comprehend the complexity of bringing the vision to life and managing multiple stakeholder points of view, including that of the customer. These leaders also are able to participate in "silo busting," or breaking down the walls between departments in service of the customer.

Research and the latest thinking on leadership development help us understand levels of maturity and development for successful leaders and organizations. When undertaking a customer-centric transformation, the transformation leaders must be able to embrace a level of complexity while working across multiple areas and disciplines within an organization to embed a customer mind-set in the leadership, managerial, and employee groups of an organization. This mind-set will then align the decision making, allocation of resources, and internal motivation of all within the organization around the customer. Research has shown that aligned values, leadership, and culture are much more likely to drive high levels of organization performance.

(*continued*)

(*Continued*)

[a]Sonja Lyubomirsky, Laura King, and Ed Diener, "The Benefits of Frequent Positive Affect: Does Happiness Lead to Success?" *Psychological Bulletin* 131, no. 6 (2005): 804. Also see Scott Lochridge and Jennifer Rozenzweig, *Enlightenment Incorporated: Creating Companies Our Kids Would Be Proud to Work For* (Dragonfly Organization Research Group, 2009), and Robert Kegan and Lisa Laskow Lahey, "The Real Reason People Won't Change," *Harvard Business Review* 79, no. 10 (January-February 2001): 87.

[b]Richard Barrett, *Building a Values-Driven Organization: A Whole System Approach to Cultural Transformation* (Burlington, MA: Elsevier, 2006), p. 85.

[c]Jay R. Galbraith, *Designing the Customer Centric Organization: A Guide to Strategy, Structure, and Process* (San Francisco: Jossey-Bass, 2005), pp. 15–21.

[d]Ranjay Gulati, *Reorganize for Resilience: Putting Customers at the Center of Your Business* (Boston: Harvard Business Press, 2009), pp. 19–31.

[e]Barrett, *Building a Values-Driven Organization*.

[f]Roger Martin, "How Successful Leaders Think," *Harvard Business Review* 85, no. 6 (June 2007): 60–67.

[g]Note: The term *Individualist* has also been termed *Pluralist*, acknowledging the skill of a leader at this stage of development to hold two opposing views simultaneously. This type of thinking often is called "and/and" thinking versus the "either/or" thinking prevalent in earlier stages of development.

[h]Jim Collins, *Level 5 Leadership: The Triumph of Humility and Fierce Resolve*, HBR On-Point Enhanced Edition (Boston: Harvard Business Press, 2009).

[i]Susanne R. Cook-Greuter, "Making the Case for a Developmental Perspective," *Industrial and Commercial Training* 36, no. 7 (2004): 275–281.

Relationship Governance

One of the biggest single difficulties in making the transition to an enterprise that pays attention to its relationships with individual customers, one customer at a time, is the issue of **relationship governance.** By that we mean: Who will be "in charge" at the enterprise when it comes to making different decisions for different customers? Optimizing around each customer, rather than optimizing around each product or channel, requires decision making related to customer-specific criteria, across all different channels and product lines. When Customer A is on the Web site or on the phone, the enterprise wants to ensure that the very best, most profitable offer is presented *for that customer*. The firm's call center shouldn't try to compete with its own stores to try to get the customer to buy from them, nor should the product manager for Product 1 compete with the product manager for Product 2 and try to win the customer for one product line or another. What the customer-centric enterprise wants is to deliver whatever offer for this customer is likely to create the most value, overall, without regard to any other organizational or department goals or incentives that might have been established at the firm. This, in a nutshell, is the problem of *relationship governance*. The challenge most companies face when they make a serious commitment to managing customer relationships becomes obvious once the firm pulls out its current organizational charts, which usually are set up to manage brands, products, channels, and programs. Most companies have organized themselves in such a way as to ensure that they can achieve their objectives in terms

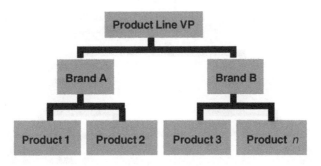

EXHIBIT 13.1   Product Management Organization

of product sales or brand awareness across the entire population of customers they serve.

But in the age of interactivity, managing customer relationships individually will require an enterprise to treat different customers differently within that customer population. Inherent in this idea is the notion that different customers will be subject to different objectives and strategies and that the enterprise will undertake different actions with respect to different customers. So, we ask again: With respect to any particular customer, who will be put in charge, and held accountable, within the enterprise, to make sure this actually happens? And when that person is put in charge of an individual customer relationship, what levers will he control in order to execute the strategy being applied to "his" customer? How will his performance be measured and evaluated by the enterprise, for the current period as well as the long term? (Recall the Canadian bank example we cited in Chapter 11, a company where customer portfolio managers are measured in the current quarter for the current revenue by the bank of the customers in their portfolios and for the three-year projected value, as of today, of that same group of customers.)

This is the problem of relationship governance. It's one thing for us to maintain, safe between the covers of this book, that in the interactive age a company should manage its dialogues and relationships with different customers differently, making sure to analyze the values and needs of various individual customers, adapting its behavior for each one to what is appropriate for that particular customer. It's another thing to carry this out within a corporate organization when, at least for many companies at present, no one is actually in charge of making it happen.

Exhibit 13.1 is an oversimplified example of a "typical" Industrial Age organization chart. In such an organization, each product or brand is the direct-line responsibility of one individual within the organization. In this way, the enterprise can hold particular managers and organizations responsible for achieving various objectives related to product and brand sales. The brand or product manager is, in fact, the "protector" of the brand or product, watching out to make sure that it does well and that sales goals or awareness goals are achieved. The manager controls advertising and promotion levers to ensure that the best and most persuasive message will be conveyed to the right segments and niches of customers or potential customers. This is all in keeping with the most basic goal of an old-fashioned Industrial Age company: *to sell more products.*

The most basic goal of the customer-strategy enterprise, however, is to increase the long-term value of its customer base, by applying different objectives and

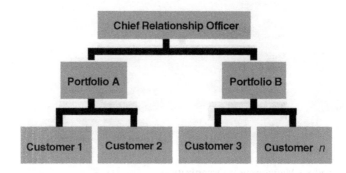

EXHIBIT 13.2   Customer Management Organization

strategies to different customers. Yes, in the process it's practically certain that more products will be sold in the short term. But in order for the primary task to be accomplished, someone within the organization has to be put in charge of making decisions and carrying out actions with respect to each individual customer.

In Exhibit 13.2, a different organization chart is drawn for the customer-value-building company, one that emphasizes *customer management* rather than product management. In an enterprise organized for customer management, ideally every customer will be the direct-line responsibility of a single customer manager (even though the customer may not be aware that the manager is in charge, as she works in the background to determine the enterprise's most appropriate strategy for that customer and then to make sure it is carried out). Because there are likely many more customers than there are management employees, it is only logical that a customer manager should be made responsible for a whole group of customers. We refer to such a group as a customer *portfolio,* avoiding for the present the word *segment,* in order to clarify the concept. A customer portfolio is made up of unduplicated, unique (and identified) customers. No customer will ever be placed into more than one portfolio at a time, because it is the portfolio manager who will be in charge of the enterprise's relationship with the customers in her portfolio and the resulting value of that relationship. If we allow a customer to inhabit two different portfolios, then we are just creating another relationship governance problem—which portfolio manager will actually call the shots when it comes to the enterprise's strategies for *that* customer? How will we calculate that customer's value accurately? And who gets credit or blame if the customer's value rises or falls?

A customer manager's primary objective is to maximize the long-term value of his own customer portfolio (i.e., to keep and grow the customers in his portfolio), and the enterprise should reward him based on a set of metrics that indicate the degree to which he has accomplished his mission. In the ideal state, the enterprise's entire customer base might be parsed into several different portfolios, each of which is overseen by the customer manager, like a subdivided business that creates value in the long term and the short term as of today.

Clearly, if we plan to hold a customer manager accountable for growing the value of a portfolio of customers, then we'll also have to give her some authority to take actions with respect to the customers in the portfolio. The levers that a customer manager ought to be able to pull, in order to encourage her customers to attain a higher and higher long-term value to the enterprise, should include, literally, every type of action or communication that the enterprise is capable of rendering on an individual-customer basis. In communication, this would mean that the customer manager would control the enterprise's addressable forms of communication and interaction: direct mail as well as interactions at the call center, on the Web site, and even (to the extent possible) in face-to-face encounters at the store or the cash register. In effect, the customer manager would be responsible for overseeing the enterprise's continuing dialogue with a customer. In terms of the actual product or service offering, ideally the customer manager would be responsible for setting the pricing for her customers, extending any discounts or collecting premiums, and so forth. The customer manager should own the offer,[2] and the communication of the offer, with respect to the customers in the manager's portfolio.

> The customer manager should own the offer, and the communication of the offer, with respect to the customers in the manager's portfolio.

The enterprise will still be creating and marketing various programs and products, but the customer manager will be the "traffic cop," with respect to his own portfolio of customers. He will allow some offers to go through as conceived, he will adapt other offers to meet the needs of his own customers, and he will likely block some offers altogether, choosing not to expose his own customers to them.

In a high-end business or personal services firm, such as a private bank, the role of customer manager is played by the firm's *relationship manager* for each client. The relationship manager owns the relationship and is free to set the policies and communications for her own individual clients, within the boundaries set by the enterprise. The enterprise holds her accountable for keeping the client satisfied, loyal, and profitable. The company probably does not formally estimate an individual client's actual LTV, in strict financial terms; more than likely it has a fairly formal process for ranking these clients by their long-term value or importance to the firm. A relationship manager who manages to dramatically improve the value of her client's relationship to the enterprise will be rewarded.

However, most businesses have many more customers than a private bank, or a law firm, or an advertising agency. For most businesses, it would simply be uneconomic for a relationship manager to pay individual, personal attention to a single customer relationship, to the exclusion of all other responsibilities. Realistically, then, the way most of the addressable communications will be rendered to individual customers, at the vast majority of companies, will be through the application of business rules. Just as business rules are used to mass-customize a product or a service (see Chapter 10), they can be applied to mass-customize the offer extended to different customers as well as the communication of that offer. Thus, one of the customer manager's primary jobs will be to oversee the business rules that govern the enterprise's mass-customized relationship with the individual customers in his own portfolio.

In addition to customer relationship managers, the one-to-one enterprise will need *capabilities managers* as well (see Exhibit 13.3).[3] Their role is to deliver the capabilities of the enterprise to the customer managers, in essence figuring out whether the firm should build, buy, or partner to render any new products or

---

[2]The phrase "owns the relationship" disturbs some people; after all, a relationship can't be "owned." Within the context of this book, "owning" a relationship means "is accountable for," in the sense of "owns up to."

[3]From B. Joseph Pine II, *Mass Customization* (Cambridge, MA: Harvard Business School Press, 1993).

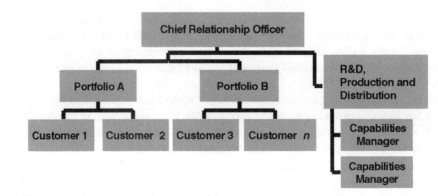

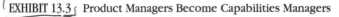

EXHIBIT 13.3 Product Managers Become Capabilities Managers

services that customers might require. We could think of capabilities managers as being something like product managers at large. The products and capabilities they bring to bear, on behalf of the enterprise, actually will be marketed not directly to customers but to the customer managers in charge of the enterprise's relationships with customers.

None of this is to say that companies can afford to forget about product quality, or innovation, or efficient production and cost reduction. These tasks will be just as important as they always have been, for the simple reason that few customers would choose to continue relationships involving subpar products or service. However, as we've already discussed, product and service quality by themselves do not necessarily lead to competitive success, because no matter how stellar a company's service is, nothing can stop a competitor from also offering great service—or a great, breakthrough product, or a low price. In the final analysis, the most important single benefit of engaging a customer in an ongoing relationship is that the rich context of a Learning Relationship creates an impregnable competitive barrier, with respect to that customer, making it literally impossible for a competitor to duplicate the highly personalized service the customer is now receiving.

Customer Experience Maturity Monitor: The State of Customer Experience Capabilities and Competencies

Jeff Gilleland
Global Strategist for Customer Intelligence Solutions, SAS Institute

Most marketers acknowledge that today's big challenge is managing the customer's experience across products, touchpoints, and channels . . . and over each customer's life cycle. This goes beyond the kind of *customer relationship management* (CRM) that focuses too much on a single product or channel transaction—the *short term*. Alternatively, **customer experience management** (CEM) requires designing an experience for each customer based on knowledge of that customer, delivering it across products and channels, and measuring individual outcomes that enable improvement of future interactions. Simply stated, CEM is about creating learning relationships—and setting up those relationships to build customer equity and shareholder value—over the *long term*.

But where are companies on their journey toward CEM and creating learning relationships? What capabilities do companies have in place to manage the customer's experience across products and channels? What benefits accrue for companies with the most mature capabilities?

The research done as part of the Customer Experience Maturity Monitor (CEMM),[a] an ongoing research project jointly conducted by SAS and Peppers & Rogers Group, has shown that a company must have more than the desire to manage the customer experience; it must have enterprise capabilities that leverage customer *insight* to better manage individual customer *interactions* and continuously *improve* results. Importantly, for these capabilities to work, the company must have a *customer orientation*—a culture that focuses on the customer and builds trust.

Research Dimensions

The research measured organizational capabilities and competencies in four categories: customer *orientation*; customer *insight*; customer *interaction*; and *improvement* (see Exhibit 13C). In total, respondents rated their companies on 58 individual variables; key learning highlights are discussed in the following section.

INSIGHT: TRANSFORMING DATA INTO ACTION   Differentiating the customer experience for competitive advantage begins with customer *insight*. This is not about uniformly enhancing customer satisfaction. It is about designing an experience for each customer that is based on knowledge of that customer, delivering it across products and channels, and measuring individual outcomes that enable improvement of future interactions.

Manage Data   CEMM research revealed that companies are good at managing customer data at the aggregate level but not at the individual customer level. For example, 52 percent of respondents rated the performance of their company as *good* or *excellent* in using customer satisfaction as key performance indicator (an aggregate measure). However, only 30 percent rated their performance as *good* or *excellent* at creating a complete view of each customer across multiple products and channels or at making a current view of customer information available to all customer touchpoints.

Predict Behavior   Of course, managing customer data is necessary but not sufficient. To manage the customer's experience successfully, you must be able to predict individual customer behavior, including next purchase, channel preference, loyalty, and profitability. Increasingly, as the price for their loyalty,

(continued)

(*Continued*)

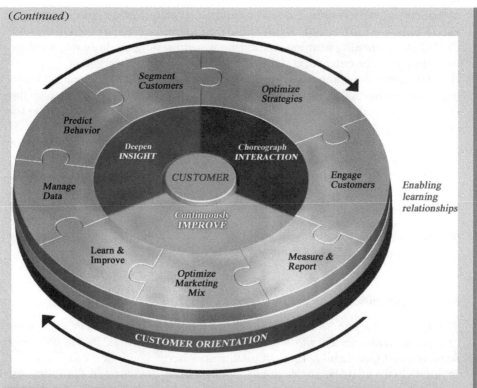

EXHIBIT 13C   CEMM Measured Customer Orientation and 3-I Capabilities

customers are expecting companies to understand their needs and to be treated as individuals.

Using customer *insight* to demonstrate that your company better understands a customer's needs is fundamental to differentiating the customer's experience for competitive advantage. This one-to-one understanding creates customer intimacy and loyalty. CEMM research revealed that only 38 percent of companies rated their performance as *good* or *excellent* in anticipating customers' likelihood to purchase, cancel, or leave.

Segment Understanding differences between customers is made easier through segmentation. This is an important practical step toward enabling the enterprise to manage customer interactions based on insights about individuals—which is the ultimate goal of one-to-one marketing.

CEMM research confirmed that sophisticated segmentation remains elusive for most companies. Fewer than half are *good* or *excellent* at even segmenting customers based on demographics, one of the most basic dimensions to consider. And a mere 42 percent rate their performance as *good* or *excellent* in calculating customer profitability.

INTERACTION: OFFERING CUSTOMIZED TREATMENT Marketers like to talk about personalized marketing: "treating customers as individuals based on their unique needs" and delivering "customized treatment." In the CEMM study, 62 percent of respondents agreed with this statement: "My company treats customers differently, based on an understanding of the needs of each one individually." On the surface, 62 percent seems pretty impressive—and perhaps a bit high. To get the real story, you have to look a little deeper.

Differentiating the customer experience for competitive advantage is about designing an experience for each customer that is based on knowledge of that customer, delivering it across products and channels, and measuring individual outcomes to improve future interactions. Done well, CEM will guide investment to higher-potential customers, provide a richer experience that engenders loyalty, and turns customers into advocates. Here's the deeper CEMM learning.

Manage/Optimize Strategies   Many companies use loyalty programs to differentiate and manage the customer experience. In the CEMM research study, 35 percent of respondents rated their capabilities as *good* or *excellent* in response to the statement: "Rewards and loyalty programs are used to encourage loyalty among high-value customers." However, only 17 percent rated their capabilities as *good* or *excellent* in response to the statement: "Individual 'treatment tracks' are created to manage the customer experience across products and channels."

Engage High-Potential Customers   In the CEMM study, only 26 percent rated their company's performance as *good* or *excellent* at orchestrating outbound customer contact across products and channels. Although this problem is easily solved with today's campaign management and marketing automation technologies, enterprise contact management capabilities remain elusive for most companies.

For inbound interactions, 32 percent of respondents rated *good* or *excellent* their ability to use customer insight to guide pricing, service and product suggestions. Fewer still, at 16 percent, rated *good* or *excellent* their ability to calculate real-time best outcomes during customer sessions.

Perhaps the biggest opportunity for improvement, for both outbound and inbound engagement, is behavior triggers. Only 20 percent of respondents rated *good* or *excellent* their ability to create triggers for systematic response to significant changes in customer behavior. Engaging customers when they have changed not only produces significantly higher response rates, but it also demonstrates to customers that their relationship matters to the company.

IMPROVEMENT: CREATING A "LEARNING RELATIONSHIP"   One of the golden rules of marketing has always been "Know your customer." Historically, doing this required deep knowledge about a market segment. It included understanding the unmet needs and wants of a particular target market, including demographics, attitudes, consumption patterns, media habits, lifestyle, and other dimensions that enabled you to define a homogenous group. And then you tailored the 4 *P*s of marketing based on your knowledge about this market segment. This approach to "target marketing" worked pretty well for decades. It enabled marketers to develop products, value propositions, advertising creative, and media

(continued)

(Continued)

buys that were well targeted to a particular market. But, in today's world of CEM, how does this approach stack up?

A Critical Gap: 62 Percent versus 29 Percent   For success, CEM requires a company to learn *continuously* from individual customers and to demonstrate, to each customer, that it is listening to them. One of the big CEMM findings around customer *improvement* (à la learning from customers) was this gap: A total of 62 percent of respondents agreed with this statement: "My company treats customers differently, based on an understanding of the needs of each one individually." However, only 29 percent rated their capabilities as *good* or *excellent* in response to this statement: "Customer profiles are continuously updated to reflect all customer activity (purchases, returns, etc.) as well as outbound (campaigns) and inbound contact (channel visits, call center, web, stores/branches, etc.)."

Do companies really understand the changing needs of each individual customer if they are not updating customer profiles and learning?

Improvement: Measure and Report   The CEMM research revealed that customer metrics are on the marketing dashboard. For example, 38 percent of respondents rated the performance of their company as *good* or *excellent* in using customer metrics (e.g., customer profitability, campaign response, channel behavior) to measure organizational performance. Importantly, 29 percent rated their performance as *good* or *excellent* in aligning incentive programs to customer metrics. In addition, 28 percent rated highly their use of customer metrics to measure individual employee performance.

But many companies are still struggling with marketing measurement basics. Only 38 percent rated their performance as *good* or *excellent* at measuring campaign return on investment (ROI)—a surprisingly low statistic, given all the great marketing automation technology that can easily solve this problem. Equally surprising is that only 29 percent rated their performance as *good* or *excellent* at measuring marketing mix ROI—which is where marketing resource management (MRM) easily optimizes marketing dollars between the plethora of advertising and promotional options.

Improvement: Learn and Improve   Learning about individual customers is difficult! CEMM research revealed that only 28 percent of companies rated their performance as *good* or *excellent* in capturing a customer's expressed needs during live customer interactions. Imagine this: A customer is on the phone with a call center rep (or on the Web site or some other touchpoint) and is giving the company the information required for success but, unfortunately, the company is failing to capture it.

But some companies are not missing the opportunity. In fact, 19 percent of CEMM respondents rated *good* or *excellent* their ability to change customer interactions based on changes in a customer's profile. So one out of every five companies is, in fact, learning from customers and improving customer interactions based on this knowledge. This one-to-one understanding creates customer intimacy, loyalty, and advocacy—the goal of CEM.

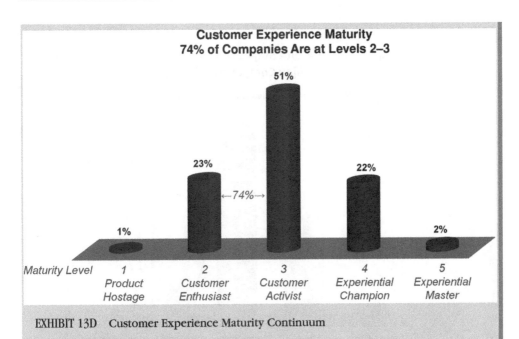

Customer Experience Maturity
74% of Companies Are at Levels 2–3

Maturity Level	1	2	3	4	5
	Product Hostage	*Customer Enthusiast*	*Customer Activist*	*Experiential Champion*	*Experiential Master*

EXHIBIT 13D   Customer Experience Maturity Continuum

CUSTOMER ORIENTATION   Although capabilities to manage the customer experience lag, a customer orientation is emerging. In the CEMM survey, 75 percent agree that their company motivates employees to treat customers fairly. And 66 percent agree that their company takes the customer's point of view when making business decisions. Also encouraging, 69 percent agree that their company considers the impact that business decisions have on the future value of its customers.

Customer Experience Maturity Equals Competitive Advantage

So where are companies in their customer experience maturity? Composite scores were created for each company based on how it rated its capabilities across 58 variables—which placed each company on a maturity continuum from 1 to 5. As you can see from Exhibit 13D, 74 percent of companies scored at Levels 2 and 3.

Companies were also asked to rate their overall competitiveness: *worse; same; or better than their key competitors*. By comparing the maturity of capabilities with relative competitiveness, the research could determine the value of improving CEM capabilities.

COMPANIES WITH MATURE CAPABILITIES ENJOY TWO TO THREE TIMES THE COMPETITIVE ADVANTAGE   The research findings revealed a direct link between the maturity of a company's customer experience management capabilities and its relative competitiveness. For companies that have progressed to the highest levels of maturity (Levels 4 to 5), the advantage is twofold to threefold (see Exhibit 13E).

(continued)

(Continued)

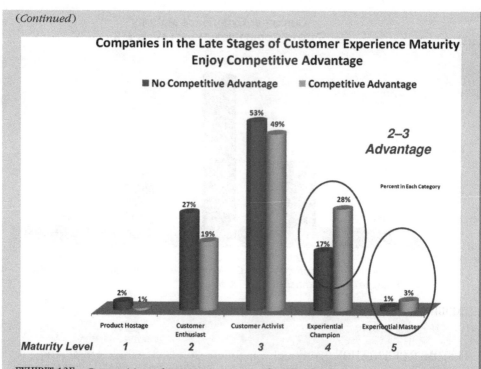

Companies in the Late Stages of Customer Experience Maturity Enjoy Competitive Advantage

■ No Competitive Advantage   ▪ Competitive Advantage

2–3 Advantage

Percent in Each Category

	Product Hostage	Customer Enthusiast	Customer Activist	Experiential Champion	Experiential Master
No Competitive Advantage	2%	27%	53%	17%	1%
Competitive Advantage	1%	19%	49%	28%	3%

Maturity Level   1   2   3   4   5

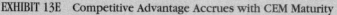

EXHIBIT 13E   Competitive Advantage Accrues with CEM Maturity

CEMM Summary

Many companies have made great progress in their journey toward managing the customer's experience for competitive advantage. They are building enterprise technologies that not only manage customer relationships across products and channels but also learn from individual customers. These companies are evolving their business models *from* using insight just for better target marketing *to* using insight to provide perceptible value to customers through a richer experience.

Customers are rewarding these companies not only with their loyalty but also with their advocacy. And in our new world of social media, customer advocacy can be a powerful force.

---

[a]*Customer Experience Maturity Monitor (CEMM)*: a global research study initiated in 2008–09 by SAS Institute and Peppers & Rogers Group. The initial research included responses from 434 companies. The first phase of the research involved in-depth interviews with over 50 companies focusing on the activities and programs they engage in to ensure a positive experience for their customers. This information was combined with surveys among 384 companies worldwide, which audited their customer experience practices and customer orientation philosophies. The results of this project serve as the benchmark data for the CEMM and provide the foundation for the analysis of ongoing research among companies in different countries and industries as well as in individual companies wishing to understand their customer experience maturity levels. For updated results, see www.peppersandrogersgroup.com/CEMM. "SAS" and all other SAS Institute, Inc. products or service names are registered trademarks of SAS Institute, Inc.

Summary

Now that we've described the larger-scale processes needed to transition from a product-centric to a customer-centric enterprise, we need to get specific: What needs to be done throughout the organization to make this transition? Part 2 of our discussion of managing the customer-centric enterprise in Chapter 14 covers just that.

Food for Thought

1. Choose an organization and draw its organizational chart. How would that chart have to change in order to facilitate customer management and to make sure people are empowered, evaluated, measured, and compensated for building the value of the customer base? Consider these questions:
   a. If a customer's value is measured across more than one division, is one person placed in charge of that customer relationship?
   b. Should the enterprise establish a key account-selling system?
   c. Should the enterprise underwrite a more comprehensive information system, standardizing customer data across each division?
   d. Should the sales force be better automated? Who should set the strategy for how a sales rep interacts with a particular customer?
   e. Is it possible for the various Web sites and call centers operated by the company to work together better?
   f. Should the company package more services with the products it sells, and if so, how should those services be delivered?[4]
2. For the same organization, consider the current culture, and describe it. Would that have to change for the organization to manage the relationship with and value of one customer at a time? If so, how?
3. At the same organization, assume the company rank-orders customers by value and places the most valuable customers behind a picket fence for 1to1 treatment. What happens to customers and to customer portfolio managers behind that picket fence?
4. In an organization, who should "own" the customer relationship? What does that mean?

Glossary

Customer experience management (CEM)   The integrated process of designing an experience for each customer based on knowledge of that customer, delivering it across products and channels, and measuring individual outcomes that enable improvement of future interactions. The goal of CEM is to create Learning Relationships with customers, thereby building customer equity and shareholder value over the long term.

---

[4]Don Peppers, Martha Rogers, Ph.D., and Bob Dorf, *The One to One Fieldbook* (New York: Doubleday Books, 1999).

Customer portfolio A grouping of customers based on value and understood by the needs they have in common as well as the needs they have individually expressed by their interactions and transactions through various touchpoints over time. In contrast to grouping customers by *segments*, where customers are treated as look-alikes within the segment (meaning that segment marketing is really mass marketing, only smaller), the customer-strategy enterprise will work to manage portfolios of individual customers.

Relationship governance Defines who in the enterprise will be in charge when making different decisions for different customers, with the goal of optimizing around each customer rather than each product or channel.

CHAPTER 14

Organizing and Managing the Profitable Customer-Strategy Enterprise: Part 2

The human mind treats a new idea the way the body treats a strange protein; it rejects it.

—P. B. Medawar

It should go without saying that an enterprise will not simply be able to paste a customer-management organizational structure atop its existing organization. Moreover, the change, in terms of success metrics, management roles, and responsibilities, and the required capabilities of the enterprise, are profound. In truth, the transition never actually ends, because there will always be additional steps the enterprise can take to improve its relationships with its customers. Nevertheless, when starting as a well-oiled, product-marketing organization, taking the first tentative steps toward customer management requires a good deal of planning. In this chapter, we address the evolutionary reality of organizational change as well as practical guidelines for each department during the transition.

During the transition to a customer-centric model, enterprises frequently under- *gradually* estimate the degree to which all facets of the business will be affected by the changes and the ongoing efforts that will be required to achieve full business benefits. The organizational and cultural transition to customer management represents a genuine *revolution* for the enterprise, but it is more likely to be successful when it can be treated as an *evolution* within the organization. Here we discuss three ways to speed this evolution process, any or all of which can be adopted by an enterprise:

> The organizational and cultural transition to customer management represents a genuine *revolution* for the enterprise, but it is more likely to be successful when it can be treated as an *evolution* within the organization.

1. Pilot projects and incremental change
2. **Picket fence** strategy
3. Segment management

Pilot Projects and Incremental Change

Most companies launch their customer initiatives in a series of pilot projects. There are so many things to do, if a customer-specific perspective is to be adopted, that usually it is a relatively simple process for a company to "cut and paste" various self-contained customer initiatives into the enterprise's current method of operating. The objective, over the longer term, is to accumulate a large number of small improvements.

It is not necessary to resolve the customer-governance problem, in order to launch a pilot project or to make an incremental change. Instead, the IDIC (Identify-Differentiate-Interact-Customize—see Chapters 3 to 10) implementation process itself is an ideal vehicle for conceiving and executing incremental changes. A small change might involve, for instance, obtaining, linking, and cataloging more customer identities, using a sweep of existing databases containing customer information. Or it could involve setting up a prioritized service level for customers now identified as having higher long-term value to the enterprise, or higher growth potential. Many incremental change initiatives are also likely to involve streamlining the customer interaction processes, so as to cut duplicative efforts or resolve conflicting communications.

Particularly for large and complex organizations, often the most direct and immediate route to a broad transition for the overall enterprise is to implement a series of incremental changes, one small step at a time. Hewlett-Packard (HP), for instance, began trying to wean its corporate culture away from the simple worship of products in the 1990s, launching an effort to create a better balance for the enterprise, in which both customer growth and product excellence would be prized.

According to Lane Michel, at that time a marketing manager at HP (and later a partner at Peppers & Rogers Group), staying focused on incremental gains helped HP win acceptance for its overall program. "We try to avoid boiling the ocean," says Michel. "Then again, it's important to show immediate results. Those early successes earn you the right to take bigger steps."[1]

One example of such an incremental step was the customer-interaction program engineered by the Barcelona Division of HP's Consumer Products Group, which produced, among other things, the DesignJet high-end printer. In order to make it possible to have a continuing dialogue with its customers, the division developed a Web site, HP DesignJet Online, to serve as a user-friendly channel for interactive customer communication. The password-protected site offers self-diagnostic tools to DesignJet customers as well as a quarterly newsletter, a user feedback section, new product notifications, and an upgrade program. The division is counting on the site to increase market share, reinforce customer loyalty, and provide a steady stream of timely market knowledge.[2]

---

[1] Don Peppers, Martha Rogers, Ph.D., and Bob Dorf, *The One to One Fieldbook: The Complete Toolkit for Implementing a 1to1 Marketing Program* (New York: Currency/Doubleday, 1997). Updated by Lane Michel, 2010.
[2] Ibid.

Another incremental but important step taken by HP was the development of a central and global electronic customer registration system, along with a master set of questions and a master customer database to store the information. The initiative was born from ideas and feedback generated across several of the company's groups and geographies. The new system replaced paper registration, which had proved a poor method for collecting usable customer data.

Over time, baby steps like these can add up to great strides. By 1999, HP had roughly 100 such incremental initiatives under way at various locations around the world, which it called "one-to-one campfires." Each was being tracked and monitored centrally, with information made available throughout the HP enterprise on the firm's intranet at a special relationship marketing section. Nearly every one of these initiatives, also, could be categorized easily in terms of which aspect of the IDIC implementation process it represented. Some of these early initiatives blossomed into major programs causing the reformulation of product designs, operational retooling, customer interactions, and management roles accountable for returns on investments made.

Keeping the process going required champions and leaders of change. At HP, these leaders initially had titles such as relationship marketing manager, customer advocacy manager, and installed base loyalty manager.[3] Over time, vice presidents and marketing managers across HP took leadership of the company's drive into customer experience, measureable results, and segment-wide changes.

A large number of incremental changes can add up to big change. In addition, an incremental change project itself could serve as a pilot for rolling out a particular idea or strategy across an entire division or enterprise. Pilot projects are a common method many companies use to make the kinds of changes required in the transition to a customer-strategy enterprise. But a pilot project differs, slightly anyway, from other forms of incremental change. A pilot project is, in essence, a feasibility study. It usually represents a test bed for trying out a new policy or strategy that, if successful, will be rolled out in a broader application. Therefore, the success metrics of the individual pilot project will have less to do with the actual profitability or business success of the pilot itself and more to do with an assessment of whether the idea represented by the pilot project would be beneficial, if it were rolled out to the broader organization. And pilots have a built-in advantage when it comes to metrics. Because, by their nature, they usually involve only a selected portion of the enterprise, it is easier to measure the pilot's performance against a "control group"—meaning, in essence, the rest of the enterprise, doing business as usual.

Incremental change projects are rarely undertaken to resolve the problem of relationship governance for the enterprise. One of the key benefits, in fact, of concentrating on the IDIC process implementation methodology is the fact that significant progress can still be made without having to come to grips with this very thorny problem. At some point, however, any enterprise that wants to begin engaging customers in actual relationships, individually, will have to deal with the issue of relationship governance, and there are at least two methods for dealing with it on an incremental or transitional basis.

---

[3] Ibid.

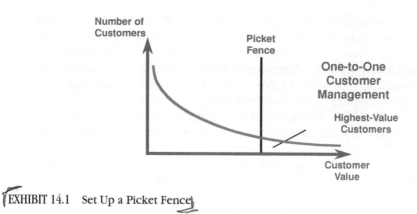

EXHIBIT 14.1   Set Up a Picket Fence

Picket Fence Strategy

The right way to transform a company gradually into a customer management organization is not to do it product by product or division by division but customer by customer. And one way to begin such a transition is by placing just a few customers "under management," then adding a few more, and a few more (see Exhibits 14.1 and 14.2). In order to make this type of transition successful, it must be recognized that the enterprise will be operating under different rules with respect to the customers under management than it will be with respect to all other customers. In essence, the customers under management will be fenced off and treated differently from the remainder of the customer base. As the transition progresses, the number of customers behind this "picket fence" will increase. As the portion of the customer base behind the picket fence continues to grow larger, the enterprise will be effecting a gradual transition to a customer management organization.

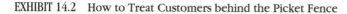

■ Link individual data over time.

■ Calculate individual share of customer and lifetime value.

■ Establish and maintain dialogue—get them off the mailing lists.

■ Mass-customize to meet individually expressed needs.

■ Allocate resources to this customer relative to this customer's value.

■ Find products for customers.

One-to-One Picket Fence

EXHIBIT 14.2   How to Treat Customers behind the Picket Fence

If an enterprise has ranked its customers by value, it can prioritize its transition in such a way as to place the more valuable customers behind the picket fence first. When customers go under management, the implication is that a customer manager in the enterprise will be setting objectives and strategies for each of them individually. The objective and strategy set for any particular customer should reflect the entire enterprise's relationship with that customer. For this reason, at least with respect to the customers behind the picket fence, the customer managers must have not only an integrated view of the enterprise's offering to and interactions with those customers, but they also must have authority to make policy and implement programs, on behalf of the enterprise.

The picket fence transition strategy is especially compelling for companies that already identify their customers individually, during the natural course of their business, and differentiate them by value. This would include banks and financial services firms, telecommunications companies, personal services businesses, some retailers, and most business-to-business (B2B) companies with internal sales organizations. The highest-value customers at many companies like these are already being singled out for attention. If a retailer, for instance, has identified any customers who merit special treatment, it is likely they are the store's very high-volume, repeat spenders; the "special treatment" might include assigning personal shoppers or relationship managers to watch over the individual interests of such customers. Because the picket fence strategy is already in place at such a firm, the enterprise's goal should be to extend the idea and automate it, by codifying the business rules that are being applied and ensuring that proper metrics are in place.

Remember that the customer manager should own the business rules for determining all of the communications that her customers receive. This means that the enterprise's general direct-mail pieces would not go to customers behind the picket fence without the initiation or approval of the customer manager responsible for them. For each customer behind the picket fence, there should be a particular objective and a strategy for achieving that objective, set by the customer manager. In fact, the customer manager will herself be rewarded and compensated based on her ability to meet the objectives set for each of her customers, one customer at a time. Over time, as technology makes it better and more cost-efficient to process customer information, and the enterprise gains more knowledge and confidence in the process, it can expand the picket fence and put more people behind it.

Although the transition involves expanding the area behind the picket fence (i.e., placing more and more customers under management), the enterprise most likely will never actually place all of its customers behind the fence. Some customers, for instance, may not be willing to participate in a relationship of any kind. Moreover, no matter how cost efficiently the enterprise has automated the process, there will always be customers who are not financially worth engaging in relationships.

Segment Management

Another way to begin the transition to a customer management organization is with segment managers. The picket fence transition is a customer-specific process that places an increasing number of individual customers under management; the segment management transition is a *function*-specific process that gives segment managers an increasing number of roles and capabilities with respect to their segments.

Remember that we chose the term *portfolio* rather than *segment* with deliberation, when we introduced the concept of customer management. The primary reason for this choice was to convey the thought that, in a customer portfolio, the customers themselves are uniquely identified and unduplicated: no customer would be in more than one portfolio at a time. And just as you manage each stock in your stock portfolio individually, you would manage each customer in your customer portfolio individually.

But even if an enterprise has not identified its customers uniquely, it still can differentiate them approximately, using survey-based consumer research and other tools. Even though the enterprise might not be able to classify any specific customer into a particular segment with certainty, the segments themselves represent different types of customers who have needs and values that are different from the customers populating other segments.

Segment management is particularly appropriate for the types of businesses that have greater difficulty identifying and tracking customers individually. The picket fence transition works best for companies that either identify customers in the natural course of their business or can easily do so, whereas the segment manager transition works for all other companies. A consumer packaged-goods company, for instance, might have a highly developed customer management organization already in place to ensure that its relationships with its retailer customers are managed profitably, but the company is unlikely even to have the identities of more than a microscopic fraction of its consumer-customers. Such a firm might establish an organization of consumer segment managers who are responsible for shaping the firm's advertising and promotion efforts with respect to particular segments of consumers, across a variety of different products and brands.

A *segment management* organization, therefore, can be thought of as a transition state somewhere between product management and customer management. The most critical missing ingredient in a segment management operation is likely to be the capability to identify individual customers and track their interactions with—and individual values to—the enterprise over time. Until the enterprise is able to add this capability, it will not be able to move from segment management to true **customer portfolio management**. But even in the absence of customer-specific capabilities, a segment management organization still can be a useful tool for an enterprise to begin treating different customers differently and for creating the value proposition for the relationships that eventually could come.

Customer Portfolio Management

At the heart of the customer management idea is the concept of placing customer managers in charge of *portfolios* of separate and individually identifiable customers who have been differentiated by their value to the enterprise and grouped by their needs. It is these customer managers who are charged with managing customer profitability. This is the core structure of the customer management organization, one in which each individual customer's value and retention is the direct responsibility of one individual in the enterprise. Managers may each be in charge of a large number of customers or portfolios, but the responsibility for any single customer is assigned to one customer manager (or, in a B2B setting, often to a customer management team). That manager is responsible for building the enterprise's share of customer (SOC) for each of the customers in his portfolio and for increasing each customer's lifetime value (LTV) and potential value to the enterprise (see Chapter 5).

The responsibility for customer management may spring from the marketing department, or sales management, or product development, or even, occasionally, from the information-technology department, where the customer data are housed. Wherever in the organization customer management resides, however, it must have a clear voice in the enterprise and have enough power to make decisions and influence other areas of the enterprise. One difficulty for this group is that the enterprise might try to hold it accountable for increasing the value of customers but fail to give it the authority to take the appropriate actions with respect to those customers. In the customer-value-building enterprise, the customer strategies should become the unifying theme for the organization; other areas of the enterprise should be made to understand how their own departmental goals relate to the customer strategies developed by the customer management group, and these other departments should be held accountable for executing the strategies ultimately designed to increase customer equity.

Transition across the Enterprise

> Many organizations learn the hard way that customer portfolio management cannot be installed; it must be *adopted*.

Many companies believe that the biggest hurdle to becoming a successful customer-strategy enterprise is choosing and installing the right software. This unfortunate outlook has led to poor results on customer initiatives. Many organizations learn the hard way that customer relationships cannot be installed; they must be *adopted*. The biggest hurdles to successful customer management have little to do with technology. The greatest obstacles are a firm's traditional organization, culture, processes, metrics, and methods of compensation. The transition needed will affect not just the whole enterprise but each of its parts as well. Let's take a look at the changes that the enterprise will face.

Transition Process for the Sales Department

The sales force plays a critical role in the customer-strategy enterprise. As the "eyes and ears" of the organization, salespeople often interact with the customer at the customer's place of business. It is during these visits that salespeople develop an information-rich point of view of the customer. Using sales force automation (SFA) software, sales reps now can easily share customer learning with their firms.

Some of the sales force is focused on driving transactions for lower-volume customers, and the skill sets of these salespeople are well suited for these activities. Other salespeople have different skills, working with customers across all levels of the customer organization and focusing on maximizing share of customer. Once considered the "lone wolf" of the organization, these salespeople effectively divide their time among sales calls, analysis of customer information, and participation in internal customer-strategy development. Regardless of position, however, salespeople understand how to develop customer insights and to provide customer information to the enterprise in an actionable way. Some information is entered into the SFA tool, and other information is shared during customer review meetings or via communications with the research and development department, customer service, or other departments.

The transition to a customer-strategy enterprise will be easy for some salespeople, whereas it will challenge the skill sets of some of the top sales performers. These principles will make a great deal of sense for salespeople who have already been practicing visionary selling, consultative selling, or strategic selling, and they probably will embrace these ideals readily. But the salesperson who relies, for example, on retailer business customers to "buy forward" in order to make quarterly product sales quotas may find the transition more difficult. Applying customer management principles requires taking a long-term view of the customer, a view that conflicts directly with the short-term focus that prevails in many sales organizations.

The sales team can help confirm that those selected as most valuable customers (MVCs) are indeed the best customers. The sales team can also find most growable customers (MGCs) that have been missed. It will be important for the organization to provide the sales team with information across other touchpoints in the organization, such as the Web and the customer service center. Real-time information is required to coordinate all interactions with a customer, and feeding in this information can be a significant change for many salespeople. The trade-off is that the enterprise can handle a lot of the most tedious record keeping and servicing very efficiently, freeing up the salesperson for real relationship building and customer growth.

One of the most significant changes for a newly automated sales force is that the daily life of salespeople will wind up on-screen for all to see. In addition, fewer salespeople will have greater responsibility,[4] putting pressure on all sales personnel to conform and adopt new policies and procedures. During this transition period, therefore, it is important to negotiate some key agreements when implementing new policies and programs:

- *Prioritize key information that is needed about customers.* Salespeople should not be spending their time typing. They should be interacting with customers and learning more about customer needs.
- *Address ways that salespeople can save time and earn higher commissions.*
- *Integrate customer information wherever possible.* Some salespeople spend significant amounts of time typing the same information into applications that have different purposes (order entry system, billing system, forecasting reports, etc.).

---

[4]Michael Ahearne, Douglas E. Hughes, and Niels Schillewaert, "Why Sales Reps Should Welcome Information Technology: Measuring the Impact of CRM-Based IT on Sales Effectiveness," *International Journal of Research in Marketing* 24, no. 4 (December 2007): 336–349; Richard A. Lee, *The Customer Relationship Management Survival Guide* (St. Paul, MN: HYM Press, 2000).

■ *Negotiate which information is for enterprise use and which information is "for their eyes only."* It is important for the salesperson to remember key customer information, such as family member names, spouse's birthday, and so on, to create a personal bond; but this may be interesting to others in the enterprise only if someone has to substitute for the sales rep in a personal meeting.

MULTIDIVISION CUSTOMERS Knowledge-based selling traditionally has occurred in B2B scenarios but has not always been applied across divisions of a company. One reason a customer-centered approach to doing business is so compelling is precisely because it enables an enterprise to leverage a single customer relationship into a variety of additional profit streams, cross-selling many different products and services to a customer in a coordinated way. The sales function plays a critical role in this relationship but is not alone in executing it.

Customer-strategy enterprises rarely isolate their customer initiatives within a single division. In a multidivisional enterprise, the divisions sell to overlapping customer bases, doing business with a single customer in several different divisions. Enterprise-wide cross-selling is not possible if the pilot project is limited to a single division and if the division databases are not integrated to facilitate a one-customer view.

In many cases, a B2B enterprise that sets out to transform itself into a more customer-oriented firm will end up restructuring the sales force entirely, in order to ensure that the sales of different products to the same customers will be better coordinated, and appear more rational to the customer.

Using Up Customers

We know a multiline insurance company in the United States we'll call Company X. It sells auto, property, life, and health insurance through a network of its own agents, each having the authority to sell any of the company's products. Some of these products generate more profit than others. Life insurance, as one example, tends to sell at a higher margin and is less subject to fraud, when compared to auto insurance. To protect agent profitability and maintain order within the distribution channel, Company X doesn't allow any of its own agents to solicit clients from any of its other agents. So once an agent lands a new customer, no other agent from that company can ask that customer for additional business.

The problem is that for a variety of reasons—background, predisposition, expertise—some agents simply don't sell all of Company X's insurance products with equal enthusiasm and effectiveness. Consider an agent who has a fine track record for recruiting new auto insurance customers but then rarely, if ever, elects to sell any other line of insurance product to them. She has found that she can build herself a bigger book of business, faster, simply by concentrating on acquiring more and more auto insurance customers, a task she is exceedingly good at, rather than spending time and energy learning how to sell property or life insurance, or some other product to her existing customers. Of course, every new customer she recruits won't be buying any other type of insurance from Company X,

(continued)

(Continued)

because no other agent is allowed to solicit, while the agent herself is unlikely to suggest other products.

In effect, Company X is "using up" a whole customer whenever it sells an auto policy through this agent. If there were an unlimited supply of new or prospective customers, this wouldn't be a problem, but the supply is not unlimited. Even putting aside the fact that a single-product customer has a greater proclivity to wander away to a competitor, the real issue here is that every time the company gets a customer and does not get the most possible value from that customer, the company loses a real monetary opportunity. And it cannot simply make this opportunity up by finding more customers.[a]

With the right metrics and a thorough analysis, Company X might discover that the value this agent leaves on the table with each new customer recruited is more than the value generated by each auto policy sold. If that were the case, then this particular agent is not creating value for the company at all but destroying it. That's right: Company X may actually be destroying value every time this particular agent recruits a new customer. Company X's business is based on the belief that as long as its sales and marketing effort is effective, it can always acquire more customers from somewhere. But this is a false assumption. Instead, to make the right decisions as a business, you must always take into consideration the population of customers and prospective customers truly available to you. After considering the whole population of customers and prospects, your job is to employ that population to create the most possible value for your firm.

Because customers are scarcer than other resources, using up customers is more costly than using up other resources.

If you let this thought sink in for a minute, you'll realize that it requires you to adopt a different perspective on your business, and this perspective will lead you to make different decisions. Evaluating your business model, or your company's various sales and marketing and other activities, from the standpoint of return on investment or payback ratio or some other financial metric, is important, but it's even more important to evaluate every action you take based on how many customers you have to use up to achieve the financial results you want.

---

[a]Sometimes companies use up customers with technology. Jill Dyché, author of several excellent books on customer data coordination and management, including *Customer Data Integration: Reaching a Single Version of the Truth* (Hoboken, NJ: John Wiley & Sons, 2006), which she cowrote with Evan Levy, explains how CDI (customer data integration), would help distinguish between John Smith (the very valuable customer) and John Smith Jr. (the deadbeat) so we don't turn down the former for a high-profit loan. Getting the process right is as important as getting the philosophy and the compensation right.

Source: Adapted from Don Peppers and Martha Rogers, Ph.D., *Rules to Break and Laws to Follow: How Your Business Can Beat the Crisis of Short-Termism* (Hoboken, NJ: John Wiley & Sons, 2008), pp. 43–45.

COMPENSATING THE SALES FORCE   Sales force compensation is often one of the most important drivers of change, partly because the salesperson's salary and bonus usually depend on product sales results. One challenge facing the enterprise is deciding how to compensate salespeople and others for encouraging and ensuring customer loyalty and growing the long-term value of a customer, even when there may be no short-term product sale involved. The fact is that many salespeople are compensated in ways that make them indifferent to customer loyalty. In some cases, new-customer incentive programs actually *benefit* the salespeople when customer churn increases, enabling them to resell a product or service to a relatively educated customer. If customer loyalty and profitability are the objectives, then the enterprise needs to explore compensation systems that reward sales reps on the basis of each individual customer's long-term profitability (or LTV). There are at least two ways an enterprise can accomplish this:

1. *Value-based commissions derived from customer, rather than product, profitability.* The enterprise identifies certain types of customers who tend to be worth more than others and pays a higher up-front commission for acquiring or selling to this preferred type of customer. It considers lower commissions for "price" buyers or returning former customers as well as other variable commission plans that emphasize acquisition and retention of customers whose value is greatest to the enterprise overall, not just to the salesperson.
2. *Retention commissions.* The enterprise pays a lower commission on the acquisition of a customer. Instead, it links compensation to the profitability of a customer over time. For example, instead of paying a $1,000 commission just for landing a customer, the company pays $700 for a new account and $400 per year for every year the customer continues to do business with the enterprise.

Transition Process for Marketing

The marketing group is responsible for traditional marketing activities, including creating brand image and awareness, communicating with the customer, utilizing the Internet and other old and new channels, and, often, creating communications within the enterprise (e.g., an intranet, company newsletters, and project communications).

In the customer-strategy enterprise, the marketing department will perform these traditional roles for customers who remain outside of the picket fence. It also may help to prepare communication messages or even business rules for customer managers who are building relationships for customers under management. In addition to deploying the traditional instruments of marketing, such as advertising and promotion, a number of other functions for the marketing department to perform are unique to a customer-specific approach, including:

- Customer analytics (see Chapter 12), a specialized skill set that involves building customer LTV models, gathering and manipulating data, and programming. The customer analytics group also may be responsible for tracking and reporting the internal metrics needed to measure the effectiveness of customer programs.
- Establishment of test cells and control groups.
- Campaign development and management, including dialogue planning.
- Offer specification, designed to appeal especially to higher-value customers and prospects.

- Customer management, as a line-management function, which has been described previously.
- Insight into short-term profitability and long-term customer equity and TSR (total shareholder return). ⌐

Transition Process for Customer Service

A service organization might be the appliance repair personnel, the hotel staff, operators answering the 800-telephone number, or the delivery crew. Every product manufactured and sold has a service organization associated with it in some way, whether customers obtain the product directly from the enterprise or through a channel organization. In the customer-strategy enterprise, the service organization has access to more customer information than in other traditional enterprises, and uses this information to deliver a valuable experience or to collect information (or both). For example, in a customer-strategy enterprise, the delivery driver might be asked to survey a customer's warehouse informally and take note of the number of competitors' cartons that are stacked within view of the delivery door. This information can help an enterprise begin to understand its share of customer.

Ironically, as pressures mount for enterprises to cut costs and improve efficiency, the customer service area may be squeezed in the process. In the customer-strategy enterprise, the customer service area plays a key role in executing customer strategies while servicing the customer. Customer calls are routed based on value and need, and the most appropriate customer service representative is assigned the call based on the skills of the rep. During the call, customer-defined business rules are applied to maximize the impact of the interaction with the customer, and the reps have been trained in how to interact most effectively with various customers. Also, the individual needs, talent, and experience of the reps are considered in the routing decisions. Reps are encouraged to enhance the skills needed to serve each customer efficiently and effectively. As customer needs change, the skills of the reps also must evolve.

What follows are two views—deep insights—about the role of service in customer relationships.

Customer Service Starts when the Customer Experience Fails

Christopher J. Zane
President, Zane's Cycles

Zane's Cycles is a bicycle retailer similar to the one just down the street from you. So why would you be interested in Zane's Cycles and my style of doing business? Everyone believes their own organization offers great customer service, but how can you know for sure that your customers won't get the "It's-not-my-problem" attitude I recently experienced with the staff at the lost baggage department of a major airline? I can say with authority that I can.

I founded Zane's Cycles in October 1981 as a junior in high school at the age of 16. I was working at a bike store in summer 1981, and the owner decided to liquidate the inventory because of high operating costs (the prime interest rate at the time was 21 percent). This gave me the opportunity to purchase an operating business for the cost of the inventory. I first had to convince my parents that it was time for me to operate a storefront business. I figured I could persuade them because I also had been running Foxon Bike Shop, a bike repair business, from our garage since I was 12. Let me tell you, this took a lot of convincing. After agreeing to personally pay back a $23,000 loan with interest to my grandfather, regardless of the success or failure of the business, my parents endorsed my desire to become a small business retailer. First year's sales—a respectable $56,000. This year's sales—an even more respectable $15 million.

As I'm sure you can imagine, this growth was not without its bumps in the road or, better stated, those huge, teeth-rattling, "am-I-going-to-come-out-alive?" potholes that suddenly appear from underneath a truck traveling in front of you on the highway. These experiences, however, have made Zane's Cycles a unique and successful retail environment. Zane's Cycles is more than a bicycle store, and I want to share the concepts that helped build the environment my customers enjoy. Please keep in mind that not every business needs to implement these specific programs, but the idea is to create something new, different, and exciting for your customers and staff.

I would much rather spend my day among customers and staff who are laughing and genuinely having a good time than addressing issues from customers feeling they have been mistreated or are unappreciated for their patronage. This is why there is constant communication with the staff about embracing a customer experience culture. The following are a few quotes that are constantly reinforced and are top-of-mind throughout the Zane's organization:

- Customer service starts when the customer experience fails.
- The only difference between us and our competition is the experience we deliver.
- We want our customers to have more fun here than at Disney World.
- And finally, from my friend Len Berry's book, *Discovering the Soul of Service* (New York: Free Press, 1999), great service not only improves business, it improves the quality of life.

In order to build and sustain a culture that lives up to these simple ideas, the employee responsible for delivering the experience needs not only to be passionate but also to be empowered to deliver the dream—constantly.

Probably the most important tool in the customer experience toolbox is understanding the customer lifetime value. It's easy to deliver on the promise of a unique and enjoyable experience when the customer you're working with is buying a bike for a few thousand dollars, but when you are trying to juggle five customers and the sixth needs help getting a bike out of her car for a free service adjustment and it's raining—well, that's when knowing the customer LTV provides the discipline to maintain the focus to ensure a unique experience. At Zane's Cycles, starting with the first bike at age 3 and ending with your last bike, usually the retirement present to yourself, our customer LTV is $12,500. Simply, the customer with the free service today is as valuable as today's few-thousand-dollar bike purchaser over a 60-year relationship.

(continued)

(Continued)

Customer service starts when the customer experience fails. If you, as a customer, are greeted by a friendly and upbeat employee at the start of your search for a product or service, and throughout your interaction with the business continually experience a positive and honest exchange regardless of the staff member with whom you're engaged, the need for resolution diminishes and your loyalty strengthens.

The only difference between us and our competition is the experience we deliver. When it comes to products or services, the true difference between similar offerings is hard to determine. Bikes are bikes, televisions are televisions, oil changes are oil changes, and dry cleaning is dry cleaning, and usually the prices are very similar as well since everyone has the same cost of doing business. We choose to support one business over another because this one helps me load the bike in the car, or explains why I should select a smaller screen because of the size of the room, or there is a cover over the seat and steering wheel so my interior doesn't get soiled, or the collar tabs are in the short pocket. The experience determines decision.

We want our customers to have more fun here than at Disney World. The Magic Kingdom is exactly that: expensive, crowded, hot, loud, but it's still a magical place because what's most important is that the people there want us to have a good time. Every interaction exceeds our expectations, and the constant innovation of the experience is the foundation on which they were created. Being constantly focused and driven to create a positive and fun experience for our customers that exceeds their expectations will make us better then Disney because we're not expensive, crowded, hot, or loud.

Great service not only improves business, it improves the quality of life. In an environment where delivering great service to the customer is the single focus, many things happen: Satisfied, happy customers are nice to the employees; happy, intrinsically satisfied employees are nice to each other; happy teams are successful, justifying higher pay and benefits; families of well-paid employees are happy; and our quality of life has improved. If we're going to spend 2,000 hours a year doing anything, why not spend it in a fun environment with people we enjoy?

Obviously none of this is possible if your team is comprised of people who don't have the personality to deliver the experience. I have built my team with genuinely nice people and then provide the tools and training to guarantee their success. Once there is an understanding of the customer LTV, and employees embrace the attitude associated with the principles above, it's time to empower them to deliver a unique experience in a way that is consistent with their unique personality. Let the fun begin!

At many firms, the "customer service" function is thought of as a cost of doing business rather than as an integral part of the products or services actually being sold to customers. It is easy to spot an enterprise with this attitude. This is the company that hides its toll-free number on the Web site and that has an impenetrable Interactive Voice Response (IVR) system (see Chapter 7).

Increasingly, customer transactions are moving to an e-commerce model, and transactions normally handled with a phone call are now being done electronically, via the Web site. In many customer service areas, this has changed the mix of calls that are handled by the customer service rep. "Easy" transaction (order-taking) calls are now being replaced with more difficult customer situation calls (complaints, inquiries, billing and invoicing questions, etc.). This can increase the level of stress experienced by the customer service reps.

Traditional measures for customer interaction centers have focused on "talk time" and "one and done" measures. (See a more complete discussion about the customer interaction center in Chapter 7.) As we dig deeper into customer metrics, we start measuring average talk time for valuable customers versus customers who call into the customer interaction center frequently and yet do not generate enough revenue to warrant high levels of service. We begin to understand which customers are buying a wide range of products and services offered by an enterprise and which customers should be but aren't. Many customer interaction center managers are left to fight a battle to increase talk time for the customers who warrant more attention, but they lack the analytics and resulting insights ("the facts") to be able to justify that decision. This is where partnering with the customer manager is key: The justification for these measures should be in the customer strategies.

The fact is, however, that a customer-strategy company often can keep its costs down by centering on customer needs. Calls are more often resolved in one session and in less total time. Customer service reps do not "chase down" information or transfer customers from department to department. Voice response unit options are reordered to present the most likely option desired by *that* customer as soon as the customer is identified. This process can significantly decrease phone costs for an enterprise maintaining a toll-free phone line. And it requires that people within the enterprise start thinking like customers, or taking the **customer's point of view** during key interactions (such as a sales call or customer care call), and combine this point of view with the customer strategy and business rules that have been identified for this customer. Change often demands new skill sets. As the enterprise begins to define specific roles and responsibilities (or job descriptions) for various customer care representatives, it also will need to develop training and development plans and recruitment and staffing plans. These descriptions include competencies and behaviors that will be required of all employees—things like customer empathy—and skills associated with different roles. Employees might determine how they "touch" the customer directly or indirectly by supporting another department.

An often-neglected step in this process is planning around the way customer care representatives are supported, measured, and compensated to reinforce the new behaviors, which should incorporate the customer-centered metrics described earlier. Unfortunately, the reporting capabilities in many enterprises are not up to the task, and some great customer-oriented efforts have gone awry because this last step was not implemented. Employees often want to "do the right thing" but are not supported or measured adequately or correctly. More important, many companies equate customer relationship management with "customer service," when in fact customer service—important as it is—is *not* the same as relationships, customer experience management, or customer equity building. The heart of a Learning Relationship is a *memory* of a customer's expressed needs so that this customer can be treated in a way that works for him without his having to be asked again.

Customer service, in contrast, is often more like *random acts of kindness masquerading as customer relationship management.*

How Do We Fix Service?

Bill Price
President, Driva Solutions

David Jaffe
Consulting Director, LimeBridge Australia

Let's look at the issues that have prevented significant improvements in service. Here we identify seven reasons that service isn't getting better and seven responses, the Best Service Principles:

Principle 1: Eliminate Dumb Contacts

Customer demand for service equals the volume of requests that customers make of companies when they need help, are confused, or have to change something. In most companies, demand is a given; lots of time and effort go into forecasting demand based on past demand, measured in 30-minute increments across a range of contact channels. Then companies work hard at matching their resources to this demand: putting people on the right shifts at the right time, finding partners if needed, and so forth. These companies are so busy trying to manage the demand and their "service supply" that few, if any, question why the demand is there in the first place. For example, how many companies report that they have made themselves easier to deal with by reducing the demand for contact? How many boards of directors monitor their rate of contact as well as the speed and cost? Very few companies think this way (although Amazon comes close by proclaiming year-by-year reductions in contacts per order). There is an unfortunate obsession with how quickly phones and e-mails are answered. The standard across most service operations is to report and track how quickly things were done, not how well they were done or how often, or why they needed to be done at all.

This issue of demand for contact is fundamental to our thinking. If companies want to rethink service radically, they need to rethink the *need* for service. Our book is titled *The Best Service Is No Service* because too many service interactions aren't necessary; they reflect, instead, as we've begun to show, the dumb things that companies have done to their customers: processes that customers don't understand, bewildering statements, incorrect letters, badly applied fees and charges, or services not working as the customer expects. Fundamental changes in service require companies to question what has driven the demand for service.

Principle 2: Create Engaging Self-Service

How often have you given up on a Web site or gotten lost in one? Have you ever listened to a set of toll-free menus and been overwhelmed by the choices, and tried desperately to find the option that lets you talk to an operator? How often have you filled out an application form online and then been told that you don't meet the criteria for an online application? How often have you searched for an online service and found that it is no longer available? How often have you been flummoxed by the operating manual for a new electronic device or for your new car? These are just some of the examples of the dumb things that organizations do or don't do in self-service.

When self-service works well, customers love it. Companies like Amazon. com and firstdirect.com couldn't have grown the way they have if customers didn't like well-designed self-service. ATMs took off because they were much more convenient than queuing in a branch. Internet banking is so convenient that it has increased the volume of transactions and inquiries that customers perform.

Why do so many companies get it wrong? Our perspective is that they understand neither the need for self-service nor how to create self-service solutions that their customers will embrace.

Principle 3: Be Proactive

The reason why companies have to invest so much time trying to predict demand and then supplying appropriate resources is that the *modus operandi* is one of reactive service: If the customer calls, the company is there to deal with it. But in many cases the company knows that there is a problem yet still waits for the customer to contact the company to fix it.

Take product recalls, for example. Recently a leading company that had no idea which of its customers had the affected product needed to wait for customers to try to figure it out and then call the company, sometimes in panic mode.

Principle 4: Make It Really Easy to Contact Your Company

Do you ever get the impression that some companies would rather not hear from you? Have you ever been on a Web site and searched in vain for a phone number to call? Have you ever found that companies expect you to get service only when they want to give it to you? If any of these situations seems familiar, it's another example of a company making itself hard to contact.

Principle 5: Own the Actions across the Company

A bizarre myth has grown up in many companies that the head of customer service is responsible for customer service. Although we recognize that someone needs to be held accountable and be dedicated to service, we do not believe that the service operations can fix service without the help of all the other company departments and, increasingly, outside partners in the supply chain or in other functions. Although the head of service does need to forecast the demand for service, and handle those contacts well, many other areas of a

(continued)

(*Continued*)

business cause the customer contacts that drive the demand—for example, billing, IT, marketing, credit, and finance. IT and process and product areas can also influence how well the customer service area can service the demand. The norm is for the head of customer service to be held accountable for the standard and methods of service. Our perspective is that responsibility for service must be spread across the whole organization.

Principle 6: Listen and Act

Some companies have millions of contacts per year with their customers, yet they still spend considerable money and time researching their customers. In fact, head-office functions such as marketing, product design, and IT have gotten further and further from frontline delivery, the information gap has increased between the head office's understanding of the customer and the behaviors and wants of customers as expressed at the front line. The interactions that companies have with customers today offer an amazing amount of insight about customers, the company's products and services, and even competitors—if companies can tap into what their customers are telling them. Unfortunately, most companies have not even thought to "listen" to their customers in this way when these interactions occur.

This disconnect is illustrated by the gap between the perceptions of CEOs and those of customers in general. . . . Over 70 percent of CEOs believe that their companies provide "above average" customer care, but nearly 60 percent of these companies' customers stated that they are somewhat or extremely upset with their most recent customer service experience.[a]

Unfortunately, CEOs and board members are cosseted—they often fly first class, have "personal" or "relationship" bankers, get queued faster, and rarely set foot in a branch or pay their own bills. Because they have become disconnected with what their own customers experience, they will have to listen even harder.

Managers in larger companies who control market and customer research or set the budget for service rarely, if ever, spend time with the frontline staff who are dealing directly with customers. In small businesses this isn't the case—an owner who runs a restaurant or cafe doesn't need to conduct research into what his customers like or dislike. He hears it directly from customers: If customers are asking for cake or health food or gluten-free products or soy milk, the restaurant owner can respond quickly, or quickly be out of business. It's too bad that many companies have forgotten how to listen in this way.

Principle 7: Deliver Great Service Experiences

Companies have created large centralized contact centers or service functions, separated service from sales or production, added lots of new technology, deluged themselves with meaningless or misleading metrics, and built walls around the customer service functions. They have then become stuck delivering service experiences that have forgotten the customer; stuck obsessing about speed, not quality; and stuck thinking that faster is more efficient. It is hardly a surprise that many customer experiences disappoint customers.

Companies Are Stuck with Service Experiences that Have Forgotten Who the Customer Is

Customers are often expected to navigate the organization and repeat account information and what happened ad nauseam, from agent to agent. The processes simply haven't been designed from the customers' perspective, and it shows. For example, customers are justifiably miffed when companies (still!!) ask them to repeat their credit card number, frequent flyer account number, or order identification number after just having done so in an IVR or with another agent or, as is increasingly the case, after doing so online. "Don't you know me?!?" they might say. Then companies add in complexity for customers, such as by asking them to repeat data the company already knows or to provide information to comply with a procedure that someone in the legal department dreamed up. These are just two illustrations of experiences that haven't been designed with the customer in mind.

Examples of Getting It Right

The good news is that there are many shining lights—companies that are getting service right, with benefits for the companies and their customers.

ELIMINATE DUMB CONTACTS: BRITISH TELECOM   In 2001, British Telecom (BT) was receiving 2.4 million customer contacts each day; over 35 percent were repeats, and many were unnecessary. BT set about reducing these and other forms of unwanted contacts systematically, and by 2004 had reduced the contact volume to only one million per day, a 60 percent reduction; at the same time, customers were more satisfied, the BT staff was happier, and the cost savings proved that better service was also cheaper.

CREATE ENGAGING SELF-SERVICE: eBAY   EBay represents one of the finest cases of customers' desire and willingness to use self-service. Not only do customers willingly buy directly from vendors, but the sellers themselves learn through various forms of self-service how to set up their stores on eBay, how to use eBay's payment and other services, and even what software is available to help them run their sales businesses. EBay also opens the communication channels between buyers and sellers through their seller and buyer ratings systems. If customers were unwilling to use self-service, eBay and the thousands of businesses that it supports would not be in existence today.

BE PROACTIVE: NOVADENTAL CLINIC   Dentistry is not an industry most would associate with great service. The Novadental clinic in Australia is run by one of Melbourne's leading dentists, whose consultancy firm advises other dental

(continued)

(Continued)

practices in how to run their businesses. The clinic demonstrates how to be proactive at every level: (1) promoting dental hygiene services to patients as a form of preventive dentistry; (2) monitoring that customers are getting checkups and hygiene services at regular intervals; (3) calling each customer more than twenty-four hours in advance of each appointment to ensure that he or she will be coming; and (4) maintaining a waiting list of other customers willing to "backfill" anyone who cannot keep his or her appointment. This is not only good service for the clinic's customers, ensuring that they remember their appointments, but also prevents costly no-shows for the dental practice.

MAKE IT REALLY EASY TO CONTACT YOUR COMPANY: USAA INSURANCE One of the more successful U.S.-based property and casualty insurance companies is USAA; it also has the highest loyalty rate in the industry. (The biggest reason that USAA loses "members" is death, not switching to the many other choices that members have.) USAA has always made it really easy for members to contact it for service, change their addresses, and learn about new products. The company publishes different toll-free numbers prominently on its Web site, in monthly magazines, on invoices and other notices, and in many other media. USAA will transfer its members to other services, but it always tells the member what that number is so that the member can call directly the next time he might need help.

OWN THE ACTIONS ACROSS THE ORGANIZATION: YARRA VALLEY WATER Award-winning utility Yarra Valley Water (also in Melbourne) was determined to reduce the number and cost of complaints. To do this, the company established a "complaints council" that met each month to review the ownership and cause of any complaints that had reached the regulatory body (the industry ombudsman). After the council assigned ownership of each complaint to a particular department, it charged the new owners not just with ensuring resolution of that complaint but also with reporting back to the complaints council about underlying causes that led to the complaint in the first place, and how they could be addressed. This systematic process meant that all of Yarra Valley Water's departments were drawn in to tackle service issues and forced to acknowledge and act on their impact on service contacts. The company has recognized the value of taking a strategic perspective on complaints, and the process has resulted in a significant reduction in complaints, according to the industry ombudsman, Fiona McLeod. Pat McCafferty, the general manager who established the process at Yarra Valley Water, says, "What made this process powerful was that it drew together the key players across the business into the issues that impacted customers. We recognized that we couldn't solve these problems without ensuring all those who impacted service had a seat at the table."

LISTEN AND ACT: AMAZON.COM All contact centers hold team meetings, usually weekly one-hour sessions that bore the agents with the latest policy changes, next work-shift details, and perhaps new company product releases. Amazon decided to inject life into these weekly sessions by asking the agents, "What have our customers been saying to you this past week?" which quickly became known as WOCAS (what our customers are saying). The company produced a weekly WOCAS report that quickly became popular reading for departments outside customer service.

In one of these weekly sessions, a customer service representative mentioned that in the middle of a call about a lost password, the customer told her that she really liked Amazon's 1-Click™ service (which enables customers to click only once with a preset shipping address, shipping method, and credit card to speed the order on its way); however, she said that she often shipped to different addresses and had two credit cards, so for any shipments other than her 1-Click settings, she had to navigate through the additional checkout process, easy to do but still time consuming. Another agent remarked that he too had occasionally heard customers talk about how cool it would be to have multiple 1-Click combinations, so the first agent asked if she could lead a task force to study how this could be done. (This was a frequent process at Amazon: engaging and encouraging Amazon agents and supervisors to launch or participate in cross-company task forces.)

After a couple of months, Amazon quietly launched drop-down 1-Click, "quietly" being another of Amazon's methods. Instead of announcing that customers could register additional shipping addresses, shipping methods, and credit cards beside their current 1-Click setting, Amazon (1) researched all previous multiple combinations, (2) preloaded them into this new feature, and (3) let customers discover it, allowing the "serendipity" for which Costco is also well-known in its warehouse stores. The result? Increased customer orders and more convenience for customers.

DELIVER GREAT SERVICE EXPERIENCES: UNION SQUARE CAFE   Successful NYC-based restaurateur Danny Meyer has had hit after hit, the earliest and best known being Union Square Cafe. In his recent memoir, *Setting the Table: The Transforming Power of Hospitality in Business,* Meyer echoes Best Service when he defines "enlightened hospitality" that "stands some more traditional business approaches on their head." Among the elements that Meyer carefully plants and then allows to flourish in his restaurants and catering businesses, all completely applicable to the broader topic of customer service in our book, are (1) creating a dialogue with guests and ensuring that they feel you are doing something *for* them and not *to* them; (2) choosing to look for new ideas and "tuning in to the feedback"; (3) hiring and nurturing "agents" instead of "gatekeepers" who share optimistic warmth, intelligence, work ethic, empathy, and self-awareness; and (4) embracing mistakes with awareness, acknowledgment, apology, action, and additional generosity. Pursuing these guest-centric processes means taking time, not hurrying the guest or the meal because they blend to become one—the experience.

Source: Adapted from Bill Price and David Jaffe, *The Best Service Is No Service: How to Liberate Your Customers from Customer Service, Keep Them Happy, and Control Costs* (San Francisco: Jossey-Bass, 2008), pp. 8–19.
[a]Accenture, 2007.

Improving Customer Service at an Online Financial Services Firm

In one instance, an online financial services firm was reengineering the customer interaction center to implement many of the aforementioned principles. The firm separated its customer base into four groups based on key customer characteristics (assets and use of the services). Once it identified its customer groups, it was easy for the firm to identify the knowledge, skills, and abilities that were required to support them. The firm implemented routing technology to redirect customer calls based on the customer grouping and the skill set of the available representatives. The firm created automated business rules that could utilize the best available personnel to handle the needs of each individual customer in the call queue. Prior to this change, any customer could be routed to any customer service representative (CSR). It was not unusual, for example, to have a most valuable customer routed to a newly hired and ill-informed rep or a rep who lacked the required skills to execute particular transactions. This required a customer hanging up and (if the firm was lucky) calling again; or perhaps the customer would be transferred to another CSR. The changes resolved these problems. A key benefit for the rep was the ability to work through a learning curve—she was directed to the types of calls that she could handle, and this significantly decreased stress levels, which reduced all the company costs related to turnover.

When you *do* need customer service, high-quality customer service is one of the beneficial outcomes of adopting customer strategies. Enterprises must keep in mind the cost of *not* providing sufficient service, thereby risking the loss of customers, the cost of lost long-term customer equity, and the expensive task of acquiring new customers. General wisdom places the estimate for customer defections due to a poor sales or service interaction between the customer and the enterprise at about 70 percent. It isn't necessary for a company to make formal Return on Customer (ROC) calculations to understand the short-term losses in revenue and long-term customer equity cost to shareholders of poor service far outweighs the current perceived "savings" of reducing service quality.

Moreover, an enterprise must balance the cost of providing customer service with the needs and desires of the customer in such a way that the customer will find sufficient value in the enterprise to remain a customer. At a minimum, certain standards of accuracy, timeliness, and convenience must be in place to placate most customers. The right technology and processes must first be deployed, followed by the training and adoption of service practices by customer-facing representatives.

But what is the "right amount" of customer service? What do customers actually need and want? Are we doing the same expensive things for everybody when our MVCs would be even happier with less expensive service (think automated teller machines or Web banking versus service counter at the bank branch)? Taking different customer needs into consideration, what is the least expensive amount for the enterprise to spend on service that works for the customer? Which channel do customers want to use? Can they be easily moved to one that costs less—especially customers with low actual and potential value? And should different levels of service be offered to different kinds of customers? Might customer service mean different things to different customers? When is self-service appropriate? Certainly these and other questions should be addressed if an enterprise is to find the balance of service that serves both the customer and the budget. According to customer relationship management (CRM) experts Seth Shulman and Stanley Brown, "It is . . . essential to ensure that the balance between unassisted/self-serve (including e-mail), agent-assisted, and wholly voice calls (where the customer can dictate instructions) is carefully planned to provide self-serve maximum value to the customer, and not just to reduce costs."[5]

Is "good" customer service in the eyes of the beholder? Some criteria an enterprise could consider from the customer's perspective include:

- Saving time or money
- Accuracy of a transaction
- Speed of service
- Ease of doing business
- Providing better (not just more) information
- Recording and remembering relevant data
- Convenience
- Allowing a choice of ways to do business
- Treating customers as individuals
- Acknowledging and remembering the relationship
- Fixing problems quickly
- Thanking the customer

> Adding or upgrading customer services uniformly for everyone is an expensive way to raise the bar. Better to know what's important to an individual customer and then to make sure that customer gets the services most important to him.

Not all of these elements are equally important to all customers. Any one of these criteria could be a deal breaker to one customer and of no consequence to another. Adding or upgrading customer services uniformly for everyone is an expensive way to raise the bar. Better to know what's important to an individual customer and then to make sure that customer gets the services most important to him.

Many enterprises have learned that the integration of the contact center with all other communication vehicles may be the first step toward successful completion of the customer's mission. For example, live online customer service, text-based chat, and Web callbacks are some of the vehicles that can elevate good, basic customer service to excellent and highly satisfactory service, the latter of which translates into customer retention, growth, loyalty, and profitability.

---

[5]Seth Shulman and Stanley A. Brown, *Customer Relationship Management* (New York: John Wiley & Sons, 2000).

Transformation from Product Centricity to Customer Centricity

Pelin Turunc
Consultant, Peppers & Rogers Group, Europe

Across industries, it has been proven that focusing on optimizing customer commitment and loyalty behavior is the key to both survival and success. A best practice for achieving this is moving from product to customer centricity, through a company-wide transformation of mind-set, and the establishment of organization, process, information, and technology requirements. Challenges arise mainly during the integration and companywide implementation of customer-centric strategies. Research indicates that over 90 percent of senior executives express that having a single, fully integrated corporate view of each customer across the enterprise—which we see as the basis of customer centricity—was either critical to their organization (44 percent) or very important (48 percent). Yet only 2 percent think their organization has achieved full integration and only 10 percent think their organization has achieved even partial integration.[a] But some companies—such as Yahoo!, JetBlue Airways, Southwest Airlines, and Capital One—are noted for having built cultures, processes, and data systems so focused on customers that they are benchmarked by organizations around the world.

One of the companies that successfully implemented customer centricity is a multinational telecommunications and mobile network provider. In the late 2000s, the company was no longer the single operator in its primary region and faced competition from the second Fixed Network Operator Licensee as well as from three other mobile operators. With the saturation of the fixed-line market, decreasing revenues from traditional income sources due to increased competition, and much-criticized service quality that created significant churn risks, the telecommunications company realized the need for a comprehensive customer-centricity strategy that would protect its subscriber base while ensuring acquisition for the next-generation offerings it wanted to launch.

The company defined and began the implementation of a complete customer-centric transformation.[b] As a first step, the current state of customer centricity in the company was assessed within IDIC framework, to understand the company's capability of identifying, differentiating, interacting, and communicating with customers or customer groups. Customer insight development via data analysis and segmentation followed the assessment. At this point, the customer population was assigned to customer segments based on their value, needs, and behaviors, and integrated segments were developed. For example, "cream" was a segment within residential customers who had extensive social networks and frequent calls. Their needs were more in the area of business communication and high-speed Internet usage. Some of the other segments included "mobi," which was made up of medium-value customers with high national mobile usage; "bytes," who had high data needs; and the "move up" segment, made up of currently low-value customers with untapped potential.

Next, the company developed capabilities to lead the change via "Customer Governance and Organizational Adaptation." It wanted to move from product management to segment management in its organization to ensure that customer specific strategies were centrally developed and executed in a coordinated way across the organization. However, it also recognized that it would not be possible to make this switch all at once for all customers. As a result, the company prioritized its segments and started segment management with the most critical segments (particularly regarding industry competition) in its portfolio. Although the company started segment management implementation with high-value segments, its execution plan made sure that customer-centricity principles were implemented for all customer segments along the customer life cycle, resulting in overall service quality improvement. End-to-end customer ownership was defined, and execution took place throughout all channels and customer touchpoints, including the field technicians, contact center, marketing, and sales. Customer portfolio management for mass and business markets was launched, which enabled the company to capture synergies across products and channels, providing one voice to the customer in communication planning and centralized ownership to ensure coordination of customer experience across channels. Understanding the needs of the customers and providing differentiated treatment to all segments was critical in providing the company with a competitive advantage.

Execution included training for employees, reporting and monitoring structures, and the alignment of incentives with the new model's priorities. "Deploying agent-level customer satisfaction measurement" to all customer-facing employees effectively helped incorporate the customer's voice into measuring customer satisfaction at an operational level. Key reporting and tracking metrics and a customer-centricity dashboard were utilized to track portfolio and segment performance and link them to employee performance.

A "Customer Centricity Program Management Office" was established and led the change throughout the whole transformation with project managers and task forces. One of the challenges, which was resistance due to role and responsibility changes, was overcome by timely and frequent communication in the form of workshops and interviews.

---

[a]Forrester Research (July 2004); available at: www.marketingprofs.com.
[b]Based on a client engagement conducted by Peppers & Rogers Group. Name of client disguised for purposes of privacy.

Transition Process for Other Key Enterprise Areas

Finance, research and development (R&D), information technology/information services (IT/IS), and human resources (HR) also need to make the transition to a customer-strategy organization, but these changes are not as readily apparent as those required by the marketing, sales, and customer service organizations. All four areas are directly responsible for *capabilities building*—or how well the organization is able to adapt and change to the new processes. For now, let's look at how the transition affects these other areas of the enterprise in more detail.

Finance

As the organization moves to customer centricity, the finance function takes on new roles within the enterprise, and these are required to help implement a smooth transition:

- Many accounting systems are not set up to measure customer profitability and LTV easily, and the enterprise will need the support of the financial area to help define these metrics.
- Having measured customer value and the rate of customer value, the company will be able to use these measures to determine ROC, which will support TSR. These measures will also provide a stronger level of accountability from the marketers than basic Return on Marketing Investment (ROMI) or Return on Marketing Resources (RMR) or Marketing Resources Management (MRM).
- Having defined and learned to report these metrics, the finance leadership will work with line and staff managers and HR to develop appropriate customer-based compensation and reward systems for employees whose responsibility is to build customer equity and manage customer relationships and retention.

Building a strong customer-centric organization requires financial support to implement new programs and technology, and it requires accounting and management support to ensure costs and results are properly tracked and understood. The finance department will play a critical role in developing and evaluating the business case for implementing customer-centric initiatives.

One of the most important transitions at a customer-centric enterprise has to do with how the firm tracks, understands, and deals with the very concept of value creation. The customer-centric firm is one that understands that it is customers who create all value. But, as we learned in Chapter 11, customers create both short-term value, when they buy things and incur costs today, and they create long-term value, when they change (today) their likelihood of buying in the future—that is, when their lifetime values go up or down. In earlier chapters we also introduced the concept of "customer equity," which represents the sum total of all the lifetime values of a firm's current and future customers, and we showed that because this number actually should be the same as a firm's "enterprise value," the ROC metric, at the enterprise level, could be shown to equal a firm's "total shareholder return." At the enterprise level, the mathematical equations for both these quantities are identified.

So one very important role for the finance department at a customer-centric enterprise is to embrace the idea that the firm's customer equity is an important intangible asset, somewhat like capital. Through the budgeting and planning process, a finance department already monitors the enterprise's financial capital in order to avoid destroying value unintentionally (or using it up too fast). The same kind of discipline should be applied to monitoring the firm's customer equity. Unlike financial capital, however, with the right actions, a firm's customer equity actually can be replenished and increased, even as it is employed to generate current cash flow from customers.

If a finance department could track ROC at the enterprise level, it could help the firm avoid eroding its value as a business over time. Any firm that doesn't track ROC might easily adopt programs that lead to unintended value destruction—programs that may generate better current-period profits at the expense of "using up" even more value from the customer base.

Because customers can be thought of as a productive asset for a business, and customer equity is similar to capital, the ROC metric can be compared to another financial metric already familiar to many large enterprise financial managers, Economic Value Added. "EVA^{TM}," as it is known, is a measure used to account for the cost of the capital required by a business, in order to give companies a more accurate picture of the value they actually create with their operations. Two businesses with identical cash flows are not identically valuable, if one firm requires more capital than the other to produce those cash flows.[6] Even if a firm measures its success in terms of return on assets, its financial results still can be deceiving unless it factors in its cost of capital. According to one EVA proponent, IBM's corporate return on assets was over 11 percent when it was at its most profitable, but at the same time it faced a realistic cost of capital of nearly 13 percent. So even though it seemed "profitable," one could argue that IBM was not actually creating value for its shareholders. A company may be unaware that it is diluting its financial capital unless it tracks EVA. In the same way, a customer-centric enterprise may be unaware it is diluting its customer equity unless it tracks its overall ROC.

Thus, the finance department's role in transitioning to customer centricity is absolutely critical. The department's basic function at any company is to track and understand how the company creates value for its shareholders and then to report the information to those who need to know—including internal managers and the shareholders themselves. To compare the likely economic impact of alternative actions, a company must always know how much capital each action will require, but it should also know how much customer equity will be consumed.

Research and Development

Research and development is another key area in many customer-strategy enterprises. R&D is responsible for creating innovative customer solutions and, therefore, works closely with marketing or sales (as it has done traditionally in the past). However, in the customer-strategy enterprise, it is the depth and quality of customer information that makes the difference. The customer manager group works within its own department to understand common customer needs, and these common needs drive some of the R&D group's work. For some customers, there are needs driving the R&D efforts that will not be seen by other customers for a long time because the most valuable or most growable customers are intimately involved in the R&D work. This work will give these customers a competitive advantage in the marketplace. For example, an MGC (most growable customer) might be a service organization working with a technology supplier to create a wireless network for the sales force and service workers that will enable them to react to their customer

---

[6]Economic Value Added® and EVA® are registered trademarks of Stern Stewart & Co.

needs instantaneously. This capability to respond dynamically will have a competitive advantage.

Information Technology/Information Services

Often, there is a centralized technology function (information technology, or IT) within large enterprises that is responsible for the technology infrastructure (networks, mainframes, routers, etc.). There may be groups (information services, or IS) that are dedicated to functions within the company and that work with the departments to implement applications that help conduct business (HR applications that manage payroll and employee records, other applications that run the order-entry system, logistics and planning, customer interaction center systems, etc.). Both of these functions are directly responsible for enabling the execution of customer strategies.[7]

Many IT/IS organizations go awry when they sponsor the CRM projects. Sometimes IT specialists overestimate their own skills in business strategy, but more often than not, the IT/IS organization runs the project management office (PMO) of the CRM project. This can work when IT/IS actually understands the importance of aligning technology implementation with the business strategy. If the IT organization cannot align the technology implementation and the business strategy, the customer management effort and the entire PMO should be governed by the business end of the enterprise. That said, business units often lack the project management skills to implement large-scale projects—and this expertise is often in the IT/IS area.

> If the IT organization cannot align the technology implementation and the business strategy, the customer management effort and the entire PMO should be governed by the business end of the enterprise.

Human Resources

The customer-strategy enterprise requires knowledge workers—people who will recognize and act on relevant customer information. HR can directly influence the changes in several ways:

- *Redefining the organization.* By taking an active part in defining the new roles and responsibilities, the HR function can map out the transition plans for many key areas of the enterprise. Part of doing this requires that HR help the business define the changes and understand how employees will be affected by those changes.
- *Evaluating whether the company has the capability to change as required by the newly developed customer strategies.* Some important limiting factors may

---

[7]R. J. B. Jean, R. R. Sinkovics, and D. Kim, "Information Technology and Organizational Performance within International Business to Business Relationships: A Review and an Integrated Conceptual Framework," *International Marketing Review* 25, no. 5 (2008): 563–583; Barbara H. Wixom and Hugh J. Watson, "An Empirical Investigation of the Factors Affecting Data Warehousing Success," *MIS Quarterly* 25, no. 1 (March 2001): 17–41.

arise, such as the qualifications of the labor pool available and local salary expectations.

- *During the transition plan, addressing all of the key recruiting, training, and ongoing support issues.* Is there adequate funding to help employees migrate to these new responsibilities? Often these are "line items" in a project plan but are not incorporated into annual training and development budgets or plans.
- *Creating career path opportunities that did not exist before.* The responsibilities of customer interaction center reps or salespeople can grow over time as their skill sets can mature. For the more senior-level executives, a well-rounded employee who has worked directly with customers will become more valued in a customer-value-building organization. Customer-focused thinking will affect recruiting, too.
- *Demanding and rewarding customer-value-building successes.* The HR leaders of a customer-centric company will hold employees accountable not just for activity but for results measured in current net revenue from customers as well as current measures of long-term equity built by customers.
- *Actively trying to manage and develop the corporate culture.* Technology now enables the lowliest employee to leap tall corporate hierarchies with a single click, subverting the power of organization charts and structured personnel policies. This means that corporate culture is even more important when it comes to determining a company's ultimate success. And a corporate culture that will give a customer-centric enterprise the best chance to succeed will be one that is centered on earning and keeping customer trust.

This last point, regarding corporate culture, is worth spending some time on, because it is so critical to success. Importantly, as businesses continue to streamline, automate, and outsource, corporate culture is becoming more important than ever before. A number of factors are at work here, including the increased complexity of modern organizations, greater sophistication of the workforce, globalization, and communications technologies that are accelerating the pace of routine business processes.

We should always remember the fact that, as far as an enterprise's customers are concerned, the ordinary, low-level customer-contact employee they meet at the store, talk to on the phone, or interact with during a service transaction of any kind—that employee *is* the company. And corporate culture is the most potent tool available for ensuring that everyone at the enterprise is pulling in the same direction.

> Culture is what guides employees when there is no policy. It's what they do when no one's looking.

Culture is an elusive yet critical part of any company's nature. Everyone talks about it, but no one can really put a finger on it. You could think of a company's culture as something like the DNA of its business operation. It consists of the shared beliefs and values of managers and employees, usually passed on informally from one to another. A company's culture consists of the mostly unwritten rules and unspoken understandings about "the way we do things around here." Culture is what guides employees when there is no policy. It's what they do when no one's looking.

As a company matures, shared values and beliefs harden into business practices and processes, until workers and managers find it increasingly difficult to describe their own cultures or to separate cultural issues from organizational structure and process issues. At some organizations, managers take a proactive role in guiding or shaping their own corporate cultures, trying to ensure that the informal beliefs and values of employees and managers support the organization's broader mission. The five-part Toyota Way, Wal-Mart's "Three Basic Beliefs," IKEA's aversion to bureaucracy, and the egalitarian HP Way have all contributed importantly to the long-term success of those firms, and managers at each of these companies actively encourage an employee culture based on these value statements.

But regardless of whether a company overtly tries to manage it or not, every organization has a culture. Difficult or conflicting cultures tend to be the biggest factors accounting for why mergers and strategic alliances fail, why change management efforts don't gain traction at a firm, and why major corporate strategy initiatives fizzle. And culture is also one of the biggest single impediments to most customer-centric transitions. In fact, a culture with bad karma will impede virtually every effort a firm could make toward better and more integrated customer-facing processes.

This is because culture is propagated the old-fashioned way—by imitation, that marvelously important survival tool. A new employee comes on board and "learns the ropes" by finding out just how things are done around here. When she encounters a new situation, she'll ask someone who's been around for a while. Successful behaviors are those that are rewarded by the organization, so how an enterprise provides recognition and incentives is important, but just as important is how the employees already working within the firm tend to socialize the values, processes, and rules when it comes to teaching newbies how to fit in.

The culture at an enterprise will reflect how it measures success, how it rewards people, what tasks it considers to be important, what processes it follows to accomplish those tasks, how quickly and effectively it makes decisions, and who approves decisions. The culture will reflect how friendly or competitive employees are with each other, how trusting they are, how much disagreement is tolerated, how much consensus is required, what privileges go with rank, what information is available to whom, what customers or suppliers are the most valued, and what actions are considered out of bounds. Although any enterprise can write down the values it aspires to and post those values on the wall, if the values are to become part of the real culture, then all the company's systems, metrics, processes, rewards, and HR policies must be aligned with them too.[8]

In terms of ensuring success for a customer-centric transition, the HR department needs to take a proactive approach to the enterprise's corporate culture, dealing directly with the many values and issues that lie beneath the surface of the firm's organization chart. Employees view many HR functions unfavorably: HR "polices" the rules and procedures, or it is viewed as a purely administrative function. The transition to customer management can serve as an opportunity for HR to address proactively the many issues that arise in the transition, because the changes are wide and deep. Directly or indirectly, though, they all echo back to the basic relationship issue of trust: Do things right, and do the right thing.

---

[8]Don Peppers and Martha Rogers, Ph.D., *Rules to Break and Laws to Follow: How Your Business Can Beat the Crisis of Short-Termism* (Hoboken, NJ: John Wiley & Sons, 2008), pp. 98–101.

HOW

Dov Seidman
CEO, LRN, and author of HOW

In a rules-based society, we often choose efficiency over value, but, while rules-based governance systems may often serve well the values of fairness and representation, their seeming efficiency hides a deep and important flaw: *We often rely on rules when they are not, in fact, the most efficient or effective solution to getting the result that we desire.* Understanding that flaw is vital to thriving in a world of HOW.

Another problem with rules lies in the fact that they are not created in a very efficient, or systematic, way. Elected bodies, vulnerable to the demands of the political process, write them; those who wield or seek to wield power over others, either militarily or professionally, write them; owners or boards of companies, or manager, chosen by professional meritocracys, write them. William F. Buckley once joked that he would rather be governed by the first 2000 people in the Boston telephone directory than the Harvard faculty—and those Harvard folk are pretty smart people.[a] Despite the best of intentions, people create rules variously and often in *reaction* to behaviors deemed unacceptable to the larger goals of the group. That is why we often find ourselves revising the rules when new conditions reveal their loopholes. Again, let me share a couple of examples.

In 1991, the U.S. Congress issued federal sentencing guidelines to incent good corporate behavior.[b] At that time, the Congress laid out a number of steps and programs corporations could adopt to mitigate their potential liability should they be found guilty of criminal violations. It was a rules-based solution proposed by a rules-based organization: the U.S. government. In response, companies spent enormously on compliance programs (proxies for good behavior, really) and grew large and costly bureaucracies of compliance in an attempt to inoculate themselves against future penalties. This carrot and-stick approach, however, did not lick the problem. Companies added more enforcement, more penalties for getting it wrong, and more incentivizing rewards for getting it right; and yet they did not see substantially more compliance. Despite this huge investment in more compliance programs, since 1991 there have actually been more companies that have run afoul of the law. In 2003, the ad hoc advisory committee to the Federal Sentencing Commission concluded, after studying these compliance programs, that they failed to achieve "effective compliance."

In the wake of a seeming abundance of corporate scandals at the turn of the twenty-first century, the U.S. Congress hastily wrote a new set of rules to govern corporate conduct, the Sarbanes-Oxley bill (commonly called SOX), and revised the sentencing guidelines to react to those transgressions. Corporations again immediately allocated billions to figure out how to comply with the new regulations, just as they did a dozen years before.[c]

(continued)

(Continued)

Consider this smaller example of the same phenomenon: A manager puts up a sign in your company lunchroom that says, "Please Clean the Microwave after You Use It"; then another, "Do Not Put Your Feet on the Tables"; then a third, "Don't Eat Other People's Food." All these rules, and the myriad more little lunchroom dos and don'ts that your manager madly prints out and posts, attempt to codify a single value, *respect*. Rather than declare a common value, such as "Respect Our Common Spaces," most rule makers spend their time chasing human ingenuity, which races along generally complying with the rules while blithely creating new behaviors that exist outside of them.

What do the persnickety lunchroom manager and his signs have in common with the U.S. government and Sarbanes-Oxley? Both reveal a startling truth about rules: Rules respond to behavior; they don't lead it. *Rules don't govern human progress; they govern the human past.* This essential truth shapes our thinking about rules: To succeed, it seems to imply, we must learn to dance with the rules. . . .

> Rules don't govern human progress; they govern the human past.

All organizations of people need a way to govern (companies, societies, and even families are alike in this way), and most governance systems benefit from the inclusion of at least some rules. Let's use a workgroup-as-stadium metaphor. We might agree, for instance, that everyone needs a ticket to get in, people will sit in their own seats, and the game will start at 9 A.M. Without some rules, anarchy rules; fans rush the gates and sit where they please, and people come to work when they feel like it with little regard for the work schedules of others. The game is never played. Most groups articulate their system of governance as a code of conduct. Some of these codes read like the tax code, a set of rules designed to anticipate, prescribe, and proscribe certain behaviors. "Clean your cubicle at the end of every day." "Always wear blue pants." They, like all aggregations of rules, seem at first blush to be an efficient way to codify and communicate the floors of human conduct throughout the hierarchy of the company. Other codes of conduct read more like constitutions, filled with the values and principles that propel the company's efforts. Clothing maker Levi Strauss's code of conduct states, "We are honest and trustworthy. We do what we say we are going to do. Integrity includes a willingness to do the right thing for our employees, brands, the company, and society as a whole, even when personal, professional, and social risks or economic pressures confront us."[d] These general statements of principle can, at first, seem vague and not immediately or easily applicable to the various day-to-day decisions a worker must face. The nature of the language a group chooses, however, exerts a remarkable and powerful influence on the conduct that follows from it.

The language of policies and rules is the language of *can* and *can't, right* versus *wrong*. It's a binary language with little room for nuance or shades of meaning. That is why it is inadequate to describe the full richness of human behavior. We are, as people, so much more than right or wrong. When you get stuck in the language of permissibility and prohibition *(can* versus *can't)*, you get stuck thinking in relation to rules rather than in the realm of true human potential. You can discuss a lawsuit in terms of utility—*"Can* we fight this effectively in court?"—but it is quite another thing to discuss it in terms of your values—"Given what we believe, *should* we fight this in court?" The first approach prompts thinking in relation to rules and codes; the second opens up thinking in relation to what is most important to an organization's or individual's core values and long-term success. In that difference—the difference between *can* and *should*—lies an extraordinarily important step toward thriving in a world of HOW: *True freedom lies not in the absence of constraint; true freedom lies in the transcendence of rules-based thinking.*

> True freedom lies not in the absence of constraint; true freedom lies in the transcendence of rules-based thinking.

Thinking in the language of *can* versus *can't* predisposes you to perceive challenges in a certain way and respond within narrow avenues. Thinking in and speaking the language of values—the language of *should* and *shouldn't* instead of the language of *can* and *can't*—opens up a wide spectrum of possible thought, a spectrum that encompasses the full colors of human behavior as opposed to the black-and-white responses of rules. This spectrum can lead to truly creative and innovative solutions to challenges.

RULES ARE EXTERNAL

They are made by others.

They present us with a puzzle to be solved and loopholes to be found.

WE ARE AMBIVALENT ABOUT RULES

*We know we need some and we want others to play by them,
but we say, "Rules are meant to be broken."*

RULES ARE REACTIVE

They respond to past events.

RULES ARE BOTH OVER- AND UNDERINCLUSIVE

Because they are proxies, they cannot be precise.

(continued)

(Continued)

PROLIFERATION OF RULES IS A TAX ON THE SYSTEM

Few people can remember them all. We lose productivity when we stop to look them up.

RULES ARE TYPICALLY PROHIBITIONS

They speak to can *and* can't.

We view them as confining and constricting.

RULES REQUIRE ENFORCEMENT

With laxity, they lose credibility and effectiveness.

They necessitate expensive bureaucracies of compliance.

RULES SPEAK TO BOUNDARIES AND FLOORS

But they create inadvertent ceilings.

We can't legislate "The sky's the limit."

THE ONLY WAY TO HONOR RULES IS TO OBEY THEM EXACTLY

They speak to coercion and motivation.

The inspiration to excel must come from somewhere else.

TOO MANY RULES BREEDS OVERRELIANCE

We think, "If it mattered, they would have made a rule."

Source: Reprinted with permission from Dov Seidman, *How* (Hoboken, NJ: John Wiley & Sons, 2007), pp. 85–86, 90, 95–96.
[a]Jeffrey Hart, *The Making of the American Conservative Mind: National Review and Its Times* (Wilmington, DE: ISI Books, 2005).
[b]United States Sentencing Commission, "Organizational Guidelines"; available at: www.ussc.gov/orgguide.htm.
[c]Laurie Sullivan, "Compliance Spending to Reach $28 Billion by 2007," *Information Week*, March 2, 2006.
[d]"Levi Strauss & Co," www.levistrauss.com/Company/ValuesAndVision.aspx.

Managing Employees in the Customer-Strategy Enterprise

The road to becoming a customer-value-building enterprise is fraught with speed bumps. We have shown so far how the transition requires a new organizational infrastructure—one that is populated by customer managers and capabilities managers who fully support the migration from day one. The enterprise moving to a customer-strategy business model will likely require new capabilities for relating to customers individually. It will need to assess where the gaps lie in its established capabilities so it can improve its focus on customers, not just products, and build profitable, long-term customer relationships.

Organizations used to be simpler to manage, because most tasks were routine, most problems could be anticipated, and desired outcomes could be spelled out in official policy—the "rules" we just read about in Dov Seidman's section. An employee's job was to follow the policy. But with the advent of new information and communications technologies, more and more of these routine tasks have been automated or outsourced, and the resulting organizations are slimmer and more efficiently competitive. What remains at most firms, and will continue to characterize them, are the functions and roles that cannot be automated or outsourced. These are the kinds of jobs that require employees to make decisions that cannot be foreseen or mapped out and therefore aren't spelled out in the standard operating processes. These jobs require nonroutine decision making. Many of them involve high-concept roles and other functions that simply can't be covered by a rule book.

In *A Whole New Mind*, author Dan Pink persuasively describes this new, postautomation, postoutsourcing "Conceptual Age." It may once have been true that information workers would inherit the world, but today's information workers can live in Ireland or China, and even doctors and lawyers are finding their jobs increasingly threatened by computers and online substitutes. Indian technology schools turn out some 350,000 new engineers a year, and most of them are willing to work for $15,000 annual salaries. So what type of work can't be outsourced or automated? Pink says the type of work that will characterize successful executives in the future (at least in the United States and other advanced Western economies) is work that involves creativity and sensitivity and requires skills in design, entertainment, storytelling, and empathy. This idea makes sense. Consider lawyers, for instance: Legal research and paperwork can be outsourced to Ireland or India, but cases have to be argued to juries in the courtroom, in person. Or doctors: X-rays can be evaluated remotely and diagnoses rendered, but bedside manner has to happen, well, bedside.[9]

This trend is already showing up in employment figures. At least within the U.S. economy, production and transactional jobs, which recently made up about 60 percent of the workforce, are being automated rapidly, while the other 40 percent of jobs, involving nonroutine decision making, have grown two and a half times faster in recent years and pay 55 percent to 70 percent more than routine jobs.[10] These nonroutine jobs require workers to deal with ambiguous situations and

---

[9]Daniel H. Pink, *A Whole New Mind: Why Right-Brainers Will Rule the Future* (New York: Riverhead, 2005), pp. 36–37.
[10]Bradford C. Johnson, James M. Manyike and Lareina A. Yee, "The Next Revolution in Interactions," *McKinsey Quarterly*, no. 4 (2005): 21.

difficult issues—problems that often have no direct precedent or at least no "correct" solution.

A company can automate the contact report a sales rep has to file, but it can't get a computer to look into a client's eye and judge whether to push for the sale right away or ask another question first. Jobs like this require judgment, creativity, and initiative on the part of the employee. As a result, according to one study, many companies are turning their attention to "making their most talented, highly-paid workers more productive," because this is the surest way to gain competitive advantage.[11]

Companies have spent the last several decades economizing, streamlining, and automating their more routine, core processes, but the cost and efficiency advantages they secured from these activities were short-lived, as the benefits of automation quickly permeated whole industries and their competitors became equally efficient. Efficiency, cost cutting, running lean and mean—these are just the greens fees required to remain in the game. By contrast, when a company gains an advantage by making its nonroutine decision-making employees more productive and effective, that company is building a competitive advantage described by three authors writing in the *McKinsey Quarterly* as likely being:

> ...*more enduring, for their rivals will find these improvements much harder to copy. This kind of work is undertaken, for example, by managers, salespeople, and customer service reps, whose tasks are anything but routine. Such employees interact with other employees, customers, and suppliers and make complex decisions based on knowledge, judgment, experience, and instinct.*[12]

If an enterprise can figure out how to manage these "conceptual age" employees better, in other words, it will have an advantage that is hard for a competitor to see or imitate. The secret, however, is not technology and process, because it just can't be spelled out like that. If it could be documented in advance and defined as a process, then it could be automated, right?

Just as the customer-strategy enterprise strives to keep and grow its customers, so too must it seek to keep and grow its best employees. The truly customer-centric organization will be better able to do this, however, because of its very corporate mission. If the firm's mission is encapsulated by earning the trust of customers, always acting in the interest of customers, this philosophy itself can provide the underpinnings for a culture of trust to permeate the entire organization. If employees are taught that every problem at the firm needs to be tackled from the standpoint of respecting the interests of the customer involved, then it is only a very short step to suggest that employee problems should be addressed from the standpoint of respecting the interests of the employee.

Jonathan Hornby, visionary and performance management expert at SAS Institute, cites an example of a bank in which Department A believed Department B was a drain on resources (and this attitude was likely a drain on company culture). Their manager used a tool created by Joel Barker called the Implications Wheel®, where employees were prompted to specify the first-order, second-order, and third-order

---

[11]Ibid.
[12]Ibid.

implications of a certain action—in this case, eliminating Department B. By the time both departments completed this exercise, Department A realized that their potential customers came directly from Department B, and they changed their position of their own accord. Strategic managers will come up with similar creative ways to encourage trust and transparency between employees as well as with customers.[13]

Trustworthiness is not an elastic concept. It doesn't stretch. No one ever has just "some" integrity.[14] You either have integrity or you don't. You are either trustworthy or you are not trustworthy. And if earning the trust of customers is the central mission at a company—the primary way it creates value and grows—then it is highly likely that this business will also enjoy the trust of its employees. And earning and keeping the trust of employees may be the single most critical step to having a productive and value-creating organization.

Never forget, also, that employees are not only networked with each other, they're networked with the rest of the known universe. The same interactive technologies that empower customers to share their experiences electronically with other customers also empower the employees at any firm to share their own experiences with the employees at other firms. The old "command and control" philosophies of management—philosophies that might have worked reasonably well throughout most of the twentieth century, are no longer very effective. In November 2003, for example, Doug Monahan, founder and chairman of tech marketing firm Sunset Direct, sent this charming message to employees:

> *I expect my computers to be used for work only. Should you receive a personal call, keep it short. Should you receive a personal email, I expect the email either not answered, or a brief note telling whoever is sending you emails at work to stop immediately. Should I go through the machines, which I assure you, I will be doing, and I find anything to the contrary, you will be terminated immediately. For those who think I am kidding, and do not get with this program, I promise you that by Christmas Eve 8:00 you will be gone.[15]*

Not surprisingly, it's difficult for a company such as Sunset Direct to trust employees. And for good reason. In such a setting, it's nearly impossible for anyone to feel good about anybody; and, whatever culture develops, it certainly won't be based on trust. Soon after this ominous threat was issued, however, and in direct violation of the edict, a Sunset Direct employee used one of the company's computers to post Monahan's message on InternalMemos.com, where it has now become a legend. Doug Monahan has realized immortality on the Web, as Scrooge.[16]

---

[13]Jonathan Hornby, *Radical Action for Radical Times: Expert Advice for Creating Business Opportunity in Good or Bad Economic Times*, (Cary, NC: SAS Institute, Inc., 2009), 10-13.

[14]We are indebted to Lt. Gen. (Ret.) J. W. Kelly, who made comments about the inelasticity of integrity in his commitment dinner speech to USAFA Class of 2007, August 9, 2005, USAFA, Colorado Springs, as reported in the *Association of Graduates Magazine*.

[15]Adam Horowitz, "101 Dumbest Moments in Business," *Business 2.0* (January/February 2004): 81.

[16]This section was adapted from Peppers and Rogers, *Rules to Break and Laws to Follow*, Chapters 6 and 11.

Contrast that with the leaders at the companies that have made the lists of "The 100 Best Companies to Work For" and "100 Best Companies for Working Mothers." Carlson Companies has been on both lists. Marilyn Carlson Nelson was at the helm of Carlson, Inc. as its chief executive officer from 1998 to 2008. Here are her views about it.

The Everyday Leader

Marilyn Carlson Nelson
Chairman, Carlson, Inc.

A favorite quote of mine is "We are defined by what we tolerate." Leaders who forget this truism do so at the risk of their organization. Like the ever-observant child, the organization always knows when behavior is being allowed that is inconsistent with its purported values. And, ultimately, it will undermine all the good that you might do.

The only sustainable way to develop trust is for leaders to model it. It cannot be imposed. It must be inspired, rewarded, and recognized in as many settings as possible, up and down the organization.

In my book, *How We Lead Matters*, I set out to write about the leadership moments I have experienced or witnessed in others during my career. Soon into the project, I realized that leadership moments don't just happen on the top floor, they also happen on the shop floor; they happen at the board table and the kitchen table. Leadership choices are being made every day by each one of us.

The complexity of the choices made by those in charge that resulted in the Great Recession of 2009 will no doubt engage scholars for a long time to come. One conclusion, however, is immediately evident: Leadership at the top of these failed institutions can be rightly blamed for irresponsible and gluttonous behavior. But there were many others throughout these organizations who tolerated the practices—who had an opportunity to make leadership decisions on a daily basis, but who instead became complicit in their silence.

The truth is for all of us, regardless of title or position, our legacy of leadership will not be written some distant day in a moment of great triumph; it is being written with each passing day.

The Long View

It's been said that the mark of a true leader is thinking well beyond his or her years—that is, establishing a leadership culture in an organization that becomes the organization's hallmark.

When we heard the news at Carlson headquarters that the World Trade Center towers had been hit on September 11, 2001, we called immediately for a phone bridge to communicate with our employees in more than 150 countries. Our instructions were simple: Take care of each other. Take care of our customers. Take care of our competitors' customers. Take care of your communities.

Finally, we told them that if we lost communication, we were authorizing them to act according to Carlson's credo: "Whatever you do, do with integrity. Wherever you go, go as a leader. Whomever you serve, serve with caring. And never, ever give up."

I think back to an article written for *Fortune* magazine by the business author Jim Collins, who has made a career of studying companies that last and thrive across decades. . . . Speaking to his methodology, he noted that he deliberately excluded some currently prominent names from the list: Microsoft's Bill Gates, GE's Jack Welch, and others like them. His rationale: Leaders cannot be truly judged until 10 years have passed after their tenure.

Only then can a leader's impact be known. Did the company or organization stay the course? Did it produce other leaders who were just as successful?

When we think about the world's great leaders, did their impact not become better understood decades later? Only time made clear who was truly great.

Rather than expend all their energies on the short term, leaders who aspire to greatness beyond their time might well be advised to approach the world with this curiosity: What will generations say about them "years beyond their ken"?

Source: Adapted from Marilyn Carlson Nelson with Deborah Cundy, *How We Lead Matters: Reflections on a Life of Leadership* (McGraw-Hill, 2008), pp. 49, 61. Marilyn Carlson Nelson is chairman of Carlson, Inc., a global travel and hospitality company that includes such brands as Radisson and Regent Hotels, Country Inns & Suites, T.G.I. Friday's restaurants, and Carlson Wagonlit Travel.

Change is important but never easy. Many believe that change can revitalize the enterprise to compete in ways that it never could have before. Resistance to change, however, is inevitable, as many employees who oppose or resist the new infrastructure will step forward. How does an enterprise cope with these changes? How does an executive manage employees in this new business environment?

Summary

We have been reinforcing the idea that a customer-based initiative is not an off-the-shelf solution but rather a business strategy that will imbue an enterprise with an ever-improving capability to know and respond to its customers' individual needs. Executed through a cyclical process, customer-strategy principles can provide an enterprise with a powerful source of competitive advantage. But doing so requires organizational commitment, careful planning, and, ultimately, a well-orchestrated array of people, culture, processes, metrics, and technology. Successful implementation comes only with an understanding of the nature of this comprehensive business model. The transition team will have to encourage a more integrative, collaborative attitude among all employees, perhaps by establishing a multidepartment task force that can standardize a way for reporting customer information and other related issues. Ultimately, throughout the entire transition, the team will need to revisit each of the steps and refine and revise how it is executing them. After all, the transition to a customer-strategy architecture never really ends.

Food for Thought

1. Choose an organization and draw its organizational chart. How would that chart have to change in order to facilitate customer management and to make sure people are evaluated, measured, and compensated for building the value of the customer base? Consider these questions:
   a. If a customer's value is measured across more than one division, is one person placed in charge of that customer relationship?
   b. Should the enterprise establish a key account-selling system?
   c. Should the enterprise underwrite a more comprehensive information system, standardizing customer data across each division?
   d. Should the sales force be better automated? Who should set the strategy for how a sales rep interacts with a particular customer?
   e. Is it possible for the various Web sites and call centers operated by the company to work together better?
   f. Should the company package more services with the products it sells, and if so, how should those services be delivered?[17]
2. For the same organization, consider the current culture. Can you describe it? Would that have to change for the organization to manage the relationship with and value of one customer at a time? If so, how?
3. At the same organization, assume the company rank-orders customers by value and places the MVCs behind a picket fence. What happens to customers and to customer portfolio managers behind that picket fence?
4. In an organization, who should "own" the customer relationship? What does that mean?

NOTE: Because this topic spans two chapters, we have included the Food for Thought questions twice for ease of use.

Glossary

Customer's point of view   Thinking the way the customer thinks, within the context of daily business processes as well as customer interactions. *Customer advocacy* is the set of actions that results from taking the customer's point of view, or treating the customer the way you would want to be treated, if you were the customer.

---

[17]Don Peppers, Martha Rogers, Ph.D., and Bob Dorf, *The One to One Fieldbook* (New York: Doubleday, 1999).

Customer portfolio management　The deliberate management of a *portfolio of customers* to optimize the value of each customer portfolio to the firm. By utilizing the feedback from each customer, a portfolio manager analyzes the differing values and needs of each customer and sets up the best *treatment* for each customer to realize the largest return on each relationship, often in an automated way using *business rules*.

Picket fence　An imaginary boundary around customers selected for management. Customers outside the picket fence likely will be treated as customers have always been treated, using mass marketing and traditional customer care; each customer behind the picket fence, however, will be the management responsibility of a customer portfolio manager, whose primary responsibility will be to keep and grow each of the customers assigned to her.

CHAPTER 15

Where Do We Go from Here?

It is better to know some questions than to know all the answers.

—James Thurber

As long as this book is, it could easily have been longer. We are learning more every day about how to grow the value of the customer base, how to interact with customers more effectively, and how to integrate a customer-centric view of the business into an enterprise's daily operations as well as its long-term strategic planning. In this last chapter, as we close our discussion of managing customer relationships in the interactive age, we need to address one more topic: Where do we go from here? Given the difficulties of transitioning to a customer-centric philosophy of doing business that any enterprise will encounter, what are the traits and behaviors that will be needed by a company's future leaders, including its marketing, sales, and service executives? What guiding principles can help a company deal with the as-yet-unforeseen technological innovations and business process changes likely to continue disrupting the economic environment throughout your own upcoming business career? If we've learned anything from clients, research, and academia in the past 10 years, it's this: Building customer value and becoming more customer oriented is not a destination, it's a journey. And it's very, very difficult to do well. But the payoff can be huge. More and more, the question is not how much it will cost to become a customer-strategy enterprise but how much will it cost *not* to. We can't fit everything we know today about building customer value, or about how to become a customer-strategy enterprise, into this book, because—as we said at the outset of this book—we are learning more every day. Moreover, within months or even weeks of this revised edition going to press, we're certain there will be still more technological innovations in interaction, customization, social media, and peer-to-peer production that we haven't addressed. What we've tried to do so far in this text is to establish a basic foundation for understanding what customer management is, how it helps an organization, and how companies benefit from it.

A lot of "real" leadership is needed. As stated repeatedly, whether we call this customer-strategy journey CRM or one-to-one or demand-chain management, it can be a real challenge. Everybody claims to know what it is. Every consulting

> **B**uilding customer value and becoming more customer oriented is not a destination, it's a journey.

company and ad agency offers expensive advice about it. Every boss thinks she understands how to go about this. It reminds us so much of the principles first described by Geoffrey Moore in his challenging books about "crossing the chasm" and "inside the tornado" that we asked him to think of managing customers in those terms. Here are his insights.

Managing Customer Relationships: The Technology Adoption Life Cycle

Geoffrey A. Moore
Managing Director, TCG Advisors

Customer relationship management is both a business approach and a technology infrastructure. In either form, it has the potential of being a disruptive innovation, creating opportunities for dramatic increases in competitive advantage but also creating incompatibilities with existing systems. As such, its adoption can be expected to follow the patterns of the Technology Adoption Life Cycle, a series of twists and turns that can bewilder and confuse an unwary management team.

The purpose of this section is to present a summary view of customer centricity in interaction with the life cycle model, with the goal of empowering management teams to leverage it in two ways. First, we look at customer relationship management (CRM) as *a source of disruptive innovation in itself* and see, by determining where it is in the adoption life cycle in a particular industry's sector, how a firm can best take advantage of its potential to improve a company's performance. Second, we consider the use of CRM as *a tool for coping with disruptive innovation* coming from some other source, that is, as a set of facilities for managing customers and the company through a difficult technology transition. By the end of this section, the goal is for the management team to be fully versed in the ins and outs of technology adoption forces as they might impact the journey to customer-focused management.[a]

Customer Relationship Management as a Source of Disruptive Innovation: ⌈Reengineering from a Transaction to a Relationship Model⌋

Let's first think of CRM in relatively broad terms, incorporating both a software systems view, in which interactions at multiple touchpoints with the customer are automated, and a management view, in which the relationship with the customer itself becomes something to be managed (or what was called, earlier in this book, operations CRM and analytical CRM). In this broad sense, companies adopting CRM must reengineer not only their software but their entire business approach, migrating from a transaction-based to a relationship-based model.

This migration is crucial for any company that plans to serve the small- to medium-size business market. Unlike consumers, these customers spend enough on individual purchases to warrant consultative sales attention when they are ready to buy. But unlike larger enterprises, they do not spend often enough to warrant continuous sales coverage of the kind that would know when they are ready to buy. What is needed is a CRM system that continually monitors and updates the state of the prospect's purchase readiness and then alerts the relevant sales channel when it is time to call. For many companies, doing this requires significant reengineering of the current ways of doing things.

Such reengineering is disruptive to established roles and responsibilities, metrics and compensation, organizational structure, business process ownership, and planning and reporting, to name just a few. As such, it will win enthusiastic support from early adopters, skeptical wariness from conservative late adopters, and a cautious wait-and-see response from the pragmatist majority. This is the classic self-segregation of any community faced with disruption into a set of "adoption response" postures.

The end result of this self-segregation is that there are four inflection points in the unfolding of any disruptive innovation, each of which rewards a different management approach. It behooves the team implementing CRM to understand this model and to select which of the four points best represents their current situation, and thus which management approach is likely to yield the best outcome. Here's how it plays out.

1. THE EARLY MARKET The early market for adopting disruptive innovations is led by technology enthusiasts and visionaries. The former engage with a new system out of sheer love for exploring its properties. The latter engage whenever they see a chance to exploit a new paradigm to gain a dramatic competitive advantage in their line of business. The two working together create the energy behind early market adoption.

If the vendors serving a given sector or region are late to adopting CRM, then a particular company has an opportunity to get ahead of the competition and set them back on their heels. In order for this outcome to come to pass, however, the effort *must* have the sponsorship of a visionary line-of-business executive with sufficient seniority and power to drive through rapid adoption despite internal resistance from less enthusiastic colleagues. Without this support, an early market project is doomed.

With this support—typically garnered by the opportunity to create a 10X return albeit involving substantial risk—the key going forward is to treat the entire effort not as buying a product, or even as implementing a solution, but rather as undertaking a custom project. The focus of the project is the 10X return, and every vendor involved must sign up for that goal. The general contractor for the effort should be a systems integrator with strong business reengineering skills, someone who has the confidence of the executive sponsor regarding the vision but who also has the skills to win support from the pragmatic rank and file who must implement the new processes.

The desired end result of this effort is a system unique to the sponsoring customer implemented well in advance of any other company in the competitive set. It is a major undertaking, and there is no guarantee of success—hence the

(continued)

(Continued)

importance of having a genuine opportunity for getting a 10X return. This is not for the faint of heart, but it is for those who live by the saying "Faint heart ne'er won fair lady."

In each case of a company that has successfully leveraged CRM, the sponsoring company was able to leapfrog its competition by using CRM to create a compelling disruption in established business practices.

Today, opportunities to be first with basic Learning Relationships and improved customer experiences per se are not plentiful. But that does not mean there are not early adopter segments in the sector. One example involves supplementing Web-based self-service systems with avatar-based support from companies like VirtuOz or Conversive, as companies like eBay and American Express are demonstrating. Another is bringing CRM into real time by combining online sales and marketing into a single console system where agents own a campaign from lead generation through to completed sale, as companies like Genius.com and Marketo are enabling.

2. CROSSING THE CHASM   Once innovations have been deployed by the first movers, there are no more rewards for early adoption, and the enthusiasts and visionaries move on to greener pastures. The next adoption strategy to come online is that of the *pragmatists*. Their approach is to convert to new technologies as soon as they know other people like them are doing so. It is a bit like dances in junior high: Everybody is willing to go out on the dance floor, just as long as somebody else from their group goes first. This creates a hiatus in adoption that we have termed the *chasm*.

To cross the chasm means to get the first herd of pragmatist adopters to switch over to the new technology. Experience has taught us that this first group will make the move only under duress. Specifically, the classic profile is that of department managers in charge of a *broken, mission-critical business process* who have been served notice that they better fix this process soon or management will find someone else who can.

In the case of customer-centricity, a department manager could be in charge of customer service, customer support, lead generation, customer renewals, or any number of other customer-specific or general business functions. All these processes are prone to break under the pressure of overanxious product managers or sales teams. Customer service processes often break, for example, when product managers give prospects lots of options when their back-end delivery systems are not capable of handling the complexity reliably. The result is a raft of customer shipments that do not match the customer's order, leading to irate calls and returned merchandise. The advent of self-service order entry over the Web has only driven this problem deeper into many industries.

Another problem area is customer support. Here the challenge derives from the complexity of the final installed system. In the personal computer (PC) industry, for example, the total number of possible combinations of different vendors that might have component subsystems interacting inside a single PC is astronomical. As a result, when something does not work, it is enormously challenging to track down the root cause. In the early 1990s, this led to 40-minute hold times just to get hold of a customer support operator who, sadly, often had to refer the problem on to someone else, leading to all kinds of customer unhappiness.

Lead generation is a third problem area. Typically mass mailings result in weakly qualified responses that either must be further qualified at more expense or turned over to salespeople (who will summarily trash them). Each new campaign effectively starts from scratch because there is no CRM system to monitor and update the behavior of the prospect relative to prior campaigns. For consumer markets driven by product promotions, this is not a big problem, but for business-oriented markets, it is a huge drain.

Finally, customer renewals, as Fred Reichheld has been trying to teach us for the better part of two decades, are the sweet spot of all established enterprises. And yet many companies—particularly those that sell through indirect sales channels—do not invest in systems to maintain the state of the customer's current inventory. Thus when it comes time to renew, they often miss the window, leaving the transaction open to the competition.

If an industry has seen its early adopters of CRM technology but has not widely adopted customer strategy as a standard way of doing business, these kinds of issues would drive executives to make the leap. In such cases, it is key that they band together, even when they are direct competitors, to make sure that the solution vendors work together to provide what we call the *whole product*. This is a complete, end-to-end solution that addresses a common set of needs specific to a particular segment. Some will end up paying a premium to get this solution because, since it is specific to one segment, vendors cannot amortize their expenses across a large customer base. But it will be well worth it if it fixes the broken, mission-critical process once and for all. The only losing behavior here is to get 90 percent of the total solution on the cheap and never get the last 10 percent put in place.

Specialized forms of CRM these days are showing up in places you might not initially think of as customer oriented. One of these is fraud detection, a technology of "anti-customer" intimacy but one that has become increasingly critical to online businesses. Here companies like FinSphere are leveraging customer data such as the physical presence of a cell phone to help determine whether the person proffering a credit card in your name is likely to be you.

3. INSIDE THE TORNADO If a company did not choose to be an early adopter, and if it wasn't forced to be a chasm crosser, then likely that company is a pragmatist not under duress, waiting to switch to the new systems as soon as everyone else does. Well, guess what—they are! All of a sudden everyone in your sector has a project under way to do CRM, and you get the call from upstairs: *Where's ours?*

This is what defines a tornado: the stampede of the pragmatist herd. That, in turn, creates a vortex of demand that sucks every vendor in the space into a frenzy of activity, trying to create sufficient supply for what has become a sudden, overwhelming escalation in demand. Today that pressure is probably less to get on CRM per se than to get on a Software-as-a-Service (SaaS) version of

(continued)

(Continued)

CRM from Salesforce.com or Oracle or to expand your marketing campaigns to include social media, whether through blogs, or Facebook, or Twitter. One hot new property here is Big Tent, which has brought together "Moms' Networks" in all the major metropolitan areas of the United States, allowing CPG (consumer packaged goods) firms to interact with their target prospects in a variety of customer-intimate ways.

Whatever the hot new thing, the pressure to get on the bandwagon is intense, and there is little time to do a thorough review of the options. As a result, customers increasingly "ask around" to learn who is the market leader, the vendor nobody ever got fired for choosing. That company's sales go through the roof, even though it becomes increasingly onerous to deal with, simply because it is the *safe buy*.

This safety goes well beyond immediate issues of reliability. As the industry goes forward, experience shows that everyone other than the market leader has an increasingly difficult time keeping partners committed to keeping its side of the interfaces up to date. Moreover, service providers will invest the bulk of their training and development to build a practice around the market-leading system, further weakening the competitors' position. As a result, those companies' customers get a weaker and weaker whole product, regardless of how good the core product might be.

The object lesson here is simple. If a company is buying during a tornado, then it should lean heavily toward the market leader unless it's in a niche that has special requirements, which the leader is unmotivated to meet. In that case, a strong niche vendor that is willing to make a commitment to a customer firm's vertical is a better choice. Finally, if the technology is open systems, such that there are clones of the market leader that are totally compatible with its technology, a firm can afford to use them to shop price, especially for the less critical installations.

A great example of a mass market in need of CRM system support today is the small business community itself. It must squeeze every dollar out of return from its marketing spend if it is to thrive and grow. E-mail campaigns from outsourcing vendors like Constant Contact help extend their reach, and that company is being thrust forward by a tornado of demand. Right behind it are companies like InfusionSoft, which specialize in the ongoing nurturing of those prospects as well as the Rolodex of customers that come out of them.

4. ON MAIN STREET Once technology has passed through the tornado, it can be classified as adopted, and all subsequent purchases are postadoption. That simply means that the technology is assimilated and no longer poses special challenges to any customer rolling out a new system. For pragmatists, this is a time of buying more of whatever they already bought during the tornado or chasm-crossing phase. But for conservatives and laggards who held off, this is now their time to enter the market.

Why would one wait so long? Actually, if business processes can function effectively without investing in new systems, the longer a firm waits, the better the deal to be had once it buys in. Every year, that is, systems become more reliable, more highly featured, and cheaper. Moreover, if a company has a system that works today, what is the gain in subjecting yourself to a new learning curve? Better to focus that energy on some business process where you can get an immediate payback.

Eventually, however, the world comes to expect a certain minimum set of technologies, simply to get along, and, when that happens, then the conservatives must make the change. For example, increasingly it has become expected that companies maintain presence on social networking sites. Companies that are putting up Web sites for the first time this year are gaining no competitive advantage by so doing. They are not fixing a broken, mission-critical process. Nor are they going with the herd, which actually went several years ago. Instead they are simply dealing with a hygiene requirement. That is classic late adoption strategy.

If a company does choose to adopt late, the key is not to overadopt. Even though the vendors are now touting second- and third-generation capabilities, you probably want to restrict your implementation to first-generation ones. It is not that the software won't work, and not that you cannot learn how to work it. Instead it is the impact on the rest of your business processes that you need to be mindful of.

> It is not that the software won't work, and not that you cannot learn how to work it. Instead it is the impact on the rest of your business processes that you need to be mindful of.

By contrast, pragmatists who are now rolling out their second or third upgrade will be very interested in these new capabilities. The truth is, as the life cycle moves onto Main Street, most of the productivity gains promised during the tornado have yet to be achieved, in large part because the software wasn't quite there yet at the time. Well, now it is, and now is the time to actively engage the end users in picking and choosing which features would make them more effective in their work. And because the technology is more mature, it should permit greater mass customization, meaning that different groups should be able to customize the system in different ways to make their workflows more productive.

All the major CRM application vendors that rose to prominence in the CRM tornado years prior to the tech meltdown at the beginning of the new century are now on Main Street, be they Oracle's Siebel, SAP, or Salesforce.com. Their systems are now becoming platforms upon which next-generation capabilities can be built. This means they will be in place for a very long time to come.

Overall, then, the Technology Adoption Life Cycle creates four natural buying points during the evolution of a new technology's acceptance into the marketplace. Each point offers a different motive for buying in at that time, which might be summarized in this way:

1. *In the Early Market*. Go ahead of the herd for a dramatic competitive advantage.
2. *Crossing the Chasm*. Fix a broken, mission-critical business process.

(continued)

(Continued)

3. *Inside the Tornado.* Go with the herd to get on the new infrastructure.
4. *On Main Street.* Go after the herd to get better values.

Customer relationship management systems are no exception to this pattern. To be sure, depending on where they are in the life cycle in a particular sector, some of these options may now be past, but the key idea is to align corporate expectations and intentions with what is deliverable during each phase. You can't come late to the party and expect competitive advantage, just as you can't come early and expect to get better values. By taking some time to think through the various adoption points and their corresponding opportunities, a company can increase the chances that a CRM implementation is a resounding success.

> You can't come late to the party and expect competitive advantage, just as you can't come early and expect to get better values.

On Main Street: One-to-One Relationships

Technology adoption life cycles are an anomaly in themselves. In high tech, to be sure, they are frequent occurrences, but outside that sector, they are not. Oil and gas have not been disrupted in our lifetime, and even with all the emphasis on green energy, I do not expect it will be. Education and healthcare continue to be conducted in undisrupted ways. Online retail opens up a major new channel to the customer, but at the end of the day it is still retail, and the supermarkets full of consumer packaged goods of today would be perfectly navigable by my grandmother, were she here to walk their aisles. And so it is that most markets most of the time live on Main Street. And it is here that one-to-one customer relationships come into their own.

The natural target of Main Street marketing is the *conservative* in the Technology Adoption Life Cycle. This is a customer who is predisposed to keep things as they are. The key to Main Street, then, is that the core offer has become so assimilated into business as usual or life as usual that we no longer register the thing itself as innovative or differentiable. But since choice depends on differentiation from the customer's view, and since margins depend on differentiation from the vendor's view, innovation does not stop: It just relocates.

There are two classic directions innovation takes on Main Street. One is in the direction of ever-increasing operational excellence, up and down the supply chain, seeking to wring out costs so that one can squeeze out a half point of margin at the point of sale. If this seems like a lot of work for a small outcome, recognize that on Main Street, the volume of purchases can be huge, and thus even a small increment of improvement, if it truly scales across the entire market, can have major impact. This is the focus of the operations and finance people for the most part.

The second direction is championed by marketing (and the two are by no means mutually exclusive). And that is toward ever-increasing customer intimacy, improving not the product itself so much as the *customer's experience of the product*. Experience, however, lives halfway between the thing in itself and the mind of the experiencer, and thus no two people ever share the exact same experience. So, if companies are to deliver better and better customer experience, one of the things they need to do is learn more about each of their customers.

For a long time this has been the home turf of demographic information. Because human beings are social animals, and because we take a lot of our values from the community we live in—indeed, often work to conform to the community's values when they are in conflict with our own—demographics works. The big new thing here is that our demographic neighborhoods have shifted from the physical world of zip codes to the virtual world of Web sites.

If we have learned nothing else from years of living with the Web, it is to have deep respect for its potential to set up highly intimate relationships that at the same time retain anonymity. That is, while customers want what they want, they do not want to bare their private secrets in order to get it. How is that possible? One major path is through self-service. And that is what the Internet is best at (see Chapter 8).

Self-service (and crowd service) begins with options, and so in the first generation of customized marketing systems, we have seen a proliferation of *offer configuration* systems. But these systems can become so complex they can bewilder the user, and so the next generation focuses on *ease of use*. That is more or less where we are today. The truth is, however, customers don't want ease of use except in the areas they want to express a new preference. Everywhere else they want the system either to *default* to the best choice or to *remember* what they chose last time. And this is the focus of an emerging set of systems.

More recently, another dimension of Web-enabled marketing that also allows for intimacy with anonymity has come to prominence, and that is *behavioral targeting*. This is particularly strong in Web-based advertising as led by Google in Search and Yahoo! in Display. Underlying technologies from companies like Audience Sciences, Visible Measures, and Rocket Fuel allow publishers and advertisers to tag individuals anonymously such that they can be presented with advertising specific to their interests. This dramatically increases the yield of marketing spend while also improving the satisfaction of the customer.

At the end of the day, what we must succeed at is positioning *customer expertise* close to the customer. At the very high end of the market, we can do this with attentive people armed with their own diaries about past interactions with their clientele. Elsewhere, however, we need to apply *data processing skills* and *marketing imagination* to win the day.

In sum, CRM on Main Street is becoming an increasingly technology-based discipline. We are going through a Technology Adoption Life Cycle of our own in marketing, sector by sector, with financial services and retail taking the lead in business to consumer and with manufacturing supply chains taking the lead in business to business. In both instances, it is easy to overreach, and so we can expect to see plenty of false starts, but because there is such rich

(continued)

(Continued)

opportunity to eliminate waste and increase customer satisfaction, this will be a rich vein to mine for many, many years to come.

---

[a]Readers may see a parallel between the ideas Moore has expressed here, drawing from his two best-selling books and extensive speaking and consulting work, and that of Everett M. Rogers in his work from the last decades of the twentieth century on adoption of innovations. (See Everett M. Rogers, *Diffusion of Innovations* [New York: Free Press, 1962].) Moore's work, of course, is based on his experience with the disruptive forces of technology, while Rogers's work is based on a more stable paradigm of adoption. Both have helped to inform us about the challenges and methods of how to get from here to there.

Geoffrey Moore talked about how companies will adopt CRM software and move into wider and wider adoption of customer-based strategies as well. In the next section, Paul Greenberg continues the discussion with a view of how business will work when a majority of businesses take the customer's point of view, innovate their value-building strategies in ways that work simultaneously for shareholders and customers, and base progress on mutual trust and benefit.

Looking To the Future: Business Becomes Truly Collaborative

Paul Greenberg
President, The 56 Group, LLC
Author, CRM at the Speed of Light

From Aggregation to Collaboration

Procter & Gamble (P&G), a company that has over 300 brands—23 of them worth $1 billion or more—sends out new products to a social network of roughly 600,000 mothers with their own network of moms—at least 25 per lead mom. P&G calls this Vocalpoint. These moms, who are classified as "lead users,"[a] distribute the products and get feedback on their quality and a suggested price point. P&G then takes this information back to the appropriate business units and applies what it has heard. It makes improvements where necessary, adds features when necessary, and even adjusts the price accordingly. Vocalpoint has been so successful as a social network that P&G has spun it off as a profit center and handles this incredibly smart marketing and product feedback effort for other companies—for a fee, of course.

Business models that were considered appropriate until the early part of the millennium would see Vocalpoint as a great marketing tool—with a huge reach because it theoretically could touch 15-million mothers who were targeted with specific products—something that investments of traditional advertising dollars couldn't even dream of.

But those traditional models were hurt by the communications revolution brought on by the evolution of the Web and the 3.3 billion cell phones that inhabit the ears of the earth. That revolution changed how individuals interact with each other and with institutions, giving rise in the business world to *social* customers who were demanding far more involvement with companies than ever before and demanding control over their own experience with the companies that mattered to them.

Disney Destinations, the travel arm of Disney, understood this in 2006 when it realized that customers weren't that interested in dealing with travel agents all the time to handle their complex vacation planning. Consequently, it created tools that would allow a family member to plan the travel online and actually lock down the reservations and the schedules and the events that they wanted—all done when they wanted in the way that they wanted. They still had access to agents but only if it was something that made sense—not because they *had* to deal with them.

Business was changing. No longer were just the sale of products and services sufficient for companies. They had to provide the products, services, tools such as the online vacation planner, and consumable experiences to allow customers to sculpt their relationship the way that they wanted. Otherwise, customers would go elsewhere to get the products that they are looking for. This is business based on an aggregation of components that customers need to be engaged with that business—necessary at a time when companies no longer compete just with their direct competitors but also with the 3,000 messages a day each person receives.

But is a model that aggregates assets that the customer needs enough for business? If a business hands the customer these keys, will it be sufficient for it to maintain a strong relationship with that customer over the next five or so years?

The answer to that is no.

Business Transformation Continues

Business transformation isn't stopping. We are at a juncture when over three fourths of all Internet users are participating in a social network, and for the first time in history, more people are communicating via social networks and communities (66.8 percent) than via e-mail (65.1 percent) according to Nielsen's "Global Faces on Networked Places" survey.[b] This transformation has empowered customers and created a substantial number of "social customers"—those customers who see companies as components for solving parts of their personal agendas and those who trust their peers more than they trust anyone else.

The proof of trust is borne by the annual Edelman Trust Barometer survey—the trusted source for who your trusted source is. From 2004 through 2009, the Trust Barometer showed that the single most trusted source for the respondents is "a person like me"—someone of like mind and interests.[c] That idea hasn't wavered. Peer trust drives how consumers think. Peer product reviews are trusted by 90 percent of respondents in one survey while advertising is trusted by 14 percent in another.

(continued)

(*Continued*)

These customers, bolstered by having access to their peers, conversing about the companies outside the corporate firewall via the channels like Twitter and Facebook on the Web, are now controlling their own destinies when it comes to how they interact with the businesses they choose to interrelate with.

Which means businesses that are attempting to differentiate themselves will have to redefine how they do business with these social customers.

Currently, the more forward-thinking businesses like P&G are using the aggregation model mentioned earlier. But this model has its limits, and already there are indications that the future rests in a more evolved model.

Collaboration, Co-Creation, and the Social Business of the Future

Businesses that aggregate the products, services, tools, and experiences still are operating from a culture that even at its best says the company unidirectionally needs to respond to customers by giving them these assets. The company is providing the assets; the customer is using them. Although that's certainly a step forward, for the future to be what the revolution in communications we've experienced over the past few years demands, the social model for business has to evolve well beyond that.

If companies are to respond to the changed expectations and demands of this increasingly social customer, they are going to have to develop business models and cultures based on co-creation. /collaboration

What is that? Put simply, it's the cooperation of the customer and the company in developing value that provides mutual benefit. It might sound complicated, but it isn't.

For example, if you're acquainted with the "modding" world in PC and video games, you know that there are vast company-supported forums and communities that consist of customers who are using source code and/or authoring tools to modify the games that the game company releases. These communities are in constant discussion over the modifications they are making, sometimes creating almost entirely new games. Sometimes they are directly altering the game itself. Valve's Counter-Strike, a counterterrorism first-person shooter, one of the most wildly popular online games in history, was a complete alteration of Half-Life, which was sci-fi based. The modification was so popular that it and subsequent add-ons had sold over 9 million copies by 2008.[d] It has a community of developers and scriptwriters to continue its expansion.

This is co-creation in short. A community of gamers, interested in making the game exactly as they wanted it, took the game and altered it to their satisfaction with the support of the company. This led to commercial success.

What's important to recognize here is that the customers/gamers were doing what they wanted to the game, not creating a product per se. Their interest was to make it playable to them personally. Part of the benefit of a social business model based on co-creation is that it allows customers to satisfy something of their personal agenda, not simply apply new sets of tools and products to their company experience. The benefit to the company is that it gets innovative products and results that it couldn't have gotten even if it had spent millions on research and development. It also gets customers who are committed to the company because of how much they participate in the company's development.

Samsung does something similar with its customer advisory boards. It is willing to open up its intellectual property to "lead customers" and in return is getting feedback on existing products that it then applies or getting new product ideas.

Case Study: Procter & Gamble Connect + Develop

The folks at P&G, who led the way to the business models being developed now, are also the harbinger of the success of co-creation as the future. In the early part of the millennium's first decade, they developed a key performance indicator for how much of their innovation will come from external sources. Back then, they set their objective as 50 percent by about 2010. Their approach to getting there became the poster child for co-creation as the future's business model.

They did some of the things that you would expect. They reached out to key scientists and engineers who didn't work for P&G. They connected to research and development networks like Innocentive, which solve R&D problems for a fee considerably lower than the internal cost of what the research would be.

But most germane to this new business model was the creation of the P&G Connect + Develop program.

P&G realized that to reach this 50 percent goal, it had to develop a culture that was dramatically different from the one available to most companies of its magnitude. That was task number one. A.G. Lafley, then CEO, understood that: "I think it's value that rules the world. There's an awful lot of evidence across an awful lot of categories that consumers will pay more for better design, better performance, better quality, better value, and better experiences."[e]

To get to that point with its customers, the culture of P&G had to be more open to supporting what the customers actually wanted. What better way than getting them to work with P&G to develop the products? Connect + Develop was the result.

Connect + Develop is an organization that provides a place for anyone who has an appropriate idea to reach out to P&G to see if the idea will be funded and acquired. The site for registered members (you don't have to be a P&G customer) lists hundreds of areas and specific products that P&G is interested in. If you can provide the idea for the product to P&G, and the product is seen to have some popular support, not only will the company fund the product, but, if it doesn't distribute it as a P&G product, it will work with you to comarket it to some other company. Products like Olay Regenerist and Swiffer Dusters are from external inventors via Connect + Develop. In its first two years, over 100 products were spun from Connect + Develop.[f]

Will we see this business model in our lifetime? In a way, we're already seeing it, but widespread support and adoption would involve cultural changes that are substantial enough to prevent most companies from supporting it right now. In the next few years, however, this model will not only be more easily adopted but more predominant, to the degree that companies realize that the

(continued)

(Continued)

social customer is not only here to stay but is far more responsive than the traditional customer to this new approach to business—a social, collaborative approach that demands time and investment.

---

[a]Eric Von Hippel used this term in *Democratizing Innovation* (Cambridge, MA: MIT Press, 2005).

[b]"Global Faces and Networked Places: A Nielsen Report on Social Networking's New Global Footprint" (March 2009); available at http://blog.nielsen.com/nielsenwire/wp-content/uploads/2009/03/nielsen_globalfaces_ mar09.pdf, accessed September 1, 2010.

[c]2009 Edelman Trust Barometer; available at: www.edelman.com/trust/ 2009/, accessed September 1, 2010.

[d]Dustin Quillen, "Valve Reveals Sales Data for Half-Life, Counter-Strike, and More," 1UP, December 3, 2008; available at: www.1up.com/do/newsStory? cId=3171638, accessed September 1, 2010.

[e]A.G. Lafley was quoted in Jennifer Reingold, "What P&G Knows about the Power of Design," *Fast Company*, June 1, 2005; available at: www.fastcompany.com/magazine/95/design-qa.html, accessed September 1, 2010.

[f]See P&G's Connect + Develop Web site, www.pgconnectdevelop.com, accessed September 1, 2010.

Now let's suppose you are a newly minted MBA and have taken a position as a customer relationship manager at a product-centric enterprise: We would expect that many of the ideas and tools you have learned in this book would help. But what should a manager of customer relationships expect to find in her briefcase? In other words, what are the leadership qualities of an effective manager in a customer-strategy environment? We start the discussion with the answer to a question we are asked all the time: What will be the characteristics of those who first manage customer relationships for a firm?

Leadership Behavior of Customer Relationship Managers

When a firm undertakes a customer-focused effort, a great deal of integration is required in all aspects of the enterprise. The management team has to buy in at the very top; and, if it does, we should expect certain types of activity and behavior at the leadership level. The leaders of any enterprise engaging in a transition to a customer-strategy enterprise will accumulate expertise about managing customer relationships and will become cheerleaders for this new business model. They will highlight it in company meetings and in business gatherings; they will openly share their expertise in and around the organization; in sum, they will become authorities on the relationship management business model.

In a leadership role, a manager must be capable of sponsoring a customer-focused project and sheltering the people involved in the pilot project. One of the easiest ways to make progress in the journey toward customer centricity is to engage in a series of increasingly comprehensive pilot projects. But a pilot project does not necessarily make money on its own. Most small pilot projects, in fact, never even have the possibility of making money. They are proofs of concept for larger projects that will be rolled out only if they make sense on the smaller level. The pilot project might be an operational test of a customer-strategy program, or a test of the value-building effectiveness of the program, or a test of the accuracy of a metric or predictive model.

Because the participants in a pilot project are exposed in the business financially—that is, they don't have enough profit underlying their activity to justify their existence—they are supported only by the learning they will gain from the pilot project. It is up to the leader, therefore, to shelter them from any economic downturn that might affect the enterprise from keeping them onboard. Ideally, a pilot project needs to be funded at the beginning, then given some running room—often one or two years—before any future decisions can be made.

A leader will measure her own success and the success of her people differently, establishing new types of metrics for the enterprise's activities and accomplishments. But she will also create a new set of rewards structures. We know from previous chapters that one of the central goals of managing customer relationships is to improve the value of the customer base, over time—that is, to conserve and increase the enterprise's customer equity. This value is nothing more than the sum total of lifetime values (LTVs) of all customers; but the problem is that LTV is a future number based on future behaviors of a customer. It's a number that has to be predicted or foretold, and it is impossible to measure exactly. Thus, a leader has to figure out what the leading indicators are of this future customer value that can be measured, and determine how a firm can tie organizational performance and compensation to those metrics this quarter.

> The customer's relationship with an enterprise will be based on the customer's view of the business, not any particular product or division's view of the customer.

A leader should be willing and able to cross boundaries to generate enterprise-wide results. One thing we know about customer-specific initiatives is that, precisely because they are customer-specific, they are neither division-specific nor product-specific. The customer's relationship with an enterprise will be based on the customer's view of the business, not any particular product or division's view of the customer. It is a relationship that might go across several different divisions and encompass the purchasing of several different products and services. The organization of the enterprise is almost certainly along product and service lines, and that means those divisional structures will have to be crossed to serve a customer across several different divisions. Taking a share-of-customer approach to a business inherently means crossing boundaries. The leader is constantly on the lookout for ways to expand the scope of her customer relationships beyond her own product or division and to reach out and encompass aspects of that relationship that go beyond her particular domain. Crossing boundaries is one of the main reasons to engage the senior leaders at a customer-strategy enterprise, and their involvement is critical because they can cross boundaries more easily and more effectively.

Good leaders will insist on having direct contact with customers. They will attend the focus groups, do phone interviews, listen in at the customer interaction center, and have meetings with business executives at the customer organization.

Leaders *want* to be directly connected to customers in as much detail as possible. Leaders *want* to have a realistic picture of what it is like to be a customer of their enterprise. Seeing their enterprise from the customer's point of view is one of the key tasks of making this kind of transition successfully.

For all the practical advice about crossing boundaries, supporting pilot projects, and coming face-to-face with customers, however, the fact is that on this never-ending journey toward customer centricity, every future manager should keep two all-important navigational tools in mind for guidance in difficult situations. As executives struggle to apply the principles in this book to new problems and unanticipated technologies in their own roles at work, they should think of these two navigational tools as lighthouse beacons, shining through a dense fog of unforeseeable economic disruptions and ever more rapid technological change:

1. Strive to always maintain and increase the trust of customers.
2. Innovate, innovate, innovate.

Maintain and Increase the Trust of Customers

Customer trust may just be the next "big thing" in business competition, and the rise of the Internet has given us all a taste of its genuine benefits.[1] Essentially, rising levels of trust have the effect of reducing the heat and friction generated by economic activity, so businesses can focus more on genuinely-value-creating processes and less on paperwork or administrative and security tasks. This is a critical idea. Technology and rising levels of trust go hand in hand. Trust of others is all the more important in a more networked and interconnected world. But a more interconnected world will tend to produce higher levels of trust as well.

Throughout history, the capacity for human beings to trust others has expanded, and been expanded by, commerce and trade. In his book *The Wisdom of Crowds*, James Surowiecki argues that the spread of Quaker philosophy hastened the rise of a flourishing trade in England and America in the 1700s and 1800s. The Society of Friends places a strong emphasis on integrity and honesty, which are core tenets of their religious beliefs. Quakers subscribe to a "Testimony of Integrity" based on the belief that people should live their lives so as to be:

> *true to God, true to oneself, and true to others. . . . Friends [Quakers] do not believe that one should trick others by making statements that are technically true but misleading.*

Quakers prospered as traders largely because they were able to trust each other. Among other innovations, they introduced practices such as public-stated pricing to improve the transparency of their dealings. Over time, the Anglo-American economy as a whole became more transparent and trustworthy, as non-Quakers preferred to

---

[1]The following section is adapted from Don Peppers and Martha Rogers, *Rules to Break and Laws to Follow: How Your Business Can Beat the Crisis of Short-Termism* (Hoboken, NJ: John Wiley & Sons, 2008), Chapter 7.

trade with an expanding population of Quaker traders in order to be sure they got a fair deal.[2]

It is clearer today than ever before that fairness and honesty are more likely to characterize developed societies with market economies and free commerce.[3] We might associate capitalism with selfishness and greed ("Greed is good," to quote Gordon Gekko, the hero of the 1987 movie *Wall Street* played by Michael Douglas), but the actual truth is that the success of capitalism owes much more to the fact that our society considers trust and fairness to be important social norms. Trust makes it possible for you to eat prepared food right up until the printed expiration date without fearing sickness, to shake hands with a fellow businessman to cement a deal even before it is written down in precise legal terms, or to write out a piece of paper called a check and know you'll be credited with making the payment because of it.

Capitalism and free markets have increased the importance of trust and fairness, but the new technologies that free markets rely on have contributed even further to this importance. As the frictional cost of moving goods and information from one locale to another has declined, the sheer volume and rapidity of interpersonal communication has skyrocketed, so that the importance of a merchant's "reputation" is greater than ever before. Three hundred years ago, perhaps, if someone were ripped off by an unscrupulous merchant who didn't live in his own community, he might have told a few friends. But they may not even have been able to recognize and avoid the devious merchant in the future, and in any case this would be as far as the news was likely to travel. In those days, gross generalizations with respect to class or tribe were the most common methods used to enforce fairness. If a merchant from Greece scammed someone in the community with barrels of bad olives, then the whole town would simply shun dealing with Greek merchants in the future. Sounds harsh now, but it worked for townspeople at the time.

Before the rise of electronic communications technologies, the best defense against unfair dealing was simply to do business only with family members or relatives, personal friends, or neighbors and town residents. As commerce developed and communication became easier, however, people began sharing evaluations of the businesses they dealt with and warning others of unscrupulous vendors. Organizations such as the Better Business Bureau came into existence not just to protect customers from being ripped off but also to protect honest merchants from being tarred by the actions of the unscrupulous.

Reputations Go Online

These days, computer technology and inexpensive connectivity allow a merchant's reputation, for better or worse, to be shared much more rapidly and widely, in much richer detail than ever before. Any number of detailed, up-to-date evaluations of a seller's reputation can usually be found posted on various online review sites. People today can easily get the skinny on merchants they've never dealt with before, without even personally knowing anyone who has ever dealt with them. Amazon.com's

---

[2] James Surowiecki, *The Wisdom of Crowds* (New York: Doubleday, 2004). To see the complete Quaker "Testimony of Integrity," see http://en.wikipedia.org/wiki/Testimony_of_Integrity.
[3] Arthur C. Brooks, "Charitable Explanation," *Wall Street Journal,* November 27, 2006.

book reviews and eBay's ratings of individual sellers are both good examples of business practices that empower consumers themselves to maintain the quality of the business offerings—in effect "co-creating" the product information necessary to inform other consumers prior to making purchase decisions. There are dozens of well-known Web sites where the reputations of different kinds of businesses and products can be updated or modified as consumers experience them, and then freely viewed by other consumers. Hotel reputations for service, convenience, and pricing can be probed on TripAdvisor.com, for example, and home-improvement or repair contractor reputations for competence and reliability can be found on Angie's List. At most of these kinds of sites, other customers have posted their reviews of various products, and the more capable review sites allow a consumer to search not just by product category but by reviewer type—that is, to find reviews that are done by people whose past reviews have been rated the most helpful by other consumers, or even by reviewers who have similar tastes as the consumer. "Rating the raters" is an increasingly important mechanism for ensuring a robust and generally accurate review site, and over time we should expect review sites to become even more sophisticated and accurate in their assessments of businesses.

Largely because of cost-efficient interactive technologies, untrustworthiness is now something few businesses can keep secret. Any company that is unscrupulously exploitative of its customers will be quickly and efficiently outed, and its business will suffer. So it's more and more financially risky to take short-term advantage of a customer, even in situations where it might seem easy to get away with. Once. But then a scorching exposé could easily go online where it could be downloaded by others, for years, and perhaps forever.

> "You can't un-Google yourself."
> —Linda Kaplan Thaler, CEO,
> Kaplan Thaler Group

One of the very first online word-of-mouth episodes, in fact, is known as the "Yours is a Very Bad Hotel" case, and it is still making the rounds on the Web. It seems that late one night in November 2001, two businessmen were due to check in to a hotel in Houston, but when they arrived all the rooms were already taken. Apparently the hotel's night clerk was so surly and dismissive that these businessmen took the effort to create a hilarious 17-slide presentation about the incident, titling it "Yours is a Very Bad Hotel" and e-mailing it to the hotel company. Now, years later, you can still find this presentation being passed around on the Web. Bloggers proudly point to the fact that they were officially warned by the hotel's parent company to take its brand name off their Web site,[4] but it is, of course, way, way too late for that. If you want to see this example of "permanent" word of mouth for yourself, just go online and search for the phrase "Yours is a very bad hotel" and count the entries. That should tell you just how successful any company can be at cleaning up the customer's milk once

---

[4]See www.craphound.com/misc/doubletree.htm for an example of an attempt by Double-tree's parent company to contain the problem. Of course, it's still easy to get a copy of the PowerPoint deck, and this kind of heavyhanded effort just makes Doubletree looks even worse. The original disaster could be construed to be the responsibility of poor local customer service at one unit. But this threat is from corporate headquarters. We should all take a lesson.

it has been electronically spilled. One advertising executive's succinct advice: "You can't un-Google yourself."[5]

The demand for more and more trustability in business is being facilitated by the increasing use of social media, coupled with the dramatic expansion of peer-produced products and services. Social media interactions and collaborative, open-source developments of software and other information resources are governed by an ethos that is separate and distinct from the ethos governing more traditional, production-for-money economics. Although there is no formal code of conduct, and certainly no regulatory framework proscribing any particular types of activities or messaging in the arena of social interaction and production, there is nevertheless a very strong and fairly cohesive set of expectations as to what behaviors are acceptable, and the "crowd" is more than capable of enforcing these standards. The result is that peer-produced, community-owned products are thriving, in ways no one would have predicted a decade ago. As Yochai Benkler says in his book *The Wealth of Networks*:

> *About 70 percent of Web server software, in particular for critical e-commerce sites, runs on the Apache Web server—free software. More than half of all back-office e-mail functions are run by one free software program or another. Google, Amazon, and CNN.com, for example, run their Web servers on the GNU/Linux operating system. They do this, presumably, because they believe this peer-produced operating system is more reliable than the alternatives, not because the system [is less expensive.]*[6]

Moreover, there is an increasing amount of interplay between open source, community-owned products and corporate-owned, for-profit products. For example, according to Benkler:

> *[IBM] has obtained the largest number of patents every year from 1993 to 2004, amassing in total more than 29,000 patents. IBM has also, however, been one of the firms most aggressively engaged in adapting its business model to the emergence of free software, [as shown by] the relative weight of patent royalties, licenses, and sales in IBM's revenues and revenues that the firm described as coming from "Linux-related services." Within a span of four years, the Linux-related services category moved from accounting for practically no revenues, to providing* double *the revenues from all patent-related sources, of the firm that has been the most patent-productive in the United States.*[7] *(Emphasis added.)*

Overall, the increasing importance of community-owned products and services (software, encyclopedias, product reviews, etc.), coupled with the friend-to-friend ethos and rate-the-rater self-policing mechanisms of social media Web sites, has dramatically escalated the role of plain and simple *trustability* in commercial interactions. The more people begin participating in social media, the more they come

---

[5]Linda Kaplan Thaler, quoted in "What's Next?" *Fortune* magazine, February 5, 2007, p. 28.
[6]Yochai Benkler, *The Wealth of Networks* (New Haven, CT: Yale University Press, 2006), p. 64.
[7]Ibid., p. 46.

to expect trustworthy behavior from the businesses they interact with. And more people are participating every day.

> "Treat the customer the way you'd want to be treated if you were the customer."

In short, there is probably no more forward-thinking business strategy to be found than constantly seeking to act in the interests of customers. It would be hard to find any single bit of advice for today's business manager that is simpler, more straightforward, or more important in terms of the benefits provided to the enterprise. So one of the beacons any executive today should steer toward is the beacon of trust. No matter how confused the business situation, no matter how unsettled the industry, and no matter how volatile the technological landscape, one sure "safe harbor" for any business will almost certainly be that of earning and keeping the trust of its customers. Remember the mantra at USAA Insurance, established under the leadership of Brigadier-General Robert McDermott: "Treat the customer the way you'd want to be treated if you were the customer."

Innovate, Innovate, Innovate

The second safe harbor beacon on these troubled business seas is innovation—not just in developing new and shinier products, but in constantly rethinking the very business model and how we make money from customers.[8]

In his marvelous book *The Origin of Wealth,* Eric Beinhocker gives a sweeping, comprehensive review of how the thinking in economics has changed over the last two centuries, and he makes a compelling case for the idea that economic progress and development should be seen as a process of evolution. This is quite different from traditional, classical economics, which is based on perfect markets and all-knowing, perfectly rational investors. Traditional economics thinking is based on the constant equilibrium of supply and demand. But Beinhocker's argument is that, in just the last couple of decades, there has been a tectonic shift in thinking, as economists have increasingly glommed on to the fact that "equilibrium" is not a realistic way to describe how the economy works.[9]

In reality, the economy is never in a state of equilibrium. Economic activity is driven by change—by a constant flow of new products and services created by self-interested but not entirely rational people seeking a profit. As new products and services are produced, old ones fail and disappear. New companies come into existence constantly, replacing old ones that sink into business oblivion.

Increasingly, economists are coming to think of the economy as a different kind of evolutionary system. Under this theory, it is progress, creativity, and innovation that are the real drivers propelling economic activity. People create new things and devise new technologies in order to make a profit by meeting some need. The innovations that make the most profit are the most "fit" for survival, so they are likely to have a larger impact on overall progress as the economy continues to evolve into higher and higher technological states.

---

[8]The following section is adapted from Peppers and Rogers, *Rules to Break and Laws to Follow,* Chapters 10 and 11.

[9]Eric D. Beinhocker, *The Origin of Wealth* (Boston: McKinsey & Company, 2006).

Changing technology and constant innovation make it extremely difficult for companies to survive and prosper over any substantial period of time. One comprehensive study examined thousands of firms in 40 industries over a 25-year period in order to understand how long the most profitable ones could maintain their superior economic performances—which the researchers defined in terms of a statistically significant difference relative to their peers. The study revealed that the periods during which any single company can consistently maintain above-average results are decreasing, regardless of industry, size of firm, or geography. Using a series of rolling 5-year periods for their analysis, the researchers found that just 5 percent of companies are able to string together 10 or more years of superior performance, and less than a half percent of their sample (only 32 firms out of the 6,772 analyzed) performed above their peers for 20 years or more.[10]

⌐The truly outstanding performers in this study were those able to string together a series of short-term competitive advantages rather than maintaining a long-term advantage.⌐You can gain a short-term advantage with a differentiated product or service, but to survive the evolutionary process you need the ability to respond to change and string a number of these advantages together. In Beinhocker's words, the truly successful firms are those that "rise into the top ranks of performance, get knocked down, but, like a tough boxer, get back up to fight and win again."[11] This is certainly how Apple could be portrayed. And 3M. And GE. But note carefully: If this evolutionary view of economic progress is correct, then there really is no such thing as a "sustainable" competitive advantage for a business. Instead, success in business, as in the natural world, comes to those "most responsive to change."

This is not Lake Wobegon, folks, where all the children are above average. Here on Earth half of all businesses are below average, and because of the increasing pace of change, it takes less time than ever to slip below the line.

Economist Paul Romer suggests one way to understand the role that innovation and new ideas play in an economy is to think of an idea as a kind of product. In contrast to a physical product, however, every newly created idea-product becomes virtually free for anyone to use (not just its creator). Even when patents are plentiful and well written, this is still true. Consider the flurry of accessories businesses that support iPods and all the non-eBay employees getting rich from eBay—all without violating a single patent but using someone else's very good idea. Because every new idea has the potential to lead to additional ideas, the more there are, the faster they come. This means the business of creating ideas is subject to increasing returns to scale, in sharp contrast to the diminishing returns that characterize traditional economics.[12]

However, while the possibility of increasing returns might lead us to conclude that creating a new idea should be a very profitable activity, we can't forget that if

---

[10]The short-lived success period of companies is mentioned in Robert R. Wiggins and Timothy W. Ruefli, "Hypercompetitive Performance: Are the Best of Times Getting Shorter?" paper presented at the Academy of Management annual meeting 2001, March 31, 2001, cited in Michael J. Mauboussin, *More Than You Know: Finding Financial Wisdom in Unconventional Places* (2006), pp. 120–121. Also see Beinhocker's *Origin of Wealth*, pp. 331–332.

[11]Beinhocker quoted from his *Origin of Wealth*, p. 333.

[12]See Paul Romer, "The Growth of Growth Theory," *Economist*, May 18, 2006.

anyone can use a new idea, then it may be difficult for us to make much money from it ourselves, even after going to all the trouble and expense of having come up with it in the first place. True profits can be generated only during the time periods that lie between when a new idea is devised and when it is duplicated by competition. And as the pace of change and innovation continues to accelerate, these time periods are getting shorter and shorter.

But here's the real point: Instead of counting on making money from every new idea, a successful enterprise in the future must be able to *produce more new ideas*, constantly. Innovation, creativity, and adaptability are traits that are more important than ever, precisely because they're more common than ever. A business's most successful competitors have these traits. Business conditions change with every new innovation, and you will survive as a business only if you can adapt (i.e., innovate). Although technology has always marched steadily forward, the pace of this march seems to have accelerated in recent years to such an extent that the actual *character* of business competition has undergone a qualitative shift.

Note carefully, however, that innovation's role is to help *customers* create value. Innovation, by itself, has no value. It can even be destructive. There is already a great deal of hype surrounding innovation, but to create real value for a business, innovation has to involve more than just coming up with cool new ideas for their own sake. That's the kind of "innovation" that brings to market a remote device for home theater systems that can't be decoded without a geek license. Innovation that isn't wanted or valued by customers is just self-indulgence, and many of the most "innovative" technology companies in the world are guilty of it.

To overcome the hype and to focus on *profitable* innovation, we have to keep the customer's future behavior firmly fixed in our minds. We have to constantly be aware of what it is actually like to be that customer; and we have to be willing to act in the customer's interest, even when it sometimes means giving up short-term value for the enterprise itself. But if the whole organization isn't already tuned to the customer's wavelength, this just isn't likely to happen.

Economist Romer suggests that if a government wants to promote economic growth, then it should create what he calls a "climate of innovation." It could do this by, for instance, improving education, subsidizing research, bringing in new ideas from other societies and geographies,[13] and enforcing legal protections for intellectual property rights (interestingly, Benkler would disagree with Romer's last point, arguing that patent protections today actually inhibit more innovation than they encourage).

Trying to create a climate of innovation is good advice for a business as well. For a business to grow, or even just to survive, it must be able to adapt to change and innovate. So how can an enterprise get better at coming up with new ideas and innovations and then putting them into production or operation? How can it turn employees into more flexible, adaptable, and creative people? And how will you architect your own firm, if your goal is to be adaptable, inventive, and responsive to change?

Apple, regarded as one of the world's most trusted brands, also has a reputation for creativity, consistently ranking first in polls of the world's most innovative

---

[13] Ibid.

companies, even with an occasional disappointing product launch. According to one assessment, four factors drive Apple's inventiveness:

1. It relies on "network innovation," regularly involving outsiders in its creative process, from technical partners to customers and others, rather than simply locking engineers away in the research and development (R&D) department.
2. It is ruthless about designing new products around customer needs with as much simplicity as possible.
3. It understands that customers don't know what they don't know; that is, breakthrough innovations will often fly in the face of what "the market" is saying. The iPod, for instance, was originally ridiculed when it was launched in 2001.
4. Apple has learned that one secret for constant innovation is to "fail wisely." The iPhone rose from the ashes of the company's original music phone, designed with Motorola. The Macintosh sprang from the original Lisa computer, which failed.[14]

Failing wisely. That's an important clue for setting up a climate of innovation, because every new idea has a high probability of failure, but without making the attempt, the small proportion of successes will never be discovered, either. As hockey superstar Wayne Gretzky once said, "I never made a shot I didn't take." James Dyson, the British vacuum cleaner magnate, claims he built 5,127 prototypes of his revolutionary new vacuum before one of his designs made him a billionaire. The Wright brothers tested some 200 different wing designs and crashed seven of them before successfully lifting off at Kitty Hawk. And WD-40 is called "WD-40" because the first 39 "water displacement" formulas tested by the Rocket Chemical Company in 1953 failed.[15]

To keep the company's chief financial officer from going apoplectic at the thought of supporting a froth of "creative destruction" and intrepreneurship, we should probably classify business failures into two different categories:

1. *Fiasco failures* are the result of stupid mistakes, lack of homework, laziness, misguided decisions, or incompetence, but
2. *Wise failures* are the result of well-executed smart ideas, based on carefully considered risks.

One of the obvious first steps, to encourage innovation, is to staff the company with more creative people, either by hiring more creative people in the first place or by teaching people to be more creative, if that's even possible. The problem is that no one really knows what creativity is or how it happens. Don't let anyone tell you otherwise. Just think about it: If we could define creativity and map out exactly how it occurs, it wouldn't really be "creative," would it? Nevertheless, anyone who thinks or writes much on the subject will agree that one secret to creativity seems to be

---

[14]"Lessons from Apple: What Other Companies Can Learn from California's Master of Innovation," *Economist* (editorial), June 7, 2007.

[15]For failures that led to success, see www.wd40.com/AboutUs/our_history.html, accessed September 1, 2010. Also see Jena McGregor, William C. Symonds, Dean Foust, Diane Brady, and Moira Herbst, "How Failure Breeds Success," *BusinessWeek*, July 10, 2006.

crossing boundaries, cross-pollinating or combining different concepts, and taking new perspectives on old issues. A creative idea is usually the result of a single human brain making a connection between two previously unrelated concepts and having some blinding insight as a result—often an insight that appears to have nothing at all to do with the original concept. Or maybe it isn't a blinding insight but just a glimmer of understanding, or even a suspicion of something sort of interesting. This is certainly one reason why economist Romer says the rate of innovation and change is accelerating in the world—because the more new ideas there are, the more combining and cross-pollinating can take place.[16]

In Walter Isaacson's richly documented biography of Albert Einstein, he catalogs a number of factors behind the man's extraordinary creativity, including that he was naturally rebellious and anti-authoritarian; that he was well read not just in physics but in philosophy, psychology, and other disciplines (he borrowed the term *relativity* itself from the budding field of psychoanalysis); and that he drew constant analogies between physics concepts previously thought to be unrelated (acceleration and gravity, for instance). To top it off, of course, Einstein was also a German Jew during the Nazi era—claimed by his home country as a celebrity but shunned by it at the same time.[17]

By most accounts, highly creative people tend to be intelligent and intellectually curious as well as flexible and open to new information. But they are also prone to be intense, motivated, mentally restless, anti-authoritarian, unorthodox, and often (as in Einstein's case) a bit rebellious. For business, a productively creative person must also be extremely goal oriented, able to recognize and define problems clearly, and capable of putting information together in many different ways to reach solutions.

Regardless of how creative the individual employees are, no enterprise can simply command people to "innovate." It doesn't work that way. All a firm can do is create an environment in which innovation is encouraged to flourish—a climate of innovation. To facilitate this, an enterprise may decide to organize somewhat differently, and it should encourage creativity and experimentation with its policies, in addition to hiring people who are more likely to be original thinkers in the first place. But in the end, no firm's creativity can be commanded. It must spring up from the culture.

Uh-oh. There's that word again. But hey, guess what? *The same corporate culture that will help a company earn the trust of its customers will also help it remain adaptive, resilient, and innovative.*

---

[16]It goes without saying that the more innovative you are, the more you will have to deal with change. See Ranjay Gulati and James B. Oldroyd, "The Quest for Customer Focus," *Harvard Business Review,* Reprint R0504F (April 2005): "Getting close to customers is not so much a problem the IT or marketing department needs to solve as a journey that the whole organization needs to make." The article identifies four stages of customer focus: Communal Coordination (collate information), Serial Coordination (get insight from customers' past behavior), Symbiotic Coordination (understand likely future behavior), and Integral Coordination (real-time response to customer's needs), citing Continental Airlines, Royal Bank of Canada, Harrah's, and SBC.

[17]Was Einstein creative because he was a "German Jew" in an era when that was an oxymoron? See Walter Isaacson, *Einstein: His Life and Universe* (New York: Simon & Schuster, 2007).

The Importance of Corporate Culture

Harvard Business School professor Clayton Christensen (of "disruptive innovation" fame) suggests that any company's ability to innovate and adapt depends on how it defines its capabilities, and that a company defines these capabilities differently as it goes through its life cycle. For a young firm, the *resources* it has available—things like people, technologies, expertise, or cash—represent its capabilities. During a company's growth phase, these capabilities begin to morph into well-defined and understood *processes*—including processes for product development, manufacturing, budgeting, and so forth. Then, when a company matures into a larger firm, its capabilities will be defined by its *values*—including things like the limitations it places on its own business, the margins it needs before considering an investment, and its corporate culture. According to Christensen, the reason younger companies are more flexible, adaptable, and inherently innovative is that "resources" are simply more adaptable to change than are "processes" or "values," which, by their very nature, are designed to turn repetitive activities into more efficient and predictable routines, and to minimize variation.[18]

In Christensen's hierarchy, it is clear that he regards a company's values and culture as the most hardened of capabilities, and we certainly agree with that. Nothing is quite so difficult to change as a company's culture, and once "the way we do things around here" becomes "the way we've always done things around here," a company already has one foot in the grave. Christensen's argument also implies that a company simply cannot become large without losing its innovativeness.

However, what if the culture that hardens into a company as it becomes mature is a culture that celebrates change, creativity, and innovation applied to the business? What if the repetitive activities and routines that a firm's culture enshrines have to do with a constant exploration for innovations and improvements? Some established, mature companies really do seem to have cultures that allow them to innovate and adapt more effectively, even while adhering to efficient business practices. Apple is not the only large firm with a track record of constant invention. GE, Disney, 3M, Google, and Toyota also come to mind.

Nevertheless, regardless of these successes, there does seem to be an inherent conflict between the process of constantly innovating new ideas and the process of operating an efficient, clockwork-like production organization. An interesting psychological study of professional football players once revealed some telltale differences between defensive and offensive players, by examining their lockers. Apparently, offensive players' lockers were found to be neater and more orderly than those of defensive players, as a rule. Now, there may be many reasons for this, but the most obvious inference is probably right: Offensive players succeed by following well-crafted plans, executed flawlessly. Timing, position, and order are everything to them. Defensive players, in contrast, get ahead by wreaking havoc with others' plans. They are simply more at home with disorder, chaos, and unpredictability.

A similar dichotomy seems to plague business when it comes to managing both execution and creativity. Efficient execution requires order, routine, and invariability.

---

[18]For a complete overview of Clayton Christensen's "Disruptive Innovation" theory, see www.12manage.com/methods_christensen_disruptive_innovation.html, accessed September 1, 2010.

But creativity and innovation involve disorder, randomness, experimentation, and failure. Few companies have resolved this inherent conflict successfully, although there are a few, just as there are a few pro ball players who can star on either side of the line. As the pace of change continues to accelerate, however, it will be increasingly important to navigate frequently between the close-ordered drill of efficient production and the chaotic experimentation of innovation.

A business enterprise is an organization made up of individual employees and managers who interact with each other and, while pursuing their own individual objectives, produce a collective outcome. Academics call this a "complex adaptive system." Beehives are complex adaptive systems, too, as are economies, social networks, governments, and even weather patterns and galaxies. The behavior that emerges from a complex adaptive system is often different from what you'd expect if you observe the actions of any single member of the system. You could watch a honeybee's actions all day, for instance, and still not be able to predict the shape, texture, or social structure of the hive.

Every year a business makes a profit or incurs a loss, and it builds or destroys customer equity. These events are the collective results of the individual actions of all the employees who make up the company. Like honeybees, the employees are each pursuing their own objectives, but the overall outcome of all the employees working together is the short- and long-term value that the firm creates for its shareholders. And this outcome itself becomes additional feedback driving future employee behavior.

Sometimes the behavior that emerges from a system can appear irrational or counterproductive. For example, if managers and employees can get ahead by achieving immediate, short-term results in their own particular areas, then the firm's overall behavior may be characterized by a lack of coordination among various silos of the organization, coupled with frequent abuses of customers, perhaps in direct violation of the company's written mission statement to "act in the customer's interest at all times." Even though no single manager thinks she is undermining the trust customers have in the firm, the overall behavior of the company might still have that effect.

The success of a complex system—beehives and businesses included—depends on its being able to strike the right balance between exploiting known food sources and exploring for additional sources. Honeybees are great exploiters, doing complex dances for the other bees that direct them to any new food source. But in addition to exploiting known food sources, bees are constantly exploring for new food, even when they already have more than they need. And they are excellent at it. Scientists have shown that bees will find virtually any viable new food source within about two kilometers of their hive with great efficiency, regardless of the nectar resources already available.

The analogy with business is clear. When a business is exploiting its known sources of income, it is living in the short term. Long-term success requires exploration as well as innovation. But one of the biggest problems with most businesses is that they just don't do as good a job as honeybees do when it comes to constantly exploring for additional income sources. The way businesses are organized, financially measured, and rewarded simply makes most of them better at exploiting than exploring.

⌈Not giving enough priority or attention to the "exploration" side of the business is the biggest strategic mistake most companies make.⌋Dell had a marvelously large food source in the form of its novel business model: direct to consumer computer sales, generating revenue even before incurring inventory costs. For years, Dell was the only major personal computer manufacturer making any money, with profit margins 10 points higher than its rivals. In Chapter 11, we talked about how Dell focused on the short term at the expense of the long term. In some ways, we can think of this as Dell's focus on exploitation at the expense of exploration. For Dell, as with most other firms, the tension between exploration and exploitation is complicated by two factors: (1) the ruthlessly short-term dynamic introduced by the expectations of the world's financial markets and (2) the fact that the financial metrics used by most companies are plainly inadequate when it comes to tracking the daily up-and-down changes in the long-term value of a business (i.e., its customer equity).

Suppose, in an experiment, we could alter the DNA of a hive of bees, genetically programming them to focus exclusively on exploitation rather than exploration. Then we put that hive of bees down in the middle of a large field of flowers. What would happen? Over the short term the hive would grow much more rapidly than the surrounding hives, because every available bee would be put to the task of exploiting the field. But what happens next? Once the field is fully exploited, the growth in nectar supplies would tail off, and soon the hive would have to fire its CEO, get in a new management team, and try to move the whole operation into a different field somewhere.

To balance exploitation and exploration, an enterprise must be willing to devote resources to both activities. Google maintains its innovative edge by encouraging employees to dedicate one day per week to exploring innovative or creative initiatives of their own choosing. Think about it: That's an investment equivalent to 20 percent of the company's overall personnel budget. Emerson Electric has a strategic investment program that allocates as much as $20 million a year as seed capital for employees' various unproven but potentially lucrative concepts.[19] Traditionally, 3M's researchers have been encouraged to spend 15 percent of their time on unstructured projects of their own choosing.

No matter how we define it—exploitation versus exploration, production versus innovation, or selling more today versus selling more tomorrow—it ought to be clear that a business will always experience some tension between short-term profit and long-term value creation. And we've already talked extensively about how important it is for a customer-centric company to balance short-term results and long-term value, optimizing the blend of current sales and changes in customer equity.

But besides the conflict between short-term and long-term measurement of value creation, there is another conflict as well—one that has been identified in a wide variety of both popular and academic business books.[20] This is the conflict that arises when managers must choose how much to concentrate on operating a business for the present versus innovating for the future. Operating a business as flawlessly and

---

[19]Emerson Electric: Jeffrey Rothfeder, "The CEO's Role in Innovation: Can a Leader Personally Drive New Ideas? Yes," *Chief Executive* (November 2005).

[20]Eric Beinhocker summarizes some of the leading thinking on this subject in his article "The Adaptable Corporation," *McKinsey Quarterly*, no. 2 (2006), 76–87.

efficiently as possible requires setting up fixed routines and repeatable processes while innovation requires you to encourage the nonroutine. To operate efficiently, a manager must eliminate variances, but innovation thrives on variances, at least insofar as they lead to more creative thinking.

This conflict has been sharpened immensely by the radical improvements in information technology (IT) we've seen over the last few decades. These technologies have fueled a global rush of efficiency-improvement and cost-reduction initiatives, as processes are more easily automated, routines are codified, and the everyday frictions of ordinary commerce melt away. The result is that while companies were always better at exploiting than exploring, technology has now made them even *better* at exploiting.

Exacerbating this problem is the fact that while efficiency-improvement programs, such as Total Quality Management, ISO 9000, or Six Sigma, can significantly improve a company's operational execution and streamline its cost structure, they also may tend to limit a company's ability to think outside the box, reducing or eliminating altogether the chance a firm will be able to bring to market a truly breakthrough idea. According to Vijay Govindarajan of Dartmouth, "The more you hardwire a company on total quality management, [the more] it is going to hurt breakthrough innovation.... The mind-set that is needed, the capabilities that are needed, the metrics that are needed, the whole culture that is needed for discontinuous innovation, are fundamentally different."[21] The problem, according to one IT industry analyst, is that innovative ideas can easily meet a roadblock when up against a "long-running, moderately successful Six Sigma quality effort led by fanatics."[22]

Thus, as more and more companies have used technology to streamline and accelerate their operations, they have become either less capable or less willing to consider game-changing innovations, which means the innovations most firms do come up with today tend to be more incremental and short-term in nature. These types of innovations involve less risk and are more likely to return a profit in the short term, of course, but they also have much less upside. The truth is, tiny or incremental improvements in a product barely qualify as real "innovation," but that seems to be the type of innovation preferred more and more.

One academic study, for instance, found that the proportion of truly new-to-the-world innovations under consideration has declined precipitously in recent years, shrinking from 20 percent of all innovations in 1990 to just 11.5 percent in 2004.[23] Another study, focused specifically on the types of patents issued in the paint and photography industry over a 20-year period, showed that after a company completed a quality improvement initiative, the proportion of patents based on prior work (i.e.,

---

[21]Govindarajan was quoted in Brian Hindo, "At 3M, a Struggle between Efficiency and Creativity," *BusinessWeek*, June 11, 2007; available at: www.businessweek.com/print/magazine/content/07_24/b4038406.htm?chan=gl, accessed September 1, 2010.

[22]The analyst was quoted by John Parkinson, "The Conflict Between Six Sigma and Innovation," *CIO Insight*, July 23, 2007; available at: www.cioinsight.com/article2/0,1540,2159181,00.asp, accessed September 1, 2010.

[23]"New to the world" stats from Robert G. Cooper, "Your NPD Portfolio May Be Harmful to Your Business Health," *PDMA Visions 2004* (January 2005), cited in George S. Day, "Closing the Gap: Balancing Big I and Small i Innovations" (July 2002).

incremental innovation rather than breakthrough innovation) went up dramatically.[24] Still another study found that 85 to 90 percent of the innovation projects in a typical company's pipeline today represent purely incremental improvements rather than creative breakthroughs.[25]

Is it possible to be both efficient and innovative, both disciplined and creative? Can the *order* of execution coexist with the *chaos* of creation? This problem has always plagued businesses but has been brought into sharp relief by new technologies, which can automate and streamline operations in ways that were just not possible before. There's hardly a management book written in the last several decades that doesn't make at least a passing reference to this problem, whether it's *Creative Destruction*,[26] suggesting that there is a tension between operating and innovating, or *In Search of Excellence*,[27] advocating that businesses need to be both "tight" and "loose," or *Winning Through Innovation*,[28] arguing that a company must be "ambidextrous" to be successful both as an operator and an innovator.

But probably the single best overall description of the organizational traits more likely to succeed both in operating their current business and in innovating for the future can be found in Jim Collins and Jerry Porras's classic 1994 best seller, *Built to Last*.[29] Collins and Porras identified a number of companies that have been consistently more successful than others in their competitive set not just for a few years but for decades. Then they directly compared the philosophies, policies, and characteristics of these long-lasting companies with other, not-so-successful firms, in order to uncover the secrets of long-term corporate success. What they found was an incredibly resilient ability to hold on to a core set of values while simultaneously tinkering, exploring, and experimenting with new ideas.

Above all, companies that prosper over the long term will almost inevitably have an extremely strong *corporate culture*. At most of the durably successful companies Collins and Porras studied, including Hewlett-Packard, Wal-Mart, Nordstrom, General Electric, Walt Disney, Johnson & Johnson, 3M, and Marriott, among others, the culture is something almost tangible. It is a quality that infuses the employees at these companies with a sense of purpose, a mission that goes well beyond simply making a profit or building shareholder value. The cultures at these long-lasting companies are "almost cult-like"—so strong that a new employee either fits in well or is "rejected like a virus."

---

[24]M. J. Benner and M. L. Tushman, "Process Management and Technological Innovation: A Longitudinal Study of the Photography and Paint Industries," *Administrative Science Quarterly* 47 (2002): 676–706, cited in Hindo, "At 3M, a Struggle between Efficiency and Creativity."

[25]Incremental versus breakthrough study: Day, "Closing the Gap," p. 2.

[26]Richard Foster and Sarah Kaplan, *Creative Destruction: Why Companies That Are Built to Last Underperform the Market – and How to Successfully Transform Them* (New York: Doubleday, 2001).

[27]Thomas J. Peters and Robert H. Waterman, Jr., *In Search of Excellence: Lessons from America's Best-Run Companies* (New York: Warner Books, 1982).

[28]Michael L. Tushman and Charles A. O'Reilly III, *Winning Through Innovation: A Practical Guide to Leading Organizational Change and Renewal* (Boston: Harvard Business School Publishing, 2002).

[29]Examples and quotes in this section from Jim Collins and Jerry Porras, *Built to Last* (1994), pp. 37–38, 43, 55, 71, 147, 162.

While respecting their core ideologies, long-lasting companies constantly experiment with new ideas and innovations, failing frequently but keeping what works. R. W. Johnson, founder of Johnson & Johnson, famously claimed that "failure is our most important product." Motorola's founder Paul Galvin encouraged dissent, disagreement, and discussion at the company, in order to give individuals "the latitude to show what they could do largely on their own."

Experimentation, trial and error, and accidental innovation play a big role at most of the built-to-last companies studied by Collins and Porras. And this pattern of random-but-successful innovations is the unmistakable hallmark of a growth process based on an evolutionary model. "If we mapped 3M's portfolio of business units on a strategic planning matrix, we could easily see *why* the company is so successful ("Look at all those cash cows and strategic stars!"), but the matrix would utterly fail to capture *how* this portfolio came to be in the first place." In other words, 3M's innovative success is yet another example of how a network of innovations grows over time. Its current set of businesses and products was not carefully planned in advance and then developed in an orderly way. Rather, 3M (and most other long-lasting, constantly innovative companies) arrived at its present state as the result of constant tinkering and experimentation, with the best, most desirable innovations claiming more and more of the firm's resources over time.

> A climate of innovation starts with a culture of trust.

One final thought about innovation: The corporate culture that is most likely to stimulate and encourage innovative ideas is one that tolerates dissent and celebrates respectful disagreement. This is a culture in which employees *trust* each other, and they trust management. People in an innovative organization won't always agree, nor should they, but they must disagree respectfully. Handling disagreement in a respectful way holds a lot of implications for the type of workplace that best facilitates a climate of innovation. It means the boss shouldn't just squash conversation by issuing edicts. It means setting up a "zing-free" workplace, where it's not okay to make snide comments about coworkers, either in their presence or behind their backs. It means assuming that people who work together deserve explanation and clarity about what's going on behind the scenes. It means rewarding people who work with others and serve as catalysts for group action, and not just the lone rangers who succeed because they trounce everyone else. It means no one at the company pulls the rug out from under people. What it means, in other words, is that a climate of innovation creates better customer experience, which builds customer equity. And it starts with a culture of trust.

Summary

It's clear from the experiences of traditional companies trying to make the change from the Industrial Age to the Information Age, and from new companies run by people born and raised in the Industrial Age (that's everybody above grade school), that using information as the heart of competitive advantage is *hard*. Many companies have gone awry. Some firms aren't trying. But payoff is happening, for the companies that redefine their core business opportunity as growing the value of the customer base. We learn more about how to do it everyday. And the field is growing into one that offers new career opportunities to those who become fluent in a decision-making approach that puts growing the value of the customer base ahead of other tactics.

There's a lot of work to do. Every company on the planet that succeeds in the next two decades will do so because of its ability to concentrate on getting, keeping, and growing the best customers in its industry.

Food for Thought

1. Imagine you have been assigned to change a currently product-oriented company to a customer-oriented firm. Select one. What is the first thing you do? What is your road map for the next two years? The next five?
2. Name two or three different industries. For each, consider completely different business models that are sustainably successful and that would be based on more collaborative and trust-building ways of creating value from customers in the short and long term.

Name Index

Term Index